THE COLLECTOR'S HISTORY OF DOLLS

BY THE SAME AUTHOR

TOYS AND DOLLS FOR COLLECTORS

DOLLS AND DOLLSHOUSES

The Collector's History of
DOLLS

CONSTANCE EILEEN KING

ROBERT HALE LIMITED

LONDON

ST. MARTIN'S PRESS

NEW YORK

© CONSTANCE EILEEN KING 1977
FIRST PUBLISHED IN GREAT BRITAIN 1977
FIRST PUBLISHED IN THE UNITED STATES OF AMERICA 1978

Robert Hale Limited
Clerkenwell House
Clerkenwell Green
London EC1R 0HT

ISBN 0 7091 5142 X

St. Martin's Press, Inc.
175 Fifth Avenue
New York, N.Y. 10010

Library of Congress Catalog Card Number: 77-6095

Library of Congress Cataloging in Publication Data

King, Constance Eileen.
    The collector's history of dolls.

    Bibliography: p.
    Includes index.
    1. Dolls—History. 2. Dolls—Collectors and
collecting. I. Title.
NK4894.A2K56   745.59'22   77-6095
ISBN 0-312-15025-3

Printed in Great Britain by Jarrold & Sons Ltd, Norwich

For my Father
whose curiosity about the past is so infectious

CONTENTS

ILLUSTRATIONS

COLOUR

with paper neatening strips. Original striped dress, printed with a
feather pattern. 10½ in. high.

12 Very large papier mâché lady *c.* 1825. Moulded hair drawn to a
plaited bun at the back of the head. Blue painted eyes. Blue heel-
less slippers. Red bands between leather and wood sections.
Wearing dress of eighteenth-century silk. 31 in. high.

13 Fine large Grödnertal-type carved wooden doll. Pierced ears,
jointed at waist. Very fine painting of hair. Wears original pink
silk and muslin costume with a chatelaine hanging from belt.
Extremely rare to find such a large doll of this type. Photographed
against linen-fold panelling at the Strangers' Hall, Norwich. *c.*
1812. 40 in. high.

14 Waxed composition with wired blue sleeping eyes and linen,
sawdust-filled body. Brown hair, knotted wig. The pink leather
lower arms match the pink silk cape, which is lined with dark
pink. Cotton dress, probably made from eighteenth-century
fabric. Petticoat and chemise. Straw bonnet with quilted lining
decorated with ribbons and flowers. Dated by costume *c.* 1818.
Marked on foot in ink "C/IT". 21 in. high.

15 Costermonger and his girl with a cart of vegetables. Marked on
case "G. Ivory Modelmaker 1898". Lady has bisque head with
painted eyes, man has carved wooden face. Both with carved
bodies. Very well-made cart with leaf springs. Donkey carved
from the solid. 20 × 10¼ in.

16 Two pedlar figures with an interesting assortment of wares. Later
figure with composition head and spectacles carries ribbons and a
peacock fan. 12½ in. high. The other with papier mâché head and
moulded ringlets *c.* 1840. 12 in. high.

17 Composition soldier, whose clothes form the body. Moulded
moustache, glass eyes and red wool wig. A Scottish soldier was
also made using this head. 11¾ in. high. Lady-doll in original
costume. Composition head with glass eyes. 12 in. high. Both *c.*
1908.

18 Large waxed composition girl doll in Victorian child's pushchair.
Hand-sewn linen body, sawdust-filled. Waxed composition
hands, blue sleeping eyes. Wearing velvet coat. 33 in. high.

BLACK AND WHITE

xiv

XV

xix

PICTURE CREDITS

Bayerisches National Museum, Munich: 31, 32.

Bethnal Green Museum, London: 41, 42, 43, 47, 53, 56, 59, 60, 63, 65, 70, 72, 77, 81, 90, 93, 98, 99, 100, 104, 105, 107, 111, 113, 115, 116, 129, 130, 131, 132, 133, 136, 138, 141, 142, 172, 173, 178, 179, 182, 191, 213, 215, 217, 220, 226, 231, 235, 239, 240, 248, 249, 267, 271, 304, 319, 341, 372, 390, 396; colour, 38.

Bramble, Nicholas: 193, 230, 258, 263, 266, 305, 320, 416, 417, 418, 435, 436.

British Museum: 36.

Brooks, Dorothy: 60, 333, 340, 342, 352, 358, 362, 363, 364, 367, 375, 377, 378.

Bull, Tilly: 224, 228, 229, 234, 238, 241, 243, 247, 269, 272; colour 32, 33.

Byford, Angela: 22, 69, 73, 75, 76, 83, 102, 139, 149, 157, 165, 170, 174, 184, 185, 194, 214, 219, 222, 244, 260, 285, 287, 294 a and b; 298, 303, 306, 315, 325, 327, 328, 329, 334, 335, 336, 361, 366, 369, 376, 379, 380, 381, 383, 384, 420, 423, 428, 433; colour, 18.

Christies, King Street, London S.W.1: 49, 55, 82, 103, 187, 189 a and b, 232; colour 9.

Deans Rag Book Company, Rye: 345, 346, 347, 348, 349, 350, 351, 354, 356, 357, 438.

Germanisches National Museum, Nürnberg: 33.

Goldscheider, Garby: 91.

Gordon Victoria: 279.

Hardwick Hall: 30.

Holly Trees Museum, Colchester: 144, 216; colour 16.

Horniman Museum, London: 1, 2, 3, 4, 5, 6, 9, 10, 11, 12, 13, 14, 15, 16, 17, 18, 19, 20, 21, 28, 40, 110, 126.

Karslake, Rachel: 360.

King, Constance E.: 23, 24, 25, 26, 27, 39, 46, 68, 71, 74, 78, 79, 80, 84, 86, 87, 88, 94, 95, 96, 102, 106, 108, 112, 114, 118, 119, 120, 125, 127, 128, 146, 148, 150, 151, 152, 153, 154, 155, 156, 158, 159, 160, 162, 163, 164, 166, 167, 168, 171, 175, 176, 180, 181, 188, 192, 195, 196, 197, 199, 200, 201, 202, 203, 204, 205, 206, 207, 208, 210, 211, 212, 221, 223, 225, 227, 233, 237, 242, 245, 246, 250, 251, 252, 253, 254, 255, 256, 259, 262, 264, 265, 268, 270, 273, 274, 275, 276, 277, 278, 280, 281, 282, 283, 284, 286, 288, 289, 290, 291, 292, 293, 295, 296, 297, 301, 307, 308, 309, 310, 311, 312, 313, 314, 316, 317, 318, 321, 324, 326, 330, 332, 353, 355, 365, 368, 370, 371, 373, 374, 382, 385, 386, 394, 395, 397, 398, 399, 400, 401, 402, 403, 404, 405, 406, 407, 409, 410, 411, 412, 413, 414, 415, 419, 420, 421, 422, 424, 425, 426, 427, 429, 430, 431, 432, 434; colour, 1, 2, 4, 8, 11, 12, 14, 15, 17, 19, 20, 21, 22, 23, 24, 27, 28, 29, 30, 31, 34, 35, 36, 37.

Museo Capitolini, Rome: 8.

Museum of the City of New York: 145, 331, 339, 343, 344.

Olsen, Jan: 169, 198, 300.

Palmer, Georgia: 408.

Smith, Myrtle: 135, 359, 437.

Smith, W. H. & Son: 323, 324.

Sotheby's, London: colour 3.

Strangers' Hall, Norwich: 52, 54, 58, 67, 101, 109, 121, 124, 140, 143, 147, 161, 209, 218, 257, 337, 387, 388, 389, 392; colour, 7, 13, 25, 26.

University Museum, Philadelphia; 7.

Victoria and Albert Museum: 34, 35, 37, 38, 44, 45, 48, 50, 51, 122, 123, 177, 186; colour 5, 6, 10.

Worthing Museum: 29, 57, 62, 64, 66, 85, 89, 92, 97, 137, 183, 190, 236, 261 a, b and c, 299, 302, 338, 391, 393.

ACKNOWLEDGEMENTS

I would like to thank the many collectors, dealers and curators of museums who over the past years have assisted my study of dolls, and the many members of the public who have talked to me of their childhood and their toys. While it is not possible to list all those who have helped me in compiling this book, I would make special mention of the following:

The curators and staff of the Bethnal Green Museum, the Horniman Museum, the Strangers' Hall, Norwich, the Victoria and Albert Museum and the Worthing Museum and Art Gallery.

Chad Valley Toys, Sylvia Willgoss of Dean's Rag Book Co. Ltd, W. H. Smith and Son Ltd, Richard Spear of J. W. Spear and Sons Ltd, the late Miss Nora Wellings and the staff at Christies and Sotheby's.

Members of the Essex Doll Club, including Angela Byford, Myrtle Smith, Nicholas Bramble, Jan Olsen, Dorothy Brooks and Rachel Karslake, who allowed their dolls to be photographed. Also the late Miss M. Macalister, Georgia Palmer, Victoria Gordon and Tilly Bull.

I would also thank 'Nick' Nicholson, who patiently arranged and photographed the dolls while enduring hours of doll talk in the background; Gail Plumb, who bravely typed the handwritten pages; and above all, my husband Andrew, who read the manuscript, and without whose complete participation in collecting and restoration my task would have been more arduous.

PREFACE

The author of any book on antique items of collectable value has to guard continually against current tastes and escalating prices being allowed to affect her judgement of the broad patterns of development. Some indication of the speed at which fashion changes is given by the fact that since the completion of this history, dolls in the adult style have again become very popular and the character babies, for instance, so coveted in Britain just a short time ago, are now much less highly regarded. Poured-wax dolls were also considerably under appreciated at the time of writing but are now commanding prices more in accord with the craftsmanship of their construction. Such evidence of the whims of popular taste indicates that the collector with a real regard for the subject, rather than an investors interest, should follow her own preferences with conviction.

There were still some lingering doubts in my mind as to a possible Continental manufacture of dolls of the 'Queen Anne' type when that section of the book was written but I am now convinced, after further European research, that dolls of this type are of purely British origin as those of proven Continental manufacture exhibit very different characteristics.

Continually, new material and revised opinions on the evolution of the less documented types of doll come to hand and the firmly-held opinions of generations can be shattered on the discovery of an old trade catalogue or a marked doll of a usually unclaimed type. It is the continual mystery of research into a collector's field that is still in relative infancy that makes the study of dolls so absorbing.

C. E. K.

INTRODUCTION

From the points of view of both the collector and the social historian, the history of the doll is both interesting and attractive. The doll, in its most basic form as a simple representation of the human figure, appears to have been as necessary to mankind as the vessels from which we drink. In times of great national distress, the individual child still had need of a companion figure upon which to vent not only love, but also extreme hate and anger. Fortunately for collectors, many dolls appear to have been treated with consideration, and sufficient examples still exist for the study of the development of the doll from its most embryonic state to the full flowering in the late nineteenth century.

Perhaps because of the uncertainty and insecurity of modern life, an increasing number of people are joining the ranks of collectors. One man is attracted perhaps by eighteenth-century porcelain, and another by finely-bound books, but such collections may often seem to have little relevance to the ordinary person. This is seldom the case with a collection of dolls. The warmth of the exhibits and the associations of childhood almost always render them objects of immediate and direct interest. There are few people who can walk past a collection of toys and dolls with no more than a glance.

Along with the increased interest in doll-collecting among all sorts of people has been a surprising lack of knowledge and documentation, which has led, for instance, to some very bizarre cataloguing of exhibits in provincial museums. An excellent Encyclopedia of Dolls now exists for the attribution of acquisitions (Coleman, *The Collector's Encyclopedia of Dolls*, Robert Hale and Co. London, and Crown Publishers, New York), but in the writing of the present book an attempt is made to give as full an account as possible of the chronological history of the doll. The doll's evolution cannot be discussed merely in the cold terms of 'schools' or 'periods', but must be related to the social context of the lives of the children who owned them; and it is hoped that the book will be of some interest to educationalists and sociologists as a study of the state of childhood reflected in the dolls young people owned.

Though usually thought of as a child's toy, the human figure in a doll-like representation has reappeared throughout history as an object of amusement for adults. The Jumping Jack or *Pantin*, which caused such amusement in the eighteenth-century French court, the well-dressed costume dolls which modern adult tourists collect, and the amusing 1920s pincushion dolls with their raddled faces and provocative poses all have a part in the history of the doll. Just as in the eighteenth century a toy was an object of frivolous amusement to a person of any age, and could take the form of almost anything from a silver snuff box to a porcelain pug, so the doll has come to be regarded in its wider sense as an object made either to divert the adult or to involve the child, and is of great interest from either point of view.

Man's fascination with the miniature has led him to use small figures for the enactment of events of importance. The church in particular made use of the immediate impact of related groups of figures in the round to create interest and participation in the great events of the Christian year. The crèche figures of eighteenth-century Italy are finely executed craftsman's dolls and in no way aspire to be works of fine art. Many collections include among the dolls of childhood such crèche figures, which are good illustrations of the capabilities of the modellers of the period. The fact that children's dolls made at exactly the same time are of a completely different standard makes them much more interesting, and raises the question of why no effort was made to be more realistic – a question which is often asked not only in the study of dolls, but also in that of painting, as two completely different sets of standards operated side by side.

Accurate representations of the figure continued to appear in the seventeenth and eighteenth centuries in the fine Pandora or mannequin figures, which, beautifully made and exquisitely dressed in fine detail, were used to illustrate current fashion to ladies of foreign courts. The nineteenth-century child's doll, which portrayed a lady of fashion, was very much the successor in this field, and although the purpose was changed, the good finish and detail of the figure continued. Modern fashion dummies are often extremely high quality, but we are too close in time to such objects to attempt a realistic assessment. Many modern dolls, especially those which reflect precise contemporary fashion, will probably one day be collector's items, but it is impossible to tell which particular types will hold an appeal to collectors of the future. This book therefore deals mainly with dolls that were made before the Second World War, which helped to disrupt the social structure, particularly in England, and made ordinary children able to possess dolls of a reasonable quality. Of necessity, the history of the doll is connected, especially in the nineteenth and early twentieth centuries, with the lives of the middle class and wealthy children who would have owned them. Regrettably, few items remain from the rag and bone toy boxes of the very poor child. Where they do, they are discussed and illustrated, but their appeal is to the more socially-minded collector. A pathetic bundle of rags wrapped in a filthy shawl would have little appeal to the cabinet collector, who is at pains to collect status-advancing investment pieces.

As this book is intended to be a comprehensive study, every effort has been made to include the dolls which mark stages in the historical development, and some of the most famous and often-photographed dolls have been included, especially those of the pre-nineteenth-century period. A very large number of previously unpublished photographs of dolls are reproduced in the nineteenth-century section, as it is felt that many famous museum exhibits are too often used, and may tend to offer only 'the recipe as before'. It is hoped that by the reproduction of many photographs from private collections, the collector will be stimulated and the ordinary reader diverted. In many previous books on dolls, the illustrations come from museums or collectors of long standing. The examples shown here are frequently from the acquisitions of people whose interest has developed within the last ten years, and whose financial means are moderate. My own collection was built on a teacher's salary, and this in itself should indicate that the beginner need not be put off collecting by a few high prices achieved for extremely rare dolls at auction. The collecting field is also continually widening, so that, for instance, nineteenth-century German dolls are now treated with respect, although ten years ago they were considered rather outside the scope of good collections.

The inclusion of several hundred photographs of dolls unknown outside a very small circle should be of interest to the established collector, for whom the captions give complete descriptions of marks and characteristics. The remaining photographs, which are of more basic interest in a comprehensive history of dolls, will, it is hoped, give an adequate photographic record of chronological development, for the use of both the collector and the student. Though not aiming to be a 'coffee-table' picture book so much as a basic history of dolls which will be of use for many years, the photographs are important and every effort was made to ensure a high standard, while posing the figures in a way that gives the maximum information. In preparing this history of dolls, the author has talked to all sorts of people about the background of the dolls which they own, as well as experts on costume and manufacturing processes, and this study has made me even more aware of the hold which a simple effigy can exert. The student of costume is intrigued by the fact that an early doll, whose clothes have been left untouched, may show the exact manner of wearing an item of costume, or perhaps a doll is discovered wearing drawers of a period in the history of costume where it had no right to be doing so!

I have frequently purchased dolls from families who have kept the toy of a sister (or child who died in infancy) for sixty or seventy years, as the glass eyes of the small object, perhaps of wax and cloth, exerted its personality upon them to such affect that they could not bring themselves to discard it casually, but searched for a collector who would care for the item and relieve them of its presence. Though it is easy for the sophisticated to dismiss an object as 'just a doll', one can begin to understand how a witchcraft representation can effect such awe, when a commercially-made, mass-produced china doll can force a sharp-tongued old bachelor to carry it shamefacedly in the bottom of a suit-case from one flat to another, because it once belonged to a sister who had died before he was born.

The doll cannot, therefore, be dismissed lightly, and an attempt is made in this book to study it in a wider context than by simply giving a date on which, for instance, a sleeping eye mechanism was introduced. The people who owned the dolls and the lives they led are often very relevant to the appearance and method of manufacture of the doll. As it was obviously impossible to relate items to the international conditions of children at a particular time, they have been set mainly against the lives of English and in some cases American and French children.

It is hoped that the presence of this book on library shelves will be of use in protecting the interesting toys which still remain in private hands from thoughtless destruction. It would be of great help to the doll historian if owners of old toys and dolls would give details of interesting objects in their possession (not necessarily those that they wish to sell or donate!) to specialist toy museums or serious collectors, so that an even greater knowledge of the doll's history may be achieved.

As remaining examples of the doll-maker's art are predominantly from the nineteenth century, this period forms the largest section of the book, and successive individual makers are discussed in detail and doll-making methods described. For precise patent dates and specifications, the reader has available a good encyclopedia, and I have therefore avoided pointless repetition of data regarding unexceptional French and German makers. Since there has previously been very little coverage of English dolls, the work of companies such as Deans and Nora Wellings are discussed at some length, as the information will be new to collectors.

I have endeavoured to avoid the whimsy that adults so often employ when talking or writing about dolls. The only whimsical dolls are those which were made specifically for adults. To the child the doll is a natural companion in everyday life and has a dignity of its own.

From the sophisticated Bru dolls of the late nineteenth century to bundles of corn carried in harvest rituals, the subject is of perpetual interest, and the enthusiasm of the author will, it is hoped, transmit itself to the reader, and encourage both the established collector and the novice to learn more about the subject they have chosen to pursue.

THE COLLECTOR'S HISTORY OF DOLLS

1 The Corn Maiden of Oats, which is found in all primitive communities. Decorated with sequins, beads and lace. A sprig of holly at the neck. Montenegran. 29 in. high.

ONE

THE FIRST DOLLS

The problem of attempting a definition of a doll is one that has taxed those who have traced the evolution of these ephemeral objects, from the time of the German writer Max von Boehn in the 1920s to the present day. To some historians, the doll is a subject to be considered in its widest form, ranging from a lump of clay, roughly fashioned into a dumb-bell shape, to a fine statuette of porcelain from the Meissen factory, made for the pleasure of an elegant court lady. Every collector has an idea, perhaps not consciously formulated as a policy, of the type of object that is to be included among his acquisitions. While one person excludes any figure that was not actually played with by a child, another will feel that, for instance, Victorian dress-makers' dummies are part of their collecting field, and will eagerly purchase any that are offered to them.

In the narrowest sense I would define a doll as a representation of the human figure to be played with as a toy by a child. Within the scope of this definition are all the treasures of the nineteenth century, when the doll-maker's art reached its peak, and objects of fine and detailed workmanship could, because of the cheap skilled labour easily available, be made in vast numbers for the amusement of the children who could afford them. The definition would also include all those simply-shaped objects which the child of a primitive tribe would accept as a companion. It is, however, a definition that has become too narrow for the present-day collector, who often includes dolls made especially for adults or even figures made originally for use in church festivals. As this book is intended for those who collect, those whose interest is in antiques and those whose interest is that of general curiosity regarding the subject, the history of the doll will be dealt with in this widest sense.

The collector of twenty years ago had no need to buy printed or celluloid dolls, as there was a wealth of good nineteenth- and early twentieth-century material which could be bought very cheaply, but the present-day collector of modest means has been forced to examine the subject more widely, and has often included dolls made as recently as the 1930s within their range of interest. It is easy for the long-established collector to disparage many of the items that are now collected as dolls by the novice, but it is well to remember that only within the last twenty years have German bisque dolls become generally accepted as collectable. Prior to this, the French doll, in all its expensive perfection, was the only late nineteenth-century doll worth including in a good collection.

Despite the fact that the collector is now unlikely to be able to obtain any very early dolls for himself, they can be studied in museums, and this study makes for a vivid awareness of how little the basic doll has changed throughout the course of history. The jointed clay doll from an Egyptian tomb could have been made quite recently by some tribal craftsman, and the basic skittle-shaped doll, to be found in most civilizations, is still played with by modern children simply as a nursery toy.

In considering very early examples, the often tenuous evidence that links the doll with the life of a child has to be continually borne in mind. It is tempting to consider every item that was found in the tomb of a child as a toy, but, as it was often the custom to include miniature representations of everyday objects in the grave, some reservation has always to be observed. Though von Boehn claimed that "the doll form, the more or less complete representation of man, existed for thousands of years before the first child took possession", it would appear to be far more likely that the doll was played with from the beginning of society. As in primitive tribes of today the children will create a simple image from sticks or even from a daubed stone, so the child in the dawn of history would have found the need for some simple object to share his existence.

Much surviving prehistoric statuary is of small size, and is often found at some distance from the places of origin, which suggests that some early exchange of these small doll-like figures took place. The simple design of many pieces suggests that they could possibly have been played with as toys, though the original intention of the person who fashioned the model was probably directed towards fertility or ancestor-worship. There is, however, little doubt that such figures would have appeared attractive to a child, had he discovered them by chance for himself. To a very great extent this is the area of 'perhaps', and most scholars prefix their comments on the so-called toys of this early period with some type of reservation.

Just as in cave paintings the artist would allow some suggestive cracks or chance geological formation to suggest the outline of an animal, so the early sculptor took pieces of bone or stone, and in their basic shapes saw a vague indication of the human figure. A smear of blood or clay for hair, and a few charcoal lines to indicate the eyes, and a manikin emerges. This is an essentially child-like process, and it seems unlikely that the child, no matter how sleepy he was at the awakening of civilization, would have failed to experiment in this basic way with the natural materials that were around him. It is in the creative play instincts of the young that man transcends the purely animal state, and we should not be too eager to claim that children in very early society were motivated in a completely foreign way to the child of today, who plays without any prompting.

The extreme scarcity of any representations of the male figure before the first Iron Age gives weight to the supposition that most of the surviving figures were made to aid fertility. A statue such as the Willendorf Venus, in all her ample motherly richness, cannot by the widest stretch of the imagination be classed as a toy, yet traces of an attractive red colour still survive on the figure, and even this Palaeolithic sex symbol might, at some state of her history, have appeared amusing to a child. It is as tempting for the ethnologist to label anything he does not understand as an idol as it is for the toy collector to see an embryonic doll or model soldier in every piece of prehistoric statuary.

This early period is of special interest in that we are given an indication of the evolution of man's representation of himself from the natural materials that were around him. The flat bone idols originating in Troy show an acceptance and use of a simple suggestive form, in much the same way as the Board Idols of the Neolithic Age emerged from the suggested shapes of flat pebbles. The earliest known statues in human form date from the Aurignacian civilization, and ethnologists indicate that the lower limbs were defined on statuary some time before the upper. The presence of legs rather than arms on figures that were intended to be naked again suggests the sexual connotation, as in many primitive toy dolls the legs are completely ignored and the major area of concentration is on the head and torso.

The Dolls of Egypt, Greece and Rome

Early figures which are often recognizable as dolls date from around 2000 B.C. and were produced by the Egyptian civilization. The wood from which they are made is cut into a simple paddle shape, which gives this type of doll its common name. Though the Paddle dolls are colourfully decorated with gay geometric designs, and have hair made from rough clay beads strung into ropes and fixed to the head with paraffin wax, fertility emblems have been found scratched on the reverse side, which again makes their use quite clear. They must certainly have appeared attractive to children, and their size – from 7 to 10 inches high – combined with their shape, which would have made them so easy to carry, makes them promising candidates for inclusion in a history of dolls. Dr Manfred Bachmann has indeed categorized them as such.

Other well-made wooden figures dating from 2000 B.C. have been found in the Nile Valley, where the hot dry soil has ensured their survival. One figure with jointed arms, which is only 7 inches high, is very doll-like, but as small figures known as Ushabti or Answerers were made to impersonate slaves and workmen for the after-life, probably such figures were made for use in tombs.

Some dolls of wood and linen stuffed with papyrus leaves were made by the Egyptians, and with their embroidered faces and hair made from fabric threads they represent a type of doll which has continued to be made throughout the years. Some of these dolls wear dresses and loin-cloths, so that the child could, if she wished, have changed the doll's costume. Extra detail was sometimes added to the figure in wax, which was an easy material to use, as it could be moulded or carved into the desired shape. Many of these dolls are so rudimentary in shape that they could not have been accepted by an adult as a model deity, for the standard of modelling for this purpose was by now well advanced. The study of Egyptian masks and figures evidences this skill; they had learned how to insert eyes into a model face in a very realistic manner, and their modelling of the human figure in its stylized form was remarkable. It is when this divergence of standard appears in a civilization, between the images made for adults and the toys made for children, that the study of the doll is facilitated. It has always been extremely rare to produce dolls for children using the highest skills available at the time, so that the fine crèche figures of the eighteenth century, for instance, were made alongside stick-like toy dolls for children.

Presumably simple jointed dolls similar to those produced by the Egyptians existed in other civilizations, but they have been without the hot dry climate that was so favourable to their preservation. Wooden dolls must certainly have been made by the early Greeks, but the surviving examples are all of clay. Probably dolls of bone, ivory, wax and fabric were often made, as individual examples have been found. Plutarch mentions the fact that his two-year-old daughter Timoxena, who was to die in childhood, played with a doll and begged her nurse for milk for the doll as well as herself. This same child, out of her love of life, asked her mother for more dolls so that she could share her joy with them. In the sad story of this little Greek girl is a foretaste of the angelic ailing children of the nineteenth century.

The custom of dedicating toys at a temple, when children passed from childhood to marriage or puberty, has ensured the survival of dolls from the Greek civilization in the remains of such shrines. The girl's doll might be dedicated to Hera, protectress of marriage, or to Aphrodite, goddess of love. A Greek epigram tells how one girl named Timarete dedicated her doll and all its clothes to Artemis. The poetess Sappho when young dedicated her doll to

(*above left*) 2   The Ushabti or Answerers were placed in the tomb to represent the servants of the deceased. Both faces show some slight effort at characterization. Clay. Finished with a thin green glaze. 4¾ and 5¾ in. high.   (*above right*) 3   Paddle doll. *c.* 1500 B.C. Fertility symbols painted on reverse in black, red and brown. Decorated with clay beads and string. Ancient Thebes. 7 in. high.   (*below left*) 4   Carved wooden Ka figure of 2000 B.C. Placed in the tomb to serve as an abode for the Ka or double of the deceased. Lower part originally fabric covered. Large white and black irisless eyes. 11 in. high.   (*below right*) 5   Pottery doll. A.D. 200. Ancient Mexico. The cord jointing makes the figure dangle effectively when moved. 8½ in. high.

Aphrodite: "O Aphrodite, despise not my doll's little purple neckerchief. I, Sappho, dedicate this precious gift to you." This custom of dedicating dolls has meant that the Greek doll can be studied in some detail, and the disparity of standard is here shown as wide as it later became in other civilizations.

Many of the dolls are made of clay, with the head and torso moulded in one piece, while the straight arms and legs swing from simple pivot joints of wire, string or gut. A few fine examples have quite ornately moulded hairstyles, some incorporating a head-dress or a ribbon decoration. The figures sometimes hold clappers or cymbals in their hands. As dolls of this type are never found in the tombs of adults, but only those of children, the indication is that they were positive toys, and not simply companions for the after-life as were the Egyptian Ushabti.

The peculiarity (shared by dolls throughout the ages) of being modelled with very short arms was in evidence even during the Greek period. This is a tradition continued to the present time, except in the case of dolls made in a purposeful representation of the adult figure, such as teenage dolls, where more natural proportions are used. When children are studying figure drawing, they are reluctant to draw arms to the correct length, as in their eyes these appear much too long. Perhaps natural proportions appeared equally unsatisfactory to the probably uneducated makers of simple dolls throughout the ages.

A Greek word for doll is 'kore', meaning girl, and there appears to be no known surviving representation of the male figure of this period in doll form. An interesting survival, however, is a rattle in the shape of an exquisitely-modelled crouching negro boy from the first century A.D. Some seated male figures from Attica, Boeotia and the Greek colonies are also known, but despite their frequent inclusion in the history of early toys they are more likely to have been made for an ornamental purpose. Small figures on simply-moulded horses are also known, but would fall rather more neatly under the heading of model soldiers than of dolls. Though many of the Greek dolls are rather sexless, others are very realistically modelled, with beautifully-detailed and finished heads on well-made torsos. One very Amazonian figure dating from the third century B.C. wears a fine helmet and in her original condition would have worn a draped tunic. There is a great deal of detail lavished on the torso which would have often been visible. In writing of the Spartan adolescent girls, Ibycus referred to them as 'bare thighed', as they did not bother to sew the side of the peplos to waist level as did most women who wore this Doric dress.

6   Despite the fairly detailed carving to the front of the figure, the back is left quite flat. Wooden doll 1500 B.C. Kahun. Ancient Egypt. 8½ in. high.

Generally the draping of the peplos would have exposed at least some part of the breasts, which is why the model bodies had to be finished with care, if they were quality dolls. There are, of course, many Greek dolls that are little more than stick-like objects, while yet other dolls of rag and wood or combinations of materials have not survived. It is in the dolls of clay, marble, alabaster and bone that we have to trace the development of the doll during this period.

With the Greek adulation of physical fitness and finely-made bodies went a desire to regulate the whole of life to conform to a pattern of perfection. In the life of a Greek child, little was left to chance. The Spartan child was taken before a group of experienced old men when a few days old for examination to decide on his fitness to live. If in any way weak, feeble or deformed it was ordered to be taken away and exposed on Mount Taygetus. In this way the Greek ideal of a beautiful people was upheld, and the suffering of unhealthy children, who were in any case unlikely to lead happy lives, avoided. In some parts of Greece, the child led an idyllic life. In Sparta for instance all types of swaddling clothes were banned on the grounds that they would interfere with the development of the young body. The girls were allowed to grow up in comparative freedom and were allowed to play with boys of other families as naturally as other girls. Spartan children usually went naked, although they occasionally wore a single, rough, sleeveless garment which reached only to the knee. Plutarch states that girls were made to take all types of exercise so that their offspring might issue from strong bodies and the girls might have strength for labour and childbirth. The actual education of children was rigidly controlled, the boys often being taken from the parents at the age of nine to begin their training for adulthood, though the girls remained at home until, at the age of eleven or thirteen, they renounced their childhood by the dedication of its amusements such as their dolls. Artemis, for example, was worshipped in her sanctuary at a type of initiation ceremony, part of which entailed the girls's wearing yellow-brown robes and playing at being a she-bear. If a girl died before marriage, which took place at puberty, she would be represented on her tombstone playing with her dolls, instead of the babies which were the prerogative of young married women.

Most Greek girls would have been able to possess a doll, as they were sold in the market-places and by street vendors, who often travelled with their goods over the whole area of Greek civilization. Sardis, capital of Lydia, on the trade route to Persia, is recognized as the centre of this Greek doll-making industry. The dolls were quite well equipped, as apart from clothes, they were sometimes accompanied by small items of table ware and even model rooms. Items of furniture large enough for a doll to sit in have been found and in the Temple of Zeus, a doll's bed was discovered among other offerings.

Doll-making was also an industry in the Roman era, and the products of

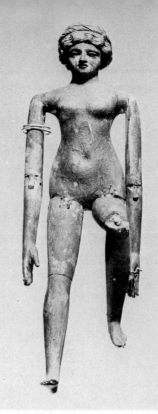

(*above left*) 7 Greek doll made in the fifth century B.C. Jointed terracotta. 5 in. high. (*above right*) 8 Girl doll of first-century Rome. Jointed body carved in some detail. Wears a gold bangle and ring. (*below left*) 9 The Kachina of the Hopi Indians were gaudily painted and decorated with feathers. After initiation ceremonies, they were used for the instruction of children. 10½ in. high. (*below right*) 10 Figs, strung on cord and decorated with scraps of fabric, create a doll-like toy. Sheerga village, Kandahar, Afghanistan. 14 in. high.

11 The clever weighting of this doll from Tanganyika makes it realistic to handle. Decorated with colourful beads and sequins. Some of the decoration covered by the fabric clothes. 16 in. high.

this industry are found in most of the Roman-occupied lands. The dolls made of the more weather-resistant materials have survived in some number, such as those made of bone, lead or terracotta. In appearance, the Roman and Greek dolls are similar, though there is a particularly fine Roman doll made of oak which has survived to give an indication of the skill of the Roman craftsmen. This doll, which was found in a tomb of the second century B.C., is most skilfully articulated with mortice and tenon joints, not only at shoulder and thigh but also at elbow, and marks an important stage in the development of the basic doll shape. The figure has also a well-carved hairstyle and the body is made to a high degree of realism. The arms are interesting, as they are made even longer than life. As the doll was found in the tomb of an adolescent girl and represents a girl of that age, I find some question as to whether the figure is really a doll, or some sort of specially-made grave companion. The remarkable coincidence of the represented age of the doll combined with the extremely well-made body – even the fingers being jointed – would suggest a purpose other than pure play. The gold bangles and ring which the figure wears would also have been rather expensive for a toy, though the doll could have been made especially for young women as are modern fashion dolls. Throughout the history of dolls, such examples of high workmanship occur in otherwise unexceptional periods, and while it is pleasant to claim that they are dolls of childhood, reservations have to be made.

In the Saturnalia at Rome the giving of dolls to children was a special feature, and these dolls were dedicated in the manner of the Greek girls at puberty, though if a girl died, her toys might be offered to the gods of the underworld. The Roman girls dedicated their dolls to Mercury, Jupiter and Diana, while the cradle toys of infancy were dedicated to Bacchus. The most famous of all Roman dolls is that rather pathetic object of coarse fabric dating from 300 B.C. Only 7 inches high, it still retains the look of a much-loved and well-handled toy, and probably has more personal relevance to the modern collector than many of the figures of terracotta or ivory which are always rather tomb-invoking. Rag dolls were probably extremely common, but they were even more perishable than wood and could only survive if left, as this doll was, in the dry, hot Egyptian soil (it dates from the Roman period in Egypt). The wooden dolls which were also very common were painted to make them more effective. One doll, as large as 24 inches high was found in the grave of a girl in the Prati del Castello at Rome. This doll was very simply carved, in comparison to a beautifully-ornamented small ivory doll which was found in the sarcophagus of the Empress Maria. In the tomb of a girl who died in the first century B.C. was discovered not only her dolls but cosmetics for their use. Several of the dolls mentioned and the circumstances surrounding them would indicate that

(*above left*) 12   Carved wooden doll, probably an ancestor representation, said to be associated with rain festivals. Bachokwe People. Holes at ears, nostrils, front and back passage. 15 in. high. (*above right*) 13   Wooden doll of religious significance. Unpainted wood. Colombia, Choco Indians. 16½ in. high.   (*right*) 14 Biteke, boldly carved, to protect a child before birth and during childhood. Some of the afterbirth was mixed with ground Cam wood and placed in the cavity. The figure was then laid over the buried remainder of the afterbirth. 15 in. high.

doll-figures might have accompanied Roman girls in the grave much as effigies were placed above the grave at a later period.

Toy furniture of the usually accepted doll's-house size is often found dating from the Roman period, and by the tone of contemporary writings playing with dolls and toys was as commonplace in the life of a child as it is today. Ivory dolls have been found frequently, not only in the tombs of young pagans, but also in the catacombs, accompanying young Christians in the grave. Possibly the doll was intended to survive long after the earthly remains of the child and to continue to represent her. Male dolls as well as female are found in Roman remains, though whether they were made especially for boys is not known. The Greek and Roman civilizations seem much nearer when the toys of children are studied, whereas the classical statues of antiquity in their cool perfection seem to us aloof in our struggle to gain some concept of period and time. At Herculaneum, a little girl's figure with a doll tightly clasped in her hands was discovered just as she had protected it when the lava and ashes destroyed her city. Not a situation or a subject about which a cold dispassionate air can be maintained with ease.

Early Automata

The idea of a representation of a god that could answer questions requested of it in a favourable manner is one that fascinated man, not only in the ancient civilizations but also in modern primitive tribes. The need to make a request or have a problem answered simply by standing in front of an effigy has held continuous appeal. As Christians of today find comfort in being able to seek help before the High Altar of Christ, so the ancient Egyptians found solace in the oracle figures which appeared actually to speak.

Authors of antiquity speak of many automata in human form. Aristotle mentions an automatic Venus which must have held great attraction, while Ptolemaeus Philadelphus is said to have shown an automaton as early as 280 B.C. at the Bacchanalia, and Petronius writes in his *Symposium* of a silver doll that could move.

It is from the writings of Hero of Alexandria, which were rediscovered during the Renaissance period, that much of our knowledge of automata of this early period depends, for because of their complexity and the secrecy surrounding methods of construction, none survived. Philosophers and poets were eager to keep secret these skills of mechanical science, as it was upon such skills that much of the power they wielded over unsophisticated minds depended. Both Hero and Philo of Byzantium constructed automata, and wrote about their inventions. Hero describes machines for turning and moving, while poets refer to the models of Vulcan among which were golden statues of apparently living

15 A gourd doll decorated with beads, leather thongs and string. The arms made of two rolls of leather. To be carried on the back and treated as a child by a Bechuana or Basuto woman who wishes to become pregnant. 8 in. high.

maidens. There were also moving statues in the temple of Hieropolis, according to Macrobius. There is a traditional belief that Daedalus made self-moving statues, which Plato claimed "would have run away if they were not fastened". Aristotle believed that these statues were activated by mercury, though Bishop John Wilkins in his *Mathematicall Magick* of 1648 states, "This would have been too grosse a way for so excellent an artificer, it is more likely that he did it with wheels and weights."

Most of Hero's models operated by the action of water, but he also used heat to obtain an increase in air pressure. A metal ornament of a priest and priestess is typical of this method. When a fire on the altar, which stood between them, was lit, the two draped figures poured their libations on the sacrifice. The altar was an ornamental box shape, made of metal, which communicated by a tube with a larger box forming the pedestal. Into the reservoir, contained in the lower box, wine or other liquid was poured through a hole in the base. When the fire was lit the air in the altar box expanded, and pressed on the surface of the liquid in the lower reservoir, forcing some of it through the tubes passing through the bodies and down the right arm of each figure, causing the arm to fall.

Another doll-like figure was that of Hercules armed with a bow and arrow. This figure worked on a combination of hydraulic, pneumatic and mechanical actions, to make Hercules shoot his arrow at a dragon which lay beneath an apple tree. The dragon, when shot, began to hiss for a few minutes. This model worked by means of a double tank which was connected by a valve which was, in turn, attached to an apple by a cord. Another cord passed over a pulley and connected the apple with a trigger in Hercules' right hand. Upon lifting the apple the trigger was released, and at the same time the valve opened which permitted the water in the upper tank to flow into the lower, thus forcing air through a tube in the dragon's mouth which hissed as it was emitted. The hissing continued until the upper tank was empty.

These two examples of ancient mechanical dolls serve to illustrate the degree of skill attained, though it should be remembered that these were not children's toys, nor is there any evidence that such toys in simpler form existed for the amusement of children. The most that a Greek or Roman child would have owned might have been a toy operated in some way by a simple pull movement, such as a tiger that opened and closed its lower jaw by the pulling of a string knotted beneath it, which ran through a hole cut in the immobile upper jaw.

Automata have always held a place on the borderline between toys and adult amusements, and many of the ingenious and colourful examples from the Victorian period were also made for adults rather than children. After the death of Hero, nearly a thousand years were to pass before any new advance in mechanical toys was recorded, though the fascination of a model able to move with apparent independence, was an idea that continued to intrigue and frighten men for many centuries, before education displaced awed innocence.

Indian Dolls

The step from the ancient to the modern is often not great in countries whose traditions and way of life have changed little through the centuries; so that in the study of dolls of, for example, the Indian civilization, we see not only the doll of today, but also an object in an almost unchanged tradition. The genuine dolls of India, as opposed to the cheap tourist dolls that can be found in craft shops all over the world, have a charming and colourful simplicity. They are as alive as the simple pottery figures made by young children and as excitingly decorated, with a juxtaposition of gaudy primary colours. Very few Indian toys are made only for amusement, but nearly all indicate some stage or story in Indian history, so that even very poor children, who cannot afford books, are able to learn the traditions and folklore of their country through playing with miniature representations. The dolls are often given as gifts on festive occasions, particularly Gokulashtami celebrating the birth of Krishna, the child god, which is primarily a children's festival. A representation of Krishna is put in a toy cradle, and songs are sung to the figure rather as carols are sung over a Christian crib at Christmas. After the singing, sweets and small gifts are given to the children.

The Indian girls have their own Gudiya festival, though the old tradition of the Dolls' Wedding, which was an occasion when the adults joined forces with the children to arrange the ceremony to the best advantage, is no longer popular. In the same way that Greek and Roman girls surrendered their toys at marriage, it is the custom for dolls and other small toys including miniature pots and pans to be included in the dowry of an Indian bride.

Many Indian dolls bear resemblance to ancient dolls found in Egypt and Crete and again, as in the dolls of the Egyptians, magic and toy are often difficult to separate. The Kalighat doll, which is basically a rectangle narrowed at the lower end and colourfully decorated, is similar in shape to the outline of an Egyptian mummy and is said to have its origins in that country. The use of many of the figures is not actually predetermined by the maker, as is the case with European dolls. If it is placed with reverence under a special tree by an adult, it is a votive offering asking for gods for food or rain, but given to a child, it is merely a toy for play. Ajit Mookerjee in his book *Folk Toys of India* describes how a woman might make an image of Gasthi, a household deity, and while she is making it,

16   Buckskin couple with child in cradle. Wax heads with hair roughly inserted. Horn hands. Man 12 in., woman 9½ in. high.

17. A buckskin doll of the Klikitat Indians. North-west coast of North America. Decorated with beads and human hair. 14½ in. high.

18 Cloth doll from Indore, Madyha Pradesh, India. Made of two rolls of fabric. Embroidered features. Bead decoration. 6 in. high.

she will explain the story of the deity to the children around her, so that when they are given the image as a toy, the figure has added significance as they know all about its background.

The dolls are made in the age-old potter's method of moulding simple conical shapes into an abstract representation of the figure. As in other ancient civilizations, it is female representations that predominate, though the mother and child combination is more in evidence in India. The dolls are often bell-shaped, so that they stand more securely, a method of construction that was popular in the primitive figures of the eighteenth-century Staffordshire potteries. The rough clay figure is either allowed to bake naturally in the sun, or fired in a kiln. The dolls have an attractive colour range, due to the different clays used and the variety of firing methods. If a very dark colour is required, the toy is put in an earthenware pot and covered with husk before it is burnt with charcoal. The woman and children often work together in the production of such dolls which, although made in the traditional manner, have interesting new additions to shape and decorative finish in each generation. The potter is an essential person in the Indian village, and is given land in exchange for his goods, which include a very large number of dolls and toys.

18

The gum of the bel fruit or paste of tamarind seed is often used to colour the figures. An extra protective varnish is sometimes given, which is made of incense, resin and lac. The old tradition of keeping the back of the figure unshaped is one that is shared by many civilizations, particularly the American Red Indians. It was believed that the plain back would help the child owner attain long life. The plain back is much in evidence in eighteenth-century European dolls. Was it perhaps some vestige of this early pagan belief that still lingered in another civilization?

Though clay is the most popular Indian doll-making substance, others were made of pith, papier mâché, cowdung, bronze, rag and vegetable fibres. The makers of wood and bronze toys are usually men who belong to guilds – an interesting parallel with the medieval European turners of wooden dolls, who also formed guilds to protect themselves.

Some of the ancient types of Indian dolls are now dying out. The Masulipatam doll, made of cowdung, sawdust and wood, is now only made by three Chitrakara families. It is a pity that tourists prefer the dolls from Rajasthani, which are well

(*below left*) 19   Simply-made clay figure, typical of those made by local doll-makers. Carries a child. Decorated in a thin watercolour that rubs away easily. Poona, Bombay. 5½ in. high.   (*below right*) 20   Carved doll from Poona, Bombay. Decorated in some detail with attractive red and brown shades. A completely flat back. Eyes indicated by a black spot. 7 in. high.

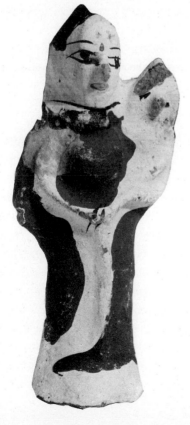

costumed and made of cloth rather more in the European manner, to the more genuine folk dolls of India. Even in these rag dolls, however, individuality is maintained, and in the dolls from Bengal, traces of the Mongolian features of the makers' ancestors can still be seen. Distinctively attractive rag dolls are made in other parts of India, notably Indore, and it is the dolls of this type that most frequently appear in European collections.

Among Indian dolls, examples continually occur that are reminiscent of other ancient civilizations. A representation of Krishna in his childhood is extremely sphinx-like, and it is only the brilliant colours that give the unmistakably Indian appearance. The tradition of playing with dolls is deeply rooted in Indian culture, and is depicted in sculptural reliefs from Amaravati and Nagarjunakonda dating from the second and third centuries A.D. The fact that the genuine Indian doll tends to be of an abstract nature, while those intended for European sale are realistic in detail, says little for the imaginative power of the European purchaser, who buys not a true Indian doll but simply a figurine of an Indian woman, which has little traditional significance.

Japanese Dolls

The European doll appears a particularly purposeless object when compared to the dolls of ancient civilizations. In Japan, as in India and quite probably ancient Greece, the doll was not only an object to be played with, but also represented a story which helped inculcate the cultural traditions of the country in girls, and the brave war-like tradition in boys. The most primitive Japanese doll-like toy is the Somin-Shorai, made of wood with six faces each inscribed with the words Somin-Shorai. These doll-like symbols were used to drive off evil spirits, and are still sold at New Year's Day celebrations.

It is believed that healing dolls were originally made of paper for the amusement of adults, and developed into a miniature figure which could be used by parents to protect their children. The Japanese had great faith in these Hoko-san, or servant dolls, which were believed to be capable of taking the sickness from a child suffering from an incurable disease. The dolls, usually of papier mâché and measuring from 3 to 6 inches, were placed at night in the bed of a sick child, and the next morning thrown in the sea, taking with them the illness which, it was believed, now inhabited the dolls.

Though doll-making did not become commercially established in Japan until the seventeenth century, doll-like figures were of course made before this date. A document from the Heian period (A.D. 794–1192) tells of a straw doll which could attract diseases to itself, and both the Boys' and the Girls' festivals, which are centred around a large number of doll-like figures, date from before the seventeenth century.

21 Group of figures from Japanese Girls' Festival. The Emperor and Empress, in ceremonial robes as worn on the occasion of an accession to the throne or an imperial wedding, are shown at the apex of the group. Below, three maids of honour, five musicians and two imperial Guards in the style of the Heian Period (794–1185), and three equerries.

The Boys' festival (or Musha Ningyo) takes place in May, the month of the Iris Flower, and the boys bathe in water in which irises have been boiled, in the belief that they will gain the attribute of the flower, which is a symbol of knighthood. A warrior doll, made with shields and helmets and with a ferocious visage, is the centre of this festival, which endeavours to teach the boy the intense patriotism that should motivate the Japanese warrior. Outside the house a carp banner hangs, indicating how, when death is near, the carp in the hands of the killer does not flinch at the knife bringing death. The figurines of the Samurai, the warrior caste, are brought out each year together with weapons and miniature armour. Stories are then told to the listening boys from the code of chivalry which is closely related to ancestor-worship.

In Japan, doll-making is an art which is handed down in families. The court dolls, for instance cannot be bought from ordinary shops but have to be made by a craftsman specialist. One family would make one special type of doll, the technique of which would be handed down only to their children. There is great emphasis on the making of elegant dolls which form an artistic representation of the figure, and to this end various techniques were used to arrange the clothes of the figure so that it was not distorted by ungainly folds. In some dolls, small slits are cut in the actual body and the cloth is neatly fixed into these, while in other examples the fabric which would be out of sight is cut away, so that the outline of the figure remains elegant. Typical of these gracious dolls are the Court Dolls of the Edo period (1615–1868) which are unsurpassed for austere perfection. The gosheningyo were popular as presents among the nobility, as they were thought to be symbols of good fortune. They usually took the form of a boy child wearing only a little belly cloth. The child's face was as round and shapeless as a moon and these figures make an absolute contrast to the other court dolls. The gosheningyo can be made of clay, papier mâché or moulded composition, and the boy figure usually carries some sort of toy or fan in one hand. He is an attractively robust figure, reminiscent of the Indian images, and is completely unlike most other Japanese dolls except the servant dolls, which are made by, and for, the less sophisticated, and have an affinity with primitive toys from all over the world.

Many Japanese dolls are considered to be works of art, and the degree of perfection is very high. The Japanese have an inherent love of the miniature, evidenced in particular in the fine inro and netsuke which are known to all collectors of antiques. This love of the miniature has encouraged the dolls' popularity, and there are over 300 different types of doll made of a variety of materials such as cardboard, paper, papier mâché, bamboo and various composition substances made mainly from sawdust. The papier mâché doll appeared in Japan in the seventeenth century, long before the substance was utilized by European doll-makers. A very fine finish, closely resembling porcelain, is given

22   A Japanese doll *c*. 1900, of the type often played with by European children. Beautifully articulated and given a porcelain-like finish by a layer of gofum: Of a type known as Yamato ningyo. This example with penis. Fine detail to hands and feet. 14 in. high.

to many good dolls. The face was covered by a mixture of pulverized oyster shell known as gofum. Rag dolls were also made in large numbers. They were constructed on a wooden foundation and called amakatsu or otagiboko. These dolls, though played with by children, were originally used to give the owner an easy confinement and are a type of doll fetish figure found in nearly all communities.

Though doll-making was mainly a household industry, certain areas specialized in the making of particular types of dolls. Cotton and paper dolls were made in the region of Osaka, while porcelain dolls were centred around Kyoto. In this century, Tokyo became the centre for dolls of rubber, metal and celluloid. Modern Japan produces more toys than any country except America, and it is interesting to note that the majority of these toys are not exported but are made for the home market.

The Japanese doll was introduced commercially into Europe in the late nineteenth century and prints and postcards of the period show how popular they became. The dolls that so attracted the European children were the 'three bend' dolls or Mitsuore Ningyo, which had upper arms and legs and the waist part of the torso made of cloth and limbs of composition. The cloth insets to the body made the dolls much more mobile than the contemporary European dolls, and with their realistic faces and black hair they had the extra appeal of an unknown race. The European dolls shown in the exhibitions which were popular after 1850 looked stiff and unreal in comparison, and they inspired the Sonneberg manufacturer Charles Motschmann to make a European doll on similar lines. Many of the Japanese dolls of this 'three bend' type can still be found, as they became established members of the toybox.

Clockwork toys were made in Japan as early as the eleventh century. These toys stood on a wooden box with a handle at the side which worked threads to make the toy, such as a juggler or a drummer, appear to move. Paper dolls were also very popular, and were used to teach girls how to use cosmetics and wear the traditional dress in an appropriate manner.

The girls of Japan were also instructed in the well-known Doll Festival or Festival of the Peach Blossom, which was held on the third day of the third month, on which it was traditional for Japanese parents to pray for the protection of their young. In poor families, the dolls can take the form of cheap paper examples, though in families of wealth, dolls and accessories are added to each year until, at marriage, the girl takes with her, as part of her dowry, the cere-monial dolls. Some family sets have items dating back several hundred years alongside very recent acquisitions. This juxtaposition makes the tableau more interesting to the individual child, who knows the items bought especially for her. Families often begin to buy extra dolls at the birth of a girl and continue

(above left) 23 Modern Japanese souvenir doll with silk-covered face. Carries a warrior's head. Gaudy colours but skilful use of form. 10½ in. high. (above right) 24 Cleverly-stylized modern Japanese tourist doll. 5½ in. high. (below left) 25 Japanese-made 'Parian' head of good quality. Early twentieth century. Made in imitation of and as a competitor to German-made dolls of the same period. Pierced ears. Unmarked. Glazed porcelain heads were also made from this mould. 3 in. high. (below right) 26 Modern Japanese figure of wood and bisque made in imitation of the decorative bisque heads made in nineteenth-century Europe. 9½ in. high.

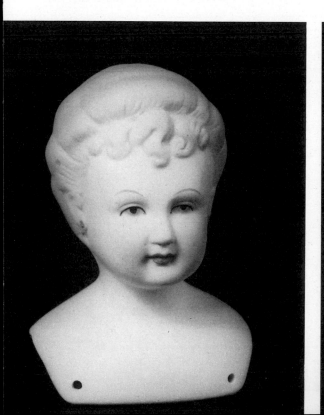

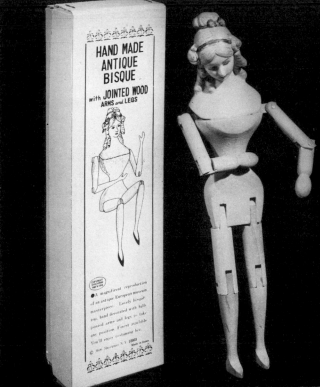

this each year, also including miniature tea sets, pieces of furniture and other small accessories.

For the day of the ceremony, the girls are given new kimonos and hair ribbons in which to pay homage to the dolls. After the ceremony, they entertain their families and friends with food eaten off miniature dishes. The festival is one of great visual appeal, and has fascinated those interested in dolls throughout this century. The ceremony is an example of the tremendous power that the doll can possess, as it is a continuous tradition, often said to date from around 70 B.C.

It is a pity that an orthodox method of setting up the tableau has now developed, as the degree of freedom which characterized it in the past contributed to keeping the ceremony alive.

The Emperor and Empress have always formed the centre point of the arrangement, which was traditionally displayed on a red-covered frame set up in the best room of the house. (When not in use, the often valuable dolls were kept in a brick building in the garden for protection from fire and earthquake.) Beneath the Emperor and Empress in order of precedence stand ministers, ladies in waiting, actors, court musicians and, last of all, girls. If the family can afford it other supplementary characters can be introduced.

The success of the Japanese doll-maker is said to stem from the skill of the artists who made Noh masks and Buddhist images in the seventeenth century, and later turned their skill to the commercial production of dolls. Kyoto became a centre for the production of heads for other doll-makers, in much the same way that Thuringia became the source of supply for heads of German dolls. Many Japanese firms had American controlling interests by the twentieth century, which encouraged the production of imitation European dolls during and just after the First World War, when German dolls' heads were unobtainable and unpopular.

Most collectors own one of the little bisque European-type girl dolls marked 'Nippon' or sometimes simply 'foreign', which were popular Japanese export wares during the early years of this century. Some of these are of a good standard, wear bonnets and have well-moulded hairstyles, while others were imitations of the Kewpie dolls, now very popular among collectors. Morimura dolls were made in direct imitation of European dolls, though again the quality is very varied, as the artisans were attempting to create a type of doll that was outside their experience, and the more interesting show the Japanese influence, especially in the slant of the eyes.

Though dolls are still made in Japan in small folk-type factories, these are usually associated with large firms to assist in marketing and distribution. There are now over 1,000 factories, one of which is able to offer over 2,500 different types of doll!

Fine traditional Japanese dolls are still made by such artists as Juzo Kagoshima and Goyo Hirata, who bases his dolls on wood block designs of the eighteenth and nineteenth century, while other producers make high-quality costume dolls to traditional designs. The Japanese lady dolls, often representing the Empress Jingu holding ceremonial wigs, are popular as colourful souvenirs with collectors of all ages. Genuine antique Japanese dolls fetch disappointingly low prices at auction in England, perhaps because they look too perfect to be considered as dolls. This lack of identification with the Japanese doll, after it has lost its novelty value as an ornament, is probably the reason they are so often found in jumble sales and on bazaar stalls. Many collectors are so sensitive of the need to identify their own background with that of the dolls they collect that they buy only European dolls. Though making for a narrow collecting field, it does contribute to the effect of a unified and harmonious whole.

Chinese Dolls

There are few genuine antique Chinese dolls, as the doll was given magical significance and it was not thought suitable for a child to play with such an image. The word doll in both the Korean and the Chinese languages derives from the same root as the words for idol and fetish. Gustav Schegel went as far as to observe that "little girls in China never played with dolls", but in the silk painting *The hundred Children*, dating from the sixteenth or seventeenth century, is a little girl nursing a doll, indicating that, though few dolls are recorded, some at least must have been played with alongside the popular marionettes.

Archaeologists have discovered doll-like grave figures of ceramics and wood with moveable limbs. Such figures were substituted for the sacrifice of living relatives and attendants after the time of Confucius (551–478 B.C.). Simple dolls of plaited straw had sometimes been used in rituals even before this date, and no good Chinese house was without its own altar on which stood deities, usually carved in soapstone, to which gifts were given in order to bring good fortune. The better of these figures date from the sixteenth and seventeenth centuries, and are collected as fine art objects together with such figures as the Eight Immortals.

The doll-like figure was always represented in an ideally realistic form, and was held in great awe. In 100 B.C. a prince was charged with having injured the Emperor by the power of wooden dolls dressed in paper, which had been endowed by a sorcerer with evil spirits. The idea of a doll to wreak vengeance on an enemy was popular throughout Chinese society, though most people made use of a straw doll dressed in blood-stained paper, which was pierced with needles to mystical incantations. This belief in the power of an image was further exemplified by a prince who pierced to the heart a doll representation of his father and buried it, as he felt his father had lived overlong.

Throughout the history of China, the importance of the human image is great. In order to bring good fortune to the occupier, an honour doll would be hung on the house door on the seventh day of the New Year. The marionettes and shadow figures which often appear in Chinese paintings are an essential element in the Chinese tradition, and the tilting toy, based on the tradition that Buddha cannot fall, has been popular for several hundred years. A weighted toy known as *Daruma* or 'fall down little priest' has been variously ascribed to both Japan and China, as the toy is derived from a monk who introduced Buddhism into the two countries. The monk allowed his legs to wither away during a nine-year penance, and as he was wrapped in a blanket against the cold, his outline was very suitable for a tilting toy. Another, more typically Chinese, toy is made of paper and thin cardboard with two sticks forming the body of the doll. This tilting toy is so finely balanced that it will always return to an upright position. It is sometimes called To-pat-to, meaning 'struck not fall', and is said to originate in South China.

The Chinese wedding procession is an ornament rather than a toy, but is composed of doll-like figures. The bride is accompanied by over forty attendants, including musicians and servants, as she is depicted travelling from her home to that of her bridegroom. As the Chinese colour suggestive of happiness is red, many of the dolls are dressed in this colour. Other doll-like figures are associated, such as a lady doll whose hands are hidden by her kimono sleeves indicating that she has just been married. This particular type of doll often has a wax head, a substance which despite its apparent lack of suitability to the climate is popular in many hot countries.

Funeral procession dolls are often seen, and with their solemn faces and clothes made of coarse fabric, they come much closer to the spirit of China than the costume dolls cleverly dressed in silk and paper that can be bought as souvenirs. The dolls found in both the wedding and the funeral procession are characterized by their long limbs, which are loosely jointed and have long pointed fingers. A constant source of inspiration to the more recent doll-makers are the characters from the Peking Opera, which are both interesting and colourful.

Although toy dolls were not popular with Chinese children, some were manufactured for the export market. Europeans were obviously considered to think more highly of children and it is noticeable that paintings of children appear far more frequently on export porcelain than on that made for the home market. Dolls were produced in Kiangsi and assembled at Kauchau, though most of the dolls made were for ceremonial purposes and it is unusual to find good Chinese dolls in the Occident.

27   Skilfully-carved wooden doll costumed in some detail. Made by the Door of Hope Mission. 9 in. high.

28   Late nineteenth-century Chinese lady "from Foochow". Beautifully dressed in the costume of a married woman. Cloth body, wooden legs and lower arms. Wears bangle and ear-rings. 9½ in. high.

Dolls of Primitive Races

It is in the sphere of magic that the dolls of primitive races are most easily distinguished. The term primitive is now used to refer to early stages of development, though it would be a brave art historian who would suggest that the products of such races are less aesthetically pleasing than the creations of so-called civilized man. Many plastic toys produced today are so simple in construction and direct in visual impact that they more closely approach the dolls of Africa than do any since the medieval period. In the simplicity of modern toys we may be searching, though probably fruitlessly, for a doll that has an age-old universal appeal for a child. The genuinely primitive doll has an abstract quality which is naturally imposed upon it by the basic materials that are at hand. It is not a doll that is consciously, and therefore untruthfully, made primitive, as many *avant-garde* dolls are today.

Every primitive race, whether from the South Seas, Asia or Africa, has developed a specific style by giving preference to certain shapes and arrangements of lines and colours that have special magical significance. There is a remarkably conservative tendency in most of these dolls, which makes dating without specialized equipment difficult, as the materials and methods of construction have often changed little over the centuries. The materials used by the peoples that were outside the sphere of contemporary European civilization were basically those that were used by the developed countries until the twentieth century. Bone, ivory, clay, wood, metal and a variety of rock-like substances have been used by all races for toy-making, but it is in the characteristic utilization of these natural substances that the primitive dolls exhibit their particular vigour.

Many dolls, even those given to children as toys, have a magical background. The Atutu tribe of Africa is particularly logical about its customs. A barren woman may be helped by the village magician's giving her a doll to carry on her back, but if the image magic is not successful, she is free to give the doll to a child as a toy, or she can even sell it to someone else who presumably might have more success. A similarly casual approach to magic is given to fetishes that are carved if a member of the tribe is in trouble. The fetishes are propitiated by the sprinkling of flour or an offering of an animal, but if this is unsuccessful, they are discarded without further thought and can become toys for children. Other figures are made by the Atutu which can be toys to amuse children or adults, and on feast days it is the custom for men of the Southern Atutu to lay out well-carved figures which they appreciate in the way a collector of sculpture might admire and enjoy his acquisitions; not for any magical significance they might hold, but purely from the pleasure of possession.

The dolls of the Hopi and Zuni Indians serve a similarly dual purpose, and after use by tribesmen in the ritual dances they are given to children. The figures are made of dry cottonwood root, and are painted in exact imitation of the masks worn by the tribesmen who impersonate kachinas, supposedly supernatural beings, at the annual tribal dances held in underground caves. The doll's origins can be identified by the painted decoration, which copies the masks. Literally hundreds of kachinas exist, representing the warm and soft rain, the rainbow and the sun gods. The Zuni Indians, who have similar rituals, also make kachinas, which are extremely difficult for anyone who is not an ethnologist to tell apart. It has been observed, however, that the Zuni kachinas tend to be taller and slimmer than those of the more famous Hopi Indians.

Their variety of decoration including feathers and beads makes the kachinas particularly collectable, and large numbers are now produced especially for sale. The old dolls have a soft, mellow appearance and were painted with natural colours, while the modern examples are finished with commercial paints.

Originally it was forbidden for kachinas to leave the village, and better examples were sometimes hung on the walls of houses. The children, by playing with these dolls, learn the names of the different characters and begin to appreciate the significance of customs into which the male children are initiated at puberty in underground caverns. The incantations that accompany the ceremony are not understood by the modern tribesman, as they are believed to have their origins in antiquity, though it is possible that they date from the nineteenth century!

The majority of primitive dolls are associated with a woman's life-pattern. The exact function of some dolls is debatable, and differences of opinion may be due to the different localities which were studied. The Suahali girl for instance is said by some authorities to carry a wooden doll on her back during menstruation, and by others to carry it on her back continuously once she is of child-bearing age. The Fingo girl in the Orange Free State carries a doll from the time she is marriageable until she produces a child, while some negro tribes of South Africa have dolls that are carried on the back, nursed, suckled and even given names. Male children are greatly desired, as they are closely linked with ancestor-worship, and in the area of the Torres Strait, a pregnant woman will play with a male doll in the hope of producing a son. The giving of a doll to a sterile woman in order to increase her fecundity is evidenced in many primitive races.

The creation and care of these doll-figures gives great comfort to the unsophisticated mind which can sublimate anxiety and distress in the care of a simple image. The Ojibway Indians have dolls known as 'unlucky figures', each of which represents a dead child. The mother, by placing one in a cradle by the fire and caring for it, is comforted by the belief that she has assisted the child's soul into the safety of the world beyond. In Nigeria, when the death occurs of a twin, the mother or surviving twin carries for ever the image of the dead child. This image is bathed and dressed at the same time as the living child and the spirit of the dead twin is thus given a place to live. The Yoruba believe that the souls of twins are indivisible.

The nineteenth-century Europeans had a similarly positive approach to death, which in its manifestations of memory rings and effigy children we now find distasteful. But it was perhaps a more sensible way of dealing with death than attempting to accept it immediately, as we often do now. Many European women still carry fetishes or amulets connected with their lives, but the primitive figures are more spectacular and are carried with greater confidence.

Some primitive carvings are made to protect the child in life. The Biteke tribe carve a doll of undetermined sex with a section cut away from the stomach. The figure is carved at the beginning of the pregnancy, and after the birth of the child a portion of the afterbirth is mixed with ground cam wood and packed into the cavity in the doll. The remainder of the afterbirth is buried in a corner of the mother's hut with the doll-figure. This ritual is believed to help in the protection of the child as he grows, by imitating the way he was nurtured by the placenta in the mother's body.

Among the methods of making simple dolls, gourds fixed together with a wooden stick are very popular. The figures are then decorated with beads, grasses and leaves to make an attractive representation. The women of the Wapogora and Wagindo tribes carry dolls made in this way when they desire children. The lower gourd is often inscribed with the tattoo marks of the tribe and an indication of the sex of the wanted child. If, after being successful and making the woman pregnant, the doll is damaged or lost, great fear will surround the child, who would then (it is believed) be more vulnerable to sickness.

The Barundi girls from the East African veldt make dolls from the flowers of the banana tree, or from the gourd which they decorate with fringes of raffia and cut holes in the foundation gourd for eyes and nose. The corn cob and corn husk have served children of many countries as a basis for a doll. The hair is an obvious form of decoration and beads and feathers can also be added. One type of corn-cob doll from Angola has the addition of wax breasts and is dressed in rag. Mexican corn dolls are made of two cobs which enables the figure to have two legs for greater realism.

In an interesting letter, a member of an English doll club recalled her childhood in Africa:

> I disliked the cob-doll at one stage and told my nurse Nhompoonsy why I didn't like them. They had only one leg. So she made long skirts for them and they took on a new appeal. The cob-dolls always took on a new look for me at harvest time, for then the maize beard made long hair for them, but with the heat, it soon shrivelled and became quite coarse and fell off. In the summer, Nhompoonsy would use sheep's wool. I knew she didn't like my dolls very much because when we went for walks with me on her back she would make excuses about how cold my celluloid doll was on her back and that a cob one would be much better.

The attractiveness of the primitive doll lies in its being constructed out of easily available materials, for because of the harmony of nature which produces the raw materials, their combination in a doll has to be successful. It is when imported materials begin to be used alongside natural substances that the cheap tourist doll, of little interest either to a collector or an ethnologist, emerges.

The Eskimos have made fine dolls with faces carved from walrus tusks, driftwood, reindeer horn and bone. These dolls, dressed in animal skin, can date from the late nineteenth century, though most have been made more recently as souvenirs. Fortunately, the modern dolls are still made of the traditional materials and the figure of an Eskimo mother with her baby peering over her

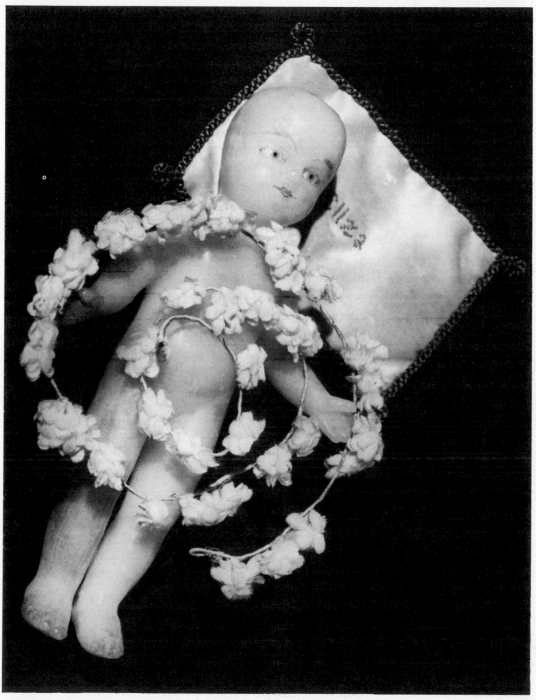

29　The "Westwood baby doll". Wax, painted features. Given by Thomas Westwood in 1844 to his wife, as he feared she would bear him no children, though seventeen were eventually born. 6½ in. high.

shoulder is a justly popular purchase. The Eskimo sometimes used a good-luck doll on fishing expeditions, when it was tied to the kayak in order to give protection.

There are still hundreds of different types of primitive dolls which can be collected quite cheaply. Providing that the only examples purchased are those made of natural materials and in the traditional manner they will be a sensible investment. 'Civilization' now spreads at an alarming rate and many of these dolls can have only a limited period in which they will continue to be made in an indigenous manner. Very soon plastic eyes and nylon wigs will be utilized in the decoration of such dolls for the visitor, and the native doll will be adapted to suit the European taste, as has happened with many Eastern dolls already.

The thread linking all these dolls of primitive regions is magic. The European doll is simply an object of amusement for the child and is usually made especially for children, whereas in countries whose life is governed largely by nature the doll has to have a purpose that fits into that scheme. The fact that magical figures are often passed on to children as toys probably gives heightened significance to the object, so that the child sees in her doll not only a toy to be enjoyed, but also a figure which was of importance to adults.

Many dolls are made of corn, an ancient tradition that still continues in various forms among the peasants of most European countries. The corn doll, in its oldest form, is in the shape of a horn of plenty, but various peoples have developed the basic idea in their own way. Figures were often made of a sheaf of wheat to symbolize the Corn Goddess Ceres, and variations of this popular form appear all over Europe. In England the figures often developed into a more accurate rendering of the female figure, such as the Ivy Girl of Kent, which is decorated with straw braids to give a very Grecian effect to the dress; though in the late eighteenth and early nineteenth centuries the figure used to be dressed in contemporary clothes complete with cap, ruffles and shawl made of paper.

The genuine dolls made for harvest celebration have to be the height of a sheaf of corn, though small examples are now made by folk industries. The Whalton Kern Babby is often dressed in actual clothes and is carried on a pole to the church, where it traditionally remained until a new doll took its place the following year. The custom of dressing a doll-figure made of corn to form the central figure in the procession of 'the last load' appears in many countries. In England, the effigy of mother earth would be carried to the harvest field and then brought home on the last waggon load, gaily decorated with flowers and accompanied by a sheaf of corn.

The Romans celebrated the festival of Floralia, the goddess of flowering and blossoming plants, towards the end of April, which developed into a festival stretching from April 28th to May 3rd, and became the May Day festivals which were an excuse for much romping and merriment. The central emblem of the festival, which is the maypole, has descended from the Roman traditions, and the festivities have often been accompanied by the creation of a May Day garland centred around a doll, elaborately dressed and festooned with flowers as a symbol of plenty, which would be carried on top of a pole to the village green where the festival centred.

There is little difference between such customs and those associated with primitive countries except that, where such customs still exist in countries such as England, they are now maintained by preservationists, and are no longer a natural expression of simple man's attempt to placate his basic insecurity.

The collector of eighteenth-and nineteenth-century dolls often becomes over-insulated against the force of the universal miniature image, which is not the pretty toy of childhood we would wish it to be. The doll can instil cold fear into strong men when it has associations with witchcraft and voodoo. The waxen image, stuck with splinters of glass and nails and hung with loathsome intent, is a filthy and frightening object in its proper environment, though it can be taken lightly enough when viewed through glass in the rational atmosphere of a museum.

It is only the 'civilized' races that think of the doll image purely as a toy, and though we take them lightly, it is well to remember that in the lives of many people the doll can reassert itself as a primitive force. In the lives of one young middle-class couple, a Victorian china doll exerts this force as strongly as the doll of the Ojibway Indian woman. The doll has its own chair, table and crockery, and is changed into a night-dress at night. It has a wardrobe of lovely period dresses for day wear and a trunk to keep them in. Though admitting to being slightly afraid of the doll, which they have called Unity, they have created a daily ritual connected with looking after the effigy child, and they are deeply concerned if they break the ritual by coming home late from a dinner party.

A doll dealer told me how one customer visited her shop each week and began by buying Victorian baby gowns and christening robes. Another week she bought an Edwardian doll's pram, and on another occasion a cradle. The dealer had failed to connect the purchases, thinking the women to be a toy collector, until one day, very cheerfully, the customer arrived and stated that today she would buy the life-size baby doll!

The instinct of a 'civilized' person is to be sickened by such substitute images, but these effigy children probably give as much comfort to their owners as the crudely-carved doll gives to a primitive African tribeswoman, and it is possibly we who shudder that are at fault for wearing too thickly and consciously our veneer of civilization.

30   Portrait of Lady Arabella Stuart by an unknown painter. The two-year-old child, who was eventually to end her life in the Tower of London, carries a lady doll in the adult costume of the period. Painted in 1579. Hardwick Hall, Chesterfield.

TWO

MEDIEVAL AND RENAISSANCE DOLLS

Before the Fourteenth Century

Several writers on toys give the impression that after the fall of the Roman Empire, children ceased to play with dolls: a statement that would appear to be highly unlikely, and based not on intimate knowledge of the period, but simply on the lack of surviving references or examples. The doll would have been a commonplace object in its most basic form, and would hardly have warranted recording in a period when the ability to write had degenerated into the prerogative of a few. Folk art changes little over the centuries, and is affected only in a very minor way by national events, so that if a merchant who sold toys ceased to visit a community, that community would in all probability make and improvise dolls for their children, despite the tribal wars and scarcity of materials which characterized the Dark Ages.

The Christian Church bears the greatest responsibility for the shortage of surviving evidence of toys from this early period. The history of the doll in ancient society is based, in the main, upon images and toys found in the graves of young pagans, and the Christian Church obviously sought to suppress such practices. More success appears to have been achieved in persuading parents to bury their children without their toys than in convincing the same parents that it was unnecessary to make votive offerings at the shrines of saints – a custom which continued far into Christian times. The figures dedicated by the early Christians were usually about 9 inches high, and were roughly modelled in the round from clay. The sharply-projecting breast and nose were features characterizing such figures. One unusual example is completely flat and reminiscent of the Paddle dolls of the ancient Egyptians. Decorated freely in earth colours, it is a piece of typical folk art. The hands of the figure are upraised in prayer, which establishes its use as a votive offering of gratitude for some favour. Were the hands not raised, there would be no difficulty in describing it as a Coptic doll, as it must be typical of thousands of similar doll-like figures made at the time. This doll, from the collection of the Recklinghausen Ikonenmuseum, originates from Behnasa and is about 9 inches high. The figure must have been stamped out in large numbers from a simple shape, rather as gingerbread men are made. The costume is a painted tunic decorated with a border pattern, which creates an attractive figure and gives some idea of the dolls that must have been sold in large numbers, not only to pilgrims but also, in a more secular form, for children. The head-dress worn by this Coptic doll has holes pierced in the position of the ears, through which glass and cornelian beads are threaded on leather thongs. As such figures were fairly thin and made of brittle clay, their survival in large numbers would have been unlikely.

The toys of European children in the medieval period would have been made mainly of wood, linen or wool, and their survival would again be unlikely in the unfavourable climate. Vast areas of England were uninhabited after the Romans left, and the native population did not, as one would have expected, move into the vacated towns, but lived in more primitive conditions in settlements alongside the fast-decaying buildings. The skills which the Romans had taught the native population seem only to have been maintained by that people while the Romans were in occupation, so that, for instance, when the early Church began to build in England, it was forced to import labour from the Continent, where traditions of craftsmanship had been kept more alive. Some skills were maintained in England, such as the goldsmith's craft used for religious purposes as well as for personal adornment. Before Norman rule, however, there are few records and little is known of the social history of the period.

The heathen belief in amulets and votive offerings survived in strength alongside the small pockets of Christianity, and must have supported some trade in such objects, to foster the belief in incantations and magic which appeared to these simple people to rule their lives. It should also be remembered that countries were not isolated completely from one another, as merchants and foreign ambassadors ensured that some degree of culture was kept alive, and examples of craftsmanship from other countries were still available.

Anglo-Saxon children were usually brought up at home, though a very noble child might be sent to court to grow up in a suitable environment for his eventual station in life, or boys destined for the priesthood might be sent to a church establishment when young. Children who were left unprotected by the death of their father would be guarded by the strong feeling of kinship which existed, and this would extend until the children reached majority. Life in the more wealthy homes was not as spartan as one might suppose. Glass was imported from the Rhineland and silver from the Eastern Mediterranean, and articles of ivory, brass and gold were quite common forms of decoration. If there was time

31   Fragment of a clay doll from Nürnberg with similarities to ecclesiastical statuary of the period. Fourteenth–fifteenth century.

32   Limewood figure in the dress of about 1530. Was once brilliantly-coloured. Discovered in 1966 behind the panelling of a Rhenish castle. 9 in. high.

33   A group of Nürnberg toy figures dating to the fifteenth century. Note the skilful use of simply-modelled shapes to create costume detail.

for personal adornment, there must also have been time to amuse a rich child with a doll, carved perhaps from alabaster, which had been used for doll-making since the Roman occupation. Poorer children would have owned wooden or rag dolls, and a rag doll is actually mentioned in the *Indiculus Superstitionum* of the ninth century. Such simple dolls, apart from being made by peasants for their children, were probably sold in a more finished form by merchants and pedlars, who continued to trade their wares.

The setting up of groups of figures to represent the Holy Family was established as early as AD 354, when Pope Liberius encouraged crèche arrangements, which were to become so popular, especially in Italy, by the eighteenth century.

Coral, shell and horn were often used to make rattles, and were sometimes carved into simple shapes, while a wolf's tooth fastened to the rattle would be considered to be of great efficacy in warding off illness. These simple toys, such as ninepins and wooden dolls, would have been bought at fairs, which were becoming a feature of life. Monsters with snapping jaws would chase the unfortunate in mummers' plays, while the Punch and Judy show also had its English origins in the Anglo-Saxon period.

The Graeco-Roman tradition of funereal sculpture continued into the Middle Ages, and establishes the ability of craftsmen of the period in fashioning realistic images. This was a custom fostered mainly by the high aristocracy of France and England, and involved the making of life-size images of the dead. The figures were constructed over a frame of wickerwork and leather, which was left hollow to minimize the weight. The figure would then be covered with plaster and painted. The heads and hands were often made of coloured wax, a medium which had also retained its popularity from ancient times, as it was freely available and easy to carve. Pivot joints at the shoulders enabled the arms of these funerary figures to move, and human hair would be added to give realism. Dressed in costume from the dead noble man or woman's wardrobe, the figure would provide an interesting spectacle for the people. In France, the image would sometimes be set on a bier, and a table laid near, from which food was ritually served daily before the interment of the actual corpse. The earliest known example of such a figure is that of Edward III of England, who died in 1377, but earlier figures of French kings and nobles were unfortunately lost in the Revolution. It is a pity from the viewpoint of the student of costume that some of the 'Ragged Regiment' in Westminster Abbey were re-dressed in the seventeenth and eighteenth centuries, as the respective Deans were ashamed of their shabby condition and re-clothed them for royal visits.

Though most figures of this type were made by craftsmen, some artists turned their attention to them, such as Jean Perreal and François Clouet. The custom continued in France until the time of Louis XII, who was the last monarch to have his death solemnized with all the traditional ceremonies of the *chambre de parade*. The English custom lasted rather longer, and Pitt, and even Nelson in his Trafalgar uniform, were perpetuated in a similar way; while the Italians maintained the custom to the death of King Victor Emmanuel in 1878, whose figure was represented life-size and leaning against a wall at his funeral!

Life-size figures were also used for the more robust activity of practice for tournaments. A fierce Saracen-like figure, jointed like a puppet, would be made to move freely on a pivot. This quintain should be struck with the lance in the centre of the chest or face. If, however, the young jouster missed the central point, the figure would swing around and hit the back of the mounted attacker, to the amusement of spectators, who would be even more diverted when he was actually knocked off his horse. Such figures were common in the eleventh century, and the making of their joints presented little problem to country craftsmen.

Many of the amusements of children at this time were robust to the point of cruelty. Cock-baiting was still a child's pastime rather than an adult amusement, and as a favour, young boys were allowed to take their fighting-cocks into school on Shrove Tuesdays. In comparison with the cruelty of cock-baiting, the practice of putting live birds and small animals into grotesquely-shaped containers so that their terrified efforts to escape would amusingly contort the appearance of the creature, seems quite tame. Many a little girl's doll must have suffered in the hands of an aspiring young warrior who, if sufficiently wealthy, was used to playing with wooden or metal knights controlled in combat by strings. Such a pair of fighting toy soldiers are illustrated in the twelfth-century *Hortus Deliciarum* of the Abbess Herrad. Had this illustration not survived, it is doubtful whether any toy historian would have believed that children's toys of such complexity were available at this time. It is probable that girls' dolls of a similar character were also available, but to date there is no record of them, merely the likelihood that this illustrated boy's toy was not an isolated example.

It was in the twelfth century that the Great Fairs became really popular attractions, and many quite poor people travelled long distances to buy and sell. Ordinary children would have been familiar with the puppet shows which were a feature of such gatherings, and many girls must have longed for a beautiful doll dressed like the heroine in the puppet play. One owner of a marionette show in the eighteenth century sold off her marionettes as 'jointed babbys' (jointed dolls), and it is very doubtful that she was the first insolvent showman to do so. Many a worn-out marionette, no longer of use for performances, must also have ended up in the arms of some little girl.

The gingerbread doll was a popular gift to be taken home from the fairs. Lavishly decorated with gilt, these edible dolls were made to represent both male and female characters, and were understandably popular, as a child can hardly become bored with a toy it can eat. Many of the wooden dolls of the period probably resembled those of gingerbread. The old Middle German word for doll, *Tocke*, means literally a little block of wood, and dolls as simply cut from a block of wood as is the gingerbread man from the dough were probably the most common. In the thirteenth century, however, poets refer to "the heavenly and beautiful *Tocke*", suggesting that in some examples a high-quality finish was obtained. A great part of the beauty of the early wooden doll would have depended on the lavish decoration of the costume and skilful painting of the features. So finely were some of the dolls dressed that the Strasbourg preacher Geiler von Kaiserberg accused contemporary parents of allowing their children to become overproud of their dolls. A small girl who might be placed in a hot oven to cure a fever, and married off at the age of seven, would appear to be in need of some frivolity in her life.

The girl of this period was of very little account until she reached marriageable age, when she could be utilized as a pawn in the land game. As a very young child, she would have to take her chance in the communal hall where her family and their retainers lived in close proximity. If she fell ill it did not matter much, as there were probably several more daughters who could take her place. The tradition of the Great Hall, with its continual activity and lack of privacy, did little to encourage parents to take a loving personal interest in their children. Individual parents must have existed who were exceptionally fond of their offspring, but for the majority the young child was of little consequence, and her care and amusement would be left to any servant who could be spared. The amusing of the child might have been assisted by such toys as a clay rattle in the form of a smiling woman, while boys were encouraged to play with small tin and wooden figures, often in the form of soldiers, to prepare them for their role in later life.

Bread dolls were eaten on saints' days, both by adults and children, in order that some of the sanctity of the saint might thus be transmitted to the eater. Gingerbread dolls were as popular on the Continent as in England, but medieval German cooks also made dolls from a mixture of sugar, meal and gum tragacanth. These confectioner's dolls were sometimes moulded in two halves, so that a small gift could be concealed inside before the final decorations were added.

The craftsmen of the period protected their own interests by the formation of trade guilds. In the early medieval period, the members of these guilds were all of one class, sharing their meals together and treating each other as equals. It was natural for an apprentice to graduate to being a journeyman and travel the countryside selling his master's wares, and, in time, he too became a small master. There is no evidence of there having been a doll-makers' guild in England, but the German makers, who worked on a much larger scale and exported their products all over Europe, were formed into groups for the making and marketing of dolls. The guilds had become much more rigid by the late medieval period, and the distinction between master and apprentice was much greater. There were complaints that the apprentices were becoming outrageous in their demands and counter-complaints that the masters were causing un-employment. The aristocracy, who were supplied with the quality products of these guilds, remained completely aloof and took refuge in the old code of chivalry, which was by this stage mainly an outward show but provided some guidelines for the education of boys.

Girls of the period were sometimes sent to song schools, but were rarely educated alongside boys, on whom they were thought likely to be a corrupting influence. The young girl would learn at home how to cook, sew and embroider, and would be taught the social graces. There was a vogue for books that taught deportment and manners, among which the Book of the Knight of La Tour-Landry was very popular. The language of tuition in England until the end of the fourteenth century was French, and the girl might, at the end of her instruction in her father's house, be sent to another noble house where she could learn the quite complicated craft of running a household.

Though contemporary German writers extolled the beauty of dolls of the medieval period, the surviving examples of thirteenth-century dolls are extremely rare and decidedly plain. The doll in the form of an earthenware rattle referred to earlier is of no great beauty, and other thirteenth-century dolls found in the remains of old Strasbourg are just simple clay shapes, though presumably they were originally decorated with some paint or colour that has not survived. One clay doll in the form of a mounted lady carries a hunting hawk in her hand, while other figures of the period depict knights in armour, indicating that the code of chivalry still maintained its outward show. The embryonic wooden doll, if placed in the hands of a skilful craftsman and painted and decorated with care, can look very beautiful, and a judgement of the toys of the period should not be based on the few surviving examples made of clay, which to many collectors look more like figurines than the toys of childhood.

Late Medieval Dolls

The fourteenth century saw the beginning of a change in the child's role in society. The old custom of wealthy nobles and yeomen living communally in the Great Hall was changing, as the nobles became more interested in beautiful clothes and luxurious furnishings. Such objects would have been out of place

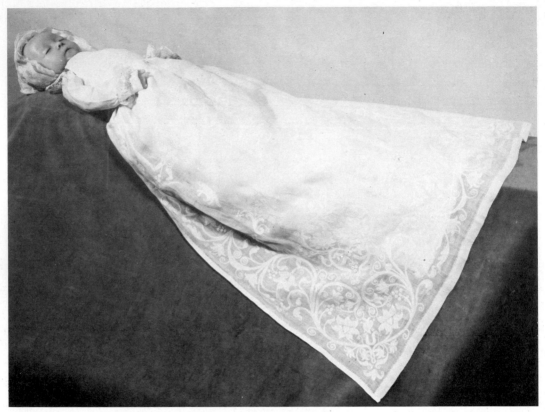

34 Wax model of a baby *c*. 1700. Robe embroidered "Don Santia Gode". A custom is said to have been prevalent in the Spanish peninsula of modelling the last member of a noble family.

in the bawdy atmosphere of the hall, and noblemen began to remove themselves and their families from the traditional mode of life. Wealthy men now became more interested in their surroundings, in the smaller apartments in which they lived in greater privacy with their children. These feudal lords spent vast sums of money in decorating not only their persons, but also the rooms in which they lived, and this outlay of money encouraged the rise of the merchant classes, who were to form the nucleus of the middle-class society. It is on the toys of this fast-increasing middle class that the toy collector depends. As the merchant classes increased in size, so the surviving number of good period dolls grows. The very poor child's doll of rag or wood was fragile and liable to be discarded, while a fine-quality doll of obvious worth would be treasured, if not by its owner, then by a servant or child who inherited it.

44

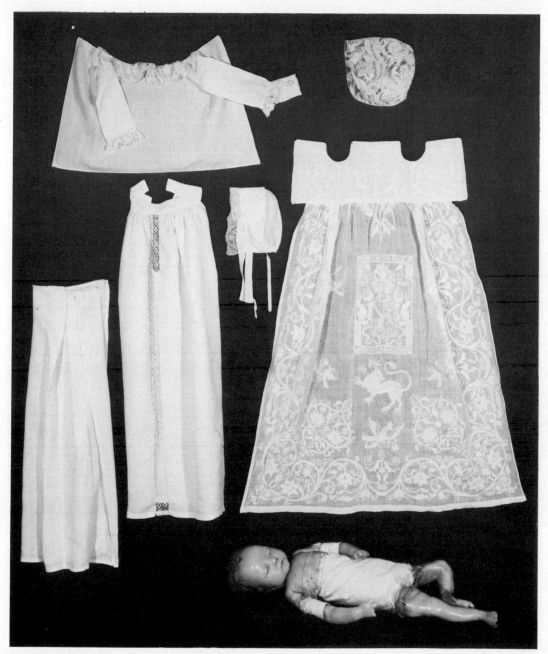

35   Wax baby in undress showing the realistic modelling of the limbs and the costume.

The late medieval period was much more colourful and lively, and the lot of the child seems much improved, apart from the obvious benefits gained from living in close proximity to the parent. There was now an even greater interest

45

in marionette shows, and these were often held in the great halls to amuse the workers, while the children of the lord might be taken to watch. A painted illustration in the Romance of Alexander shows glove puppets performing for the amusement of courtiers, though both types of puppets appear to have been popular. The fourteenth century also saw a great increase in the number of schools, and it became possible for poor children who were unusually intelligent to have some means of raising their status through education. The great fairs held on church feast days, such as those of St Denis and St James, were still very popular, and as people travelled across the country to visit the fairs, the speed of the spread of new ideas increased. The traditional dolls of bread and ginger-bread were still popular, though wealthy children might now be bought dolls such as those sold at the annual fairs in Venice and Florence, where dolls of wax, wood and composition are recorded as being offered for sale.

These fourteenth-century composition dolls were probably made of a pressed and moulded substance of waste matter, such as had sometimes been used in the making of life-size funeral images. None of these dolls have survived, and our knowledge of their existence depends completely upon written records. The wax dolls were almost certainly made of solid wax, carved and pressed into shape, rather in the manner of the cheap doll's-house dolls of the seventeenth century, which depend for their realism on the skill of the costumier. The common availability in the fourteenth century of the three types of doll which retained their popularity until the end of the nineteenth century is interesting, as it would suggest that similar dolls of wax and composition probably existed much earlier, but were only produced on a fairly large commercial scale in the fourteenth century.

Traditionally, Sonneberg and Nürnberg are said to have established them-selves as great toy and doll centres at this time, while Augsburg and Judenberg made similar products. This area became a toy-making centre, as it was close to the trade routes, and was fortunate in the enthusiasm of its merchants, who were prepared to export the wares all over the known world. Nürnberg had been famed throughout the medieval period for the skill of its craftsmen, and had already become an important centre for general commerce. The success of the toy industry depended on the proximity of areas where simply-made wooden toys were produced on a folk basis, such as Oberammergau and Gröden. With the increase in commerce between European countries in the fourteenth century, these toys, which had previously been made in some number in the preceding century, became widely disseminated.

The rapid increase of literacy in the fourteenth century has meant an increase of documentary evidence, and instead of depending on archaeological finds, the collector is able, from this period onwards, to rely on written references to toys and dolls. The number of references suggests a product that was more common-place than one is often led to believe. One writer suggested that: "No mother in the Middle Ages would have allowed her child to play with a doll unless it had first been blessed by a priest." Judging by the number of examples and references, the priests of the period would have been kept very busy! Though lifelike figures were connected with witchcraft, and some country people might have held some doll-like figures in awe, there is no evidence to suggest that in European society the child's doll was ever generally regarded with fear. The doll of evil cults and witchcraft must have been an object easily distinguished by an adult. In the Middle Ages, representations of the figure no longer inspired awe, as they were too commonplace. The young knight tilting at the quintain that swung provokingly in front of him hardly felt in awe of the figure. Individual instances might have occurred of a doll being blessed, but it would have been very much an exception. The traditional edible dolls sold in vast numbers at fairs were still popular with poor children, while the wealthy child might see, beside these rather mundane toys, a spectacle which delighted the eye during a banquet. At the end of each course, a dish called a subtlety was served. Made of jellies, con-fectionery and gum tragacanth, the subtlety represented curious figures, often of an allegorical nature, besides the more common forms of animals and men. The popularity of such edible figures contributed to a fantastic demand in the fourteenth century for gold leaf and powder gold, which was used for the decoration of such frivolities intended for adults as well as children.

The mannequin doll also makes its first recorded appearance in this century. When Queen Isabella of Bavaria married Charles VI, she ordered a mannequin doll to be made in Paris and dressed in the new fashions which had been intro-duced. The clothes for this doll were made by the valet to the King. When completed, it was sent to England to show the Queen the contemporary fashion of the French court. The court valet to Charles VI also received 500 francs for dressing another doll in 1396, which was used to illustrate costume in a similar way. Max von Boehn suggests that, as the price of these costumes was so high, the probability is that they were made life-size so that they could be worn. It is unusual to find reference to size in descriptions of medieval dolls, as figures of all sizes were referred to in the same way. In referring to 'dolls' such as the one purchased by Isabella, we have, therefore, to bear in mind that this was no small play object, but an adult toy or foible constructed in the most lavish way possible.

The most frequently described and photographed dolls of the fifteenth century are made of white pipe clay, and were discovered under a pavement in Nürn-berg in 1859. The dolls were found in a group, and are commonly believed to have formed part of a merchant's stock or, possibly, to have belonged to a shop. Similar dolls have been discovered elsewhere in Germany during excavations, such as at Tannenberg, which would suggest that they were quite common. The figures wear moulded clothes and represent ladies in court dress, monks, and babies in swaddling-clothes. The baby doll is often considered as a nineteenth-century development but, in the doll world as in most other art forms, there is little that is really new. These Nürnberg dolls often have a round hole cut in the chest, which German writers suggest was made to hold a small coin, possibly given as a baptismal gift. The figures, though attractive and retaining a tremendous sense of period, reminiscent of Chaucer and medieval churches, would have hardly made satisfactory toys. They were probably far more in the nature of Staffordshire chimney ornaments, to be enjoyed by a child, but at a distance. The figures could not have been dressed, cuddled or dropped, and certainly appear more in the nature of ornaments than as a development in the history of the doll. If a child could, quite commonly, see jointed marionettes at fairs, she was unlikely to be satisfied for long with a stiff figure, more like a pilgrim's offering than the rag dolls which she would have found more satisfying.

The pipe clay figures, which vary between 3 and 6 inches high, do indicate the type of clothes which other dolls of the period would have worn. The variety of head-dresses and the detail of different costumes gives an awareness of the large number of moulds that must have been available. The Finland National Museum has a fragment of a clay doll of this type, which was probably originally made in Cologne, and taken to Finland in a merchant's stock.

Doll-making was, by the fifteenth century, very firmly established in Germany, and the first-recorded makers of dolls, Ott and Mess, make their appearance in 1465 as *Docken macher*, a term used at the time for makers of toys in general, though the two named makers are believed to have made dolls. Regrettably there is no mention of the type of dolls which these two men made, but it is possible that they were makers of figures similar to those illustrated in the *Hortus Sanitatis* of 1491, which shows a Nürnberg doll-maker at his work. One man handles the torso of a doll while appearing to be in the process of fixing on an arm, indicating joints at the shoulder, while another unfinished doll lying on a table is still without its lower legs, indicating jointing of the lower limbs also. The obvious conclusion is that wooden jointed dolls were commercially produced in large numbers by the middle of the fifteenth century.

The making of German dolls at this time was, according to Dr Mannfred Bachmann, a free craft, not limited by very tight guild rules, so that dolls were often made as a minor industry by craftsmen of various trades. The members of the guilds were naturally only allowed to make dolls from their own special material, so that the joiners made wooden dolls, the potters clay, and the metal workers tin figures.

From the fifteenth century onwards, merchants depended to a much greater

1   Thai dancer
2   Seventeenth-century wooden torso
3   Pair of seventeenth-century wooden dolls

extent on luxury needs. As most countries produced their own basic necessities, the foreign merchant was welcome only as a supplier of spices, textiles and jewels that gave country life some magnificence. The French in particular had a good reputation for luxury goods, among which were beautifully-made dolls. "Charming and attractively dressed dolls" were seen by Antoine Astérau, a contemporary traveller, in shops at the Palais de Justice, where they were offered for sale alongside other expensive frivolities. In 1455, Raoulin de la Rue was responsible for providing the daughter of Charles VII with a doll which represented a woman on horseback accompanied by a footman. The idea of a life-size Pandora to illustrate fashion was still very popular, and Ann of Brittany commissioned a large doll for Queen Isabella of Spain to show her the French mode. These *grandes Pandores* were as much symbols of the status of the giver as functional objects, and the costumes were decorated with great ostentation. As the clothes were quite probably worn by the recipient, there appear to be no surviving examples, but judging by their cost they must have been extremely splendid.

Though children during the medieval period were frequently neglected and often learned little, there is scant evidence of actual physical cruelty. The Tudor period sees a very different state of affairs. The noble child, who might be given a luxury doll from the Palais de Justice, might suffer like Elizabeth Paston, who did not want to marry an old and ugly widower of fifty, and was consequently beaten for nearly three months on end "once in the week or twice, sometimes twice in one day and her head broken in two or three places". It is salutary to note that her mother was a highly-respected woman of religious principle. The 'belashing' of boys and girls in an effort to make them receptive, either to learning or their parents' wishes, was quite common, and they also suffered under a hard home and school discipline. From being lightly regarded, education had become extremely important, especially to children of the merchant classes, as it was by such learning that the families' business prospects could be improved. Very little was spared in forcing such knowledge into an unwilling child. Girls were still sent to other households as they had been in previous centuries, and were often pledged in marriage at six or eight years old, so that many were said to go to their bridegroom clutching a doll, which they found far more absorbing than the equally bored boy. Just as the old code of chivalry had little in common with real life, so late medieval love poetry had very little relevance to the girl, who was simply an inheritance symbol. If her family was unsuccessful in mating her, they would relieve themselves of the responsibility for the girl by placing her, on payment of a dowry, in a nunnery. Many of the females in convents at this time were very young, and were even seen to play with dolls, to the disgust of thinking churchmen.

4 Eighteenth-century carved doll

The inculcation of fear, both into the father-child relationship and into that of the master and servant, was a reflection of the attitude of the European church of the period. Christ was represented as an awful and terrible judge, and this fear encouraged the late medieval cult of Mary and the Saints, who might be persuaded to intercede for unworthy man. This cult led to an ever-increasing number of images, made in particular from alabaster, which was quarried in England in Derbyshire and Nottingham, and sent to London to be carved. Small alabaster figures were made in the tradition that had existed since the Romans. This need to see actual images of the saints encouraged the popularity of the crèche, even in remote country districts, where they provided yet another spectacle for the people. At Witney in Oxfordshire, a play was performed each year which portrayed the Resurrection of Our Lord, and the priests would arrange the puppets to represent the characters. The most interesting of these was the 'waking watchman' who, on seeing Christ arise, would begin to cluck like a hen!

Such folk figures were quite commonly seen, and must have provided a guide to many a country craftsman making simple jointed dolls for sale at local fairs; for though the Dutch and Germans were exporting dolls in quantity, it is unlikely that they supplied all the cheap dolls sold at fairs.

The Renaissance: The Sixteenth Century

The standard of dolls had improved during the late fourteenth and fifteenth centuries, and the quality dolls that are referred to appear to have been sumptuous. The dolls of the Renaissance are perpetuated by such paintings as Cranach's *Charitas*, showing a little girl clutching a rather stiff doll, and the painting by an unknown artist of Lady Arabella Stuart, who carries a doll dressed very lavishly in Tudor dress. Lady Arabella's doll appears to be jointed at shoulder and elbow, and the face was painted realistically. It is unlikely that the painters would have idealized the appearance of the dolls, so that we must conclude that the dolls of wealthy children were artistically finished and actually beautiful in their original state. A doll painted by Cranach the Younger also appears to have good articulation in the upper part of the body, though the skirt area is as stiff as that of the doll held by Arabella Stuart. Possibly the petticoats were made very stiffly or, as has been suggested by other writers, the legs and lower torso were dispensed with, and the figure rested on a conical framework or shaped wooden base. The doll painted by the younger Cranach has the most beautifully-detailed carved hands, and the figure appears to wear a wig. The dolls carried by all these noble children are in lovely pristine condition, and it is possible that the dolls were bought especially for the child to hold in the picture, as they show no signs of having been played with. The frequent inclusion of dolls and toys in paintings of this period indicates that the doll was quite commonplace, in the lives of wealthy children and of little peasants as well. Despite the number of dolls illustrated in paintings, disappointingly few actual dolls remain: an oak stump doll, a few fine wooden dolls and one of rag are all that are known to survive from an age that produced the dolls of great artistry which can be seen in prints and paintings.

Despite the notion that the spirit of the Renaissance was one that manifested itself mainly in artistic expression and scientific discovery, a greater awareness of the needs of children did develop, and adults of the period appear to have found children more interesting. The sixteenth century saw the publication of the first book on paediatrics, *The Boke of Chyldren* by Thomas Phaire, which described the many "grevous and perilous diseases" which commonly affected children. His awesome list includes "terryble dreams, styfness of limmes, bloud-shotten eyes, scabbynesse and ytch and Colyke and rumbling in the guttes". These rather worrying complaints were rivalled by remedies such as the brains of a hare mixed with honey and, as most diseases were conveniently attributed to teething, a wide variety of aids to help the teeth come through were suggested. The first cast tooth of a colt set in a silver mount had apparently proved useful, as was a piece of red coral hung about the neck, on which the child could "labour his gummes". Ignorance and neglect caused a high mortality rate, so that Montaigne could remark that he had lost three children at nurse "not without regret but without grief".

Though there was more interest in children, it should not be thought that they were treated more gently or with greater consideration. The child had to apply himself completely to his learning, which began very early in life, so that prodigies of ten or eleven wrote Latin letters and entertained visitors with their fund of classical knowledge. Girls as well as boys from noble and wealthy merchant families were now educated. "A little girl ought to learn Latin. It puts a finishing touch to her charms", wrote Cardinal Bembo. One little girl, Lucy Apsley, could read fluently at the age of three, and liked only academic subjects. When forced to play with other children "I tired them with more instructions than their mothers and plucked all their babies to pieces" – a reference to the rag dolls which are known to have been common but have not survived.

Not all children thrived on the academic discipline; some positively wilted, such as Massimiliano Sforza, the little Duke of Milan, who had one aim in life – not to go to school. He refused to be interested in the beautiful miniatures that were especially painted to illustrate his school books, and, after an enforced stay in Germany, he returned to Milan with shocking and gross manners and a convenient forgetfulness of both reading and writing! Apparently the elegant Renaissance spirit was weak in Germany.

Continental parents were very strict with their children, but the English were reputed to be quite brutal. Birch rods were sold in the streets by pedlars crying "Buy my fine Jemmies; buy my London Tartars", and as a final insult to the child, these birches were added to his school bill. An Italian traveller visiting England in the reign of Henry VII commented:

> The want of affection in the English towards their children is a marked feature. Having kept them at home until the age of seven or nine, they then board them out, both boys and girls, to hard service in the houses of other people. Few are born who are exempted from this fate. For everyone, however rich he be, sends away his children into the houses of others while he in turn receives the children of strangers into his own. On my enquiring the reason for this severity they said that they did it in order that their children might learn better manners.

Renaissance paintings suggest an idyllic childhood. A plump little girl dressed in a practical short dress peeps from behind a door; the children of a Swedish count play with war toys in an allegorical manner, and happy-faced little girls clutch dolls. It should, however, be remembered that such paintings probably had as little relation to actual childhood of the period as had medieval love poetry to men and women of the time. In studying the paintings and prints of the period, the conditions, often of positive cruelty, under which many of these children lived should not be forgotten. There are of course some attractive customs relating to childhood in this period, such as the rolling of newborn infants in red rose petals, and the strewing of sweet-scented flowers on the floor of the lying-in room, customs somehow more evocative of the Renaissance than the fact that nearly half of all children died in their first few months of life.

The making of fine-quality luxury dolls, such as those sold in the Palais de Justice, continued into the sixteenth century, when even greater detail was given to the figures. Fortunately, one such doll of the period survives dating from 1590. This doll, now in the Royal Armoury Collection in Stockholm, is reputed to have belonged to one of the daughters of Charles IX, and reflects precisely the fashionable ladies' costume of the period. Though fashion dolls are known to have existed before this time, no known examples have survived, which gives this particular figure importance in the documentation of the history of the doll. It illustrates how deceptive the description 'rag doll' can be, as this is not the cheap and tatty object conjured up by the description, but a princess's gift, and it raises the possibility of other dolls of comparable quality having been made earlier in time out of this humble substance.

The construction of the Stockholm doll is interesting, as the figure is built up over a wire armature swathed in unspun rose and yellow silk thread, which creates a small figure rather like the pin men we drew as children. The real hair is braided and decorated with a diadem of pearls, and the features are

36 Print of a sixteenth-century Dutch market place. The doll-seller offers a good variety of well-costumed wares.

37 Few early rag dolls survive, though many were made. This figure, mounted as a decoration to a needle-case, dates from the late seventeenth century. The costume is possibly an attempt to represent court dress. Figure built up over an armature of thin stick. Hair made of silk threads. Embroidered face. Silver brocade dress. $2\frac{1}{4}$ in. high.

embroidered on the fabric of the face in what appears to be a humble manner for so costly a doll. The luxurious costume consists of a skirt and bodice, together with two petticoats. One petticoat is of cut and uncut velvet, while the other is made of silk taffeta. The loose sleeves of the costume are embroidered with real pearls and the doll carries an embroidered muff. A simple linen chemise is all that is worn as underwear. This doll is a joy to the student of costume, as it has been left untouched, and gives a precise description of the fashion of the period and the method of wearing it.

It appears strange that such an expensive costume doll should have been made on a comparatively poor figure, when finely-made artists' lay figures, usually of beech, were quite freely available. These figures, which were in general use by the sixteenth century, were fully articulated, and could bend and turn not only their limbs but also the torso and head by means of skilful jointing at these points. Dürer was once considered to have carved the lay figures which he used for his paintings himself, but they are now thought to have been made by the woodcarvers of the Regensburg Salzburg School. Such finely-articulated lay figures would appear to have been ideal for use as fashion dolls, but apparently were not utilized in such a way. Some of the lay figures were reputed to have been made by artists such as El Greco, and were usually of wood, though there are references to some with heads and hands of wax with the usual ball-jointed bodies. Max von Boehn suggested that as similar figures were often found in pairs, they were of an amorous nature, but it would seem more likely that an artist found it useful to have a lay figure of either sex.

The lay figure can always be distinguished from both dolls and crèche figures by the complete realism of proportion and the accurate articulation, not necessary in a doll, which, for instance, usually has feet and hands that are much too small. The heads of lay figures are often left completely plain, though presumably the examples with wax heads were carved to represent specific characters. I have on several occasions been offered lay figures as 'very early dolls' but, though a delight to handle, they cannot be classified as dolls in the truest sense, so that quite respectably early lay figures can be bought comparatively cheaply, and are often utilized by interior decorators as decorative objects.

Paris continued to be of great importance in doll-making during the sixteenth century. Many foreign nobles and rulers ordered dolls to be made as gifts. In 1571, the Duchess Claudia of Lorraine ordered four to six of the most beautifully-dressed dolls that could be found for the daughter of the Duchess of Bavaria. The agent was instructed that the dolls should not be too large, as they were intended for a new baby. The six dolls bought by Henry II for his daughters cost him 9 francs, which was then a large sum, and in 1530 the Emperor Charles V had spent 10 francs on one similar doll for his daughter. The figures mentioned are all play dolls, and despite their high cost were intended for the amusement of the recipients. As some of the surviving dolls of the period are of cabinet size, it is probable that some were made for the diversion of adults or older children.

The dolls of the nursery were more cheaply made, and included stump dolls carved from one solid piece of wood, a technique popular since ancient times. As some of these stump dolls are primitive in the extreme, they are occasionally confused with dolls that originated in more modern primitive tribes, and extreme scepticism needs to be exercised when such an object comes up for sale. The problem is further complicated by carved figures, usually of women, taken from sixteenth- and seventeenth-century furniture where they originally formed perhaps an arm support or the decoration of a court cupboard. The collector is unlikely to be offered a genuine stump doll, and should be very wary of any dealer who claims to possess one. A good genuine example of such a doll is in the London Museum and dates from 1600. The figure wears a long dress and a small ruff around the neck. The doll is shaped rather like a skittle, but the torso has more shape than would be found on actual skittles, which also sometimes masquerade under the title of embryonic dolls. Gouged-out grooves suggest the folds in the dress of the museum example, and when painted, such a doll could have looked attractive. The doll indicates the construction of many of the beautiful stiff wooden dolls seen in paintings and prints of the period, sometimes accompanied by a toy cradle.

Male dolls appear to have become more popular during the sixteenth century, and several are recorded. These male dolls sometimes took the form of jointed knights, mounted on horses that were also jointed. In an example in the Bayerisches National Museum, Munich, the knight wears a black leather jacket with long sleeves over very well-made armour. In a French woodcut of 1587, another jointed knight doll is illustrated, which has been placed astride a dog by the children who owned it. This figure again wears armour that is beautifully constructed.

There was a renewed interest in automata, and Bernadino Baldi perfected a means of constructing figures that worked on a hydraulic system. In Italy also, another fine spectacle were the grottoes made by Thomas de Francici which contained moving figures, and were a great attraction for children. Peep-shows, where the objects were carefully arranged to give an illusion of the depth of perspective, were also very popular, as were the Jumping Jacks, the poor child's automata, simple examples of which could be bought at fairs, together with puppets and Jacks-in-the-box.

Pipe clay was still a popular medium for the construction of dolls, and one elegant lady with a draped head-dress and a low-cut dress dates from 1525. Some of the pipe clay dolls are almost as simple as those made of wood, despite the fact that, being cast from a mould, a detailed finish could more easily have been given. A fine limewood doll, measuring 9 inches high, was discovered as recently as 1966 behind the panelling of a Rhenish castle. With a high domed forehead and round face, the doll epitomizes the middle-class German woman of the period. Such wooden dolls were made in large numbers in Germany and Holland, and in Nürnberg there were seventeen workshops devoted exclusively to the manufacture of dolls. One Bamberg maker was a woman named Barbara Beuchin, and she was given permission to sell the dolls that she had made in the market-place. A woodcut of the period shows a stall run by a woman in a Dutch market. The woman offers an astonishing selection of dolls and toys to the apparently bourgeois customers. Apart from some small and rather stiff dolls, such as are often seen in woodcuts of the period, the stallholder is also selling fine jointed dolls about 36 inches high, that could sit and appear to have been quite realistic. Small male dolls are also displayed for sale wearing military costume. The standard of all these dolls appears to be very high, especially when it is considered that they were being sold to poorer children. Were such dolls discovered now in good condition, they would no doubt be classed as 'fashion dolls' of the period. Perhaps the doll in the Stockholm Museum is not quite as unique as collectors like to think.

An interesting doll is shown in an illustration for *Kunst und Lehrbüchlein*, published in 1580. A girl carries a doll which appears to have been made of a substance other than wood, as the arms hang limply. Possibly the doll was constructed partly of fabric or leather. The print also illustrates the custom of dressing a doll in a miniature replica of the clothes the child owner wears, which is also seen in sixteenth- and seventeenth-century portraits.

Earthenware dolls were now becoming much more common, and were imported into England from Germany and the Low Countries by the beginning of the century. A book of rates for 1550 quotes a set rate for: "Babies and puppets for children, the groce containing twelve dozen, thirteen shillings and fourpence and babies heads of earth the dozen ten shillings." Despite the large number of earthenware heads that must have been sold, to the time of writing none are known to have survived; they appear to have been as elusive as dolls of alabaster which have also, despite their apparent durability, disappeared.

Though wood was the most popular doll-making material, it was followed by dolls of a composition substance, which was cheap to produce and simple to mould. In his *Traité d'Architecture* of 1567 Philibert Delorme describes dolls made of paper paste pressed into hollow moulds. Such dolls were not made exclusively of paper pulp, and often all sorts of waste materials such as bran, vegetable matter and sawdust were combined to make a pulp. Another, more sinister, ingredient of such moulded figures was arsenic, used to prevent the mixture being eaten by rats. In 1564, 2s. was paid for sufficient arsenic to treat paper-pulp figures that were being constructed for a pageant, and the arsenic appears to have been a recognized ingredient of the mixture. Most dolls made in this way were produced in Nürnberg and the surrounding area, as the doll-makers utilized the waste materials from the paper mills, and had the skill to create out of this cheap product attractive dolls that were exported across Europe to France and England. As dolls made of composition substances are even more fragile than wood, and prone to distortion by heat and damp, it is little wonder that no surviving examples are known.

Cabinet collections have already been mentioned as enjoying popularity in the sixteenth century, and whereas some were in the form of peep-shows, others were more in the nature of the doll's house as we know it today. One particularly fine house is known to have existed. It was commissioned by Albrecht V, Duke of Bavaria, in 1558 for his daughter. Our knowledge of the contents of this house is derived from a printed inventory made before the house was destroyed by fire. The chapel was complete with priests and musicians, and the sewing-room peopled with ladies at work. It was probably for art doll's houses such as this that some of the fine small dolls such as that in the Armoury collection were made. Wax was also used for cabinet dolls, and some wax heads were made in such a way that the substance was rock-hard, according to a contemporary source.

The waxen figure has been connected with witchcraft from ancient times, though actual toy dolls do not appear to have been used for such purposes. As early as 1441, the Duchess of Gloucester was charged that, by sorcery and witchcraft, she intended to destroy the King, by making a waxen image of him. The English and Scottish witch trials are rich in references to 'waxen images', and in 1609 Frances Lady Essex employed a witch to make her husband impotent, and so secure an annulment of marriage. Small wax images were used to this end. One figure was that of a naked woman 'spreading and laying forth her hair', and another was sumptuously dressed in silks and satins. Both sound more aphrodisiac than otherwise.

Waxen images were also recommended for the use of priests in exorcism. The priest would make an image of the possessing devil, and adding a suitable epithet would throw the figure into the flames. Though figures connected with witchcraft are referred to as dolls, and one unfortunate woman suspected of witchcraft was burned because she had some children's dolls in her possession, they appear usually to have been figures specially constructed for magical purposes, incorporating some tissue of the person to be bewitched. No confusion of the two appears to have arisen except in the Ingoldsby Legends, when a little girl finds an image of her father stuck with pins and plays with it as a doll.

Another sixteenth-century development was an increase in the number of available doll accessories, so that children are illustrated changing their dolls' clothes, feeding them from miniature dishes and putting them to bed in cradles. There was a much more varied pattern to the dolls that were produced, and though German makers still led the field, dolls are known to have been made elsewhere. The rigid regulations of the trade guilds were a hindrance to the toy-makers; one rule, for instance, was that dolls' heads could only be finished by craftsmen painters, which meant that the product had to be passed from one worker to another, and could not be completed in one workshop. Consequently, though the industry was expanding, it was hampered by its self-imposed restrictions.

The Seventeenth Century

Our knowledge regarding the variety of toys available in the early seventeenth century depends largely on the memoirs of Dr Jean Heroard, the Physician in Charge to the little Dauphin, later Louis XIII of France. Though the toys described by him are obviously of a more exotic nature than the average merchant-class child of the time could have owned, they do indicate the range of toys that were available for wealthy children. Among the more unusual toys was a fountain made of glass, that could pump up water, and a small drum beaten by a lady-doll worked by strings. The doctor paints an attractive picture of the young Louis, dressed in his own miniature suit of armour, and pulling along a silver cannon tied to his pinafore with one of his garters. His toys included earthenware figures, lead and pewter soldiers, drums and swords. The toy knights that were popular in the sixteenth century also had their place in the royal nursery, and the Dauphin owned not only a knight on horseback, but also a similarly-mounted Turkish trumpeter. The making of pairs of dolls representing Christians and Infidels was popular, and the costumes offered splendid opportunities for the toy-maker. So good, indeed, was the armour on such toy figures, that early collectors of militaria classified the armour they had worn as miniature suits in the nature of apprentice pieces or traveller's samples. Their frequent presence in prints of the sixteenth and seventeenth centuries and their description by Heroard as playthings of the Dauphin classifies them as dolls' costume.

One of the male dolls, similar to those that had been sold on stalls in the sixteenth century, was also owned by the Prince, though his doll was predictably well dressed, wearing a scented ruff embroidered with gold thread, and matching tights. The Dauphin was so pleased with this particular doll that he said that he would marry it to his sister's doll, possibly the beauty that the Count d'Osni had given her. The Duke had sent the Dauphin at the same time a coach in which rode several dolls, including one representing 'my mistress the Infanta'. The coach was accompanied by another male doll in armour, which the Dauphin could use for his war games.

The younger sisters owned several miniature rooms which contained dolls. One bedroom showed a lying-in scene, apparently a popular subject for such rooms, with a midwife supervising the mother and child who lay in bed. Some of their miniature rooms contained dolls enacting scenes, such as Holofernes with Judith in the act of slaying him: not a subject that would appeal to a modern parent! The Prince and Princesses also owned plaster dolls and a little earthenware monk which probably resembled the pipe clay baptismal dolls discussed earlier.

The lot of the Continental child had improved, and by the end of the seventeenth century it was thought that forcing a boy to submit to beating was degrading to his dignity, though unfortunately no such scruples affected the new-found puritanical zeal of the English parents, who continued to treat their children as harshly as ever. The fate of the poor foundling child was, paradoxically, better than it was to become in the eighteenth century. Fed, clothed and looked after by the benefactors of the various charitable institutions that had been set up, his lot was probably much better than it would have been in a peasant home, especially as he would later be trained in a useful skill such as spinning.

Many English children were infected by the unhealthy puritanical zeal of their parents and teachers. One child of four "became very solicitous about her soul and everlasting condition, weeping bitterly to think what would become of her in another world."[*] The children of that century were continually reminded of the brevity of life, and a proper awareness of the trials of death and hell fire was given by taking them to executions and showing them corpses. In some households, toys of all kinds were forbidden, and the children were expected to stop their friends from enjoying themselves too much. Books such as *A Token for Children; being an exact account of the conversation Holy and Exemplary Lives and Joyful Deaths of Several young Children* were studied, so that the child would be given an awareness of how he should live a life of religious ecstasy and die 'with the Saviour's name on his lips'. In another book of 1672, a little girl looks sadly at her reflection in a looking glass and comments,

> "What a pity such a pretty maid
> As I should go to Hell."

John Bunyan wrote of the terrible visions of hell that were made to haunt the dreams of his childhood. One little child prayed "with such extraordinary meltings that his eyes have looked red and sore with weeping by himself for his sins".[†] Encouraged by their parents' praise for their piety, these children apparently wallowed in weeping for their little transgressions.

[*] Quoted by Pinchbeck and Hewett in *Children in English Society*.   [†] Ibid.

Death was, however, always very near, and brothers and friends were often lost during childhood, so that the constant admonitions of their nurses and tutors fell on ears that already knew something of the fraility of life. Mrs Thrale, in a letter, regarded the death of her various daughters at school with "great equanimity", and Sir Charles Verney remarked that though he had lost several children, he still had left a baker's dozen. Despite the fact that parents prepared their children to be carried off to the next world at any moment, this does not appear to have made them more lenient in their treatment. Fathers often flogged their children regularly for the good of their souls and for the wrongs that had not been discovered.

> Remember that when no one else watches,
> The angels are still there.

Against the cruelly religious upbringing of the seventeenth-century English child, the sentimental religiosity of the Victorians seems flabby and harmless.

This century is a period of great contradictions: on one side rigid puritanism, and on the other excesses of behaviour both sexual and moral. The simple life purposely led by an English Puritan contrasted strongly with the ostentatious display of Continental merchants, typified by the mania for collecting costly objects to be included in cabinet collections. This collecting craze reached its peak in the construction of display cases in the form of miniature houses to contain small items of silver and porcelain. These 'doll's houses' were exhibited as status symbols in the homes of wealthy merchants, and being adult toys not prone to the devastation of the nursery, the figures they contained have often survived intact.

Probably the best known art cabinet at the time was that given by the town of Augsburg to King Gustavus Adolphus in 1632, which included a pair of dolls that have survived. These dolls measure about 10 centimetres and represent a cavalier and his lady dancing. The mechanism by which they worked is now broken, but they stand hand-in-hand waiting to begin. The male doll is dressed in silks and lace and can move his head, while the female, whose head is lost, is dressed in yellow and rose-coloured silk. The figures are made and dressed in great detail, considering their size, and it is thought that they represented the best dolls available in Germany at the time.

Some rooms were made to contain models of characters known personally to the recipient, such as the wax dolls which inhabited a *Chambre du Sublime* given as a gift to the Duc du Maine in 1675. This room was gilded, and contained a likeness of the Duke himself and his court friends diverting themselves by reading poetry.

One German lady became financially embarrassed through spending too much money on her art doll's house, while Anna Köferlin of Nürnberg assembled a fine house which she exhibited with an accompanying pamphlet, in which she explained how children could learn how to run a house by playing with such a toy. The dolls included in such Nürnberg houses were usually made of wax, and were about 9 centimetres high. Despite their small size, the finish of such figures was so good that they were necessarily expensive.

Dolls were still a very popular gift among the nobility. A woodcarver, Mathias Schutz, worked especially for the court at Munich, making and mending quality dolls. Royal children were presented with dolls that could be dressed and undressed, and others were accompanied by huge wardrobes, such as that given to the future Duchesse de Longueville. The larger dolls now appear to have become the preserve of children, and references to dolls given as gifts usually apply to cabinet dolls, except in the case of the genuine fashion figures.

The doll's house that belonged to Margaretha de Ruyter, now in the Rijksmuseum, contains wax dolls that are very beautifully made. Ranging in size from 12 to 20 centimetres, their modelling is of excellent quality, and the different characters inhabiting the house are virtually small portraits in wax. The lady-dolls wear the precise costume of the period, and there are even child dolls wearing the ribbons from the back of the dress known as leading strings, which would be held by an adult when the child was learning to walk. The head would be protected by a padded cap in case of falls. A baby doll also lies in a wicker cradle, showing again that baby dolls have been made for centuries.

Wax was still used popularly for the making of dolls. A German maker, Daniel Neuberger, was praised for the strength and realism of his dolls, while Mrs Goldsmith in England was famous for her life-size waxen models. The Duchess of Richmond, known as La Belle Stuart, was among many famous people that she modelled, and this particular effigy cost £260. It was also a popular custom among wealthy people to have their favourite dead children modelled in wax and the figures, if they were of babies, would lie in the vacated cradle. Waxworks were popular fairground attractions for the people, and shows such as the Temple of Diana occupied a pitch in the centuries-old Bartholomew Fair.

Prints of the seventeenth century show that quite ordinary children played with dolls as a matter of course. An engraving of 1665 illustrating children's games shows two little girls playing with dolls, toy crockery and a cradle, while other engravings include children playing with dolls as an ordinary event. When Lady Jordan, who was at Cirencester when it was besieged, became deranged and returned in mind to her childhood, the servants "made Babies for her to play withall", just as she had done each day when a child. Surprisingly few actual dolls have survived from this period, considering their commonplace nature, presumably because the dolls were thought to be of little value and discarded like outgrown clothes.

The fascination of mechanical figures to the common people was still very strong, and they were delighted by such figures as one shown in fairs which opened and shut its mouth and rolled its eyes grotesquely. Many good mechanical figures were made by German craftsmen, such as those taken to the Court of Peter of Russia, to whose instincts such play figures held great appeal The German craftsmen took him canaries that sang, as well as walking dolls, the first reference to dolls capable of this feat, apart from the dancing pair that belonged to Gustavus Adolphus. The method by which these dolls walked is unknown, but it was probably some sort of a wheeled system. Peter's own favourite toys were a pair of lions that stood either side of his throne and rolled their eyes, wagged their tails and opened wide their jaws. These figures were skilfully operated by a pair of bellows.

Papier mâché dolls were becoming even more common, and were now made not only in Nürnberg, but also at Sonneberg, whose industry had been less affected by the Thirty Years War. Another reason for the emergence of Sonneberg as a great toy centre was the fact that the makers were given an exemption from taxes and duties which equalled that given to the Nürnberg merchants at public markets. There were now seventeen specialist doll-makers in the Nürnberg area alone, and, due to the availability of the waste materials from local industry, it is likely that many of these made composition dolls. An illustration in Weigel's *Haupstande* of 1698 shows doll-makers working on this substance. Some of the heads they are producing appear to be of a grotesque nature and intended for pageants and carnivals, but smaller heads intended for dolls are also shown. These heads were made by pressing the pulped waste matter into a greased mould and simply removing them after they had contracted because of the drying process. Very early dolls of this type, of which no known examples have survived, are thought to have had heads that were smooth and round and to have been made with nicely-moulded breasts. A late seventeenth-century swaddling baby in the Museum of Decorative Art in Paris was given a fine plaster finish before it was painted. This beautifully-decorated Italian figure wears a glass necklace and a somewhat incongruous cloth bonnet. Apart from the making of swaddling babies and crèche figures out of this substance, small statuettes of saints, such as St Nicholas were also made, intended to be given to children on church feast days and played with as toys.

Christoff Weigel discusses in his book the various types of dolls made during his lifetime, and includes, apart from dolls of wax and paper pulp, the edible toys of gum tragacanth that had been popular in the previous century. He is full of praise for the wood turner, and comments that this craftsman was able to make many attractive dolls in the form of rattles, which were made in particular in Thuringia, though of course simple turned dolls were produced in most countries, especially Russia and Sweden. There is an interesting reference to wooden Nürnberg dolls of the period that were covered in cloth and had painted faces, but once again no examples of the type are known. The early seventeenth-century Sonneberg dolls were of simply-painted wood and had carved wooden limbs. The Sonneberg carvers gave their dolls small waists and slim hips, in contrast to the less shapely early dolls from the Alpine countries. According to some authorities glued-on noses have also been added, which enables them to be distinguished from the French and English wooden dolls of the period. The dolls that were made sound very like the Penny Woodens the Victorians knew, or the Flanders babies of the eighteenth century.

So fine was the woodcarving produced in the Oberammergau area that, in 1681, the craftsmen formed themselves into a carvers' guild and styled themselves artists rather than craftsmen. Wooden dancing dolls were made at Berchtesgaden, which was famous in addition for miniature ivory toys. These dancing dolls were also a speciality of the Sicilians, who brought them to England to perform in the streets and markets.

The doll by the end of the century had become an accepted article of commerce, even as far afield as America. A few dolls had previously travelled to this new country as gifts for the Indians, but with the rapid increase of emigration from Europe, children of the new country wanted dolls of their own. In 1695, Higginson wrote to England for dolls that he wanted to sell in America, and presumably others were imported from Europe. The most famous early doll connected with America is that taken by William Penn when he went to Pennsylvania in 1699, which has the typical, slightly-slanted eyes of the early wooden dolls now wearing eighteenth-century costume. American settlers also began to produce dolls of their own, as there were in their number craftsmen who had worked in Europe making wooden articles. Pinewood was obviously a popular medium, and the dolls were often made with the bonnet in one piece with the body, like a stump doll. One extremely unusual early American doll represents a negro boy, who was given pearl buttons for his eyes.

Throughout the century there is an interesting contrast between the richly-dressed dolls that are recorded, and the rather spartan lives led by the children who owned them, more especially in England. The only doll that really appears to retain the spirit of England in the seventeenth century is that often-photographed Puritan lady of oak, carved in the form of a stump doll. We have to conclude, however, that such dolls were not really typical, and that children's toys closely reflected the wealthy society of the period, even when they were intended for middle-class sale. The puritanical zeal of the seventeenth-century

English does not appear to have had much effect upon the dolls that were made and dressed in beautiful clothes. The most finely dressed figures of the late seventeenth century are the pair of jointed wooden dolls known to the family that once owned them as Lord and Lady Clapham. With their over large heads that are carved with some realism, the dolls conform to the seventeenth century English style, seen also in engravings, of carving the heads on a larger scale than the bodies. These dolls are of great importance as, seen in conjunction with the carving of the Old Pretender figure they set a definite native style for the period. Among the taxes levied to protect British industry was one relating to wooden dolls, so that the manufacture must have been well established.

The importance of Lord and Lady Clapham as costume documents is discussed in a short paper which was issued by the Victoria and Albert Museum, and which commented on the almost total lack of any other good visual source material of the period. They wear semi-formal Fashionable Undress and are accompanied by a wardrobe of 'undress' robes. The man wears a red woollen coat with silver tissue cuffs and buttons that matched the material of his waistcoat and breeches. Well made leather shoes were worn with metal buckles affixed with buttons. The shirt was provided with long tails that could be wrapped around the thighs as men of this time did not usually wear underpants. He was also provided with a nightshirt, kid gauntlet gloves, and a banyan of salmon pink satin of French or Italian origin.

Lady Clapham wears a mantua with the train held in place with loops and buttons, a garment of great importance as it stands at the beginning of the evolution of the eighteenth-century gowns. A cap with lappets has a frill that is given vertical emphasis by a wire support. Right at the back of the head can be seen a knot of coiled hair twined with pink ribbon, known as a choux. This doll is also accompanied by an undress gown that indicated the move in fashion towards the later sack. Until the museum saw this miniature it had been unaware there was any difference in cut between the undress gown of men and women.

The 'Old Pretender' doll now at the Bethnal Green Museum is another fine example of the period, the hands being particularly stylised. On the face the doll wears the patches that had been a popular decoration since the middle of the century when, in a book called *The Artificial Changeling*, it was commented that: "Our ladies have lately entertained a vain custom of spotting their faces, out of an affectation of a mole, to set off their beauty, such as Venus had: and it is well if one black patch will serve to make their faces remarkable, for some fill their visages full of them, varied into all manner of shapes." Though the patches worn by the doll in question are round and few in number, some took the form of a coach and horses, and could be seen driving across fashionable society faces.

THREE

THE EIGHTEENTH CENTURY

It is fitting that a century which saw a much greater interest in childhood and methods of up-bringing should offer to the modern collector some of the toys and dolls that the children of the eighteenth century owned. Though many dolls have survived from this period, most have already been absorbed into good collections, and only occasionally come on the market; and naturally when they do, they command high prices, if in an acceptable condition. It is fortunate that an increasing number of dealers now specialize in dolls, so that the collector is able to acquire interesting dolls without years of searching market stalls and junk shops in the rather vain hope of finding a really early doll. The specialist dealers have contacts who scour shops and sales over the whole of Europe to provide them with their stock, so that the individual collector has to have a great deal of luck to find early examples very cheaply. It is probably more economical in the long run to pay the often high cost the dealer requires, rather than spend fruitless years in hunting for a specific type of doll.

The wealthy eighteenth-century child was often pampered and indulged to an absurd degree by its parents who, perhaps with little understanding, tried to follow the strictures of educationalists. Though Montaigne was read on the Continent, he was not widely followed in England, but his ideas filtered into the down-to-earth policies of Locke, who advised such startling innovations as allowing the young to wear comfortable clothes and take outdoor exercise, including swimming and games. In the previous century, children had been kept indoors a great deal and dressed in tightly-fitting, restricting clothes, which were often removed only when the child's presence became offensive. The new idea of bathing children regularly was one that took two centuries to become thoroughly established in English-speaking countries! Some of Locke's ideas were hardly conducive to the happiness of children as, among others, he advocated that the child should be fed very irregularly, in order that he should become used to going hungry for long periods and eventually learn to transcend the pangs of hunger entirely.

He was scornful of the parents who indulged their young by buying them elaborate and expensive toys, and thought that children should be encouraged to create their own toys out of what lay at hand. The English pedagogues, Maria Edgworth and her father, were influenced by the ideas of Locke, and suggested such modern-sounding toys as pieces of wood cut into squares and triangles, with holes drilled into them, so that the child could learn how to construct interesting forms or buildings. They also advised that children should be allowed to play with delightful substances like modelling clay and wax, so that their creative instincts would be encouraged. In some of their ideas the Edgworths were of course influenced by Rousseau, whose *Emile*, sometimes called the children's charter, was a book that was read by fashionable parents. Harriet Wilson the courtesan talks scathingly of her fashionable sister's children, who ran about the house naked, behaved as the mood took them and explored one another's sexual organs with a lively interest, because their parents wished to be thought progressive and follow the 'noble savage' ideal of Rousseau. Some of his ideas when put into practice were extremely destructive, as he believed that children should only learn when they wanted to, and there should never be any punishment. Fortunately, his theories were too obviously damaging to society to be adopted by many sensible parents, who found the ideas more palatable when watered down by the Edgworths.

Rousseau did believe, however, that little girls should be encouraged to dress dolls, as "In due time she will be her own doll", and have learned how to dress herself by her play dress-making. The Edgworths also commended dolls, as they considered that they would inspire girls to neatness and good taste in clothes, and so encourage them to "make those things for themselves for which women are usually dependent upon milliners". The love of 'finery and fashion' which playing with expensively-dressed dolls encouraged was predictably frowned upon, as were the beautifully-made and furnished doll's houses of the period, which to the Edgworths were only good if empty, thus encouraging the child to furnish them and make various items herself. A coach and horses with doll passengers, a popular toy of the period, was similarly disparaged – far better a no-nonsense wheelbarrow that could be played with inventively and usefully. Though their strictures were probably excellent as regards the child's development, it is fortunate for the collector of toys and dolls that their ideas for 'rational toys' did not become too popular. The very articles which they despise are those for which the modern collector searches avidly.

It should not be thought that the lot of the child, so downtrodden in the

38 Fine wooden doll, dating from the end of the seventeenth century. Known affectionately by collectors as 'The Old Pretender doll'. Said to have been given by the family of James Stuart to the family of a supporter. Painted upward-looking eyes. Delicately-painted cheeks.

seventeenth century, changed suddenly: the new ideas obviously spread very slowly, and though embraced by many members of fashionable society, percolated hardly at all into the lives of children of the lower middle classes, while the lot of the poor unprotected child became even worse than it had been in the previous century, when at least some effort had been made to fit the child for his future work. The eighteenth century is the period when a man could be hanged for stealing trifles, but only given a short prison sentence for putting out the eyes of a foundling child so that it would be a more pathetic begging figure.

The old Puritan ideas were also very strong, and strict Nonconformist families would have had little patience with such outrageous ideas as those suggested by Rousseau, though some of Maria Edgworth's moral tales, which sought to enact in words what Rousseau had advocated being learned by experience, were thought suitable nursery reading. Mrs Wesley, though not a cruel mother, gave each of her children exactly one day to learn the alphabet at the age of four, and taught her wailing babies of a year old to "fear the rod and cry softly". Child prodigies were adored and flattered, and memory feats were accomplished which severely tried the child, so that several of these infants who could speak in several languages and recite long passages in Latin did not live to reap the fruits of their early endeavour. Henry Longden's father explained the omnipresence, omniscience and omnipotence of God, rather hopefully it would seem, to his five-year-olds! The back-board, which was strapped over the shoulders and fixed to an iron collar, was a commonplace piece of nursery equipment, and many a child did all its lessons from early morning until seven or eight at night standing upright in such a contraption. This harsh attitude to the children of over-large families, whose parents found restraint easier to impose than the dangerous freedom of the new ideas, encouraged the development of people who would themselves grow up harsh and dictatorial. These were the children who, despite their blue sashes and golden curls, grew up to be the demanding employers of the industrial revolution.

The Georgian Englishwoman had much more freedom than her contemporaries on the Continent, and ordered her own life and children according to her own ideas. These ladies talked and read on the same footing as men and hunted, shot, rowed and enjoyed ribaldry equally with the opposite sex. The eighteenth-century woman was not the obsequious, cringing creature of many a nineteenth-century novel, but a person respected as an equal both for intelligence and ability. It was her sound common sense that caused her children to be dressed in a simple style of their own, and dispense with the periwig, sword and long coat that had been the lot of small boys and the tight lacing and heavy adult-style clothes of little girls in the early years of the century. By the second half of the eighteenth century, children wore simple loose dresses with sashes

39   Engraving from *Galerie des Modes*. 1780. The doll's costume precisely reflects the child's.

41 Wooden doll dating to the 1760s and dressed in Spitalfield silk. Flat back. Upper arms made of the dress fabric, and nailed to torso. 14½ in. high.

42 Poured-wax figures dating to mid-eighteenth century. Cloth bodies. Lady wears moulded-wax high-heeled shoes. Costume of Netherlands. Dutch. Ornamental statuettes rather than dolls. 9 in. high.

(*above*) 40 The skittle-shaped torso is the base of most wooden dolls made in the seventeenth and eighteenth centuries. The arms, made of wood, leather or linen would have been nailed in this instance. The enamelled eyes are set well into the wood. Nail holes where hair was once attached. 13 in. high.

and ribbons, or loose shirts and pantaloons, instead of being dressed as miniature adults. The *Ladies' Magazine or Universal Entertainer* which appeared in 1749 had no recipes, fashion notes or household hints, and appealed to a sensible person, rather than a society decoration. Many of these ladies perhaps allowed their children too much freedom, which they were unable to restrain when they were sent to school, so that uprisings, riots and drunken brawls were commonplace in educational establishments for young gentlemen. Whenever George III met an Eton boy he would always ask, "Have you had a rebellion lately, eh?"

The girls were either educated at home, or sent to a girls' seminary, while those lower down the social scale went to dame schools or even the charity schools, which were encouraging the spread of literacy in the working classes. The girls were taught mainly the social graces and skill in needlework, though some schools attempted to instil knowledge by fearsomely rigid discipline. There was, however, some loosening of the tight-lipped seventeenth-century ways, and the more emancipated children of the Age of Reason enjoyed brightly-presented picture books of their own, and an ever-increasing assortment of toys from which to choose.

Even the young baby was beginning to emerge from the tight swaddling-bands that had imprisoned it for generations. Bandages were still often used, but babies of rational mothers no longer had their whole body from neck to thigh kept still and stiff within swaddling-clothes. A doll in the Gallery of English Costume, Manchester, is dressed in baby clothes dating from the first quarter of the century. It wears an open gown of cream satin over a blanket-stitched cream flannel petticoat, an open linen chemise and a linen napkin. The only remnant of the old swaddling is a binder at the waist. Many superstitions did linger in the nursery. Pins put in a baby's cap were believed to keep away the fairies, and the baby's right hand was often left unwashed so that it would acquire riches in life. There was a gruesome, but successful, trade in selling the hands of men who had been hanged on the gallows, as the touch of such a hand was thought to have excellence in curing childish ills. An equally unlikely remedy was one used for the 'curing of whooping cough' which involved tying around the child's neck the staylace of its godmother which had been knotted nine times. Snail broth and fried mouse were still used as time-honoured remedies for childish ailments, as was powder of dried toad or even mistletoe. The Age of Reason was not allowed to take over the nurseries completely.

The increasing parental interest in children can be seen by the more frequent inclusion of children in paintings, in which they are often represented playing informally, quite unlike the stiff miniature adults of sixteenth- and seventeenth-century paintings. It is also seen in the fact that specialist toyshops were established for children, notably the 'Noah's Ark' in High Holborn, which was opened by a Cornishman, William Hamley, a surname well known to the London child of today. Though there are frequent references in eighteenth-century literature to 'toy shops', it must be remembered that these refer to shops selling china and trinkets for the amusement of adults, and not children's toys. There were also specialist toy stalls for children at the great fairs, and one print of Bartholomew Fair shows a pickpocket at work while a man pays for playthings for his children, who are offered a good selection of toys and dolls.

The fairs did a great trade in Gingerbread Husbands (as they were now called), and a particular favourite was a gingerbread representation of George III on horseback, wearing a tailed coat and a flowing wig. Other edible toys, made of marzipan or even bread, were also sold to children, who saved up for weeks before being taken to such events as the Gingerbread Fairs held twice a year in Birmingham. A description of such a fair is given in *Rural Scenes* written at the end of the century: "This is fair day and all the little boys and girls dressed in their Sunday clothes are bustling about, enjoying the crowd and noise and music. Some are pushing up to the toy stalls, viewing the gay rows of painted dolls and bright tin tea kettles." And, "Here there are some little fellows spending their grandpa's new sixpence at a show box where they may see Windsor Castle or the King going to Parliament."

Puppet shows, which were a regular source of amusement at the fairs, deteriorated during the eighteenth century, according to Strutt, who, writing at its end, commented on how marionettes had fallen on evil days and were now badly made, with the wires that communicated the motion to them appearing at the top of the heads. It was presumably the deterioration of realism that caused the public to lose interest and led the woman mentioned in the previous chapter to sell off her puppets as 'jointed babies' to the children.

Though the Great Fairs were a source of toys, the chapmen and pedlars who travelled the country also took dolls in their packs, together with battledore and shuttlecock, toy soldiers and the new attractive books for the instruction and amusement of 'Little Master Tommy and Pretty Miss Polly'. Through most of the children's books of this period runs the idea that if the child is good it will be happy, but the publishers were beginning to attempt to attract and please the child by the method of presentation, some even giving a small free gift with the book. The pedlars carried a wide variety of dolls from materials that were cheaply available: wood, wax and even cheap earthenware. The term 'bagman's baby' is a misleading one, and has been used to describe most types of eighteenth-century dolls, from the small woodens a Spitalfields merchant used to advertise his silks to little waxed compositions. In actual fact, the term was used simply to indicate the source of the doll's purchase rather than its type.

Large country estates had their own craftsmen's workshops, and it is from

43   Carved wooden doll costumed in *Fashionable Undress for Spring*, 1755. One of the dolls dressed by the Powell family. 10½ in. high.

44 Late eighteenth-century French wax doll with fabric body.

45 Wax lady-doll dressed in green brocade. Could possibly have represented a court lady in a crèche setting, as the feet are similar to those commonly found on such figures. Eighteenth century. Well-modelled hands, white wig. 13½ in. high.

46 Carved articulated eighteenth-century torso. Probably a figure for the display of costume. Green and brown decorative border revealed where later blue paint has rubbed away. Torso would have been mounted on a rod or a skirt-shaped wooden frame. Brown painted hair. Realistic brown eyes. 14 in. high.

these that many of the fine English doll's houses are thought to have originated. Probably some dolls were also made on the lathe in the carpenter's shop, though the known surviving eighteenth-century examples have a marked affinity to one another that would suggest that they came from a limited number of makers, though the movement of labour was now much faster, and it is probable that the methods were simply passed from one craftsman to another. Making a basic jointed wooden doll is not difficult, and would have been child's play to an eighteenth-century carpenter.

There was no sudden peak demand for dolls, such as developed with the Victorian-style Christmas. The eighteenth-century festival was not a children's feast, though they would enjoy its accompanying festivities, such as the mummers' play and the feasting. Twelfth Day was kept for the children, and parties were given and special cakes made, decorated with sugar figures representing the Magi. Gifts were given on Twelfth Day, but to nothing like the extent of the nineteenth century, though Continental children might be given dolls representing saints, and rather more presents than a contemporary English child. Dolls were usually given as birthday gifts or brought back from occasional visits to town, but the cheap dolls would be bought by the child herself from the fairs or the bagman. In the more puritanical homes, all such festivals were frowned upon as frivolous time-wasters, and the children were fortunate if they owned even one commercially-made doll. Jane Thackeray, whose father was a well-to-do doctor, wrote: "My play things were few, a doll that I fondly loved, and who was undressed every night and put into her cradle, and two magnetic fishes with a fishing rod and a green and white skipping rope." Even these few possessions would have appeared sinful to the more narrow Nonconformist families, though surprisingly, Mrs Sherwood confesses to having once owned a fine doll with "a paper hoop and hair of real flax".

Plaster Dolls

The alabaster dolls were still popular, though the term in the eighteenth-century sense is believed to refer to dolls made of plaster of paris, which was easy to cast, rather than the genuine doll of alabaster which had to be carved. There are no known surviving plaster dolls, though they would have been cheap to produce and were presumably very popular. Dorothy Herbert wrote that: "We have another addition to the family which afforded the young folks much amusement. This was a large alabaster doll I brought over – we christened her Miss Watt." There are records of dolls of this substance being bought in Bristol, and as alabaster was mined in England, it would appear likely that there was some native production of such dolls. Other comments in eighteenth-century literature about dolls that broke easily would suggest that the dolls referred to were of this substance, sometimes even used over a central wooden core. The fragile nature of plaster would have meant that a doll's useful life would have been very short, and is probably the reason why no cast heads of the material are known.

Fournier, writing about French dolls made in the nineteenth century, praises their beauty and compares them to those of the eighteenth century which he considered to have been poorly made and badly dressed. The heads were made of Spanish White, the equivalent of plaster of paris. He complained that nothing had been done for 200 years either to improve them or to decorate them more artistically: "The doll-maker has confined himself to that humble *mélange* of earth, paper and plaster which was spoken of in the account of 1540. The same stuff that had served instead of *carton pierre* for ornaments on cornices and ceilings."

Dolls of China and Earthenware

Earthenware dolls, which had been imported into England presumably from Germany since the seventeenth century, were still popular, but another type of doll, potentially much finer, was beginning to emerge – the doll of porcelain. Hard paste porcelain was first made in Europe at the Albrechtsburg at Meissen in 1710, and was used for making both decorative trinkets and household items. Derby, Meissen, Höchst and Chelsea were among the factories that produced statuettes of children, some even represented as playing with dolls. One doll in the hands of a child wears a very fashionable dress with panniers, while swaddled figures of babies were still popular in earthenware as well as porcelain. The primitive, slip-decorated, earthenware cradles are well known, and though believed to have been intended as christening gifts, were probably frequently utilized by a child as a toy cradle. None of the great English porcelain factories are recorded as having made dolls, as the products of such factories as Bow were always expensive, even when they took the form of adult 'toys', and would have been considered far too good to give to children. Early doll-collectors erroneously used the terms Bow or Chelsea to apply to heads of different types, a charming and exciting idea but extremely unlikely, as there are no records or even fragments of dolls. The porcelain doll of the eighteenth century is very much a German preserve. A fine Sonneberg doll, believed to date from the late eighteenth century, is known. This doll wears the sickle-shaped roll, which was a popular form of hairdressing, but apart from this example there are only a few dolls that can even tentatively be regarded as eighteenth century, though they are known to have been manufactured then. It is interesting to note that several

47 Undressed eighteenth-century wooden doll to show the construction of the more common figures of this type. Linen upper arms tied to the torso. Lower arms white leather. Hoof feet. Known as Sophie. 24¾ in. high.

48 Eighteenth-century doll's-house figure, with face and hands of black velvet. Embroidered features. Made to represent the 'decorative' black slaves found in elegant homes of the period. 3½ in. high.

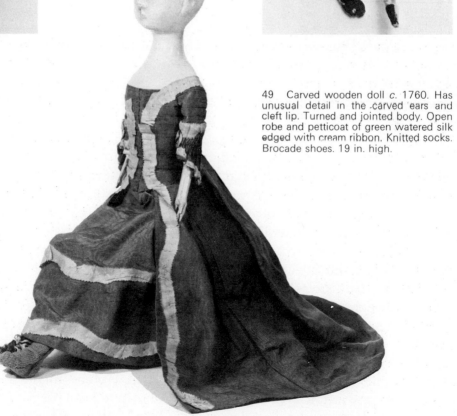

49 Carved wooden doll c. 1760. Has unusual detail in the carved ears and cleft lip. Turned and jointed body. Open robe and petticoat of green watered silk edged with cream ribbon. Knitted socks. Brocade shoes. 19 in. high.

firms, such as Limbach and Greiner, who were later to become famous for doll-making, were already producing porcelain at this time. It is probable that dolls' heads were made at other Continental factories, but at present conjecture has to be relied upon.

Papier Mâché Dolls

Composition dolls were much stronger than dolls of plaster, earthenware or porcelain and had the added advantage of being very cheap to produce from mainly waste materials. Paper pulp was becoming an increasingly useful waste product, because of the rapid increase in the number of books produced, especially in the Sonneberg area. Though most surviving eighteenth-century dolls are made of a paper-type mixture, some were made of a combination of rye or meal with glue size to form a modelling material known as brotteig. The mixture was highly malleable, and could be used for the construction of individual heads, though its qualities were more frequently utilized in moulds. It was also used to create the features on wooden dolls. Many wooden heads that appear to have intricately-carved hairstyles are in fact moulded out of this or a similar substance, as individual carving of delicate curls and fine features would have been too time-consuming. The reason for the great lack of early examples of these dolls lies in its obvious attraction for vermin, and though the makers attempted to use various materials such as garlic, tobacco or even arsenic to make the articles unattractive, they do not appear to have been successful.

The fact that the heads of the dolls were eaten and disfigured quickly in the rat- and insect-ridden houses must have been very upsetting to the child owners, and the makers experimented with various substances until a material similar to that which was later used for papier mâché furniture was developed, being a mixture of waste materials, glue size and flour, with only a small quantity of the latter used. The doll-makers of Sonneberg and Nürnberg made their individual mixtures from ingredients such as white lead, pitch, brick, gips and quartz, in an attempt to create a strong doll's head that would remain attractive.

Very few eighteenth-century composition dolls remain. The known dolls have heads that were moulded bald, so that a wig could be attached, though the smooth pate does sometimes have the suggestion of a hairstyle roughly painted on. Some are moulded to waist level and made from a simple two-part mould. Leather was usually used for the arms, lower trunk and legs, and was sometimes nailed to the torso and the join neatened by a strip of tape or leather. Breasts are indicated on the dolls known, as they were intended to represent ladies, and were attractively dressed. One interesting head has jewels painted on the moulded hairstyle. This doll is in the collection of Estrid Faurholt and

50   Mid-eighteenth-century rag doll probably made as an inhabitant for a doll's house. Features were once painted. 3½ in. high.

deviates interestingly from the usual rule of heads of this period which are moulded plain. The doll has a painted 'powdered wig' and wears a choker-type necklace, which is also painted on the papier mâché. A small hole is pierced through the head, just above the ear, presumably where a jewel once hung. The body is also unusual for the eighteenth century, as it has garters painted on. The doll is apparently dated by the hairstyle, but it is possible that it was modelled retrospectively and belongs in fact to the nineteenth century.

Lower arms and legs were sometimes made of wood, with fork-like hands and simple feet. In better examples, glass was sometimes used for eyes, though the substance was still fairly expensive. The glass-makers of Lauscha near Sonneberg had been able to supply eyes for dolls from the middle of the century, though economy had limited their use. They discovered how to blow round glass eyes, which were cheaper to produce than those of the paperweight variety which are found on most dolls of this period. Some of the paperweight eyes in eighteenth-century dolls are so dense in texture and colour that it is difficult to tell without removing them if they are made of porcelain or glass.

The rough finish of the papier mâché moulded head was made smooth by a coating of gesso, a mixture of whiting and size, which produced a good surface for the painting of the dolls' features. Cloth was occasionally used to reinforce heads as was traditional on many Italian crèche figures and swaddling babies. American collectors use the term 'carton' to describe these early papier mâché dolls, as the insides of the heads resemble grey egg-cartons. Jo. E. Gerken suggests, after considerable research on the subject, that it is possible that some very early dolls were made of carton to the hips or even the knees, but with cloth backs to the heads, though this seems to have been an unnecessarily complicated method.

One papier mâché doll originating from Sonneberg has an open-closed mouth, revealing two upper teeth. All the known dolls of the period have brown or black eyes, sometimes pupil-less. One doll made at the end of the eighteenth century wears patches, though these were no longer worn by fashionable ladies. It is not easy to date these early dolls unless they are in original clothes, as it is on the costume and hairstyle that dating often depends. The standard of painting, the moulding and finish often vary greatly, as does the size of the dolls: known examples range from 14 to 23 inches high.

An interesting group of papier mâché dolls, dating to the first half of the century, came up for sale at Sotheby's, London, in 1974. As they all retained their original costume, dating could be quite precise. The finest doll represented a fashionable lady, and wore a fair wig and a lace and ribbon fontange. The heads were made of wood and the arms wired. Body, legs and feet were made of papier mâché. A later example, dated to the 1730s, was given inset blue glass eyes and a brown wig.

5 Eighteenth-century wooden group

Two of the dolls were dressed in the costume of nuns. One represented a Canoness of St Augustine, and the other a choir nun of the Benedictine order. They both had papier mâché bodies with wooden hands, and the knee joints were given hinged metal hooks, to enable the legs to be held straight. Though of great importance in the history of the papier mâché doll, the figures were strangely unattractive, and held little of the instant appeal that dolls of the eighteenth century usually command.

Pantins

Another toy that reflected the increasingly cheap production of paper and card was the *Pantin*, known also to children as the Jumping Jack. These were flat, cut-out figures which were swivel-jointed and operated by strings which ran across the back from limb to limb, causing the figure to move amusingly when cleverly operated. The more complex versions could be controlled rather like marionettes, so that one leg or one arm could be moved, but the cheaper versions sold for children had all limbs operated by a single thread. Though usually associated with the eighteenth century, the Jumping Jacks had their origins in antiquity, and are known to have been made in Germany on a small commercial scale from medieval times. During the eighteenth century they were produced in the Erz Mountains.

Originally the *Pantins* were made as children's toys, but they had a great appeal to eighteenth-century French adults as salon amusements, where their use gave satirists great scope both in words and drawings. The French of the period believed that the novelty originated from a village near Paris, which was famous for its dancing, and many of the figures do in fact look like drawings of dancers. Such characters as a shepherd or shepherdess, Harlequin, Scaramouche or even soldiers lent themselves to caricature in this manner. One *Pantin* was commissioned by the Duchesse de Chartres who paid Boucher, the fashionable painter, 1,500 francs to paint a very special figure for her. Other less affluent enthusiasts painted their own. The figures could be bought engraved on paper or card ready to paint, cut out and assemble at home, or they could be purchased ready coloured and made up. Though most of the *Pantins* were under a foot high, some were as tall as 28 inches.

They were popular with the French aristocracy, as they often represented famous people. Even the sophisticated adult of today could hardly fail to be diverted by the capering of a Jumping Jack caricaturing well-known public figures.

The *Pantin* was never popular with the more sober English aristocracy, who considered it strictly a child's toy, and even as a toy it does not appear to have been as popular as it was in France. There is a belief that the *Pantins* lost their popularity in France after the law intervened to prohibit their use, as they were believed to excite women and cause them to give birth to crippled children, though in fact it is more likely that the adults became bored with the craze, and the *Pantin* reverted to its place as a child's toy.

Fashion Figures

It was another peculiarly eighteenth-century fashion for ladies to have wax dolls made as portraits of themselves and dressed in fashionable clothes, possibly in imitation of the fine mannequin dolls that were sent from Paris to show the civilized world the current modes. The fashion figure was popularly called a Pandora at this time. Two figures were often displayed; one, known as *La Grande Pandore*, dressed in *grande toilette*, and another figure, *La Petite Pandore*, wore *negligée*. There were special costume exhibitions in Paris which used doll-figures for display and Rose Bertin, milliner to Marie Antoinette, made fashion dolls for the Queen and her mother. She is recorded as having made dolls other than for display purposes, such as one supplied in 1788 for Madame Dillon's daughter. The doll in question sounds fascinating, as it was a large doll "with springs, a well made foot and a very good wig". It wore a linen chemise, silk stockings and a well-boned corset. So popular was Rose Bertin that she was able to survive the Revolution and opened a shop in London for the emigrée nobles.

Ladies, such as the novelist Mlle de Scudéry at the beginning of the eighteenth century, used to stand the two Pandoras in their rooms, so that the current fashion could be examined and admired. The coming of the fashion doll was an event eagerly awaited, even by ladies as far away as America: in New England Miss Hannah Teatts, a Mantua maker, displayed "a baby dressed after the newest fashion of Mantuas and nightgowns and everything belonging to a dress. Lately arrived on the Captain while from London." At the Sensa, a fourteen-day Venetian fair, a doll was regularly exhibited dressed in the height of French fashion. So seriously did the French take the construction of fashion figures that a bureau of registry was set up to regulate the styles sent out, so that all the makers would follow the same design. This bureau was possibly a defence measure against some contemporary criticism that the French were making use of such figures to get rid of old stock! The example sent by Rose Bertin to the Court at St Petersburg is almost disappointingly simple. Another contemporary title for the Pandoras was 'Poupées de la Rue de Saint Honoré', the street that was the centre of Parisian tailors.

The Pandoras were specially manufactured for their purpose, and Robert Culff states that a number of patterns were reduced in scale so as to be shown to advantage on such dolls. One French duke is reputed to have owned twenty-five life-size mannequins on which his own wardrobe was set out, though the actual Pandoras were much smaller but probably at least half life-size. Madame Eloffe supplied a customer with a fully life-size doll in court dress, and the Contesse Bombelles was also supplied with a life-size figure in 1788 which cost 409 francs. There is one tradition that *La Grande Pandore* was almost life-size and the other much smaller, but as there are no documented examples we are again in the realms of conjecture.

So luxurious were many of these dolls, that they caused contemporary writers to expostulate at the expense of adult toys, and it was by the flaunting of vain follies such as these that the French nobility fanned the Revolutionary spirit. The French were complacent about their pre-eminence in design: "The chic imparted to fashion by French hands is imitated by all nations, who obediently submit to the taste of the Rue Saint Honoré".★

Though English fashion figures were sent to America and even Russia, the English court ladies were to be satisfied only with the genuine French designs. In 1712, Betty Crosstich, a milliner, declared that she had received the French baby for the year. "I have taken the utmost care to have her dressed by the most famous Mantua makers and tire women in Paris." Another milliner stated that her doll was always ready to serve: "If you come, it will cost you two shillings, but if you would send for it, seven shillings." If the dolls were sent out by the dress-maker to clients it is little wonder that so few are known. Despite the fact that hundreds of Pandoras were made, only a few figures which can be described as 'probable' mannequin dolls remain. The fashion dolls became superfluous after the introduction of the ladies fashion magazines, which could give detailed instructions and sketches regarding design. Another reason for the discontinuance of their use was the French Revolution, which removed Paris from its position as the Mecca of fashion. *Le Cabinet des Modes*, published in 1785 with hand-coloured plates, stated that subscribers "need no longer be obliged to maintain commission agents at great expense or to have dolls made, puppets always inadequate and yet extremely dear, which give at best merely a hint of our new modes."

The few apparently genuine Pandora figures that remain are those made of wood. Some were undoubtedly made with plaster heads on a roughly-constructed base, as in the seventeenth century, but the fragility of the plaster gave them little chance of survival. As many of the figures would have been given to children when disfigured or the garments damaged, it is little wonder that few remain. There are a number of figures that are quite small but beautifully dressed, which will be discussed later, but they are unlikely to have been genuine

★ Merciel, *Tableau de Paris*.

Pandoras, as the doll would not have been large enough to show off all the relevant details of the costume. Estrid Faurholt illustrates an early Pandora in her collection, which is carved of wood and has a well-modelled face with painted eyes. The figure wears a simple, long garment which is carved from the solid, and which would have provided a good foundation for the skirts of a dress. The neckline of the doll's robe is cut low and square and the wooden arms are jointed at wrist and elbow. The complete figure stands 18 inches high. The head bears traces of a wig which was once attached. A figure very much in the same manner is illustrated by Carl Fox in *The Doll*, where it is described as an eighteenth-century Flemish manikin. This figure stands 27 inches high and has well-carved hands and face. The torso rests on a wooden stand, which is constructed to show the flare of a dress. This figure, though again it has no look of religiosity has a hole drilled through one of the hands which is disconcerting. Was the figure made for religious use and a rosary fixed firmly on this way, or was a saint's symbol attached to the hand? Perhaps the hole was drilled to enable the hand to be held in position for display purposes or to attach a fashion accessory.

Another doll of a similar type was recently on sale in a London market. It stood about 24 inches high, and the head had once been gesso covered and painted as a lady. The torso was realistically carved and the arms jointed. From the waist down the figure was constructed of flat wood cut in the shape of the outline of a crinoline dress, in the manner of a dummy board. Accompanying the figure were roughly cut but authentic patterns for seventeenth-century dresses designed to fit, while the figure wore a simple dress of coarse linen.

Surviving figures of this type all pose many problems, but a common theme runs through the three examples discussed and the one illustrated. The articulation and proportions are not good enough for an artist's lay figure and the forms are represented simply dressed which would have made them useless in the studio. Secondly, the figures have nothing of the appearance of religious carvings, as they have very earthbound faces, and the jointed limbs would not usually have been necessary on a statue which would have retained one pose. Two of the figures are rather large to have formed part of a crèche group, and in any case, crèche figures, except those made in the Tyrol, are not usually jointed. Court ladies did often form part of the group in a crèche setting but the scenes were usually on the much smaller scale. On the balance of probability it would, therefore, appear that the figures were intended for secular use, probably to be dressed and used as display figures for costume.

The illustrated torso is unusual, as the hair is beautifully carved, though the core of the head was lathe-turned before the craftsman carver began work. The old lathe-mark can be seen amongst the carved hair. The brown glass eyes are inset into the gesso covering the carved face and indicate a quality figure, as

51 Wax and rolled paperwork portrait of Queen Anne, 1709.

they are extremely realistic, in contrast to the dense eyes seen on eighteenth-century play dolls. The question of religious or secular use, Pandora or statuette when applied to such figures is fascinating and discussion of more examples when discovered will, it is hoped, shed more light.

85

Doll-dressing was cultivated as a craft by ladies and their daughters in the eighteenth century, and excellence of costume should not lead the collector to believe that a doll-like figure is necessarily a Pandora. It is, more correctly, a doll dressed in the costume of a fashionable lady. Many of the dolls given to children were very magnificent. An engraving dated 1800, *New Year's Presents at Paris*, shows dolls, beautifully dressed, that are nearly as large as the children to whom they are given. Louis XV gave the Infanta an exquisite doll which cost 20,000 livres, and other fortunate children were given dolls of a high standard. Elizabeth Craven was given a doll on her tenth birthday which was modelled to represent her, with blushing cheeks and averted face. Her uncle defended his extravagant gift on the grounds that each time he gave the good-natured child money, she gave it all away to the poor. In the *Anecdotes of Mary, or the Good Governess* we are told how the heroine spends 6 guineas on a doll which was dressed by a court dress-maker in full court dress. Georgianna, Duchess of Devonshire, sent home to England a doll she had dressed in detail for her daughter, with three costumes in the style of the French provinces and capes of gold and silver that the doll could also wear. Her son was sent a boy doll dressed in the style of a page of the Doge of Venice.

The dolls made by the English Powell family were specially dressed to record contemporary changes of fashion, but are by definition dolls in fashionable dress rather than Pandoras or fashion dolls, which would have been circulated by dress-makers. Some of the Powell dolls are unreliable, as new heads were substituted in the Regency period for the original wax. Several sources describe a pair of male dolls measuring 11 inches as manikins, though their mere size would have made this unlikely. These dolls wear court dress, with silk shirts and breeches. One of the figures wears leather riding boots and the other indoor shoes with bows on the front. The figures are ball jointed and once carried swords, and it is probable that they were doll-figures, such as those dressed as knights and played with by noble children in earlier centuries. The standard of costuming is thus deceptively high in good dolls, which often leads to the incorrect supposition that they were made to be copied by a dress-maker. Another fine, beautifully-articulated eighteenth-century doll is dressed in a robe of silver brocade stiffened with red baize, gold and silver embroidery on the bodice and embellished with real pearls. This particular doll has a well-modelled, expressive woman's face but is not a fashion doll as such.

Even the very much occupied Mrs Delany turned her skilful hands to doll-dressing. "Miss Dolly Mode's box just packed up to go to the carrier next Friday containing imprimis: a lady à la mode in accoutrements but in every other respect toute au contraire, for she can neither rouge nor giggle nor run away, she is nailed down to her good behaviour." This doll was preserved for many years not only as an example of the fashion of the time, but also to illustrate the maker's skill and ingenuity. The collector should not, therefore, even when dealing with eighteenth-century dolls, be too eager to claim ownership of a fashion doll. It is more likely that he possesses a fashionably-dressed doll of the period.

Paper Dolls

Another method of studying and examining costume *à la mode* was by the use of paper figures. The ladies' heads were sometimes painted in the manner of a miniature, and this could be put behind an oval-shaped hole in a piece of paper, on which was painted a fashionable costume or even a fancy dress. Some miniatures of ivory and even copper were painted in this manner before the eighteenth century, but the use of cheaper paper examples appears to have become popular at this time.

The more common method was to have a painted dummy figure 5 or 6 inches high and an assortment of dresses painted to fit that dummy. An interesting group of drawings came up for sale in 1973 at Christie's. They showed dresses worn by the family of the Reverend Robert Johnson (Rector of Wistastowe, Shropshire) and their friends in the years 1787–99. The designs included a wedding trousseau as well as morning dress, slight mourning dress and court dress. There were also accompanying hats and capes.

It was a pleasant and fashionable pastime for ladies to create such figures, just as they amused themselves with silhouette cutting and rolled paper work, but the information which they give to the student of fashion is invaluable. In 1775 Parson Woodforde was shown some paper dolls which he evidently considered unusual. They were "quite flat and about six inches long with several different dresses to clothe them". He seems to take their availability much more for granted by 1780 when he records that he gave a child a "very pretty doll cut out of paper with several dresses".

Flat paper or card dolls became popular in Europe from about 1790 and were sold in sheet form. They were made representing professions and traders as well as fashionable dress. Wood engravings of a similar kind had been sold in Germany since the Middle Ages, but these new paper dolls appear to have derived in the main from English sources, as they are referred to as 'English dolls'. They were however also produced in other Continental countries: Bertuch and Gavarni both printed a series of such figures in imitation of the English product. The genuine English paper doll was popular, as it contained so many different possibilities and changes of costume. In the *Journal des Luxus und der Moden* of 1791 is the comment:

> A new and pretty invention is the so-called English doll which has lately arrived from London. It is properly a toy for little girls, but is so pleasing and tasteful that mothers and grown women will also likely want to play with it, the more since good or bad taste can be observed and so to speak studied. The figure is a young female painted on cardboard and cut out. It is about eight inches high, has simply dressed hair and wears underclothes and a corset. With it go six sets of tastefully coloured and cut out dresses and coiffures.

The costumes included hats, negligées, caracos, chemises, furs and hats that "could be tilted or set back at will". The dolls were packed in neat paper envelopes that could be easily carried in a portfolio or working bag for amusement at parties, as well as to occupy children.

Wax Dolls

The fashion for ladies to have wax models made of themselves encouraged artists in this medium, who often received very high fees for their skill. Apart from making models of fashionable people, the craftsmen in wax also made anatomical models, such as those made by an ancestor of Madame Tussaud. Mrs Salmon's waxworks were very popular with visitors to London, and she also taught the art and sold all sorts of moulds and glass eyes. George IV's mother commissioned a portrait model of him in wax from another artist when he was a baby, which she kept in her room on a velvet cushion protected by a bell glass. Hair skilfully inserted into the wax scalp either in groups or singly was known at the time, and some play dolls are believed to have been made in this way. The most common method of dealing with the hair, both on models and dolls, was still the wig, but some examples exist where the hair was modelled in the wax.

The bodies of wax dolls were either jointed and made of wood, or made of linen stuffed with sawdust or tow, while some were still made in the traditional way of wound silk or cotton over a padded armature. An interesting German wax doll of the middle of the century had a thin fabric laid over the face between the layers of wax to give added strength, a method which used also to be used occasionally to strengthen papier mâché figures. The two media merged in the late eighteenth century to give a new doll-making method – waxed composition. The date usually given for the first examples of this technique is 1784, but as one sees more examples of dolls of this type in original eighteenth-century costume the date is probably much earlier.

The eighteenth century saw the establishment of most of the doll-making methods which were not perfected until a hundred or so years later. As early as 1701 a Dr Claver Morris visited London and bought a doll for his daughter, "a wax Baby with an invention to make it cry and turn its eyes". This doll was quite expensive for the time, costing 5s. Dolls that 'walked' on wheels were shown in fashionable salons, and the 'open closed' type of treatment for the mouth was popular. One German doll dating from 1730 represents a girl showing just the tip of her tongue. Inset hair, glass eyes, jointed bodies and waxed composition were all known in the eighteenth century. There is a wide variety of standard of eyes for dolls of this period; they could be extremely realistic or merely little round beads of wax, such as were used on doll's-house dolls.

A doll of exceptional quality was that given by the Duchess of Orleans to the young queen. The doll was a "wax baby three foot high with diamond earrings, a necklace of pearls and a diamond cross. With furniture of plate for a toilet and two Indian chests full of linen and several sorts of clothes for the Baby. The whole for that Princess to play with."

Shops specializing in the sale of toys and dolls were becoming more common, such as A. Loriot of New Bond Street, the Noah's Ark, and the toyshop run by William Deard at 'The Sign of the Golden Door over against Suffolk Street'. The Deards also had a toyshop in the Strand, but it should be remembered that, though styled toyshops, they only included 'fine toys for juveniles' in their stock, which was mainly composed of trinkets and china. John Mason's shop in Philadelphia advertized 'drest dolls, Naked ditto and Lilliputian dolls', and he was also able to supply new wigs.

Wax lent itself well to the making of small heads for doll's-house dolls, and several eighteenth-century houses are still inhabited by dolls of this substance. The head was sometimes even hammered with nails on to a wooden body, as the Lilliputian dolls usually had heads of solid wax. An interesting group of dolls, all about 8 inches high, are reputed to have been taken to Salem, Massachusetts, from Portugal by Captain Cheever in 1795. These dolls, whose gaudy appearance must have shocked the provincial townfolk, were given heads and exceptionally well modelled hands of wax. The bodies were of wood, and the legs of the same material ended in high-heeled shoes. It was fashionable to exhibit dolls in show boxes, and in this case they could perhaps be intended to represent the characters in a play. The wax doll's-house dolls with beads of wax for eyes are not easy to date, as the moulds for their manufacture continued to be used into the 1830s.

Folk and Novelty Dolls

Alongside the more elegant dolls of china, papier mâché and wax were produced the folk dolls that had been constructed in a similar way from ancient times. The skittle-shaped birch dolls had long been made in Sweden, and appear in other countries, while rattle dolls, made rather in the skittle shape, appear to have been made in most central European countries but especially in Thuringia and Berchtesgaden; turned wooden swaddling babies were made in particular at Oberammergau. The early dolls carved by American settlers were made of the wood that lay at hand, mainly pine and maple. One such doll, in the New York Historical Society collection, has a painted dress with red and black polka dots. Many wooden folk dolls are so embryonic in nature that they are very difficult to date, except by carbon 14 analysis of the wood, and it is possible that the dating of many of these early woodens is actually over conservative.

As few rag dolls have survived, some writers on dolls have been led to suppose that they were rare in the eighteenth century. Though clothes were expensive, cheap woollen fabrics and rag were almost always available in sufficient quantity to make dolls at home. Some rag dolls were also made to be sold commercially; for instance the Noah's Ark in High Holborn stocked rag dolls. The rag doll becomes a sad object after only a few years, and presumably they were discarded when no longer attractive.

Though the rattle is common to most civilizations, it reached its climax in the *poupards* of the eighteenth and nineteenth centuries. The *poupard* is a doll's head mounted either on a stick with a squeaker or rattle or, in later versions, on a musical movement. Napoleon's son, the little King of Rome, was given a rattle in the form of a Punchinello with the face of Napoleon, made at the Emperor's command. This *poupard* was mounted on an ivory handle and decorated with bells. Other simpler versions were made with wooden or composition heads, though the making of such toys did not reach its peak until the nineteenth century.

Other novelty dolls available included wooden dolls whose skirts opened to reveal a well-equipped kitchen, and monks made on a similar principle whose habits opened to reveal an altar. Some of the tumblers and playing tops of the period almost take the form of dolls. One tumbler wears a cocked hat and a coat shaped nicely down over the weighted ball-shaped base, while a playing top casts the shadow of Marie Antoinette on the ground when spun.

Wooden Dolls

The type of doll most commonly associated with the eighteenth century by collectors is the jointed wooden doll often called (erroneously) a Queen Anne by English collectors and (cumbersomely) a Maryanne Georgian by Americans. It is basically the type of doll which was made in the seventeenth century, and that continued to be made well into the nineteenth. Though incorrect, the term Queen Anne will be sometimes used for ease of expression, as it is known and understood by collectors.

It would seem probable that dolls of this type were made and decorated in England in some considerable number. Imports of toys, including dolls, were

52   An extremely fine pair of mid-eighteenth-century doll's house dolls. Lady in maroon and white. Man wears purple coat and brocade waistcoat. The limbs are carved in the manner of the later Grödnertals, but the bodies are simply roughly-cut rectangles of unfinished wood. Lady wears a patch. Man carries spyglass. 4½ in. high.

53   Room of Nürnberg doll's house showing early eighteenth-century figures with wax hands. Faces were presumably once wax masks that have fallen away.

taxed at sixteen pence of every pound of their value, and extra protection was given to the home industry by the prohibition of the import of painted dolls in 1747. Dolls were sent to America from England, including some of "Lilliputian size" for baby houses. Dolls seen in the Ann Sharp and the Nostell Priory baby houses, both of which originated in Yorkshire, are roughly carved with some individuality and are completely unlike the usual type of Queen Annes, suggesting possibly, local manufacture. Those seen in other houses however are simply miniatures of the normal type. The fact that most dolls of the Queen Anne type have been found in England does not completely preclude German manufacture, for the bisque dolls that were made in vast numbers in Germany in the nineteenth century are now easier to find in England and America, as they were primarily intended for export.

Some English makers are on record as having made jointed dolls, such as the wood-turner William Higgs, who was involved in a court action over the theft of some of his dolls: "14 naked babies, and two dozen dressed babies and one jointed baby." The maker was able to distinguish dolls he had made himself from those of other makers, and he usually sold them to shops, one in St Catherine's Lane and another in Whitechapel. He was paid 2½d. each for them. The dolls were made entirely in his workshop, and his wife dressed them before they were sold by a journeywoman who worked for him. The unjointed dolls were possibly of the 'bedpost' type, with arms and legs of leather or fabric. Though we can therefore be sure that these dolls were made in England, it is less easy to identify them.

A few collectors suggest that wigs were only worn on English wooden dolls, but this would appear unlikely, as the Continental makers put wigs on almost every other type of doll. A similar comment is also made about the larger heads originating in England but, while it seems applicable to the early years of the century, the heads are not noticeably large in comparison with others by the middle years, when the English products appear indistinguishable. The similarity between the dolls of Queen Anne type is interesting, as presumably the makers were aiming at a more or less uniform product, possibly because of the movement of workers. The carved dolls of indisputable German origin show greater characterization than the English, with the exception of a few made for dolls houses.

In structure, the eighteenth-century jointed doll continued in the age-old tradition. Good examples were given ball joints and well-carved hands, while cheaper versions might have only the body carved of wood, the arms and legs often being made of simple stuffed cylinders of leather. The fingers were made of a variety of materials: straw, bamboo, wood or little rolls of leather. The arms, whether of wood, leather or fabric, were often attached by leather hinges, except in the good-quality dolls, where a joint was used. The back of these dolls is often flat, perhaps because of the method of fixing to the lathe, or perhaps to make the doll easier to clamp down to a work bench to carve the features. A flat-backed doll would also lie better in a toy cradle than a round one, which would tend to roll about. Not all have the flattened back, and the degree of flatness varies also between examples. Breasts were sometimes indicated on better-quality dolls, and the wigs could be attached to the pate by nails or even pins. Few dolls of this type retain their original hair, though the nails which once fixed it in place often remain and are a help in dating.

One peculiarly eighteenth-century advance was the application of a moulded mask of brotteig on to the turned plain head core, which saved time, as it dispensed with the services of the craftsman carver. Heavy gesso or plaster was also sometimes used for this purpose. Mrs Delany mentions a doll she had been dressing which was dropped by the friseur who was making its wig, causing the nose to break. This break would not have been very likely in a doll with a completely-carved face. This doll appears to have been quite prized, as the lady comments that: "It will be some time before I get another doll that will do" – a comment that suggests that good jointed dolls were not all that easily available, even to court ladies who were close friends of the royal family.

The seventeenth-century Queen Anne type is usually represented by the lovely example in the Victoria and Albert Museum, which gives the impression of having been especially carved and decorated as a gift for a wealthy child. The eighteenth-century examples, in comparison, seem very much less magnificent and more in the nature of children's toys, even when they retain their original clothes. It is doubtful, therefore, whether one should state that all early eighteenth-century dolls were of a very high quality, as a variety of standard must have also existed in the seventeenth century, and it seems wrong to judge the quality of dolls of that century by so few examples.

There are some apparent differences in standard between dolls that can be fairly accurately dated. The early eighteenth-century examples have some specially-painted detail, such as patches on the face or highlights to the painted eyes, which are less likely to be found in later dolls, possibly because glass eyes became the tradition for the later top-quality dolls. Several writers on dolls comment on the 'stitched' appearance of the eyebrows of eighteenth-century examples, but even study of the few exhibited at the Victoria and Albert Museum indicates that this was not always so. Certainly the cheaply-made embryonic eighteenth-century doll often has eyebrows that are treated in an almost mass-production type of painting, but other examples show a variety of treatment. One method was lightly to paint in the shape of the eyebrow and then indicate the hairs of the brow by slanting parallel upright lines in a much darker shade. Another was to paint the brow line and then put the hair strokes above the line. The latter is the method used on the 'Old Pretender' doll. An example dating from 1735 has a strong brow line painted with hair strokes almost converging from either side, while a doll of 1763 has a softly painted brow line with upper eyebrow strokes, but here the lower strokes are omitted and small dots substituted.

There are examples that can be fairly positively dated but there seems no definite similarity in the craftsmen's painting of the brows, so that the conclusion has to be drawn that the various decorators simply treated the painting of the eyebrows in the way they thought best, and that the 'stitched' eyebrows so often talked about were used on cheaper eighteenth-century dolls but were more common in the nineteenth century, when such dolls were less fashionable and owned by more ordinary children.

A more positive difference appears to be in the articulation of the legs. Early dolls usually have the upper legs set into the hips with mortice and tenon joints, a system which obviously demanded some care in cutting, and was consequently replaced, as the mass production of dolls increased, by the use of a simple pointed torso through which a wire, dowel rod or even string could be threaded to hang the legs.

Glass eyes increased in popularity as the century advanced and they became cheaper. They sometimes have extremely large pupils, which makes it difficult to say whether they are made of china or glass. The treatment of the painting of the face of cheap dolls developed into a pattern as the century progressed, so that tiny rows of dots became the standard method of representing lashes, and a fine line reflected by a row of dots became the established treatment for eyebrows. Very late dolls of this type have pinched features with eyes, nose and mouth concentrated on a small area of the head, whose only carved detail was on the nose. Known as 'bedpost' dolls, examples of this type much more frequently have the blue eyes that were becoming more popular.

The surviving Queen Anne types whose faces were given the plaster-mask finish tend to be much smaller, but unless the doll is badly chipped, it is often very difficult to know whether the features are wood or not, as the surface is usually given generous coats of gesso and varnish. The attractiveness of the Queen Anne dolls lies in the fact that they are the earliest variety still available to collectors, and they retain their primitive appearance, which makes them look even older than they actually are. The crèche figures and automata of the eighteenth century show the quality of figures that the doll-maker was capable of achieving, but the makers of wooden dolls obviously chose to go their own way, and create a doll that would appeal to children, be cheap enough to be dispensable and yet be capable of showing off clothes in the style of a lady. These dolls appear ill at ease

54 Artist's wooden lay figure, dating to the eighteenth century. The fine articulation of this figure was necessary and can be compared to the simpler method used for Pandoras and the rudimentary construction of play dolls. Well-made miniature clothes 16½ in. high.

55 A mannequin with eight dresses in a folder inscribed "Dresses for 1786 and fashion of 1786". Painted.

against an eighteenth-century background of elegant furniture and delicate jewellery. They are almost a culture of their own, which has a more direct primitive influence still at work.

Most of the observations made with regard to the dating of such dolls can only be taken as very general guidelines, as there are exceptions to almost every rule in doll-collecting. Some apparently late dolls are found with good heads on crude bodies, and some well-carved faces are found with a very poor finish and poorly but originally dressed. An unusual example of this type of doll is believed to have been made to represent a negro and still bears much of the dark paint. Another has a slit cut in the top of the head for the insertion of the hair, so that continually slight variants are found: which is, after all, what makes the study of dolls so fascinating.

Not all eighteenth-century wooden dolls are in the manner of the Queen Annes. Many more realistically-finished examples are known. Some of the carved Bavarian wooden dolls have bodies stuffed with tow, and are beautifully dressed, such as a lady and manservant who ride in a sledge. The latter figures have only the heads, hands and feet made of wood, while the bodies are again tow-filled. The National Museum of Finland has a doll of carved wood that 'walks' on wheels concealed under its skirt. The mouth of this doll is slightly open, and its teeth can be seen.

Several German toy-makers of the eighteenth century are known, and as the makers became more conscious of themselves as part of an industry, they showed their products at the big trade fairs such as Leipzig, which was becoming almost as important a centre as Nürnberg. Johann Demetz became well known as a carver of dolls and Christian Friedrich Hammer was working in Nürnberg in 1730 as an art turner, making brotteig-overlaid dolls over which he broke guild rules by painting them in his own workshop, thus causing a long battle with the bismuth painters. This battle meant eventually that doll-makers were able to finish the dolls they had made themselves, which saved the expense of moving the dolls to another workshop for finishing. This method of working was peculiarly Continental, as the English makers had freedom to finish their own dolls. The freeing of doll-makers in Germany from trade guild restrictions meant that doll-making factories became viable, and families such as the Dressels of Sonneberg were quick to take advantage of this new freedom. Prior to this, documents show that there had been considerable movement in dolls between turning and sale, so that they were sometimes taken quite long distances to be painted, which was not only time-consuming but expensive.

Costume

A doll cannot be dated purely on the evidence of its clothes. Some have been

re-dressed recently in old fabrics, others wear dresses that once belonged to dolls of a different period, while others again were re-dressed by the families who originally owned them in order to keep the doll fashionable. The costume can, however, be taken as an extra piece of evidence in dating a doll, and a few general observations on eighteenth-century dolls' costume may be useful.

The inspiration for the dress of a noblewomen in pre-Revolutionary Europe came exclusively from Paris. The *sacque*, an overdress that hung full and loose from the shoulders, became fashionable for all sorts of occasions, and was worn over the very full-skirted silk gowns that were supported by round hoops which were in fashion until about 1730. Hoops are quite often found on dolls where the underwear (being made of linen or flannel) has survived, in contrast to silk dresses, which have often almost completely disintegrated. The hoop consisted of a canvas petticoat into which were sewn horizontal circular bands, made of whalebone or metal in adult costume, but sometimes simply of cane or even thick card in hoops worn by dolls. Pocket slits are nearly always found on both dresses and petticoats of dolls dating from the first quarter of the century, and fine quilted examples of hanging pockets to be worn under the hoop are some-times found. The early eighteenth-century bodice was still tight-fitting and made with pointed fronts, which set off the low necklines edged with frills and flounces. Sleeves were three-quarter length, and finished with matching frills. Long decorative aprons were worn at the start of the century by all kinds of women, because of the popularity of tea-drinking, which made some garment to protect the expensive clothes of the lady necessary when she served the beverage.

Pastel colours were considered to be the most effective, and they were printed, woven or even painted with the popular flower motifs. To achieve a high-busted, narrow-waisted effect, corsets were always worn. When corsets are found on dolls, they are usually of linen, but leather was sometimes used. Tiny caps with hanging lappets were often worn on the head, but most women chose to wear only a few jewels or ribbons on their simply-dressed hair. The presence of silk ribbons hanging from the shoulders, and known as leading strings, is not a reliable indication that a doll is intended to represent a child, as they were worn by any dependent female.

Dress after 1730 became much more heavily ornamented, and all the available edges were decorated with ruffles and flounces. The *sacque* gown was modified into an overdress that was lightly fitted at the front and fell gracefully at the back in regulated pleats from the shoulders – a style known as Watteau pleats. The shape of the hoop itself was also changing, until by 1735 the front and back was flattened and the width was only at the sides, which made it easier for women to enter narrow doors. This type of hoop was much shorter and covered the

8 Swinging Simon and Halbig

9 Five bisque-headed automata

waist and hips only, so that any doll wearing the flattened hoop can be dated as after 1735.

The influence of the French court encouraged the reintroduction of the bell hoop, which supported dresses that were incredibly complex and decorated, not only with the customary frills, but also with feathers, beads and any other novelty the dress-maker could procure.

The hoop was finally ousted and replaced by bustles in the 1780s, when the high ornamentation of costume also declined. Waistlines were no longer quite so low and narrow, though corsets were still worn. The change towards a new and simpler style of dress was led by English society. The English gown was a simple satin dress with elbow length sleeves, which was sometimes set off by large picture hats made of fabric or even straw, the material frequently found on dolls' hats of the period.

Close examination of the dress of eighteenth-century dolls is always necessary, as a reconstructed costume obviously detracts greatly from the doll's value. No matter how threadbare or tattered the dress of such a doll might be, it must be preserved, as dolls of this period dressed in more recent fabrics never fail to look ridiculous, apart from the fact that the collector who re-dresses such a doll is deliberately vandalizing an object of great interest not only to doll-collectors but also to students of fashion history.

FOUR

AUTOMATA AND CRÈCHE FIGURES

Automata

With the exception of the bristle dolls that appeared to dance on piano keys, moveable dolls, before the nineteenth century, were the province of gaping peasants, royal children and the elegant society which included a visit to the popular exhibitions of automata among its regular amusements. Until the mass production of the clockwork toy, the moveable figure was an expensive luxury that could only be justified if an admission charge could be obtained for its viewing, or if it was to be sent as a prestige gift to a great noble or a distant eastern prince.

The eighteenth-century public found such devices so fascinating that Cox's Museum was opened in London, where figures as tall as 16 feet could be viewed. As tickets cost 1 guinea each, it is obvious that a fashionable clientèle was encouraged. James Cox was given various commissions from the East India Company to supply luxury automata to various Eastern Princes, and eventually set up a business in Canton. Many European automata still exist in China, and the Peking Museum has several good examples dating from this period.

In ancient times, the use of moveable figures was purely for the awe they would inspire in the unsophisticated minds of worshippers. A Roman historian talks of statues which ran blood, and even appeared to sweat with anguish when sufficiently encouraged. Many of the articulated statuettes made by the Greeks are believed to have been constructed in this way, so that they would be able to move and come to life in the other kingdom. Moving statues had played their part through the ages in fertility rites and ritual ceremonies, but little advance had been made after Hero until the Renaissance, when the works of the Alexandrians were rediscovered, and inventors such as Battista and Aleothin added their ideas to the growing pool of knowledge. *The Relations of Motive Forces with Various Machines as useful as they are pleasing* was published in 1615 by

Salomon de Caws, an engineer in the service of the Elector Palatine. In this work Caws describes the grottoes set up by the nobility as pleasure areas in the grounds of great houses.

The grottoes usually included a number of fountains which, apart from adding to the effectiveness of the arrangement, also provided the motive power for the doll-like figures which moved and appeared to play musical instruments. The music was often produced by a water-wheel which operated the keys of (perhaps) a flute, by means of a train of gear wheels. The decorative effect of the grottoes must have been great, and it is a pity that they have not survived, requiring us to base our knowledge of these arrangements on written sources.

In Montaigne's *Journal de Voyage* of 1581, he describes the Este garden at Tivoli where automata, including birds and all sorts of figures, ceased their movement and music when an owl appeared, while some figures caused a diversion by sprinkling the visitors with water. Classical subjects were obviously popular themes for grottoes, and characters such as Echo listening to a Satyr playing a flageolet, a Cyclops who plays the Pan pipes or Venus riding in a shell were all created in the gardens of St Germain-en-Laye, Fontainebleau and Versailles.

The Francini family were responsible for many of these mechanisms which motivated the figures and music by water power, and were used to decorate fine gardens, especially in Italy and France. Though the grottoes must have provided a colourful spectacle, they did not retain their enchantment once the novelty had worn off, and such settings were soon seen only in simple form in public gardens and exhibitions.

Miniature grottoes, however, remained popular as items that could be constructed at home, and small dolls of the period were often used to people them. Other, better-quality miniature grottoes were made for public exhibition in such places as fairgrounds, where a coin in the slot would cause the musical box to begin to play and the small figures to move. I am reminded of a London Chinese restaurant whose window held an entrancing grotto, where oriental dolls in boats sailed amongst tawdry but exotic flowers and had the power to captivate attention amongst flashing neon lights and far more sophisticated window displays. Just as Louis XIII as a child had been fascinated by the grottoes at Fontainebleau and Versailles, so modern children are attracted by primitive but ingeniously-constructed moving displays.

Many of the ideas used in the making of mechanical figures were first discovered by the clockmakers of the sixteenth century, who made the central figure of wrought or cast iron, known as the Jack, strike the hours. Clocks of this period incorporated figures representing the Magi, Warriors or Classical figures, while Death striking the hours was probably the most popular. Augsburg

56 "The Dunce" who appears to read badly and raises his arm and lowers head in shame while kicking his heels, to the accompaniment of a slow sad tune. Composition head, china arms. Probably French, though the figure looks German. *c.* 1860. 19 in. high.

and Nürnberg were both important centres for the making of mechanical figures for clocks and especially watches. Garnier observed that Nürnberg made clocks that were more like toys, while Augsburg produced items more in the nature of works of art or science which were presumably intended for the more sophisticated market. Table clocks were often made interesting by such scenes as Mary rocking the Infant Jesus, or a group of figures from the Italian Comedy made of carved wood and dressed like dolls in fabrics.

The eighteenth century saw the peak of ingenuity in the art of the clockmaker when all sorts of musical mechanisms – clavichords, bells, flutes and even the cuckoo – were added. One clock showed a quarrelsome wife appearing to nag her husband by opening and shutting her mouth and ending the harangue by hitting him over the head with a broomstick. Court and ballroom figures were

57   "The Patent Autoperipatetikos or Walking Doll. Martin and Runyon, Office 299 Broadway, N. York." This example has a good 'Parian' head. Kid arms. Mauve silk dress covers a cardboard dome that contains mechanism. Patented 1862. 10 in. high.

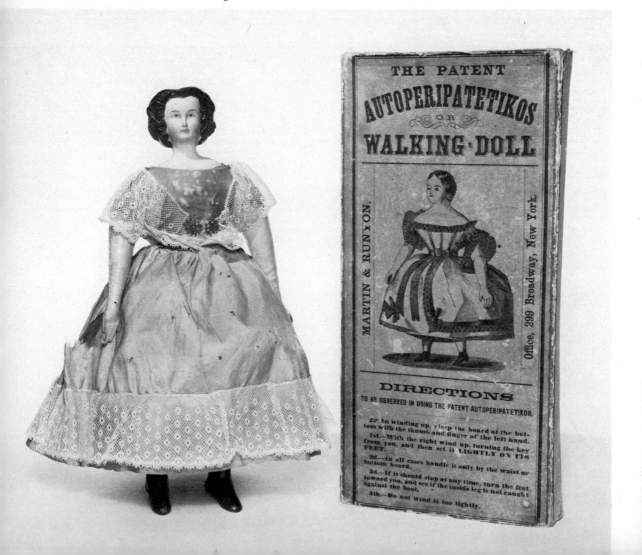

58   Group of painted wooden piano dolls. The figures stand on bristles that vibrate when the piano is played. German. Late nineteenth century. 2–2½ in. high.

the most popular, but some clocks held scenes as prosaic as figures greedily eating meat balls.

It is by the study of such clocks that the collector of automata is made aware of the standard it was possible to achieve at the time, but it was not until the late seventeenth century that mechanical dolls appear as toys, apart from those made for the children of the French kings. André Bigue, who ran a shop at Lille in Flanders, sold all sorts of novelties, including an interesting coach with numerous figures. The coachman and footman both had their own special movements and the coach and horses moved several times around its cabinet when wound up. A lady, 12 inches high, was also worked by a spring which caused her to curtsy and move a fan held in her hand in a realistic way. Other French mechanical toys of this period included a big game hunt and a working model of a blacksmith's shop.

The most famous eighteenth-century maker was Vaucanson, and, though he is popularly remembered for his duck which voided the food it had appeared to eat, his most interesting achievement to the collector of dolls was the creation of a figure that played an instrument. He had originally wanted to make a 'human anatomy' that worked in much the same way as the duck, but decided that it would not be so acceptable to the public, though he, as an ex-medical student, thought the idea a great challenge. Vaucanson presented his flute player to the Academie des Sciences in 1738, together with a paper that explained so exactly how it worked that replicas have been made. A tabor and tambourine player were exhibited at the same time, to the amazement of the contemporary audience.

At first, many people would not believe that sounds were produced by the flute which the automaton was holding. They thought the sounds must come from a bird organ or a German organ encased in the body of the figure. The most incredulous, however, were soon convinced that the automaton was in fact blowing the flute, that the breath coming from his lips made it play and that the movement of his fingers determined the different notes. The machine was submitted to the most minute examination and stringent tests. The spectators were permitted to see even the innermost springs and to follow their movements.

Vaucanson had spent a great deal of time both in the study of musical instruments themselves and in the method of playing them, and he had completely mastered the assessment of air pressure needed to secure high and low notes. He had also studied the changes of speed at which air had to enter the instrument, and all this knowledge was carefully utilized in the creation of the figure.

The flute player, which was over 6 feet high and was made of wood, was worked by a wheel train which drove a crankshaft, and the movement and music were produced by a series of cords, pulleys and three large bellows. These bellows were weighted so that air could be obtained at high, medium or low pressure. Another clever device enabled the lips of the automaton to be drawn back, opened and shut. An excellent and full description of the mechanics of this figure is given in *Automata* by Chapuis and Droz, the standard work on automatic dolls and toys, and the source on which most writers on the history of dolls have to draw for the early history of this specialized field.

Many imitations of Vaucanson's work were made after the publication of the memoir. A mechanic by the name of Defrance, for instance, manufactured a life-size shepherd and shepherdess who played thirteen different tunes. The impressario Du Moulin, into whose possession the original figures came, removed parts from the duck and the tabor and drum player to make it difficult for anyone

(*left*) 59 Bisque shoulder-head walking doll. The mechanism marked "Steiner" on the bellows. As the figure rolls along it cries "Mama" and lifts its arm. Fine-quality head with a double row of teeth. Dark blue fixed eyes. Marked "J. Steiner, Bte. SGDG. Paris". 15 in. high.

(*right*) 60 Steiner bisque-headed doll made to represent a kicking child. When wound, the figure turns head, kicks its legs and raises its arms to be picked up while crying "Mama". Kid-covered body with composition limbs. Pierced ears. Open mouth with two rows of teeth. Marked in a blue circle on back "Magasin des Enfants, Jouets et Jeux, Passage de l'Opéra, Paris". 18 in. high.

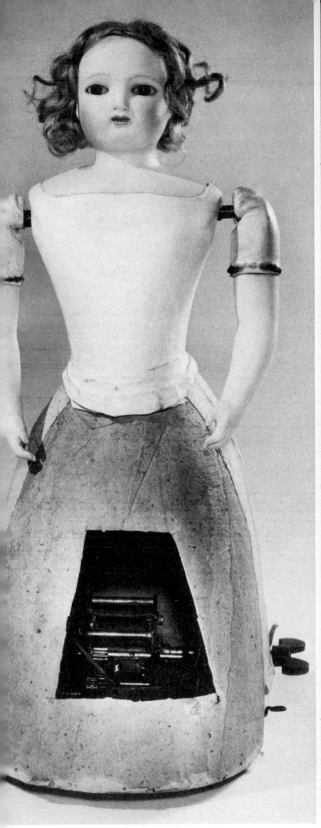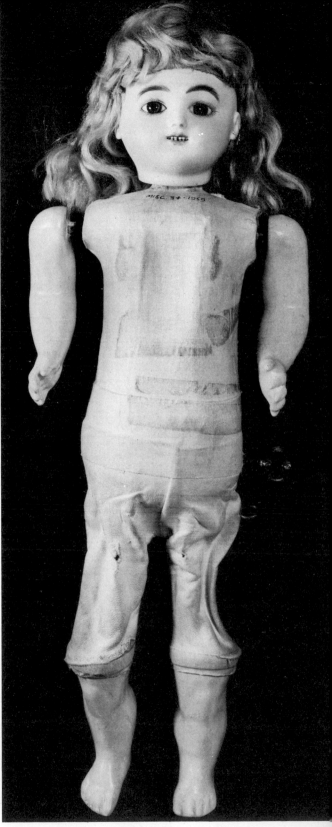

else either to repair or copy the figures. The models eventually passed at auction into the hands of people who wished only to make money out of their exhibition and cared little for their scientific and mechanical interest. Figures occasionally come to light that are thought possibly to have been made by Vaucanson, but he is recorded only as having made the previously mentioned 'human' figures. His achievement lay in his success in making a model figure play an instrument by its own movement, whereas previously, though the models moved their fingers, the music was not produced by this movement but came from another source.

Other groups of shepherds and shepherdesses playing instruments were made, but, despite the way that posters of the period eulogize their charms, it is difficult to estimate whether they performed as realistically as those made by Vaucanson. Jean Roullet, for instance, the grandfather of Decamps, made a fine model of a young negro which played a flute organ, and models of court ladies were still popular.

The main aim of all the eighteenth-century makers was the creation of a figure that appeared to be real, and probably the greatest acclaim was given to the work of Jacquet Droz, who presented his first great work in 1773 with the assistance of Leschot. Droz had previously made small objects such as snuff boxes which were made with moving figures to decorate them. 'The Lady Musician', who was represented in the work he first presented, became famous in all the European courts. The mechanism for this figure was made of four groups. One, placed under the organ, operated bellows which supplied compressed air to the flutes, while the two larger barrels operated a regular wheel train. The three mechanisms housed under the seat were linked to each other and released each other. The mechanism in the foreground caused the girl's chest to rise in breathing and governed the movement of the eyes in all directions. The fingers were worked by rods and levers, and the upper arms do not move away from the body, so that all the movement originated from the elbow. The lifelike swaying movement of the figure was controlled by a cam.

The design of the figure is very clever, as between the pieces of music which it performs, the automaton appears to go on breathing and turns her head from side to side to see how many people are watching, and then, apparently confused by the number, lowers her eyes to the instrument. The doll itself is a fine portrait figure, beautifully dressed in the height of fashion. It is generally considered that this figure represents the ultimate in man's effort to create a mechanical figure which actually plays an instrument.

Leschot and Jacquet Droz are believed to have made another musician in 1782, which represented a girl playing a harpsichord while being instructed by a teacher. When finished, this design was sold by Jacquet Droz the Younger to the firm of Jacquet Droz and Maillardet of London for £420. Known as 'the replica',

61 Fine-quality tinted-bisque head representing a Burmese girl, who gracefully pours tea while the music plays. The key marked "LB" for Leopold Lambert, Paris (1888–1923). 20 in. high.

this figure was even more skilfully made and played eighteen melodies. A poster, published in 1827, probably refers to this figure and others made by Droz.

> The nobility, gentry and inhabitants of Hull and its vicinity are respectfully informed that the grand Mechanical and Magical Theatre (from the Gothic Hall, Haymarket, London) is now open every day and will continue for a short time only at the Apollo Saloon. . . . The Automata comprise the following subjects. The Juvenile Artist, whose astonishing performance in Drawing and Writing alternately in the presence of the company defies all attempts at rivalship in regard to their beauty and correction of design and execution.

The replica girl playing the harpsichord was called 'The Fair Roxlane' by Maillardet, and it travelled all over Europe, eventually being sent to St Petersburg, since when its whereabouts has been a mystery; it remains a collector's discovery dream.

A beautiful dulcimer player was constructed in 1780 by Roentgen and a watchmaker, Kintzing, for Queen Marie Antoinette. This automaton had music especially composed for it by Gluck and can still be seen at the *Conservatoire des Arts et Métiers* in Paris. It was dressed in fabrics from the Queen's wardrobe, and wore hair made from one of her wigs. It remained the favourite of the Queen for only a few months and was then sold to the Academie des Sciences.

The figure made by Jacquet Droz which collectors regard most highly is undoubtedly his Juvenile Artist. This is a wooden model of a young and beautiful boy who sits working at a table. Droz was not the first, of course, to have made writing figures. They had been crudely made by Arab craftsmen in an earlier period, but the first which actually wrote were made by Friedrich von Knaus, who built four models dating from as early as 1735. In the first examples the letters were traced merely by a hand holding a pen, but the last device made was of a figure that held a pen and wrote the letters by the movement of the wrist. The Knaus automaton was simpler than those made by Droz, but nevertheless was able to write quite a long passage of up to 110 words. The figure could also write any sentence that was composed in advance, and it could write to dictation when manually controlled.

The Droz writer is 28 inches high and carries a goose quill in its hand. The figure dips the pen in an ink-well and shakes it twice before beginning to write. One hand is placed at the top of the page and the figure pauses once more before beginning to write. All the words are written very slowly and the automaton changes from one line to the next, putting a full stop at the end of the passage.

62 Attractive French automaton representing a young woman pushing a pram. Mechanism by Decamps of Paris *c.* 1880. When wound the legs move and balance is maintained by the pram. Bisque swivel head on shoulder plate, bisque arms and legs. The right arm once held a parasol over the doll's head — satin and velvet dress. 12 in. high.

A draughtsman was originally exhibited with the writer, and was a little less difficult to construct as it did not require as many selections of cams. The figure drew amusing pictures and also had a moving head and eyes that turned. These figures, when exhibited together, caused such great interest that an apparently clever chess player was made by Von Kempelen in 1770 which was in reality a complete fake, as it had a boy concealed in the base who was able to control the movements of the players.

Droz and Leschot built other automata, often assisted by Maillardet. A story which appeals to most collectors' instincts is that originating from the Franklin Research Museum. A machine in extremely bad condition, having been burned, was discovered in Philadelphia and restored by the museum in the belief that it was the work of Mälzel, a later maker. When restored the figure began to write and ended one of its sentences, "Written by Maillardet's automaton". The figure writes verses such as:

> Unerring is my hand, though small
> May I not add with truth.
> I do my best to please you all
> Encourage then my youth.

– copies of which are taken away as souvenirs by visitors to the museum. The figure incurred a change of sex during restoration and now represents a girl, though it was originally a boy, as is indicated by the words the automaton writes.

Walking and Talking Dolls

Attempts to make a doll that appeared to walk were usually concentrated on a doll-like figure which moved on wheels or rollers concealed under the skirt, and a similar doll dressed in Renaissance costume and made in 1764 was signed P. Gautier. This doll appears to pluck the strings of a guitar and turns and lowers its head as it moves forward on rollers. It was difficult to make a doll which moved by placing one foot in front of the other, but Charles Abram Bruguier is believed to have made a doll with a mechanism concealed in its body which moved forward a step at a time while turning its head from side to side and carrying a rake to help provide the necessary balance. This doll is believed to have been made around 1821, and there appears to have been no further advance in walking dolls until Simonet designed another similar doll in 1829. Nicholas Theroude specialized in wheeled 'walking dolls' in the 1840s and '50s, though surviving examples are not very attractive because of the rather ugly papier mâché heads he used.

The piano-dancing dolls were necessarily small, under $2\frac{1}{2}$ inches high, and were usually made completely of wood with quite skilfully-carved faces. The

63 Clockwork Juba dancers. Figures jog up and down on pins as the music plays. Painted wooden figures. Were advertised in the *Queen* for 1875 at 12s. 6d. Contains a mechanism of nice quality. 10½ in. high.

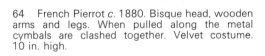

64 French Pierrot *c.* 1880. Bisque head, wooden arms and legs. When pulled along the metal cymbals are clashed together. Velvet costume. 10 in. high.

dolls were made hollow, which enabled the legs fixed inside the body by strings to move freely. The dolls stood on four bristles that provided just enough balance to keep the doll upright when the piano was played, and the vibrations caused the figure to appear to dance.

Contemporary descriptions often refer to dancing dolls, but these are usually found to have been of the type of figure that revolved on a simple pivot and had been made for several centuries. A fashion print of 1855 shows a well-dressed young woman holding a dancing doll of this type, dressed fashionably and wearing a large hat with streamers. The Bestelmeier catalogue of 1800 lists mechanical dolls dressed in the height of fashion, and these were also probably of the pivot type.

The Czar had been given walking dolls as early as the seventeenth century, but these were in all probability figures that moved on wheels of some kind, and were possibly similar to the types dressed in court costume and made for the amusement of the French court. Tilting dolls also frequently provided adults as well as children with amusement, as they were sometimes dressed to represent fat old gentlemen, with frock coats drawn tightly over the apparently bulging stomach that was in reality the round papier mâché tilting base.

The attempt to create a mechanical figure that appeared completely realistic necessitated the invention of a speaking mechanism, and Mälzel, a German who took out a patent in 1823, is believed to have been the first model-maker to have in any way achieved this aim. The doll he made appeared to say 'mama' and 'papa' when bellows concealed in the body closed and sent air into a tube of lead containing a flapping tongue. The valves in the mechanism had counter-weights which also helped control the sound made by the device. The word 'mama' was formed by the movement of a small wheel with wolf teeth.

In 1815 Leopold Robert, a painter wrote in a letter: "Some time ago we went to see the collection just come from Russia, and among many other marvels we saw a waxwork figure of a child who could pronouce all the letters of the alphabet very well. The way he expressed himself was quite intelligible." Unfortunately, there is no record of who made this doll, or of whether it was a true automaton, or perhaps just another clever trick. Contemporary accounts and advertisements for such wonders are notoriously unreliable, as like the advertisements of today, they succeed in making everything sound quite unlikely.

An almost unbelievable account of Mälzel's automata was written by Mrs Child in the *Girls' Own Book* of 1848. "First there was a chess player, an image

65   A barrel-organ player with five small bisque-headed dancing dolls. The organ player beats time and nods his head while the dolls pirouette to music. Bavarian or Swiss. 20 in. high.

(*above*) 66   Spinning-top dolls *c.* 1892. White bisque heads and arms. The base marked "Toupie Brevete SGDGEC". 3¼ in. high.   (*below left*) 67   Well-made pine Jumping Jack. Early nineteenth century. Such figures brightly painted, were made in Oberammergau. Arms, legs, beard and tongue move when string is pulled. 14 in. high.   (*below right*) 68   A wide variety of tin, doll-like figures were made. Here a Chinaman who brandishes weapons and is marked "FM" in a circle on hat for Fernand Martin and a flywheel-driven tin lady who rolls along on four wheels.

dressed like a Turk, who sat at the board and played as good a game of chess as if he had brains in his wooden skull. He shook his head and rapped the board with his fingers when his adversary made a move contrary to the game; and when he had the King in his power, he called 'Echec!'" Another automaton was a carousel which sounds equally wonderful, as it represented a circus with a fountain in the centre. A number of figures rode around the circus performing special feats. A Spanish lancer caught a cap on the point of his lance without stopping his horse, and rode off with it, while 'The Marksman of Madrid' aimed a minute pistol at a bird sitting on a post which fell off, apparently dead. A vaulter jumped great heights, while a clown pursued by a hungry horse was at last overtaken and his cap snatched from his head. Harlequin, who attempted a rescue, was eventually thrown from his rearing horse, which according to the contemporary account caused great amusement to the watching children.

The mechanical dolls that are reported to have performed obscene antics at the parties given by the Princess of Wales at Blackheath might simply have been a piece of malicious gossip on the part of an unsympathetic contemporary, though dolls of a similar type may well have been available or the story would have been too far-fetched even for the Regency period.

A series of cheap and now rather macabre figures were sold in the Regency period by 'Edlin's National Repository of Amusement and Instruction' at New Bond Street. A few of these figures used to be exhibited by Miss Blair Hickmann at her charity exhibitions of dolls. They do not appear consistent with the type of toy we now associate from their own advertisements with the Rational Toy Shops, but presumably shops in the nineteenth century were as likely to sink their principles for gain as they are now. The dolls, which depict mechanically such everyday scenes as snuff taking, spinning and a lady waving her fan while her doctor diagnoses influenza, are hinged with leather and work by a series of levers which activate wire spring-joints, which in turn enable the figures to take a pinch of snuff or work a spinning wheel. Some of the Edlin toys are found with the name of their maker, John Hempel, on the base. The dolls are made of wood with cleverly characterized painted plaster faces reminiscent of caricatures seen in *Punch*.

Collectable Automata

Most of the dolls discussed in the earlier part of this chapter have been of such a standard that they would be found now only in museums or the collections of the very wealthy. The nineteenth century was, however, slow to advance the ingenious and intricate mechanical movements which had so awed the eighteenth-century public, so that there are not as many early nineteenth-century automata available as might be expected from the glorious beginning.

The Exposition Universelle, held in Paris in 1879, was an important landmark in the construction of automata as it encouraged the inventors by rewarding them for their efforts. A swimming doll made by Martin was exhibited for the first time at this exhibition: a doll that was still being mass produced by a descendant in 1929.

Most of the nineteenth-century automata are combined with a musical box to provide an amusing family show. The cartel type of musical boxes was sold first in Geneva in 1833, and the new construction enabled advances to be made more quickly as previously only a small volume of sound could be given off. The cartel was developed by such improvements as mechanisms which enabled sound to be produced loudly or softly so that the musical box could have a much wider range of uses. The drums and bells were at first arranged in view behind the cylinder, but later they were concealed in the cases. After 1850, comb music was combined with air-vibrated reeds, which enabled a good range of sound to be produced.

The musical box on which stood a doll, which performed a few fairly simple movements, was the most popular type of nineteenth-century automaton. These figures were not intended as toys, but as items to be displayed in the parlour, for some were very expensive. The French were particularly skilful in making such groups and were fond of the apparently human figure with the head of a monkey that could preen and admire itself in imitation of a young dandy at a mirror, or take a delicate pinch of snuff. One tableau on a musical box shows dolls playing cards at a table while another drinks tea.

When dolls were used, the French makers often utilized bisque heads made by famous doll-makers, such as Jumeau, or even imported heads made by German firms, such as Simon and Halbig. The presence of these heads on the automata make the groups doubly desirable, both to collectors of dolls and automata, which accounts partly for their high price.

The collector is unlikely to find a good automaton in a non-specialist shop, and even dealers in antique dolls often have little knowledge of the mechanisms of automata, so that purchase from a dealer specializing in such figures is advisable. It is a mistake to buy any damaged automaton unless ridiculously cheap, since what can appear to the uninitiated as a simple repair can be extremely costly and difficult to effect.

A wide variety of much cheaper figures were made as shop-window display dummies, and include clowns, Father Christmasses or Chinamen, all of which had nodding heads that would rock for hours once wound up. Such figures,

69   Papier mâché Chinaman, whose head nods for a long period when key wound, indicating its original use as a display model, possibly for a tea-seller's shop window. 22 in. high.

usually made of composition, are still quite cheap, and some of the better-dressed example, such as the illustrated Chinaman, fit in well with collections of dolls. Some rather more expensive dolls of this type were also used as advertisements for shops: one example appears to drink a cup of tea, while another samples a glass of whisky.

Tin figures which work by clockwork or flywheel mechanisms, such as a lady mopping the floor or gliding sedately along carrying a fan, can still be found on antique market stalls, though often in rather a battered condition. Those that carry no maker's name are still fairly cheap, but initials such as F.M. in a circle (for Fernand Martin) pressed into the tin cause a steep rise in price. Martin made a number of small figures, usually under 6 inches high, such as a little pianist, a messenger boy, a man breaking plates or a barber's shop. These tin toys were decorated with a thin colour varnish and sold very cheaply by toy-shops and street hawkers. The American tinsmiths at the same period were making clever walking figures with loosely-riveted joints.

The famous firm of Roullet et Decamps included walking dolls among their products, and Jean Roullet, the founder of the firm, won a silver Medal at the Paris Exposition of 1878. Most automata that come the way of the average collector were made by this firm, which is still in production. Designs, if they proved successful, were produced for many years, so that automata are discovered whose appearance would suggest a nineteenth-century date yet were made as recently as 1920. Acrobats in well-made sequin-spangled costumes stand on top of many of their musical-box movements. Nursemaids wheeling babies in prams, tambourine players, groups of dolls and magicians were all made to the highest standard by this prolific firm. The large number that have survived in working order evidences the quality of the original workmanship.

One of the best known automata was made by Decamps working in partnership with Durand, a well-known inventor. The result of this partnership was 'Professor Arcadius' which was exhibited at the Exposition Universelle Paris in 1937. A rather foolish-looking old man sits ruminating at a table on which stands a pen in an ink-well. The Professor can be consulted by putting money in an appropriate slot and allowing the hand to be examined. The automaton appears to look at the questioner by opening his eyes very wide. He then reverts to his original position and writes down his prophecy. Tearing it off the sheet he gives it to his client. The comments are, in the manner of all such fairground predictions, conveniently vague. The Professor makes remarks such as: "An intelligence developing thanks to powers of observation": very much in the traditional vein of the magicians who sat on the top of seventeenth- and eighteenth-century clocks, though Arcadius has twenty phrases in his repertoire.

The first automaton made by Decamps was a snake charmer. While music

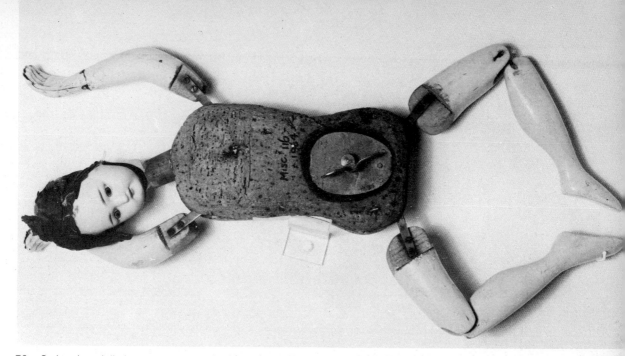

70   Swimming doll that once wore a bathing dress. Known as Ondine. Similar dolls were advertised by J. M. Theobald in the 1880s for 12s. 6d. each. "Designed by a Parisian mechanician" and suggested as an adult amusement for parties. Bisque head by Simon and Halbig. Cork body. Wooden arms and legs. Patented in 1876 by E. Martin. 17 in. long.

played, the charmer lifted a rattlesnake in one hand and a trumpet in the other. Trapeze artistes were very popular products of the firm, and a very complex equilibrist was made. Another well-known prestige piece was 'The Illusionist' which was made in the eighteenth-century tradition of life-size and lifelike constructions. 'The Illusionist' contrives to remove a female figure dressed in Oriental costume from the cabinet in which she is standing to another with which there is no apparent communication.

Though such prestige works are fascinating to the collectors of automata, they are really outside the scope of the average collector, who usually looks for the more modest, commercially-produced doll-like figures, standing or sitting on some sort of musical box and performing a few relatively simple movements, such as smoking, blowing a bugle or playing an instrument. A very elegantly-dressed lady-doll is a popular collector's piece, and this doll powders its face and appears to study the effect in a mirror. Other Parisienne bisque heads are used on figures in such arrangements as a lady and young man in court dress who dance, and a little girl who appears at a window and waters the flowers. Simon and Halbig heads were often used instead of the more desirable French heads, and were sometimes made so much in the French tradition that they can only be identified by the incised marks on the back of the heads.

One of the best-known smaller automata is a 'Seated Turk'. Dressed in silks and satins, the figure slowly turns his head to smoke a hookah and drink coffee while batting his eyelids as the music plays. Organ-grinder figures were also very popular, as the movement of the figure reflected the sound of the music in the base. Many of these fine groups were made to be preserved in cases and, with the exception of some of the dancing and walking dolls and the tin toys, they were never intended for children, except as occasional parlour amusements to be stared at in wonder.

Beautifully-made modern automata can still be seen in the windows of fashionable Parisian shops, and are made by Jean Farkas and his wife Annette. The dolls, which often represent ladies, have bisque heads and well-made wigs – some made by Annette Farkas herself, who also makes the clothes out of genuinely old fabrics. Some of the figures, which are made to represent traditional characters, such as smokers, acrobats and guitarists, can now be worked by electricity. Jean Farkas designs each part of the body with great skill to contain the movement he wishes it to make, though the heads and limbs are made especially for him.

These figures are in the tradition of luxury French toys and are very expensive, so that it would hardly be likely that a dishonest dealer would 'antique' such a figure and sell it to an inexperienced collector as antique, since some cost far more than old examples fetch in the salerooms.

The Decamps business is also still active, though it now mainly produces automated prestige window-displays for shops. The workshop of Lucien Bontems, which was established in the mid-nineteenth century, still exists, so that at least some of the old French tradition of skilful workmanship is maintained.

Marottes

Marottes fall between the categories of dolls and automata, as they are formed by mounting a musical movement on a stick and covering it with the fabric of a doll's dress. When the stick, which can be made of metal, wood or even ivory, is swung around, the musical movement is activated and produces an attractive effect when combined with the bells that usually decorate the pointed ends of the originally gaudy dresses.

A few rare marottes have a complete doll, which stands on top of the musical movement, and are dressed in clothes and ribbons which swing as the toy is turned to produce the music.

Others, sometimes now referred to as folies, have no musical box concealed, but simply a squeaker device and the marotte has to be shaken rather than turned.

(*right*) 72 In this more complicated version, the dress conceals a musical box that is activated when the marotte is swung. Probably constructed in France but utilizing a flange-necked Armand Marseille head. 12 in. high.

(*above*) 71 A folie whose blue silk dress conceals a cardboard squeeker. Bisque head impressed "Limoges 02 France". Pierced ears, brown glass eyes. 12½ in. high.

(*left*) 73 A marotte of high quality, whose musical movement is activated by a flick of the wrist. Bisque head, probably French, on a composition body. 11 in. high.

These *folies* are decorated in a very similar way to the more valuable musical versions with bells, gold fringe and braids. A padded hat shaped rather like a clown's is also common, as the shape was suitable for the attaching of extra bells, which contributed to the festive appearance of the dolls.

The Société de Fabrication des Bébés et Jouets made many of the heads of bisque that are found on such dolls, and a large number of the French heads were also made in the Limoges area. Some heads with flange necks were especially made for use on such toys, but others were simply the usual heads found on jointed dolls. Some of the heads made by Armand Marseille have this flange neck, and are to be found on *marottes* that look so completely French that at first it is hard to believe that the head could possibly be German, as some are made in the French manner, though usually without the pierced ears that are most common to French dolls.

Early *marottes* were rather dull objects of papier mâché, which usually represented a child in swaddling-clothes, rather in the manner of the doll-rattles that had been popular since the Middle Ages. Occasionally a rattle is found in the shape of a doll, but when this is so, it is usually made of tin, celluloid or silver. The exception is a rattle doll that was made by Butler Brothers. This doll had a head made of china that contained china balls which rattled when the doll was shaken, and sounds dangerously unsuitable for children.

Crèche Figures

Many collectors like to include a few crèche figures among their acquisitions, though such models can in no way be thought of as secular dolls, as they were made by artists and craftsmen purely for use as religious statues. They are the only doll-like figures of any great age that are available to the ordinary collector, as the small examples in terracotta or wood fetch quite low prices when sold at auction. The largest carved wood figures such as those originating in Bavaria do however command respectable prices, as they are of really fine craftsmanship, and are bought as works of art by leading antique dealers.

Small individual examples from the well-made crèche arrangements particularly connected with the seventeenth and eighteenth centuries are often bought by doll-collectors as samples of the standard of figure-making that could be achieved at a time when children's dolls were still extremely crude. The heads were made in very realistic detail out of wood, terracotta or plaster. Inset glass eyes are often found, though many are simply painted on, while hair

74   Carved wooden crèche figure representing a court lady. Inset glass eyes. White wool wig whose curls are stitched in place. Decorated in silver thread on cream silk. Eighteenth century. 11 in. high.

was suggested either by carving or by the addition of a wig. The intention of the craftsman was to make the figure appear completely realistic – an aim that was admirably achieved.

The making of crèche groups, at first representing only the Holy Family itself, dates to around A.D. 400, though it is also sometimes suggested, without any apparent proof, to have been instigated by St Francis of Assisi in the thirteenth century. This legend possibly arose because of the story that St Francis arranged a play about the birth of Christ to instruct his congregation in a way they could understand. This attempt to present the Christian story in a simple way was the reason for the popularity of the Christmas crib in Italy, where it was known as the *presepio*.

From a relatively humble beginning, the crèche groups became steadily more ornate, until they were items of fashionable interest set up in the great palaces in a spirit of quite irreligious competition. St Clement's Church at Prague is believed to have the earliest known crib, which dates from 1563, but many small groups, sometimes carved in high relief, were made for use in the houses of merchants. Some of these small cribs are priceless works of art made of gold and silver, but others are quite simple and carved out of wood by local craftsmen. The crèche arrangements that appeal to doll-collectors are those that held a large number of figures that were dressed in fabrics and arranged every year in a slightly different way with the addition of new figures. One such was owned in the sixteenth century by the Duchess Constanza of Amalfi, and contained 116 figures.

The crèche groups would be constructed by the most skilful craftsmen available, and in Italy many of them lived and worked in one street in Naples which was named after the craft of its inhabitants. The fashion was introduced to Italy at the beginning of the seventeenth century when a group was made in Sicily, but Naples quickly became the most important centre for the creation of ornate groups of a standard suitable for the wealthy Italian princes. Michele Perroni is known as a maker of the realistic figures that held great appeal for the Neapolitans, who each year introduced more figures and scenes around the central theme. The artist-craftsman concentrated on making heads of terracotta and the bodies were assembled by less skilled workers, who were able to repair or even remake bodies that had been damaged. This is one of the reasons why it is often difficult to be precise about the dating of such a figure, as the head is often considerably older than the clothed body.

75   Carved wooden crèche figure, whose hair is also carved. Glass eyes with a body of wound moss and tow. German in manner. 13 in. high.

The groups would be exhibited at Christmas in churches, convents and small houses, as well as in the great palaces of the Italian princes, who were so eager to outshine one another by their splendid displays. The inclusion of all sorts of bystanders including villagers, merchants, birds and animals as well as the Angelic host gave the craftsmen great scope, and a figure would sometimes be made representing the person who had commissioned the *presepio*, rather in the manner of the great Florentine painters, who often included a portrait of their patron in a painting. Individual worshippers would sometimes also commission a crèche figure for a church arrangement as an act of penance.

Giuseppe Sammartino, Giuseppe Gori and Angelo Viva were well-known makers, who appeared to specialize in the creation of figures of Orientals and nobles. When artists such as these had painted the terracotta faces with great realism in oil colours, the figures would be dressed by sewing women, who worked in and around Vico dei Figurari. Fine silks and brocades decorated with gold and silver thread and semi-precious stones were lavished on important figures, which even now, despite their faded state, retain much of their original splendour.

Charles III, King of Naples, as an act of devotion arranged a *presepio* himself, and his queen used fabrics from her own wardrobe to dress the dolls in a suitably splendid manner. This *presepio* contained 150 large angels and countless cherubs grouped around Mary and Joseph, who are always represented in a devotional pose with as spiritual an expression as the artist could create. In 1478 two sculptors, Pietro and Giovanni Alamanno, were commissioned to make a crib for the family chapel of Jaconello Pepe at St Giovanna Carbonara. The figures made were itemized as Jesus, the Virgin Mary wearing a crown, Joseph, eleven angels, eleven prophets, two sybils, three shepherds, twelve sheep, two dogs, four trees, an ox and an ass.

The Neapolitan cribs are often considered to be the finest ever made. One group, in a museum near Naples, includes 500 figures of people and 20 of animals, all made of carved wood and wax and modelled as portraits of nobles and peasants. The court figures are exceptionally well dressed, some, it was spitefully said at the time, being better dressed than the people they were supposed to represent.

Whole families and groups of nuns in convents would concentrate throughout the year on the dressing of these splendid figures, so that an effective display would be arranged for the annual Christmas visits to rival *presepios*. This rivalry encouraged the creation of a large number of incidental but interesting figures, and also ornate and complicated backgrounds often in the manner of an idealized rocky grotto. Silversmiths and goldsmiths also contributed miniature items to the arrangements, and some *presepios* included such scenes as market stalls, which provide the historian with a fascinating, if somewhat romanticized, view of everyday life of the period.

Simple mechanical movements were sometimes introduced, rather in the manner of the decorative grottoes, and, in the eighteenth century, figures such as woodcutters and musicians that appeared to move. Water, and later steam, was used to motivate such settings that were less popular in Italy than in Germany.

The more realistic groups attempted to give an illusion of perspective by placing the large central figures in the foreground and others, in diminishing size, further away from the viewer, as in a painting. The terracotta heads painted in oil colours are the most common Neapolitan crib figures. Inset glass eyes were often used and the body was built up over a wood or wire armature by wrapping tow, string or even strips of fabric around to provide a good shape. The basic figure, undressed, is often quite ugly and not very realistic, but the makers' skill was such that, when dressed and bent into a suitable pose, the figure is completely convincing. The hands are usually delicately made and quite realistic, and often carry a rosary, a flower, or even, if the figure represents a trader, some of his wares. The craftsman only put detail on the parts of the body that could be seen, so that lower legs are modelled often with sandals or shoes with buckles or rosettes, while the upper legs are just roughly wrapped about with tow.

The Neapolitan terracotta heads are usually made on a deep narrow shoulder plate, so that, for instance, a man's powerful neck and chest could be shown under an open shirt or the cleavage between a women's breasts. The shoulder plate is usually much shallower at the back, where the costume would cover more of the figure. If the head is removed from the body the initials of the maker can sometimes be found incised on the inside of the shoulder plate, but it is inadvisable to remove the fragile clothes of such a doll on the slender chance of finding a marked example. Some of the heads gave great character, with weatherbeaten faces, wrinkles and goitrous necks, while others have bald heads and gaps between their teeth.

The Neapolitan figures range in size from 8 to 18 inches, though some of the central figures are sometimes even bigger. The hair is nearly always moulded, and wigs do not appear from studied examples to have often been used, as the heads were made in the correct classical sculptors' manner with all the detail added in the same medium.

Sicilian crib figures tend to be rather smaller, and the heads are more frequently made of carved wood or wax. Giovanni Matera was one of the greatest of Sicilian crib artists and the Bayerisches National Museum, Munich, has a fine group of his in a romantic landscape setting of picturesque ruins. The figures have well-carved heads of wood and the clothes are made by the simple but effective process of dipping fabric in heavy size or light plaster and arranging it in careful sculptural folds over the figure to represent the clothes. When dry, the fabric becomes stiff and the folds of the drapery are maintained exactly as the craftsman intended.

The Jesuits spread the idea of the Christmas crib in Germany during the seventeenth century and, while not rivalling the Italian *presepio* in breadth or characterization, the German groups have a more robust appeal of their own. They are not as often the works of art the Neapolitans produced with carefully-studied arrangement and use of perspective, but are settings in a more folk-like manner, without the rather contrived effects of the Italian examples. The German cribs seem intended to appeal more to the humble congregation of a church rather than to sophisticated collectors such as the Medici family. There are, of course, splendid contradictions to this general assessment, in particular some of the prestige settings made at Oberammergau; but the German cribs do generally have a less sophisticated approach to the subject than the Italian.

The majority of the German figures have carved wooden heads and some were especially made for annual cribs on display from Christmas to Easter. Wax was also used by the German crèche makers and the work of Johann Baptist Plöderl, who worked in Wasserburg in the eighteenth century, has a high reputation. Giovanni Battista Cetto was another famous eighteenth-century maker of wax figures, who included an extremely fine miniature crèche, now in the Bavarian National Museum, among his works.

Wigs were used much more frequently on German figures of this type, and are usually made of wool or silk, though sometimes real hair was employed. The lengths of wool or hair were knotted into a small skull cap of coarse fabric. The hairstyle was usually sewn into position, as it did not need rearrangement in the way a doll's hair does each time it is dressed. Ringlets and curls are often found to have neat stitches behind them which have kept the hair neatly in its original style after several centuries.

Bavarian and Austrian crèche figures are often carved of limewood and are sometimes articulated by ball and socket joints. Some of the Tyrolean figures are particularly splendid, and as large as 24 inches high. These are often recognized by art collectors as fine statues, rather than just lay figures for church use. The woodcarvers of both the Tyrol and Oberammergau made crib figures in great numbers to the end of the nineteenth century, though the most popular were those in miniature that could be hung on a wall or stood on a small table with candles burning in front as the devotion of the humble. These two areas still produce cribs, though not usually to the standard of the church cribs of the eighteenth century. The Oberammergau Museum has a crib containing over 200 figures, most of which are about 16 inches high. This crèche was made for

10 Wooden crèche figure
11 Papier mâché Regency doll

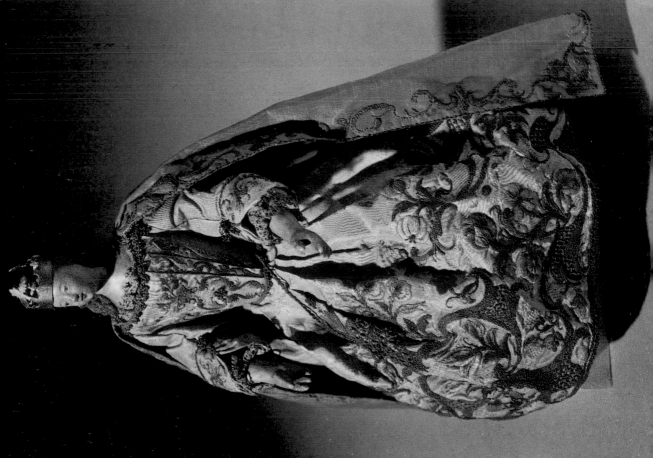

the village church by local craftsmen, who added figures to it each year between 1780 and 1860. The figures are dressed in the manner of the actors of the Passion Play of two centuries ago. This crèche setting is probably the most splendid of all, and still has the power to awe its viewers in the way that once simple country folk were awed by the crèche groups set up in their local churches.

In cribs from the Erzgebirge, mechanical movement was a speciality. The figures were at first usually worked by water or steam, but more recently smaller versions were made with a clockwork mechanism. Cheap card or paper versions of the crib setting were also made in the late nineteenth century in Germany. Some of these were quite large, and could be folded for storage from one Christmas to the next, while others were very small and in the form of a Christmas card. Variations of this old type of Christmas card are still made today, but without the fine detail that was lavished on the nineteenth-century examples usually 'printed in Bavaria'.

As the construction of crèche figures hardly changed for several hundred years, individual examples that have become dispersed from their original settings are not easy to date. Clothes, though an indication, would have probably been replaced and cannot therefore be relied upon for any more than a tentative dating of the figure itself. The wax figures, because of the incrustation of dirt that builds up on the surface, tend to look older than they actually are, while those of terracotta or wood often still look quite fresh. The wooden figures are probably the easiest to date, as they can be studied in relation to schools of carving and the fashionable manner of various periods.

Dolls of religious significance

'Christ the Good Shepherd' was a popular figure in the eighteenth and early nineteenth century, and was usually represented as a little boy with abundant curls and a rather spiritual expression. Some wax dolls are found with the hand outstretched in the position of holding a staff or shepherds crook that has long since disappeared. If the doll is obviously some sort of statuette rather than a play doll, it is likely that it was originally intended as a figure of the boy Christ, either simply as a religious figure for a convent or large private house or possibly as a devotional figure in the bedroom of a child of wealthy family. A few were probably used in churches, but the examples I have seen suggest a more intimate family setting for the figures.

'Bambino' dolls were often given to mothers in Catholic countries on the birth of a child. These were sometimes very extravagant and ornate, with gilded and flower-strewn cradles, while others were very simple and consisted of a cheap doll wrapped in swaddling-clothes lying in its wooden cradle. Various

76 Poured-wax figure with extremely beautiful face, probably representing Christ the Good Shepherd. The right hand bent to hold a crook. Inset hair. Small teeth. Moss-filled linen body. Nineteenth century. Similar dolls were often given to Catholic children as a devotional figure for their bedroom. 21 in. high.

77 Group of figures, buildings and accessories from a crèche setting. Smaller figures would originally have been placed in background to give effect of depth. Heads of wax or composition. Very detailed costumes on foreground figures.

78   Paper crèche group. Late nineteenth century. Unmarked but probably printed in Bavaria. 15½×12 in.

types of dolls were utilized for these gifts, so that they have to be individually dated. Even today, many a christening cake bears a gilded cradle containing a plastic baby doll, a variant of the old tradition.

Dolls representing church dignitaries were often given to wealthy Catholic children in the eighteenth century, so that they could learn about their church by the dress of its hierarchy. A seventeenth-century painting by Jan Steen shows a child holding a doll-statuette of St Nicholas, which she has been given as a gift, and similar dolls have continued to be made to the present day, though the modern Father Christmas dolls look hardly saintly. Nuns also made popular subjects for dolls, and Marie Antoinette bought a doll dressed as a Carmelite nun for her daughter Marie Thérèse so that the little girl would not be frightened when she visited an aunt who had taken the veil. Statuettes of nuns were often sold outside convents as dolls to be taken away as gifts for children. These figures were sometimes dressed in detail by the nuns themselves. In a painting by Chardin a girl holds a doll dressed in the Carmelite manner, while another eighteenth-century painting by Greuze shows a girl holding a doll dressed in a monk's habit. One American doll-collector specialized in dolls dressed in the robes of religious orders and had many old dolls dressed especially for her in detail by the nuns themselves.

FIVE

THE REGENCY PERIOD

The English farmer has of late years become a different character. A fox-hunting horse; polished boots; a 'get out of the way or by God I'll run over you' to every poor devil upon the road. Wine at his dinner; a servant to wait upon his table; a painted lady for a wife; sons aping the young squires and lords; a house crammed up with sofas, pianos and all sorts of fooleries.

The farmer drew all Cobbett's wrath upon his new parlour with its decanters and dinner service and "even a bell pull on the wall in true stock jobber style".

The farmer's desire to improve his condition of life was part of a general aim among people who were benefiting from the prosperity of the Napoleonic Wars and consequently sought to improve their image in society. Shopkeepers, merchants and industrialists all began to copy the way of life of the old rich merchant class and surround themselves with ornamental but unnecessary decorations. That their children should now have proper nurseries and be given toys that would not be put to shame by those owned by children from the Great House was all part of the new pattern, and has meant that many families even today retain dolls bought at this time for ancestors. The Regency period is much nearer in time than we may appreciate when we read contemporary biographies and descriptions of everyday life. A very old lady was recently showing me her interesting scrapbooks made when she was a child, and I remarked upon a lovely watercolour miniature of a little girl of the Regency period. "That – oh, that's my grandmother", remarked the lady. I was startled into the realization that a period that was labelled in my mind almost as neatly as the Cromwellian era was still, to some people, the age of their close relatives.

It is therefore little wonder that there are a considerable number of dolls of this period available, especially as early collectors often thought little of dolls of this time, preferring the perfection of the late nineteenth-century bisques.

79, 80 Many of the dolls played with by children in the first quarter of the nineteenth century were quite large. Represented in contemporary prints, "La Toilette de la Poupée" and "Les Etrennes" (*below*).

The Regency dolls retain a wonderful period feel. They can belong to no other era. Few collectors ever need to take a doll made at the beginning of the nineteenth century to a museum for an opinion as to its date. The dolls complacently state their period of manufacture by their narrow-chested and wide-hipped figures and their bland unassuming faces.

Many of the so-called progressive ideas of the eighteenth century with regard to the upbringing of children still persisted, and the erring boys of the English public schools were still a great trial to their masters. Some children still ran almost wild in the grand houses of their parents, but there was, creeping into the most cultivated of society, a new and fashionable piety, in reaction to the frivolous

134

excesses of the previous century. The English complimented themselves on the fact that the sound of the guillotine had not been heard in the city of London. The nobility felt that their way of life had remained secure because they had not behaved with the excessive foolishness and levity of the French aristocrats, and, with the French wars safely behind them, they reacted with a period of ostentatious piety. Grace and family prayers were now said regularly, even in the most sophisticated society families. In the eighteenth century churchgoing was not rigidly imposed by parents and employers, but Sunday observance now began to be applied much more firmly and all forms of headstrong behaviour were frowned upon. Young ladies were instructed to be modest, and were restrained from the mad romping and games of football with their brothers that their mothers had been allowed to enjoy.

Many children still suffered under the peculiarly English nursery cruelty and were threatened into a cowed obedience by cruel punishments. Elizabeth Grant wrote a pathetic account of her childhood in the first ten years of the century. The day began traumatically for the children of the family when they were plunged into a tub of water which stood outside the house, so that in winter the ice had to be broken before the children were pushed in the water to the accompaniment of their screams and pleas for mercy. Dry bread and cold milk were then served as breakfast. When the children refused to eat the food that revolted them, their father, Sir Peter Grant, stood over them a whip in hand and lashed them until they were forced to eat the nauseating food. All such excesses of parental discipline were excused on the grounds that it was good for the child and strengthened his character. Children's stories, which had become much lighter in the late eighteenth century, began once more to pontificate and moralize in an effort to make the child into a wise little adult. Foreign visitors complained about the strange methods of upbringing, with such comments as that of Prince Pückler-Muskau: "Such a thing can only be seen in England, where children are independent at eight and hanged at twelve."

In this effort to encourage the young to mature quickly, the children of wealthy parents were encouraged to do much more for themselves, so that the young men often helped look after the horses, and the girls washed the fine drawing-room china and even clear-starched their own decorative linen! Gainful pursuits were very much encouraged, so that flowers were drawn and pressed, scrapbooks begun and all sorts of small craftwork embarked upon to fill the long hours more profitably than by sitting around reading frivolous novels. Young ladies were also encouraged to wait upon their elders on the picnics which were becoming highly fashionable as a result of the Gothic revival. Another means of teaching deportment and adult graces was at the children's balls that were held regularly. Prince Pückler-Muskau, a visitor to England at the time, commented on a children's ball given at Lady Jersey's: "It really afflicted me to observe how early they had ceased to be children. The poor things were for the most part as unnatural as unjoyous, and as much occupied with themselves as we great figures around them . . . it was only at supper that the animal instinct displayed itself more openly and unreservedly." Presumably by supper-time hunger had reincarnated the eighteenth-century noble savage!

The same visitor comments on another "scene which could only have taken place in England": a little boy, quite alone, driving his small carriage pulled by a dog amongst the carriages and stage-coaches of the late night London streets, probably rushing home from one of the adult-style social calls that the young were expected to perform. Though no longer dressed as miniature adults, the early nineteenth-century child was now expected to behave as one.

Fashionable society did not have sufficient interest in the lives of poor children either to change their system of upbringing or to make much effort to alleviate their distress. It was the custom for country children to help their parents in spinning and farming, and there seemed but little wrong in allowing them to go into the factories and mines to work alongside their fathers. The sight of maimed and exhausted children, often hired from Poor Law Institutions, was common in the industrial areas of the country. The wealthy mill-owner would look at the filthy stunted children working in his factory for as long as fifteen hours a day, and saw no injustice that he could right in the fact that his blue-sashed children were well cared for in their clean nursery. He merely thanked a generous and understanding God for placing him in a prosperous position.

The very poor country child might have been bought an occasional toy at the hiring fairs when his parents went to obtain new work, and where gingerbread dolls and simple wooden toys were on sale, but his usual amusements would have been very meagre, perhaps a bone wrapped in a torn piece of cloth, or a piece of wood similarly decorated with rags. More poor children were now brought up in the spreading industrial areas, where depressions in industry hit very hard. The parents could not obtain the natural produce of the countryside that had helped the eighteenth-century workers over poor times, but were obliged to go hungry or else send their children, who were cheaper to employ, to the factories instead of them. The lot of the underprivileged early nineteenth-century child was a sad and bitter one.

Conditions in America were comparable to those in England. The new industrialists grew richer while the poor immigrant labourers, often from Central European countries as well as Ireland and other poor parts of Britain, were increasingly injured and exploited.

81 Leather was sometimes used for the faces of dolls, but rarely to such good effect as in this example with a swivel head made in 1828. Brown glass eyes, teeth, wig of human hair. Made for Miss Louisa Parker by the ladies of Ashburnham Place. 19 in. high.

137

The dolls that are now collected were owned not only by very wealthy families, but also by the children of shopkeepers and better-paid workers. Even these relatively privileged children did not have a life without hazards. The child was as likely to die before the age of five as to live, and smallpox scars were still considered a familiar feature on many faces. Public executions were still a practical form of cautionary tale, and as a special treat, for hilarious amusement, the children could be taken on a visit to Bedlam, where lunatics were kept. The love of the grotesque manifested itself in the popularity of German toys carved in the form of cripples and deformed people, and in the mechanical dolls which performed obscene antics such as those exhibited at the parties which the Princess of Wales gave at Blackheath. The eighteenth-century delight in simple ribald amusements was therefore still very much alive, and adults as well as children enjoyed cock-baiting, Punch and Judy shows, skittles, blind-man's buff, hot cockles and leap-frog – a game even played on the gun decks of the *Victory* at Trafalgar.

Marketing of Dolls

In the eighteenth century, dolls and toys had been distributed in the main by pedlars and stallholders, who moved from one fair to another; but by the early nineteenth century, there were more permanent toyshops, and even quite humble village stores included dolls among their stock. Bazaars were becoming very popular, and were set out as arcades of shops specializing in various items like mirrors, dresses, porcelain and toys. It was fashionable for people to drive to these elegant shopping areas in their carriages and, after completing their purchases, to sit drinking coffee on a glazed gallery overlooking the open trade area below. Such conveniently set out centres made shopping a social occasion, and many of the finest dolls of the period would have been sold from these arcades. The Old Argyle rooms were very fashionable also, and appear to have been run on similar lines; certainly dolls were sold from the stalls there.

The doll merchants were no longer content to send their wares across the country in pedlars' baskets. They now supplied toyshops with dolls made to order and published their own catalogues to this end. These early toymen's catalogues are an invaluable source of information for the collector of dolls, as the wide range of toys available is really staggering. The catalogue of Hieronymus Bestelmeier of Nürnberg appeared in 1800, and contains some 500 drawings of toys with prices and descriptions. Offered for sale among many others were English fashion dolls, presumably those made of paper, jointed wooden dolls, mechanical dolls dressed after the newest fashion and a nursemaid and child with a baby cart. Agents of the Sonneberg, Groeden and Berchtesgaden

(*left*) 82 The dolls, popularly described as Queen Annes, were made well into the nineteenth century, as is shown in this figure in contemporary dress that once belonged to Lady Anna Gore Langton, daughter of the second Duke of Buckingham. Lady Anna was born in 1821. Blue enamel eyes, fair wool wig, kid lower arms. 26 in. high. (*below left*) 83 Blue eyes, with both pupil and iris, are considered later than those that are pupil-less. The dating of this doll to the early nineteenth century is based upon this. Flat back, linen upper arms, fork hands. 21 in. high. (*below right*) 84 Illustrated from the book *Queen Victoria's Dolls*, by Francis Low, published in 1894. Showing Miss Cawse as Fatima, Lady Brighton, and Cestra, Countess Regal.

areas all produced their own brightly-coloured sample books to tempt shop-keepers and stallholders. The English makers appear at this period to have almost given up trying to compete with the Germans, as did the Americans, though Philadelphia leather dolls were advertised in 1822, and some small-scale doll-making must have continued in most countries.

The French doll-makers now usually bought their dolls from Germany and dressed them in the height of fashion in the French workshops, so that the French continued to sell beautifully-finished dolls, even though the doll itself was only occasionally made in France by such makers as Simar and Martelet, who are listed by Luella Hart as mould-makers who worked in Paris.

Nürnberg was still the distributing centre for dolls made by the folk-industry workers of Berchtesgaden, Oberammergau and Thuringia, but there was now a difference. Previously, the agents had sold the dolls that the homeworkers had made in the traditional manner, but now, with the increasing speed of communications, the agents began to ask the makers for specific types of dolls that were proving popular, so that individual regional differences between the dolls and toys produced became much modified, and a more uniform type of product was marketed, as is evidenced by the toy catalogues. It was only in a very few places, such as Oberammergau, that the distinct traditional styles were still produced.

The bismuth painters were so called because they had used this substance to prime the waterproof coffers that were popular. The term became used to describe all the craftsmen who applied paint to unprimed surfaces. It is often said by writers on dolls that the bismuth paint, which was poisonous, was used on dolls' heads, but Carl Groeber, the venerable German authority on dolls, very firmly states that the substance was not used. The confusion presumably arose among collectors as the dolls' heads were known to have been painted by the 'bismuth painters'. It would have been in any case a rather unnecessary and expensive method of treating a doll's head that hardly needed waterproofing. A coat of size would have been quite adequate for a fairly cheap toy, especially as a layer of gesso was often added.

The methods of sizing and varnishing heads differed greatly in efficacy between one area and another, so that dolls were often sent from, for example, the Grödnertal to Oberammergau to be finished by the more successful methods used in that area, though the practice was gradually being discontinued as areas became more skilful in finishing their own products. St Ulrich became the centre of the Grödnertal toy trade, and at the beginning of the century there were over 300 woodcarvers in the area, making mainly costume dolls and toy animals as well as the caricatures of beggars and cripples previously mentioned. Though the population of the Grödnertal Valley was only some 3,500 people, there were, according to Carl Groeber, some 348 Grödnertal firms, who had depots in 130 places abroad.

The Sonneberg area ran an even more efficient marketing system than that of the Grödnertal, and their agents were sent as far as Russia, so that many toys made in that country evinced a pronounced German influence. As Sonneberg was on the great highway between Nürnberg and Leipzig, it was in a good position to trade in toys, and sent many of its products to the Nürnberg area.

Some leather-faced dolls are known to have been made in England, and it is probable that at least some of the beady-eyed wax doll's-house dolls were made here also. There is a strong probability that the wooden bedpost dolls were mainly made in England as well as the waxed compositions more generally associated with Germany.

Wooden Dolls

During the eighteenth century, there had been a fairly wide diversity of standard in the wooden dolls produced, so that well-finished heads with finely-modelled faces existed alongside the simple bedpost type of doll, which had been made for the less affluent market. The early nineteenth century saw a levelling off of standard. I know of no nineteenth-century Queen Anne types which have the detailed characterization found in some of the eighteenth-century examples. This was possibly because makers worked to the merchants' orders to an increasing extent, and because dolls were very rarely made now to any individual's specific order. Even very privileged children bought their toys from shops, so that we read of Victoria, when a child, taking her own money to a toyshop to buy a beautiful doll and Albert, when he was a boy, even going to local fairs to buy his toys. The period when very special dolls were individually made for wealthy children certainly appears to have been over, and from castle to front parlour children played with very similar dolls. The little jointed 'Grödnertals' which Queen Victoria dressed and played with are still to be found in very middle-class surroundings, and were even cheap enough to be bought occasionally for the children of working men.

It is difficult to fix a date when the dolls that collectors refer to as Grödnertals were first produced. These dolls have upswept hair, often decorated with a small painted comb, and have slim delicately-jointed limbs. The faces exhibit the wide range of expressions found on most hand-finished dolls, and can resemble aged peasant women or young and elegant court ladies. This variety of expression was exploited by the young Victoria and her governess, when similar dolls were dressed to imitate court, ballet and operatic characters of the time. The better peg woodens have expertly-carved heads, and the hair is skilfully painted, often with quite detailed treatment of small ringlets that sometimes fall to the cheeks.

There is a very large variety of sizes, from about 1 inch high to as large as 40 inches. The quality Grödnertals have the addition of a waist joint, and very occasionally a swivel neck, rather in the manner of an artist's lay figure, from which it is sometimes suggested that they have descended. The very large dolls were articulated by ball and socket joints, but the smaller doll's-house size has simple pivot joints. The hairstyles worn by these little Grödnertals identify them as being unmistakably Regency, an impression added to by their high bustline, which accommodated the Empire style dresses they often wore. The limbs of even small examples can still be moved easily, as can the rather elderly-looking doll's-house doll illustrated. The fact that these dolls will adopt almost any position they are put in says much for the quality of the wood that was used, as underseasoned wood splits and shrinks quickly, and these Grödnertals are very rarely found in bad condition.

An interesting variant on the basic Grödnertal type of doll is found with a hairstyle that is apparently intricately carved and often has pierced ears. Examination often shows that these heads are actually made of a form of plaster, as no chisel marks can be detected. Collectors often feel very annoyed to discover that what they had long cherished as an example of the skill of the doll-carver is actually mould-produced, and sometimes even refuse to believe that this is so. The collector is advised to examine the head very carefully for any remains of a mould mark, though such marks were often almost completely removed during the skilful finishing process, which added a few strategically-placed curls to mask the line. As heads of this type are usually heavily gessoed, it is often not easy to decide on the substance of the head, but the chances are that it is covered with plaster or brotteig. The time that would have been needed to carve the face and the intricate hairstyles would have made the process very expensive even using peasant labour.

Some plaster heads were also made with a black spot on the top of the head. These dolls were sold 'bald', presumably so that they could either be given a head-concealing head-dress or a wig. Such examples are very rare on wooden peg-jointed bodies, and would obviously be exciting finds. R. E. and R. C. Mathes comment that the only bald heads they have seen had ribbon lacing painted up the legs, in the manner of the satin slippers worn in the early nineteenth century. Other rare dolls in this classification would include dolls with glass eyes set into the plaster coating and any with unusual additional detail that is original, such as applied jewellery, unusual shoes and, of course, male dolls, which are virtually impossible to find, though there is one South German male doll with glass eyes which dates from 1830 and a few doll's-house size Grödnertals.

Very early nineteenth-century wooden dolls were sometimes made without combs and with the short urchin-type cut to the hair that was favoured especially

85   Papier mâché heads were sometimes applied to wooden jointed bodies, but the hairstyle was usually more ornate than on this example dating from the 1820s. The painting of the hair is very reminiscent of that used on Grödnertals. 14 in. high.

in France at the time. Children of the period also wore their hair cropped, though few Grödnertals are found dressed as children. Some dolls wear the pantalettes that were becoming very popular for young girls, and were often made in matching fabric to the dress, but for the most part, the jointed woodens seem to have been made in imitation of adults, and are often found still wearing the fashionable dress of the period with high waists and low necklines, which effectively set off the dolls' nicely-turned shoulders.

Alongside the mass-produced Grödnertals, which are so peculiarly Regency, were made dolls similar to those produced in the eighteenth century. The Queen Anne type was still manufactured, even though the fine examples are no longer seen. More common in the early nineteenth century was the 'bedpost' variety, that has limbs that are sometimes mere sticks and at others rectangular bags of sawdust. Babies' clothes are also more frequently seen on such dolls, and the general standard of clothing also appears to have dropped, as they were super-seded by more up-to-date forms of doll-making and became the toys of more ordinary children.

The Salem Institute has a group of amusing wooden dolls of this period which were produced in France. They are made very simply with a rectangular wooden body and fixed stick legs. The faces are carved, but in a very simple manner, and it is the costumes that were given most care by the maker, being made of paper and fabrics cleverly utilized to make attractive dresses. It is not easy to say whether the figures were intended as play dolls or whether they were made as amusing ornamental items; if the latter, the maker was very successful, as they still have the power to divert.

Folk dolls were produced during the Regency period as they are today, out of any materials that lay to hand. But whereas the folk dolls of today are often made of rag, the early nineteenth-century examples that have survived are usually of wood, such as a roughly-carved stump doll that was found at Vaasa when a potato field was being dug. This doll has a long jacket with buttons over a dress, while another similar doll was given rather more detail. The folk dolls can often be identified by the method of carving, as detail is often gouged out or incised, which is a much easier process than carving in the round and is the child's first natural method of indicating detail on a figure he has made of clay or wood.

86   Grödnertal with ear-rings that are attached to the head with fine screws. The hair is treated in a stylized manner with soft curls to the cheeks. Yellow comb. Blue eyes. Written on torso in ink the letters "SU". 13 in. high.

87   The articulation of the wooden arms can be clearly seen in this example, that represents an older-looking woman. On small examples such as this the hair is even further simplified. Black eyes, yellow comb and shoes. 5½ in. high.

Paper Dolls

The fashionable adult conceit of owning a small dummy of oneself that could be admired when dressed in various costumes was still popular in the Regency period. According to Lady Charlotte Bury in her *Diary of a Lady in Waiting*, Princess Charlotte, while receiving a visitor, sat "looking at a little picture of herself which had about thirty or forty different dresses to put over it, done on isinglass and which allowed the general colouring of the picture to be seen through its transparency." No isinglass dolls appear to remain, but ladies lower down the social scale used paper figures in a similar way. I was shown a miniature of a Regency lady which had fifteen different fancy dress costumes behind which the portrait could be placed so that the face could be seen. Some of the costumes were regional, while others were completely fanciful, but all were painted in watercolour and appeared to be home-made. Many ladies of this time were highly skilled in painting miniatures, which were carried out in a stylized manner which looks quite professional. Home-made examples of paper dolls of this period can sometimes be bought amongst old folios and scrapbooks at auctions, and it is well worth searching them out, as they are often considered of little monetary value.

The commercially-produced paper dolls of this period are keenly sought after by collectors of books and ephemera, as well as doll-collectors. The so-called English fashion dolls of the eighteenth century continued to be popular, and were published by, among others, H. F. Müller, who issued a book around 1812 of costumes for lady-dolls with an accompanying male figure which could be dressed as a beau, geologist, gardener or even a hermit. S. and J. Fuller in 1810 published the *Protean Figure of Metamorphic Costumes*, which was a print of a man in a scenic background, who could be dressed, garment by garment, in the costume of a knight, a monk or a French soldier. This type of paper doll was quite unlike the dolls we know today, as each part of the costume was laid over the figure individually, so that the shirt would first be placed in position, then the coat that showed the shirt beneath, and so on until the figure was complete, even to items carried in the hand.

A similar system, in which the items did not attach in any way but were just laid in position, was used by F. C. Westley, of Piccadilly, London, who published a book called *The Paignion* which included pictures of the interiors of a shop, church and a bedroom with sixty-five paper dolls that could be placed in any of the scenes to give a different effect.

S. and J. Fuller of the Temple of Fancy produced a series of cut-out paper dolls in a very similar manner, which took the place of pictures in the stories, which were sold in the form of printed boards tied together with silk ribbon, though, in this case, the dolls head slotted into the costume. The most popular

88 Paper costume doll. Watercolour and ink. *c.* 1830. The clothes can be lifted away by tabs to reveal the figure wearing knee-length chemise. 6½ in. high.

89 *The History of Little Fanny* published by S. and J. Fuller, of the Temple of Fancy, Rathbone Place, 1810. A story accompanied by an assortment of hats and costumes.

90 *La Poupée Modèle* published *c.* 1830 by R. Ackermann Jnr of London. Figure measures 8½ in. high.

book issued by Fuller was the famous *History of Little Fanny* which ran to four editions in the first year of issue. Fanny had six different outfits which illustrated part of her story, and she is the paper doll with which collectors are most familiar.

91 *Les quatre Ages* published by Alphonse Giroux, Rue du Coq, St Honoré. The more unusual male dolls are accompanied by a variety of hats, heads and costumes. Early nineteenth century.

Other titles were published by the same firm, such as *Phoebe the Cottage Maid* and *Hubert the College Boy*, but the most avidly searched for by modern collectors tells the adventures of *Young Albert the Roscius*, the boy actor who had taken the London stage by storm in his portrayal of Shakespearian tragic characters. Many such publications fall very much on the border line between dolls and children's books, and only rarely come the way of the doll-collector.

The Continental makers appear to have made more paper figures in the authentic paper-doll style, such as a Weimar maker who produced a doll with two wardrobes with six different costumes, which was sold for a crown. A French woodcut shows ladies of the period displaying a doll with cut-out costumes following contemporary fashion. It was a peculiarity of the period to make the dresses and costumes include the arms in a variety of positions, rather than have the arms of the dummy showing as is the case with modern paper dolls. The dummy is usually represented in a low-necked petticoat, and the dresses fit over the shoulders, as backs as well as fronts were often given. Ballet and theatrical costumes were among the most popular, and such dolls appear to have been particularly in favour in the States.

The Regency period is the time when paper became really cheap, and it was utilized for all sorts of home-made dolls, which have only rarely survived, as they were often made in the round. Such frivolous amusements as the paper-doll books must have been severely frowned upon by Mrs Trimmer, the educationalist whose favourite words were 'improving' and 'exceptionable'. This lady, whose moral books had such an effect on the youth of the period, even considered that plays should not be acted lest the child should adopt the bad character he was portraying. What she would have considered of the practice of dressing up dolls as ballet dancers and Catholic monks would be fascinating to read.

Papier Mâché Dolls

The dolls of papier mâché, whose manufacture was begun in the eighteenth century, really came into their own in the Regency period, the hairstyles of which lent themselves so well to a moulded treatment. Dolls with all sorts of extravagant hairstyles were made, sometimes out of eight- or ten-part moulds which were skilfully joined in the finishing processes. The figures are usually dated by the period of the introduction of the specific hairstyle, but the catalogues of the period show a wide variety of styles, some of which were out of fashion ten or more years before the date of publication. The date of the hairstyle's introduction can therefore only be taken as the date on which the mould was first made, rather than the actual date of the doll's manufacture.

A few papier mâché dolls have hair wigs, which are intricately plaited and arranged, and were probably treated with some sort of size or lacquer which has kept the arrangement rigidly in place. Some of these wigged examples have survived with the hair in such good order that in photographs they often look like moulded styles. Such dolls are great rarities, as are dolls of this type with inset eyes, since it was obviously a much easier process to simply paint them on. A few papier mâchés were also made with the black 'Biedermeier' spot on the top of the bald head and these too are quite rare.

A bald-headed man with side whiskers was shown in a toy catalogue of this period, though none are known to have survived. The same catalogue shows heads of young children which would also be great rarities, as the known examples are all lady-dolls. Interesting mask-type heads appear in this catalogue, which were presumably meant to be used (much as craftshop dolls' masks of today) with a rag backing, though it seems an unnecessarily complicated method for a doll assembler to use. One very rare doll of a similar type that has survived has a braided upswept moulded hairstyle with real curls applied at the front. Possibly the mask-type heads were treated in the reverse manner, so that the hair could be attached to the rag backing.

Most dolls of the papier mâché type were made by pressing the pulp into metal or plaster moulds, so that an even thickness was applied. The German term for this process is Drücken, or pressing, and this squeezing and pressing was usually done by children working in extremely bad conditions. The method of making a papier mâché head is basically that experimented with by almost every school child of today. A mould is made; the mixture is pressed in and allowed to contract slightly in drying, lifted out, and placed on racks which allow an even circulation of air so that the model dries without warping. The parts of the mould are then stuck together with a strong glue, and any unevenness of the join disguised by the use of a filler such as plaster of paris, gesso or even a very fine form of the basic mixture that was used for the head itself. The rough cast, when completely dry, was covered with an even layer of gesso or plaster to fill in any slight imperfections of the surface and provide a good ground for the painting of the face. This ground coat could be applied either by dipping the shoulder head into a bath of plaster, in which case great speed would have to be used in order to dip a sufficient number before the mixture began to harden, or by application with a knife or the hands. I have found it easier to apply this type of coating by hand, as even a pliable palette knife does not adequately follow the shape of the head. Some old examples have an extremely fine surface coating which could have been dipped, but others have extra detail built up in the plaster, which would have been modelled by the hands of the workers whose labour was so cheaply obtained, despite the fact that the mixture often contained substances such as lime which must have caused them injury.

The painting of the heads was carried out by more experienced workers, who succeeded in giving even dolls made from the same mould slightly different expressions, by a painted highlight to the eyes or a slight twist to the lips. The papier mâché dolls were really the first mass-produced dolls, as dolls' faces of wood had needed much more hand-finishing. Different areas of Germany are thought to have favoured different shades for the painted eyes, but this is not easy to prove. When the painting was complete, the heads were usually lightly varnished if they were of reasonable quality, though some cheaper dolls of the period were made without this surface covering, which makes them almost impossible to clean successfully.

The shoulder heads were attached, usually by glue, to bodies which were made of leather, fabric or even wood. The leather body, however, appears to have been the usual type used. A simple, almost abstract, representation of the figure was cut from four pieces of leather, which were seamed together to give a wide-hipped and narrow-waisted effect. Heavy wire was sometimes used as an extra support inside the sawdust filling, as is the case with the undressed doll illustrated. The wire in the doll continues into holes drilled in the wooden lower limbs, which enables the doll, despite its 32 inches, to stand almost as rigidly as it did when new. The joins between the simply-turned legs and arms and the leather body were tidied by strips of paper or leather in red, blue or brown, which gave the undressed doll a good finish.

Most of the dolls appear by the catalogues to have been sold undressed, though the individual toy-sellers might have dressed them before sale in up-to-date costume, as they did in France. Some very small examples have heads that were cast solid, as their size made it difficult to dry them without some warping, which was difficult to disguise on a small and detailed head. Some of the large versions did need some strengthening, which was given occasionally by the insertion of a layer of cloth inside the cast head before drying had begun, a method similar to that used in eighteenth-century church swaddling figures. Another method, more frequently used, was to strengthen delicate areas of the head, such as the nose, with cloth or paper soaked in glue and pressed firmly into the cavity. Such reinforcing was not often needed on the fairly simple moulded dolls, but is often found on those with very well-defined features or complicated hairstyles. The dolls with the more ornate styles which made the head itself heavier were made with slightly shorter and much thicker necks to take the extra weight. There seems to be no connection in time between these thicker-necked examples, merely the fact that the construction of certain types of doll necessitated this thicker mould.

The feet of these characteristically Regency dolls were carved and fixed to the turned legs by a simple dowel joint, though in very small examples it is some-times carved in one with the leg. Coloured slippers are usually worn, and do appear to follow the general fashion guidelines of the period, so that early nineteenth-century examples have pointed toes, while by about 1820 the toes have become squared. The feet of dolls made after 1830, however, have much more realistically rounded toe-lines.

The toy catalogues show how deceptive old line drawings of dolls can be. The articulation often appears much better than it could ever have been, and hands and feet appear to be far more realistically carved than extant specimens imply. Obviously, the maker had to show the dolls in their best light, but the difference is a caution against relying too much on artists' impressions of dolls when studying their history.

Wax

The Regency period, with its rapid industrial expansion leading to a much larger market for the toy-makers, was rich in new techniques and styles. More advances were made in doll-making during these early years of the nineteenth century than in several hundred years preceding it. Another of the kind of doll associated with the period is the waxed composition doll, which is attractive to collectors, as examples can still be bought frequently even in the foremost salerooms.

The composition substance which forms the foundation layer of the heads of these dolls is almost identical to the carton or papier mâché that was used for the classical papier mâché dolls. This similarity in the method of construction has led to many dolls of this type being attributed to Germany, even though dolls of this type were also made in England.

The English doll and effigy-makers had always held a particular fondness for wax as a medium, and it seems strange that this particular method was not exploited more, especially as a cheap type of papier mâché was made in quanti-ties for the decorative moulding on cornices and ceilings which had remained popular since the mid-eighteenth century. The difficulty of obtaining labour cheaply enough to mass-produce toys was the main drawback for the English makers, while the Germans had vast numbers of people who would work very cheaply, if not in factories then on a folk basis, to make cloth bodies and dress the dolls. The cheapness of the German product made it uneconomical

92 Papier mâché head of the style sometimes referred to as 'Queen Adelaide'. Leather body with strips of blue paper at joints. Wooden lower arms and legs. Red and yellow gauze dress. $9\frac{1}{2}$ in. high.

for English manufacturers to attempt to compete in selling to toy dealers, who would obviously buy the dolls with the greatest profit.

These early years of the nineteenth century, despite all the technical advances, were lean years for the producers of quality dolls. Attention seemed to have turned towards dolls that could be very cheaply produced to please the new expanding market, and even examples from this period owned by the English Royal Family are quite humble. Princess Charlotte owned a doll that she called 'the great doll's baby', but its only claim to splendour is in the baby clothes and the velvet cover which bears an embroidered crown on the initial 'C'. Possibly some poured waxes were made, such as one in the Finland National Museum which has unusual bent arms, but few have been discovered that can be positively dated to these years. The notable exceptions are the wax heads made for leather bodies, such as were usually used on papier mâché dolls. These heads were of solid wax with glass eyes and they wore very ornately-coiffured wigs. There is some suggestion that they could have been used as hairdressers' models, but this is unlikely, as they are typical dolls of the period, apart from their wax heads. Such dolls are extremely rare, and are usually to be found only in museums, but they are interesting in that they show how adaptable the doll-makers were. Presumably these heads were made for the very best-quality dolls of the type, which is why so few have survived.

The papier mâché bases of the waxed composition dolls were made in simple two-part moulds. When dry, the head was joined by glue, and an even coat of pink watercolour paint applied. The eyebrows and mouth were also painted on at this stage. Not all dolls of this type were given the pink flesh tone; some were left grey, and only the details of the features were painted on.

Most dolls of this type have glass eyes, usually large and dark with huge pupils and no iris, though more natural eyes with both an iris and a pupil were used at the time. The eye sockets were cut out before the coat of flesh-coloured paint was applied, and the head was dipped in the bath of wax. Some heads were given several dippings, and the lines of the layers can often be seen at the edge of the shoulder. Most dolls, however, only merited a single immersion in wax, and some were dipped so inefficiently that parts of the shoulders never received their proper coating. The wax had to be allowed to cool completely and harden before it was re-dipped, so this process was reserved for the more expensive dolls. In the examples I have studied, the blue eyes also appear to have been used on those dolls of slightly better quality and with more realistic limbs.

If the eyes were to be worked by a sleeping mechanism, the top of the head was neatly sliced off at this stage of manufacture. There was enough room for ordinary fixed eyes to be positioned through the hollow neck, but the wire-pulling device that worked sleeping eyes needed more room to enable the parts

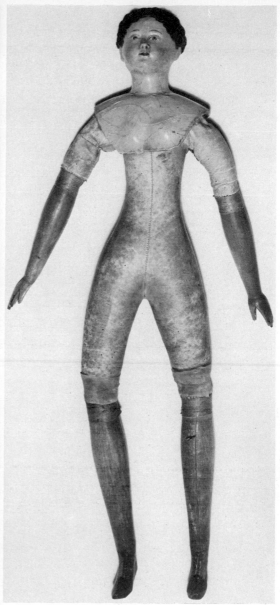

93 Good contemporary dolls' heads were often utilized in the making of work bags and pincushions. Brown eyes, well-painted ringlets to cheeks. Pink silk bag. 12¾ in. high.

94 Papier mâché doll in undress to show the typical construction. White leather body, sawdust-filled over wire armature. Ends of heavy wire fit into holes drilled in wooden lower limbs. Red bands at elbow and knee. Blue shoes with flat heels. c. 1820. 31 in. high.

to be assembled. Not all dolls of this period have the flat paperweight eyes, for some are found with round blown glass eyes which were necessary in a sleeping doll. These dolls were a novelty at the time, and were often referred to by contemporary writers in tones of admiration. Little girls began to demand dolls with eyes that opened and closed, rather than the usual fixed-eye type. Since sleeping dolls were recorded in the early eighteenth century, it appears likely either that their use was discontinued because the method was unsatisfactory, or that there were very few made, as the writers of the early nineteenth century do not appear to have been familiar with them.

The waxed composition shoulder heads were sometimes given wigs of flax or hair, knotted on a loosely-woven mesh fabric or (more frequently) attached to the head by pulling it through a slit several inches long, which was cut from just above the hairline to half to three-quarters of the way down the back of the head. The hair was fixed back on the inside of the pate with glue and arranged neatly on the outside of the head, and the hair was curled into ringlets with heated tongs. This method of fixing the wig has led dolls of the type to be known as 'slit heads', or even 'old split heads', not over-attractive names but convenient as they exactly describe the type.

The waxed composition heads were mounted on bodies that were made of stout cotton, and the basic shape was very cheaply and simply made. The arms often end with leather gloves, which reach to just above the elbows, and are found in a variety of colours. Many have only three fingers and a thumb, but others have the correct number. The thumb was often sewn on separately, which meant another doll-making process, so it was sometimes omitted altogether. These leather arms are part of the actual construction of the doll, and were not sewn on over the fabric, but were themselves filled with sawdust, as was the rest of the body. The legs were usually sewn in one with the body, which accounts for the turned-in toes in which this method of construction resulted. The illustrated wire-eyed doll has legs that are joined together at the knee-stitching, indicating that it was not customary to wear drawers at her time and place of manufacture. Some late waxed dolls made in this traditional manner but stuffed with horsehair had the hair inserted in groups into the waxed head, but these appear to date from the 1840s.

Better-quality examples have waxed composition arms and legs. The limbs of these better examples contrast oddly with the small, stick-like leather arms of the other contemporary dolls, as they are of a much more realistic size; in

95 Popularly known as slit heads because of the method of hair insertion, such dolls were made in large numbers in the first half of the nineteenth century. Some made in a similar way are found in eighteenth-century costume. Dark irisless eyes. Leather lower arms. Linen body with turned-in toes. 20½ in. high.

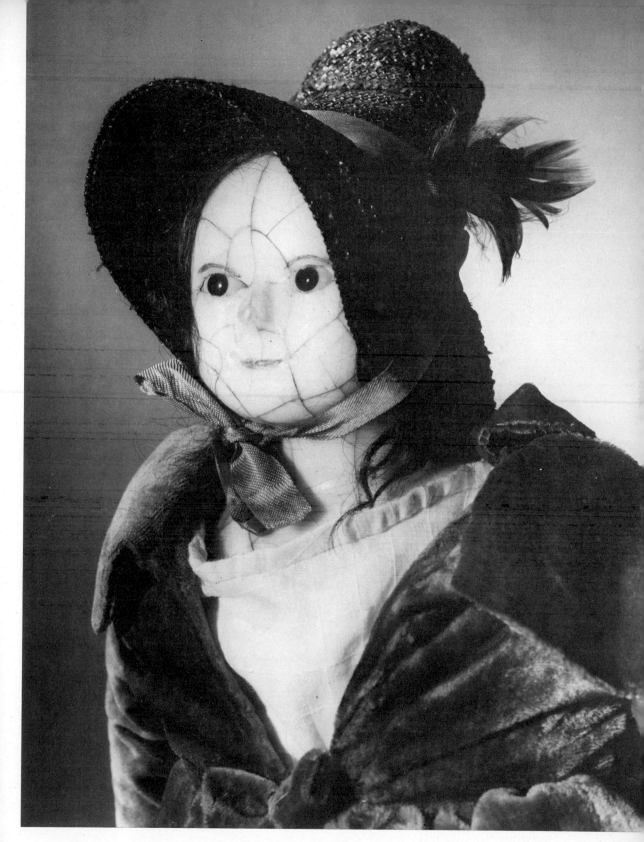

fact more natural than any dolls that had been made up to that time, as hands and feet had usually been tiny and completely unrealistic.

The beady-eyed poured-wax dolls that inhabit many Georgian dolls' houses were still made, and can be seen in Regency dress in houses of the period. Another interesting type of doll was made of wood, but had a waxed head, presumably to give a smooth realistic finish.

The mechanism that works the eyes usually emerges from the body at waist level in the form of a wire lever, which, when pushed, closes the eyes. A pull causes them to open. The arrangement is rarely completely satisfactory, as the wires running through the sawdust-filled body usually make a hole which allows the sawdust to escape, so that dolls often have to be filled with extra sawdust to make up for the quantity lost over the years. The eyes also often become jammed, and I have long since stopped fixing back the tops of such heads, because access to the eyes is so often needed to make them work well, as the wire used was often insufficiently rigid to give adequate leverage on the eye mechanism. Another method was to attach two strings which came out at the bottom of the doll's body to the wire, and this method, which allows a direct pull to be exerted, is usually more successful than the waist-level lever, as the string for closing the eyes by this method runs over a bar inside the head and a point of zero leverage cannot be reached.

Dolls of waxed composition are almost always badly cracked. This cracking often starts at the end of the slit in the head and runs down the centre of the forehead. The combination of wax and composition is not a happy one, as the composition often warps slightly, causing the brittle wax to crack. An individious practice once sprung up, actually condoned by some museums and writers on aesthetic grounds, of re-dipping these old heads. The end result was always disastrous, and looked like a reproduction head on an old body. The charm of such dolls lies in the patina which they have acquired, and while it is obviously permissible to replace chipped-off pieces of wax and clean off actual dirt, these are dolls that do not respond at all well to over-zealous restoration. Their flattened noses and prim faces look far better when left with their full complement of cracks acquired over the years.

Other Advances of the Period

The increasing skill being developed in the manufacture of porcelain offered new possibilities to doll-makers, and a few very rare dolls of porcelain are believed to date from this period. One Berlin doll with brown hair bears the factory mark on its shoulder, while other dolls reflect hairstyles that were popular in the Regency period, and, though it is more likely that these dolls were in fact made later, there is the possibility that some were made at the time. The

96 Two prints of French costume for 1830. "Chapeau de gros de Naples. Redingote de gros d'Orient", and "Chapeau de velours plain. Robe de gaze garnie de feuilles de satin."

china dolls with round black spots on the top of the head (often referred to as Biedermeiers) are thought to have been first produced at this time, but I have been unable to find any references in contemporary literature to china dolls being played with by children, so that one has to suppose that if such dolls were made, they rarely came to English-speaking countries, and were probably adult toys, as porcelain was still very expensive. An interior of a ladies' room of the period shows a doll of indeterminate substance sitting on a chair by the bed with what appears to be a purely decorative intention, and clearly a doll that was to be given to a wealthy lady could be extravagantly made. The earthenware dolls, whose import was recorded in the seventeenth and eighteenth centuries, appear to have completely left the scene, as have dolls of such substances as alabaster, though there was some fashion for dolls made of leather – an unfortunate choice as the faces of such dolls now look horrific.

D'Allemagne, that often-questioned early writer on dolls, states that at the French Industrial Exposition of 1823, there were dolls that said 'mama' or 'papa' according to which arm was raised. There was also an invention of this type patented in 1824 by Mälzel, who in another patent of 1827 created a device which emitted sounds like 'mama' and 'papa' when squeezed; but as no existing examples are known, it is difficult to surmise whether the patent was actually used. Another interesting patent of 1824 shows a weight attached to a doll's eye to effect closure, a method that was not put into general use until the end of the century. Such devices as squeaker boxes, which sounded when squeezed, were becoming part of the doll-maker's equipment, and made it possible for him to produce a wider variety of dolls.

A variation of the usual doll was those that represented old and wrinkled women: a type that was often used by the makers of pedlar dolls, though actual portrait dolls were also made, such as one representing the Marchioness of Blandford made by Richard Cockle Lucas in 1832, which exactly represents the toothless features of the old lady. Figures such as this can in no way be classed as children's toys, but serve to indicate the skill of the craftsmen of the period.

Costume

When costume has survived in good condition on dolls of this period, it is usually made of muslin or cotton, as the silks which the dolls frequently wore were too fragile to have survived years of rough treatment. Some papier mâché dolls are believed to have originally been sold wearing Empire-style pink muslin dresses, but most examples of this period are found to have been dressed or re-dressed at home, often with very great skill. Some wear quite detailed costumes, made in close imitation of contemporary adult dress, while dolls representing children are still quite rare. If a doll, dressed in the costume of around 1810, wears pantalettes which match the dress, then the doll was certainly intended to represent a child, for drawers were not worn by women, because they would have spoiled the fluid lines of their softly-clinging dresses.

By 1815, little girls' dresses had become shorter, and the ends of the pantalettes were deliberately shown beneath the hemline as a decorative feature of the costume. Shoes were made either of soft kid or of the material used for the dress, as was also the custom for ladies. The short hair that had been fashionable for children at the beginning of the century was gradually going out of fashion, and much longer hair was seen by the 1820s. Accompanying the longer hair was an increasing amount of costume ornamentation, so that bows, frills and ruching were again becoming the necessary dress for fashionable children. By the end of the Regency period, the child's dress had lost all the ease and grace it had

shown at the turn of the century, and capes, bonnets and huge collars again burdened little girls.

The boys, who had worn simple loose shirts and easily-fitting trousers from the time they were able to walk, began to be kept in skirts for a much longer period, so that one reads of boys complaining at having to wear such foolish and restricting clothes. The Prince Regent had complained of his skirts when he was a boy in the late eighteenth century, but the fashion had become much more widespread by the 1830s.

Heavy fabrics were also very popular by this time, and plaids and much deeper and richer colours set off the fur, fringing and artificial flowers that were bedecking the female form. The ladies' dress that was worn early in the century is easily recognized by its slim skirts, softly gathered in just below the bustline, with a long train added for more formal occasions. For the most part, however, ladies' dress was as unrestricting as that worn by children. The way that the dresses clung to the contours of scantily-clad women was lampooned by caricaturists, though in fact most women were forced by the climate to wear more underwear than one is often led to believe. One notable advance was that underwear was now washed regularly, and offence was given if sophisticated people smelled too strongly.

After 1820, boned corsets and starched and stiffened petticoats again became popular, and the easy lines of the Empire dress were submerged under the huge sleeves, collars and skirts which effectively concealed the female figure. Horsehair, whaleboning or even small cushions or wicker baskets were used to make the full sleeves maintain their correct shape, which is an extremely unnatural one.

The Parisian doll costumiers obviously sought to dress their products in the height of fashion, but those dressed at home were usually at least four or five years behind society fashion, and their dresses are most frequently made of cotton. Despite the fact that ladies are said to have worn little underwear, dolls that are still in their original dress often wear not only a chemise but several petticoats. All these original clothes should be kept safely, even if the doll is so unsightly that it has to be re-dressed in old fabrics, because they are of great interest to students of fashion.

14   Waxed composition doll, c. 1818
15   Costermonger and his girl

SIX

VENDORS AND ORNAMENTAL DOLLS

Pedlar Dolls

Despite the fact that pedlar dolls are thought to have been made before 1800, I know of no English examples that can be positively attributed to the eighteenth century, so that from the point of view of the collector the pedlar doll is very much of the Regency and early Victorian periods. Almost every book on dolls and every doll museum includes pedlar dolls within its range of photographs or exhibits, though in truth they were never intended as children's toys. The fact that they offer wares for sale has often led them to be classed in much the same category as toy shops, which were used as a means of basic instruction in shopping, but there is nothing to suggest that pedlar dolls were anything other than adult toys, to be admired on the sewing table or parlour mantelpiece. Probably more old dolls than we realize were used purely as ornaments, as is evidenced in Laura Trowbridge's reminiscences of the period around the middle of the century, when she and her family left their old home and were told that they could each choose a present.

> Sad to say we asked for some silly object of our childish imagination. I asked for a wax gipsy figure with a tray of tiny toys to sell, that lived under a glass case – I thought it rather like a doll, and Vi set her heart on three little wax babies on three gilt chairs also under a tiny glass case that she used to be allowed to play with sometimes in my mother's room.

How many of the dolls that we now think were cared for lovingly by children were in fact kept purely as ornaments for mothers' amusement, while the children played with the more sturdy toys? Certainly the pedlar figures look far

97   A pickled apple made an effective head for a pedlar doll. Added realism was given by the insertion of glass eyes. Carries a range of lace and wool in a basket. 12 in. high.

more at home when museums exhibit them in reconstructed parlour interiors than they do in nursery surroundings. Such a doll as that reputed to have been made up by Queen Adelaide would have given rise to all sorts of childish nightmares had it shown its spectacularly ugly face in the night-nursery.

The pedlar figures can be considered the successors of the doll's houses, which so amused adults of an earlier period, as they too pander to the adult's fascination with the miniature, though the pedlars are of course on a much more humble scale. The lock which protected the valued contents of eighteenth-century doll's houses from the prying hands of the young is now replaced by a glass shade, which shows off such a figure well.

Though pedlars are usually considered to be a particularly English frivolity, some appear in the toy catalogues of Hieronymus Bestelmeier, at the turn of the century. This marketer of toys offered 'Woman pedlars with moveable heads', for sale, though there appears to be no surviving example. These German toys with moveable heads were very popular, and the Prince Consort, when a child, wrote a very appealing letter to his father asking for a doll that nodded its head. Presumably some of these dolls were sold with items which they offered for sale, as in the same catalogue is also listed a dealer in fashion goods with a boutique. It is always romantic to imagine that some ancestor made such figures in the leisurely nineteenth-century evenings, but, as more examples are found that are similar to one another, it is becoming probable that many of the dolls we once considered home-made were in fact assembled commercially. There are some examples that do appear to have been constructed at home, and these usually include a large number of needlework items among their wares such as socks, scarves and shawls which would have been simple to make. The way that the arrangement of pedlar doll and shade often perfectly complement one another is a further indication of the professional hand, as anyone who has attempted to fit a shade to such a doll will testify. The frequent inclusion of reasonably-scaled, small, commercially-made objects would also have been much easier for a toy-maker than for a country lady to supply.

Many such dolls represent old gnarled features in wax or papier mâché. These would have had little popularity in the nursery, and are unlikely to have been specially made from a mould that was only to be used once, so we have to conclude that heads of this kind were made in some number, presumably for use on pedlars and the like. There is the possibility that some of the labels found under the base of the domes which protect the pedlars belonged to the firm that fixed the figure in position in a shade perfectly suiting the arrangement; but until more actual facts are discovered and more examples found, we are still in the realms of conjecture.

Almost every type of early nineteenth-century doll was used for the

98   Pair of pedlars exhibiting the fine range of well-made wares we now associated with the dolls made by
C. and H. White of Milton, Portsmouth, whose label is on the base. The use of kid faces is also typical of White.
Woman carries ballads, skimmers and graters; the man beads, braces, purses and a razor strop. 11 in. high.

manufacture of pedlar figures. The wax dolls that represented old women were obvious favourites, while others of wood and waxed composition were also utilized. Porcelain dolls, though sometimes used for bazaar stalls, were much too pretty to be used to represent weatherbeaten crones, whose features could in fact be more effectively portrayed by (for instance) a dried apple. Bisque dolls were never used to make pedlars, as this type of ornament had passed out of fashion long before bisque dolls became popular. There were selling figures made with bisque dolls, but these cannot be defined as pedlars in the true and narrowest sense: that is, a figure carrying a number of items on a tray or in a basket in the manner of the old hawkers.

In a period when people living in country houses tended to be isolated from the fashionable influence of the town, the coming of the pedlar was viewed with some excitement, as he not only brought items which they could not buy in the small village shops, but also carried news and fresh ideas. With his cry "What is't you lack? What is't you buy? See fine bands and ruffs!" he was greeted with enthusiasm by the young women, from cottages and farms, and from the great country houses too. These travelling salesmen usually carried needlework materials, braids, laces and small decorative additions for ladies' dress, but others known as chapmen carried small books and pamphlets, which discoursed, often libellously, on matters of current interest.

Though the hawkers were welcomed for the frivolities that they brought, they were often viewed with great distrust, as they had a bad reputation for stealing. In a contemporary book, *Pedlar Ann*, children were told how a pedlar stole the silver from a country house while the ladies were busily looking through his wares.

It was often the custom for pedlars to travel in pairs, and sometimes even their children were taken along, so they could learn the trade. Stories abounded of apparently penniless hawkers who, at death, were found to have hidden away vast sums of money which they had amassed by devious means. The public was therefore understandably nervous of such people, while welcoming them for all the extra items they provided. In an effort to regulate the behaviour of these traders and protect householders, the pedlars were made to carry certificates of good character signed by a clergyman. After 1810, licences were also issued, so that any model carrying a card proudly stating 'Licensed Hawker and Dealer in Small Wares' can be dated as after this time.

Curiously, it is only the country hawkers that were used for inspiration for these figures, despite the fact that all sorts of interesting salespeople were to be found in town streets, selling almost everything from prints in an upturned umbrella to sheep's feet in a basket or dolls in a wicker carrier. There is an understandable similarity in the way that pedlar figures are dressed, often in a red

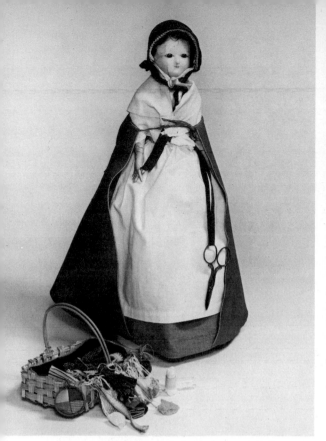 

(*left*) 99   Waxed composition figure of the typical 'slit-head' type used for a pedlar selling sewing items from a basket. Blue leather lower arms. Typical red flannel cape. 13 in. high.   (*right*) 100   Fortune-telling sewing companion. Bisque head with painted eyes. Very fine hands. Came originally from a doll's house. 7 in. high.

flannel cape over a dark patterned skirt. The red cape was almost a uniform for women pedlars, and helped protect them from harm when travelling along country roads with their boxes of lace, dresses and millinery. The evenings were spent in country inns, where the wives of the pedlars made caps and frills to sell the next day, and the dishonest pedlar would dispose of the trifles picked up on the journey.

The maker C. and H. White of Milton, Portsmouth, assembled many pedlar figures. One pair, in the traditional manner, is in the Bethnal Green Museum, London, while another pair came up for sale in 1972 at Sotheby's. The second pair mentioned is rather more unusual, in that it represents a market gardener and a poultry seller. All the dolls used by this firm for making the pedlars themselves are similar, having heads of kid leather. All the known White dolls have wooden bases covered with marbled paper and sellers of a wide variety of country goods were made. The costumes of the dolls and the items they carry are, however, completely dissimilar, and some of the items on the trays and baskets have an amateur look, as do booklets with titles made up of strips cut from contemporary books, with subjects ranging from *Views* and *Sketches* to a *Reign of George IV*.

167

(*left*) 101   Pedlar with carved wax head, under glass shade. Hair simply inset into one roughly-cut slit. A good assortment of wares including a violin, bear grease, rose water, cold cream and the "Ballad of Lord Bateman". 10 in. high.   (*right*) 102. Two souvenir figures representing Boulogne fisherwomen. The larger has a good-quality F.G. head with glass eyes. Small figure has bisque head of coarse quality with moulded black hair. Ear-rings fixed to cap. Terracotta limbs to both figures. Larger doll 12 in. high.

The lady poultry-seller wears a white dress with a chintz cape, and carries her poultry in two large baskets, while the traditionally-dressed pedlar woman carries a storm lantern and a candle in one hand and in the other a basket containing skeins of wool, cards of buttons, pincushions and needle-cases. Hanging from the basket is a lace sampler on a blue card, a skimmer, skewers and a nutmeg grater. The male pedlar carries trouser braces, strings of beads, ribbons, needle-cases, net purses, a book entitled *Favourite Walzes*, a box of tooth powder and a package with the proud title 'Packwoods Incomparable Razor Strop'. All these are miniature items unlikely to have been made by a lady of the period, but very likely to have been made by a small manufacturer with a good eye for novelty value. The scale of the items in relation to one another is also really too exact to have been achieved at home.

The Sotheby's pair with their chicken skin faces are very typical of C. and H. White. The male doll carries his basket on his head, and is skilfully dressed in a red waistcoat and brown canvas trousers, protected by a long apron. The seller of seaside produce in the Tunbridge Wells Museum and once thought especially constructed is in fact seen in several collections. In the past the majority of these dolls were considered home made, a belief often fostered by the statements of vendors and donors, who are apt to repeat the claim that great-great-grandmama made the pedlar when she was a girl – a claim that is often very hard to substantiate and often merely a family tradition. I have bought several doll's houses in the certain knowledge that they were commercially made, but the sellers have given me the most exotic histories for them, usually culminating in an ancestor who was a cabinet maker. After a while, the collector learns to treat all such claims with concealed scepticism, and only accept them if they can be backed by personal judgement.

The leather-faced dolls utilized by C. and H. White are rarely found on any other type of doll and were fairly obviously made by this particular maker for use only in his own workshop. Other professional makers used standard dolls that were available.

Several of the wrinkled and gnarled character wax heads used on pedlar dolls also give an appearance of having been made specifically for the purpose, as do the composition dolls in the Stratford on Avon Museum. Such heads, being mould-made, are unlikely to have been made only once, despite the fact that only one surviving pair is known; but whether such dolls were sold to be assembled at home or to the manufacturers of novelties is a problem that will only be resolved through further discoveries.

The penny-wooden doll, when made up as a pedlar, does tend to give a much more amateurish appearance, especially as the items for sale are usually of the wool and cotton variety, including handknitted gloves, hats and purses. Small items such as these are quite easy to knit on dress-makers' pins, if rather tedious, and are the most likely sort of item to be found on the trays of good fake pedlars; so that great care has to be exercised in the purchase of such dolls, even from reputable antique dealers, who, not being specialists, are often deceived by well-made reproductions.

Despite the fact that there is almost a tradition among doll-collectors that pedlar dolls are always dressed in a long red flannel cape, an apron and a little bonnet, examination of a variety of such figures reveals the fact that is usually the more 'home-assembled' figures that are dressed in this way, while those apparently commercially made are dressed in the variety of clothes one would have expected hawkers to wear.

Sarah Thrifty of the Manchester Art Gallery, made on a Grödnertal-type doll base, wears a cotton bedgown printed in blues and greens, a black woollen petticoat and a blue and white checked apron. The clothes were then protected by the traditional cape. This doll is very much in the home-made category, as is the papier mâché pedlar of the Holly Trees Museum, Colchester, who carries a group of home-made wares and is also dressed in a red cape. Several of the dolls in the Bethnal Green Museum, believed to have been dressed by ancestors of donors, are also costumed in this traditional way.

A very popular method of making a realistic model of an old crone was to fix an apple to a stick and roughly carve out the main features. After dipping in vinegar, the head would be allowed to dry naturally so that a rather ugly old face would be suggested. Women's magazines were explaining this method of making a gipsy doll well into the 1920s, especially in America, where the method remained in vogue for much longer than it did in England.

There are no known examples of genuine Continental pedlar figures. Wax street vendors with excellently-modelled features were made in Mexico until fairly recently. These figures have a look of great antiquity, because of the tremendous realism of their features, but they are as yet of little value in comparison with the pedlars of European origin. Bunches of fruit, sacks of grain, sieves and parcels are sometimes fixed to their backs and contribute to their ancient appearance. A toy museum dated a pair I once owned as rare eighteenth-century Neapolitan figures, and I, being in my first year of doll-collecting, believed it. Experience teaches that neither doll museums, catalogues of respectable salerooms nor old-established collectors can always be relied upon, and eventually the more experienced collector has to fall back on his own judgement. I discovered the true provenance of my figures much later, when a Guyanese friend recognized them as having been made in a part of the world he knew well. Apparently, the Amerindian craftsmen who made them had learned the skill from Italian émigré workers in wax, which accounted for their excellent finish. It is one of the paradoxes of the collecting world that despite the fact that these figures are far superior in workmanship to the European pedlar figures, their value is as yet unrecognized.

Fake pedlar dolls are often seen for sale in antique markets. They are usually made up from a 'wooden-top' doll of a type still made, and dressed in the usual long black clothes and red shawl. A small tray is easily made, as are tiny wire items such as spectacles and toasting forks. With the aid of a few hand-made woollen items, these hawkers can look quite effective. Though ingenious they are of no value – only a guaranteed trap for the unwary. A superior kind of fake pedlar is made by equipping a battered small wax doll with the usual miniature wares supplemented by a few pieces borrowed from the contents of old doll's houses. When sprayed with dust, such forgeries can look authentic, and can only be detected if the seller is willing to allow the items to be examined very closely for fading or warping. These are most definitely not the type of doll for the novice to risk money in buying from a dealer, unless he will allow the item to be returned if found to be unauthentic.

The most desirable pedlars to buy are those commercially made in the very early nineteenth century, when pedlars would visit country mansions and barter their wares for the fine thread spun by the ladies of the house. With cries such as "Pretty maids, pretty pins, pretty women", the pedlar would conduct his business after showing the householder his certificate of good character. The pins that are often found holding the items on the doll's tray in place, or even offered for sale, are another help in dating. The Tudor method of constructing a pin from two separate pieces of brass wire, one piece being coiled into a brass head, was still in use in the nineteenth century, until it was superseded by a method of one-piece construction which retained the coiled end. In 1830, solid-headed pins were introduced by Taylor and Company, and it is this type that is most often found. The early pins were expensive, which was why, for instance, the wife of George III was so miserly over pins and arranged them in geometric designs on her pincushions. The pin-seller himself, with his box and a long paper of pins in his hand, would have made a delightful pedlar figure, as he cried: "Three rows a penny, shorts, whites and middlings."

Reels of cotton would also be out of place on the tray of an early pedlar, as cotton was still sold in hanks at this time. By examining the objects such as razors, tapes, boxes and books on the tray, an approximate idea of the figure's date can usually be arrived at, on the supposition that the figure is in its original state. Many families have added items to the pedlars' trays over the years, which makes exact dating difficult. A good general knowledge of small antiques and an interest in the introduction of various items into general use is also helpful, although the best evidence to the more experienced collector is the 'feel' of age that an untampered-with figure has. The items that the figure carries on the tray, and the clothes worn, have settled down into very positive positions over the last century, and the impression given is that even the least attempt to move one of the objects would disrupt the group.

A few black-faced pedlars are known, though their features tend to be European. An example claimed to be eighteenth century in an American museum has a black wax head on a wooden body, while a more recent negro flower-seller has a face of black cloth.

Although there is a tendency to categorize all figures who 'sell' as pedlars, the word is really too general, and many dolls and doll groups were made which cannot logically be classified in this way.

Stall-holders and Vendors

The gracious lady who presides over a colourful and well-stocked charity bazaar stall is well known to almost every reader of books on dolls. Wearing a blue silk dress typical of the 1830s and an elegant bonnet on her 'coiffure' hairdo, she performs her duty to society most elegantly. The stall includes a wealth of small frivolities, such as pictures, mirrors, trinkets, vases, a draughtsboard and a miniature doll's house. The scent bottles are cleverly made by fixing beads of different shapes together, to give the effect of the ornate cut-glass Victorian scent bottle. The items do not all come from the same period, and most appear to be of the late nineteenth century. It has been suggested that the older doll was placed behind a stall made up around 1875, and certainly the style of the wares accords strangely with the dress of the doll. Nevertheless an attractive group has been created and, after all, a group 'faked' in the nineteenth century is now respectable.

Another group, also in the Bethnal Green Museum, represents a female pedlar who sells lace and sewing accessories from a booth, and has a lady and child as customers. Dating from about 1830, the group is arranged in a box-shaped wooden frame representing the stall with a green cotton awning spread over the top. Around the sides of the stall hang knitted shawls, scarves, parasols, a walking stick, bag and apron, while larger shawls hang on the sides of the booth. On the stall itself are pinned small bags, buckles made of tiny beads wired together, and small sketches. Again a few of the items seem to be later than the date of the doll, though most of the wares appear Regency. Presumably many such stalls lost some of their stock through the years, and had it replaced by new owners, which is why stalls that are a little contradictory in appearance are usually dated by the dolls used.

Glazed porcelain dolls were sometimes employed when the items offered for sale were rather more feminine, since the pretty face of a girl obviously looks very wrong on a traditional pedlar. Flower-sellers are frequently represented in this way, and even wax or composition dolls dating from the end of the century are sometimes to be found with baskets of fish or other items for sale.

The illustrated costermonger and his girl appear to have been specially made as an individual piece, as there is far too much detailed work in the construction for the group to have been made commercially in any number. A bisque shoulder head of the type that could be bought very cheaply for home assembly was used for the lady's head, while both bodies were carved of wood, as was the man's head, and dressed in contemporary costume. The wares in the cart are cleverly made from carved wood, stiffened paper and fabric. The maker, G. Ivory, was evidently proud of his work, as he fixed a plaque to the base of the case which held the group to inform posterity that he finished his work in 1895.

The fish-seller in the Tunbridge Wells Museum dates from around 1835, and is seated at a table on which is spread seaweed with crabs and shrimps offered for sale. Baskets containing other items, made mainly from sea shells, are arranged around the central figure, which is a wooden doll of the period, dressed in a

103 Wax-headed pedlar dolls. Man wearing black tail coat, wife in green check dress carrying a face screen. Mid-nineteenth century. 10½ in. high.

104 Green-curtained market stall with Grödnertal figures. Books, laces and needlework items for sale. Among the books *Milner's Church History*. 14 in. high.

fashionable tall hat and a small shawl. This figure was made possibly as a seaside souvenir or memento, as were the commonly-found Breton fisherwomen. These figures usually have bodies roughly made of terracotta with heads of porcelain or bisque. A few have heads of a quality more usually associated with French lady-dolls, and many collectors are tempted to fix such heads to a leather body to create a 'fashion doll'. It is a pity when this is done, as an authentic item is thereby sacrificed, and this can only be done by a person who has little genuine concern for antiques. The Breton girls usually carry baskets and, perhaps, a shrimping net. They fall very much on the border line between statuettes and dolls, but usually appear in doll collections.

Some toy shops were made purely to display dolls and their accessories. The boutique with its fashion-doll customers and sample dresses displayed on stands is the ambition of most collectors, though shops selling meat or groceries were not intended to hold a figure, but in others the doll is as essential a part of the construction as it is in a stall or pedlar figure. Almost any doll of a suitable size was used by the shop makers, though the manufacturers of butchers' shops usually used figures carved of wood, as the meat was often also represented in this way. Many doll-collectors consider shops and bazaar stalls as toys rather than dolls and do not include them in collections, while others accept them on the grounds that the doll is an integral part of the whole.

Fortune-telling Dolls

The pedlars who roamed the countryside were often prepared to look into the future for a small fee, and there was a great fascination among people in all walks of life with clairvoyants who broke the day-to-day monotony. Fortune-tellers were an accustomed part of the country scene, and were often represented in dolls. Professional fortune-tellers were frequently consulted by wealthy clients, while the fortune-teller's booth was always popular at country fairs. Even the Princess Victoria had a fortune-telling doll in her collection, which gave sound advice, such as "Happy and blest with the man you love best", or "You'll have a boy to bring you joy".

The penny-wooden dolls were ideal for conversion into such figures, as they were light and had small waists to which the leaves which bore the messages could be attached. The usual method of construction was to cut a series of pastel-coloured sheets into an attractive scalloped design and thread them together at the narrow end. When tied around the doll, the leaves represented the full skirt of the dress.

105   Charity bazaar lady with papier mâché head and hair wig, dressed in the costume of the 1830s. Contents of stall much later than doll, but an interesting assortment. 10 in. high.

Contemporary girls' magazines gave instructions for the making of fortune-telling figures, while in 1891 B. Voight patented an 'Oracle Doll' in Germany, though I have never seen an example of this doll. The most frequently found are those with full skirts of paper using any available doll. Fortune-tellers were clearly popular amusements, as their state when discovered is usually very bad, and there is not a great deal that can be done to restore them without renewing the paper which would destroy the authentic doll.

Sewing Dolls and Pincushions

Though the making of pincushion dolls reached its peak in the 1920s, examples occur from the beginning of the nineteenth century. As pins were expensive, devices for protecting them were necessary, and pads filled with sawdust or even emery powder were made which kept the pins free from rust. The bags were formed over pieces of circular card or wood, which provided a firm base, and the tops were gathered in to the waist of the doll. Almost any type of doll could again be used, and I have examined several where a broken child's doll was utilized to make the figure. Similar examples are sometimes found which suggests that some were made commercially, but most are obviously home-made. When the figure was completed, pins could be fixed into the skirt in patterns, so that names or flower shapes could be outlined, and the disappearance of even a single pin noted.

Such figures were most useful in the early years of the century, when pins were in short supply, but they had become such an accepted part of dressing-table accessories that they continued to be made even to the present day.

Some of the more ornate pincushion ladies were kept under glass shades for protection, but the needlework companion dolls were purely utilitarian objects. Again a variety of doll types was used for their construction, varying from Grödnertals to chubby little bisque figures by the end of the century. Some doll shapes were specially made flat, to be made up into needle-cases, but although I have found examples of these in metal, rubber and tin, I have not found any made of china.

The *Englishwoman's Domestic Magazine* for 1865 published drawings of a 'Work Table Companion' designed especially for their readers. Many dolls were constructed according to the suggested design, and small porcelain dolls were usually used as the base by the maker. The doll wore a padded hat, which acted as a pincushion, and carried a ball of thread slung over her back. The patch pockets of the skirt were made to carry packets of needles, while a pair of scissors was slung from the back of the waist.

Many such home-made dolls were extremely complicated and are sought by collectors of needlework accessories as well as dolls. One popular idea was to attach a very long gown with open sides to a doll's-house size doll. Underskirts were made in the same way, so that six or eight layers could be used as the pages of a needle-case. Personally I feel that the claim of the collector of needlework accessories is stronger than that of the collector of dolls, but few can resist a good-quality miniature doll, to whatever use it has been adapted.

106   German print, dated 1880, showing beautifully-dressed children with their nurse. Taken from *Illustrierte Frauen-Zeitung*.

SEVEN

THE VICTORIAN ERA

"I have always maintained", wrote Sir Walter Besant in 1897, "that the eighteenth century lingered on in its ways, customs and modes of thought until the commencement of Queen Victoria's reign." Certainly after 1837, the changes which had begun to alter the face of England and America were much accelerated, so that within fifty years a completely different mode of life was established. It was not only the countryside that became transformed, with the ever-widening industrial areas, but also customs, manners, standards and even ways of considering the world to come were revolutionized.

Great disquiet had been expressed in the eighteenth century over the exploitation of poor children, and a series of commissions were rather tentatively set up to enquire into the lives of slavery which were led by so many. The Children's Employment Commission of 1842 astounded Parliament with its revelations, and legislation was begun with the aim of easing the condition of those who worked in the coal mines. The wretchedness of these boys and girls had been shown up in the Commission's report, and the Government was at last shocked into some action. Because of the conditions under which most children lived, their life-span was often pathetically short, and it is always salutary to remember, when considering the nineteenth century, that the average age of the population was around twenty-five!

The rapid changes effected during the period were the work of a predominantly young society, though it is often difficult for us to realize today how youthful were many of the men and women who, dressed in ageing garments and wearing staid, tightly-buttoned expressions, stare at us from the pages of Victorian albums. The greatest culling of the population took place before the age of five, and the death-bed scenes which are described with great sentiment in many children's books must have been a normal part of a child's life.

The English middle class had established for itself strict codes of behaviour, deviation from which meant social ostracism; so that people quickly assumed the comforting security of a set way of life, and the respectability that was accredited by both society and the Church to the upholders of this creed.

There had never before been such a sharp distinction between the lives of poor children and those who came from comfortable homes with enough money to educate and clothe them well. Many good men who wanted their children to be educated were so poorly paid that they were forced to keep their children from school in order that they might earn the 1s. 6d. or 2s. a week that would so usefully supplement the family income. The number of schools had increased very sharply, but most charged a few pennies for the education they gave. Many parents found even this token payment too high. At one school in the Cotswolds, a mother withdrew her children because another had fractionally lowered its charge, and had the added attraction of a willingness to keep the children until six o'clock, when she finished work. Often, if the children had not paid their pennies by Tuesday morning, they were asked to leave, so that the progress of their education was directly influenced by the fortunes of the parents.

The Census Report of 1851 stated that many country children obtained employment at the age of nine, but in mechanical employment in towns labour began much earlier, from the age of six upward. Few parents would have wanted to see their children's bones eaten away by phosphorus in the poisonous atmosphere of a match factory, but, as there were always younger children to feed, this way of life was accepted with a dull resignation. A father who worked as a nail-maker was questioned by a member of one of the commissions, and his answers make sad reading. He talked of working from 5 a.m. to 10 at night, and added:

> Some children begin at eight years old, but I should say not many before nine and most at about ten. I should not like my little boy there, now five, to begin before nine, and he sha'n't if I can help it, but, if I am in any way obligated, he must. He is but a little mossel, and if I were to get that little creature to work, I should have to get a scaffold for him to stand on to reach, and with that it would be like murder work, as you might say. . . . It is quite right that the young ones should not work as long as they do, and should have some teaching. I am certain I should like my children to have an easier time of it . . . four of my five children go to the Church Sunday School.

Not all parents were as concerned for their children's welfare, and many were exploited so cruelly by them that the parents themselves must have been reduced to an almost animal state by perpetual deprivation. There was a great feeling of hopelessness among the poor. One fourteen-year-old boy who worked in a

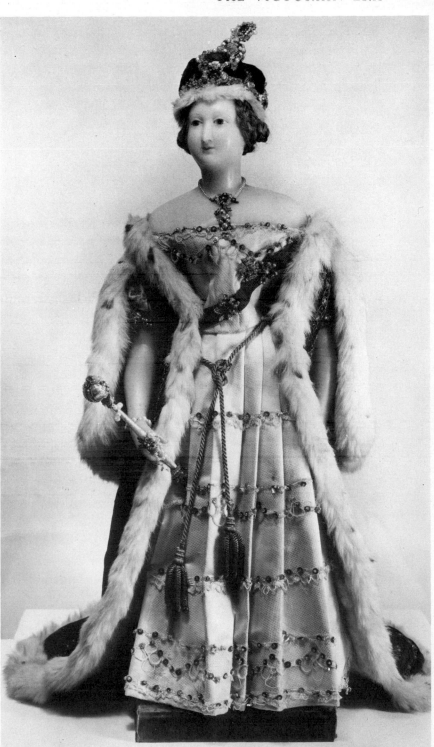

107 Poured-wax portrait model of Queen Victoria in coronation robes. Costumed *c.* 1840. Glass eyes and a hair wig. Blue velvet cape. 24 in. high.

glass warehouse saved 17s. in the bank over a four year period by working over-time. "When my little sister died, they buried her with it. I have not put by any money since."★

A master sweep who felt that it was wrong to take small boys and girls from their parents to clean chimneys used one of his own children for the work, but eventually "I felt that we could not stand it any longer, and that we would sooner go to the workhouse than suffer what we did from it." This man was upset by the fact that although he offered a mechanical cleaning service, it was refused by the very magistrates and ladies who professed to pity the lot of the climbing boys. In their own homes they felt the child sweeps would be cleaner and more efficient.

"No one knows the cruelty which a boy has to undergo in learning. The flesh must be hardened. This is done by rubbing it with brine close to a hot fire. You must stand over them with a promise of a halfpenny etc. if they will stand a few more rubs." Some of these children were purchased from their parents as early as the age of four. "At first they will come back from their work with their arms and knees streaming with blood, and the knees looking as if the caps had been pulled off. Then they must be rubbed with brine again and perhaps go off to another chimney. In some I have found that the skin does not harden for years." These boys and girls slept in their filthy clothes, with their bleeding wounds under sacks and straw made foul by soot and damp; many simply 'fell asleep' in the night and never had the energy to wake up again. Such children, who were deprived of the natural freedom of childhood, would hardly ever have played with toys or nursed dolls. They were so exhausted on finishing their work that they often drifted into sleep while eating.

The children of the class who continued to live at home fared a little better, as they were often not put to work at such an early age, and did have some time when they could play naturally. The small dolls of wood could be bought very cheaply from swagmen's bags, and it was these that were most frequently found in poor homes. An improvised doll of rag would perhaps be made, if the mother had the time and skill to embroider the face, but more often a wooden spoon, a large bone, a roll of paper or even an old shoe would be wrapped around with cloth to make a simple doll that could be nursed. These dolls are now the hardest for the collector to find, because most were thrown away as being of no value, except to the child who once owned it. A few museums have examples, and they are a more revealing commentary on the lives led by the majority of European children in the nineteenth century than the china dolls, which would have belonged to the children of parents with some money to spend on toys.

★ This, and three following quotations from *Report of the Children's Employment Commission*, 1865.

108 By the end of the nineteenth century, the china-headed doll was an essential part of the nursery scene. Two dolls by Cuno and Otto Dressel. Boy has good-quality gusseted leather body with composition lower arms, brown eyes. Marked with the Mercury sign. Girl with blue eyes has bisque lower arms on gusseted kid body. Marked on shoulder "COD 92—4 DP". 23 and 21 in. high.

109 Mothers took great pleasure in sewing fine outfits for dolls, and a good range of commercial patterns was available by 1900, such as these "Penny Dolls' Paper Patterns" produced by Blackmore.

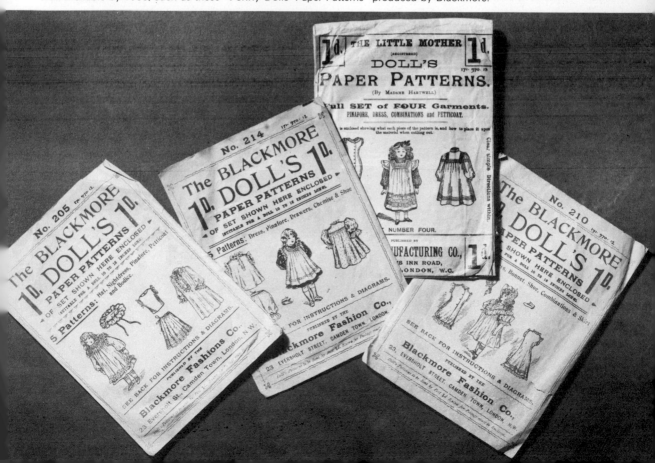

Clothes-peg and wishbone dolls were made and played with by children from all kinds of homes, not only the very poor, as they became traditional doll-making methods. Some examples are found dressed in unbecoming tatters that some workman once wore, and others wear fine silks and lace from quality evening gowns. Even the wealthy young Sebastian in *The Edwardians* by V. Sackville West amused himself with these commonplace objects when he was bored.

Small china dolls were so cheap by the middle of the century that they were carried in the baskets of most 'penny-a-piece' men. They were often of a type described in contemporary writings as 'armless' though presumably this only meant that the arms were moulded in one with the body, rather than being jointed as were the wooden dolls. Such items would have been impulse buys, obtained perhaps on the way to or from work by a kind parent as he passed the street seller of dolls with her basket of wares. Mayhew comments on the squalid surroundings in which many dolls were assembled for street sale. The importers sold the small dolls by the dozen to the women who hawked them, or to the stallholders in the markets. Some stalls obviously attempted to cater for a rather wider market, as they displayed dolls costing as much as 6*d*.

In the 1850s, the majority of dolls were sold from baskets which were carried into the richer suburban areas. A vendor of the period commented:

> Spoiled children are our best customers. Whenever we see a likely customer approaching, we always throw ourselves in the way and spread out our dolls to the best advantage. If we hears young miss say she *will* have one and cries for it, we are almost sure of a customer, and if we see her kick and fight a bit with the hussmaid, we are sure of a good price.

It is refreshing to be shown that the writers of moral tales were not always effective in controlling the behaviour of young Victorians!

The dolls that were sold in the London streets were usually assembled at Alfred Davis's and White's at Houndsditch, and at Joseph's in Leadenhall Street, while Clerkenwell was also known as a doll-making area. The heads were imported into England from Germany, as they were to America and France, though all three countries produced some quality dolls of their own. The German makers were popular because of the cheapness of their products in china, as well as the traditional wood, and their readiness to accept deferred payment for goods. It has long been rumoured that china dolls' heads were made in the Staffordshire potteries, but there appears to be little evidence to support the idea, though there is some similarity between the faces of many of the small black-haired dolls and the chubby-faced children of many a Staffordshire chimney ornament. No shards, patterns or catalogue references have been found regarding this manufacture, so that it seems likely that the English potters of the period decided that the making of such absurdly cheap products could not show them a profit, as the market was already adequately supplied by the German makers. The French porcelain decorators are reputed to have considered the painting of dolls' heads beneath their dignity, though it is more likely that the lack of mid-nineteenth-century French dolls' heads resulted more from their low potential as a commercial venture than on the artistic qualms of the workpeople.

The lives of wealthy children, though by no means idyllic, were now coloured by rather more indulgence, and many autobiographies reflect the happy hours spent in playing with the dolls and toys that were a natural part of nursery life. With the increase of the middle classes, the toy-makers were presented each year with an ever-widening market for their products, and as a variety of dolls was expected in the nurseries, the doll-makers were forced to create better and more ingenious dolls than had satisfied the children of the early years of the century. The mid-nineteenth-century girl, restricted by her heavy clothes and strict discipline, played with dolls for a long period of her life. Clothes could be made from illustrations seen in ladies' magazines, underwear was stitched carefully in miniature as needlework practice, and neat repairs were made to damaged skirts. Many of the china dolls of this period when in original state present the appearance of a needlewoman's sample that must have taken many weeks to complete.

> The young lady of 1837 has been to a fashionable school, she has learned accomplishments, deportment and dress. She is full of sentiment; there was an amazing amount of sentiment in the air . . . she likes to talk and read about gallant knights, crusaders and troubadours. She gently touches the guitar – her sentiment or her little affectation has touched her with a graceful melancholy, a becoming stoop, a sweet pensiveness; she loves the aristocracy, even though her house is in that part of Bloomsbury, whither the belted earl cometh not . . . on Sunday she goes to church religiously and pensively followed by a footman carrying her prayer book . . . she can play on the guitar and piano a few easy pieces which she has learned; she knows a few words of French which she produces at frequent intervals; as to history, geography, science, the condition of the people, her mind is a complete blank. She knows nothing of such things. Her conversation is commonplace as her ideas are limited.*

A fashionable education aimed at the creation of this kind of vapid personality in a girl, in whose presence men talked trivialities, because they felt that she was incapable of understanding constructive thought. The girl's energy was channelled from early childhood into the pursuit of time-filling, embroidery, shellcraft, bead-work or painting in watercolours: all occupations which have

* Sir Walter Besant.

provided the present generation with a wealth of attractive period frivolities, but which could have done little to awaken the intellect of the girls who produced them. Victorian dolls are often found with dozens of items in their wardrobe, all carefully stitched by the young owner and her mother or nurse, and while we exclaim upon their perfection, we should also regret that they were given nothing better to do after the perfunctory lessons of the morning were finished.

Sickly and sentimental poems and stories were read, and dainty tears were dabbed becomingly with a lace-trimmed handkerchief when the lot of the poor chimney-sweeps was mentioned. It became fashionable for a young girl to have a hectic bloom in the cheeks, to cough and to swoon, so as to be considered romantically consumptive. Much time was spent, from the age of five, in doing good works; and a great deal of energy was expended on making articles for the poor, who they pitied, but saw no other comfortable way of helping. The children's books of the period abound with stories of well-dressed ladies and their children visiting the poor-but-clean, and sending the child's best doll to cheer the sick child whose lot they found so heart-rending.

At Christmas, huge parties were given in the great houses for estate workers' children, and many sentimental tears were shed over the obvious pleasure given by the toys and dolls handed from the tree. The Victorian Christmas did much to boost the doll-makers' sales; in the eighteenth century, though a branch of a tree was occasionally decorated, Christmas had not been a festival aimed at children. The marriage of Queen Victoria had caused a German custom to be introduced by the Prince Consort into his adopted country, and he wrote exultantly to his father, "Two children of my own to give presents to at the German Christmas Tree and its radiant candles – it is like a dream."

Fine toys were sent to Windsor from the Princess Augusta of Prussia, who included among her gifts small model greengrocer's shops and model soldiers 'for Bertie'. Each of the royal children was given a table laid out with their toys, and we are given a charming description by an eye-witness of Christmas 1847, when little Prince Alfred "in a glorious tinsel helmet that almost covered his face was shooting us all with a new gun, and Princess Alice was making us admire her dolls. They had one Christmas tree among them but the Queen, the Prince and the Duchess of Kent had one each."

The splendour and merriment of the young Royal Family at Christmas spread very willingly throughout English society during the middle years of the century, so that by the Edwardian period, the English regarded Christmas almost as something they had created along with the Empire.

The angel doll which had adorned the top of many German trees was con-

110   The underprivileged child was forced to make her doll from the materials that lay at hand. Here a mutton bone was wrapped in rag to make a doll. *c.* 1850. Arms made of a roll of fabric. 6 in. high.

sidered unsuitable for Protestant England, and a silver star was substituted, though by the 1880s the German wax and tinselled angels were decorating our trees after all, having become 'fairies' on their journey. Many of these fairy dolls, in their bedraggled and tarnished finery, look more like little chubby barmaids than the elegant fairy folk exemplified in the drawings of Walter Crane and Kate Greenaway.

The pride which was fostered in all well-brought-up children regarding the glory of their country, and its benevolent interest in the people of the colonies, was reflected in the increasing variety of dolls dressed in the costumes of distant lands. Eventually china and wax heads were made in imitation of the features of people as distant as China or Africa. As the makers of bisque dolls became more skilful, they were able to create attractive dolls that represented Oriental or Indian children, and colour the bisque so artistically that the dolls were very convincing. At the Great Exhibition of 1851 were exhibited wax dolls especially made in the costumes of all nations – a great attraction to the younger visitors, who often had not seen 'foreign' dolls before. Children were also encouraged in their reading books to admire the soldiers, missionaries and explorers who spread the British way of life over the globe.

There was great emphasis upon duty: 'May filial love repay thy parents' care'. Such sentiments are constantly repeated in the carefully-worked samplers, which continued to be a popular form of needlework exercise for children. The girl must have felt quite weighed down with the duty she was constantly told was owed to friends, school, home, Church and country, as well as by the actual weight of the garments in which her body was encased. Many girls refused to take advantage of more interesting ways of life offered to them, as they had been made to feel from their earliest years that their principal duty was to their parents. Many intelligent girls were prepared to waste their lives away in the day-to-day trivia of arranging flowers, or carrying soup around to the poor.

Despite these oppressive bonds of duty, many children had gay and happy lives, surrounded by the closely-knit family group with its continual additions. They were often treated very indulgently, and were showered with the dolls and toys that are now so collectable, since they were made to a high standard for a middle-class market of discernment. Novels and biographies of the period tend to present the repressive side of a nineteenth-century childhood, but many children must have grown up in an idyllic atmosphere, as did the grandchildren of the painter Burne-Jones who, with great understanding, painted a cat, a kitten and a flight of birds in an alcove where naughty children were put to stand in the nursery.

111 The nineteenth-century child was encouraged to admire not only the Queen but soldiers and statesmen. This figure closely resembles the models of Lord Roberts made as a play doll by the Pierotti family. Inset hair and whiskers. 18 in. high.

A great treat for many children in the second half of the century was a visit to the Lowther Arcade, just off the Strand in London.

Dolls that smile and dolls that cry,
Soldiers ready for parade,
All are here for you to buy
In this wonderful Arcade.

Toys are hanging up on strings,
Toys are laid in tempting rows,
And each shop with pretty things,
Is so full it overflows.

The poem was accompanied by a drawing by Walter Crane showing an assortment of the delights that could be purchased in this fashionable toy bazaar. Well-dressed and prosperous parents are shown taking their excited children around the stalls. The readiness of these parents to accompany their offspring on such expeditions is an indication of the gradual change of attitude to the relationship of parents and children. A child's infancy in the eighteenth century and the Regency was a period that had of necessity to be endured by the parents, if possible at some distance. By the late nineteenth century even fathers were prepared to be amused by the toys that were to be seen running across the floors of toyshops. The toy-makers had a hand in this. Many of the dolls and toys made after 1880 are constructed and decorated in a way that would have held a direct appeal to the adult, who, after all, was the person holding the money. This applied far more in the field of mechanical toys than dolls, but certainly many of the elegantly-dressed lady-dolls must have held great appeal for the fashion-conscious mother or elder sister.

One of the most reputable London toyshops was Cremer's of Regent Street, founded in the Regency period, and still a favourite at the end of the century. So keen was Henry Cremer to obtain good stock that he made a rushed visit to Paris in 1870 in search of the last dolls and toys he might obtain for some time, because of the impending Franco-Prussian War. The Soho bazaar, though it did not rival the Lowther Arcade, was another source of quality toys for English children, though some of the best were sold in the Burlington Arcade. Prior to the First World War, London was known as the greatest doll market in the world, and millions of German dolls were imported for distribution not only around England, but as far afield as America and the Colonies. Hamley's was known as 'The European Toy Warehouse' because of the number and variety of toys imported and exported. Charles Morrell also sold dolls, and the firm's mark is often seen stamped on the bodies of wax dolls made by the Pierotti family. Mrs Jane Morrell operated a dolls' warehouse at the same address, and

112 Mother and daughter in Public Promenade Dress of the late 1830s.

113 Especially-dressed shop-display figure in fashionable red velvet outfit known as 'The Gordon'. Unmarked head with fixed glass eyes. Composition body. 7 in. high.

PUBLIC PROMENADE DRESS.

their stock was mainly imported from Germany, Austria and France. Most of the department stores, such as Mortlock's, included dolls among their stock, though there were many specialist shops such as F. Aldis of Belgrave Mansions, Edward Smith of Cheapside and, probably the best known to collectors of dolls, Mrs Lucy Peck of 'The Doll's House', Regent Street.

French children were encouraged, to want not only dolls but also beautiful costumes and accessories for them, by the doll competitions and exhibitions that were staged by the foremost makers. Hordes of chattering, well–dressed little girls were paraded with their dolls, often before a wistful audience of children from nearby orphanges. Some of these dolls were purchased from the fashionable doll shop *A La Grande Duchesse*. Doll repair shops were becoming much more common both in France and England, and it is because of the work of these repairers that so many dolls of the period present problems of attribution. As some bodies were subsequently fitted with several heads (because of breakages), not all of the same type or even coming from the same country, what can at first glance appear to be a doll of some interest is often discovered on closer inspection to be a skilful repairer's combination of parts. They were not always over-fussy about supplying spares of the same material, so that sometimes an early bisque will be found with replacement glazed porcelain legs, or a composition body repaired with celluloid hands.

Beautiful clothes could be purchased at such shops as *A La Poupée de Nuremberg*, again in Paris, while most of the doll distributors, such as Gesland, were able to supply lavish trousseaux, often in trunks. Gesland was proud of the fact that he could repair in ten minutes *bébés* and dolls of all makes, and maintained a large stock of replacements heads. Many of the doll factories situated outside Paris felt it worthwhile to maintain a showroom in the city, where not only children but also foreign buyers could examine their dolls, beautifully arranged, often in miniature rooms. The distributors of German dolls usually exhibited at the numerous trade fairs, though the Parisians themselves were very disparaging about their standard. The French doll-makers were not always so critical, and often used German-made heads on dolls that were marketed in boxes which suggested that the assembled doll was completely French.

America became the doll centre of the world as a result of the Great War, though there had been a doll-making industry since the Civil War. Many of the American firms, such as the Jointed Doll Company of Springfield, or Lacmann of Philadelphia, used heads made in Germany on bodies they manufactured themselves. The first well-known commercial dolls manufactured in America were made by Joel A. H. Ellis of Springfield, but the centre of the American doll trade became New York and its surrounding area. The death-knell of the lovely ephemeral dolls was sounded in 1892, when Solomon Hoffman began to manufacture 'Can't Break 'Em' composition heads. Both the dolls made at home and those imported from Germany and France were distributed by firms such as the Baltimore Bargain House, Schwartz Bros and Montgomery Ward. The mail order business for dolls was great, as were the distances many people lived from large towns, and these catalogues are a rich source of material for the doll-collector, especially regarding the costumes in which the dolls were originally dressed and their prices. Many small town stores and village shops, both in England and America, ordered their stocks from the pages of these

16 Pedlar figures, *c.* 1840
17 Composition soldier, *c.* 1908
18 Composition Victorian girl doll

catalogues, for the sale of dolls was becoming an increasingly attractive business.

The Rational Toy Shops were a curiosity that first appeared in the eighteenth century, and again became popular during Victoria's reign. These shops sold only toys that had a useful and constructive purpose, so that there were no baby houses or well-dressed dolls, as children were encouraged to construct such items themselves. Undressed dolls would have been sold, as they would have encouraged the girl's creative skill, and judging by labels found on toys, items that did not exactly conform to their criteria were sometimes sold too. These shops do not appear to have maintained any lasting popularity, as they aimed at the taste of the progressive parent rather than the wishes of the child.

By the last quarter of the century, even very poor neighbourhoods had shops which set out attractive displays of toys at Christmas, and groups of cheap dolls to tempt the child with a few small coins to spend. The small jointed German dolls, such as those made by Armand Marseille, cost only 2s. at the end of the century, and were sometimes purchased in pairs, often the sole difference being the colour of the hair.

Toy gingerbread was only occasionally found in the London streets in the mid-nineteenth century, though the traditional figures were still to be found at fairs. Gingerbread dolls of brown and white were sold, depending on whether sugar or treacle was used in the mixture. The figures were decorated with the gilt and tinsel that had so attracted generations of children.

Another toy that was peculiarly Victorian was to be found in the baskets of street sellers: the gutta-percha doll. These elastic dolls, which could be squeezed into grotesque and amusing shapes, had been quite expensive when first intro- duced as a novelty, but had become the property of the poorest child by the mid-century. Mayhew states that the dolls of this type, sold in the London streets, had no actual gutta-percha in their composition but were made of a mixture of glue and treacle. Even by the 1880s these amusing figures were disappearing from the street markets, and they are now virtually impossible to find. Some genuine gutta-percha heads are known, but these will be discussed in the section on rubber dolls, as it is impossible without chemical analysis to tell the two substances apart.

Poor children could sometimes buy quite good toys from the 'swag' shops, in whose windows were displayed a miscellany of objects, ranging from old clothes and razor strops to musical boxes and 'French toys with moveable figures'. These second-hand shops often used a doll as their symbol which was hung outside. They were always black and had two faces, so that they faced up and down the street at once, and were dressed in a discarded child's dress of white. None are known to have survived, and indeed they must have been frequently replaced, as the effect of the weather must have been destructive to a rag doll.

19   Pair of poured-wax English dolls

20   Pierotti-type poured-wax doll

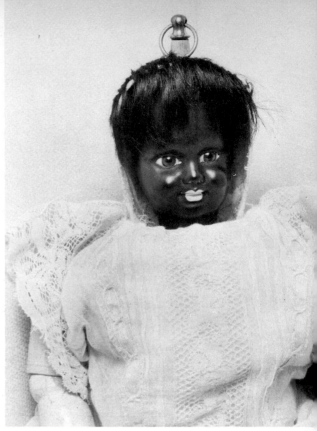

114   Coloured dolls were especially made for children with colonial interests. This doll was probably made for the French colonial families of the period and locally dressed in Morocco before sale. Brown painted eyes, black well-moulded hair, *café au lait* tint to shoulder head and arms. Cloth body, very narrow waist. 12 in. high.

115   A wealthy family might buy a two-faced doll such as this, thought to represent Topsy and Eva in *Uncle Tom's Cabin*. 13 in. high.

The toy-makers were encouraged in their efforts by the great trade fairs which were becoming a traditional feature of the years after the successful example set by the 1844 Berlin Exhibition. At this fair were shown dolls of all nationalities, made of wax and papier mâché. The firm of Löwenthal was remarkable in the success of its stand, and the same firm staged an effective display at the English Great Exhibition in 1851. The Paris Exposition of 1855 is memorable because Greffier displayed Japanese dolls that were to be the inspiration for the Motschmann patent for a realistic baby doll. The comments of the juries at these exhibitions are of great help to those interested in the history of dolls, as they often indicate when innovations took place. The 1844 exhibition, for instance, records that dolls with glass teeth as well as the more usual eyes were on display. These comments cannot always be taken at face value, since they are often coloured by an over-zealous nationalism, which causes some loss of judgement. This applies particularly to the French judgements at the end of the century, which spoke disparagingly of any dolls made outside that country. They congratulated the principal manufacturers on making dolls

116 At the end of the century elegant and 'progressive' ladies dressed in the aesthetic style. Brown silk dress worn by wax doll 13½ in. high.

117 Though idealized by artists, the genuine child of the period was as scruffy and untidy as the child of today at play. In this photograph the children might have been loaned the good toys especially for the occasion.

118   Contemporary artists often parodied the manners and dress of aesthetic families, as in this illustration from *Mrs Leicester's School*.

that imitated nature so precisely that they were unrivalled. The progress of many of the great French doll-makers, such as Bru and Jumeau, can be followed in the extravagant praise of juries at exhibitions, not only in France but also (for instance) at Philadelphia in 1876 and Vienna in 1873, where their superior taste and workmanship was commended.

Mass-production methods were becoming commonplace in the industry by the end of the century, so that quite a large number of all the different types of dolls manufactured at the time are now available to collectors. So many different kinds of dolls were made that it appears more logical in this book to deal with

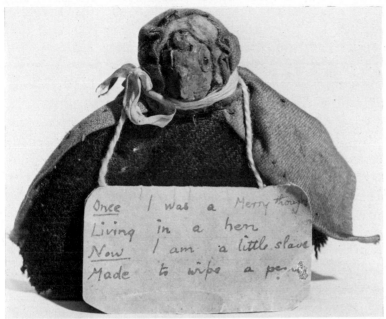

119 Children from all types of social background made wishbone dolls. This late nineteenth-century example was given a sheet of blotting paper to act as a pen wiper. Beads for eyes. 3½ in. high.

120 Children often accumulated a large number of miniature dolls, such as these French examples with composition bodies and bisque heads. Doll with black hair 5½ in. high.

them separately, though in some chronological sequence, in the next chapters. As most dolls now procurable by collectors date from the Victorian and Edwardian eras, the discussion of these examples forms the main section of the book.

The mass-production methods meant that some women only painted dolls' eyebrows, while others only curled wigs. The man who actually strung the dolls was considered to be very important, though to the modern collector this seems one of the less skilled processes. The majority of dolls' clothes were made by outworkers, to patterns carefully worked out by the designers. The outworker received the pattern, usually in the form of a buckram template, which could be re-used. Some of the big firms had their own dress-makers, who worked in the factory itself on clothes and miniature accessories. So successful was the effect of the beautifully-dressed French dolls that they ousted the German-made products which had relied upon cheap but well-constructed items. The French makers produced luxury dolls for the increasingly over-indulged children of the wealthy middle classes.

These children of the second half of the century were regarded with a great deal of sentiment, as can be seen in the popular prints and paintings of the period, which depict children, romantically or classically dressed, playing with flowers, dogs or pretty toys. Possessions had become all-important to the newly affluent, and as their children were part of their worldly goods, the children's nursery was equipped with all that was considered beautiful and new. It is revealing that the first commercial nursery wallpaper was designed by Walter Crane in 1875, and was highly successful, whereas previously nurseries had been decorated very economically, often with pieces of furniture that were not good enough for other rooms. Whereas in the eighteenth century only aristocratic children would have owned luxury toys, in the nineteenth century they were now owned by a vast number. Childhood was also a much less boisterous time than it had been in the previous century, and children were persuaded to take good care of their toys so that they could add to their store of possessions.

The children were encouraged to want new dolls by exhibitions such as that held in the Albert Hall, London, in December 1896, when hundreds of dolls were displayed, all beautifully dressed and representing various countries. A group of dolls dressed in imitation of characters from paintings by Millais won much admiration. After looking at the dolls, the children were presented with sixpences fresh from the mint and 'crackers galore'. A large attendance must have been expected, as 11,000 sixpences were ordered for this purpose. Similar exhibitions of dolls were held all over Europe and America, and sometimes included sections for home-made examples. Girls were encouraged to demonstrate their skill as needlewomen in dressing of dolls for entry in competitions

121 On long carriage journeys, a child could play with tiny wooden dolls that fitted into a leather case. Very well made and obviously a gift for a wealthy child. Mid-nineteenth century. Case $2\frac{1}{4}$ in. long.

organized by girls' clubs and magazines; the dolls were given away to hospitals and charitable institutions after the event. An exhibition of between 300 and 400 wax dolls was organized at Charing Cross Hospital, London, in 1890. The exhibits were dressed in the costumes of sisters, nurses and probationers who worked in the various hospitals throughout the kingdom. At the end of the display, the dolls were to be put on permanent exhibition in a Nurses' Home. I once tried to locate this interesting group, but even the Charing Cross Hospital where it was held knew nothing of it, though they found my information interesting for their archives.

Publishers also were taking a great interest in dolls by the 1880s, and patterns for dolls' clothes were often added to the pages of magazines as an inducement to buy. Readers of the *Ladies' World* were apparently quite prepared to pay

1s. 6d. for a doll's dress pattern, at a time when patterns for ladies dresses cost only 6d.!

The dress of fashionable children and their dolls had been much influenced in the seventies by the flowering of the Aesthetic Movement. 'Aesthetic' parents like Ellen Terry allowed their children to be surrounded only with items in the best taste, so that nursery walls were decorated with Japanese prints and they were made to wear little kimonos to blend artistically with their surroundings. They were allowed to read only the most artistic of books, such as those illustrated by Walter Crane and Kate Greenaway, and were dressed in close imitation of the costumes devised by the latter. When one of Ellen Terry's children was given a doll dressed in a brilliant-pink frock, the child was shocked by its vulgarity.

The fashionable aesthetic mothers dressed their children in delicately-patterned dresses, made of fabrics obtained from the newly-opened dress department at Liberty's, which catered for their taste. Artistic clothing was available here for ladies, as well as their children. Du Maurier mocked the children of the Aesthetic Movement in a series of cartoons depicting a family known as the Cimabue-Browns and their aesthetic friends. One cartoon showed the young Cimabue-Browns dressed in Kate Greenaway costumes with peacock feathers in their hats and solemnly carrying the large sunflowers that were symbolic of the movement. Less *avant-garde* children were dressed in similar fashion until the 1890s, and dolls of this period are often found dressed in imitation of the clothes worn by their young owners.

Throughout the century, attempts had been made to create a doll with an indestructible head. Various substances, such as rubber, tin or glued layers of felt had been tried, but although the dolls did not break as easily as china, they became crackled or defaced after a few years' wear. Nevertheless, the doll-makers were proud to announce the patenting of any new materials, though to our eyes they appear regressive. It was when such substances as plastic were discovered that dolls lost the ephemeral quality which makes them so attractive to collectors.

The education of girls of all classes had slowly improved during the century, but the process was much accelerated in the closing years. As early as the 1880s clothes had begun to be more practical, and such alarming garments as the Reform bodice were accepted wear. By the 1890s, the girl was considered in a completely different light to that in which she had been pictured in the 1830s. The *Girl's Own Paper* for 1894 commented:

> The young lady with sloping shoulders gazelle-like eyes and unchanging amiability would find no place in the present world. A course of gymnastics would be ordered as an antidote to her tendency to faint at critical and uncritical moments, and her frequent weeping would arouse irritation rather than sympathy among her friends. . . . Where there was weakness there is now strength of purpose.

122 Large numbers of specialist toyshops were established by the middle of the century. In this interior drawn in 1845, some idea of the range of toys stocked is given.

123 The exterior of the London Toy Warehouse. Illustration from *Wonders of a Toy Shop*, 1845.

The problem of 'what shall we do with our daughters' was by this time as pressing a question as 'what profession shall our sons enter'.

While the children of the 1920s and 1930s obviously continued to play with dolls, the doll had by this time returned to its place as a toy for the young child, with the obvious exception of art dolls. The golden age of the doll-maker had been the 1870s and 1880s, when the dolls were exhibited as status symbols by girls as old as twelve or fourteen. From the point of view of the collector the golden age was ended when dolls again became the property of children, and were no longer manufactured for young women of some taste and discrimination.

EIGHT

NINETEENTH-CENTURY DOLLS OF WOOD AND PAPIER MÂCHÉ

European Wooden Dolls

The most famous group of early nineteenth-century dolls are those played with by Queen Victoria as a child. Dressed in court costume or as actresses of the time, these cheap little wooden figures from Germany assumed a glamour of their own. Similar dolls were for sale in the streets until the 1840s, despite the fact that their upswept hairstyles with neat combs were rather out of fashion by this date. It was perhaps the marketing of dolls such as these, made from an unfashionable model, that caused Margaret Howitt in 1875 to comment in *Leisure Hour*, "The Grödner, left to himself, is not inclined to keep up with the Age."

The wooden dolls that were found in both England and America in the early nineteenth century are almost exclusively from Germany, and were often referred to as Nürnberg toys, though in fact this town was merely the distributing centre for the thousands of toys that were produced weekly in the surrounding areas of Oberammergau, Berchtesgaden and Grödnertal. Hieronymus Bestelmeier claimed that all the wooden dolls found in his trade catalogues were made in Nürnberg but, as many of his illustrations are to be seen in other contemporary distributors' catalogues, his claim is usually considered to be that of an over-enthusiastic salesman, though it should of course be remembered that most dolls were made to very similar specifications. Some wooden dolls were made in England in the 1840s by such makers as Robert and Henry Jones, but the number produced must have been very small and examples are not known.

The method of sending direct orders to the woodcarvers of the Sonneberg area, as well as the Grödnertal, did much to stamp out any individuality that the items once held, though the specifications were useful in setting out the standard of manufacture that was acceptable. For example, the toy distributors were very proud of the fine articulation of their products, and in their trade magazines the dolls are shown in a variety of rather unlikely but presumably desirable positions.

St Ulrich became the distributing centre for the dolls produced in the Grödnertal, and the merchants of this south Tyrolean town claimed to have had little, if any, contact with the Nürnberg merchants who would have been their rivals. The production peak of classical Grödnertal dolls was reached in 1820, and, though large numbers continued to be exported into the mid-forties, they had become the province of the poorer child, who was of necessity less fashion-conscious.

The fine large Grödnertals with their haughty faces and elegant air are the last of the quality wooden dolls that were produced in Europe. Trade schools were set up in Germany at the end of the century in an effort to encourage the making of quality dolls from the wood that was so freely available, but their success appears to have been negligible, and by 1900 the manufacture of wooden dolls on a true folk basis had almost disappeared except in Russia.

The elegant, slim-waisted and high-busted Grödnertals had degenerated by the 1850s into a much more stolid version. The bodies were no longer beautifully designed to resemble ladies, but were skittle-shaped with flat backs and round chests above low waists. The limbs were still jointed in the traditional way, but the arms now had little shape, being merely sticks with pink paint applied where the hands were indicated. These dolls were still made to represent women, so the flesh-coloured paint was usually taken down well below the bustline, and in some better examples the bust and shoulder area is carved in the manner of the earlier Grödnertals. It is in the treatment of the head that the greatest difference between the Grödnertal and the early Penny Woodens lies. The latter have simple round heads with the hair painted on, whereas the earlier dolls had hairstyles that involved some carving and ornamentation.

In some early Penny Woodens, there is a double hairline, indicated by the use of first a transparent and then an opaque colour. The lighter paint appears to have been used to suggest the part of the hair that is drawn back while the solid colour is applied to the top of the head. Some dolls made before 1875 do not have this second line, but it is a good indication of a respectably early doll of the type. Sometimes an extra curl will be painted just in front of the ears in a simplified version of the Grödnertals' hairstyles. In the example I have before me as I write, this curl was neatly applied on one side of the face and forgotten on the other because of the speed at which the decorators worked.

J. P. Purger of St Ulrich handled such wooden dolls as these, arranging their delivery to the decorators and eventually their export. This firm worked from 1851 until 1896 in the merchandizing of dolls, and exhibited some of their wares at the Great Exhibition, though it is likely that the dolls displayed would have been specially-made prestige pieces. The commercial dolls were carved in one area, and then sent in large consignments to peasants for decoration. The

(*left*) 124 Unusual carved wooden man-doll. Body typical of the Grödnertal. Painted eyes, carved beard and moustache. Dressed in mid-Victorian costume. 7½ in. high. (*right*) 125 Mid-Victorian wooden doll, here described as 'penny wooden' type. The two-tone painting of the front of the hair is often a characteristic of the nineteenth-century dolls of the type. Well-made very narrow-waisted body. 9 in. high.

faces of these wooden dolls are suggested by a few deft strokes. In small versions, both the eyes and the brows are painted black, with red mouths and red spots for nostrils. In some large examples, the iris is given some colour.

A contributor to *Leisure Hour*, writing of a visit to St Ulrich in 1875, described the traditional local method of working, as learned from the words of a peasant girl who ran a fruit stall in the market. This girl painted dolls' faces in quiet trade periods, and succeeded in painting one hundred dozen every week, though she claimed that the number would have been much greater had she been able to work at home. The dolls decorated by this girl were supplied by Herr Purger, who paid a farthing a dozen for the work. Decorators like her would one day apply dabs of colour to the cheeks of dozens of dolls, and on the next day the lips, shoes and stockings would be painted. The finishing process was the painting of the black eyes, eyebrows and hair. In this simple way, an embryonic mass–production method was created, which would have been very necessary to a worker who was supplying her own watercolour paints, and would not have wanted to waste any precious colour by continual washing of brushes. The protective varnish that was applied to the painted parts of the doll on completion had also to be supplied by the worker, and paid for from earnings.

Johannes Demetz of St Ulrich is generally believed to have initiated doll-making in the area. At first he carved only religious figures, but by about 1710 he was making toys as well. It is believed that at this early period the dolls were sent for finishing and decoration to Thuringia and Bavaria, but by the nineteenth century the dolls were completed in the one area, through the work of Franz Runggaldier, who is thought to have started the doll-painting side of the industry. Georg Lang of Oberammergau is another of the handful of makers whose names we know.

Many writers on dolls as well as collectors have grouped together several distinct types of doll made in this century and labelled them Penny Woodens, Dutch Dolls or Peg Woodens, according to their fancy. Examination reveals, however, that the Regency Grödnertals were succeeded by three distinct categories: the Penny Woodens already discussed, the Dutch Dolls and the Wooden Tops.

The Wooden Top is the most commonly-found wooden doll of the period, and is in fact still being manufactured today. These folk-made dolls were carved out of pine in a similar manner to the Penny Woodens, except that the bodies are much thicker and less shapely, and the features, instead of being merely painted on the skittle-shaped head, are often carved in some detail, and the nose is always represented in high relief. Very large dolls were sometimes given ball-and-socket joints, and feet were either carved, attached to the ankle by peg joints, stuck or nailed on. A few quality examples have the waist joint sometimes found on Grödnertals. Examples of the type as large as 24 inches are found, and the heads of these are carved roughly but effectively. Ears are often indicated, and the eye sockets gouged out to give the face a more sculptural quality than is seen in the small versions. Hands are usually spade-shaped, and the individual fingers are ignored. When dressed, some of the very large dolls of this type, such as the pair dressed in Welsh costume from the Horniman Museum, can hold their own against the classical woodens of the previous century.

Small examples often do not have applied feet, but the arch of the foot is indicated by a notch cut at the end of the stick-like legs, though old Wooden Tops over 9 inches high usually have the carved feet. As there are a large number of modern dolls of this type on the market, made in the traditional way, a few suggestions for identifying genuine examples would seem helpful. A clever faker finds it quite easy to distress a modern doll and create an appearance of great age, so that scarred and flaking paint is only of help to the collector who is used to looking at genuinely old examples, and has learned to recognize, almost by instinct, the look of old paint. Early dolls usually have carved and applied feet, whereas modern Wooden Tops, even when quite large, have notched hoof feet. The modelled 'shoes' are usually painted black or blue, but the notched feet of those made more recently are simply dipped at the end into pink or white paint. Old examples have hands that are carved into a spade shape, but modern dolls have stick-like hands with no additional detail. A few small mid-nineteenth-century Wooden Tops have stick-like hands, but in this case it was the small size that made the carving unnecessary. The lower legs and forearms are often painted in flesh colour on old dolls, which adds to the realistic effect, while more recent dolls have limbs that are left plain or painted white. The double line of clear and opaque paint is often found on the hairline of old dolls, but this is by no means always the case. Ears never appear on modern versions, though a few older dolls are known which actually have pierced ears. The modern Wooden Tops are very light in weight, whereas mid-nineteenth-century examples are often quite heavy.

A quaint version of the doll was known as a Wooden Kate and was sold in markets at the end of the last century. This type of doll had a carved bun at the nape of the neck and was made in Austria and Hungary. It is thought that dolls of this kind sometimes had leather joints instead of the wooden peg jointing. A few similar dolls made in the same area were given coloured torsos, though the reason for this variant is unknown.

Many wooden dolls found in Holland have heads that are mounted on cloth bodies, and are similar to specimens offered for sale in the catalogue of a Swiss manufacturer dating from the middle of the century. These dolls wear simple hairstyles, and look very sensible and motherly with their no-nonsense faces. Except for a few very small examples, all the illustrated heads have pierced ears. These shoulder heads are intended to fit cloth bodies made either by doll-makers or the child's mother. Similar dolls were probably made in the St Ulrich area, as it is recorded that their larger dolls heads were destined for Amsterdam, where they were to receive bodies before continuing their journey to England under the title of Dutch Dolls. It seems very possible, therefore, that these were the original Dutch dolls often referred to in Victorian nursery stories, though the term later came to be used to describe almost any wooden doll. The traditional explanation for the term is the etymological theory that Dutch is a corruption of Deutsch, as most wooden dolls were made in Germany.

There is little evidence of any large-scale wooden toy-making in Holland, yet so strongly was the belief held in England that the toys came from Holland that a little rhyme was made to criticize the destructiveness of English children when compared to the industry of the children of Holland. Some of the genuine

shoulder heads that were assembled in Holland have very finely-carved hair, and in good examples the shoulders too are well finished. Similar heads were sometimes sold for use on puppets: until a few years ago a long-established London toyshop still had a few old specimens for sale. The main difference in the carving of the head between these and the Wooden Tops lies in the fact that in these the hair is actually carved rather than merely being painted on.

It is surprising that the type of doll played with by almost all children before 1914 is the least well documented, and very few makers are known. J. D. Kestner is one of those recorded and he made dolls which were lathe-turned and known by the firm as 'Täuflinge', meaning babies ready for christening. This name was used by other makers to describe various types of doll, though Kestner's dolls were probably made of one piece of skittle-shaped wood, which was painted to simulate swaddling-bands. The faces of such dolls nearly always bear a close resemblance to those of Wooden Tops, and were probably painted by the same outworkers. Swaddling babies similar to these were made in Russia, Sweden and Czechoslovakia. Julius Dorset, Fleischmann Crammer and Zeuch and Lausmann all made, or at least handled, wooden dolls, while Rudolf Schneider in 1914 registered a German trademark for an all-wood articulated baby doll. A few wooden dolls of the Motschmann type are known, but these are very rare.

By 1875, there were eight or ten principal dealers in St Ulrich, who made weekly payments to outworkers on delivery of goods and managed the exporting of the products. The writer in *Leisure Hour* attributed much of the success of the trade to Herr Purger, who improved the standard of work in the area by bringing from Munich good models which could be locally copied. In the warehouses of Herr Purger and Herr Insam there were rooms full of toys in white wood. "Here are billions of wooden dolls, flung down helter skelter, paid for by Herr Insam at five farthings the dozen", wrote Margaret Howitt. Apparently nearly all this vast stock of toys was destined for Britain, with the exception of the shoulder heads that were going to Holland for completion.

The warehouse of Herr Insam was in operation until 1925. He relied completely for his supply on the patient industry of local people. At first, doll-carving was a masculine occupation, but after the introduction of machine-made lace the women were no longer fully occupied in their traditional craft, and they too made dolls. Whole families would sit until late at night around the work-bench, carving hundreds of dolls to be taken on Saturday in baskets or small carts to the distributor's warehouse. Large crates stood waiting at the wholesale exporters to be filled with the five-farthings-a-dozen dolls, brought on foot by

126   Pair of wooden dolls in Welsh costume. Good quality for the 'wooden top' type, as they have carved ears and shaped faces. Dolls date to the mid nineteenth century. 22 in. high.

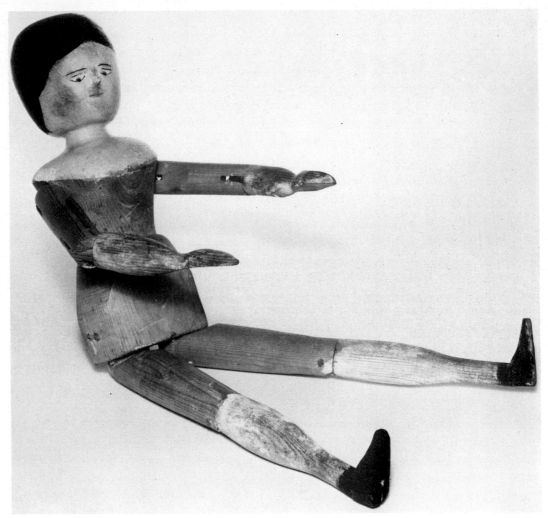

127　A well-made wooden doll of the mass-produced type made *c*. 1840. The shaped legs and spade-like hands are typical of early dolls of the type. Blue eyes, black boots. 19 in. high.

the workers. The exploitation of this cheap folk labour was the basis upon which the German exporters based their reputation for cheap but well-made toys.

Herr Insam exhibited his folk-made dolls at both the Paris Exposition and the Vienna Exhibition of 1878. He had agents who worked in Paris and London on the marketing of dolls made in St Ulrich. The introduction of the mechanical lathe increased the area's production potential, and one carver is recorded as having made one hundred dozen dolls in twenty-five hours using a mechanical lathe.

Wooden folk dolls have been made to some extent in almost all countries, and the skittle-shaped dolls of Sweden, for instance, are only a little different

(*left*) 128   Carved wooden shoulder head of German or Swiss origin, mounted on a home-made body. Similar heads were also utilized for puppets. Cream and brown silk dress. 13 in. high.   (*right*) 129   Carved wooden swaddling babies with painted decoration. 10½×11 in. high.

from examples made of oak and found in early eighteenth-century England. The brightly-painted wooden dolls made in Russia in the nineteenth century have their own particular character and look at first glance more like ornaments than toys. They are carved from triangular sections of wood and represent (for example) a standing woman wearing a hat and carrying a dog. All the folds in the clothes of such figures are roughly but effectively carved, and the contours are heightened by painting in bright colours. The turned wooden nests of dolls are a familiar sight in Russian gift shops, and they appear to have maintained their popularity with children despite competition from modern plastics.

American Wooden Dolls: The Springfield Manufacturers

The first American-made wooden dolls were those made by early settlers for their children. Carved from the solid wood, some of the early nineteenth-century examples show quite a high degree of craftsmanship. A character known as Schimmel is believed, in Pennsylvanian Dutch country, to have travelled around making wooden toys and dolls for children, but there appear to be few facts available concerning this character. The folk dolls, carved from pine or maple, are the true early American dolls, as distinct from the Queen Anne types that were imported from England and Europe.

The only positive advances made in the construction of wooden dolls after 1830 were made in America. At a time when European makers were losing interest in the traditional material, the inventors of the new country were able to take a fresh look at the possibilities of wood when combined with the mechanical advances of the middle years of the century. Whereas in the Regency period wooden dolls had to be carved by hand, they could now be pressed into shape, using methods that were similar to those employed in making furniture, and laborious and expensive handwork was made unnecessary.

Joel Ellis of Springfield, Vermont, is generally considered to have been the first producer of a commercial American doll. The basic construction of the simple peg-jointed doll was brought up to date and improved to create a shape that at a glance more closely resembles an artist's lay figure. Ellis was a man of great ingenuity who apart from his doll innovation patented thirteen other items, one of which was a pram or 'cab' which caused him to be nicknamed 'Cab Ellis'. A bad flood in 1869 ruined his original business and he established the Vermont Novelty Works to manufacture wooden dolls. The first patent related to a doll made of green rock maple, which was steamed to make it malleable, and the steam-moulded by a hydraulic machine. The dolls were actually manufactured at the Vermont Works by the Co-operative Manufacturing Company under the presidency of Joel Ellis. The patent states, "In the manufacture of dolls it is important to secure sufficient friction at the joints of the limbs to hold the limbs and body in any desired position, so that the doll may stand erect, or in an inclined position, or be supported on its head by the arms." The mobility of the doll can still be seen in surviving examples. "The tendency for two parts of the tenon to spread when compressed in the slot is constant, and compensates for wear and affords the necessary friction."

The dolls made by the Co-operative Manufacturing Company are very much lady-dolls, and wear a prim hairstyle of the 1860s. Flesh-coloured paint was applied to the head and well down over the shoulder, in some examples almost to waist level, so that the dolls could wear fashionable low-necked dresses. The lower arms and legs of these Joel Ellis dolls were dipped in flesh-coloured paint, in the style of contemporary porcelains. Metal hands were used which were fitted into the turned wooden arm at a point about half-way between wrist and elbow, the paint helping to conceal the change of material. Dolls with both fair and dark hair were made, and some were even painted black to represent negroes. Only one mould was used for all the dolls that were manufactured,

130   Advertisement for Schoenhut Art Dolls.

UNBREAKABLE "SCHOENHUT DOLL" ALL WOOD

The All Wood, Steel Hinge and Spring Jointed Perfection Art Dolls

WITH CHARACTER HEADS

"Schoenhut Dolls" are really Classic Figures of Children

"Schoenhut Doll" is a real manniken, a fully jointed artistic figure, not only the strongest and most indestructible Doll that was ever made in the history of Dolls, but also a Doll that will be indispensible to artists and instructors in Art Schools, being **superior** to any **jointed figures** ever produced.

The Body, Head, Arms, Legs, Hands and Feet are made from **solid wood**; these parts are painted in **enamel Oil colors and can be washed.**

The **Head** is artistically modeled in real character style, more natural and life-like than anything ever attempted. It is not a "Doll Face" head, but a production of art, executed and criticised by the most distinguished artists.

The figure is **jointed** with our new **Patent Steel Spring Hinge**, having **Double Spring Tension** and **Swivel connections.** The parts are held tightly together, although flexible enough to be placed in any correct position, and will stay in any position placed. **The joints move smoothly.**

NO Rubber Cord whatever is used in this "Schoenhut Doll" it will never have **loose** joints and will **never** require **restringing.**

The "Schoenhut Doll" can be placed in any natural position, incorrect position being almost impossible. Being fully jointed at the **wrists** and **ankles** as well as the other regular joints, the most graceful poses can be made. It can also be used for demonstrating exercises in physical culture. The most elaborate window decorations can be made with them. By grouping and dressing them accordingly, the most artistic tableaux can be set up.

To execute the most difficult poses, we furnish free with every Doll, a unique, practical metal stand, with a post that fits into the sole of the foot, the foot being especially made to receive the post.

but it was adapted by painting in a variety of ways. The dolls' quite shapely lower limbs were encased in side-buttoning boots, which were again painted to conceal the change from wooden legs to metal feet. The features of the Joel Ellis dolls were painted in the main by women, two of whom are believed to have been Ellis's cousins. The paint is the weakest part of the design, and has often flaked away, making the dolls attractive only to enthusiasts.

The turned body sections were fitted together by mortise and tenon joints, and the head was attached by a large tenon that fitted into a hole drilled in the head. The feet were jointed, so that the doll could assume any position, and were actually made of pewter or iron. These metal parts did not respond as well to the jointing method as the wood, and have often been lost. Though the 12-inch size is the most commonly found; it was also made 15 inches and 18 inches high. The dolls were sold originally at $9 to $13 the dozen, and the 1869 price list of Ellis Britton and Eaton, his partners since 1858, stated that dolls were distributed by Ellis and Jacquays in New York. It seems possible that, like many other manufacturers, Ellis marketed his dolls for some time before registering a patent, though the price list could refer to some other type of doll that is not recorded but was made or assembled by the firm.

The 1873 depression meant that there was little money available for spending on children's toys, and the firm's order books fell so low that the making of dolls was discontinued. The industry did not die in the area, as a few years later the partnership between Luke Taylor and Henry Mason was formed.

The Mason and Taylor dolls are again made of wood, but the head has a layer of composition substance over the wooden core. The distinctive feature of the product was the swivel head, claimed by the applicants for a patent as new and "constructed with a flange which forms the neck of the doll, and a bearing for the head on the body, and a groove in combination with a pin, whereby the head is fixed to the body and permitted to turn therein, substantially as and for the purpose described." An opening was apparently allowed in the composition of the head to allow the entry of air to dry the head out.

Like Joel Ellis, Luke Taylor was an inventor, and it was he who made the machines for the manufacture of dolls. The bodies were similar to those made by Joel Ellis and were also lathe-turned. Again like the Ellis dolls, the hands and feet were of metal, but the latter were usually painted bright blue, whereas the Ellis doll usually had black feet. Early Mason dolls, according to Eleanor St George who knew Luke Taylor's son, had stationary heads, wooden spoon hands and metal feet. After 1882, the swivel head of which the firm was so proud

131   The skilful jointing of the Schoenhut dolls means that they can still assume the advertised positions. Boy doll with moulded hair. 16½ in. high.

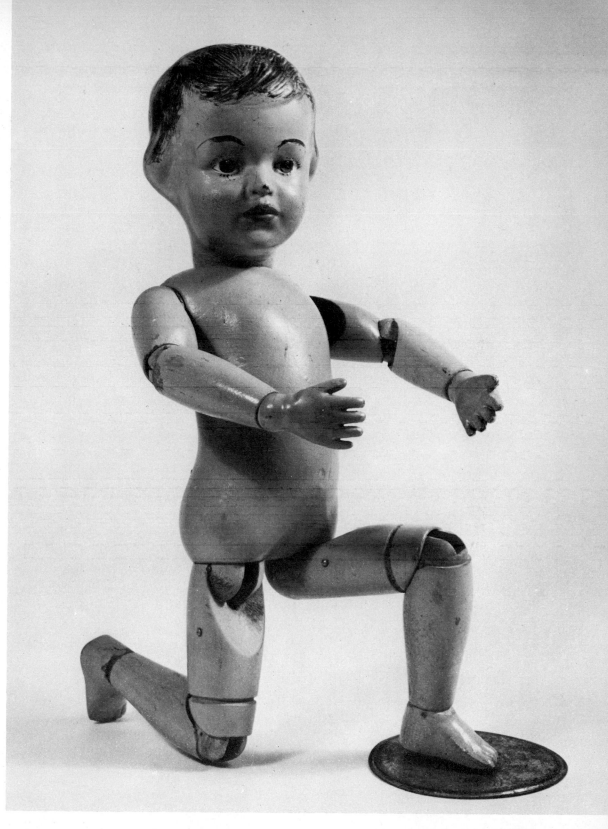

was used. One of the best-documented of the firm's products was the Witch or Wizard doll, though other novelty products such as a bald-headed infant were also made. The Witch or Wizard doll was especially made for export to Japan, and was accompanied by a knife so that the head could appear to be severed. There were no arm or leg joints on this doll, and the face was painted to resemble an Oriental's. The slippers were of the usual Mason and Taylor blue. Some black dolls were made by the firm, but as was the case with the Ellis dolls, they were merely the standard head painted black. "To have made negroid faces", said Mr Taylor, "would have necessitated new moulds, and moulds are expensive."

The products of the area are often so similar that they are simply described as 'Springfield dolls' though study does reveal the differences between makers. Though these dolls can still occasionally be found in America, they are virtually impossible to find in Europe, even in doll museums, and they usually have to be studied through illustrations and patent drawings. The Jointed Doll Company marked their dolls with a black band around the waist, which listed the patent date 'Improved Jointed Doll Patent April 29th 1879'. These dolls are very similar to the Masons, and have swivel necks and composition covered heads, though a few examples with stationary heads were also made. In 1879 Martin, one of the partners in the firm, obtained a patent for ball-and-socket joints secured by rivets. These dolls are about 12 inches high, and a contemporary advertisement stated:

The head can turn in any direction, the arms can be placed at any angle. It will stand alone, sit up or kneel down. The following important merits the doll possesses over all other dolls for small children will, when it becomes universally known, make it one of the staple toys. First – it being all solid wood – the head is solid wood, except a light plastic surface to form the finish – it will not break so readily, and in the hands of small children will last much longer than any doll. Second – by the movements of the joints and the positions it can be made to assume, it possesses more novelty and will amuse much longer. Third – it is the cheapest to the purchaser when all its movements are taken into consideration. One of its chief merits is, the novelty is greatly enhanced by not dressing it, as the movements of the joints are more readily seen and therefore will interest small children more than if dressed, while the cost and trouble of dressmaking can be saved.

The patent sketch shows a drawing of a doll that looks typical of those made by most of the Springfield makers. The advice to the buyer not to clothe the doll

132   Schoenhut advertisement, showing the method of attaching the doll to its stand and the jointing method

INGENIOUS CONSTRUCTION OF THE
"Schoenhut Doll"

SEE the patent STEEL SPRING HINGES having DOUBLE SPRING TENSIONS and SWIVEL connections

NOTICE—NO rubber cord is used. NO more loose joints. NEVER needs restringing. NO broken heads.

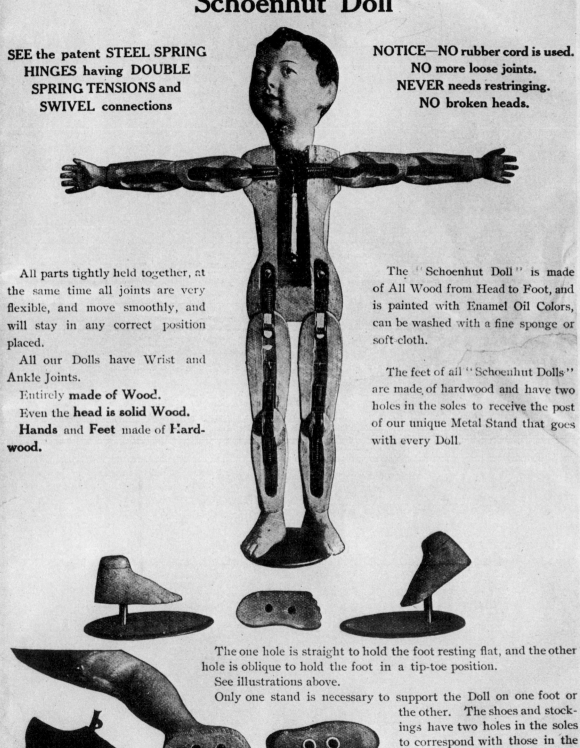

All parts tightly held together, at the same time all joints are very flexible, and move smoothly, and will stay in any correct position placed.

All our Dolls have Wrist and Ankle Joints.

Entirely **made of Wood.**

Even the **head is solid Wood.**

Hands and **Feet** made of **Hardwood.**

The "Schoenhut Doll" is made of All Wood from Head to Foot, and is painted with Enamel Oil Colors, can be washed with a fine sponge or soft-cloth.

The feet of all "Schoenhut Dolls" are made of hardwood and have two holes in the soles to receive the post of our unique Metal Stand that goes with every Doll.

The one hole is straight to hold the foot resting flat, and the other hole is oblique to hold the foot in a tip-toe position. See illustrations above.

Only one stand is necessary to support the Doll on one foot or the other. The shoes and stockings have two holes in the soles to correspond with those in the feet.

is, however, extremely interesting, as it seems a progressive attitude for a period not noted for its aesthetic appreciation of simple form.

Though all the known examples of the work of the Jointed Doll Company have moulded hair, the patent drawing shows a doll that wears a wig, tied back at the nape of the neck. It appears that the American maker was using as much creative licence as the German catalogue artists.

Paint used on dolls of the Jointed Doll Company was guaranteed not to wash off, and the 12-inch dolls were advertised as a good buy at $12 a dozen wholesale. It is interesting that these early doll-makers of a fast-developing country should have devoted their energy to the creation of 'unbreakable' dolls, while at the same time the European makers were quite happy to sell replacements for their fragile products. The attempted permanence of the dolls reflected the desire of a nation which was very literally on the move to obtain security and stability in at least some facets of its life. Later, when the people were more settled, the ugly philosophy of built-in obsolescence emerged.

The Schoenhut Company

The Schoenhut products follow the method of the better American dolls, according to which an old material was utilized in an up-to-date way. There is a tradition that the grandfather of Albert Schoenhut taught his son the craft of doll-carving, which he had practised in his native Germany. Albert emigrated to America at the age of seventeen, and by the time he was twenty-two in 1872 he was able to start his own toy-making factory, which at first mainly made well-finished toy musical instruments. The very famous Humpty Dumpty Circus, which when it began included about twenty figures and animals, was patented in 1903. Every figure had six joints, which enabled it to assume almost any position. The clowns had slots cut in their hands so that they could balance on chair backs or on ladders. These are now the easiest of the figures to find, and were made in the greatest number. Later other circus characters, such as a lady acrobat and a ringmaster, were made; others, like a negro dude and a Chinaman were constructed simply by attaching different heads to the figures and costuming them appropriately. Some were given bisque heads, but most were of wood. At least one Schoenhut circus character is included in many doll collections, though it is often felt by purists that their rightful place is in a collection of toys.

The first spring-jointed doll made by the Schoenhut Company was included in a set called 'Teddy's adventures in Africa' and was a portrait doll of Teddy Roosevelt. The spring-jointed doll which established the company's fame was patented in 1909, but was not on general sale until 1911. These dolls were marketed under the impressive title of 'Schoenhut all wood perfection art dolls'.

George W. Schoenhut stated in a letter to J. P. Johl:

The principal feature of the doll was the unbreakable nature of the parts, and the indestructible metal joints. The joints were so mounted that the springs in them would compress if they were pulled rather than stretch. This made the life of the doll almost endless. After his original concept of the dolls' construction, Albert Schoenhut employed Italian sculptors to mould the faces of the dolls.

The enamel paint used for the dolls' faces was very effective when new, but has now assumed the rather worn look that is the fate of most late wooden dolls. The eighteenth-century makers used a much more satisfactory lasting medium. The hair was either of 'carved' wood or was provided by mohair wigs. The first examples were 16 inches high. The dolls were sold complete with a metal stand, and the feet were holed to enable the doll to be posed in a variety of positions. Even the shoes and socks were made with holes, allowing the peg of the stand to pass through them into the feet. The patent drawings show how complicated was the design for the doll, which makes all other wooden dolls appear primitive. The ball-jointed body was strung on a series of rods, pivots and metal springs for each joint. The idea which was particularly revolutionary was that in pulling the joint apart, the spring was put into a state of compression, rather than the anticipated expansion. This was achieved by attaching a spring, the natural state of which was open to a rod which kept it closed and under pressure from the jointing of the doll. The complicated method meant that it was almost impossible for a piece to fall off the doll, as could often happen with elastic-jointed composition bodies.

The Schoenhut firm was justly proud of its dolls. An advertisement which dates from about 1915 reads:

Never were dolls like these before. So Beautiful. So Durable. So Artistic – So Sanitary. An American invention made entirely from wood. Even the Head. Perfectly jointed with steel springs. No elastic cord used.

The Body, arms and feet are made from solid wood; these parts are painted in enamel oil colours and can be washed. Some of the heads are modelled in the regular doll face effect to imitate the finest imported bisque heads.

Character heads are artistically moulded in real character style, more natural and life-like than anything attempted. It is not a doll face Head, but a production of Art, executed and criticised by the most distinguished artists.

The figure is jointed with our new patent steel spring hinge, having double spring tension and swivel connexions – the parts are held tightly together, though flexible enough to be placed in any correct position and will stay in the position placed. The joints move smoothly.

No rubber cord whatever is used in this Schoenhut doll. It will never have loose joints and will never require restringing. Established 1872.

The dolls' bodies were lathe-turned, and the heads were machine-carved from

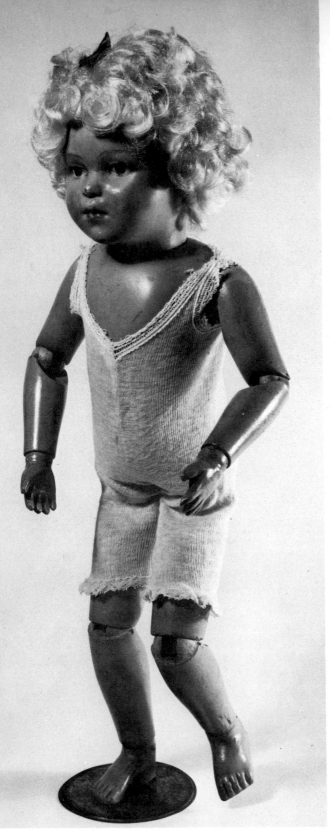

133 Schoenhut girl doll wearing a wig. Though hardly the most beautiful of dolls, they do exhibit the standard of workmanship. 19 in. high.

(*below*) 134 a and b Springfield wooden dolls in fair condition and positioned to show the clever articulation.

(*opposite*) 135 Carved wooden shoulder head of fine quality for the early twentieth century. Probably Swiss. 5 in. high.

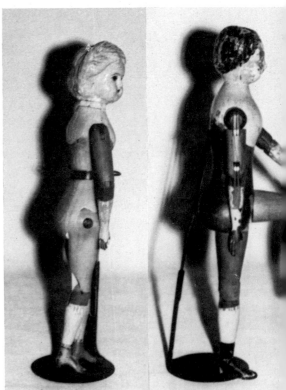

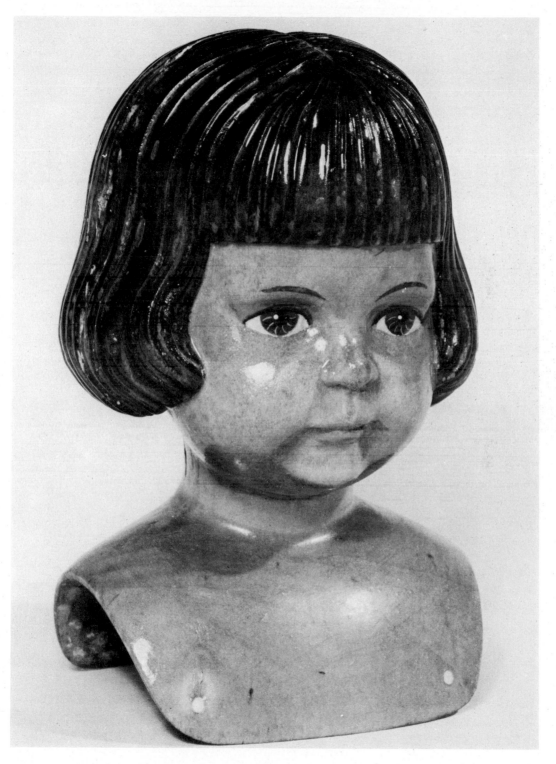

221

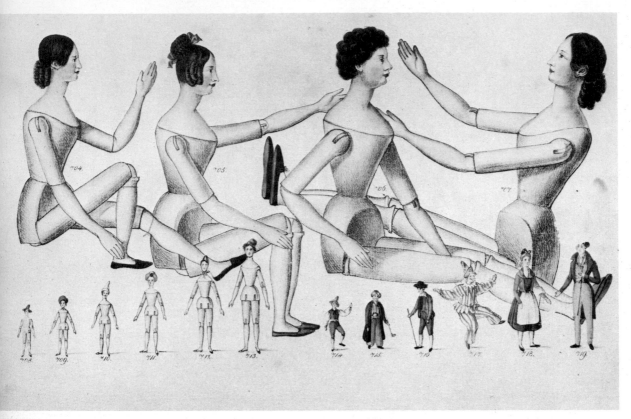

136 Page from a Biberach catalogue *c.* 1836, showing the good articulation of their dolls. The faces were either *brotteig* overlaid or carved and the dolls appear to wear wigs. The costumes available are also of interest.

the solid wood and hollowed out. It is interesting that as many boys as girls were made, because most manufacturers of the period found that boy dolls did not sell so well. The dolls were sold dressed in effective but simple contemporary clothes, though toyshops also stocked costumes specially made for them. One particularly fine doll was sold dressed in the kit of an American footballer.

The Schoenhut Company differed from the other American makers of wooden dolls in that it continued to introduce different models almost every year. The early types have closed mouths, which give the dolls an attractively pensive look. Even the manikin footballer looks far too soulful ever to be engaged in any rough and tumble. This particular doll has a very finely-constructed body and was used for 'Artists and Window Displays'. The manikins measured from 19 to 21 inches. Eleanor St George stated that only about 1,000 manikins were made, and many were destroyed when the company was dissolved, so that they are the rarest of the Schoenhuts.

137 A large papier mâché bust with the hairstyle of 1835. Once made, the moulds continued to be used for many years. 14 in. high.

222

223

A variety of children's heads were produced, some of which again had carved hair while others wore mohair wigs. A bent-limbed baby with interesting dowel-jointing was made to compete with the character dolls from Germany that were flooding the American market. H. E. Schoenhut obtained a copyright on the head of the baby on whom this character doll was based, and this model is known to collectors as the Copyright Baby. It was made in sizes ranging between 9 and 17 inches. A walking doll was made in 1919 with the copyright head. Though most of the dolls had closed mouths, some had teeth made of metal. The dolls were designed by Harry Schoenhut after 1916, and he was responsible for the introduction (amongst other things) of the walking doll with shoes specially constructed to enable the doll to keep its balance.

The firm insisted on attempting to compete with bisque dolls that were imported, rather than exploiting the possibilities of the wooden dolls they could make so well. Frequently in advertisements they claimed to make dolls that were just like bisque, and they even made a copy of the Bye-Lo Baby, which was the current rage among doll buyers. They also attempted to make imitation glass eyes in their effort to compete with French and German dolls that could be made so cheaply. The depression of the 1920s caused the bankruptcy of this firm and of so many others.

None of the American doll-making firms can be praised for their longevity, but they are noteworthy for their contribution to the development of a medium that was almost ignored by European manufacturers, in the second half of the century.

Papier Mâché Dolls

A doll made of a waste mixture pressed and moulded into shape would appear to us today to be potentially a cheaper product than a figure of hand-carved wood. This was not so in mid-eighteenth-century Germany. Wooden dolls could be carved, assembled and painted at home, so that the merchant had no overhead costs apart from storage and distribution, while dolls made of paper pulp, in any one of its number of varieties, had to be factory-made in moulds. Despite cheap labour and the exploiting of child workers, the cost of manufacture was higher than that involved in the making of wooden heads.

Though millions of papier mâché heads were made, good examples are not found very often, as they were subject to damage from vermin and also from damp and heat. Even papier mâchés that are prized in collections are not always safe, as central heating can cause a shoulder head to warp very badly. The wooden doll has a much sturdier construction.

21 Wax Lucy Peck doll

The coiffure dolls or 'milliners' models', which are so particularly associated with the early years of the century, continued to be made until the 1840s, and even later examples in original clothes are occasionally found. As in all spheres of doll-making, the manufacturers are unlikely to have discontinued a line simply because a hairstyle became outmoded; although the model might no longer sell in Paris it would still have charm for a country child. A number of dolls with hairstyles similar to that popularized by the young Victoria are known, and are sometimes dated to the period of her coronation, but as Victoria wore her hair in the German manner, it would appear unlikely that the dolls of this type were modelled to represent her.

Papier mâché dolls with a black-painted spot, the suggestion of a hairstyle or a painted arrangement on a plain egg-shaped skull are common from the mid-nineteenth century. The description 'Biedermeier' is sometimes applied to dolls of this type, but the term is used by collectors to describe various types of doll and has become misleading. German collectors use the term Biedermeier to describe almost any mid-nineteenth-century china doll; English collectors use it to describe bald-headed dolls with a small round spot on the top of the head; while others, most correctly, use the term simply to refer to the years 1815–48.

Papier mâché dolls are known with a black spot painted on the head, in a similar manner to porcelains. An old doll-collectors' theory was that the black spot indicated the point at which the wig was to be fixed, an expedient that would appear to be somewhat unnecessary! It appears more in the manner of a traditional method of treating the head. The decorator usually painted on hair, but in the case of dolls that were to be wigged, he simply painted a circle on the top of the head to show that the decorating was complete. In a similar way, sew holes continued to be placed in bisque shoulder heads, though the shoulder plate was almost always stuck to the body. Tradition among German toy-makers seemed to die hard.

The suggestion of painted hair allowed the doll to be costumed as a male or female. Some have quite well-painted short hairstyles, and old examples can be seen still in their original male attire. Many are found with the nails that once fixed the wig on lady-dolls still embedded in the papier mâché. The versatility of the method would have been to the advantage of both manufacturer and doll-dealer.

When the French doll-maker Soret obtained a patent in 1847 for making pressed paper dolls, he was proud of the fact that his dolls would compare very favourably with those made in Germany. His patent stated that up to that time the French products had been inferior to the German. Despite the pride of this inventor, the French doll industry does not appear to have benefited greatly, for despite the fact that some papier mâché heads were made in France, the monopoly

22 Parian doll with moulded turban

138 Page from Biberach catalogue, showing the wide available range of papier mâché dolls. Some are probably intended to represent boys.

was still held by the Germans. In making dolls' bodies, however, the French makers were unsurpassed. D'Allemagne stated that the French and German makers were complementary to one another, the one making excellent heads and the other excellent bodies. This co-operation ceased at the end of the century, when the German government prohibited the sale of doll parts to other countries, in an attempt to give protection to the native industry.

The typical early nineteenth-century German body was made of pink or white kid, sewn in four sections to give a rigid and unnatural form. Arms and legs were turned and finished with spoon-like hands and simply-carved feet. The French style body was an object of much greater sophistication. Gussets were added at hips and knees, so that the doll could assume a seated position, and the arms were attached separately, so that they would move easily for dressing. In comparison the old-style German body was as stiff as a wooden doll. These French bodies made for German papier mâché heads were the forerunners of the

139 Mid-nineteenth century doll of the Franco-German type. German papier mâché shoulder head mounted on a French pink kid gusseted body. Bamboo teeth, glass irisless eyes, well-painted curls before ears. Stuffed with bran. 31 in. high.

226

beautifully-sewn ladies' bodies that were to be used, in the last quarter of the century, for the bisque lady heads that established French supremacy in making quality dolls.

The rather ugly mid-nineteenth-century German papier mâché heads look out of place on the French type craftsman-made bodies, but presumably the French industry was forced to accept these Sonneberg heads if it wished to keep alive. Though ugly to non-collectors, the dolls do have some charm to the initiated. Their grinning mouths often exhibit a row of rather discoloured teeth, made of bamboo, glass, porcelain or wood. The necks are much thicker than on earlier dolls, and some resemble children rather than the traditional ladies, but the intention always seems rather tentative, as though the makers wished to produce a doll that could be anything the buyer wished, from a young girl to a society gentleman.

The eyes are usually of the all-pupil type without an iris, although in versions that have painted eyes the treatment is realistic. There is a great variety of finish to the painted hair. Some have merely an uneven patch roughly shaped to indicate the hairline, while others have delicately-painted curls and waves. Pierced ears are sometimes found, but these usually appear to be an afterthought, applied if the character the doll was to assume needed ear-rings.

It is probable that such heads were made by (among others) Fleischmann and Dressel, though no marked heads of the type are known. The bodies, though well made, have not the firm feeling of the later lady-dolls, but similar processes for making the bodies were used. The leather was well stretched before sewing so that the possibility of legs with an uneven appearance was eliminated. The body was held open at the neck over a metal ring, and a filling of cork, sawdust, hair or even straw was forced in with a variety of specially-made tools. Complete families would work to assemble the dolls, but though the families themselves are sometimes well documented, their products are not.

The second half of the century saw yet another advance in the design of papier mâché dolls' heads. These were heads made in the traditional manner, but with simple everyday hairstyles and round peasant-like faces. The dolls of this type were at first made alongside the Franco-German dolls, but appear to have remained popular for a much longer period. Their genealogy is apparent in their spoon-like hands and turned legs with neatly-painted boots, though their finish is much poorer than that of the coiffure dolls. A few samples still carry their makers' mark, such as those of the Dressel factory, though again attributable examples are very rare.

140   Pair of papier mâché dolls c. 1840. Kid bodies with red paper bands. Larger doll has yellow shoes and the smaller green. 10½ and 13 in. high.

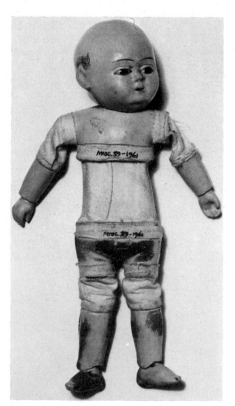

(*top left*) 141 Papier mâché head with inset glass irisless eyes. Hair-stuffed cotton body. Pink kid arms. Shoulder head modelled to waist at front. Face left unvarnished. Moulded hair drawn into bun. 31 in. high.

(*top right*) 142 Papier mâché boy with moulded hair. Detail as previous illustration, but face varnished and blue kid lower arms. Black irisless eyes. Scottish costume with brown jacket and red cravat. 31 in. high.

(*left*) 143 Motschmann based his European-made dolls on the Japanese figures seen at the 1855 Paris Exposition. Jointed composition figure with insets of fabric. Dark irisless eyes. 8 in. high.

(*opposite*) 144 Composition doll with moulded hair, wearing Dutch costume and holding bonnet. Dark irisless eyes. Fabric body, realistic limbs. Figure indicates the trend away from the stylized figures of the Regency period. Wears blue knitted stockings, black and white striped petticoat. *c*. 1850. 24 in. high.

These are the forerunners of the attempt to create a child-like figure, and some have, concealed in the torso, a simple press-action voice box. The Motschmann-type baby dolls were quite revolutionary, as commercially-made baby dolls were almost unknown (except in baby houses) before this time. Charles Motschmann of Sonneberg is believed to have been so impressed by the Japanese baby dolls he saw at the 1855 Paris Exposition that he worked at improving on the basic idea of a doll whose limbs were joined by cloth sections. These cloth insertions made the doll pliable and very realistic to handle. Many of the heads found on early Motschmann dolls are typically German, with bamboo teeth and painted hair, though a few wear wigs. Motschmann-style dolls were made of waxed composition, wood and even porcelain, as well as papier mâché, though the latter appear to be the earliest.

These loosely-jointed babies represented an important advance in the history of the doll, as they sought to represent a young child, whereas previously lady-dolls were the only type of figure worth producing commercially. They also reflect a change of attitude in the buying public, who previously had thought of children almost as miniature adults, but were now beginning to appreciate childhood as a state that was interesting in itself.

The Motschmann dolls were cheap to produce and were made in great number, becoming popular, inexpensive nursery gifts. The inserted pieces of cloth were fixed to grooves cut in the lower limbs, so that the German-made babies were less likely to fall apart than the originals which had come from Japan. Despite the quantity manufactured, dolls of this type are now hard to find, and it is surprising how many good representative collections are without an example of a doll that was originally so common.

Throughout the century, attempts were made to create a substance that was both strong and capable of detailed moulding. All sorts of variants on the basic mixture of paper pulp, glue size and plaster were tried, and manufacturers claimed, erroneously, that their own particular dolls' heads were unbreakable. In earlier papier mâchés it is sometimes possible to see the actual lines of the pressed grey paper pulp, but the late nineteenth-century examples are made of a much denser mixture, often containing so much plaster that it can be scraped away with a finger-nail. These dolls of debased papier mâché are usually referred to by collectors as 'composition' dolls, though the difference is often based on age and quality rather than on any analysis of the mixture.

The Franco-German papier mâchés were the last European quality dolls made of the substance, which came to be superseded by china and wax. After 1855, dolls made of the debased papier mâché did continue to be made in the old idiom, with a shoulder head and with lower arms and legs attached to a cloth body – but the makers were no longer content to sell the dolls as papier mâchés;

145 It is rare to find papier mâché dolls in this excellent condition. The figure bears a label reading "Greiner's Patent Doll Heads, No 10, Pat—March 30 (18) 58. Ext '72".

their sales literature instead described them as similar to dolls of china. The era of the truthful papier mâché was over.

The composition dolls, as collectors now refer to them, have limbs made of the same material as the head. These were fitted to the body (often straw filled) with a groove around which string could be tied tightly. As the clothes of children became shorter, it became necessary to show the dolls' feet, and chubby, realistic feet begin to appear under full-skirted dresses. The top of the head often has a roughly-shaped hole, through which a bunch of hair to arrange on the outside of the head as a wig could be pushed. The eyes are similar to those of blown glass in the heads of china dolls, and sometimes weighted sleeping eyes were added, though this type of eye mechanism is mainly found on composition dolls made after 1890. A few male dolls with moulded moustaches and beards were made, but these are rare, the majority of late papier mâché dolls being made to represent young girls.

A useful method of dating dolls of composition and papier mâché is by the shape of the shoulder plate. Early dolls have a generously wide plate, because low-necked dresses were the fashion. The breasts are often moulded also, so that very low ball-gowns could be displayed on a doll. As the century progressed and a more modest neckline was adopted, deep shoulder plates became unusual, since it was only necessary to show the chest and shoulders. By the end of the century, the shoulder plate had shrunk to such small proportions that it was often little more than a scarcely-disguised means of attaching a head to a cloth body.

Few composition dolls are marked, but most were actually made in Germany, with the obvious exception of American dolls. I have found several marked 'O.X.O.', but this would appear to be a size rather than a maker's mark. Dolls marked in this way were also made to be wax dipped, resulting in a slightly more expensive doll; this manufacturing method accounts for the similarity between many composition and waxed composition dolls.

The finish on many early compositions is often very poor and easily becomes marked. The heads were dipped in flesh colour, the detail of brows, mouth and cheeks painted and a very light varnish added for some protection. When new, the dolls very closely resembled the bisque dolls with which at the end of the century they competed. Although they tend to be dismissed lightly by collectors as undesirable because of their often spoiled complexions, these were once attractive dolls. One purchased recently was still in its original box, and showed how effectively eye-catching these cheap dolls must have been. Over-zealous cleaning by collectors has often taken off the protective varnish, and left the

146 By 1870 the makers of composition dolls were also turning towards a more child-like figure. Fixed realistic blue filamented eyes. Fabric body, composition lower arms and legs. Green silk dress. 19 in. high.

complexion spotted and powdery. Re-varnishing is never successful; even diluted picture varnish gives the wrong effect.

In the early twentieth century, a series of lady-dolls were made to be dressed in fashionable costume, and when this is intact they make quite desirable acquisitions. Baby dolls of this powdery composition are not often found, as they did not come into their own until after 1900, when shoulder-headed dolls were used much less. The substance remained popular for a long time as a medium for creating a light but strong head for use on clockwork figures and automata.

The original clothes for the girl dolls most frequently found by collectors consisted of a chemise and a pair of drawers made of heavily-stiffened muslin. The bodies are often also made of muslin, which has been treated with a stiffener to give it more weight. A surprisingly large number of the voice boxes that were inserted still work. This type of doll, unless beautifully dressed at home, has a low monetary value in itself, unless it is of some rarer variety, such as a man, a lady-doll or a baby. Many well-known makers made some dolls of composition, as an alternative to bisque heads, which could be sold to a less affluent public, though after the middle of the century they were never again quality dolls in their own right.

American Papier Mâché Dolls

Papier mâché was used for doll-making comparatively late in America, and the method was taken to the country by such émigré craftsmen as Greiner, who appears to have gone to America with the intention of setting himself up in business as a maker of dolls. The home product, up to the middle years of the century, had been made of wood or rag, and imported dolls were comparatively expensive, so that there was a rapidly-expanding home market for attractive and well-produced items.

American papier mâchés are very rarely seen in Europe, and English collectors' knowledge of such dolls is of necessity at second hand. Few museums possess examples of a type of doll that was almost exclusively made for home sale, and dealers appear loth to import examples despite the apparent European interest.

(*top*) 147   The basic composition Motschmann baby was made with several variations, as seen here in the undressed figure which has the impressed letters "SCJ" or "T" on the back. Both have squeakers in fabric inset torsos. 7 in. high.

(*bottom left*) 148   By the 1920s, the cheaper type of composition was used only for inexpensive dolls. The construction was adapted for costume so the legs were modelled higher to allow for short trousers. The small shoulder plate typical of dolls of this period. Painted brown eyes. Voice box. Marked "M & S". 21 in. high.

(*bottom right*) 149   Correctly-dressed First World War soldier of composition with painted hair and features. A variety of soldier-type figures was made, but this has more realism than most. 16 in. high.

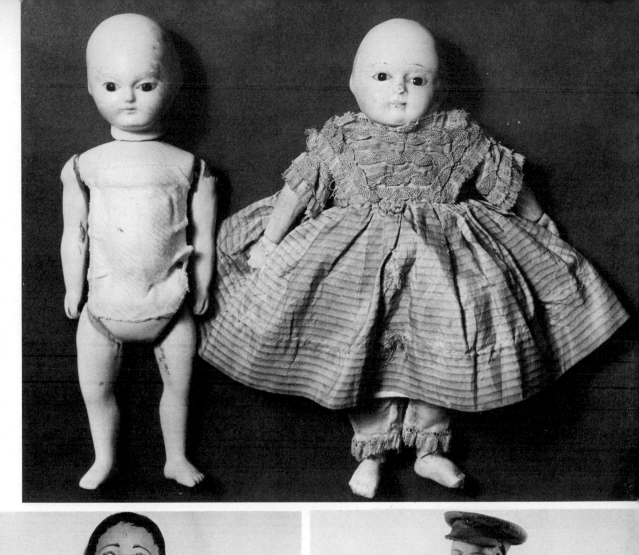

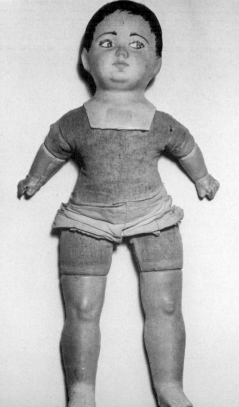

Like many other German immigrants, Ludwig Greiner and his family choose to settle in Philadelphia, among many of their own countrymen. The availability of those raw materials necessary for the manufacture of dolls also made the area attractive. Leather, animal hair, textiles, varnishes, plaster and colour were all close at hand. The entire Greiner family became involved in doll-making, and had the co-operation of other German families in the district, such as the Lacmanns. Greiner imported German toys for sale in his novelty store, but was quick to realize the need for a cheap home-made product.

It is believed that the family made dolls for some time before the registration of the first patent for an improved dolls' head in 1858, as a few heads are known that bear the 'patent applied for' mark. These heads are very much in the manner of the authenticated products, and are generally considered to be early Greiners. The early heads made by the firm were composed of equal quantities of paper, whiting and rye flour, mixed with glue and strengthened at weak points with linen cloth. As German doll-makers had been reinforcing heads with fabric for some time, it seems rather strange that the method of strengthening was especially patented. It might have been merely a sales ploy, to make the product appear more desirable with its black and gold label proudly announcing the patent date.

The early Greiners have black hair, parted demurely down the centre in the manner of German porcelain dolls. The eyes are usually painted blue, though set-in glass eyes are sometimes found. The dolls have a slight, comfortable double chin and are made in the old style to resemble ladies, but a much more down-to-earth type of womanhood than that characterized by the elegant German dolls with coiffure hairstyles.

The Greiner dolls were made in a wide variety of sizes from 13 to 35 inches, and many heads were sold separately to be attached to home-made bodies. Those most desirable to collectors are mounted on bodies made by Lacmann, who produced well-made bodies of cloth with leather arms. The arms were an innovation, as a core of a composition substance was moulded into shape and then covered with leather or fabric, which gave a firm and well-modelled effect. Earlier Lacmann hands had been made over a wire armature that enabled children to place the hand in any desired position. Though the Lacmann patent for the moulded hands was secured after the death of Greiner himself, collectors believe that the hands were used by the firm before the actual registration of patent.

150 By the last years of the century weighted sleeping eyes were used for composition dolls. The more realistic approach to the modelling of the face was evidenced in the making of wax and composition dolls before those of bisque. Blue eyes, open mouth with two lower teeth and tongue. Pink cotton sawdust-filled body. Realistic bare feet. 17 in. high.

239

The original 1858 doll's-head patent was extended in 1872, and there appears to have been a greater variety of heads made at this date, including a number of fair-headed dolls. Though the most common Greiners have the centre-parted waved-and-curled hairstyle, a few marked examples are known that appear to represent boys. There are also variations in the hairstyles and, not surprisingly, in the finish and quality of the face. The heads were lightly varnished before sale, and this protective layer has sometimes become very discoloured. Despite the patents for reinforcing parts of the head likely to sustain damage, many of the noses and chins have become rubbed with age.

Various attempts were made to overcome the fragility of the composition substance by (for example) Carl Wiegland of New York, who attempted to strengthen a doll's head by placing a layer of paper between two of cloth. Other American makers such as Phillip Goldsmith, Lerch and King, Hawkins and Reichman made moulded heads that look similar to the Greiners. The salesmen for Horsman and Michton, who marketed the 'Can't break-em' heads, used to bounce the heads on the floor to show their strength! Dolls marked 'M & S Superiors' have often been found in the United States, though it appears likely that they were actually German dolls, as they bear a strong resemblance to marked Dressel products. A label bearing the words 'Indestructible Heads – Superior' was on a doll made by the Dressel firm, and exhibited at the 1884 New Orleans Exhibition, but there is still considerable controversy over the origin of the heads.

My own favourite American papier mâchés are those made by Judge and Early. Their 1868 patent attempted to give the dolls a good finish by coating the mould with glue and whiting. Some of the heads made by the firm are rather in the manner of the staid Greiner, while a few charming examples were made with unusual moulded long blonde hair drawn back in an Alice band, so that the hair appears to fall loose over the shoulders. While the quality of the Judge and Early dolls is not remarkable, heads moulded in this way make a complete change from the usual upswept hairstyle, and are very desirable to the collector.

151   Large Edwardian composition child doll in original boxed state. When new, such dolls had a most attractive complexion and must have proved severe competition for the dearer bisques. Pink, straw-filled cotton body. Voice box. German, though there were English makers of composition dolls. 26 in. high.

152 Waxed composition slit head with very dark blue eyes wired to sleep. Wire lever to side of hip. Sawdust-filled body with legs held together at knee level by a few stitches. Blue leather lower arms. 24½ in. high.

NINE

DOLLS OF WAX

Waxed Dolls

"A row of small children stood gazing with admiring eyes at a large wax doll displayed in a window, dressed in an apple-green coloured silk dress, pink sunshade in hand. 'Price one and five three, it's marked!'" The rather surprising fact about this description is that it was written in the Playbox Annual of 1918, a period when it is popularly thought that the wax doll was long eclipsed, except in its finest and most expensive poured versions, which would not have been sold for such a small sum in a back-street shop.

It is rare to find a waxed doll whose original clothes are in the post-war fashion, yet there was evidently still a good trade in them. The likelihood is that the majority of those made at this time were constructed and dressed retrospectively, so that we now tend to date them as earlier than their actual time of manufacture. Children themselves were often dressed in an apparently outmoded style of clothing, and in many photographs dating to the 1920s, the children still look from their costume to belong to the nineteenth century. Many dolls, it would appear, suffered similarly from the outmoded ideas of their owners.

The poured-wax doll and that of waxed papier mâché, which are particularly typical of the period under discussion, developed alongside one another in the nineteenth century. The waxed doll, with its hair set into a slit in the head and its large all-pupil eyes, had its origins in the eighteenth century, and continued to be made until the late 1840s, when cheap versions under 12 inches high were still being sold to the crowds at fairs and race meetings.

A more expensive doll of similar type was made with large hands and feet of more realistic proportions. The heads are very similar to those of the cheaper and earlier version but tend to have wigs attached in a more conventional way with glue. The eyes are also of a much better quality. The main difference between

(*above*) 153   A page from a Victorian scrapbook, showing a group of children playing with their waxed composition dolls.   (*below left*) 154   Probably because they were rather unwieldy, the 'pumpkin' heads often retain their original clothes. Large black irisless eyes. Sawdust-filled cotton body with voice box. Painted orange boots. Red and white dress. 26¾ in. high.   (*below right*) 155   Granny Sidebotham's pumpkin head. Showing the crazing that is frequently found on dolls of the waxed composition substance. Black irisless eyes. Has jointed hands that are unusual in dolls of this type. Blue boots. Black velvet coat over yellow and cream dress. 28 in. high.

the two types lies in the fact that the quality dolls have waxed composition limbs, which would have given them an air of reality when compared to the slightly older dolls with their mean, narrow, leather arms. These moulded and wax-dipped limbs were attached to the cloth body by sew holes through the composition. It is a method that has been proved satisfactory, as most of the examples I have handled still have their original cords fixing the limbs.

The hair was usually knotted into a cap which fitted well down over the 'ears'. When curled, the hair covered the cotton mesh of which the cap was made and formed quite an effective hairstyle. Wigs so fair that they were almost white were popular, and perhaps show an odd lingering of a long out-of-date fashion for powdering the hair. A few dolls of this type wear wigs that are simply a length of hair stitched to a strip of cloth, in the semblance of a parting, and then glued to the scalp, with the ends curled into ringlets. Better-quality waxed dolls were still occasionally given inset hair, and one very unusual man-doll of this type in the Norwich Museum collection has not only inset hair but also whiskers and the remains of a beard. It is very rare to find any doll of this waxed type without the cracks that are common to all dolls of waxed papier mâché, and collectors have to accept these imperfections as evidence of respectable age.

Eyes that were made to open and close by means of a wire that protruded from the body at waist or crotch were a frequent feature of dolls of this kind. It was a method that continued to be used throughout the century on a variety of dolls, but is usually primarily associated with those of wax. Lucy Peck, a creator of quality English poured-wax dolls, made use of this same method as late as 1900.

As most papier mâché heads were made in the Sonneberg area, it is generally assumed that the waxed heads originated from the same source though several makers of English waxed compositions are recorded, and advertisements frequently refer to the English made dolls of this type; but the doll-making methods used are so traditional that it is impossible to state the accurate source of a particular doll. Waxed dolls were also made in France, often, it is believed, over a plaster base, but tantalizingly few authenticated examples have been reported. Several English makers of poured-wax dolls also made some of composition, and the two methods were sometimes combined as in the work of the Wheelhouses of the Waterloo Road, London. It is therefore an oversimplification to state that all waxed compositions originated in Germany.

Several coats of wax were sometimes given to the papier mâché shell, in order to create a top-quality waxed doll that looked like the expensive poured versions. The hair was occasionally set into the wax coating of the head to create a realistic wig: this was a method later exploited by the makers of poured dolls, but seen quite often in these top-quality waxed products. It is easy to be misled by the outward appearance of these dolls into thinking that they are poured, but the faces lack the precise modelling seen in the better dolls, and often have a rather softened and blurred look. Some examples of the type are very large, and it is possible that this was a method favoured by the makers of big dolls, as the head would appear to be rather stronger than a shell of wax alone.

Though most of the slit-headed type of doll are found dressed in ladies' clothes, a few examples of the plumper, realistically-limbed dolls are found dressed in the clothes of young girls, and a few baby dolls are known, though these often formed part of a baptismal gift rather than being actually used for play. Waxed Motschmann-type baby dolls were made as toys, but they are often very disfigured and are not very popular with collectors.

The standard of costuming these early nineteenth-century waxed lady-dolls is almost always very high. Garments, though simple in shape and made of linen or flannel, were most beautifully stitched. There is little of the ornamentation for its own sake that is found on later dolls, and the costumier appears to have relied more on shape and good seaming to achieve the desired effect. An occasional doll is found whose owner obviously had access to good-quality silks and brocades, but the majority are found simply dressed in the white fabrics that were available to all but the poorest of women by the middle years of the century. Dating of the dolls has to be achieved by reference to their original clothes, as the various types of doll were made for considerable stretches of time, and do not themselves provide a precise guide for the collector.

By 1830 the softly-flowing skirts gathered to fit the body just below the bust-line had almost disappeared, and very full skirts gathered to the natural waistline, the forerunner of all Victorian fashion, had become popular. Dolls do not often wear crinolines, so that their dress has to be dated by its decorative detail, the way in which the fullness of the skirt is disposed, and the skirt's length. A good illustrated guide to nineteenth-century fashion is a necessity to any serious doll-collector. It is as essential as a good encyclopedia of dolls' marks, both for judging the date of costumes and for making reconstructions when a doll is purchased without clothes.

Some wooden dolls were given a waxed surface, to act as a seal to any imperfections in the wood. At times, the coating is very thin, but sometimes a moulded wax mask would be fitted over a wooden core. One unusual doll of the latter type has hair set into the wax. Waxed woodens are very rare, and are unlikely to come into the possession of collectors, as it was not a popular doll-making method. Another interesting type of doll, obviously not as rare as the previous one but nevertheless very collectable, is the three-faced doll made by the

156   By 1840 the early 'slit heads' had developed into a rather more realistic figure with modelled limbs. Bald head, fixed blue eyes. Heavy, sawdust-filled body. Replacement wig. Original was white and tightly knotted on a mesh cap. 24½ in. high.

247

Bartenstein firm. The faces turned under a bonnet, and showed a baby in three moods. It is a rather unsuitable construction for a doll whose fragile surface is likely to be damaged by continuous turning, but some examples have survived quite well, as have wax dolls on swivel necks.

Multi-headed dolls of waxed composition were made around 1900, again in what would appear an unsuitable medium for interchangeable parts. They were usually of the cheaper type and fitted into a waxed shoulder socket. It is obviously very unlikely that many would have survived with their complete complement of these quite fragile heads, and few are found today.

The slit-headed doll, with its all-pupil eyes and leather or waxed arms, was made alongside a type of doll whose direct origins can be seen in the papier mâché coiffure dolls that were themselves sometimes waxed. The turned and painted legs found on coiffure dolls can be seen in a rather shortened form on dolls made up to the 1880s. Similarly, the early wooden arms ending in simple spoon-like hands were made, though of lighter wood and less realistically painted, up to the same period. The slim and elegant heads of the coiffure dolls developed into more homely-faced ladies with all-pupil eyes and rather characterless expressions. The same dolls were made to be sold either in the waxed or the composition state, and a few boy dolls, also with moulded hair, were sold. At this stage the waxed composition with moulded hair was still fairly realistic, and the hair was even painted in a dark colour over the wax. Early examples of the type have a thin layer of tinted wax, which gives an attractive bloom to the face, and does not obscure much of the modelling, as do those made with moulded hairstyles after 1860. Extra decorative detail such as a comb or ribbon were sometimes added to the hairstyle and of course included in the mould. Dolls of this type are quite rare, but are interesting in that they mark a transitional period. A press voice box was often added to the torso to make the doll more appealing to a child, though to the adult these prim ladies who squeak when their stomach is pressed always appear delightfully absurd.

The delicate features of these transitional dolls became much simplified for cheaper productions, and consequently the detail of the faces became less precise. Collectors refer to mid-nineteenth-century waxed dolls of this type as squash or pumpkin heads, because of their round, moon-like faces that are very narrow from back to front. The heads were narrow so that they could be produced from shallow moulds, which meant that drying was accelerated and the danger of warping became much less. As the detail of the head was only slightly raised, the papier mâché did not need extra strengthening, as had been necessary in the more

157   Large good-quality heavily-waxed composition with inset hair and eyelashes. A pinker wax than usual. Shoulder head glued to body, but eyeleted limbs are sewn. Realistic blue glass eyes. 30 in. high.

248

249

three-dimensional coiffure heads. Making a pumpkin head only required a two-part mould, whereas the coiffure heads were sometimes made of four or more parts. Another economy was the fact that the colour was now applied to the papier mâché shell itself, and an ordinary white wax was used to cover both hair and face, thus saving several finishing processes. These pumpkin heads are a good example of how a fairly sophisticated prestige product can become simple, mass produced and eventually quite primitive.

It is because of their primitive appearance that I find the pumpkin heads appealing. Most collectors like to own at least one example of the type, and as they are not highly priced, this is usually possible. The wax has often contracted unevenly with the composition shell and cracking has occurred, though to nothing like the extent of the slit-headed type. The price of such dolls is kept low, as they all tend to look rather alike, and collectors rarely want several dolls that are almost identical. Thousands of these squash heads must have been imported, since there are still a large number that come regularly on the market. The probable reason for their survival is the fact that they made most unsatisfactory play dolls. The body was tightly packed with sawdust or straw, so that it was quite unyielding, and the large waxed head was cold and unlovable. The sharply-pointed feet and hands must also have made the doll an unsuitable bedfellow. Its lack of warmth is also evidenced by the large number that are found in their original clothes, as though the doll was stood in a chair to be admired but rarely played with. When most dolls are purchased privately, they are usually sold in an untidy and dishevelled state, with an assortment of garments acquired during some hundred years of family life. This is not so with the pumpkin dolls. They are found dirty, and sometimes damaged by the climate, but rarely with that loved and battered look that is seen in other more yielding dolls.

The standard doll of the type has blonde hair, quite ornately moulded in a waved and upswept style, with a rather Germanic-looking roll of hair at the back. Combs and ribbons are frequently indicated in the mould, though quite often the maker did not bother to paint in the detail. The heads were dipped in bright flesh colour, and the hair was painted brilliant yellow before the head was immersed in hot wax, which softened the crude colour and made it fairly realistic. Usually only one immersion was given, or else the ground colour would have become too obscured. The detail of ribbons, combs, lips and brows was added by the decorator, who sometimes also tinted the cheeks. The detail has often been rubbed away, as the paint did not adhere well to the wax, especially the black that was used for combs and ribbons.

158   Waxed Chinese doll with black irisless eyes. Once wore ear-rings. Pigtail emerges through hole on crown. Pink fabric body. Voice box. Waxed lower arms and legs that are barefooted. Size 12¾ in.

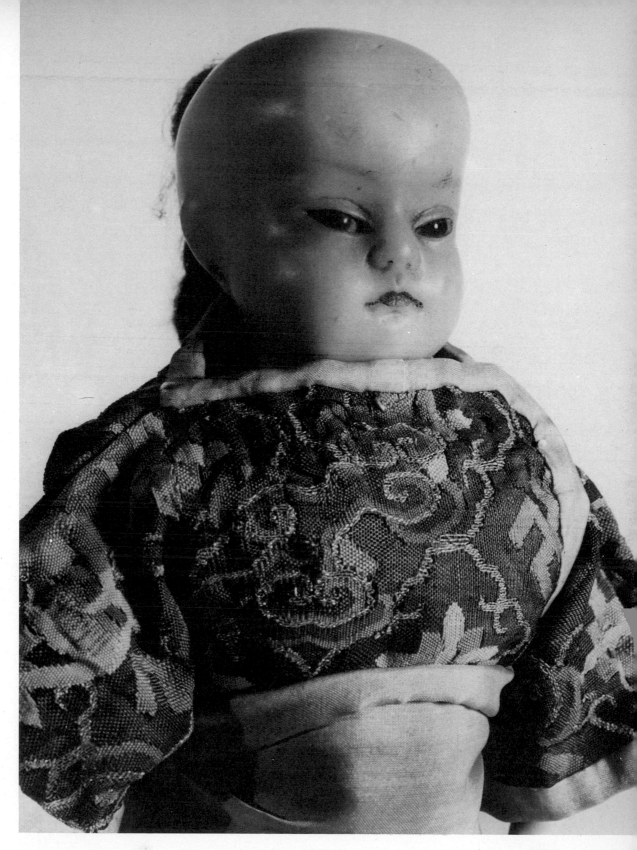

251

The eyes of pumpkin dolls are usually of the black, all-pupil variety, though one is known with eyes that move by means of a balance weight. Contemporary dolls were often given quite realistic glass eyes, and the use of the old-fashioned all-pupil variety is another indication of the cheapness of the product. Later versions have simple, wrist-jointed lower arms instead of the older turned variety, but there is otherwise little difference between early and later dolls, whose dating must depend on the style of their costume. A wide variety of sizes was made. The smallest I have seen was about 9 inches long, but no doll's-house dolls of the type appear to have been made. The largest size made in any number was about 26 inches, though it would be interesting to learn of any larger examples in collections.

Pumpkin heads are rarely found in costumes of later than 1870, and it seems logical to conclude that this type of doll was not made after this date. Another doll of the same lineage then took over, in the form of a cheap bonnet doll. Some made in small sizes were obviously intended to be sold very cheaply, and are tawdry in construction, though interesting for the variety of headgear they exhibit. Some wear flat hats with stiff feathers, all of course moulded in the wax, while yet others wear bonnets of quite ornate design. The head-dress is usually worn well back on the head, for otherwise a mould much more complicated than two or three pieces would have been required. One large example wore an ornate blue confection, decorated with flowers and feathers and held under the chin with a large bow, all the detail being moulded in the usual manner. A few had mohair glued to the head just beneath the brim of the hat, but this was an unsatisfactory method, and the heads look best when all the work is executed in the same manner.

Most of these bonnet dolls descended from the pumpkin head appear to have been made between 1865 and 1885, and I have found none that I can positively date as either before or after this time. One amusing example in the Worthing Museum wears spectacles. When the squeeze box in the torso is pressed, the head turns to one side and the arms are raised, in imitation of the action of shaking an apron. The bonnet heads are rather more desirable than the standard pumpkin heads, as they were made in a much greater variety, which makes them potentially saleable to a wider range of collectors.

Very fine lady-dolls of waxed composition were made in the Sonneberg area in the middle years of the century, and they are model dolls in the truest sense, with beautifully-arranged, heavily-powdered wigs and exquisite clothes. The

159 Waxed bride doll with cobweb over face. Very yellow wax. Blue fixed eyes. Fair mohair wig. Black boots with fixed fabric stockings and gold paper garters. Sawdust-filled body. Voice box. Very detailed original clothes, including a corset. 24 in. high.

ears were often pierced, and they had bodies that were jointed and made of leather, including the forearms. These dolls were obviously closely related to the Franco-German papier mâchés, with their fine gussetted bodies, though in this case the German manufacturers were able to make the bodies themselves, probably from French designs. It is possible that the bodies were imported from France, but not very likely as the trade was usually the other way. These dolls are rarely seen in English and American collections, and were probably made as prestige products for the German market, being more like fine miniature fashion figures than play dolls. They demonstrate that dolls of very fine quality could be made by this method, though to see them it is necessary to visit German museums.

Baby dolls of waxed composition are found much more frequently to have been made after 1860. The Motschmann type had long been popular as were the small Sonneberg babies with the all-pupil eyes. A few baby dolls were now given sleeping eyes, worked usually by the wire-eyed method. Small baby dolls also continued to be used as baptismal gifts, and as figures to decorate boxes and other decorative arrangements. There is often the question with waxed baby dolls as to whether they are actually play dolls or figures taken from such an arrangement. One thinks particularly of the babies made in the form of a box to hold sugared almonds. The legs kick and the head turns when a string in the side of the box is pulled. Doll or box? The item could fit equally well into a collection of either sort.

The Develas firm of Paris made wax figures of children for various purposes, including effigy figures that were probably portraits, wax figures, and the figure quite commonly found in Continental museums, the Infant Jesus, often in the manner of the Good Shepherd.

The slit heads and pumpkin heads were not sufficiently attractive to continue to appeal to children, and a new type of waxed doll evolved that resembled the expensive poured-wax figures. These new waxed compositions were often dipped two or three times to give a thick dense coating of wax. The body of the wax itself was tinted so that it was not always necessary to apply a layer of paint to the composition shape before dipping, though in most cases the traditional method was maintained. These late nineteenth-century waxed dolls have a much more realistic appearance, and have what we now think of as doll-like faces, with big eyes and slightly upturned lips. They rarely have much character or

160   Unusual waxed doll with black painted hair swept into bun at nape of neck and decorated with long comb. Black irisless eyes. Shoulder head modelled with small breasts. Ends just above waist at front. Voice box. Wooden lower limbs. Brown and yellow painted boots. 20¼ in. high.

255

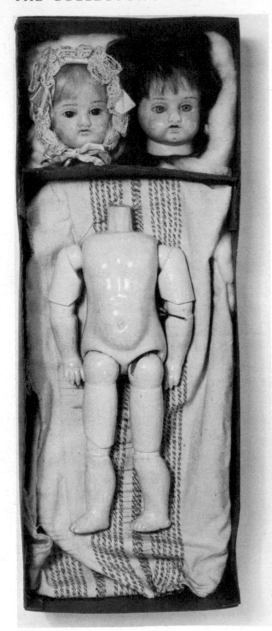

161 Good-quality ball-jointed composition and wood body with interchangeable cheap waxed heads. One head missing. Original box. Strings to back of torso for voice box. Stamped on body "M.Sch." 11 in. high.

162 Better-quality waxed compositions were given inset hair, as in this example with a slightly-turned head. Horsehair-stuffed body. 16½ in. high.

expression, but are liked because they have the kind of face that is immediately visualized when one thinks of Victorian dolls. Quite splendid mohair wigs were often made for the better dolls, while cheaper versions wore hair pushed in a bunch through a hole roughly cut in the top of the head. Blonde hair with blue eyes was the most popular colour combination, but a reasonable number have

brown hair and eyes. Black hair was most unfashionable in dolls, reflecting the taste of the age.

More expensive versions had arms and legs that were also made of waxed composition, but the limbs of cheap dolls were left undipped, and were merely painted. Some of the dolls have plump, well-moulded toddler-type feet, while others wear a stylized black boot with a small heel. The moulded boots and shoes worn by these late waxed dolls are an aid in dating, as current fashion is again reflected in their design. Boots and shoes of some variety appear, ranging in shape from calf high-buttoned or laced boots to dainty slippers with a thin strap. Coloured boots are much rarer, but orange was popular, in particular with the Dressel firm, which marked many of its dolls. An effective method of applying a stocking to such legs was used by this firm, though it is also seen on dolls that are unattributable. The fabric for the stocking fitted into a groove at the level of the boot top, and the top of the stocking was tied into another groove at the top of the lower leg. The fabric of which the upper legs were to be made was then applied and covered the top join. The lower join was marked by a strip of gold decorated paper. Tassels in imitation of bootlaces were sometimes added as a final touch. The better the quality of the doll, the more likelihood that the limbs will be waxed, as is the case with the marked Dressel dolls, some of which have inset hair. Many firms (such as Kestner) made waxed dolls, but as they rarely marked their products, most dolls of this type are classified only according to their date and quality. Even the country of origin is often uncertain.

Most of the waxed compositions are attributed to Germany, though it is known that some were made in England. John Edwards, for instance, better known as a maker of poured-wax dolls, also sold dolls of composition, and it seems likely that a cheaper-quality waxed doll would have been useful for his wholesale business. Henry Pierotti also made composition dolls, and it would be strange if the two media were not combined occasionally.

Strange anomalies are continually found in the examination of dolls of this type. Inset hair seems an expensive method to use for cheaply-made dolls, but it is sometimes found on examples that are otherwise of fairly low quality. Wigs knotted into a cap in the old manner are also found. This is a method of wig making that generally ended after 1855, yet a few late waxed dolls wear them, presumably utilizing old stock, or the product of a rather old-fashioned maker. A method used quite often to attach a conventional wig was to nail it to the head with half-inch nails. Four or five was the usual number. It is remarkable that the heads did not shatter when the nails were driven in, but they caused as little damage as they did to the wooden-headed dolls on which this traditional method of attaching a wig was first used. Economies were sometimes made in the amount of mohair used: some dolls have very short hair that is tightly curled to cover as

27 Bisque shoulder head with moulded flowers in hair

much of the head as possible. A few of the bodies are very well made, with shaped waists and plump upper arms filled with animal hair. Others are merely a series of rectangular bags, roughly filled with straw and joined together in the semblance of a figure. The straw has often become broken over the years, which causes the doll to fold over slightly with the weight of its head.

The most attractive heads were made with a high proportion of beeswax in the mixture, and these have a soft and rather yellowed look. After 1880 paraffin wax was used to a greater extent. Paraffin wax sets harder than beeswax, but it also has less adhesive power, and once the wax begins to crack away from the head the whole face soon disintegrates. As the wax was often tinted before use, it is difficult to ascertain whether beeswax or paraffin wax was used. Some writers suggest that beeswax can sometimes be detected by its smell, but though a lump of pure beeswax has quite a strong smell, I have never been able to detect it on a doll. From experiments carried out by pouring paraffin wax and beeswax on to a sheet of thin cardboard, it would appear that the beeswax was more suitable for doll-making. The paraffin wax set white and hard on the surface, and did not allow any ground colour to show through. The beeswax formed a soft brownish cover through which the colour underneath could still be seen. The disadvantage of the beeswax in not setting as hard as the paraffin wax was offset by the fact that while a scratch on the latter scarred the surface with a white mark, a nail driven across the beeswax merely left an unevenness of surface, and no ugly mark. When the cardboard was bent back, the paraffin wax cracked away, but the pure beeswax remained firmly attached, even when the card itself cracked through being folded back. The sensible doll-maker would have combined the two to gain the best properties of both, but collectors always enjoy speculating as to which of the two substances was used.

A variety of wax mixtures was used, probably including Chinese spermaceti wax which sets very hard, though beeswax must have been used in a large proportion. The melting-point of the later waxed dolls appears to be much higher than that of the old slit-head type, whose wax will begin to melt if placed against a window, even in English winter sunshine. Several of the later dolls, some of which wear labels 'Warranted to Stand Any Climate', have been quite undamaged when I have left them even in the summer sun for some hours. It is

(*top*) 163   Pair of late nineteenth-century waxed dolls in original costumes. Larger doll has orange, black and gold waxed high-heeled boots. Blue fixed eyes, voice box. Pink velvet costume. Doll to right wears a blue dress with yellow-trimmed straw bonnet. Blue sleeping eyes. Horsehair-stuffed body. Bare feet. 22 and 20½ in. high.   (*below left*) 164   The Christmas tree fairy made its first English appearance in the mid-Victorian era. Wax, plaster-reinforced shoulder head. Sawdust-filled body. Brown fixed eyes. 11¼ in. high. (*below right*) 165   Small waxed bonnet doll with dark irisless eyes. Feathers to moulded hat in green and orange. Wooden lower arms and legs. 8 in. high.

166 Waxed doll in green woollen dress and bonnet. Has large blue fixed eyes. Composition lower arms and legs. Was originally purchased in France. 17 in. high.

167 Pair of plaster-reinforced wax dolls. Doll with hat has fixed blue eyes and open mouth with teeth. Composition lower limbs with black ankle-strap shoes and white moulded socks. Doll in red silk dress has bare feet, blue eyes. 14 and 9¾ in. high.

obviously inadvisable to leave any type of wax doll in the sun at all, but I have at least learned something from my carelessness. Presumably the parents of the late nineteenth century remembered how the dolls of their youth had distressingly melted away, and the labels which the dolls sometimes wore were intended to reassure such people that no such fate would meet these new dolls, probably of a much harder type of wax.

A few of these late dolls were even guaranteed washable, but water running over the shoulder head and into the stuffed body must have caused great damage. There are many cautionary tales in Victorian children's books regarding the fate of dolls that were carelessly treated, but as it was the custom to refer to all dolls as 'wax', it is difficult to surmise which type of doll is referred to, though a story in the *Juvenile Instructor* of about 1885, written by Mrs Walton, does appear to describe dolls of the waxed type. The story was called (in typical late Victorian fashion) 'Do Try', and described a toyshop in a poor area of a town under the shadow of a gateway.

> There sitting in a row and looking out at her were a number of dolls – beautiful wax dolls with curly hair and blue eyes and pink cheeks. And Poppy had never had a wax doll of her own. Her only doll was an old wooden creature, with no hair and with long straight arms; She could never even sit down, for her back and her legs would not bend, and when Poppy came home and looked at her after she had been gazing in the toy shop window she thought her very ugly indeed.

The waxed dolls, such as those gazed at in such wonder by the poor child, were very attractive when new, but unfortunately suffer the fate of most combined substance dolls and are often badly cracked. At the end of the century, weighted sleeping eyes were often put into these dolls in imitation of those in bisque heads, with disastrous results. The lead weight, as it swung to and fro in the head, was bound to eventually cause damage, even when the inside was protected by a piece of cork; and in some very cheap dolls even this elementary precaution was dispensed with. Tiny teeth were also put into late dolls of the type, again in competition with bisques, but they always look rather ugly and unsuitable on wax dolls.

As good dolls become more difficult to find, the waxed compositions have increased greatly in popularity, despite their frequently-damaged state. The more unusual types have long been popular, such as the illustrated European 'Oriental' doll. The doll has a completely bald head with a pigtail protruding from a small hole cut in the crown. Perhaps once the remainder of his hair was painted on, rather in the manner of the early coiffure dolls, which had combined hair treatment both real and painted. Certainly there are no remains of any glue,

THE twelve Miss Pelicoes
   Were twelve sweet little girls ;
Some wore their hair in pigtail plaits,
   And some of them wore curls.

The twelve Miss Pelicoes
   Had dinner every day ;—
A not uncommon thing at all,
   You probably will say.

The twelve Miss Pelicoes
   Went sometimes for a walk ;
It also is a well-known fact
   That all of them could talk.

The twelve Miss Pelicoes
   Of course, to school were sent ;
Their parents wished them to excel
   In each accomplishment.

The twelve Miss Pelicoes
   Played music—*Fal-lal-la !*
Which consequently made them all
   The pride of their papa.

The twelve Miss Pelicoes
   Learnt dancing and the globes ;
Which proves that they were wise, and had
   That patience which was Job's.

The twelve Miss Pelicoes
   Were always most polite,—
Said "If you please," and "Many thanks,"
   "Good morning," and "Good night."

The twelve Miss Pelicoes,
   You plainly see, were taught
To do the things they didn't like.
   Which means, the things they ought.

Now, fare ye well, Miss Pelicoes,
   I wish ye a good day ;—
About these twelve Miss Pelicoes
   I've nothing more to say.

K.C

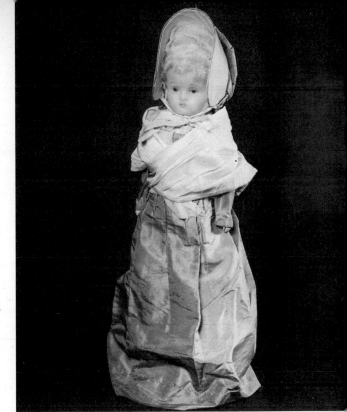

nails or hair on the head now, and the doll was completely untampered with when it was purchased with a group of French dolls.

The lady-dolls, made mainly in the Edwardian era, are very collectable if in nice condition, but often their faces are very badly cracked. These so-called 'Gibson Girls' wear very detailed and correct costume, and form an interesting commentary on the changes of fashion at the time. Though the heads are all very similar, with rather haughty narrow faces, they are clothed in all sorts of outfits, from walking-out costume to one in mourning such as was worn at the funeral of Queen Victoria. These dolls were dressed before sale, and though the clothes are often sewn in place, they exhibit skill and a good sense of design. Their glass eyes are usually of the fixed variety, and they have abundant mohair wigs. Amusingly, feet made for use on child dolls were often used, and the rather grand Edwardian lady with upswept hair and substantial breast looks absurd when her dress is lifted to disclose fat little feet wearing short white socks and black strap nursery shoes. Fortunately, not all the heads were fixed to children's bodies, and some have quite well-shaped legs and feet that are left bare. Being fairly cheap dolls, most have mohair wigs that are glued in place, but a few examples of better quality have set-in hair.

Waxed dolls were not made exclusively by the European makers, as a few were made in America. The Webber Singing doll, originally made with an imported French waxed head, contained a voice box fitted into the torso. This

263

264

doll, which was an innovation in the waxed-doll field, was produced from 1881 and contained a perforated music sheet to produce sound. Among the songs that could be chosen were 'Yankee Doodle', 'Home Sweet Home' and, retrospectively, 'God Save the Queen'! One doll bore the words 'I sing I want to be an angel', and quite a good range of tunes was offered. The later dolls were given heads made in Germany, which were probably cheaper than could be obtained from other American makers. Musical movements always appear out of place in a waxed doll, as the substance looks a little fragile to support the mechanism, but aesthetic scruples were unlikely to have deterred the enthusiasm of the young owners.

In order to produce waxed dolls even more cheaply, the French and German makers developed a new method whereby cheap plaster was substituted for papier mâché. The dolls were never very satisfactory, as the core was very fragile and broke quickly. Many Christmas-tree fairies are found that were made by this method, and the manufacturer must have maintained a steady trade in replacements each year. Some very large dolls were made, occasionally on quite good bodies. Sleeping eye mechanisms were put into some, with the usual disastrous result of broken plaster. When cracked, very little can be done to these waxed plasters, repair being difficult because the plaster has often fractured, giving the restorer no base upon which to work.

Despite their cheap construction, most surviving dolls of this kind obviously found good homes, and the excellence of their costume is often a little incongruous. The poor mother, who could not afford a fine doll for her child, seems to have compensated for this by dressing the doll to the best of her ability, so that good lace and well-stitched underwear often grace a doll that cost very little. I tend to keep any well-dressed doll of this type as, despite damage, they can present an effective appearance when arranged in a group.

Experiments were made throughout the century at waxing all types of materials to create a realistic doll's head. An English firm, Baly and Baxter of Longton, Stafford, patented a rather peculiar process in the early twentieth century whereby unglazed china dolls' parts were coated in wax, allowed to cool and then dipped again and immersed in cold water in order to give a glossy finish. I have seen no actual surviving dolls of the type, and the method does appear to have been unnecessarily complicated, though indicative of the lengths to which manufacturers were prepared to go in order to create a realistic effect.

170   Few waxed dolls are marked, but this example, always protected under original glass shade, carries the mark of Ernst Friedrich Dressel. Wig, ears pierced for ear-rings, slightly open mouth with small teeth. Horsehair-stuffed body. Lower legs with moulded orange boots with tassels. 27 in. high.

171　Scrapbook page showing a well-dressed child playing with a fine doll.

Poured-Wax Dolls

Wax dolls of strangely-mixed methods of manufacture are often seen on display in museums, having perhaps a wax head and porcelain lower limbs. Though the museums are right to display the doll in the state they received it after years of use by children, the collector should not assume that the dolls came from the manufacturer in this way. Though the seller or donor often in all innocence swears that the doll looked just like that when she was given it, examination always reveals that the limbs were replaced because of damage. Toyshops were often prepared to sell dolls they had themselves mended, though at a reduced price, and the manufacturers supplied them with spare parts. The owner of a toyshop that was closed in 1935 told me that he used to replace any broken bisque head with one by Armand Marseille, as he was always able to obtain these in a wide variety of sizes. Dolls were sometimes damaged before they reached the toyshop, and the young child was unlikely to be put off a doll by the fact that it had china legs and a wax head! Early doll-collectors often claimed that such marriages of parts were correct, but a little thought shows how complicated would have been the manufacture of a figure from parts obtained from different factories. Great suspicion should, therefore, be aroused by a doll whose head differs in substance from the limbs, except in the case of those made of composition, which were used with waxed heads as well as on bisque dolls.

A doll with a poured-wax head and limbs of waxed composition would be especially suspect. The makers of these high-quality dolls were proud of their product, and very unlikely to have made use of a type of limb found on very cheap dolls. If the doll is attractive and the limbs are not recent replacements, it should still be purchased, but only in the knowledge of the fact that for a somewhat hybrid doll the price should be quite low.

The English supremacy in making poured-wax dolls was acknowledged all over Europe. Several of the families who created such dolls were Mexican or Italian in origin, and brought their native skill in making church figures of wax with them. Dolls of poured wax were still made on the Continent, but those of good quality are almost always attributed to English makers. The exceptions are some beautifully-dressed lady-dolls that are German in origin, and portrait dolls such as one representing Josephine that is indisputably French. The Spanish also had great skill in the making of poured-wax figures, especially infant dolls, for memorial as well as church purposes, but few authenticated nineteenth-century examples of play dolls can be found.

German makers, when creating poured-wax dolls, appear to have concentrated their attention on lady-dolls to which grand wigs could be applied, and they did not spend time in inserting hair skilfully into the pate, as was common with English makers. After this statement no doubt some German collector will

267

produce an authentic German doll with hair inserted in this way, but to the time of writing I have not recorded any.

The custom of having an effigy of a child modelled in wax as a remembrance continued late into the nineteenth century, and however unappealing we may find the tradition, the skill learned in what must have been a fairly brisk trade in a time of high infant mortality, even among rich people, probably aided the modellers skill. One London doll-dealer found the presence in her shop of a doll called 'Eva', which stood about 36 inches high, most disconcerting, as she felt that the doll had been modelled as a portrait of a lost child. I must confess that I find some of the life-size wax figures rather macabre, and they are not objects that I would like in my home despite their admirable craftsmanship.

When the son of Queen Victoria's eldest daughter, who was married to Frederick of Prussia, died of meningitis in 1866, his mother had a wax model made of the child. The effigy was placed in the baby's empty cot, and a ball and a rattle were laid on the floor where the child used to throw them in his play. His slippers and toys were placed at the foot of the cot by his mother, and the whole group became a private memorial to her grief, keeping the dead person with the living for a little longer. By the end of the century, such manifestations of grief were becoming less popular, and even the Queen herself in old age, after her splendid excesses in this direction, reflected that there might be little merit in such practices.

Something of the old effigy tradition lingers over the poured-wax dolls even among the investment-eyed collectors and dealers of today. Several will not buy wax dolls as they find their presence too disquieting. This aversion has contrived to keep the price of dolls that are skilfully and individually made down to that commanded by the mass-produced bisques of the early twentieth century. As I find these dolls very beautiful, it is an unpopularity that aids my collecting. There is also concern felt among American and Japanese dealers at the thought of transporting dolls often considered very fragile. Recently, German collectors have succumbed to the charm of these particularly English dolls, so presumably this territory of the native collector will not remain long without competition.

Apart from effigy figures some commemorative dolls were made, ranging from a model of Queen Victoria in her coronation robes to a much later model of Lord Roberts made by the Pierotti family. The Royal Family were an obvious inspiration for portraits, and Madame Montanari is believed to have made a baby figure as a representation of Princess Louise. Victoria was commemorated in her wedding dress, and doll-makers are reputed to have made baby dolls in imitation of the quickly-increasing royal children. The doll-makers also claimed in their advertisements that they made 'wax figures' as well as dolls, but no surviving attributable figures of ordinary people are known.

There were several makers of quality wax dolls working in the London area in the middle years of the century. Many of their products are unmarked, but a few makers stamped or incised their trade names on the cloth bodies or wax heads, and other dolls with similar characteristics are attributed to these makers.

All the doll-makers worked in a similar way, by pouring delicately-tinted wax into a mould and allowing it to cool and harden before another layer was added. Some dolls were made with only one pouring, but four is not uncommon, as a large doll had to be made much more thickly. The Pierotti firm tinted the wax of the last pouring more heavily so that the colour would glow through attractively. Arms and legs were sometimes given several pourings also, though they are often not as thick as the head. The moulds used were usually made of metal, but wood, plaster or even clay could be used for dolls of a limited number.

The artist modeller would create a head out of clay, and a plaster or metal cast would be taken of it in two or three parts. The pieces of the mould would be fixed together before the pouring began. Modern wax doll-makers usually simply tie the parts together with cord so that they fit perfectly. The wax was then heated, and when very hot the colouring agents were added. A large number of heads would be poured at one session together with the accompanying arms and legs, since otherwise colour variations in the wax might have occurred. The moulds would be stood upside-down in rows, and the workman would fill them. After a very short period for cooling, the wax that still remained liquid would be poured off. The heads would then be allowed to set and become quite cold before the second pouring was made. This method meant that the parts of the doll likely to have most wear were given the thickest layer of wax, resulting in feet and hands that are often almost solid.

The moulds were taken apart when the heads were cold, and any unevenness left by the mould's edges was cut away. A mild solvent such as turpentine was then used to rub over any slightly uneven parts of the head and give a good uniform finish. At this stage the eye sockets, which had been filled with wax, were cut away, and glass eyes were inserted, either by warming the eye and allowing it to slightly melt the wax around it, or by fixing it in with a little melted wax. The doll's complexion, rather glossy by this time, was made less hectic by a powdering of potato meal, plaster of paris, talc or violet-powder. Sometimes the mould lines can just be detected on a doll's head, but the finishing was usually so skilful that the construction method cannot be seen.

Glass eyes were obtained in the main from Lauscha and Walterhausen, but in the middle years of the century English manufacturers had used eyes made by the two principal doll and human eye-makers in London. The eye manufacturer who talked to Mayhew said, "There are two sorts, the common and the natural as we call it. The common are simply small hollow glass spheres made of white enamel and coloured either black or blue, for only two colours of these are made. The bettermost dolls' eyes, or the natural ones, are made in a superior manner." The eyes which are now referred to as having *yeux fibres* were presumably the 'bettermost ones' – so much for present-day pedantry! French eyes of good quality were also imported into England, despite the claims of Mayhew's eye-maker who stated that French eyes were very inferior. It seems unlikely that a country with such a fine decorative glass-making tradition would have been unable to produce good dolls' eyes. Though eyes were usually fixed in place in heads of poured wax, a few with sleeping eyes are found, but the wire-eyed method of fixing sleeping eyes was the least likely to damage the substance of the head.

The insertion of hair into the scalp was an effective but laborious process. The hair, either human or mohair, was inserted into the wax either singly or in small groups. Different makers used slightly different techniques, but most used some sort of metal gouge for the incision and a heated tool or roller for sealing the wax back into place over the cut. It took a considerable time for even an experienced worker to insert hair in this way, and the insertion of delicate eyelashes was an even more skilled operation. Eyebrows were often suggested by laying hairs along the brow line and lightly fixing in place with wax or varnish, but they have frequently been worn away. Some firms were prepared, for a small extra fee, to implant the hair of the recipient into her doll's head – a service which must have saved the shedding of many tears when the child's long curls were shorn.

The holes left at the lower edge of the shoulder head for fixing it to the torso were protected in better-quality dolls by metal eyelets. A thick, soft, white cotton was usually used for sewing the wax parts to the body so as not to cut into the wax. The body was made of good-quality cotton or linen and filled with animal hair, or even a kapok-type filling after 1900. Sawdust was hardly ever used in quality wax dolls after 1885.

The maker's name was stamped on the body after the hair had been curled, though the majority were not stamped until they reached the shop where they were to be sold. The doll was then costumed, either by outworkers of the doll-maker or sometimes by people who worked for the toyshops. Some were sold at a much cheaper price, dressed only in a simple chemise, and these would be dressed at home before Christmas by loving relatives or nursemaids. Much fine work was lavished on the costumes of these dolls, and good fabrics made up in imitation of fashionable children's clothes of the era are seen. The purchasers of these quality dolls were of necessity fairly rich, and consequently the dolls exude an air of luxury and care. They are often dressed with an attention for fashionable detail, and a delight to the student of costume.

The names of the artists who modelled the dolls' faces are not recorded, and

172　Poured wax with fixed eyes and inset hair. Dressed by Lady Cave in 1900 to represent her grandmother, Sara Penfold, who died in 1856. 20 in. high.

173　Poured wax with wired sleeping eyes and tongue. Both moved by a wire lever that protrudes from body. Dark brown eyes. Hair wig. *c.* 1860. 24 in. high.

271

even many of the firms which made the dolls are only known by name, as no records have been found. The great English porcelain factories kept detailed pattern and order books, by which the development of their products can be traced, but dolls' price lists and catalogues have usually been discarded, as the doll was considered with little interest once its type went out of fashion. The only firm that is quite well documented is that of the Pierotti family, who produced dolls until the 1930s in a charmingly British anachronistic way.

The Pierotti family is recorded at Great Ormond Street and Argyle Street in the 1850s, though most attributable surviving examples of the firm's work dates from after 1880. Giovanni Pierotti, is believed to have come to England from Italy in the mid eighteenth century and married an English woman. It was his son, Domenico who was the first wax doll-maker. Around 1850, his son, Henry Pierotti was making dolls of wax and papier mâché or composition, though there are no surviving examples of the papier mâché dolls that he made. Collectors are fortunate in having at the Rottingdean Museum, Sussex, a set of tools and examples of the work of the firm, which they were given as a gift by Mrs Muriel Pierotti. The doll-making family ran a gallery in the famous London Crystal Palace Arcade in Oxford Street, from which were sold not only beautiful dolls but all sorts of good toys as well. They were proud of the 'Royal Model Dolls', which they manufactured, but it is debatable whether they were actually made in the likeness of the Royal Family, though it would be pleasant to attribute some of the figures of Queen Victoria, for instance, to this great firm. A few miniature dolls were produced, such as those made for the wedding cake of one of the Royal Dukes, but apparently no doll's-house figures.

The exhibits at the Rottingdean Museum show that both moulded and blown glass eyes were used in the dolls, and they also reveal the number of gouges and knives necessary to make even a quite small doll. The Pierotti dolls are usually characterized by a head that is slightly turned to one side, and has well-detailed, delicate features. The hair used for the wig is usually fair, and inserted into the head in groups that are very close together, so that the dolls often still have a quite abundant wig. The heads were cut off at the crown for the insertions of the eyes, but the thick hair concealed the join that occurred when the two parts were heated and fixed together again.

The bodies of Pierotti dolls are much slimmer and more shapely than those made by either Lucy Peck or the Montanari family, and present a rather better-finished look. Bodies used by other makers often look rather lumpy, but the Pierotti usually has all its stuffing still neatly disposed and in place. The body is often stamped on the torso with the name of the retailer, so that names like Hamley's, Morrell's, Mortlock's or (lovely title) 'The Beaming Nurse' at Peacock's might be seen. The actual maker's mark is very rarely found, but

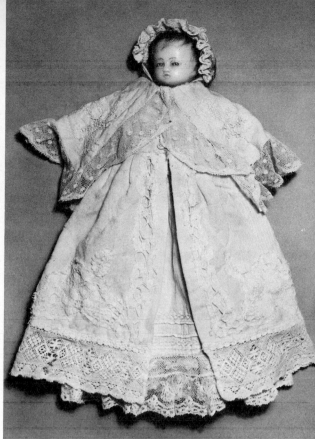

(*left*) 174 Realistic poured-wax baby doll with rattle. Head turned to side. Very yellow wax. Inset hair. Large realistic hands. Hair-stuffed body. 26 in. high. (*right*) 175 Short-coated baby made by Pierotti. Poured wax, inset hair, lashes and brows. Hair-stuffed body. Marked in oval on body "Hamleys, Regent St. Dolls repaired". Original owner was taken to the shop to purchase the doll. 11½ in. high.

when it exists, it is incised on the back of the neck and simply reads 'Pierotti'.

Some fine portrait dolls representing men as well as women were made by the Pierotti family, as well as some rather oddly-shaped baby dolls with bent limbs on cloth bodies. The bent wax limbs do not suit the traditionally-shaped fabric body, and the end effect of these dolls with their downward-turned heads is extremely strange. The well-known portrait doll of Lord Roberts is a delightful piece of craftsmanship, and his whiskers inset into the face always arouse admiration, despite the effect of his rather brightly-hued complexion. The purplish tint to the wax, which is very evident in examples such as this, is seen to some extent in many of the firm's dolls, and is one of the features by which they are recognized. It should however be remembered that some Pierottis are found made of quite pale wax, and others that exhibit none of the Pierotti characteristics are found with a puce tinge.

One lady-doll's shoulder head measures 6¾ inches high, and is of a type usually associated with figures that were especially dressed by large or exclusive shops to display the current fashion in their windows. There are several very beautiful dolls of this type in the Victoria and Albert Museum, and the Pierotti family probably made dolls of a similar quality, though only the one authenticated bust is known.

The Pierotti dolls are a favourite, as quite a number have survived, and many collectors have examples of a type of doll that was made in the same manner for three-quarters of a century.

Marked dolls by the Montanari firm are even rarer than those actually marked Pierotti. A few dolls are known that bear the maker's signature written in ink on the lower part of the torso. It sometimes simply reads 'Montanari' and at other times 'Montanari, 180 Soho Bazaar, London'. The name was not always spelled correctly. An example in the Strangers' Hall, Norwich, is authentically signed 'Montanary' and a fairly typical Montanari in my own collection is incised 'Mty'. It is interesting to note that many of the signed dolls exhibit none of the characteristics associated by collectors with the products of the firm, some being of quite poor quality. A Montanari that was still in its original box, as sold at the Great Exhibition, came up for sale recently and was mainly remarkable for its lack of quality. Many of the doll-makers had galleries in the fashionable shopping bazaars, and the Montanaris used the Soho Bazaar as one outlet for their products. The family also worked from 251 Regent Street, and this fact is also sometimes recorded in a mark. Madame Montanari first sold dolls from Soho Square, and she must have been still working at this address when she gained such praise (in the *Jury Report*) for her exhibits at the Great Exhibition of 1851. She submitted a group of dolls representing all ages from infancy to womanhood, which she arranged in several family groups. "A variety of expressions are given to the figures in regard to the ages and stations which they are intended to represent."

One aspect of her work did worry the jury. They were concerned that her dolls were so lifelike that they did not encourage a child's imaginative powers in the way that other stiff and almost symbolic dolls of the time did. They were also a little tart at the prices of the dolls, which they felt were too high for most children. Undressed dolls were sold between 10s. and 105s., and dressed dolls were considerably more expensive. The dolls that were dressed by workers of the Montanari firm itself are very characteristic. Fringe is often used as trimming and boat necks on waisted dresses with full puff sleeves were the standard design. The dresses showed off the plump arms and shoulders of the dolls admirably and a doll still in its original Montanari costume is very desirable.

176.   Seated, poured-wax lady-doll. Inset fair hair. Blue fixed eyes. Hair-stuffed body with very small waist and large hips. Maroon velvet and silk dress. 23 in. high.

Madame Montanari displayed her dolls at other exhibitions, including that at Paris in 1855, where she claimed that all her dolls would stand all types of climate and could be washed in alkaline water. The firm was typical of the age, in that it not only sold from a bazaar, but also followed the great trade fairs that could boost sales.

Napoleon Montanari is mentioned in records after 1860, when Madame Montanari had moved a few hundred yards into Oxford Street itself, though by 1870 they had moved from the prestige address back into Fitzroy Square, where Richard Montanari was working as a 'manufacturer of exhibition prize wax and rag dolls'. It is difficult to gauge whether these were all members of one firm working from different addresses, or whether the whole group moved together from one place to another. All the addresses are within a few hundred yards of one another, so it is possible that different lines were made at the various addresses. Richard Montanari is described, for instance, not only as a doll manufacturer but also as an 'artist and modeller in wax'. The Fitzroy Square address would have been very suitable for an artist's studio, where clients could have come to have a likeness modelled and casts taken in wax, as it housed some of the rather bohemian characters of the time.

The dolls made by the Montanari firm are believed to include a portrait doll of Princess Louise, and presumably other model portrait dolls were made on commission. Certainly at the Great Exhibition several portraits of the royal children were included in their exhibits. One of the Queen Victoria portrait dolls looks more typical of the work of the Montanari than the Pierotti family. It is unfortunate that even portraits of the period were often rather stylized, so that examples may often not be recognized by present-day collectors.

Napoleon Montanari, in addition to his more decorative work, made anatomical wax figures for hospitals. At the Great Exhibition he exhibited a wax figure portraying 'the last hour in consumption'. It was also Napoleon who arranged the collection of wax figures illustrating the different characters in Mexican town life, which aroused great admiration for his skill in modelling. His expertise in anatomical work must have stood him in good stead for one of the groups – an Indian scalping a white traveller.

The Montanari dolls are characterized by their plump, rather short necks with a roll of fat at the front, and a slight bulge of fat at the back. Arms and legs are also very chubby, again with the rolls of fat at elbow and ankle. The eyes are often of an attractive violet colour, not often seen in dolls of other makers, and the hair is of course set into the scalp. Genuine human hair is usually found on Montanari dolls, and it is rarely as densely inserted as in the Pierotti. Dark hair was popular with this maker, though it is usually dark or mid-brown rather than black, which would have been unpopular with the buyers. One interesting

English Model Dolls, Dressed and Undressed.

No. 11634. English Model Dolls, dressed in long robes as babies, clothes made to take off, size 1, 10/6; size 2, 14/; size 3, 18/; size 4, 24/; size 5, 33/; size 6, 30/; size 7, 42/; size 8, 54/; size 9, 66/; size 10, 72/; size 11, 100/; size 12, 110/ each.

No. 11635. Model Dolls, wool costume, boy and girl, the pair in box complete, 4/6.

No. 11636. Gutta Percha Dolls, dark or golden hair, dressed, 8/6, 12/6, 18/, 24/, 36/, 54/, 60/ per doz.

No. 11637. Dolls' Costumes, set consisting of hat, muff, shoes, collarette; in wool, 9/ per doz. sets; in satinette, 8/6 and 12/ per doz. sets.

No. 11638. Composition Dolls, imitation human hair, 2/6, 3/6, 4/, 4/9, 5/6, 6/6, 7/, 8/, 10/, 12/, 13/6, 15/, 18/, 21/, 24/ per doz.

No. 11639. Model Composition Dolls, flowing hair, wool bodies, 7/, 8/6, 11/, 12/, 14/, 16/6, 18/6, 21/, 24/, 27/, 30/, 36/ per doz.

No. 11640. English Model Dolls in fancy wool costumes, size 1, 1/6; size 2, 2/; size 3, 2/9; size 4, 4/6; size 5, 5/0; size 6, 7/0; size 7, 9/0; size 8, 10/6 each.

No. 11641. English Model Dolls, dressed in Llama costumes, size 1, 12/; size 2, 15/; size 3, 24/; size 4, 27/; size 5, 30/; size 6, 34/; size 7, 45/; size 8, 50/; size 9, 60/; size 11, 72/; size 12, 84/ per doz.

No. 11642. Mother Hubbard Rag Dolls, 8/6 per doz.

No. 11643. Dressed Rag Dolls, 3/, 4/6, 8/6, 12/, 10/, 24/, 36/, 48/, 54/ per doz.

No. 11644. Dressed Rag Dolls, short costume, 18/, 24/, 30/, 39/, 54/ per doz.

No. 11645. Dressed Exhibition Rag Dolls, long or short robes, made to take off, 4/, 6/, 8/, 9/, 10/, 12/ each.

No. 11646. Gutta Percha Dolls, glass eyes and wool bodies, 4/, 8/, 12/, 16/, 24/, 30/, 36/, 42/ per doz.

SILBER & FLEMING,

Manufacturers,
Importers, Warehousemen,
and Agents,

LONDON.

When ordering, please state the amount desired to be paid for dressing, as a small doll can be well dressed for 1/9 up to 30/ each; a medium size doll from 3/6 to 40/ each; a doll of No. 11663 size, *represented in drawing*, from 20/ each, or as shown in drawing, 60/ each, according to the quality of materials used.

No. 11663.

No. 11663. Dressed.

English Model Dolls, with inserted hair of light golden colour. The head, arms, and legs are made of fine wax, the body is stuffed with wool, and covered with fine cotton cloth, the whole doll being proportionately and properly shaped so as to fairly represent the human form. The drawing represents a doll photographed wrapped in paper, as usually supplied to the trade. This doll is made in 20 different sizes or varieties. The smallest size, No. 11647, is 13½ inches in length; No. 11656, 22½ inches in length, and the doll here shown, No. 11663, is 32½ inches in length. The prices are not regulated entirely by the length of the doll, but also by the size of the head. No. 11647, 1/4; No. 11648, 1/9; No. 11649, 2/; No. 11650, 3/; No. 11651, 3/6; No. 11652, 4/6; No. 11653, 5/6; No. 11654, 6/6; No. 11655, 7/6; No. 11656, 8/6; No. 11657, 10/6; No. 11658, 12/6; No. 11659, 15/6; No. 11660, 18/6; No. 11661, 21/; No. 11662, 24/; No. 11663, 30/; No. 11664, 40/; No. 11665, 50/ each.

177   Interesting advertisement by Silber and Fleming for English-made dolls, indicating the range and prices.

Montanari has the lips slightly parted and shows its teeth, a type of modelling that is very rare in wax play dolls, though window models of wax, sometimes even had china teeth implanted.

The colour of the wax used by the Montanari family is much softer and more mellow than that used by the Pierottis, and more opaque than that used by, for instance, Lucy Peck, but these comments can only be generalizations, and exceptions are always discovered, as each batch of dolls poured would have differed slightly in colour. The cloth bodies are much plumper than those found on Pierotti dolls, and of course they are hand sewn, whereas late Pierottis were stitched on a machine. The hands are larger and modelled to a much higher standard than those on Pierotti dolls, though the feet are often not as good as the delicate, well-defined feet that the latter made.

Montanari dolls are the most desirable of wax dolls as they were made for a much shorter period, and therefore there are fewer available. The firm also manufactured a very strange line of dolls known as English Wax Dolls that were awarded a prize medal at the 1851 Exhibition. These wax dolls had muslin stretched across the face to act both as a protective layer and to give a soft, natural effect, though to the modern collector it is difficult to believe that the lifelike effect of wax could have been improved on. The muslin was cut away around the eyes, and fixed down neatly around the lid so that the effect was realistic. These dolls did not withstand the ravages of time very well, and few are reported in private collections. The often-quoted *Playmates* of 1879 describes these 'London Rag Babies' as being quite strong enough for a baby to play with. It approved of the muslin-covered heads, which gave the dolls a soft, babyish look. The London Rag Babies, which were probably made by other firms as well as the Montanari family, were exported to America, though again few are preserved because of their poor condition.

The last quarter of the nineteenth century saw sixteen makers of high-quality wax dolls in London alone, and there must have been several others that went undocumented, in addition to provincial makers. As so few wax dolls are marked, they all tend to be attributed to one of the few makers whose dolls have some particular characteristics. The doll-maker to the Royal Family was Herbert Meech, and, like many other makers of quality wax dolls, he advertised that he was able to clean and repair dolls. The known Meech dolls have rather unattractive faces, and the hands and feet are less well modelled than those found on Pierottis, but as so few marked examples are known, it is hardly fair to judge the firm's standard. John Edwards made exhibition rag dolls and dolls of wax and composition. The best known of his achievements is the kneeling wax doll that was made for the 1871 Exhibition. Once again, though the name is often used 'knowledgeably' by collectors, we do not know of sufficient marked

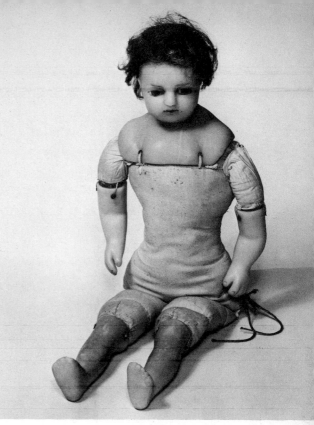

(*above left*) 178   Early nineteenth-century wire-eyed poured-wax head showing wire lever to crotch. Black irisless eyes. Inset hair. 14½ in. high.   (*above right*) 179   Poured wax stamped "H. J. Meech" in oval on torso. Auburn inset hair. Fixed blue eyes. The string protruding from hip works the 'Mama' mechanism. 20 in. high.   (*below*) 180   Montanari-type doll showing the typical fringed costume favoured by the firm. Photographed from side to show the characteristic modelling to the back of the neck. 18½ in. high.

examples of his work to be able to attribute unmarked dolls to his firm.

Charles Marsh supplied poured-wax dolls to C. Gooch of the Soho Bazaar, who cleaned and repaired dolls besides running a toy gallery. More Marsh dolls are known that are marked, but the complication here is that they are all quite dissimilar. One marked doll has the soft expression, blue eyes and fair hair of a typical Pierotti, while another has round features and soft brown hair reminiscent of Montanari dolls. The known dolls all, however, have a face that looks almost straight ahead, and all are pretty dolls, though they help little in attributing unmarked dolls.

Santy, Bazzoni, and Thomas and Marian Betts were all makers of good poured-wax dolls, but their products are indistinguishable from those of the makers discussed, and a marked example of any of these dolls would be a treasure.

Lucy Peck advertised that she ran a 'Dolls' Home' at 131 Regent Street in 1901, and she claimed to be a maker of quality English model wax dolls. She also advertised that she would insert real hair into wax dolls and models, and she was one of the makers who was prepared to implant hair brought in by her customers. Mrs Peck was one of the few who obligingly stamped her dolls with an oval or rectangular mark on the stomach. She is interesting as being the only known maker to use a wired-eye mechanism on dolls of poured wax made as late as this, and indeed the method was out of date on almost every other type of doll. Other manufacturers experimented with such devices as flirting and sleeping eyes, but this maker used a method that had been proved successful over the years, and the mechanism usually still works well. The eyeballs have a layer of wax painted over them top and bottom, as in early nineteenth-century dolls of the wired-eye type. Little girl dolls with fairly thick bodies and limbs are most often found, though beautiful lady-dolls, tall enough to be used as fashion display figures in shops, were also made to an extremely high standard.

The colour of the wax is of little help in identifying a Lucy Peck, as all shades were used from quite a dark colour to her more usual pale pink. The hair is very thickly inset, and was obviously intended quite often to be short, as several are known with short hair cut in the one style. The hands and feet are poorly modelled in comparison with earlier doll-makers in the medium. A characteristic of the dolls is the very long upper arm. The wax part of a doll's arm usually ends at, or just slightly above, the elbow, but the Lucy Pecks' extend to within about 1 inch of the end of the shoulder head on a doll measuring 20 inches, and the cloth arm is really only a means of articulation. The sew holes

181   Poured wax with blue fixed eyes. Inset hair. Marked "Mty" on foot. Typical Montanari roll of fat under chin and to back of neck. Plump limbs with bracelets of fat to wrists. 22½ in. high.

282

are usually eyeletted, a precaution against damage that was sometimes dispensed with by both the Montanari and the Pierotti family. The advantage of the arms that were modelled well above the elbow was that the doll could wear a dress with extremely short sleeves, and the costumier did not have the irritation of an arm that continually revealed its cloth upper parts.

The costume display dolls that were made both by Lucy Peck and the Pierotti family are typical of many that were made not only for fashionable London dress shops but even for provincial drapers, though in the last case the figure would often be more like a basic dress-makers dummy with a wax head attached at the neck. Some of these heads were made with a great deal of characterization and represent grinning, rather wicked-looking boys as well as the more conventional ladies and stern gentlemen for the display of tweed jackets in country tailor's shops. At the other end of the range were exquisite figures, such as that dressed by Frederick Bosworth of 9 Burlington Street in 1903–4, to display a blue crêpe de Chine dress trimmed with velvet – the height of fashion for the year. These figures range in size between 20 and 30 inches, though the more usual type of dummy was naturally life-size. Such figures could make an interesting collection in their own right, as even some of the common drapers' versions are very well made. Unfortunately, many have been destroyed by shops, and costume museums are also eager to acquire them. When they come up for sale in provincial salerooms they fetch very little, though a 30-inch figure dressed in miniature clothes of the period would command a high price in any saleroom, since it would rightly fall into the classification of a fashion doll.

When buying wax dolls, some degree of damage has to be accepted, as absolutely perfect wax dolls are rare. A doll with limbs that are slightly damaged is far preferable to one with replaced parts, though some restoration, if well done, helps the doll retain a pleasing effect. Wax does sometimes fade, so suspicion should not necessarily be aroused by a doll whose legs differ slightly in colour from the shoulder head, if it has been exposed to the light for many years; though if the colour is very different, the cord sewing on the legs should be compared to that fixing on the other wax parts, and the suspect limbs should be examined for a too-pristine condition.

As the makers of these wax dolls were eager to maintain a high reputation, the quality of the whole doll should be good. Reproduction replacement limbs usually lack the crisp finishing of the genuinely old. The prime value of a doll lies in the head, and if a doll with a fine head has lost its limbs, it is quite legitimate for a dealer to use replacements, as long as this is clearly stated on the doll's price ticket. It is better to accept a crack that runs down the face than to attempt a

182 · Poured wax in bridal dress marked on torso "Charles Marsh". Inset hair and brows. Fixed blue eyes. Pierced ears. 19 in. high.

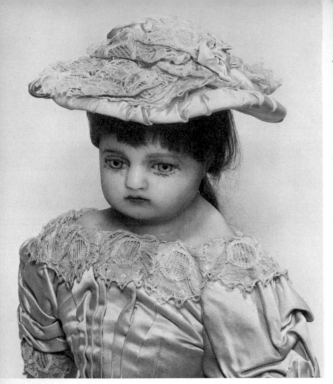

183 Poured wax with inset hair and lashes. Printed oval mark to back right thigh "H. J. Meech, Kennington Rd, London, S.E." On left thigh in circle "Dollmaker to the Royal Family, 6 Prize Medals Awarded". 23 in. high.

184 Poured wax with sleeping eyes. Hair is mohair and inserted in large groups. White dress. 20 in. high.

restoration that is likely to prove unsuccessful, as poured-wax dolls, once fractured through, will always show the crack. Many casual sellers of old dolls will assure the buyer that such cracks can be sealed with a warm needle, but workers in wax are quite emphatic about the fact that, though cracks can be made less noticeable, they can always be seen unless a complete new section is put into a head. As wax is almost impossible to match perfectly, this is a course to be attempted only if one is faced with a crushed head!

The fashion for re-dipping waxed dolls is fortunately becoming less prevalent among collectors, but many dolls are still unnecessarily restored. I have known people to obtain a complete replacement arm because a few fingers were broken. Such practices are vandalism rather than restoration. As wax dolls become rarer, the collector will be forced to accept inevitable damage in the way museums do. Though wax dolls are not as fashionable as bisques, it should be borne in mind that they are much rarer, and more to be respected as antique objects of individual craftsmanship.

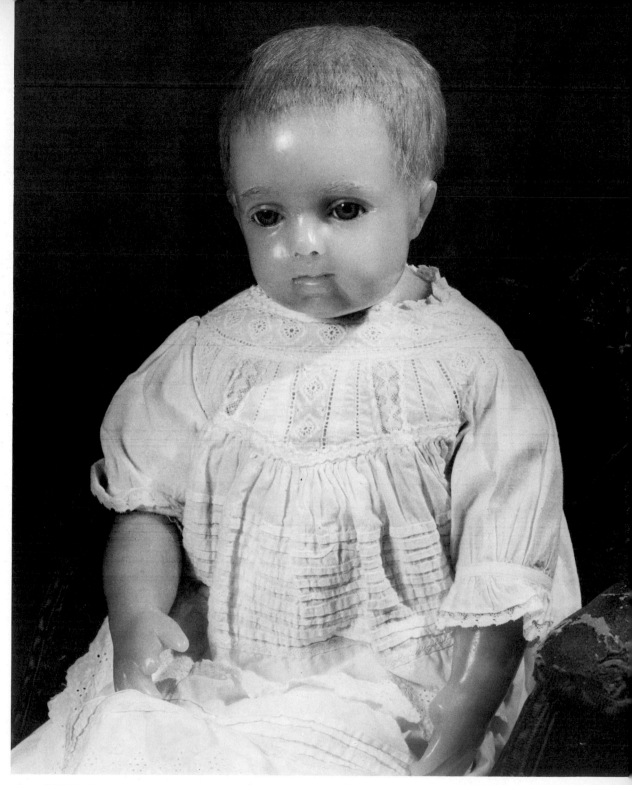

185 Realistic poured-wax baby doll seated in a child's pushchair. Very well-modelled head with inset hair, lashes and eyebrows. Eyeletted wax parts. A very realistic doll, as the head is very heavy when carried. 23 in. high.

186　Extremely fine-quality pink-tinted porcelain lady-doll with blue eyes. Slight lustre to dark brown hair. The porcelain shoulder is unusually low at the back. Brush marks to nape of neck. Simple, ungusseted leather body. 18 in. high.

TEN

PORCELAIN AND PARIAN DOLLS

Porcelain Dolls

So fine is the quality of some nineteenth-century dolls that, at first, doll-collectors were bemused by their high standard and made fanciful claims regarding their origins; some heads were labelled Bow, others Chelsea and those that were rather unremarkable were given the comforting description of Staffordshire. Despite the protestations of regional historical experts, ceramic collectors and the archivists of various china factories still in existence, it took many years before doll-collectors were prepared to accept the fact that their very beautiful and skilfully-made acquisitions were primarily the work of unnamed and otherwise quite unmemorable German porcelain factories.

Fine toy tea sets and dinner services had been made by great factories, such as Wedgwood, Bow and Caughley in the eighteenth century, for very rich children to play with under supervision; but the substance was still too expensive to be used as a material for dolls' heads, which would break with predictable speed. It was not until the mid-nineteenth century that the cost of porcelain became low enough for it to be used on a large commercial scale as a doll-making material. Most of the china dolls were made in Germany in one of the hundreds of porcelain factories that made all types of household china as well as frivolous items. It is possible that a few were made in France or England, as some bodies bear the French patent mark on the torso but the German makers were able to sell small articles of china so cheaply that there was little business sense in attempting manufacture in competition with the much cheaper source.

An interesting reference in the *British Toymaker*, which was published for a short period during the First World War, refers to the manufacture of china heads in the Staffordshire potteries, which had been 'increased' due to the shortage of dolls that had previously been imported from Germany; but as no wasters or shards that can be identified as doll's parts have been found, despite

287

frequent excavations, we have to conclude that it is unlikely that heads were commercially made on any scale before 1900.

Even in the middle years of the century, china was still expensive. A familiar scene in St James's Park was of children very carefully carrying their china mugs as they were taken by their nurses to the milk-seller, to be given milk, warm and fresh from the cows that were kept there. The nurses were always very frightened in case one of the mugs should be broken – a fear that extended to the nursery, and caused the china-headed doll to be put in a cupboard out of reach of the child's eager but clumsy hands.

The making of fine porcelain objects had reached its peak in the eighteenth century, when the taste for the rococo had stimulated great craftsmen to produce exquisite work. With the decline of rococo fashion, the use of porcelain became more mundane and the substance, though expensive, did not retain the exotic appeal it had held in the middle years of the century. Many porcelain collectors spurn items made after 1800, when hundreds of minor factories were set up, especially in Bohemia, to manufacture more utilitarian wares. Though beneath the notice of the aesthetic collectors of fine porcelain, it is the products of these small factories that concern the collector of dolls.

It would appear appropriate at this stage to distinguish between the various types of body used in the manufacture of china dolls' heads. China is a blanket term that includes earthenware and hard and soft paste porcelain. Earthenware dolls were made during the medieval period and were imported into England during the eighteenth century, but few were made after this date, for despite the fact that they were cheap to produce, being fired at a lower temperature, they were much less durable. Interestingly, one firm was still making earthenware dolls at Ilmenau at the end of the nineteenth century, and one English firm made some during the Second World War.

Many of the products of the Staffordshire factories, including the well-known groups and figures, were made of earthenware, which can be easily distinguished from porcelain by the fact that light cannot penetrate the body. If china heads for dolls had been made in the middle of the last century in Staffordshire, they would have probably been made of this cheap material, which was used for the well-known chimney figures to which dolls used to be compared. I have not, to date, found any white china dolls' heads that are not translucent, and any discovered would be interesting and extremely rare.

Although it is quite simple to distinguish between pottery and porcelain by holding an article close to a powerful light source, it is less easy to tell the difference between hard and soft paste porcelain. Soft paste porcelain dolls' heads are very rare, but a few are known to collectors. Some experts claim to be able to distinguish the two by the composition of the body when held to the

28 Group of 'blonde bisques'

(*left*) 187 Porcelain shoulder head with five ringlets falling to shoulder. Peg joints attach the china limbs to the wooden body. Mid-nineteenth century. 11½ in. high.

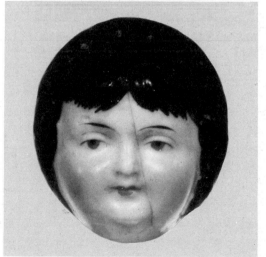

(*right*) 188 Black-haired porcelain in original dress. Pink lustre to head. Original coral necklace. Blue eyes. Flat black boots. Pink garters, tied in bow. 21 in. high.

(*bottom*) 189 a and b Two-sided porcelain doll, representing age and youth. Probably originally made up as a pincushion. 8 in. high.

light, but neither I nor any of my porcelain collector friends have found much success with this method, as regards porcelain items made in the very late eighteenth or early nineteenth century. The soft paste is however generally accepted as being rather more translucent than hard paste when held to the light. The hard paste is, as the name implies, hard to the touch when a finger is rubbed along the unglazed edge. In the case of dolls, the base of the shoulder would be the spot to test, but plates are obviously tested on the foot rim. The soft paste body will hardly drag the fingers at all and is velvet-like to the touch, while the hard paste feels sharper. Collectors, in the days before they knew better, would go around antique shops armed with a triangular file, which they drew across the unglazed foot of an object. If an incised mark was left, the body was soft paste, but if it was resistant to scratching then the paste was hard. Another test is by judging the amount of grime that has accumulated on the unglazed lower edge. A hard paste item can be wiped clean fairly easily, but the soft paste, which is more easily penetrated, is more difficult to clean.

Soft paste dolls are rarities, as comparatively few factories used this substance in the nineteenth century. It was discovered originally in Florence in the sixteenth century, but was perfected only in the eighteenth. The paste is made of a mixture of vitreous substances, a grit containing sand or flint, saltpetre, sea salt, soda, alum and alabaster. The constituents are fused by heat, and marl containing gypsum and clay are then added. The mixture is then ground and filtered until it is suitable for moulding. Glazed pieces were often given a second firing to ensure the merging of the glaze with the body. Soft paste porcelain would have been very suitable for the detail on dolls' heads, for it was a joy to model, as is seen in examples of figures made at Sèvres. Rouen, St Cloud and Vincennes, which was later taken over by the Sèvres factory, all worked in this substance. After 1800, the Sèvres factory was completely redesigned to make only hard paste porcelain, and it was of this hard paste that the experimental dolls now in the Museum of Decorative Art, Paris, were made at the beginning of the twentieth century. There are no known soft paste dolls, and the factory does not believe that any were made there.

Early doll-collectors attributed their ornate but decidedly hard paste dolls' heads to the Bow and Chelsea factories, which worked in soft paste. Heads with obviously nineteenth-century hairstyles were optimistically attributed to these factories, despite the fact that they had ceased operation before 1800. The idea that the factories could have made dolls' heads probably arose because of the

190   Fine mid-nineteenth-century porcelain doll, made in Germany. Well-modelled shoulders and hairstyle. Unmarked. Sawdust-filled body. China limbs with heel-less boots, painted garters. 20 in. high.

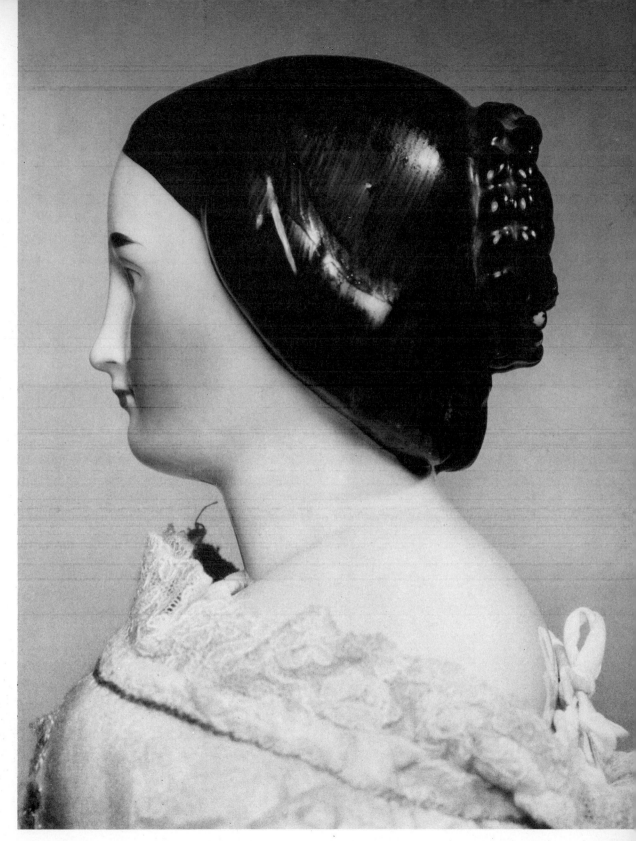

number of 'toys' in the form of patch boxes, cane tops, scent bottles and the like that were made, particularly by the Chelsea factory. Despite the term 'toys', these objects were luxury trifles made especially for the amusement of adults, rather in the manner of the creations of Fabergé.

All the nineteenth-century German porcelain factories worked in hard paste – with the exception of Volkstedt in Thuringia, which made soft paste but only for a short time. This fact often makes me question the dolls that are claimed by collectors to be soft paste, but without taking the heads off the bodies to make a proper investigation, one cannot refute the assertions of well-known collectors. A respected ceramic expert, who is curator of a museum with a renowned collection of soft paste porcelain, assured me that one of the dolls in a travelling exhibition that was housed in his museum had a head of soft paste, and I would not doubt his judgement; but lesser experts are advised to test dolls' heads very carefully before advancing claims, which can be very misleading for the serious student.

A few very well-known factories, such as the Royal Copenhagen, made marked hard paste dolls' heads of high quality in the mid-nineteenth century. Hard paste porcelain is made by fusing white china clay or kaolin and an easily-fusible rock (such as feldspar) with quartz or sand. The more china clay contained in the mixture, the more difficult it is to fuse, but the end product will be much harder. The mixture can be poured or pressed into moulds, and as the glaze is made of the same substance as the body, though of different proportions, it is usually applied before firing, so that only one process is needed. Hard paste heads give a good 'ring' when tapped, and was the substance of which dolls' heads were generally made.

Most of the advances in the European manufacture of hard paste porcelain were made at the Meissen factory in the Dresden area during the eighteenth century. In the nineteenth century, the Meissen factory was prepared to make all sorts of bijouterie, and appears to have included dolls' heads among these products. The well-known crossed-swords Meissen mark does not always indicate that the head was made by this famous firm, as other smaller porcelain factories copied the mark and some complete forgeries are known. The attributed heads that have been carefully vetted by experts are of a high standard and represent rather more mature women than the typical mass-produced round-faced German doll. The china is flesh-tinted in a delicate soft pink, and the hair is made more realistic by painting on streaks of a darker colour. This hair treatment is never found on cheap dolls, as it involved another painting process that meant extra cost. The hair is often arranged neatly in a plaited bun, and one doll with moulded ear-rings is known. Three sew holes, on both the front and back of the bust, are found on the attributable examples, though

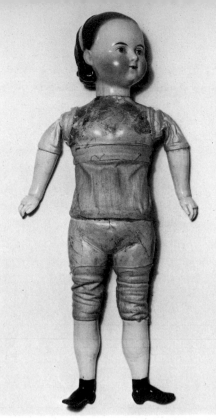 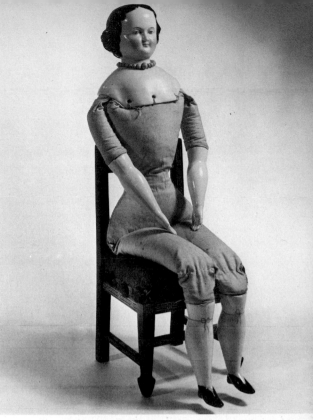

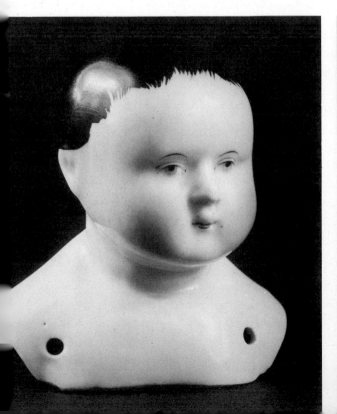 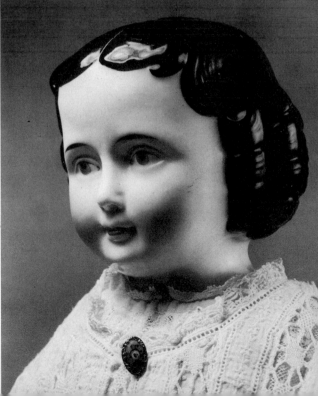

(*above left*) 191   Unusual swivel-headed Motschmann-type porcelain. Composition torso with fabric insets. Voice box. Very delicate shading to front of painted hair. 15 in. high.   (*above right*) 192   Seated porcelain doll in undress to show the typical body construction. 21 in. high.   (*below left*) 193   Fewer boy dolls were made of porcelain. This example has a slight lustre to head. Blue eyes. Hair painted and without any moulding. 3½ in. high.   (*below right*) 194   Porcelain heads were made in a very wide size range, some as large as 8 in. This quite large doll has well-modelled ringlets and a little more expression than is often found in dolls of the type. 24 in. high.

obviously the presence of these sew holes by themselves would be no indication of origin.

A fabulous marked Meissen doll in the collection of Frau Estrid Faurholt has golden hair streaked with a darker colour, and brown eyes. This particular doll is dated as between 1830 and 1840. The known Meissen dolls have hands of a very fine and realistic quality, not at all like those found on mass-produced china dolls. It is surprising that more manufacturers did not make use of the idea of moulded ear-rings on glazed porcelains, as ear-rings were traditionally given to good dolls. The only reason for their omission by the makers was that the glaze would have run into the pierced holes and filled them! Unglazed heads made at the same time often have pierced ears.

It is fashionable at the moment to attribute any good-quality doll with a pink glaze to the Berlin factory, whether or not the shoulder bears the correct K.P.M. mark. The known and marked examples of the Berlin factory are enamelled in soft pink flesh colour, and are characterized by their slim appearance, which is increased by their elegantly long necks. With the exception of an unglazed boy's head, the dolls made by the Königliche Porzellän Manufaktur are of women rather than girls, and the faces are modelled with character.

The other dream piece for which collectors search is surely a marked Copenhagen doll. These heads again represent mature women, wearing their hair upswept into a bun much as did the young Victoria when she came to the throne, a fashion that had been popular for some time in Germany. The Copenhagen dolls are understood to have been made only with brown hair, but so few marked examples are known that few conclusions can be drawn as to the general quality of the dolls made at the factory. Casts of heads made at the factory during the mid-nineteenth century show a series of lady-dolls, all with hair dressed in the Copenhagen manner, and an interesting boy's head that has much of the quality associated with a portrait bust.

Most porcelains that are found by the average collector are cheerfully unmarked, except by numbers, and almost completely unattributable, except as to their country of origin which is almost invariably Germany. Interesting exceptions are those made at Fontainebleau by Jacob Petit, in an attempt to compete with the ever-increasing use of German dolls' heads on French bodies. Despite the fact that he patented the heads in the 1840s, the hairstyles are those that were fashionable in the 1830s, indicating how retrospective were the fashions for dolls' hairstyles. Many of the great German porcelain factories such as Rauenstein are thought to have included glazed porcelains among their

195 Porcelain doll of the 'bald head' type wearing a mohair wig. Blue eyes, light brown painted eyebrows. Sawdust-filled body. Black high-heeled boots. Late nineteenth century. 14¾ in. high.

products, but the collector searches in vain for marked examples, and all we can conclude is that few of the German factories felt it beneath their dignity to manufacture dolls' heads among their other products.

Another type of pink finish is given to the faces of dolls by the use of a pink lustre. This must be distinguished from the pink enamel that was used for instance by the Berlin factory, which gave an even flesh tone to the head. The lustre effect is much softer, but considerably less even in tone. If such a head is tilted slightly, the pink colouring will catch the light and give the characteristic lustrous glow. Lustring of earthenware was first carried out in Egypt, and although by the fifteenth century the technique had been developed to quite a complex standard, it was not sufficiently cheap to be used on dolls until well into the nineteenth century. The glazed surface of the head was covered with a thin film of prepared metallic oxide. If the metallic oxide had been added thickly, it would have simply given another layer of solid colour. The skill of the craftsman lay in its extremely fine application, so that the most delicate sheen would be transmitted by the finished head. Gold and platinum were used as a source for the lustre, as they both oxidize very little under atmospheric influence. Gold was used to create all the soft colours from bronze to the most sensitive pink.

It is unlikely that any dolls with a lustre finish will be found dating from before 1845, as it was after this date that the technique became widely used. The heavy gold finish that is sometimes found decorating the head-dresses of porcelains was usually simply gold paint, and has often rubbed away, though the lustre technique was used very heavily to achieve the gold detail on some heads. Some lovely purple and pink lustre colours were used to decorate not only the heads but also the dolls' boots and shoes.

Any dolls that are lustre-decorated are worthwhile acquisitions, though the heavier forms of the lustre were not used as often on glazed porcelains as on the Parian dolls that were made when the technique became even cheaper. The lustre on porcelains is usually simply to achieve a delicate flesh tone, and decorative detail on the head-dress is more often given with ordinary enamels. Porcelains with lustre-decorated head-dresses are therefore especially desirable.

The basic porcelain doll has black moulded hair and blue painted eyes, and is attached to the sawdust-filled body by two or three sew holes at the front and back. The lower arms and legs of commercially-assembled dolls are also of porcelain, but since many heads were sold loose to be assembled at home, some

196 Porcelain bonnet doll with fair hair and blue eyes. Remains of lustre to bonnet and bow. Light brown eyebrows. Blue bonnet. High-heeled purple lustre boots. 14½ in. high.

297

very grotesque bodies can be found that are completely original. Dolls' heads were often sold in drapers shops and country stores, and the more thrifty house-wife bought these and made up the complete doll herself. Some of the makers of these home-made bodies evidently had so little idea of proportion that they were probably children, especially as the needlework often leaves much to be desired.

The sewing of the body is an indication of a doll's date, as the sewing machine was not in general use until around 1870, and even after this date many clothes, even those purchased from drapers' shops, were made entirely by hand. It would be unusual to find a commercially-made doll sewn by hand after 1890, though of course heads were still sold separately for assembly at home, where there was often no sewing machine.

Porcelain dolls usually wore some kind of a boot or shoe as they represented ladies or young girls. Obvious exceptions to this rule are the Motschmann-type babies that were made of porcelain, and a very rare boy doll is also known that has moulded bare feet. The type of footwear is often taken as an aid in indicating date: flat heel-less boots or slippers were worn by dolls made before 1875, and after this date, high heels, or at least some suggestion of a heel, are usually found. Boots and shoes were enamelled black or brown and have light brown soles. Blue, pink or lilac garters were painted as bows, tying just below the knee. More unusual treatment of the legs would include moulded garters of unusual design, and boots that were coloured and had moulded decoration.

Since many makers used a basic body and limbs and merely manufactured different heads to keep up with fashionable demand, the indication of date given by footwear is usually only slight. Even men-dolls were given the standard body with tiny waists and elegantly-turned ankles; matching the parts obviously bothered the makers very little! The only real guide is the presence of heels on the shoes, as a child of the century's late years would have felt dissatisfied with a doll wearing flat slippers that were many years out of date.

Very few male dolls were made. A lady who remembered her childhood in the nineties told me that she and her friends quite simply did not like boy dolls. Some porcelain boy dolls were made, and one man-doll with a moustache who wears a type of clown's hat. The illustrated doll's-house man with an almost abstract treatment of moustache and beard is also interesting, but I know of no porcelain man-dolls with moulded detail. The porcelain boy dolls have lightly-modelled hair, sometimes given more realism by individual brush strokes at the forehead.

Many heads were made that could be used on a doll dressed as a girl or boy. These heads were modelled with a short hairstyle that fell close to the head. An example of this type of unisex hairstyle is seen in the photograph of the porcelain doll's-house dolls and in the interesting male 'Frozen Charley' – a doll that bears out the fact that fairly feminine hairstyles were intended for representations of boys as well as girls.

A few white-haired dolls were made for doll's houses as a variant on the basic head. One has a bright pink lustre face, and was obviously intended as a doll's-house grandmother. I have not seen any black-glazed porcelain dolls, possibly because the German makers were not concentrating as much on the American market in the middle years of the nineteenth century, when this type of porcelain doll was most fashionable, though quite a large number of black-glazed Frozen Charlottes were made later. An American doll-dealer told me recently that she had a black porcelain doll in her stock, the first she had owned; it was on a cloth body with the usual glazed arms and legs, and was made to represent a negro.

China-limbed dolls on the wooden bodies more usually associated with Grödnertals are now very difficult to find, but they are beautifully made when compared with the cloth-bodied porcelains, for they are fully articulated and can assume any position. The china limbs were made with special holes through which the usual wooden pegs could be pushed, at the knee and elbow joints. The head was attached to the wooden body by wooden pegs that were pushed through the 'sew holes' at the front. The back of the china shoulder head was cut in a special way – very narrow at the back with one central hole for its single wooden peg. China heads that were intended for use on wooden bodies can be thus distinguished if they are found separate. The wooden pins that attached the parts were kiln-dried to reduce their size, and then pushed through the holes in the wood and china that they fitted. After absorbing moisture from the atmosphere, the pegs became swollen and could not fall out as the shape became exactly filled. Although any doll of this type is desirable, those that have unusual hairstyles are particularly so.

The potteries relied greatly upon the labour of children for their ability to produce items cheaply. Children began work in England at around the age of eight, though even younger children were employed in some German factories. The children helped the workmen wedge the clay before use and kept the factory tidy, though their most useful work was carrying moulds into which the clay had been pressed or poured. The clay was either rolled out thinly and pressed into the plaster mould, or mixed to a liquid consistency that could be poured. Most dolls' heads were made by the second method, but some, especially earlier dolls, were made by the pressed technique. Plaster of paris moulds were used because the substance was quick to absorb moisture, and a layer of dry clay quickly formed on contact. The moulds would be left until a sufficient thickness of dryer clay had formed and then the surplus was poured away – a similar method to that used by the makers of poured-wax dolls.

Examination of the inside of a head soon reveals the method of manufacture. Pressed heads have slight ridges and are uneven, while those that were poured are quite smooth. Though the pressed heads generally appear to be rather earlier, some with the short boyish hairstyles dating from the end of the century are found.

The child workers carried the poured or pressed heads into the drying-rooms, where they were laid out on shelves to dry and contract away from the mould. The two halves of the head were then lifted from their moulds and skilfully joined together by a craftsman known as a 'repairer'. The join between the two parts can always be seen, which is why it was made to run down the head unobtrusively behind the ears. A porcelain head made from more than two parts would be very unusual, for surprisingly-complicated effects can be achieved by this simple method.

Great care had to be taken that the parts of the head dried evenly, to prevent warping, which would have made the joining of the two parts difficult. Many stories exist about German potters who made the heads in their own 'back-yard kilns'. While possible, it is very unlikely that they would have had much success. Any potter working in a small studio will testify as to the difficulty of making (for instance) tiles without the advantage of a large, carefully-regulated drying-room. Unless the back-yard kilns were very well equipped, their success rate would have been small. This is not to say that small potteries did not make dolls, but there is a great deal of difference between a small, properly-run pottery and the German and Staffordshire back-yard kilns so often mentioned by collectors.

The drying-rooms in the nineteenth century were about 13 feet square and were filled with shelves. In the centre of the room was the stove, often red hot. The temperature in these rooms, into which the child ran with the pressed or moulded heads, was between 120 and 148 degrees, which meant working in an extremely unhealthy atmosphere. The bad conditions led to a noticeable stunting of their growth, and the potters' journeymen were remarkable for their short stature, induced by a childhood spent in such heat.

After the 'repairers' had finished work, the completed heads were placed in 'saggars', vessels of fine clay which held a large number of items. These saggars were placed in a kiln heated by several fires, and served to protect the wares from kiln-staining caused by impurities in the air or from specks of grit.

Hard paste items were often fired and glazed in one operation, but soft paste had to be glazed as a separate process. The dangers involved in working in the atmosphere of the dipping house were considerable: the lead used in the glaze created a poisonous atmosphere, and the children who carried the wares from the dipper were brought into physical contact with this lead. Few adult dippers were able to continue this work for many years as they suffered from 'painters'

Colic' or paralysis and were often crippled at an early age. But because the boys who worked in the dipping houses earned more than the other children, there was never any shortage of recruits, especially as the work was less physically arduous.

After the firing was completed, the kilns were allowed to cool and as soon as was possible the unloading or 'drawing' began. The speed at which this could be effected was crucial, as the pottery, to be economic, needed to keep its kilns continually in operation, so that many burns were sustained in the effort to empty the kiln as fast as possible. A human chain of children was often made, and the hot wares thrown quickly along. The workers were only able to stand the heat inside the kiln for a short time, but the effort was deemed worthwhile for higher wages.

Any roughness was filed off the lower edges of the doll parts, and the heads and lower limbs were sent to the painting-rooms, to be decorated by women and children under the supervision of an overseer. Though the decorators worked in close proximity, the work was not unpleasant. Some heads are painted with such assurance and skill that it is hard to believe that their decoration was the work of children. Some decorators gained more skill than others, and their work can be seen on heads that have an extra flourish: perhaps a ringlet that artistically strays forward, or a clever painting of the lips or eyes to give added expression. The occasional carelessness of the worker is also interesting to note. A line is sometimes omitted over one eye, a garter might have part of the bow missing or the pupils might be painted of unequal size. All collectors know the difference of expression that can be given to heads taken from one mould, and it is worth noting any differences between heads that at first glance appear identical.

White-glazed porcelain heads were decorated with overglaze colours. A large range of shades was available, but their disadvantage was that they could rub off if handled or washed frequently, despite the fact that they were fired again at a low temperature. Many old heads are found that have been left out of doors, and much of the decoration has been worn away. Heads that are now found by amateur 'diggers' often suffer in this way. The decorator sometimes painted her number inside the head, but most were the product of mass production which allowed no time even for this. Some heads have incised numbers, and a few have been found with letters similarly incised, but these were used by too many factories to be much help in attribution. Since dolls' heads were sold so cheaply, the factories did not consider it worth marking the items properly, as they did crockery. It is amusing to reflect that the dolls' heads are now worth several times as much as an ordinary cup and saucer, fully marked, from one of these minor factories.

Some of the finished heads would be supplied to shops to be sold for home assembly into dolls, pincushions or tea cosies according to the whim of the buyer. The remainder were commercially assembled and sometimes dressed before sale. The bodies were made by outworkers out of materials supplied by the manufacturer. To have sent the porcelain limbs to these outworkers seems to have been an unnecessary and time-consuming hazard. The limbs could not be filled with sawdust until they had been joined to the hands and feet by the ridges left for this purpose, and we are thus forced to presume that these quite delicate parts were sent to the outworkers with the fabric, and many breakages must have occurred. It appears likely that more dolls than we like to think were wholly assembled in one place, and that doll-making was less of a folk industry than we in our romanticism like to believe.

Irrespective of whether they were made at home or by small doll-making firms, the bodies are assembled in a very uniform way and tightly packed with sawdust. It is possible to estimate the date of the doll by studying the shape of the body in relation to the fashionable outline of various periods, though the small doll's-house doll retained the simple hourglass body throughout the century. Early dolls' heads are small in relation to the total height of the body, but those made after 1880 make less attempt to copy the correct adult proportions of the figure.

Some commercially-made dolls were given leather arms, with the amusingly-shaped hands that are always associated with this method. The arms are made completely of leather, not just to the elbow as on the waxed dolls. A wide variety of colours was used, but from the collector's point of view, it was an unsatisfactory technique, as the arms have usually become marked and disfigured with wear.

Dolls made of porcelain but without the usual moulded hair are always of interest. Mohair wigs were often used, giving an odd, half-realistic effect. Later dolls of this type represent girls rather than ladies, and have the round faces and short plump necks of children. Some early examples have real hair wigs fixed into the tight arrangement sometimes seen on papier mâché dolls. The bald-headed porcelains sometimes have a black spot painted on the head, and dolls of this type generally tend to be earlier (though not as early as the Biedermeier period with which they are commonly associated, but which had ended by 1840, when china dolls began to be made in quantity). The bald 'black spots' almost always represent ladies, and usually have the very sloping shoulders and rather slimmer faces associated with dolls made between 1840 and 1860. Some, possibly made to represent boys, have a painted area on the head that is partly spot and partly suggested hairstyle. The genuine porcelain boys often have the slim, sloping shoulders of women.

197 Pair of shoulder heads indicating the difference between early and late dolls of the porcelain type. The larger head, which is pressed, has the very sloping shoulders and well-painted eyes typical of dolls made before 1865 while the smaller head that is poured has squarer shoulders and much cruder decoration to the eyes. In this case the red line over the eye is omitted. $4\frac{1}{2}$ and 3 in. high.

198 Porcelain head with well-modelled hair swept into a bun at the back. Exceptionally well-modelled ears for this type. Leather arms with well-made hands, fabric body. 16 in. high.

303

199   White bisque doll described as 'Parian' with chestnut-coloured hair. Brush marks to forehead. Blue eyes. Turban decorated in blue and pink, with gilt lustre decoration. 16 in. high.

200   Back view of turban head showing the care the decorators were prepared to expend on heads. Parian lower limbs. Black heel-less boots. Sawdust-filled body.

201   Ladies of 1844 in evening and opera dress. The figure on the left wears a turban similar to that seen on 'Parian' dolls of the period.

Some collectors claim that early dolls have a red-painted line that reflects the eyelid, and that this decoration is not found on late dolls. All the large dolls I have seen have this red line, which was a traditional decorative technique irrespective of age. It is sometimes omitted in small doll's-house dolls and on a few very poor-quality heads, but little that is constructive can be deduced from its presence on a doll.

Eyes are almost always blue, as the colour livened up the face and suited the dead white better than brown. A few brown-eyed porcelains are known, but these are quite rare, especially when compared with the later tinted bisque jointed dolls that were made in equal number with brown and blue eyes. A few very special porcelain dolls were made with set-in eyes, one very exciting example even having eyes that sleep.

The early dolls often have more care given to their decoration, as they were fashionable and popular toys; but as they became outdated, they were made for a poorer market and the quality inevitably dropped. Eyebrows were often painted with little thought of the shape of the brow beneath, and colour was given to the cheeks in two bright dabs, rather than being blended in. Several well-known doll-makers made white-glazed shoulder heads, but their work was un-marked and impossible to attribute. Dolls can most safely be dated according to their hairstyle, and, while not a completely accurate guide, the study of fashion-able hairstyles does give an approximate date within a range of about fifteen years.

Blond-haired porcelains were not often made, possibly because the colour looked too insipid against a white face. Brown-haired porcelains, especially if they are of a very light tone, are even rarer. A few very fine lady-dolls with heads that swivel at the base of the neck in the shoulder plate are known, and often attributed to a French source, as they are found on the typical gussetted French kid body and dressed very fashionably. These porcelain lady-dolls with swivel necks appear to date from around 1870, and certainly look more French than German in features, though it is possible that they were made to French specifications. Swivel-headed dolls were made in an attempt to give dolls greater realism, and the earliest method on porcelains was to make the head only swivel on the neck which remained static. Though dolls of this type are a delight to the collector, they did not give a very realistic effect, and were produced in very small numbers. Any swivel-headed porcelain is of interest, as it was a type of mechanism that was not fashionable when porcelains were in their heyday, and it is always unusual to find a quality product made at a time when the substance was no longer popular with the fashionable and progressive makers. Some lady-dolls of this type have the name 'Madam Rohmer Paris' stamped on the bodies, and these are the very lovely luxury items more usually associated with tinted bisque heads.

Glazed porcelain heads used on the early dolls made by Huret in Paris differ considerably from the German product as the top of the head is cut away and a cork pate inserted, to which the wig was fixed. The heads were mounted on beautifully-made gussetted bodies. The dolls are interesting as marking the transition between the old stiff china dolls and the more realistic French ladies. The trend towards realism marked the decline of china dolls, with their stiff poses and heads that only very occasionally tilt to one side.

Glazed porcelain was very rarely used for multi-faced dolls, but one nice example came up for sale at Christie's in 1973. It represented a very young girl and an old and wrinkled woman, one face being represented on either side of the shoulder head, so that the doll had to be completely turned to change the character. The vendor, who is a doll-collector, had never liked the head, considering the one side too sickly and young and the other too old and ugly to identify with. The head nevertheless found an eager buyer, despite its damaged state.

Dolls that have some sort of hat or head-dress moulded in one with the head are referred to as bonnet dolls, and could form a fascinating collection in their own right. Some are found with attractive pastel-coloured bonnets and blonde hair, while others wear quite sophisticated hats decorated with bows. A few early bonnet-type dolls are known, but these wear very simple headgear, rather more like caps with ribbons tying under the chin. Most of these dolls date from the period after 1885, and very similar heads are often seen on china figures made in Germany at the same time.

At the end of the century, some amusing heads with a moulded flower worn in the manner of a bonnet or cap were made, and are generally referred to by collectors as marguerite or flower dolls. Some of these flower heads were made as late as 1910, but are pleasant acquisitions. Fewer are found in England than in America, as at the time of their popularity, the American market was taking most of the better-quality German products.

The value of a porcelain doll depends partly on age and partly on the rarity of the hair treatment and colouring. Dolls with moulded breasts tend to be more interesting than those with shallower shoulder pieces, as they are much earlier and of good quality. Various claims have been made that certain moulds were intended as portraits of characters such as Jenny Lind or even Queen Victoria, but there is little to substantiate this, apart from a fleeting resemblance. A few late dolls were made in porcelain with moulded necklaces and the name 'Bertha' or 'Ethel' moulded on the shoulder, so that they would be given a character of their own as soon as the child saw them. It is difficult to estimate the popularity

202   Parian with black hair moulded in ringlets that fall well down over shoulder. Moulded Alice band. Blue eyes, very sloping shoulders. Black heel-less boots. Very correctly-made original costume of the late 1850s. 17 in. high.

of white china dolls with children, but as they are rarely mentioned in auto-biographies, perhaps they always held more appeal for the adult, who could dress them in the fashion of the period. Old ladies (from whom I have bought such dolls) had usually inherited them, and they had never been played with, but kept in a drawer or wardrobe out of respect for their age, and given little affection.

Dealers sometimes claim that dolls with a large number of black specks in the glaze are much older, and are so disfigured because "the makers were inexperi-enced". In fact these were probably faulty dolls that were sold off cheaply in the way 'china seconds' are today. The potters were sufficiently experienced to make a perfect china head long before they made the majority of china dolls.

Emma Clear of California made reproduction glazed china dolls of the highest quality, one of the first being a copy of a so-called Jenny Lind doll. Reproduction china dolls are now being made again in kit form in the antique manner, and those made small enough for doll's houses are especially popular. It is a pity that dolls of this type are always so imitative; it should not be difficult to make a modern doll in the traditional manner but in the current idiom.

Parian Dolls

Genuine Parian china was used as an expensive medium for minor art objects, and was not used for the manufacture of dolls' heads. Several doll experts state that there is no difference between Parian and ordinary porcelain, but as porcelain-collectors and experts recognize the difference, it seems strange that writers on dolls set themselves on high and state that the recognized substance does not exist!

The white biscuit porcelain dolls with unglazed faces have been termed 'Parians' by doll-collectors for so long that we may use the term here, although strictly it is incorrect. The fact that the makers of white biscuit heads were aiming at a product that closely imitated the fashionable Parian ware is however inescapable. The doll-makers employed similar decorating techniques, and even constructed shoulder heads that are very reminiscent of busts made to represent famous people.

No dolls' heads are recorded as having been made by any of the great English porcelain factories which have precise lists of their products after 1850. The true Parian ware was made only in England, though a debased form was manu-factured in Europe. The Sèvres factory, as well as other Continental factories,

203 Parian dolls of this type were once believed to have been made in France but are now considered to be mainly of German origin. Blue eyes, fair hair. Marked on shoulder "12.B". Heel-less black boots. Sawdust-filled body. 11¾ in. high.

204 Side view of 207 showing hairstyle and original ear-rings.

205 Back view of 203 showing hairstyle.

206 With fair hair and blue eyes, this doll's head, with slight variations, is the most commonly-found Parian. Lilac dress decorated with black. Head marked "16". 14½ in. high.

had produced white, unglazed porcelain biscuit figures as early as the eighteenth century, as had the famous Derby factory, and it was during experiments made in the 1840s attempting to rediscover the formula used by the latter that the new Parian substance was invented by (it is generally believed) John Mountford of Copeland. The material was at first variously referred to as Stone china, Statuary Porcelain or Carrara, according to the whim of the individual factories which all claimed to have invented it. It was greatly admired for giving an effect of marble. The Victorian loved marble in classical statuary, ornately-carved fire-places and tombstones, and were delighted with a ceramic substance that could be produced comparatively cheaply and used to make busts and figures in the manner of carved marble for the decoration of reception rooms.

True Parian has a soft, ivory tone and is like silk to the touch. It is made of an especially highly-vitrified form of bisque porcelain, and the earliest experiments were made with soft paste versions. It is semi-translucent, so that some direct light can be seen through even the thickest part. It was used to best advantage as a modelling material, because of its peculiar crispness on complicated groups. A more commercial application lay in modelling famous contemporaries in classical poses. The fairly wealthy people who bought the Parian figures would have felt more inclined to buy a doll that was made in this very fashionable manner, and the doll-makers were quick to realize the potential of an 'art' product. The fact that many of the dolls made in this way were able to be sold very cheaply does not detract from the makers' original intention of creating an artistic object that was to appeal to the fashion-conscious mother rather than the child. These dolls are important, as they were the first conscious 'art' product.

The attractiveness of these heads for women is evidenced by their frequent use on pincushions and other needlework trifles, a use that would appear to account for the large number that are found without bodies. Parian dolls were popular between 1855 and 1885, thus falling neatly into the period slightly behind the zenith of the Parian ornaments, and into the period when copies in white bisque had become popular with the lower middle classes.

The early white bisque dolls are often quite heavy, especially in comparison with those of ordinary porcelain which could be cast much more thinly. White biscuit products were traditionally more expensive than glazed porcelain, as great care was needed in the composition of the clay and in the firing: any slight cracks, impurities of surface texture or kiln-stains could not be disguised with colour or a heavy glaze. The number of wasters from each firing must have been quite high, despite the care taken by the craftsmen.

Since white bisque was such a lovely material for detailed moulding, the German doll-makers took pride in creating unusual hairstyles, ornate head-dresses and decorations such as flowers, combs and bows. There is a tradition that some Parian dolls were made in France, but there are no marked examples to substantiate this, and I am inclined to think that almost all the bisque dolls with white faces were made in Germany.

The artist doll-maker made a model shoulder head out of wax or even alabaster, and as he was usually modelling the head of a woman, he was naturally influenced by the current ideal of female beauty, as seen in drawings, prints and (at the end of the period when most 'Parians' were made) photographs. The Empress Eugenie had caused a great stir by her cool beauty, and modellers, while not actually copying her features, were obviously influenced by the type of beauty she represented. The same ideas of classical beauty can be seen in numerous unnamed statuettes and busts. A few heads have become particularly associated over the years with various famous characters, so that the lovely doll with the plumed snood is now referred to as 'Princess Alexandra', and another is known as the 'Countess Dagmar'. As long as collectors use these resemblances simply as convenient distinguishing terms for various types of moulds, little harm is done, but it is misleading to label them as character dolls when they are merely contemporary representations of an ideal of feminine beauty.

If the Empress Eugenie doll had been a true portrait, much greater attention would have been paid to her particular characteristics, outstanding among which was the 'Empress's signature'. This referred to a peculiar method Eugenie used of emphasizing her eyes, which were rather pale, by the use of heavy black outlines, a remarkable characteristic in a period when make-up was timidly discreet. One of the English court ladies at the time of the Emperor and Empress's State Visit wrote complainingly, "If only she would not paint her eyes and eyebrows." Her hair, at the time when she was most admired, was copper coloured, and her eyes pale blue-green, but none of these characteristics are reflected in the doll once believed to be a portrait of her. In a similar way, the 'Jenny Lind' doll is inaccurate as a portrait of the singer.

After the modelling of an elegant shoulder head, the wax or alabaster model would be passed on to a skilled workman known as a block cutter, who decided how many sections the head should be cut into to make casting possible. Dolls' heads are usually made of two-part moulds, but a few are reported to have been cast in three pieces. Extra detail, such as flowers, was usually applied by hand.

The parts of the head were slip-cast in the same manner as the dolls that were later to be glazed, and allowed to dry in an even temperature before the repairer fixed the parts together by slightly dampening them. This joining called for some skill when working in unglazed bisque that would magnify any imperfections.

312

Artistically fashionable people of the nineteenth century liked the effect given to table centres, for example, when glazed and enamelled Parian was combined with the white, so that classical white-draped ladies are sometimes found supporting gilded and painted bowls. This kind of ornamentation was extended to the white biscuit heads, and the hair was enamelled in yellow, brown or even black. The most popular colour was blonde, as the bisque (being porous) took staining quite well so that an extra firing of the more expensive enamels was not always necessary. Many cheap white figures were sold, almost as handicraft items for women to decorate at home with these stains, but I have not yet found any dolls' heads that could be described as having been decorated in this manner. Gold enamels, lovely purple, violet and red lustres and soft overglaze colours were used to decorate the Parian heads, so that many are in themselves interesting examples of mid-nineteenth-century decorating techniques.

Some large factories sold undecorated white heads to doll-makers and decorators who painted them at home and marketed the items in a small way. It is possibly from this craft carried on in 'back-yards' that the old story of German potters working at home developed.

Untinted bisque heads with set-in glass eyes are rare. Glass eyes are usually found in the Parian dolls that have the top of the head left open, though some are found in dolls with the full domed head. Swivel-necked Parians are even rarer, and male dolls of white untinted bisque are hardly ever found outside dolls' houses, though a most appealing boy with a moulded Scottish hat decorated with lustre plumes was made. Many lady-dolls have pierced ears, though the original ear-rings, when still in place, are nearly always rather uninteresting glass beads that, to the eye of the modern collector, do not look sufficiently splendid for these hand-finished dolls.

Parian dolls are usually mounted on well-stuffed cotton bodies, and given 'Parian' lower limbs and arms. Shoes are nearly always of the flat-heeled type, though some are decorated with lustre. A doll-collecting friend owns one very beautiful Parian doll's leg which he considers so lovely he keeps it in a place of honour. It certainly is a very remarkable leg, with its decoration of purple lustre gold and pink! In some of the very large dolls, such as the illustrated 'Princess Alexandra', thick wire was used as an armature to ensure that the long body kept its shape. Some heads are found mounted on commercially-made bodies with leather arms, while others have obviously been made up at home. Pincushion dolls are often worth investigating, as sometimes the complete doll was buried in sawdust to make the item, possibly after the child had grown too old for it. One very special bisque is known that has a wooden stockinette-covered body of the type more usually associated with tinted bisque lady-dolls.

207 Parian doll with pierced ears and blue band to hair that once belonged to Ann Coker, a servant girl. Marked "8" on shoulder. 8 in. high.

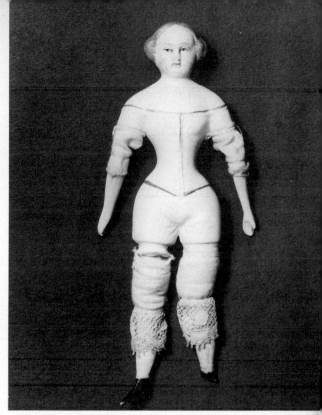

(*above left*) 208   Parian bonnet doll. The decoration in blue and pink. Blonde hair. Marked "Germany". Brown glazed boots. 7 in. high.   (*above right*) 209   Unusual Parian with fabric insets to allow for movement. Head and body in one piece. Marked "8" on buttock. Gilt decoration. 6 in. high.   (*below*) 210   "Godey's Fashions for September 1866". Page from American fashion magazine of period.

A very unusual Parian was examined recently whose head, torso and upper legs were made in one, and the moulded combinations were decorated in gilt. Articulation was given by the cloth inserts to arms and legs.

Collectors sometimes refer to these white bisques as Dresdens. Some were in all probability made in this area, as were all sorts of cheap Victorian trifles, but it is impossible to distinguish dolls from any one particular area, for they are usually marked only with a number or a letter of the type used by scores of makers. Some are also referred to as rare or even 'unique'; but it is extremely unlikely that any mass-produced item made comparatively recently could be unique, and the term is not used in this book, even with regard to items that have never been seen before, since it is probable that some collector somewhere has an identical example.

The Parian dolls have an elegance that gives them great appeal even to non-collectors. Lovers of porcelain are often surprised by the skill and artistry lavished on toys that were to be sold so cheaply. Many heads hold their own against quite respectable porcelain items. Parian dolls were collected in the 1920s and 1930s, when even French bisque *bébés* were considered quite common, and they are still sometimes bought by non-collectors simply as beautiful objects. Until recently they were comparatively underpriced in England and could often be bought for much less than German double-jointed dolls. Their quality is now generally recognized by European collectors, as it has been to those in America for some time. Writing in 1948, Eleanor St George was already exclaiming upon the 'unreasonably' high prices collectors in America were prepared to pay for these dolls: a cry which every doll-collector down the years must have voiced about almost every type of doll, yet we always go on paying. In the case of the Parians I for one feel they justify the price.

ELEVEN

EARLY BISQUE DOLLS

German Makers

White bisque, though artistic and extremely attractive to the eye of an adult, was hardly realistic, and its cold perfection was inevitably superseded by techniques that offered the child a more lifelike toy. For about thirty years the two variants were sold alongside one another, until by around 1885, the Parians finally lost their popularity altogether and only occasionally reappeared in the form of dolls'-house or small bonnet dolls. The notable exceptions are those made by the Japanese in the early years of this century in imitation of the somewhat outdated Parians. These Japanese dolls can be distinguished by their rather coarse white bisque, a loss of fine detail (especially in the moulding of the hair), and a rather too blatant use of colour for the features, so that lips, for instance, are painted in a deep red that would have been unacceptable to the more sensitive German decorator.

The term 'blonde bisque' was used by Eleanor St George to describe dolls with moulded hair, cloth bodies and pink bisque faces. Though the phrase has no technical meaning, it is still used by collectors as a simple means of distinguishing the type. These early bisque shoulder heads are of interest, as there is an even greater divergence of standard than in almost any other class of doll; they range from specimens that are really fine examples of nineteenth-century porcelain to badly-moulded, poorly-made heads whose only commendation is that they were cheap to produce.

These early bisque dolls already exhibit a pattern that was to continue until 1939. Top-quality dolls were produced by manufacturers who also made thousands of cheap items intended to earn the pennies of the poorer child. The divergence of standard is due to this very wide market that had to be satisfied.

The cheapest type of blonde bisque wore a simple hairstyle, moulded quite close to the head. The arms and legs were often disproportionately small and attached to a sawdust-filled fabric body. This is the type of doll so often seen in doll's houses, where the original owners sometimes embellished the rather uninteresting heads by the addition of a black moustache or a touch of silver paint to represent a grandmother's white hair. This simple basic doll was made in a variety of sizes, the largest being about 20 inches high. A few manufacturers at the beginning of the twentieth century used printed fabrics for dolls' bodies, presumably in an attempt to make them more attractive, as they were sold undressed. The decoration of the fabric ranges from United States emblems to simple arithmetical exercises. This fabric is most frequently seen with heads of glazed porcelain, but is also sometimes found on blonde bisques.

As many of the shoulder heads were sold loose for home assembly, an amusing variety of grotesquely-shaped bodies is found. Though heads mounted on home-made bodies are of less monetary value, they are interesting as specimens of folk craft, and often reflect the period of their assembly far more than those that were made commercially. Pieces of an outworn dress, a pair of legs that once belonged to a much older broken doll, and filling that can vary from dry grass to pieces of a worn-out blanket often combine in the creation of a cheap toy for an infant.

In direct contrast to the peculiarities of the home-made body were others finely made of leather with skilfully-inserted gussets and good-quality animal-hair filling. Sometimes a combination of fabric and leather is used, and the lower legs, that were to be covered with stockings, are made of cloth. The older type of fabric body with leather arms is also found, especially in combination with heads of a better quality. For some reason, the cheaper heads are usually found on the commercially-made bodies with bisque limbs, indicating that the ornate heads were those most frequently sold loose. The body used by Bawo and Dotter had a corset printed on the front and sometimes on the back, and although it is found more often in combination with a china head, it has been seen with bisque. The bodies used by Kling are sometimes characterized by two rows of stitches that run down the front of the body and are also occasionally found on bisque-headed dolls.

The dolls of this type divide into two main groups. The first type is simply made, while the other soars to wild heights of extravagance. Many collectors exhibit the top-quality bisque heads simply as busts, and make no effort to create a complete doll. Large consignments of these well-made heads were sent from Germany to haberdashers, confectioners and gift shops all over America

211 With slight variations, this doll typifies the basic 'blonde bisque' type with yellow hair and blue eyes. Unmarked. 17$\frac{1}{2}$ in. high.

319

and Britain. Some of them are so skilfully made that they transcend the world of the doll and become high-quality ornamental items. The tinted white bisque of which the heads were made lent itself to the detailed modelling of complicated contemporary hairstyles. Small flowers, leaves, combs and jewels were moulded by hand and applied to the head before firing. Pieces of lace were dipped in slip and applied as collars and ruffles around the neck. Fragments of glass were also occasionally embedded, to represent jewellery. Some heads were given glass eyes, and in this case the eye sockets were cut out before firing.

The heads were either sold blank to small decorating factories or completed at the pottery after firing. In either case, all the skill of the decorator was lavished upon ornamentation. Some heads were fired before and after the pink flesh-tint was applied, while it is believed that some were stained by the decorator and not re-fired. I have not seen any heads of this type made of self-coloured pink paste; this technique appears to have been reserved for socket heads, but the technique was feasible, and no doubt a rare example will sometimes occur.

Though eyes were usually painted, as on the Parians, the most desirable are those of inset glass. The eyes were held in position by a layer of plaster of paris. These pale bisque heads with glass eyes have great appeal to collectors, and dolls of this type were sought after when many of the others that now fetch high prices could be bought for negligible amounts.

The ears of good-quality bisques are usually pierced, though the original ear-rings are often very disappointing, being only simple round glass beads. Some very desirable heads have the ear-rings actually moulded in one with the ears, in which case they are often much more ornate and perhaps lustre-decorated.

Hair is almost invariably blonde, though a few late examples of more granular bisque are auburn or even black. Most of the decorative detail was lavished on the hairstyle. The dolls were made in a period when fashionable women were able to devote hours to sitting in front of a dressing table attended by their maids, who performed wonders with what was often an unpromising head! The styles were aided by false pieces and horsehair pads, and decorated with strings of pearls, flowers, feathers or jewelled tiaras. Most hairstyles were upswept, for otherwise they would have been unable to support the ornamentation, but some wore ringlets that fell to shoulder level at the back. The fashionable bisque lady-dolls very accurately reflect this period, in which the decoration of the female figure reached its peak. The rich child gazed in wonder at her mother in evening dress, who had been pushed, pulled, padded and coiffured into a statuesque representation of her husband's wealth. The poorer child admired such ladies in the street and in magazines, and joined with her richer counterpart in demanding dolls that were as decorated as the ladies on whom they looked with such wonder.

320

30 Belton type with umbrella
31 Walking Jumeau with flirting eyes

The fact that so many of these lady heads were sold loose is supported by the degree of decoration, often quite unsuitable, that was given to the shoulders. The busts were sold as decorative items in their own right and parts that in an ordinary doll would have been covered by the neckline of a dress were given applied and painted detail. Later costumiers have often experienced great difficulty in incorporating this detail into the complete dress, and some strange effects have been created. One is sometimes confronted by a doll whose rather prim, beruffled, high neckline suggests an elegant afternoon outfit, but which suddenly changes at shoulder level into a splendid evening dress, much better suited to bare shoulders. Lustre as well as the cheaper gilding was applied to the decoration, making these heads colourful objects which hardly need the clothes on which other types of dolls depend for much of their appeal.

A fine group of heads was presented to the Metropolitan Museum of New York by the Borgfeldt Company, which had been one of America's biggest doll importers. The heads show the wide variety made in this manner, ranging from bare-shouldered elegant ladies with swivel necks to rather schoolmarm-like characters with high-necked blouses, modestly tied with a bow. All the heads carry the usual type of incised number that is generally accepted to refer to the mould. Some very attractive heads are recorded with the letter 'R' on the back, and, though the possibility that this might point to the Rauenstein factory is attractive, it cannot be proved. It is more likely to be simply another means of mould identification. The swivel-necked bisque dolls with moulded hair are quite rare, especially when found on the original fabric-covered, wooden-articulated bodies.

The German porcelain factories included dolls such as those sold by Borgfeldt among their mass-produced items, and the heads were originally sold so cheaply that it was felt hardly worth marking them. Firms such as Dernheim Koch and Fischer, who made detailed and flower-encrusted figures, are thought to have also made dolls' heads, and some have been found with what appears to be part of their mark. Other firms now quite well known to collectors, such as Simon and Halbig and Armand Marseille made decorative figurines, very much in the manner of the ornate shoulder heads. It is likely that a few were made by these potteries, but so far no sufficiently marked heads have been discovered. The Simon and Halbig heads that are known are not of the very highly-decorated type and were evidently play dolls.

As young girls' dresses were worn at mid-calf length for most of the period during which these dolls were made, the treatment of the legs and feet became much more important. Stockings are sometimes indicated by ribbing moulded in the bisque, and the scalloped edge of a pair of drawers often gives a neat finish to the lower limbs. Shoes and boots are occasionally given almost as much

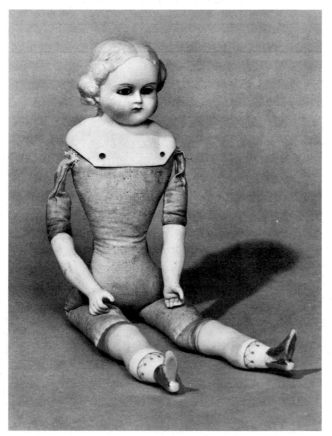

212 By 1880 women were wearing costumes that were both restricting and ostentatious as in this print from *Illustrierte Frauen-Zeitung*, 1881.

213 Bisque heads of this type are only occasionally marked. This example with inset blue glass eyes is incised "074X 6". The cross mark probably part of mark used by Dernheim Koch and Fischer, a firm that specialized in the making of Dresden-type bisque figures. 18 in. high.

214 'Blonde bisque' with inset glass eyes, in undress to show typical construction. Glazed socks and purple lustre boots. 11 in. high.

215 Very unusual pink bisque swivel head on shoulder plate. Glazed moulded hair. Inset glass eyes. Pierced ears. Exceptionally fine quality. Decorated with a beard by the manufacturer. Dressed in Indian State costume of a Rajput Court. 22 in. high.

decoration as the heads, and are improbably lustred in pinks and purples, with gilded tassels and fringes. The arms and legs are still disproportionately small, in the traditional doll-making manner, and again look slightly strange in comparison with the attempted realism of the faces, often aided by a slight turning of the head.

In the modelling of these early bisques can be traced the change from the haughty white bisque ladies to a softer and much younger-looking doll. Some of the faces of the bisques, with their piled-up adult hairstyles, do look almost too young for the grandeur of their hair. Nearly all these heads appear to have originated in Germany. There is a long tradition among doll-collectors that many came from the Dresden area; as all kinds of cheap novelties were made in this part of Germany, the tradition is probably reasonably correct.

As with the white bisques and unusual porcelains, there are various titles that have been given to the more positive models. A doll with a blue scarf draped about its neck and shoulders is popularly known as the 'Empress Louise' while Jenny Linds, Countess Dagmars and Princess Alexandras abound. As with the dolls of white bisque, the supposed characters are simply representations of the current ideal of female beauty, and any direct effort at portraiture is unlikely. The dolls of this type are sufficiently fine in their own right to avoid the need for emotive titles, except as collectors' identification jargon.

Another type of shoulder heads was made alongside the discussed ornate examples. These dolls were much more in the tradition of the glazed porcelains, with the prim faces and rather sober hairstyles associated with the more common types. The bisque faces do, however, reflect the change towards a younger-looking doll, and many with tiny waisted bodies look more like plump eleven-year-olds in the face. Eyes were usually painted on dolls of this cheaper type. A few have glass eyes, but it is even more unusual to find them in dolls of this plain variety than in the coiffured heads. Some of these cheaper bisques are too highly coloured to be very attractive to the modern collector, who prefers pale examples, though the child of the 1880s probably found these warmly-coloured dolls a welcome relief from the cool, unrealistic ladies to which she was more accustomed.

The basic dolls, with blonde hair and bisque limbs, can still be bought quite cheaply, but those with inset eyes, pierced ears or attractively-decorated boots are scarcer and more expensive. The marked Simon and Halbig heads are also interesting as examples of the factory's early work. They are sometimes of quite good quality with some extra detail, such as an Alice band or pierced ears. The Simon and Halbig heads appear to date from around 1875 onwards, and mark the transition to the period when makers began to find it useful to have their own mark incised on dolls. The Kling Company also found it useful to mark

216 Fine-quality *Parisienne* with the face of a mature woman. Pierced ears, two-tone lips. Leather gusseted body. Blue and cream silk costume. 19 in. high.

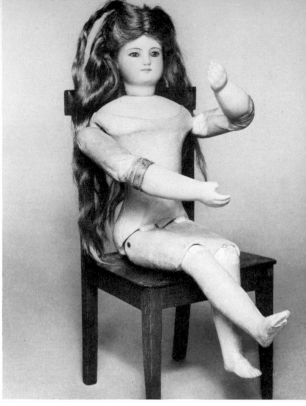

(*above left*) 217 *Parisienne* with bisque head of much poorer quality. Pierced ears. Blue eyes. Gusseted kid body with well-moulded bisque lower arms. Dress of blue satin trimmed with lace. 12½ in. high. (*above right*) 218 Beautifully-articulated swivel-necked *Parisienne* with wooden kid-covered body. Bisque lower arms. Unmarked head but of good quality. 12 in. high. (*below left*) 219 A few *Parisiennes* have the unusually large eyes often associated with the Jumeau factory, as in this example. Gusseted leather body. Marked "2" on head. 16 in. high. (*below right*) 220 *Parisienne* with metal-frame body covered with stockinette. Body often described as 'Gesland' type. Marked "F.G.", for Fernand Gaultier, on left shoulder. 18 in. high.

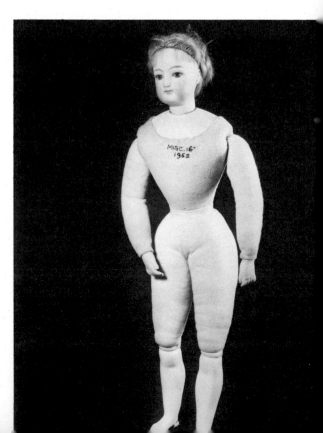

their bisque heads of this type. These heads are not very lovely, having over-full lips and being too highly coloured for the modern taste.

The 'blonde bisques' also indicate another, and more interesting, change of attitude towards dolls: there are far more male examples. Many of these fall into the classification of doll's-house dolls, as they are only about 6 inches high. They were still not made in the same number as the females, who were needed in quantity to present the satisfactory appearance of an inhabited house of the time. Cook, kitchenmaids, parlourmaids and nursemaids were necessary, as well as the lady of the house and her stay-at-home daughters. Doll's houses usually have very few men, though a butler often appears, even in very ordinary doll's houses. Doll's-house men therefore now command a much higher price than the ladies, who were made as miniature characters who could represent grandmother, an elegant young sister or a stern governess. The painting of the men is often very amusing, and ranges from black-haired be-whiskered characters who would be more at home in a Victorian stage melodrama, to blonde, weak-chinned young men with drooping yellow moustaches. None of these dolls are marked, except with a number and (occasionally) a letter, but they have as much character as the best of the lady-dolls who inhabit these late Victorian and Edwardian houses.

Larger men-dolls are even harder to find, for very few seem to have been made. A male doll that was generally acceptable to boys was still some eighty years in the future. Those that were made for the limited market that existed were rather grotesque specimens, having fine bearded and whiskered heads mounted on the standard ladies' body – slim-waisted, wide-hipped and with tiny arms and legs! I know of only one male bisque doll with inset glass eyes, and this has a moulded head-dress. The addition of glass eyes seems to have been deemed necessary only for lady-dolls.

Rather easier to find are bisque shoulder-headed boy dolls. Their faces are a little similar to the basic lady, but have a very correctly moulded boy's hairstyle. The popular original costumes for these boys included the ubiquitous sailor suit, worn by little boys from all kinds of background, and Highland dress, popularized by the royal children at Balmoral. These boy dolls have a very meek, idealized appearance with only a slight attempt at realism.

A number of bonneted dolls were modelled in bisque, and exhibit an amusing range of headgear rarely seen in costume books and probably only seen on dolls. The advice that is often given of dating a doll by its hat or head decoration is highly unreliable, as dolls' fashion, when related to moulded decoration, existed within its own world – enchanting, but hardly a matter of historical accuracy.

Some of the bisque shoulder heads are also seen in glazed porcelain versions, and are sometimes so variously decorated that they appear quite unlike one another. One doll, popularly referred to as the 'Empress Augusta Victoria' (wife of the Kaiser) because of the moulded iron cross on her chest, can be found in dark and fair versions that present a very different appearance. There must be many unphotographed and unrecorded versions of these shoulder-headed dolls which would in themselves offer a wide collecting field. Good condition, though important, is not quite as necessary as in the later dolls, and some with seriously-damaged or missing limbs can still fetch good prices at auction. Damage to the shoulder head itself has a marked effect on price, but if the head is an unusual or very beautiful mould it is still worth buying, since the supply of such dolls is limited by their fragility. The limbs may swing alarmingly together when the doll is moved, and collectors often have to admit that despite care in handling, they have been responsible themselves for cracks or chips to legs.

French Bisque Lady-Dolls

She was the most beautiful person in the world. She had brown eyes and pink cheeks, a blue silk dress and a white bonnet with orange blossoms in it. She had two pairs of shoes and two pairs of stockings and she had two wigs, a brown and a flaxen one. All her clothes took on and off and there was a complete change of them.

I saw her first at a bazaar and longed to possess her, but her price was two guineas and no hope mingled with my longing. . . . Then suddenly, one of the great good fortunes of my life happened to me. The beautiful doll was put up to be raffled and my sister won her; I trembled with joy as she and her wardrobe were put into my hands. I took her home. I dressed and undressed her twenty times a day. . . . I told her fairy tales and took her to bed with me at night for company, but I never loved her.

French lady-dolls such as this one acquired by a little English girl in the 1860s made a great impression on the minds of children. Similarly well-equipped figures are often recalled in autobiographies, when other toys have long been forgotten. The fact that the dolls were often bought complete with a travelling trunk with its own label and padlock was an added attraction, and many old ladies remembered with nostalgia similar toys of their own youth. One writer remembered a French doll so perfect that it demanded a place of great honour on the nursery mantelpiece, alongside her plaster statue of the Madonna! This awed love for a figure that was just a little too perfect is not the same emotion as the warm affection that a battered flannel pig or a rag baby arouse; the French lady-doll was stared at in wide-eyed wonder and covetousness when seen in a toyshop, but at home her perfection could be a source of embarrassment that precluded joyful play.

To the collector of today these figures are a delight, as they completely recreate in miniature the fashionable lady of the period and her necessary accoutrements.

Women's fashion has never been, and hopefully will never again be, as complex as it was in the years between 1860 and 1885, the period that exactly coincided with the popularity of the lady-dolls. Every surface of a dress was decorated in some ingenious way, as plain areas came to be considered 'rather common'. Birds, seals, mice, flowers, feathers, jewels and laces all combined to create costumes whose designs were so complex that they rendered even the fashion journalists speechless. The increase in general prosperity encouraged a more reckless attitude to the cost of clothes, and women vied with each other in presenting an appearance of expensive detail that they hoped could not possibly be copied cheaply by people lower down the financial scale. As is always the case, copies were made, and the fashionable ladies hurried on to yet another excess that was copied in its turn by the costumiers of miniature lady-dolls.

These miniature figures, when in original condition, still present the wealth, competitiveness and sheer vulgarity of the period more clearly than any contemporary fashion drawing. The artist, with some innate good taste, contrived to present a coolly elegant design for the avid readers of the ladies' journals, but the French dolls present the effect that was created by the dress-makers who copied the fashions for customers. Overdressed, over-equipped and delightfully vulgar, these lady-dolls exquisitely parody their age.

The French doll-makers, though skilful in making quality bodies, had continued to import papier mâché and china heads from Germany. From the first part of the century, the area around the Passage Choiseul in Paris had formed the centre of the French doll industry. Here were to be found the dolls boot-makers, milliners, wigmakers, corset-makers and couturiers, all combining to create a fashionable and unquestionably French doll from the unpromising German head. The trade fairs showed the world the weak points of the French doll, admired for its costume but criticized for the mediocre quality of its head.

A few improvements were made in France by such Parisian doll-makers as Ainé Blampoix, who in 1855 obtained a patent for the application of glass eyes to porcelain dolls. It is doubtful whether the heads themselves were made in France at this time, though by 1865 bisque swivel- and fixed-head dolls were being manufactured by Gaultier, along with many other French makers who had decided that the rather stereotyped German heads were no longer good enough for their luxury items. The early French bisque heads that these manufacturers created are, despite their excessive sweetness, some of the most beautiful dolls' heads that have ever been made.

These French lady-dolls, often provided with a change of wigs, were made at the same period as the German bisques with ornate moulded hairstyles. Both types pandered to the desire of the girl to own a doll that looked like a grand lady. Because of their much greater degree of realism, the French dolls were the more popular, and were sold as late as 1890, though by this time manufacturers like Jumeau were only making leather-bodied dolls of this type to special order.

The French manufacturers boosted sales by various advertising ploys, such as the publishing of small magazines for children, which persuaded them to buy at certain shops. Little Parisians were encouraged to ensure that their dolls were better dressed and equipped than those of their friends, and every new fashion item was quickly made in miniature to supply this artificially-created market. This must be one of the most distasteful periods in the history of the doll, despite the fact that it produced such fine-quality items. The picture of the rich, well-dressed, pampered little *Parisiennes* parading their competitively-dressed dolls to an audience of children from nearby orphanages is not one that can have pleasant associations. This is, sadly, the beginning of a period when advertising was aimed directly at the child. Garden parties, balls and other sponsored social events were created solely for the purpose of display, the firm of Huret in particular giving a great deal of attention to such sales methods.

Like most French makers, the Hurets had at first concentrated attention on improvements to dolls' bodies. The firm had been active since the middle of the century, and Mlle Huret's dolls were often marked with a stamp on the chest, reading, 'Maison Huret, No. 22, Boulevard Montmartre, Paris.' Several interesting advances were made by the firm, including the registering of a patent for a swivel that enabled a doll's head to turn or tilt. This invention made it possible for a much more realistic doll to be made, which could assume a varying character by the position of the head: at one time looking down shyly, at another with the head haughtily tilted upwards. The faces of Huret dolls are plumper and more child-like than those used by other makers, and are sometimes found mounted on well-articulated wooden ladies' bodies, instead of the more common gusseted kid that were cheaper.

The lady-dolls precisely reflect the period in which they were made, by the items that were thought necessary in their well-equipped trunks. Combs, mirrors, scent bottles, fans, purses, muffs and even little silver tea sets were all packed away, with the very necessary visiting-card cases, for this was a period when young girls were expected to make their own round of social calls as exercises in etiquette. In this period of ostentatious affluence, families who were fast increasing in wealth built large, pretentious houses and filled them with every conceivable type of ornamentation. Wives and children too were expected to look expensively dressed and pampered. For the first time, a great deal of money was lavished on furnishing and equipping the nursery, and the ladies' magazines gave helpful advice on how such rooms should be artistically decorated. This is the age of the great rocking-horses, big doll's houses and expensive toy prams; the French lady-dolls were simply another expensive addition, the dolls particularly suggesting the ostentation of upper middle-class social life, where display of both oneself and one's home became all-important. The 'trousseau tea' for instance, to which relatives and friends were invited to view the clothes of the bride, was typical of this type of conscious display, a display aped even by poor people in the expensive and unnecessary grandeur of their funerals.

It was once thought by collectors that these follies of French doll-making were intended as miniature copies of current French fashion, sent to dress-makers or clients as Pandoras. The fact that many of the dolls were dressed some-what retrospectively, and that it was much easier to send clients the current fashion journal, makes this hypothesis unlikely. The survival of the small children's advertising papers encouraging the purchase of new items for the dolls' wardrobes also establish the items as toys. The only true 'fashion figures' are those made for shops to display costume, or those commissioned by the eighteenth-century nobles as gifts to foreign princes. In either case, the conven-tion was that the figures should be either half or fully life-size. Despite the popular use of the term 'fashion doll' to describe bisque-headed lady-dolls, the phrase is to be avoided, as it leads to some confusion. The figures are more correctly described as lady-dolls or *Parisiennes*.

The conscious display of a girl's expensive dolls was encouraged, for the first time, by the marketing of specially-made dolls' stands. The use of these stands puts the doll into a strange limbo, between toy and ornamental figure. Shops such as *A la Poupée de Nurenberg*, *Au Nain Bleu* and *Madame Barrois* supplied dolls' wardrobes, gloves, trunks and accessories. At the outbreak of the Franco-Prussian War in 1870 Henry Cremer, of the London toyshop, rushed to Paris to buy up remaining stocks in case he would be unable to obtain the quality toys associated with his shop. He complained bitterly about the increase in price of dolls' stockings, which were apparently made not in Paris but in the provinces.

Making clothes for the figures that were equipped not only with dresses but also capes, skating costumes and even fancy dress provided work for an army of sewing women, milliners and leather workers, as the items that accompanied the dolls were made by craftsmen. The Jumeau company claimed at the end of the century that all their dolls' costumes were made at their own factory, but certainly many of the other doll-makers were supplied by outworkers, who slaved for very little in the awful conditions well known to readers of Victorian literature.

The doll-makers were passing into their most inventive period, and all types of body constructions were used. The gussetted leather body with individually-stitched fingers is the most common, as it was the cheapest. A new development was the leather bodies with bisque lower limbs that gave the figure much more realism. Others were made of beautifully-joined wood, in a much more sophisticated and updated version of the old Grödnertals. Metal-jointed armatures covered with white stockinette were used for others, which were made realistic by the use of bisque lower legs and hands. The dolls of this last type have stood the test of time most successfully, and can often be stood unsupported. The leather-bodied dolls have not fared at all well, as the sawdust with which they were often filled sometimes ran into the jointing and now forces the dolls to adopt a partly crouching position. One of the loveliest bodies was used by the Widow Clement, and was of pressed leather. The Jumeau firm used more than six different constructions, ranging from a simple cloth body to one of fine articulated wood. A rather odd combination of metal upper arms and bisque hands, together with wooden legs, was used by Terrene, while some of the Delphieu bodies were simply pink cloth.

All the French makers were keen to introduce new inventions and new materials into the construction of an already fine product. Rubber was used by several makers, as was the much older gutta-percha for limbs. From the collector's point of view these substances were very unsatisfactory, for they have often perished. A large number of patents for improvements were registered by firms such as Huret, Rohmer, Bru and Jumeau. One interesting invention from the Rohmer factory was for a head that was made to turn by a cord that ran through the head and down the body. Any new ideas were quickly incorporated by the makers, who appeared to care little for the laws concerning the use of another firm's patent. Jumeau, for instance, claimed so often that they had invented the swivel-head mechanism that for many years they were believed, and the older Huret patent was forgotten.

Fortunately for the present-day collector, many of the makers were proud of their creations, and stamped the name of their company on the chests of the dolls. A few even marked the backs of the heads. The Simonne mark in turquoise on the chest is particularly memorable, but little reliance can be placed on standard marks on the back of the head. Lady-dolls' bodies are often provided with reproduction heads, made in France and marked with appropriate stamps, usually referring to the Jumeau factory – a name which those who attempt to deceive are aware is known to almost every antique dealer. An unmarked doll is now often a much safer buy than one that appears to be fully attributable. Reproduction heads with 'FG' impressed in the china are also seen now, as the genuine dolls of this type have become popular, and the forger is never far behind.

It should not be assumed that all genuine *Parisiennes* are of good quality. Some are decidedly cheap, both in general construction and in dress. In particular I think of those dressed in the costumes of the French provinces, which often have

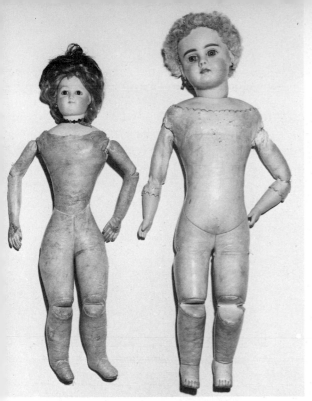

(*left*) 221 Two dolls with gusseted leather bodies showing the differences of construction between a French and a German adult type doll. *Parisienne* on left is 16¼ in. high.   222   *Parisiennes* were once thought to have been made as mannequin figures. These well-constructed model clothes are shown to indicate the standard used by dress-makers when creating working models for costume. Made at a shop in Paris known as The English Warehouse by Miss French *c*. 1900 to be sent as model to London fashion houses. 23 in.

little to commend them. Some genuine dolls are made of bisque of such poor quality that no self-respecting forger would consider using it!

Heads of very fine quality were marked 'FG', and dolls marked by this firm, or attributed to it, are current favourites. Some of these heads are mounted on the fine-quality, fully-articulated wooden bodies and are believed to have been made by Fernand Gaultier. Heads marked in this way are also found on the stockinette-covered bodies known to collectors as 'Gesland type'. As is the case with almost every type of *Parisienne*, it is also found on the basic kid body.

Though the lady-doll is usually associated with the swivel neck, quite a number were made in the old manner with rigid neck, a type of construction that is popularly referred to as 'Huret type', though usually unmarked. In the old trade catalogues, the dolls of this type were rather lower priced than those with the more realistic neck, and were often dressed as souvenir items. Quite good marked *Parisienne* heads are sometimes found on terracotta fisher-girls, that were sold particularly in Brittany. It is a temptation to remove these heads and put them on kid bodies to make the more conventional doll. If the temptation has to be succumbed to, the original body should be retained so that

333

the doll could be reassembled at a later date. It is often difficult to establish absolute originality, since if a child broke the head it would have been taken back to the shop for a replacement of the same size but (all too often) of a different make. Usually the collector has to be content with knowing that both the body and the doll are old, and that the two have been together for at least the last eighty years.

Of all the makers of *Parisiennes*, the Jumeau firm is the most famous. This maker's name is now known to every junk-market dealer. The first doll-collectors placed the products of this factory above almost every other, and made forgeries inevitable because of the good prices such dolls commanded. Fewer reproduction *Parisiennes* are seen in England at the time of writing than there were a few years ago; this is due to the fact that the basic lady-dolls no longer command such high prices in relation to other types of dolls, and also because dealers have become educated to the forgeries and no longer buy them. The current fakers of dolls have turned their attention to the very popular French *bébés*. The reproduction ladies do occasionally reappear, and are distinguished by the poor painting of the lips and brows and a lack of expression when compared with the older dolls.

The Jumeau firm was established as early as 1842, when a partnership existed with a certain Belton. By the time the firm was displaying its work at the Great Exhibition, Belton had already left. The jury thought very little of the German-made heads on the beautifully-dressed French dolls, and the Jumeau firm soon saw the advantage of manufacturing its own dolls' heads. Porcelain heads were made at the Jumeau factory at Montreuil-sous-Bois after 1873, possibly as a result of the Franco-Prussian War, which temporarily halted the supply of German heads. It is thought possible that some glazed china heads of a rather outdated style but with distinctly French faces were made by the firm at this early stage, but as none are marked this is difficult to ascertain. Some of the early Jumeau heads were made without the swivel mechanism, which the firm quickly pirated from the Huret establishment. Some early Jumeau bodies were also found with heads marked 'FG', which were probably bought from this maker either to supplement the early Montreuil heads or to predate the bisques made there.

From the 1860s to the end of the century, the Jumeau firm continued to make lady-dolls alongside the increasingly popular composition-bodied *bebés*. Both pink and white kid bodies were used, and the firm continued to use sawdust as a filling material, long after other French firms had progressed to fillings of cork or horsehair. The leather for such bodies was stretched, sometimes stiffened, and dried before the pieces were cut from metal templates. A few *Parisiennes* are hand sewn, but most were made on a sewing machine, as were their clothes.

Henri d'Allemagne described the Jumeau products as, "Dolls preserving the cachet of elegance and good taste which has always distinguished the productions of this house, in which are made not only dolls de luxe, but also ordinary dolls, with or without trousseaux, and whose prices have increased the important sale of dolls." From the period of the 1873 Vienna Exhibition, where the firm won a gold medal, the Jumeau Company continued to arouse admiration and commendation at the frequent trade fairs, culimating in a gold medal at the 1878 Paris Exhibition. The Jumeau 'Medaille d'Or' stamp on dolls' bodies refers to this award.

Though the type of body usually associated with the firm is that of sawdust-filled leather, other types were experimented with. Some were made with stockinette-covered metal bodies and others of wood, to which leather was shrunk before assembly. This last type is the most pleasing, as both the shape and the articulation have lasted well. Another version was made only of wood, with the attached bisque head, and yet another very rare type had moulded bisque high-heeled shoes. The shoulders of this rare doll were also given more detailed treatment than usual, being modelled much lower, to show the breasts and cleavage.

Many of these Jumeau *Parisiennes* are completely unmarked, or perhaps a stamped-on marking has rubbed away with time. Others probably carried paper labels which have fallen away. The completely authentic examples sometimes have some red letters or figures on the back of the head, or on later dolls of the type the 1878 'Medaille d'Or' stamp on the body. The applied-yesterday 'Deposée, Tête Jumeau' is to be avoided.

Some dealers have been known to apply a fake mark to a perfectly genuine, but completely unattributable, French lady-doll so that a higher price can be asked. Some experience of dolls of this type is advisable before buying, especially if the dealer refuses to give a receipt exactly describing both the date and the type of doll. Some claim that the reproduction dolls are over-smooth, others that they are too granular. I have seen reproductions of both kinds, and would advise extreme care in purchase. An unmarked, but genuinely old, *Parisienne* is infinitely preferable to those of spurious claim.

Large, well-made eyes are a feature of *Poupées Modèles*, and those of Jumeau in particular. The eyes were made by craftswomen who had developed great skill in making eyes from rods of glass, setting the pupils and iris into a well-shaped white. The coating of clear glass which the eye was given before annealing increased its luminosity. The most beautiful eyes were used on the *bébes*, as they were much bigger, but the smaller eyes used on the *Parisiennes* are also extremely fine.

Great care was taken in the arrangement of the doll's hair, which was made either of very fine human hair or of Tibetan goat. The heads were usually left open at the top and a cork pate was inserted. The open top allowed the workman to set in the eyes without any difficulty, and to repair them if necessary. The cork pate also provided a fine base to which a complicated hairstyle could be pinned. German bisque-headed dolls were made in this way to lower the duty cost, that was levied by weight, and this consideration must have played some part in the French use of the method.

Madame Jumeau, as well as Mlle Huret, concerned herself with both the exhibition and dressing of the dolls. Paris had hundreds of out-of-work sewing girls and milliners who had served an apprenticeship with famous dress-makers, and their skill was utilized in the creation of the dolls' stunning ensembles. The Jumeau firm in particular was very publicity-minded, and staged exhibitions of dolls in suitably-furnished rooms and miniature settings all over Europe and America. Part of the reason for their fame was the effort put into the promotion of the dolls. In 1897, Jumeau claimed that the most expensive dolls, including those sent to England, Spain and Germany every year as fashion models, were fully dressed at the Jumeau warehouse at the Rue Pastourelle.

Statements such as the above, and the report of the jury of the 1878 Paris Exposition, have misled generations of doll-collectors. The jury were sure that the pretty styles shown at the Exhibition would meet the requirements of the foreign dress-makers, who "use these little models that are so easy to transport anywhere, in order to spread the latest French fashion". The assumption was made that the dolls made by Calots, Bourgoin, Terrene and Chalte and Leborgne were intended as ambassadresses of fashion. Certainly their arrival in a provincial town must have made both the children and their mothers aware of the sumptuousness of French fashion, but the dolls were specially marketed as toys for children, and any use by dress-makers was incidental or possibly even a publicity-man's deceptive claim.

Examination of the original clothes of such dolls often reveals a lack of detail that a dress-maker would have found very necessary. The clothes were skilfully made for general effect, and many were designed in such a way that they were only suitable for dolls' wear. Edges were often very badly finished, and pinking shears were sometimes resorted to, instead of tedious hand-rolling of edges. Underwear is also usually very simple, despite the fact that by the 1860s the full-size counterpart was becoming much more decorative, and a genuine miniature fashion figure would have worn the necessary frilled and often

223   Lady-doll with jointed composition body of a type peculiar to Lanternier. Socket head modelled with great realism but in a poor-quality bisque. Open-closed mouth with moulded teeth. Head marked "J. E. Masson, S.O. Lorraine. No. 0 A.L. et Cie Limoges". 17½ in. high.

coloured underwear. A few very excellent *Parisiennes* are dressed in this way, but the majority have simple white cotton petticoats and drawers trimmed with the basic minimum of lace.

A miniature suit especially made for dress-makers use is illustrated, to show the standard that would have been necessary in a working garment. The difference between this and the clothes made purely for visual effect on a doll is obvious.

There are however some notable exceptions, such as those fine wax lady-dolls at the Victoria and Albert Museum which were dressed by Frederick Bosworth of New Burlington Street to show the fashion for 1903. These dolls are of course much bigger than the *Parisiennes*, which range in size between 10 and about 22 inches. The wax figures conform to the fashion model standard of being about half life-size.

Another exception is the dress models made to fit ordinary commercially-made dolls between 1880 and 1890 by Mrs J. A. Latter Axton, who was designer of 'styles' to Marshall and Snellgrove. One doll is dressed in a newly fashionable jersey and sash, a suit that was commissioned by Queen Victoria as a present for the daughter of the Duke of Edinburgh, and comprised a very up-to-date woollen jersey finished with a frilled and typically 1880s skirt. The ploughboy blouse of 1883 was made to appeal to ladies of an 'Arts and Crafts' inclination, and was beautifully smocked; my own particular favourite is a design for a dress for an Aesthetic lady, the mother perhaps of the du Maurier's infamous Cimabue-Browns! A few of these designs are so well executed that their intention as a detailed description of a most particular design is unmistakable.

The French lady-dolls are of great interest, for along with the ornate and tinted bisque ladies of the German makers they mark the peak of dolls made in imitation of the adult figure. After this climax, though some cheap dolls were made in the form of ladies, the attention of the quality makers passed to the manufacture of child-like *bébés*. Not all the lady-dolls were objects of great beauty: some were made of poor bisque, and others have very unlovely faces. The most unattractive have teeth, which give them an unpleasant leer, though being rare they are very desirable collectors' items. The 'Smiling Sister' dolls that are well known to American collectors are hardly beautiful, but are greatly prized for their rarity. These dolls have exquisitely-made, ball-jointed bodies, including joints at the waist and ankles, and have an incised 'J' for Jumeau on the back of the head. Not all the lady-dolls are even well proportioned; some have arms that are far too short, and others, in particular the leather-bodied Jumeaus, often have slightly over-long arms and the usual small hands. The dolls with the painted eyes also usually tend to look rather mean in comparison with the best examples.

There are only a few marked Bru lady-dolls, although the firm, which was in operation from the 1860s, made a large number. The advertisements stated that *Parisiennes* were made, but as so few are marked, they have to be attributed by likeness to authenticated items. Some heads marked 'B & S' are thought possible Brus, but there is little to prove the assumption. Those that are generally accepted as having been made by Bru have a very pale bisque in comparison with the *bébés* made by the same company, which are of a rather dark colour. In 1869 Bru registered a patent for a slim, beautifully-articulated doll of moulded rubber that was fully jointed. Dolls of this type, but unmarked, have been found, and it is difficult to be sure whether they in fact came from Bru or from one of the other makers, who were all quick to pirate the new ideas. Various collectors and dealers will assure the curious that they can always tell a Bru, but as one will claim a certain doll is definitely a Bru while another equally knowledgeable person will state that the same item is a Jumeau, the wise collector accepts as authentic only the item that carries some proof, such as a label or mark.

An extensive subsidiary industry spread around the luxury dolls. Carpenters made small well-constructed wooden wardrobes for their linen and costumes, and even small laundry trunks that often accompanied the ladies were made in a wide range, from cheap examples of cardboard covered in imitation-leather paper to brass-bound, correctly-made miniatures. Some of the clothes that appear to be commercially manufactured were made up at home, with the help of patterns for dresses and underwear which were given in children's and ladies' magazines. Patterns for all sorts of rather unlikely excursions were given and, when made up, were often of as high a standard as those made by the *Parisienne* dress-makers.

French lady-dolls used to be very expensive in comparison with other dolls, but the gap has narrowed in recent years, and other types, such as good character dolls, have almost overtaken them. In part this is due to the fact that collectors became unsure of the authenticity of examples and so began to avoid purchase, which depressed the price. Fully-marked and attributable dolls of the type command excellent prices, especially those with a trousseau. Though the basic dolls can still be purchased quite reasonably, any with an unusual body construction or facial expression are eagerly bought by established collectors.

TWELVE

FRENCH DOLL-MAKERS

The idealization of children by late nineteenth-century writers and illustrators reached most unhealthy proportions. Death, birth, beauty of nature and character were all linked to a child's supposed understanding of these things and sentimentalized beyond all reason. Books with titles such as *Jessica's First Prayer*, *Pictures for our Pets*, or *Spring Flowers and Spring Blossoms for the Young and Good* suggest the rather sickly relationship between author, illustrator and the imaginary child, whose spirit was to be a continual source of moral inspiration for world-tarnished adults. Christmas cards, scrap screens, photograph albums and workboxes all carried the beautiful and idealized childish image which the general buying public obviously much appreciated.

It was inevitable that the sugary paintings and prints of children with flowers and pets should be succeeded by child-like dolls, large eyed and beautifully dressed, which made their initial appeal to the adults who purchased the toys. The doll-makers modelled an idealized and perfected child, and many of the early French *bébés* have faces that are too stylized ever to be seen in nature. With their huge eyes and perfection of feature, they do not always appeal to the modern taste for a more lifelike doll, and many collectors claim actually to dislike the faces of the early French *bébés*.

The description *bébé* was used to refer to a doll made in imitation of a child between the age of eight and twelve. The Bru *bébé*, with its well-developed bust, would appear rather older, and some of the later dolls made by S.F.B.J. were intended to represent chubby toddlers; but generally the French makers aimed at a portrayal of a child in a pre-adolescent stage. Though various firms have laid claim to having made the first dolls of this type, it is difficult to establish the true innovator. The likelihood is that, as with the *Parisiennes*, all the firms were pirating and developing new ideas at approximately the same speed, and any

224 Variations on the sailor suit made so popular by the royal children were worn by dolls as well. This jointed composition doll with bisque socket head is marked "Ste C". Also marked for Steiner on hip. Type referred to as Bourgoin Steiner. Closed mouth, applied ears. Separately-moulded big toe that is a characteristic of the firm's work. 18 in. high.

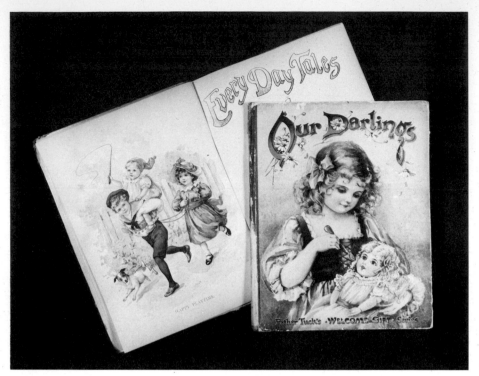

(*above*) 225 The sentimental approach to children is typified by these illustrations from late nineteenth-century books. (*below left*) 226 The Steiner label can be clearly seen in this jointed example with fixed wrists. Closed mouth, pierced ears. One brow painted higher than the other and the eyes also set unevenly. Impressed "J. Steiner, Bte. SGDG. Paris. Fre A.9". 16 in. high. (*below right*) 227 Typical early French ball-jointed body marked with the Jumeau Medaille d'Or stamp. The very cut-away head is also typical of good French bisque heads. 15 in. high.

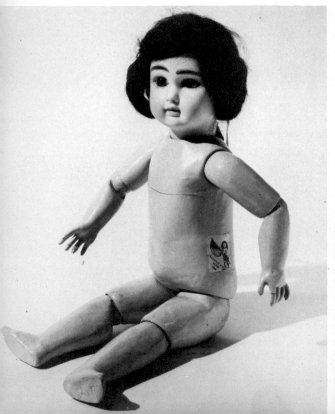

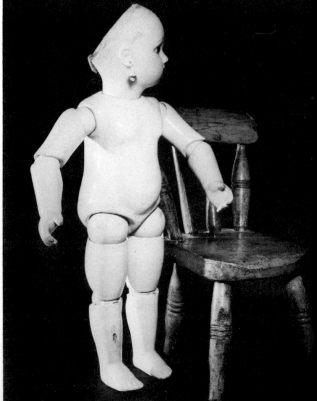

advantage would only have been held for a very short while. Steiner was among the firms that claimed in advertisements to have invented the new type of doll, but a counter-claim was made for *Bébé Bijou* that Grandjean was the true innovator.

Considerable impetus was given to the doll-makers by the very short but far reaching Franco-Prussian War of 1870–1, which culminated in the fall of the Empire. The French loathed the Germans as a result of this conclusion, and were eager to overcome them in any possible way. Even the child's doll was not considered too humble to participate in this racial hatred.

At the time of the war, both Bru and Charles Parent were making tentative experiments with the ball-jointing methods used by all the French makers in the 1880s. It is generally believed that ball-jointing of dolls' bodies with wire or cord did begin in France, though the basis of the method is logically traced back to the Grödnertals and jointed lay figures that the Germans made so successfully. The new French method used wire or sometimes pins for the articulation of joints, though these two methods were superseded by the use of rubber, which allowed a much tighter stringing of the doll than was possible with cord. Some of the early Jumeau ball-jointed *bébés* were strung with cord or wire, and were not intended to be as closely strung as modern collectors think desirable. Few dolls are found now with their original joining method left intact, as all too often the cords broke or the wire rusted, and elastic was substituted.

Some of the French vindictiveness towards the Germans can be seen in a booklet which Jumeau enclosed in dolls' packaging at the beginning of the 1880s. The book took the form of a letter supposedly written by the doll to its new owner, in which it scoffed at the ridiculously ugly German dolls with their stupid faces of waxed cardboard, goggle eyes and poor bodies. The sounds emitted by these cheap German toys were likened to the cries of an animal, and the doll considered it far better to be silent, as she was, rather than make such dreadful noises. Another example of the firm's clever utilization of packaging for the purposes of advertisement came shortly after the building of the Eiffel Tower. Dolls were sent to America wrapped in a sheet of paper that opened out to reveal a game representing a race up the new tower. The two supposed contestants in the race were a German doll carrying the national flag, and a lovely French doll who stood on a pedestal holding aloft the tricolour.

The new French dolls were items of pure luxury and typical of the beautiful frivolities that the Anglo-Saxon associates with late nineteenth-century France. Most of the doll-makers had prestige showrooms in Paris, though their actual factories were in the suburbs or even the provinces. Many of the potteries were in the Montreuil area, where skilled potters could work between factories, and similarly the costumiers and assemblers of dolls worked in one area of Paris. The makers were able to draw upon several useful labour sources for the construction of their dolls. The large number of poorly-paid Parisian dress-makers was an obvious choice for stylish costuming and equipping of the dolls, while prisoners in French gaols were used for the finishing of parts before assembly. The prisoners are also believed actually to have painted the features of dolls for some companies. Jumeau obtained worthwhile publicity by employing orphan girls and undertaking to guard their welfare, in a philanthropic manner typical of the late nineteenth century.

The very frequent trade exhibitions enabled the French makers to astound the public by the superiority of their products, and they became highly skilled in presenting their wares in the most attractive manner. Being fully aware of the fact that they could not hope to compete with the Germans in the making of low-priced dolls, they at first diverted their energy into luxury products, such as the dolls which they had exhibited at the 1867 World Exhibition, which wore cashmere shawls and cost over 600 francs each!

Despite their obvious dislike of the Germans, the doll-makers were unable to be completely independent. Some of the makers are thought to have maintained some trade links with that country, by obtaining parts or sometimes even heads for the dolls. Neither did the Parisian doll shops stop trading in German dolls, though they were often repacked in France in attractive boxes that suggested a French origin. Often the doll itself was re-dressed in the French style. Shops such as *Au Nain Bleu* and *Au Paradis des Enfants* sold both French and German dolls, though the German makers often gave their dolls titles such as *Bébé Cosmopolite* or *Mon Trésor* as an aid to the marketers, who often wished to conceal their origin.

The earliest *bébés* were a development of the kid lady-dolls and have similarly made, but very much thicker bodies. A lady-doll and a German leather are photographed alongside one another, so that the difference of shape can be clearly seen. The larger doll was cork filled for lightness, but most were still stuffed with the unsatisfactory sawdust. The wooden ball-jointed bodies freed the doll-makers from the tedious process of filling the fabric or leather bodies, and made it possible for them to create dolls that, if cared for properly, were almost indestructible. The makers thought it appropriate to term such products *Bébés Incassables* or unbreakable child dolls. The phrase was used by many of the doll-makers, so its presence on a label or stamp gives only an indication of the country of origin.

Many small firms such as Blampoix, Denameur and *Aux Enfants de France* made *bébés*, some registering patents and consequently labelling their dolls 'Bébé Breveté'. Some of these small makers ran their own shops in the city, but others provided only the stock for the toyshops that were famed for the variety and splendour of their merchandise. These toyshops remained open until late at

344

night, in order to persuade the pleasure-seeking adults to take home a gift for the children. At Christmas and holiday times, the toyshops also stayed open to catch the late custom. Most ran their own repair service, and a doll could be immediately fitted with a new wig, or a fine dress could be chosen from the wide range that was temptingly displayed.

Though the *Parisiennes* were still selling very well in the 1880s, the *bébés* were fast overtaking them, despite the fact that they were more expensive. This higher cost was incurred because each part had to be individually lathe-turned and drilled, and the whole of the assembly had to take place in the factory, whereas the old leather bodies could be sewn by outworkers. It was only when the composition substance was used instead of wood for limbs that the child dolls became really cheap.

Some of the dolls exhibit such a difference of standard and finish that it is difficult to believe that they came from the same factory. The dolls of Jules Nicholas Steiner are a case in point. Some of the heads are almost amusingly ugly, with grinning mouths revealing a double row of moulded teeth, while some of the closed-mouth *bébés* are quite extraordinarily beautiful. The Steiner Company, one of the oldest in France, was established in 1855, and from the 1860s onwards was continually registering patents, many of which related to mechanical improvements. The walking Steiner, which is key-wound and raises its arms while crying 'mama', is popular with collectors despite the fact that a very ugly head with upper and lower teeth was used. The makers' mark is not carried, as it usually is, on the doll's head, but is found on the mechanism, which is concealed under the cardboard dome which supports the skirt. The Steiner advertisements boasted of their success in manufacturing other dolls that walked and talked, as well as the very popular *bébés* which they proudly claimed to have invented.

The Steiner baby that turns its head from side to side and kicks its legs in the air can be seen in several collections, though it could hardly have been an exciting toy. A more far-reaching invention was a method of causing a doll to sleep by means of a wire that controlled the eyes, and was worked by a lever from the side of the head, just above the ears. Two turns on this lever caused the eyes to close.

After 1889, a label showing a girl carrying a banner is often found on the bodies of the dolls. When the firm was not using its various mechanical inventions, it created much more attractive dolls. Their *bébés* are very lovely, and are characterized by gentle faces with very heavy brows. Most French *bébés* wear a pate of cork, but those found on Steiners are usually of purple cardboard. A characteristic purple undercoat was used on the wooden bodies before the flesh colour was applied, and this can sometimes be seen through chips in the surface colour or around the ball-joints. Another characteristic of the Steiner dolls is that they usually have fingers of the same length. A big toe that is separated from the smaller toes is another well-known feature.

Sometimes heads are marked 'Le Parisien' and a further mark such as 'Le Petit Parisien, Bébé Steiner' is put on the body. Some of the dolls also carry the name Bourgoin. Most of the inventions were patented and the majority of medals were won while the firm was under the leadership of its founder, Jules Steiner. Like most of the other makers, the Steiners experimented with rubber as a doll-making medium, and by 1872, the firm claimed to be producing five different types of *bébé*. These included the basic *bébé* and others that slept, walked, talked or were mechanical in some other way. Despite the fact that the collector of today prefers dolls with fixed wrists, at the time of making the dolls with jointed wrists were considered more progressive.

The negro and mulatto babies made by most of the French makers were something quite new in the doll world. A few rare black dolls had been produced, but it was not until the development of the *bébé* that really lovely-coloured dolls were made. Some of the most attractive are those with a *café au lait* tinting that was intended to represent a mulatto child. These coloured *bébés* were extremely popular in the United States, and in the French colonies, though they are very difficult to find in England.

The Gesland factory made particularly sturdy bodies of wood. Though the surface paint tends to flake away, these heavy and very solid bodies have lasted in excellent condition to the present time. This firm, it will be remembered, was also responsible for some of the best lady-dolls' bodies, though it is not known for sure whether they actually manufactured heads or used those supplied by other makers, such as Fernand Gaultier. The illustrated Gesland doll has a bisque socket head, but another marked version of the same model was made in composition and mounted on a shoulder plate, so that this particular model appears to be one of the few that can be attributed to the firm itself.

The illustrated doll (237) raises the question of the dolls with solid crowns to their heads. The dolls made in this way are usually unmarked and are popularly referred to as Belton type, though no connection can be traced back to the maker whose association with Jumeau was so short. Some of these dolls have heads that are completely bald, while others can have as many as four holes in a flattened area of the bisque at the top of the head. It was often thought that these holes were for tying on a removable wig, but since many of the type have been found with their original wigs very firmly and obviously deliberately stuck in place, the explanation can only hold in a few cases. The illustrated doll has a spring at the top of the head, which links with the body and obviates the necessity for a

228   Very pale bisque, marked "Eden Bébé" with six moulded teeth. Body also marked with blue stamp. 18 in. high.

wooden disc at the neck. Perhaps at some stage in the development of the *bébé* this wooden disc was considered unsatisfactory, as it does sometimes slip from its correct position, and this alternative method was devised. No doubt eventually a description on a box or an old trade catalogue will solve this question, which is a continual puzzle to collectors.

The Huret establishment, primarily famed for the making of *Parisiennes*, turned to the construction of jointed *bébés*, and like Gesland created dolls of very high quality, those made by Huret, however, having particularly well-made tongued and grooved joints. Fernand Gaultier is yet another manufacturer whose fame lies mainly in the making of lady-dolls, but he too made some very beautiful child dolls with huge eyes and the rather petulant expression so typical of the *bébés*. 'F.G.' *bébés* are much harder to find than their lady-dolls, and they command a very substantial price.

The dolls that bear the words 'A. Marque' also present collectors with a problem. They are at present completely unattributable, and only around twenty are recorded, over half of which are in museums. They appear to be of French origin and have the typical body and pierced ears associated with that country. They are not always considered beautiful, as they have sharp faces with pointed chins and look later than the *bébés* already discussed. They are usually made with the long lower legs more typical of twentieth-century dolls, and resulted from the fact that fashionable short skirts showed up the rather unlovely jointing at the knees, and forced the makers to make adjustments in length. Whatever their true attribution might be, the dolls are desirable purely for their rarity.

The manufacturing of quality dolls in France was extremely competitive, and though prices were kept as low as possible, many makers were forced to rely on unusual inventions that would give their products 'novelty value', a phrase that appears to have been quite irresistible to our nineteenth-century ancestors. Schmitt developed a very complicated method of laying wax over bisque, a process which he obviously thought would make the dolls' heads more attractive. I cannot help but wonder what happened when the wax eventually flaked away. Did a beautiful tinted bisque face emerge, or just a dull grey china!

Rabery and Delphieu, who had made lady-dolls from the middle years of the century, also turned their attention to the making of *bébés* with, at first, white or pink kid bodies. During the 1870s, these leather bodies, with simple pin swivel-jointing methods, are often referred to by the makers as jointed dolls, and a distinction has to be drawn between these and the later double-jointed dolls of wood or composition with which collectors are more familiar. Most of the dolls that are marked 'R.D.' are typical of the better French products, with thick eyebrows, moulded teeth and a cork pate to the head; but as is the case with almost every manufacturer, there are exceptions that are of a poor standard. In

(*above*) 229　Jointed *bébé* marked "E.J." for Emile Jumeau. The blue eyes are unusual for type. Ball-jointed body fixed wrists. An unusual small size. 10 in. high.　(*below left*) 230　Coloured bisque shoulder head with swivel neck. Marked "Bru Jne". Replaced eyes. Most of the French companies made coloured dolls ranging in shade from a soft brown to an almost black colour. $14\frac{1}{2}$ in. high.　(*below right*) 231　Bisque, closed-mouth swivel head on jointed composition body. Pierced ears. Fleece wig. Marked "Déposé E 6 J" on neck for Emile Jumeau. 15 in. high.

the 1880s and 1890s, when every doll-maker turned his attention to the making of figures that could at least talk or walk, Rabery and Delphieu patented several improvements of their own. Among their other specialities were *marottes* and dolls that said 'mama' and 'papa' by pulling a string that moved a simple bellows inside the torso.

In the products of the Lanternier factory of Limoges can be studied the variety of manufacturing standard of which the French makers were capable. Lanternier at its best made good-quality dolls, with bisque of a very acceptable standard and precise painting of detail. One in my own collection bears a strong facial resemblance to dolls from the Jumeau factory, and is made doubly attractive by large green paperweight eyes. Another, in comparison, has a very poorly-made body and a face of an unpleasant white powdery bisque that has little appeal. Despite the often poor quality of the china, surprising in an area such as Limoges, the moulds used for the dolls were quite pleasant, one of their advertisements claiming that the House of Lanternier was renowned for the heads of *bébés*.

Lanternier was one of the three French companies selected by Sèvres for help in making porcelain heads, but whether the help was useful it is difficult to judge, as there appears to be no one time at which the quality of the heads suddenly improved. Frequently at small country auctions, the Lanternier dolls of poor quality fetch very good prices quite simply because they carry a French mark, for there is a general, but uninformed, belief among small antique dealers that all French dolls are worth more than those made in Germany. No doubt when the general dealers attempt to sell the poor-quality dolls to specialist dealers or collectors they are surprised to be told that the balance is now almost redressed, and a good German doll is worth far more than one that is French but of an inferior standard. This statement would not have been true as little as five years ago, which says much for the sense and taste of present-day collectors.

Fleischmann and Blodel are an interesting company, as they are typical of the trade links that continued, despite racial animosity, between France and Germany. The firm had its origins in Bavaria, but also opened a Paris branch which advertised that *Bébés Incassables* were made for export, and that samples of German articles were also stocked. Among the firm's range were dolls that slept, walked and talked, and a patent was registered in 1892 for a doll that walked and turned its head. One attractive version appeared to throw kisses when a button was pressed, and the doll also turned its head from side to side. The company is known in particular to collectors as the maker of 'Eden Bébé', a doll that, like many others that appear to be French, has been found with the Simon and Halbig mark on the head. The firm was even more active than others in the registering of patents, and was so successful that, after its amalgamation into S.F.B.J., Fleischmann became head of the French firm. As a result of the outbreak of the First World War the firm's property was sequestered and its head deported.

Though the bisque of some of the most expensive French dolls is very fine, the general quality of bisque used in German dolls is much better. Even Jumeau quite often used bisque of which both colours and texture are far short of perfection. The standard of the best German dolls is in fact often better than that of the French, though the French dolls are made very attractive because of the superiority of the huge eyes that they used. The very fine-quality bisque was made by allowing the kaolin mixture to macerate in water for an unusually long period before it was used. The Jumeau factory strained and filtered this mixture again and again through successively finer strainers, the last being said to resemble a fine silk tissue. Some of the very large French heads were made in the old pressed manner, but the majority were poured into the moulds, which was a much faster method.

After the heads had dried out and contracted a little from the plaster moulds, the two parts were joined together and the eye sockets cut out. A better-quality doll can be recognized by the care taken in the hand-finishing, such as the thinning down of the cast around the eyes to give a soft, natural effect instead of a sudden ridge. At this stage the ears would be pierced, either through the ear lobe or simply right into the head. Any collector who has been forced to remove the doll's wig simply to repair the fixing of an ear-ring will know which was the better method. Large dolls of good quality are characterized by the separate application of moulded ears, rather than those that were cast in one with the head. The applied ears can be distinguished by the very positive modelling and by the joining line that can be traced almost all around the ear, giving the impression that it could almost be lifted away.

The heads were fired for about twenty-six hours, and any irregularities were afterwards filed away before they were passed to the decorators. Two coats of colour were often applied, and the details of brows, lips, nostrils and the characteristic black lining around the eyes, as well as the cheek colouring, were added before the heads were re-fired at a lower temperature for a short while. New moulds had to be made continually, as only around forty to fifty heads could be taken from one before it became chipped or damaged.

The sewing women who had clothed the *Parisiennes* turned their attention to creating fashionable outfits for the *bébés*, for which the complicated children's clothes of the time provided good models. The large bonnets and hats, balanced by full petticoats and skirts gathered to a low waistline, are typically French. Some *bébés* in original clothes were however dressed quite simply, in frocks that fell from a gathered yoke just below the sleeves, rather like the later smocks that Edwardian children wore. Though the sewing machine was in general factory use, it is surprising how many dolls' dresses were still commercially made by hand. Probably it was felt that many of the small garments were easier to make in this way. The shoes often carry the doll-maker's name, though obviously shoes were passed from one doll to another over the years, and marked footwear cannot be taken as a reliable indication of origin. The shoes now fetch a considerable amount in their own right, as they give a touch of authenticity to a good doll.

Smaller *bébés* were often sold laid out neatly on top of their clothes in a trunk. A change of wigs and shoes as well as the more obvious dresses was sometimes given. It is now quite difficult to find the dolls complete with their trousseaux, but they were originally sold for as little as 10s. 6d. from Charles Morrell of Oxford Street, who was also able to supply a top-quality version for around £3 in 1896. Marion Howard Spring, who was born in 1890, wrote a charming description of a small red-leather trunk she was given by her mother one Christmas morning. When she opened the trunk, she found inside a lovely doll with a complete wardrobe of clothes, all exquisitely hand-made, including stockings, dressing gown and a fine brown velvet coat and bonnet.

The idea of a doll contained in a trunk is not one that can be considered as having a great deal of appeal for children. I distinctly remember as a small child being very concerned lest my dolls should suffocate under their blankets, and the thought of putting the doll into a trunk of clothes would have appalled me. No doubt the manufacturers thought more of the attractiveness of the gift pack than of its effect on the sensibilities of small girls.

Dolls became so complicated both in construction and dress by the end of the century that the jury of the St Petersburg Exhibition of 1903 were moved to criticize the over-elaboration of the French dolls, rather as the Montanari family had been castigated at the 1851 Exhibition in England. When dolls reach the stage where their main purpose is to perform some complicated and, to the child, probably uninteresting movement, they become a thing of swivel pins, rods and metal work that holds little illusion. A lady writing about her childhood in Edwardian England remembered how her own illusions about her French doll were shattered. "I never felt the same about Marguerite after her wig came off and I saw the horrid mechanism that made the lovely eyes open and shut; a crude piece of lead! My father glued the hair on again, but now I knew what was going on underneath!"

Jumeau

Like most of the other French doll-makers, the firm of Jumeau was established in the middle years of the nineteenth century. They at first made lady-dolls,

33 Fine-quality Bru doll

sometimes with glazed china heads but more often of bisque, which they produced at their factory at Montreuil. After 1875 they were rushed along, together with the other doll-makers, into the competitiveness of doll-making innovations, and became the leading French company in both output and reputation.

Jumeau operated on a modest scale at the Rue Mauconseil before rapid expansion necessitated a move to the more convenient Rue Pastourelle, in the centre of the doll-making area of Paris. The elder son, who had been expected to follow Pierre Françoise the founder, died, and Emile, who had actually trained as an architect, was to continue, expand and improve the business. The expansion of the Jumeau products which had already begun was very much accelerated after Emile took over the firm in 1876.

Some manufacturers had advertised *bébés* in the 1850s, though it is probably lady dolls that are referred to, and they were then probably of the leather-bodied type, although a few also contained voice mechanisms. Until the late 1860s the firm used either the traditional heads obtained from Germany or the bisque heads made by Fernand Gaultier; but then a silver medal was won for the making of dolls' heads, as well as the bodies and clothes which had previously won commendation. Jumeau himself stated that *Bébé Jumeau* was sold only after 1879, but earlier examples are claimed in several collections, and many of the statements made by the company in the course of advertising are misleading.

The manufacture of Jumeau dolls was described in a book written by Léo Claretie, who visited the factory in 1895 and was astonished at the complex processes that were necessary in the making of a comparatively simple toy. A few of the comments and descriptions are rather suspect, such as that relating to the cutting out of eye sockets after firing! In the main, Claretie's description does provide an interesting general survey of the factory at the time.

The metal-workers' shop was first visited, where copper wire was twisted into hooks for stringing, springs and rings. The tools and machinery necessary for the complete construction of the doll were made in a well-equipped blacksmith's shop. Here were made the steel moulds into which the composition bodies were pressed.

After the papier mâché had dried out a little, the two parts of the metal moulds were taken apart and the bodies allowed to dry slowly. The writer describes the dirty green colour of the moulded torsos before painting. This colour was in fact variable, according to the waste materials used in the mixture, and dolls are found in several shades ranging from grey to blue or brown. Hands had to be made solid, and a better-quality mixture was used, usually of brown or fawn. There is a tradition that many of the hands were stamped out by outworkers, who had their own machines, but this would appear contrary to the Jumeau policy of centralizing and modernizing all the methods of production. At the

34   Group of character babies
35   Group of Oriental baby dolls
36   Miniature German soldier

time of the visit, the hands were seen being made at the factory and lying in piles beneath the machine.

After describing the method of stringing the jointed doll, the writer passed on to the shoemakers, where the dolls were fitted with shoes of 'a beautiful reddish-brown leather', machine-stitched to imitate a real shoe. The footwear at the factory was decorated with rosettes, ribbons, cockades and imitation buttons. Some of the shoes seen were large enough to be worn, according to the writer, by a six-year-old child. These shoes were probably for the dolls which the firm sold as window models for the display of children's clothes. On the workroom wall hung a chart showing all the different types and sizes of shoes made.

An interesting description is given of how the wigs, made either of real hair or Tibetan goat, were curled. Lengths of hair were rolled on wooden curling pins, wrapped in paper and then boiled. They were dried out in a gas-heated oven, a process which fixed the curls very firmly in place. It was believed that after this treatment the ringlets and curls would never drop out of position. Some of the wigmakers were at work making wigs with plaits at the back and curls at the front of the head. Many of these original Jumeau wigs were actually

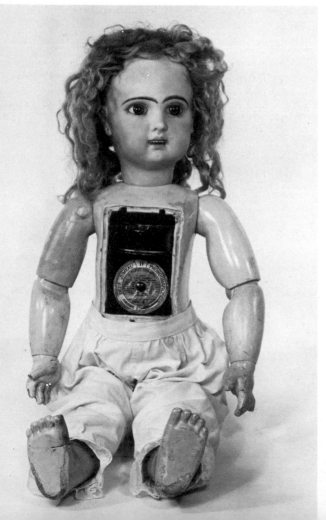

232   Phonograph talking doll. Head marked "Déposé Tête Jumeau 11." The mandrel with Lioret Jumeau label. Composition body containing movement. Winding key and stop-start lever at back. 25 in. high.

233   Edwardian postcard showing a girl of the period with an unmistakably Jumeau doll.

Mon cher bébé et sa Maman
Vous adressent un compliment

quite simple, and it always seems such a pity that in order to make the dolls more striking, many dealers substitute new wigs of long ringlets for the originals.

In the sewing-room, the walls were covered with patterns of dresses and designs for outfits. The pattern pieces were cut in metal so that they could be used without distortion. The women were seated at their sewing machines stitching underwear. All types of feathered hats, dresses, capes and coats were in process of manufacture, and one group of women spent their time in dressing the dolls and arranging their hair before they were sent off to be packed in boxes. Over the whole factory hung the unpleasant smell of dry glue and rancid paper from the area where the bodies were made, but the costuming department was evidently a colourful and attractive scene.

The finished dolls were taken from the factory at Montreuil to the main showroom at the Rue Pastourelle. Madame Jumeau was responsible for the selection of designs for the dresses, which were submitted to her from all over France. The 1879 advertisements claimed that the dresses were made of wool, foulard or silk, though some are believed to have been dressed in knitted or crocheted outfits. Among the more expensive outfits was a fur coat of Mongolian lamb, and matching hats and muffs could also be bought. Dolls dressed for confirmation, the seaside or winter with coats and matching gaiters were all made, in surprising detail. Extra dresses, socks, shoes and underwear could be purchased separately or as a complete trousseau in a small trunk. Silks, satins, lace and wool were all used in the creation of correct outfits. Though many of the dresses at first glance appear very complicated in construction, it is often surprising how simply made they actually were, and how effective were the results. It is questionable whether all the clothes were made at the factory itself, though the firm certainly claimed this, and the outworker method was never as popular in France as in Germany.

Much of Jumeau's success was due to its marketing skill. The dolls were displayed with their accessories in cases at the Paris showroom, and exhibitions of beautifully-arranged dolls were held as far apart as Melbourne, New York and London. In competition with all the leading doll-makers, including Bru, the firm won a gold medal at the 1878 Paris Exposition, and it is this medal that is referred to by the 'Medaille d'Or' stamp on the bodies of subsequent dolls. Three years after this award, Jumeau warned the public not to buy any dolls that were not marked with his name, and all the dolls were packed in boxes which read 'Bébé Jumeau, Diplôme d'Honneur, Medaille d'Or 1878.

The advertisements which the company wrote for both the French and English-speaking markets made much of the dolls' eyes, which they described rather off-puttingly as 'human'. The best-quality eyes were those with fibres which ran realistically outwards from the pupil, and are referred to by collectors

356

as *yeux fibres*. In a day's work, a skilled craftswoman could make around 120 pairs. Ordinary dolls' eyes could, in comparison, be made at the rate of about 400 a day. Earlier eyes were made by a three-part process, but a cheaper method was used after 1890. The eye-makers worked in small groups over bunsen burners with their rods of coloured glass, and were nearly all women, who were thought to be more skilled at this work.

The earliest method used by the French makers of creating a doll that appeared to sleep was by making the eyelid move rather than the eye itself. Jumeau introduced this particular improvement to dolls' eyes in 1885, and his version moved by means of a lever at the back of the head. Attention was continually given to eye improvements, and versions were made that could move from side to side, known to collectors as glancing or flirting eyes. In 1897 the commonly-found type of sleeping eyes was introduced: these worked by means of a lead weight.

The better Jumeaus are very pale in colour and made of the smoothest bisque imaginable. The huge, rather round eyes are another desirable characteristic, as the eyes of later dolls became much smaller in proportion to the face because of the trend towards naturalism. Fixed eyes are some indication of an early date, but some of the much smaller late eyes were also fixed in position. Most popular of all to collectors is the so-called 'Long-faced Jumeau', which is one of the earlier models, and is usually found on a ball-jointed body. The ball-jointing of these early French *bébés* is not to be confused with that of the German dolls, which is much more clumsy. An early ball-jointed Jumeau is shown undressed, to make this clear.

Closed-mouth *bébés* are almost invariably more expensive. The long-faced, closed-mouth Jumeau with a ball-jointed body and large eyes, such as that illustrated in colour, is the most sought-after specimen. The bodies are marked with the Jumeau stamp, the heads carrying only an incised number. Some of the early dolls, such as that illustrated undressed, have large almond-shaped eyes. American collectors sometimes refer to these as portrait Jumeaus. The English collector, however, uses the term 'portrait' for the later dolls that resemble actual children, and a good example of a portrait Jumeau is also shown. Many of the heads of the most desirable collector's Jumeaus are unmarked, except for a number, and have to be attributed either by appearance or by the mark on the body, which has all too often rubbed almost away.

In 1892, in an attempt to sell a cheaper and more competitive doll, Jumeau introduced two new models with a twenty to forty per cent difference in price from the standard dolls. These economy dolls did not carry the Jumeau name.

234 It is unusual for a doll to retain its original wig in as fine a condition as this *bébé*. Closed mouth, applied ears, brown fixed eyes. Marked "L" in red. 26 in. high.

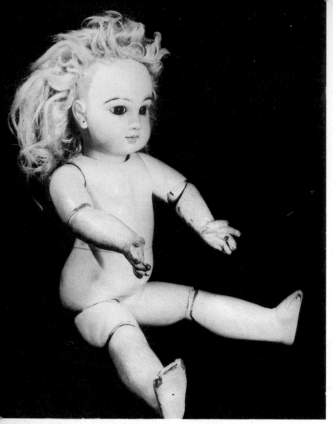

(*above left*) 235 Closed-mouth *bébé* with applied pierced ears, fixed eyes, well-painted brows. Stamped "Déposé Tête Jumeau. Bte. S.G.D.G.9." 20 in. high. (*above right*) 236 *Bébé* with large fixed grey eyes. Pierced ears, open mouth with teeth, early type of ball-jointed body. Head marked "Jullien". Paris maker, 1863–1904. 16½ in. high. (*below*) 237 Very heavy carved wooden body marked in circle "E.G.", probably for Gesland. Wig removed to show original spring to which stringing of body is attached. Closed mouth, pierced ears. Heads of this type referred to as "Beltons". 22 in. high.

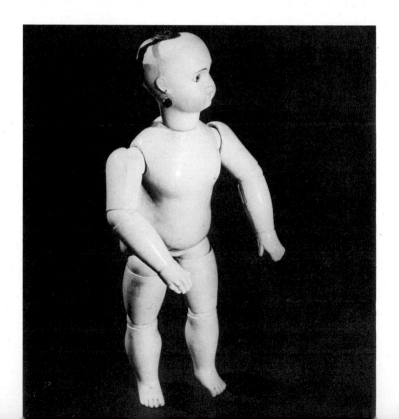

238 Closed-mouth bisque-headed doll with fixed brown eyes. Closed mouth. Impressed "E.J." on head for Emile Jumeau. 23 in. high.

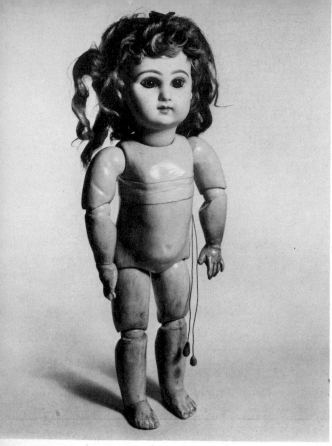 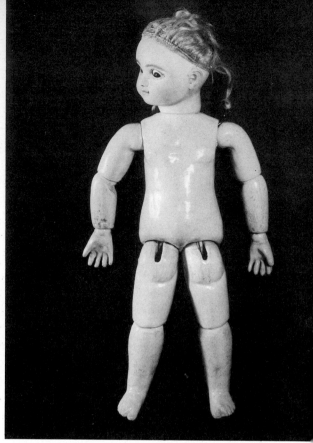

(*left*) 239   Closed-mouth *bébé* with strings to torso for voice box. Leather strip joins the cut torso together. Later type of French body with jointed wrists. 17 in. high.   (*right*) 240   Jointed *bébé* with head turned to show lever at side of head that opens and closes eyes. Marked "J. Steiner, Bte. S.G.D.G. Paris". 12½ in. high.

It is dolls that fall into this category that cause most confusion, and enable the unscrupulous to claim that any unmarked but vaguely French-looking doll is a Jumeau.

Coloured dolls were produced alongside the more conventional pink-tinted versions, and the mulatto almond-eyed Jumeau is one of the most attractive of the type. The coloured dolls are now quite difficult to find in Europe, as the majority were exported at the time of manufacture to the United States.

The dolls were made, dressed, packed and dispatched from the Jumeau factory in order, so the company claimed, that the shopkeeper might have as much profit as possible when reselling the items. At the Vienna Exhibition, there was some surprise over the good quality of the dolls in relation to their price, which was considered very attractive.

Mechanical Jumeaus have a double appeal, as dolls and automata, and are consequently expensive to buy. The best Jumeau heads are not often seen on automata, as fairly small heads were commonly used, but there are obvious exceptions. The mechanical dolls were assembled by other makers, who merely purchased the heads from the factory. There is, at present, no firm evidence to suggest that any automata were constructed by the firm itself. Among the more

360

241 Bisque *bébé*, whose body carries the Medaille d'Or stamp and whose head is maked "L" in red Brown eyes, original wig. Applied ears, cork pate. 26 in. high.

attractive is a doll-seller, which has a basket of dolls at its feet. As the music plays, the vendor turns her head from side to side, as though looking for customers. Another lovely doll also turns its head from side to side while raising and lowering a bouquet. On the doll's hand, a very realistic bird jumps up and down, singing as it does so. There is a very wide variety of automata that incorporate Jumeau heads, and they could form a collecting field by themselves, albeit a highly expensive one.

Edison's invention of a 'talking machine' in 1877 opened a new era, it was felt at the time, for the doll-maker. No longer would it be necessary to fix ineffective sound boxes in the torso of a doll, giving at best only squeaks in different tones. At last the true-to-life doll could be made! The demonstration of the American phonograph caused a great stir at the 1889 Paris Exhibition, and it says much for the speed at which doll-makers were prepared to incorporate new inventions that by 1894 the phonograph was being used by the French manufacturer.

A contemporary description of a French phonograph doll explains that it was worked by a system of cog wheels that were set in motion by the pulling of a knob. The doll then began to speak in these words: "Je suis bien contente, maman m'a promis d'aller au théâtre, je vais entendre chanter, tra, la, la, la." It then begins to sing a pretty little song, or even to laugh, and ends by saying, "Merci ma petite maman." Girls with attractive but high-pitched voices like children's were employed by the phonograph company in the recording of cylinders for these dolls. The wax cylinders could be taken out of the doll and replaced by other records.

A good example of a Jumeau phonograph doll came up for sale in 1973 at Christie's and contained a Lioret phonograph movement with a white celluloid cylinder playing 'Il Pleut Bergère'. The head was marked and a 'Lioret Jumeau' label was on the mandrel. The doll reached £750, indicating how difficult it is to find working dolls of the type. Those with their original sets of changeable records which Jumeau provided are virtually impossible to find.

The new invention proved far too expensive to use generally, despite the doll-makers' high hopes, and though it later makes an odd appearance in the catalogues of various makers, it did not have the far-reaching effects that had at first been expected. Other inventions came fast and furious in the 1880s, though the Jumeau firm never allowed itself to go to absurd excess, as did some of the other doll-makers such as Bru. As well as the supposedly ultimate *Bébé Phonographe*,

242   Two small bisque-headed straight-limbed French dolls before an open French wardrobe containing hats, negligée, dresses and cape, with neatly-folded linen on shelf. Black doll has fixed eyes and open mouth. Painted orange stockings. 7½ in. high. White doll with closed mouth and huge eyes marked "J" Paris. 8½ in. high.

there were the usual walking, talking and hand-kissing dolls, some with glancing eyes. Though the firm was willing to take advantage of new ideas, they would not allow the dolls to become so complicated that they were unsatisfactory as toys.

A contemporary described the dolls that Jumeau exhibited at the 1889 Paris Exhibition as "beautiful, intelligent and French-looking". They were also described by the same person as wearing very lovely hats and dresses of pure Lyons silk.

Despite the admiration which the dolls aroused, competition was becoming very great, expecially from Germany, but also from the other French makers; and the firm was forced to turn its attention to the marketing of cheaper goods. By 1897, it is estimated that between 3,000,000 and 4,000,000 dolls a year were made, an indication in itself of how short were the lives of many dolls, as present-day collectors have difficulty in finding nice examples. The calculation is based on a visit to the factory in 1897, when 17 different head sizes were seen and 600 or 700 of each size were claimed to be made daily. An idea of the rapid growth of the firm can be seen in the facts that around 1880 only 85,000 dolls were made each year, a number that had risen by 1884 to 220,000.

A variety of marks, both incised and stamped, are found on Jumeau heads. They range from the frequently-found 'Deposé Tête Jumeau' to 'Breveté S.G.D.G. Jumeau' or even simply 'E.J.', the last being believed to refer to Emile Jumeau, who had taken over the firm from his father. It is a great pity, from the collector's point of view, that unscrupulous fake marking of heads has meant that any stamped marks are now a very unreliable guide. Unmarked heads were made by the factory throughout the period, and in most cases the unmarked dolls that have the definite look of age are a much better buy than those that flaunt bright new marks. Suspicion should be aroused in the mind of the buyer by any dealer who offers for sale several dolls that are all identically marked, as this is straining coincidence just a little too far. Continental dealers appear to be much less scrupulous than those in England and America, and collectors often return home with a 'Jumeau' that they discover later is a reproduction. Some of these dolls are very well done and I know several collectors who have knowingly bought such reproductions, as they felt that they were buying a modern top-quality doll in the old manner. This reasoning does not hold much appeal for me, but if the collector is only searching for an attractive doll, he or she can do little better than buy an example of this type.

243   Very fine *bébé* of the type described as a 'Portrait Jumeau'. Ball-jointed body marked in blue "Jumeau, Medaille d'Or". Applied ears. Fixed wrists, closed mouth.

365

Bru

The most aggressive competitor of the Jumeau Company in the field of quality dolls was Bru. This firm aimed purely to make dolls of unsurpassable quality, and their production was much more limited than that of the Jumeau firm. Consequently, the dolls are even harder to find and command the highest price.

The Bru *bébés* are very much in the tradition of the French lady-dolls, and are extremely beautiful, but often just a little vulgar in concept. Too much conscious effort was put into the creation of items that had innovation value, and some of the results are quite repulsive, such as 'Bébé la Tèteur', who appears to drink milk from a feeding bottle that was supplied with the doll. A few drops of eau-de-Cologne were added to water to create the effect of milk, and the doll appeared to suck up this mixture. The head held a container for water which was moved by suction. A key at the back of the head was turned to the right and the bottle put into the *bébé*'s mouth. The key was again turned, but this time to the left, and the doll appeared to suck up the liquid. When the key was turned to the right the liquid poured back into the bottle in a completely repulsive manner.

The most desirable dolls made by Bru are those with well-modelled heads, often covered with sheepskin wigs, which swivel in a bisque shoulder plate. Several good examples are illustrated, so that the body construction can be studied and the excellent modelling appreciated. The Bru *bébés* have rather heavy faces, and are made of a darker-toned bisque than those of Jumeau, whose best dolls were made of a most delicately-tinted china. The slightly-parted lips, known as an 'open-closed' mouth, is also a characteristic of the earlier leather-bodied *bébés*. This was another firm whose factory was at Montreuil-sous-Bois, and they were making kid-bodied *bébés* as early as 1868. The Bru company, like the other French makers, was very conscious of the importance of dress, and any new styles were quickly copied in the best materials at the workshops, which were organized in a very similar way to those of the Jumeau establishment. Some of the Bru dolls were sold complete with a little couch and pillow on which they reclined elegantly. The shoes, which are always of nice quality, are marked either 'Bru Jne. Paris' or simply 'Bru'. When the doll was in a sitting position, the soles of the shoes could be seen easily, and this marking of shoes with the firms name was a cheap, but effective, advertising method.

Like the Jumeau factory, the Bru establishment was keen to make the public aware that it marked all products, though this was mainly after 1880, when competition became most aggressive. Some of the early Bru *bébés* are marked with only a circle and dot, though a sticker was fixed around the body just

244   Open-mouthed Jumeau with very thickly-painted brows. Pierced ears. Head marked "Déposé Bébé Jumeau". Jointed body with joint at wrists. Marked on body in green "Bébé Jumeau, S.G.D.G. Déposé". 25 in. high.

366

367

(left) 245 A much cheaper range of French dolls was also made. Firms such as Lanternier produced more economical *bébés* such as this example, marked on head "Fabrication Française A.4". Fixed blue eyes, pierced ears. Jointed body. 13½ in. high. *(right)* 246 Some of the better-quality Lanterniers are reminiscent of some of the Jumeau moulds. This example, with dark green fixed eyes of unusual colour has a voice box in the torso operated by two pull strings at hip level. Composition and wood body. Marked "Fabrication Française" in rectangle and "A.L & Cie Limoges. A.9". 24 in. high.

under the arms, carrying the firm's name. Unfortunately, these labels have often broken away, and the incised symbols have to be relied upon. The crescent and circle mark is usually found on a slight bump at the back of the neck which is a characteristic of the better dolls.

The heads fit into bisque shoulder plates on these better dolls. The shoulders have extremely well-defined modelling, and the attractive small breasts are shown. Attention was also given to the back of the doll, and the shoulder blades are beautifully modelled – details with which no other doll-maker concerned himself. The necks are often rather thick and goitrous-looking, and are probably the doll's least attractive feature. A few have moulded teeth in the open-closed mouths, while others show the tips of their tongues. The marking of many of the dolls is quite surprisingly full, and is not only on the head but also on the side of the shoulder plate. These quality shoulder heads with swivel necks are most frequently found on gussetted leather bodies, sometimes with wooden lower limbs and exquisitely-modelled china arms.

As with all the French makers there is a variety of standard, but not, it must be

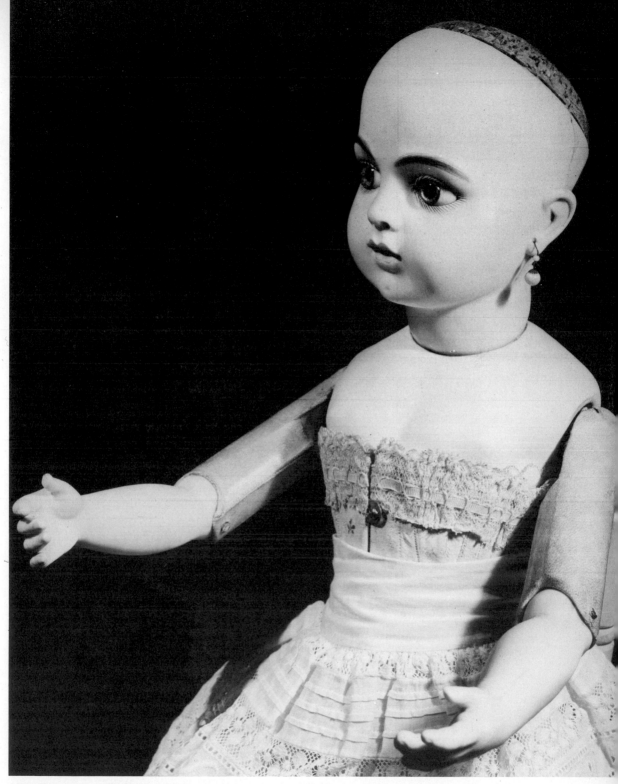

247   The work of the Bru establishment was unsurpassed for the quality of its products. This example is particularly fine, even for its type. Cork pate, applied ears, closed mouth. Shoulder plate with moulded breasts. Kid-covered upper arms, bisque lower. Metal joints. Wooden lower legs with well-carved toes. Marked "Bru Jne" on shoulder plate and neck. 26 in. high.

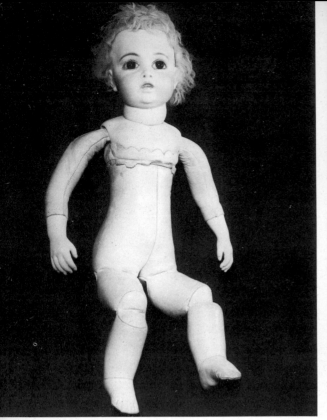 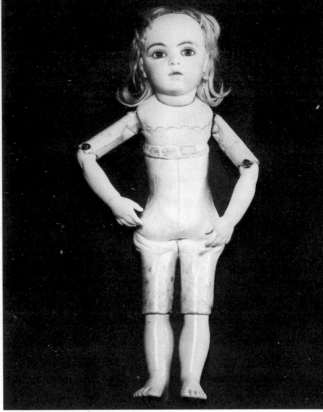

(*left*) 248   Another typical Bru with gusseted leather body and bisque lower arms. Open-closed mouth with moulded teeth. Pierced ears. The rather goitrous neck is typical of Bru, as is the sheepskin wig and pink leather body. Moulded breasts with the nipples tinted. Marked with crescent circle dot symbol. Pale colour bisque. 16 in. high.   (*right*) 249   Bébé Bru wearing original label. Open-closed mouth. Much darker-toned bisque than the previous Bru. Marked on head "BRU-Jn J", on left shoulder "Bru Jn" and on right shoulder "No. 5". Leather body, bisque arms, carved wooden lower legs. 16 in. high.

agreed, as wide in the products of this firm as in those of the others. The type of Brus mentioned above were the most beautiful, but other Brus were made of composition or even rubber. These two substances held great appeal for the doll-makers, who were continually searching for an unbreakable manufacturing material. Their ball-jointed dolls are in the best French tradition, and sometimes have additional joints at the ankle. The best Bru jointed bodies were made of turned and carved wood.

As early as 1868, the firm was reported to be making straight-limbed and jointed dolls that both cried and talked, though these were of course lady dolls of the Parisienne type. Between 1867 and 1869, Casimir Bru Jeune registered several patents, including one for a double-faced doll and a crying doll which had a rubber ball fitted with a reed inside the body; also a sleeping and awake double-faced doll, known as the 'Surprise' doll, worked by the turning of the head on a rod that ran down through the body. The head was thus turned without upsetting the doll's hair, which remained neatly in place. The jointed all-rubber doll was patented in 1880, but it is rarely found, presumably because the rubber perished. It is paradoxical that these dolls, which were intended to be indestructible, are in fact those that have most deteriorated with age.

Ordinary wooden ball-jointed bodies were made by the Bru Company from around 1870, though the joints were held together at first with pegs or pins, rather than the more familiar elastic. Some of the jointed bodies were covered with a skin of rubber, which aimed at giving a more realistic effect. The company was proud of the good articulation of their *bébés*, which they claimed could be put into any position. The best Bru jointed bodies had ankle-joints, which made the doll very different from the bodies used by the Germans or even the lesser French firms.

Much of the effort to keep ahead of the market went into the creation of novelty items. 'Bébé Gourmand', which according to the firm's advertisement both ate and digested its food, must have closely rivalled 'Bébé la Tètour' in offensiveness. A breathing Bru was patented in 1892, which contained a mechanism in the chest which pumped up and down in imitation of breathing. Several collectors who have seen working examples of this doll have commented upon its most unpleasant and eerie effect. Each year, some new idea had to be offered

250 Postcard used as an advertisement in the early twentieth century by the famous French toyshop Au Nain Bleu, 27 Boulevard des Capucines, Paris, which sold quality French dolls.

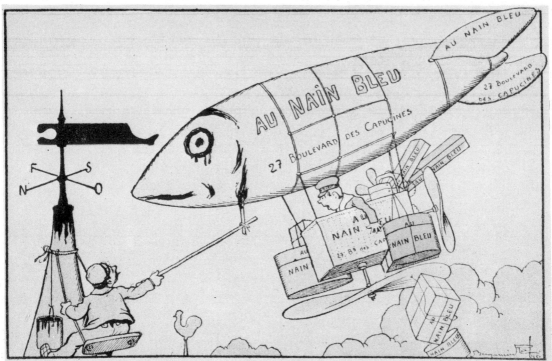

to the public, and the popular French walking, talking and kiss-throwing dolls were all experimented with by Bru, though the musical doll patented in 1872 by Madame Bru, which contained in its torso a multi-disc music box, must have been a leader.

The Bru company was founded by Casimir Bru Jeune, but the advances were continued under his successors. In 1883 the company, known as Bru Jne et Cie, had passed to H. Chevrot, who continued to trade under the old-established name. All the gold medals acquired by the firm were won under the direction of Chevrot, who was particularly skilled at promoting the firm. Advertisements carried during his period claimed that twenty-five patents were in operation, which included, besides the *bébés* already discussed, 'Bébé le Dormeur', which opened and lowered its eyelids over its eyes. This idea for a sleeping doll was much more realistic than the weighted version developed later, but it had the disadvantage that the material forming the eyelid, which was subjected to continual rubbing, became marked and unpleasant, and the lever which operated the mechanism also sometimes worked loose with too much use.

Paul Girard followed Chevrot as head of the company, and he again was active in the registering of patents, particularly with regard to improvements in eye mechanisms. The walking and hand-kissing dolls were extremely popular in the 1890s, and the early version marketed by Bru threw kisses when a string was pulled, though their later kiss-throwing doll worked by the leg movement, as did most of those made at the same time by French makers.

Possibly some of the firm's skill in mechanical doll-making derived from their other interest, the creation of mechanical toys, for which they received certificates and various commendations. Certainly, the Bru company is regarded by collectors as that which made the greatest contribution to the development of the mechanical doll. Their other primary contribution lay in the making of quality bodies for *bébés*. Their early leather-covered bodies often had metal joints connecting the wooden sections, which still work smoothly. When wood was used for the lower legs, the feet were very well carved, while the quality of the bisque limbs and heads is without equal. The whistling Bru, with its lips drawn into a whistling position, is very popular with collectors, though not as attractive as the basic leather-bodied closed-mouth *bébé*.

Later dolls of the jointed type betray the gradual falling-off in quality seen in the products of all the French makers, who were being forced to economize in the effort to compete. Some of the late Brus are quite unremarkable, and do not stand out as fine objects when surrounded by other quality dolls, as do the early Bru *bébés*. 'Bébé Bru' continued to be marketed under its original name by S.F.B.J., and it is the dolls of this period that are the least beautiful. Most collectors long to acquire a fine example of the work of this doll-maker, but as they were

251 Many firms turned their attention to the making of character dolls in the first years of the twentieth century. Smiling boy with the brilliant blue eyes that are a feature of better S.F.B.J. dolls. Marked on neck ''S.F.B.J.''. Open-closed mouth with moulded teeth. 13 in. high.

always very expensive dolls, they tend to serve as the ultimate for collectors, and several long-standing doll enthusiasts who have acquired them claim to have lost interest, as they felt there was nothing else to search for.

S.F.B.J.

The German doll-makers, by their traditional skill in mass production of dolls' parts, found in the new jointed *bébés* a type of body construction that they could easily copy. They had worked for well over a hundred years on variations of the basic papier mâché mixture, but had never been as successful as the French in making sewn leather bodies. The German makers consequently had made little effort to compete with the luxurious French lady-dolls, but the new jointed papier mâché *bébés* with bisque heads were very much within their orbit. The German doll-making industry therefore turned all its attention to the production of jointed dolls, and made *bébés* that were not as fine as the best produced in France but attractively cheap. Manufacturers in Germany were prepared to arrange credit facilities for shopkeepers, which gave dealing with the Germans an added attraction, and gave much cheaper shops, who had perhaps doubted their ability to sell the dearer French dolls, the chance to stock similar but very much more economical versions.

The French makers struggled against the German competition for several years, and in much of the Jumeau propaganda can be seen the apparent bitterness of the conflict. Eventually the cheaper articles, which were just as attractive to the children of England and America as the fine *bébés*, won; and the French doll-makers were forced to reorganize their companies or go out of business.

A company was formed in 1898 which included a son-in-law of M. Bru and two daughters of Jumeau among the directors. Many of the leading French doll-makers joined the syndicate, which was known as the Société Française de Fabrication des Bébés et Jouets (the society for the manufacture of *bébés* and toys). The original partners were Jumeau, Bru, Fleischmann et Blodel, Rabery et Delphieu and Pintel et Godchaux. A few years later P. H. Schmitz and Ad. Bouchet were added, with Daniel et Cie joining in 1911. This company was now able to reorganize completely its operations and make all the manufacturing much more rational. Popular dolls such as Bru's and Jumeau's for which a great deal had been spent on advertising, continued to be produced and marketed in the old manner, but there was even in these a gradual lowering of standard, in order to help the dolls compete with the cheap German rivals.

The new syndicate was not over-fussy about using German parts for their dolls. S.F.B.J. dolls that were sold in their own boxes and marked 'Made in France' were frequently found to have heads marked with the initials of German makers. Simon and Halbig heads, in particular, are found on dolls that purport to come from firms such as Jumeau. The policy of the company appears to have been that it was quite permissible to use German heads as long as the public were not aware of the fact. Though the first thought of the modern collector is to lift a doll's wig to examine the maker's mark on the back of the head, the ordinary purchaser of a new toy for a child would have hated to disarrange the hair in this way, and in any case the mere initials would have meant little to the uninitiated.

I bought a very French-looking walking doll recently from an old lady who had kept it all her life, as it had been given to her by an aunt who was a Carmelite nun. The doll looked French, had a French body, and was dressed in French provincial clothes, but at the top of the head was the familiar S & H mark and the word 'Germany'. From the time of the doll's purchase, some seventy years ago, this doll had been treasured as an example of French manufacture! Some of the German dolls, such as this, appear to have been purposely made to look very French, and it was natural that the French makers should overcome their pride where commerce was concerned and utilize the much cheaper source.

Fortunately, most of the bisque heads used by S.F.B.J. continued to be made at the factories in the Montreuil area, and the Jumeau showroom at 8, Rue Pastourelle continued to be used. By 1911, the syndicate advertised that they were making 5,000,000 dolls a year at their Vincennes factory, and by 1925, they had in all eight factories for the production of dolls. Output soared to around 7,000,000 dolls a year by 1922, and it is little wonder that those marked S.F.B.J. are the most commonly-found French examples.

Some of the S.F.B.J. dolls are very cheaply made, with poor-quality bisque and indifferent modelling, because of mass production and the pressure of ever-harder competition from Germany. Some of the smaller dolls are decorated badly and tinted in a strange way that gives the faces an oddly mottled effect. Despite their economical construction, many of the dolls were originally dressed quite prettily, and obviously the French at first found it necessary to maintain their standard in at least this aspect of doll-making.

Each year prizes were awarded for the design of dolls' outfits. Madame Bonneaud was the firm's chief fashion designer, and she worked in the factory on the Rue de Picpus, with her team of assistants, on the creation and adaptation of children's fashionable costume for dolls. All the pattern pieces were cut from buckram, and could be assembled in different fabrics and with various trimmings. The collector is always surprised how rare it is to find two such dolls dressed alike, unless they are in regional costume.

The difference in standard of products is probably more noticeable in the work of S.F.B.J. than in that of any individual doll-maker. The good examples are very acceptable, but the very poorly-modelled dolls with mean, featureless faces should be avoided: a well-made German doll is a much safer buy. The most commonly found are those marked 60 and 301. These are typical of the variety of standard, as some have very finely-made faces, reminiscent of the Jumeau moulds, and well-constructed bodies, while others are found on cheap stick-like moulded limbs. Some have thickly-moulded brows, pierced ears and the well-modelled teeth that are typical of the better French dolls.

The two numbers are not always found on dolls that came from the same model. Collectors of (for example) Armand Marseille dolls refer to 390s or 370s, and the type of face can at once be recognized, but S.F.B.J. does not seem to have worked in this way, and comparison of a group of dolls marked 60 quickly shows that they most definitely were not all from the same model. Some 301s are marked 'Unis France' and have composition bodies with painted socks. This 'Unis France' mark was late and was only used after 1921. It is possible that the numbers refer to a particular factory or production line, but until more research has been undertaken, the buyer will do well to avoid purchase of the dolls purely by reference to the number which appears in this case to have only limited relevance to the model or the quality.

This discrepancy between heads marked with the same number extends even into the range of character heads, but to nothing like the same extent. The 230, for instance, is usually best known as a character baby with a plump face, but it is also found marking typical *bébé* heads that are mounted on jointed or walking bodies.

At the time of writing, character dolls are extremely popular among collectors, and now almost assume the pride of position once held by the *Parisiennes*. Character dolls are those which were, or appear to have been, modelled on real children, and have portrait-like detail associated with an individual child, instead of an idealized 'dolly' version. The character dolls became popular in the early twentieth century and reflected the trend away from the high sentimentalism of the late Victorian period. The character dolls made by S.F.B.J. are the most prized by collectors, as they represent the skill of the French doll-maker combined with the appeal of a portrait doll. The S.F.B.J. characters are usually in the series 203–252, though a few are found with low numbers. Eyes were sometimes decorated in the intaglio manner and painted, or else made of glass. The fixed glass eyes are particularly effective, as they have a brilliant quality of colour not seen in the work of other makers.

The syndicate appears to have been quite casual about the type of body that they combined with the various heads. The 237, for example, which is a boy doll with flocked hair, was made with either a jointed, a straight-limbed or even a walking body. When I began to collect, I was often deterred from buying

(*above left*) 252 Dolls made by S.F.B.J. were often dressed in regional costume and sold as souvenirs. This pair measures 10 in. high. (*above right*) 253 Typical sleeping-eyed jointed doll made by S.F.B.J. Marked "SFBJ 60 Paris". 23½ in. high. (*below*) 254 Many S.F.B.J. dolls were produced in the 1920s, such as this, still wearing original green silk dress and straw hat. The upward-looking dark eyes are a characteristic of many of the dolls marked "60". 19 in. high.

377

S.F.B.J. characters, as I felt it possible that the heads were on the wrong bodies. I discovered later many more, both in museums and private collections, that were made in just the same way, though other makers tend to have reserved various types of heads for particular bodies.

Probably the rarest made was the 'interchangeable doll' that came complete with a choice of three heads. A body with three contrasting sets of clothes was provided and three of the currently popular character heads. The smiling head is usually a 235, the crying head a 233 and the boy head a 237. Each of these dolls would be a desirable acquisition in its own right, but as a complete interchangeable doll would command a very high figure.

The S.F.B.J. 226, which is a crying baby, is interesting, as it is believed to have been made as a copy of the much more common German doll, popularly referred to as the Kaiser baby. The manufacture of this doll indicates the willingness of French makers to copy German ideas, when it was felt to be in their own interest. The French version is made of very superior bisque, and often has the fixed, inset, vivid glass eyes associated with the better products of the firm. The cheaper version was made with intaglio eyes and the head was marked only 226 without the S.F.B.J. mark. This difference can be seen in several of the character dolls. The most expensive versions carried both the makers' and the design mark, while those that were cheaper, either because of the type of body used or the method of decorating the head, simply carried the number. The cheaper version of the 227, which is a smiling boy, was produced on a straight-limbed body, whereas the fully-marked version had the quality jointed body.

Several dolls marked 227 were made which could not possibly have originated from the same model, as the faces are so completely different. One has a very straight nose and an open mouth, and has hair that is only painted on, while another, completely different in modelling, was made of composition. Yet another has flocked hair and an upturned nose. It has been said in the past that all these dolls were made to look different by the skill of the decorator, but whereas hair could be treated in varying ways, no skill of the decorator's brush could alter the actual shape of the face.

As S.F.B.J. were using up the remaining stock and moulds of the several companies, it is not unusual to find a marked Jumeau body with an incised S.F.B.J. head, and of course the converse is equally true. Dolls produced after the amalgamation were still marketed as 'Jumeau', and the high standard set by the original firm was maintained as far as was possible; though as the firm was

255   Very pale bisque *bébé* marked "SFBJ 230 Paris" in circle. Blue flirting eyes. Head turns as doll walks, crying "Mama". Each hand is lifted in turn to blow kisses. Pierced ears, moulded teeth, 22¼ in. high.

forced to be more competitive, more economical types of body gradually became evident.

Some of the innovations of the Bru Company were extended to S.F.B.J., and an extremely interesting but very rare nursing doll was manufactured. The doll had a removable back to the head, and a rubber tube ran from the mouth to an opening between the shoulder blades: certainly a much more attractive method than that originally used by Bru. Coloured and mulatto *bébés*, which Bru had also made, continued to be produced by the syndicate. Some of the colouring is very effective, but on other dolls it is extremely poor.

My own particular favourite among the character dolls is the 238, which is a very appealing girl doll, with the well-inset eyes and very heavy brows that characterize these quality S.F.B.J. dolls. One wonders whether the French found heavy brows a thing of great beauty, or perhaps the decorators felt, as do collectors of today, that dolls' faces with very heavy brows actually look more attractive.

Though the clothes in which the *bébés* were dressed formed one of their main attractions, by the early 1920s the French makers had turned their attention to very cheap production methods, and the clothes, though marginally better than those of the German makers, were unexceptional. Muslin dresses with matching petticoats and knickers, all trimmed with the minimum of cheap lace, became the most popular, though occasionally a doll dressed in silks in the fashionable style of the 1920s is found. The composition pierrots which S.F.B.J. made are also very typical of this period, when the pierrot was used to decorate everything from evening bags to powder bowls.

In buying dolls made by this company, the collector should look for examples where the bisque and the decoration of that bisque are of good quality. The body should also be well made, otherwise the money would be better spent on an attractive and solidly-constructed German example. All the S.F.B.J. character dolls are very worthwhile investments, as are those made from the old Jumeau moulds. Any with very thick moulded or painted eyebrows are always very saleable, and those with pierced ears are invariably more popular than the dolls without provision for ear-rings, though of course many of the dolls with pierced ears are not of good quality.

Though firms such as Bru and Jumeau were absorbed into S.F.B.J., the dolls made by the individual firms continued to be marketed under their old names, so that as late as 1921 'Bébé Bru', 'Eden Bébé' and 'Bébé Jumeau' were still being manufactured. In 1922 the syndicate claimed that they were using 2,000 models,

256   The howling baby is one of the most effective of French character heads. Open-closed mouth with moulded teeth. Untinted hair. Brilliant blue eyes. Bent-limbed baby body. Marked on head "SFBJ 233 Paris". 12 in. high.

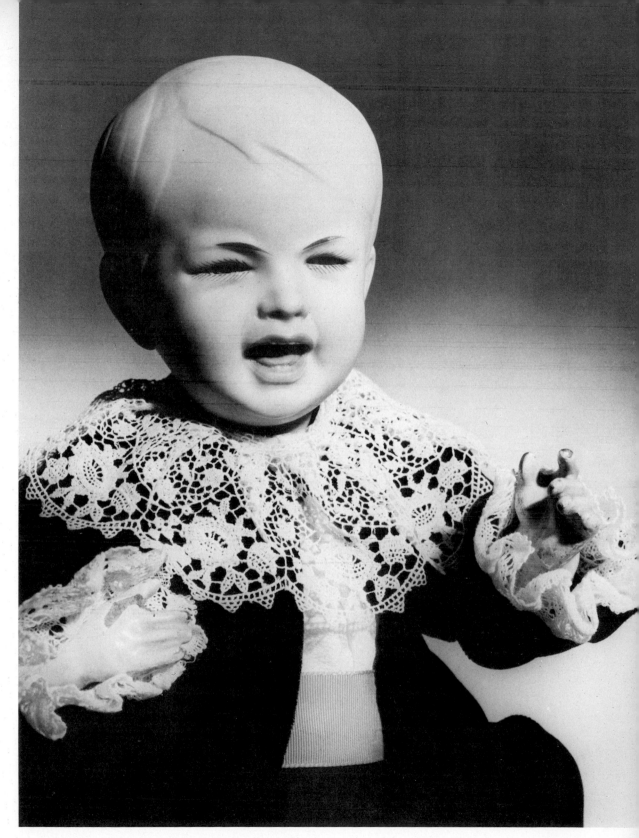

including many character and coloured dolls, as well as *marottes*. Walking, talking and hand-kissing dolls all continued to be made until the 1930s.

Possibly the most famous dolls made by the company were those that were especially created at the request of the French government as a gift for the English Princesses Margaret and Elizabeth when King George VI visited France. The dolls were 32 inches high and were given glancing eyes. Judging from photographs, the dolls were made very much in the glamour idiom of the late thirties, and are not very attractive either as accurate portraits or as objects; but the idea was both charming and traditional.

THIRTEEN

GERMAN DOLL-MAKERS

Much of the old prejudice regarding dolls originating in Germany stemmed from a misplaced contempt for mass production. In order to compete successfully with the French quality makers, the Germans resorted to the construction of very cheap items that were basically mere copies of a type of doll made very successfully by the French. When the German makers ceased to be copyists and became creators in their own right, their dolls become just as interesting to the modern collector as the majority of French dolls.

At the beginning of the twentieth century, about half the world's total output of dolls was created in Germany, mainly in Thuringia and Bavaria, the traditional doll-making centres. In Thuringia were all the conditions necessary for cheap manufacture. Skilled workers could be drawn from a large population that had been concerned with doll-making for several generations, and there was an abundance of local fire clay for the potteries. Wood was plentiful, and was used both for the turning of dolls' limbs and for heating some of the kilns, though at this time coal was becoming more commonly used. Some firms, such as Armand Marseille, are said to have imported British anthracite for their furnaces, as it gave a fierce and relatively dust-free heat which was unlikely to cause imperfections to the surface of the bisque heads during firing. There was also water power, which was utilized by some of the manufacturers. The German government viewed the doll-making industry favourably, as it provided useful revenue, and aid was given in the form of subsidies and in assistance to schools that were set up to teach the design of dolls.

Many potteries were able to produce china dolls' heads very cheaply, as they did not completely concentrate on their production. Leading French makers, such as Jumeau, claimed to make all parts of their dolls at their own factory, but German firms, such as Kämmer and Reinhardt, bought heads from potteries which also produced a wide range of household ceramic items. Armand Marseille made colourful figures, Heubach a wide range of mantelpiece trivia and Simon and Halbig included small ornaments among its range. It should be remembered that dolls' heads often comprised only a small percentage of a pottery's total production, and several factories that are well known among porcelain collectors for the quality of their ornamental items did not find it beneath their dignity to make dolls' heads. The Rauenstein, Limbach and Ilmenau factories are notable examples.

It is curious that such a wealth of detail was incised on the back of dolls' heads by firms who hardly bothered to mark many of their ornamental items, except occasionally with their initials and, after 1890, with the country of origin. It appears likely that the manufacturers were fostering a type of brand loyalty which they did not think necessary in the case of small ornaments, which would represent 'impulse buys'. It is perhaps not completely by chance that Schoenau and Hoffmeister used a symbol for their trade-mark that was so similar to that used by the more progressive Kämmer and Reinhardt that even collectors of today are initially confused. One wonders how many original sales were aided by this confusion regarding a similar trade-mark.

The first bisque heads made by the Germans in imitation of the *bébés* were mounted on leather bodies which were slimmer but much less skilfully made than those of the French. The German bodies were almost straight, with little effort made to create a waistline, but their cheapness was a great advantage, and when dressed, the poorly-made bodies were not so obvious. The shoulder heads used were often of very good quality. The Armand Marseille 370 at best is a most attractive doll, with large eyes and a gentle expression that even children of today find appealing. Though shoulder-headed dolls of this kind were produced well into the 1920s, they are generally considered to be the early type of German girl dolls. A large number of firms made heads in this traditional way, though some are of much poorer quality than those made by, for instance, Armand Marseille and Cuno and Otto Dressel. The leather bodies which were used for the latter are often of a very good standard for German dolls. Most dolls of this type were sold dressed only in a chemise, and it is extremely rare to find a doll dressed in original clothes that can be attributed to the manufacturer. They usually wear well-made but home-stitched costume. The leather bodies were usually filled with sawdust, but some firms, such as Simon and Halbig, used cork occasionally. Cheaper dolls were given bodies of pink cotton, often boldly stamped, 'Hair stuffed. Made in Germany.' Black fabric was often used for the

257   The German makers created dolls that are more true to life than those of the French makers in general. This closed-mouth shoulder-headed doll has a stuffed cloth body with bisque lower arms. Pierced ears, fixed brown eyes. Marked on shoulder "123". 27 in. high.

37   Henbach character baby

38 "The Genteel Boy and his Doings"

lower legs, presumably to represent black stockings. Dolls of slightly better quality were given composition legs to match the arms. The best dolls of the type were given arms and, very occasionally, legs of china. A group of Armand Marseille dolls with varied but authentic body constructions is shown, to give some indication of the variety of methods used.

The tariff laws of 1890, which made it necessary to mark all items with their country of origin, makes the collector's task in attributing early twentieth-century dolls much easier. The more business-like way in which the companies worked has made possible a great deal of research into dates and patents, carried out by enthusiasts such as Louella Hart and the Coleman family. The maker's mark, model number and country of origin are to be found on the back of the doll's head or on the shoulder plate. The patent number of the head is also sometimes given. Despite much research, dolls are continually found with marks that are completely unidentifiable, because of the hundreds of small factories that occasionally made dolls to order. These unattributable heads have to be valued on their quality and interest, though most conform to the basic so-called 'dolly-faced' type. For a collector to attempt to buy even one doll from each of the German factories would be a major task.

As there are such a large number of small firms, the history of the achievement of the German makers in the late nineteenth and early twentieth centuries has to be studied in relation to a few of the very famous firms, whose products are found in some quantity.

It is no accident that the more realistic type of doll was developed in a country that was sympathetic to the educational aims of Friedrich Froebel and Maria Montessori. The climate of opinion in the early twentieth century favoured a much greater understanding of a child's basic needs. There was a great upsurge of interest in psychology and teaching methods, and it became almost sinful to claim that a doll was manufactured simply as a pretty toy. Dolls, like the furniture produced at the Bauhaus, had to be designed precisely to satisfy their function. During this period the doll appears to have been almost reborn, and manufacturers commissioned artists to create dolls that would stimulate and satisfy the child. Käthe Kruse, herself the wife of a sculptor, made her first Art Dolls in 1904. These figures were aimed at "a high-class trade which has a leaning towards the artistic". Other progressive doll-makers, such as Marion Kaulitz and Paul Sanger, worked in the new creative manner, and nearly all the major doll factories began to consider the making of character dolls a necessary part of their trade.

The earliest character baby heads were mounted on very grotesquely-shaped leather bodies. These dolls often look as if the maker simply cut down the normal 'little-girl' type of body and reassembled the pieces. Some of the early

(*above left*) 258   German closed-mouth doll in pale blue velvet suit. Marked "B.S.W." for Bruno Schmidt. 19 in. high.   (*above right*) 259   Many good porcelain factories included dolls among their products. Ball-jointed body, slightly-open mouth with inset teeth. Blue sleeping eyes. Marked "Wally" with clover mark for Limbach. Very pale head. 26 in. high.   (*below*) 260   Realistic baby dolls were made in far greater number in Germany. Head marked "604.10 Otto Reinecke". Bent-limbed baby body. Open-closed mouth, two teeth.

shoulder-head character babies were probably intended for leather bodies such as these, though ordinary socket heads are also frequently found mounted on them. Early Kämmer and Reinhardt heads are also known to have been attached to double-jointed bodies when the character dolls were in their first experimental stages.

Bent-limbed composition baby bodies are described in advertisements dating from 1904, and I know of none that can be dated as before this time. The bent-limbed body was a boon to the doll-maker, as the casting was simple and assembly fast, as there were only six basic pieces to be strung together. Most represented a baby in a sitting or crawling position, though some had almost straight legs, so that the toddler-type doll could stand. The new products thus had a double appeal, in that they were economical to produce and popular with children as being fairly realistic copies of babies.

Many modern collectors affirm their dislike of the large baby dolls, and it appears that the children who once owned them found their presence a little overwhelming at times. Barbara Sleigh, writing of her childhood, recalled a Christmas in 1915 when her mother bought a life-size baby doll that she felt could do an economical double-duty both as a present for her daughter and as the Christ-child in the Christmas tableau. "I hated the doll on sight. Its very life-size emphasized its cold lifelessness. It seemed for all the world like a real dead baby. I did not want to play with it."

When I began to collect, I almost invariably exchanged my character baby dolls for what were to me more attractive, but in retrospect, much less interesting, jointed girl dolls. This appears to be a tendency among many new collectors, who only gradually acquire the enthusiast's liking for the more unusual character dolls. I now regret many of the good examples that I parted with, and attempt to replace them, but because of the tremendous current interest in dolls of this type, the reacquisition has become very expensive.

Character baby dolls can be differentiated from the standard babies produced by a wide range of doll-makers by the skilful realism that was given to the features. They have rolls of fat, dimples, uneven features and the sulky or even positively unhappy expressions of real babies, some even appearing in a crying pose. Eyes are not necessarily glass: in fact some of the best heads have intaglio eyes. The heads are made in a very wide range of sizes derived from the same basic model. Some of the large heads were made in smaller sizes by taking a cast of the fired head which would make the next size cast considerably smaller. This method, though one of the most common, was not always used, and several small heads appear to have been cast from a similar but remodelled version of the original. In some cases, the various heads have slightly different detail added, such as modelled quiffs of hair or moulded eyebrows, which could not have been

261 Three-faced German doll whose head turns within a hair-covered composition hood. By turning the ring at top the face turns. Strings at waist for sound box. Body marked "Gëschutzt". Calico-covered torso. 13 in. high.

389

produced simply by reduction of the basic model by casting.

The bodies of the quality character baby dolls are also of a better standard, and represent the child in a more natural position. Cheaper dolls have both legs and arms in the same position, whereas the characters have each limb individually modelled. One fist is sometimes clenched, while the fingers of the other hand are extended, and one leg is often bent much more than the other to give greater realism. Recently many of the auction rooms and antique-fair dealers have taken to calling even quite commonplace baby dolls by Armand Marseille 'character babies', despite the fact that they are not so regarded by established collectors and were obviously not made originally with this intention.

Kämmer and Reinhardt

Some of the finest dolls which attempted to imitate the features of a real child, either in gay or sulky mood, were made by Kämmer and Reinhardt, a firm that was established in Waltershausen in 1886. The modeller and inventor of the dolls was Kämmer, while Reinhardt had the business acumen and dealt with the practical side of the concern. In 1909, the firm attempted to boost sales, which had suffered a temporary decline, by introducing their character babies, of which the doll popularly known as the 'Kaiser baby' is the most common. Collectors once believed that this doll had been modelled on the young son of the German Emperor, but its origin was in fact much more prosaic: it was based on the child of the sculptor who was commissioned to create the doll. Early versions were sold on double-jointed bodies, but the more popular are those on bodies that can be arranged in a crawling position, which was the manner in which the firm represented the doll in its catalogues. When the Berlin artist showed his model to Kämmer and Reinhardt, they were at first afraid that it had too much realism for contemporary taste, and would not sell very well. A few dolls were included among standard orders, and were reasonably successful, which encouraged the manufacturers to continue production.

Though the progressive dolls made in the years before the First World War were usually referred to as Artistic Dolls, the Kämmer and Reinhardt company preferred the term 'character', which has been retained by collectors. Two jointed character dolls known as 'Peter' or 'Marie' and marked 101 were also made, though judging from surviving examples in nothing like the number in which the baby marked 100 was sold. The doll number 114, which is either 'Hans' or 'Gretchen', according to the hairstyle, was modelled on Reinhardt's own nephew. Other characters, such as 'Walter' and 'Elsie', are believed to have been named after the children who posed for the artists who created the models.

262 Very small character baby with laughing open-closed mouth. Blue painted eyes. Bent-limb baby body. Head marked "R 5 G". 6¾ in. high.

263 Boy doll with moulded hair that was flocked. Blue fixed eyes. Shoulder head marked "14" on neck. Blue cloth body marked "Poppy Doll". Composition arms. 10½ in. high.

264 Postcard produced during the First World War by E. Mack, King Henry's Road, Hampstead.

"ANYHOW—IT WAS

MADE IN GERMANY!"

265 The size of this character baby is indicated by the fact that it is seated in a toddler's dining chair and wears the clothes of a two-year-old Victorian child. Very pale bisque, open-closed mouth with two lower teeth. Blue sleeping eyes, original Kestner plaster pate to head. Bent-limb baby body. Marked "Made in Germany. G. 20. 211. G.D.K. 20" for Kestner. 26 in. high.

392

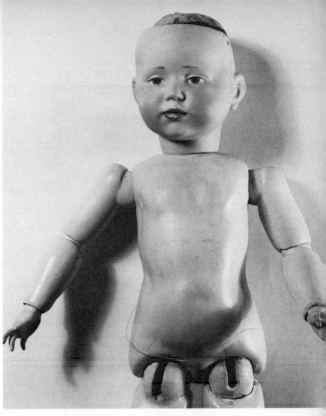

(*above left*) 266 One of the most sought-after German dolls is the jointed closed-mouth K & R marked "117A". This example in original state including label. 23½ in. high. (*above right*) 267 Closed-mouth doll with poor-quality bisque head marked "101 K & R" for Kämmer and Reinhardt. Painted eyes. Jointed body. 15 in. high. (*below*) 268 The typical toddler-type body used by Kämmer and Reinhardt with well-fitting hip sections. Head marked "K & R, S & H, 121, 62". 27 in. high.

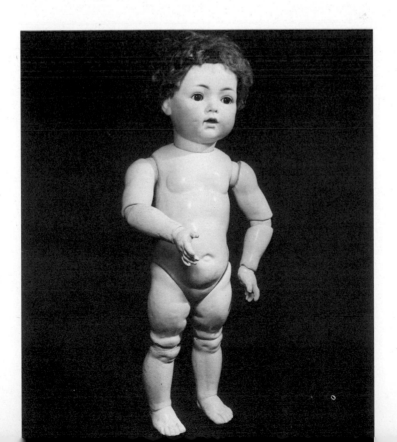

The dolls were a great success, as they were completely in the idiom of the period, and were sold dressed in the unornamented, sensible clothes that were becoming the accepted dress for the young. All the K & R dolls are desirable acquisitions, but those with a sulky expression known to American collectors as 'pouties' are the most highly-regarded as collector's items. The 117, a closed-mouth girl doll, is a particularly attractive model, as is the more common open-mouthed version of the same doll. This could be obtained in either a dull realistic finish or a very oily smooth bisque, which is less real but much rarer.

A good-quality, well-presented product was the principal aim of the firm. I was fortunate in buying one doll from a family that had once owned a toyshop, and the doll was acquired previously unsold and in its original imitation crocodile-skin box with metal protective corners. An attractive Art Nouveau brown and red label incorporated the words 'My darling' in the cartouche. Straw-filled packets of pink paper protected the doll top and bottom. The trade-mark of the company was in a prominent position on the label, which also bore the original English price of 11s. 6d.

The doll was sold dressed only in a simple chemise, with pink ribbon on the shoulders matching the bows in the mohair wig. Good-quality white shoes with pink laces and pink cotton socks were provided. I acquired a box of dolls' bodies and broken heads from the same family, who explained that a number always arrived broken because the lead weights behind the eyes smashed the heads. Usually the manufacturers tied the lead weight with string which was threaded through the two holes at the back of the head. On arrival, the shop-keeper's first task was to cut away this retaining string. Several of the broken Armand Marseille heads in the box still had the cords attached to the weights. The K & R eyes were made to a higher specification than the simple mechanism used by such firms as Armand Marseille, and most of their quality dolls did not need the eyes to be tied in transit, as lead weights were not used as often, except on small baby dolls.

The majority of Kämmer and Reinhardt heads were especially made for the firm by Simon and Halbig, and it is a very common mistake among collectors to attribute the dolls to the latter. It should be remembered that the heads were made to precise specifications from the Kämmer and Reinhardt model, and are therefore attributable only to that firm. Part of the confusion arises because the K & R mark is often at the top of the head and sometimes covered by a wig, while the S & H mark is much lower down. It is surprising how many long-established collectors still insist on calling the Kämmer and Reinhardt dolls Simon and Halbigs, despite the fact that the former, being doll-making innovators, are by far the more interesting.

Apart from the interest of the actual heads, the K & R dolls also exhibit a good range of unusual eye mechanisms. The metal device that enabled the doll to be laid down with its eyes locked in the open position was often used, particularly on the 126, which is a baby doll, and those marked 'N' for naughty, usually the 117. The head had to be sharply tilted to the side, which locked the position, and later tilted in the opposite direction to release it. Sideways-glancing eyes, known as 'flirty', were very frequently used, and give even their more ordinary dolls an added liveliness. The painted eyes which were used for baby dolls, and occasionally on the character children, were effective and very desirable to collectors when on the older dolls, as they are much rarer.

A very unusual 126 has a mechanism in the torso that enables the doll to raise and lower its arms while crying 'mama'. The regular voice box, which is quite common, was very crudely inserted by simply cutting the torso in half and then cutting a square filled with wire gauze to allow the escape of sound. To the new collector, these poorly-made voice boxes often appear to be a later addition, but they are of course completely authentic.

The changes in contemporary fashion are reflected in the body constructions of the K & Rs. When girls' skirts became shorter in the 1920s, a new type was evolved with a much slimmer body and long lower legs that allowed the joint to occur well above the knee. Ball-jointed knees were hardly decorative when revealed. Such bodies are usually referred to by collectors as 'teenage', though the firm continued to use the ordinary 'little-girl' heads for them. Very well-constructed toddler-type bodies were also made, one of which is illustrated to show the construction. When the doll is unclothed, this type of jointing looks very much more natural. Googly-eyed dolls were usually made with these toddler-type bodies, though occasionally the teenage type was used.

The firm claimed to have developed several doll-making innovations, such as the insertion of teeth, the use of oval wooden joints and stiff joints, as well as their work on eye mechanisms. It is believed that at some stage there was a merger between Simon and Halbig and Kämmer and Reinhardt, but no date is known and it is obvious that the two firms continued to preserve their separate identities. The Handwerck Company was also taken over by K & R, though again the separation of production continued. In 1916 the firm was sold to Gebrüder Bing, with Reinhardt remaining as adviser. But Bing Werke, as it later became known, again allowed the original company to operate in its traditional way. Some of these pre-First World War mergers seem to fit more into the pattern of the cartels operated in major German manufacturing industries at the time, as a method of self-protection and profit maximization.

Simon and Halbig

The Simon and Halbig Company, which was eventually taken over by Kämmer and Reinhardt, was probably the second largest maker of dolls' heads in Germany. Some of the 'blonde bisque' shoulder heads with moulded hair were discussed in the chapter on early bisque dolls, and they establish the fact that the company had been in operation for some time. The kid-bodied dolls that were given well-made shoulder heads are thought to have been originally made in the 1880s and 1890s, as they are very much in the tradition of French dolls with their large eyes, pierced ears and heavy brows. Dolls continued to be made from the original models for some considerable period, so that dolls constructed in this manner could have been made as late as the 1920s. The standard of work is very high in these early dolls, some of which were made with closed mouths. The bodies are also superior in construction to many of the contemporary German makers. A few rare dolls were made with swivel necks that fitted into shoulder plates – completely in the French manner.

It is known that Simon and Halbig heads were used by various French makers, both of dolls and automata, and their products are certainly as good if not much better than those of the average French manufacturer. Dolls with marked Jumeau bodies are often found with Simon and Halbig heads that are completely original, and it appears that the French were quite prepared to utilize this cheaper source of quality heads.

Various eye mechanisms were patented, including one similar to that used by the French makers which enabled the lid to be pulled down over the eye itself. A wire lever or sometimes strings leading from two holes at the back of the head were pulled to move the lids. Another invention enabled the eyes to move up and down and side to side by means of a single mechanism.

Relatively few character dolls were made by Simon and Halbig, though they provided them for Kämmer and Reinhardt and other firms. The products marked only S & H are usually made in a very traditional manner, but to a surprisingly high standard. The teeth, for instance, are almost always moulded rather than inserted, and consequently have not often suffered damage. Because of the quality of the heads, they were used on the Edison phonograph dolls and by Roullet and Decamps on many of their mechanicals. 'Eden Bébés' are also found with heads made by S & H.

Some very attractive coloured dolls were made, and the craftsmen were particularly skilful in tinting such heads to give a much more natural effect than is usually seen on German dolls. The Oriental double-jointed girl dolls, made to represent Japanese and Burmese, are very striking, especially when found in original condition wearing their kimonos. One character-type doll has the huge saucer-like eyes associated with the French makers, and while nothing like as beautiful as the coloured dolls, is obviously a good collector's piece.

Pensive-faced Simon and Halbigs are also very rare, though the head marked

(*above left*) 269   German doll of fine quality with slightly-pouting closed mouth and intaglio eyes. Marked ''K & R 114''. Toddler-type composition body with toes that turn in slightly. An unusually large doll for the type as it is 26 in. high.   (*above right*) 270   Two character babies. The doll with a comforter is the most famous of the K & R characters and is marked ''28 K & R 100''. Blue intaglio eyes, open-closed mouth. The girl doll with wig has blue sleeping eyes, and an open-closed mouth. Marked ''K & R, S & H 116 21''. 11¼ and 10¾ in. high.   (*below left*) 271   Jointed girl doll with blue painted eyes, wearing a wig. Closed mouth. Marked ''K & R 109''. 22 in. high.   (*below right*) 272   Jointed girl doll with fixed eyes. Unusual, as it has one wide lower tooth as well as two upper. Marked ''S & H''.

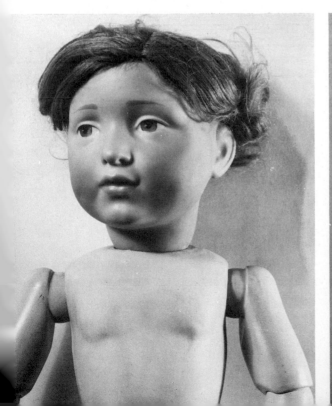

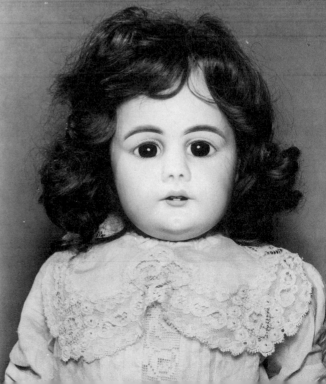

1388 is the least often discovered. This doll has the face of an older girl with a smiling 'open-closed' mouth. The heads that carry numbers ending in 'o' are usually of the shoulder-head type, while the socket heads usually carry numbers ending in '9' if they have the standard slightly open mouth with teeth. Since 'open-closed' and closed-mouth dolls were made in much smaller numbers, they were given sizes of their own.

The slim-bodied lady-dolls are also very much sought after. A few have the traditional cloth bodies with moulded composition or china limbs, but others came on slim composition-jointed bodies and have socket heads. The model numbers correspond quite closely in dolls made by Simon and Halbig, and do not have the slight differences that other makers show between one size and another. This precision was probably forced on the company by the fact that they supplied so many heads to specifications of other makers, who would not have welcomed variations.

It was German mass-produced dolls, such as those made by S & H and Armand Marseille, that brought well-made dolls within the reach of ordinary children. A lady brought up in the East End of London recalled that when she was a child, all she and her sister ever expected or received in their Christmas stocking was a cheap jointed doll. Their father bought these dolls on the Sunday before Christmas in Petticoat Lane, where, being dressed, they cost 1*s.* 11*d.* each. Undressed dolls were even cheaper. Identical dolls were always bought, one dark and one blonde, for each of the girls, who thought them beautiful, as they could move all their joints, open and close their eyes and even wore hats.

Various mechanical dolls that appealed to the top section of the market were made by the doll factories themselves, if they were fairly simple, or supplied to the makers of automata. The swimming doll, known as 'Ondine', was usually given a head made by Simon and Halbig, as were many *marottes* or *folies*. As the French walking dolls were so popular, the Germans found it necessary to make their own, some of which are very similar to those made by S.F.B.J., though the finish is not quite as good. A particularly well-constructed walker was provided with a Simon and Halbig head by its manufacturer, who covered the untidy mechanism between torso and legs with a neat pair of leather knickers. The key-wound mechanism was supplied by Roullet and Decamps, who probably marketed the doll, but since few dolls are found in their original boxes, it is difficult to be categoric.

Some attractive but rather puzzling S & H heads were used on small carved

273   Pair of Kammer and Reinhardt dolls. Both marked "K & R 117N". Both have four teeth in open mouths and brown eyes. The girl is in original boxed condition with K & R shoes and ribbon to wig. Added dress. Both have locking mechanism to eyes that enables the dolls to lie down with their eyes open. Original price of 11*s.* 6*d.* on girl's box. 23¼ and 21¼ in. high.

399

wooden dolls with blue- or green-painted legs. The style of costume suggests that the dolls were dressed in France, or certainly for the French market, and a few were mounted on musical boxes. Advertisements for similar dolls appear as late as 1910 in German trade catalogues. The dolls were fixed by the arms to a half hoop of cane. When the sides of the hoop were squeezed the doll swung to and fro and turned somersaults. Directions for making similar home-made toys are found in girls' magazines of around 1900, though a rag doll was suggested for use in the home-made version. Robert Culff, in his *The World of Toys* describes a few similar dolls as marionettes, though the catalogues that show the type appear to be simply advertising a play doll.

As Simon and Halbig maintained a high-quality product to satisfy their French customers, the price now asked for dolls of the type is higher than that of other German makers. Poor quality S & H dolls were made with badly-shaped mouths and thin composition bodies, but in nothing like the number made by the other manufacturers.

Armand Marseille

The most prolific of the German doll-makers, producing a wide range of cheap dolls, was Armand Marseille, who was established in Köppelsdorf as early as 1865. Like Simon and Halbig, the company manufactured heads for other firms so that examples are often found that were made, among others, for Bergman, Borgfeldt and Louis Wolf. Dolls marked A.M. are found in a very wide quality range, as they were made at a price to suit even the poorest of children. The cheapest have badly-made, thin composition bodies that are sometimes not even painted, and crudely-decorated heads of highly-coloured and coarse-quality bisque. The finest, such as those marked 1894 and believed to have been first made around this date, are very beautiful, with large eyes and well-modelled brows, that compare favourably with products of almost any maker.

Many collectors buy an Armand Marseille doll as a first purchase, not only because they are still relatively cheap, but also because many have very gentle and appealing faces. The most common shoulder head is the 370, and this is found on a variety of bodies, but those of gussetted leather are the most desirable, as they were originally the best quality. American cloth was sometimes used for later bodies made in the traditional leather manner, and these have often lasted in very fine condition. The most commonly-found heads on jointed composition

274 Realistic baby, complete with rolls of fat and fretful expression. Open-closed mouth, blue sleeping eyes, bent-limb body with ball joint to shoulder. Marked "1428 6". Size 13¼ in.

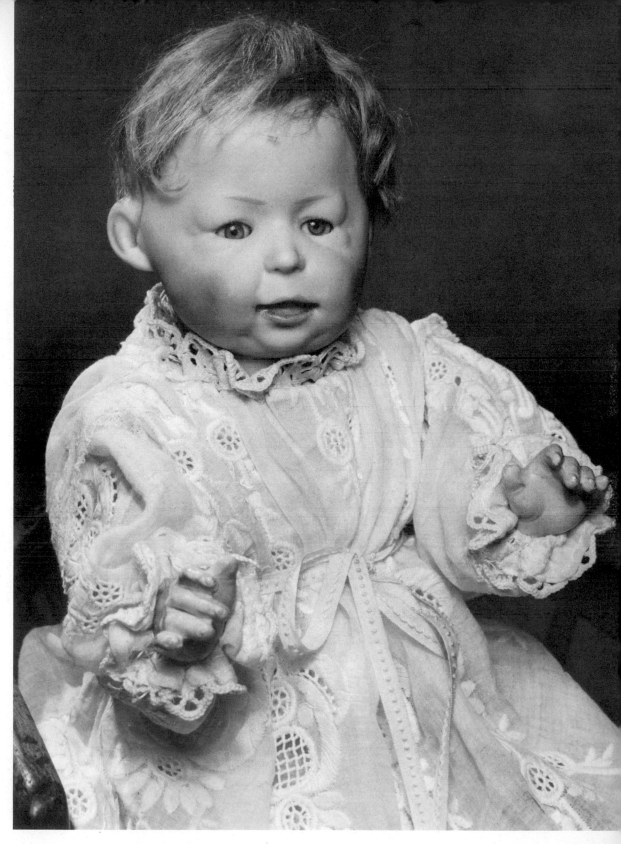

bodies are those marked 390. At present, collectors like the very pale tinted 390s, which can look very pretty when given fair wigs.

Greater realism was the aim of the makers in giving the dolls eyebrows of mohair. Slits were cut in the bisque on the brow line and mohair fixed to a cotton backing, was pushed through from inside the head. The hair has often fallen away from the canvas backing, which gives the dolls a rather macabre appearance, though when found in original state the method was very effective. Heads of this type are usually filled from crown to neck with the patent and model numbers, and obviously the manufacturer was rather proud of his achievement.

Character Armand Marseille dolls are very rare. One of the most avidly sought-after A.M.s is the lady-doll, with an elegant head, a closed mouth and rather incongruous sleeping eyes. A slim composition body was used for this doll, which is always a great favourite among collectors. As with almost every make of doll, those with closed mouths are the most expensive, but A.M.s with intaglio eyes are also very rare (though in a doll such as those made by Heubach, they would be completely unexceptional). The 550 closed-mouth 'little-girl' doll is another that is admired by collectors. At the time of writing, those with moulded top-knots and googly eyes are extremely popular.

Late dolls made by the firm often have colour that is sprayed on, rather than fixed in the normal way by firing. When in original condition, these painted heads are quite acceptable, and the eyes in particular were often given extra detail, rather like blue eyeshadow which makes them look large and realistic. It must be remembered that despite the fact that the manufacturers always claimed that the dolls could be washed, the painted heads suffer if cleaned in this way. A damp cloth only should be used to clean off marks, otherwise the paint begins to come away. The glue which fixes the wig in position has also very often damaged the surface of the paint, and the condition of such heads is frequently very poor. These lower-quality painted heads often fetch surprisingly high prices at country auctions, where local dealers appear able to resell at the current price for the fired bisque heads. Specialist dealers still sell such dolls very cheaply, as they are not popular with collectors.

The painted finish is acceptable when it is used on black dolls. A large number must have been made, but they are becoming steadily more difficult to find. The coloured dolls with the fired-on colour are the best, as they have a soft finish. The Oriental babies are also now very popular, and again there is a wide variety of tinting, from one that is almost pink to others of quite dark yellow. I consider the Oriental and closed-mouth black baby dolls among the most appealing of the type, and I find it very difficult to part with Orientals, even if I already have them in my collection, though I can muster little enthusiasm for baby dolls in general.

275 Some of the German dolls are very beautiful. This heavy-browed shoulder-headed doll has pierced ears and a slightly open mouth. Bisque lower arms. Jointed leather body. Marked on shoulder "70 S & H 8½" for Simon and Halbig. 22½ in. high.

The coloured dolls were in fact merely the basic baby heads produced in white by the firm, tinted and decorated in various ways, which meant that they could be made very cheaply and finished according to demand. The Red Indian dolls that were sold in appropriate costume are also effective, though nothing like as appealing. The Indian dolls were made mainly in small sizes, though larger examples are occasionally found; they often have the stiff-limbed unjointed bodies found on the cheapest dolls, but a few were made with small neatly-jointed bodies.

The 'Floradora' heads, which were made initially for Borgfeldt, were at first given leather bodies, though the more common are mounted on jointed composition and wood bodies. The legs on such dolls are often very gangling and amusingly spidery, having long dowel-like sections with little modelling. Floradoras appear to have been exported mainly to America, as dealers from the States affirm that they are as mundane as 390s, whereas in England they are much less common.

Some Armand Marseille dolls have the horseshoe mark which is more commonly associated with Heubach. This is because Armand Marseille and Ernst Heubach were joint owners of the Köppelsdorfer Porzellanfabrik. Most dolls were sold very cheaply dressed or wearing only a simple white chemise, as in the illustration of the Floradora doll which is still in its completely original state. As most German dolls were sold in this costume, a large number of patterns and ideas for clothes were given in contemporary ladies' and girls' magazines. Many advocated the teaching of dress-making skills to young girls, who could use their jointed dolls as models. Schools, even in quite poor areas, often requested that pupils should provide themselves with cheap jointed dolls that they could dress in miniature, sampler-like, garments in imitation of those worn by the girls themselves. An A.M. jointed 390 was dressed in 1910 by one little girl who, in addition to sewing the necessary petticoats, was also required to work a mend suitable for each material and the area of damage. In this way were created figures that are now of interest not only to doll-collectors, but also as accurate costume and needlework miniatures of the time.

The *Ladies' World* for 1901 commented that "no self-respecting mother and child could possibly take out a doll in last year's clothes. The whole effect of our costume would be spoiled." The articles goes on to comment that "As picture gowns are all the rage just now, a picture gown she shall have, in the Marcus Stone style." The advice to the mother suggested that the gown should be of pale blue muslin, with cream lace mitten sleeves. All should be edged with muslin frills, with a wide sash of blue silk around the waist. The combinations were obviously rather daring for the period, as they were made without sleeves and were only tied on the shoulder by narrow ribbon. Some additional amusing

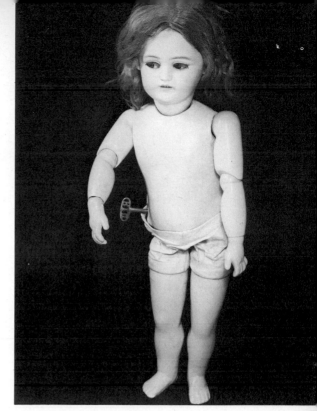

(*above left*) 276   Attractively-coloured jointed girl doll with well shaped wooden body. Eyes sleep by the lowering of the lids that are controlled by strings that lead from the back of the neck. Brown eyes. Marked "S & H 1039 7 Dep" for Simon and Halbig. Height 15 in.   (*above right*) 277   Walking doll whose mechanism is covered by kid knickers. Winding key marked "R.D." for Rouet et Decamps. Flirting blue eyes. Open mouth with moulded teeth, pierced ears. Head marked "1078 S & H Simon and Halbig, Germany". 23½ in. high.
(*below left*) 278   Simon and Halbig produced heads to the specification of several companies, in this case for Dressel. Head marked "S & H 1349 Dressel, S & H". Pierced ears, sleeping blue eyes. 19½ in. high.   (*below right*) 279   Delicately-tinted Burmese girl with original wig. Open mouth, pierced ears. Jointed body. Head marked "1329 S & H". 12 in. high.

(if somewhat sickly) advice is given with regard especially to wax dolls: "quite a lot of lace can be used, as dolls feel the heat dreadfully. It spoils all their pretty complexions too! For this reason be careful to hold a sunshade over them if out while the sun is strong, or, if they are driving, see that the hood is up." All this advice was obviously intended for quite wealthy little girls who accompanied their mothers on afternoon calls.

Gebrüder Heubach

Heubach was a very old-established firm, whose main porcelain factory was at Lichte, Thuringia. Dolls' heads were just a part of the firm's wide production. Collectors of general antiques are no doubt aware of the wide range of mantel-piece trivia made by the company, such as Easter bunnies and crawling babies. Though originally sold very cheaply, the figures were attractive, as were most similar items made by other German factories at the time. Some collectors specialize in the baby ornaments made by the company, and though they are not generally classified as dolls, they do fit reasonably into doll collections as small interest items in large cases, where they look amusing when arranged in groups.

The pensive-faced character Heubach baby is one of the most beautiful of German dolls. This character doll is made more attractive by the fact that a self-coloured pink bisque was used. This same self-coloured bisque is also found on some of the smaller closed-mouth babies with intaglio eyes. The colouring of the body of the paste gives the heads an extremely good matt finish, and means that they never shine in the rather sweaty way of many good bisque dolls, including those made by the foremost French makers.

The factory that assembled the Heubach dolls was at Sonneberg, and a very large variety of models was used, especially in comparison with many of the other German firms. Heubach obviously relied on a variety of different types for the sales appeal. One doll that was unusually grotesque, for a firm that specialized in dolls in comparatively good taste, was a clockwork walking doll that moved on wheels and cried 'mama' as it rolled along. The ultimate in character babies was also made by this firm, and represented a baby having a temper tantrum. This doll was sometimes given a wig, though the hair was more frequently moulded.

A few unusual character dolls made by the firm have the heads modelled in one with the shoulders, a type of construction that had gone out of general fashion among progressive makers before the introduction of character dolls. Some collectors like to think that any unmarked head that has highlights painted on the intaglio eyes is a Heubach. This method of painting the intaglio eyes was

(*left*) 280   Sitting in a Victorian child's pushchair, this Simon and Halbig doll wears the clothes of a four-year-old child. Pierced ears, pale blue eyes, marked "Simon and Halbig 85". 32½ in. high.   (*right*) 281   Two-faced doll with the other face smiling. Turns by pulling string leading from torso which also works squeaker voice box. Blue fixed eyes, composition lower arms and legs. Marked on body "Deutsches Reichs-Patent U.S.P. No. 243752". Made by Fritz Bartenstein. 12½ in. high.

commonly used by them, but it is extremely unlikely that all the unmarked dolls were made by this firm, and other characteristics, such as the construction of the bodies, have to be taken into account before any such attribution is made. One characteristic is the firm's method of including a loop for attaching the head to the body in the moulding of the head itself. This meant that the usual wooden disc with a metal loop was not necessary inside the head, though this latter method was the more commonly used even by Heubach.

Some of the Gebrüder Heubach baby-type bodies are very well constructed, though the heads used on these are generally unexceptional. The ordinary basic jointed dolls are often quite mean and uninteresting, but these appear to be the mass-produced dolls made for the poorer market. One doll that was made with moulded hair and bow was a reversion to the nineteenth-century type of head, and is reminiscent of the mantelpiece ornaments made in very similar fashion.

Like most other twentieth-century doll-makers, Gebrüder Heubach made googly dolls, some of which were quite large. Though too 'Walt Disney' for my personal taste, this type of doll has become highly collectable in the States and now command high prices especially those with eyes that move by the action of a wire lever that protrudes from the back of the head. Though the googlies are

407

408

now very popular, I find them rather disturbing, as they tread very uneasily on the border line between realism and fantasy.

Other German Makers

The quality products of Gebrüder Heubach should not be confused with the mundane dolls made by Ernst Heubach of Köppelsdorf. This factory made a large number of rather ordinary jointed dolls of poor quality, sometimes with very oddly-shaped limbs. They are much less desirable to collectors than those made by the Brothers Heubach. Having said this, it should also be noted that some of the prettiest German dolls were made by this company also. The bisque in the better dolls is quite fine, and the colouring very delicate. When their better heads are combined with the more solid bodies that the firm made, the result is very pleasant. As with the work of any maker, the quality of particular dolls has to be judged individually.

The straight-limbed toddler bodies made by Heubach Köppelsdorf are unusually well balanced and the dolls will stand safely. A few character types were made, and there was some association with the products of Armand Marseille, who owned part of the Köppelsdorf factory. When friends look at my own collection of dolls, it is usually a very pretty Heubach that is singled out for its pleasing appearance.

Dolls made by Schoenau and Hoffmeister are often confused by novice collectors with the work of the Simon and Halbig Company, as the initials used are the same. The Schoenau and Hoffmeister mark is SPBH with the initials P.B. enclosed in a five-pointed star, very like that used by Kämmer and Reinhardt. The P.B. stands for Porzellänfabrik Burggrub.

Though some of their products are notable for their delicacy of feature, they are not as highly regarded as those made by Simon and Halbig. Many of their dolls carry numbers on the back of the heads which appear to be the dates when the heads were made, such as 1906 or 1909, but the same models continued to be used for many years. The shoulder heads, which are rarely found, are marked with an 1800 sequence.

The Oriental girl doll made by the firm is one of its best products, though some of the closed-mouth babies are also quite effective. Baby heads marked only 'Porzellänfabrik Burggrub' were also the work of this firm and are often found untinted. There is a tradition among collectors that some of these dolls were intended as clowns, to have their white faces decorated by the purchaser.

282   This Armand Marseille head was one of the firms most attractive models. The heavy brows with distinct moulding and large dark eyes combine to give a good effect. Marked "1894 AM". Jointed composition body. 19¼ in. high.

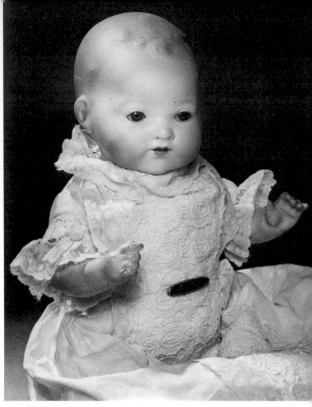

(*above left*) 283   One of the most commonly-found baby dolls marked "A.M. 996". Baby body with straight legs so doll can stand. 15 in. high.   (*above right*) 284   Known as 'My Dream Baby', this doll, in a wide variety of sizes, was probably the firm's most popular. It could still be bought in the late 1930s. Blue sleeping eyes. Marked "A.M. 351". 15 in. high.   (*below left*) 285   Armand Marseille "20", remarkable mainly because of its size. 40 in. high.   (*below right*) 286   One of the more unusual combined composition and leather bodies. Shoulder head marked "A.M. 370". Universal joint at knee, ne plus ultra at hip. 16¾ in. high.

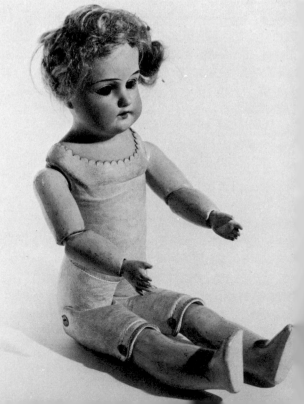

287 Unusual closed-mouth smiling Armand Marseille with intaglio eyes. Marked "A.7.M Germany". 20 in. high.

Many still bear some remnant of commercial sprayed-on colour, similar to that used on late A.M. heads, and it seems possible that the paint was of a very inferior quality, and has often washed off. Another possible explanation is that the firm sold off large numbers of undecorated heads at the end of production, but none of the explanations are completely satisfactory.

Gebrüder Krauss dolls are popular, as they closely resemble the better French dolls, with very heavy features and large eyes. Some of the jointed dolls made by this firm look so French that it is only by looking at the jointing method that the true German origin is revealed. Their closed-mouth doll is also particularly effective. The illustrated Krauss, when purchased, was trussed like a mummy in sticking plaster. I naturally assumed that the body was crushed or broken, but, after carefully unwrapping several layers of plaster, all the parts were discovered complete, if unstrung, and very sticky! Each generation had added another layer of plaster when the doll's joints began to feel at all loose!

The Kestner family had its doll-making origins in the very early years of the nineteenth century, and is one of those steadily prolific firms upon which Germany's success in doll-making was built. In the middle of the nineteenth century they were creating dolls in both papier mâché and wood, while glazed porcelain heads were made after 1860. All varieties of doll were produced by the Kestners, including wax, though the bisque dolls, being marked, are the most familiar.

Most collectors like to acquire at least one of the Kestner character babies, which are often only marked with a number. Heads have often to be identified by reference to the series of numbers produced by the firm. Though the models that bear the same number are very similar, they are not identical, for some have additional detail on the head or an extra roll of fat or a dimple. The mould number found on the head appears to refer to the type of model it is based on, rather than the mould itself. The character babies are well constructed, with rather heavy features; and although they command quite high prices, they are not rare unless very large.

The lady-dolls with kid bodies that sometimes bear the words 'Gibson Girl' stamped on the chest are also popular, as they are a late, but well-made, derivative of the *Parisiennes*. They were based on the paintings of haughty society ladies by Charles Dana Gibson. Their Oriental dolls are also greatly sought after. Many good-quality jointed dolls with heavy composition bodies carry numbers on the heads that fall within the Kestner range, and the dolls are thus usually attributed to the company, though it is not clear why such quality dolls were left unmarked. In the catalogue of Mary Merritt's Toy Museum is illustrated a doll made by Kestner with four optional heads, including one with a closed mouth and intaglio eyes. Such interchangeable heads were sold by several of the

288 In order to give added realism, slits were cut in the bisque head for eyebrows and mohair inserted. Sleeping blue eyes. Jointed composition body. Marked "DRGM 377439. Made in Germany DRGM 374830/37483". 20 in. high.

doll-makers, but are rarely found in original state. Despite the fact that the establishment was very large, and a quantity of dolls was produced, there are disappointingly few really interesting and progressive dolls in comparison with, for instance, Gebrüder Heubach. The Kestner effort appears to have been put mainly into the marketing of good-quality dolls made in a fairly limited range.

An even older-established company was that of Cuno and Otto Dressel of Sonneberg, in the heart of the doll-making area. The origin of this firm can be traced back to 1730. Members of the Dressel family married into other doll-making families such as the Fleischmanns, Greiners and Heubachs. This recorded family movement is typical of the way that various doll-making methods and improvements were passed from one group to another. Early dolls made by the firm are not marked, and it is their later dolls of bisque or wax with which the general collector is more familiar.

The trade-mark used by Dressel is more complicated than most and represents the Roman winged helmet with the caduceus, from which collectors derived the term 'mercury mark' as a descriptive definition. Papier mâché or composition-headed dolls made by the company carry the words 'Holzmasse' in the trade-mark, meaning wood pulp, a description which is of course left out on the heads of bisque. The firm is believed to have made the dolls of composition itself, while bisque heads were made to order by other companies. The bisque shoulder heads are often of very good quality, with well-moulded brows and sharply-defined features, but some of the smaller dolls are very nondescript, especially in comparison with some of the poured or waxed dolls, that the firm created. Few adventurous dolls were made, and all the products in bisque are completely in the traditional manner; even the seemingly essential character dolls were not made.

Some very progressive Heinrich Handwerck dolls were accurately modelled from life, and represented both adult and child-like faces. Many of the heads used by this company were actually made by Simon and Halbig. Early collectors thought that the name Handwerck meant that the dolls were the handwork of a particular man, because they mis-translated the word into English. It would be equally strange to claim that all Jumeaus were made as twin dolls, as the name translated means twin! The two firms Max and Heinrich Handwerck are simply the names of the companies.

Heinrich Handwerck produced both Oriental and character dolls, but these are very rarely found and the collector usually represents the firm's work by one of the double-jointed dolls that were much more common. Some leather-bodied dolls with shoulder heads were also made, but even these are comparatively rare, though they should not therefore be considered valuable! The dolls made by Max Handwerck, who also worked at Waltershausen, are of good quality but again rather ordinary.

289 Pretty A.M. 390 known as Geraldine by its original owner. Jointed body, carries night-gown in basket. 17¼ in. high.

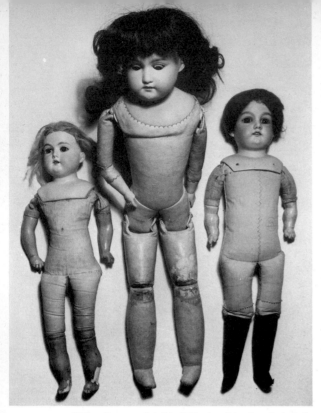

290 Group of A.M. 370 shoulder-headed dolls showing variety of bodies used by firm. The large doll, distorted because of angle, measures 25½ in.

291 Old photograph showing an Edwardian father preparing for Christmas morning.

292 Many dolls were sold dressed only in a chemise. Jointed girl doll in original boxed state. Marked "Floradora, A5M". 21 in. high.

293 Baby doll in original boxed condition wearing a lilac silk dress and bonnet of the style favoured in the 1920s. Marked "150 Welsch". 12 in. high.

294 a and b   Two faces of a three-faced doll showing Red Riding Hood, Grandma and Wolf. Ring on hood turns head. Jointed composition body. 13½ in. high.

An amusing variety of two- and three-faced dolls in various media was made by Fritz Bartenstein of Thuringia. The dolls are very cheaply constructed, but make up for their tawdry construction by their interest value. Carl Bergner also made multi-faced dolls of similar quality. Dolls of this type have a rod that runs through the head into the torso, and the head is turned either by a string that leads from the torso, or by a knob that is fixed to the top of a cardboard hood that conceals the unwanted faces. One very interesting version represents Red Riding Hood, her grandmother and a rather squashed-faced wolf!

The multi-faced dolls can be found on bodies of cloth-covered composition or cardboard with composition limbs, double-jointed or even baby-type bodies. Though adult collectors find them very interesting, children do not appear to grow very fond of them. A modern Japanese two-faced plastic doll was given to a London Museum recently because the child for whom it was bought disliked it so intensely.

417

295   Good-quality pale girl doll with huge eyes. Head marked ''50C14 R dep''. Pierced ears. Heavy ball-jointed body of French type with fixed wrists. White silk dress. 31 in. high.

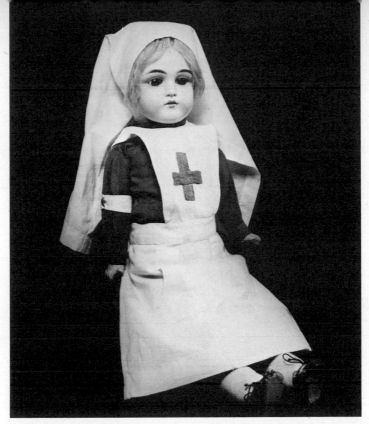

296   Nurse doll in original costume made from the uniform
of a First World War Red Cross Nurse. Very correctly-made
miniature clothes. Shoulder head marked "SPBH 1800".
Composition lower arms, hair-stuffed body. 17¾ in. high.

297   Postcard intended for children printed during the
First World War and entitled "Dress Rehearsal".

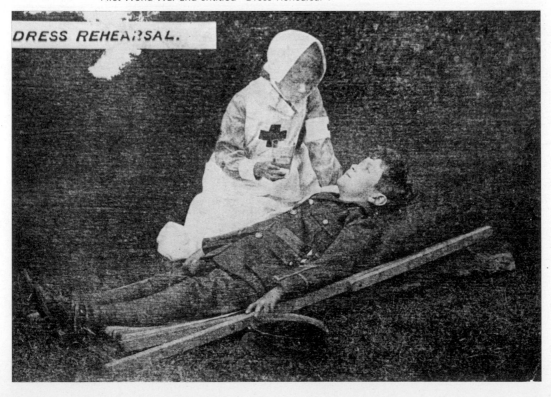

DRESS REHEARSAL.

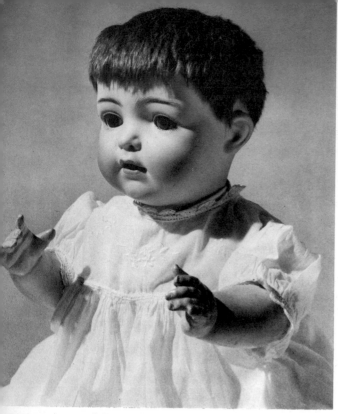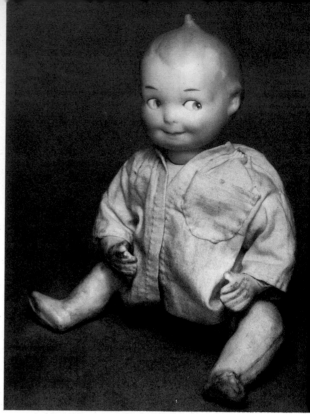

(*above left*) 298 Bent-limbed baby doll marked Franz Schmitt. Sleeping eyes. Open mouth. 19 in. high.
(*above right*) 299 Bisque-headed baby with moulded top knot. Blue painted sideways-glancing intaglio eyes. Head marked "G.B. 252 Germany. A.M. DRMR". Made by Armand Marseille for George Borgfeldt. 7 in. high. (*below left*) 300 Googlie doll by Heubach. Straight-limbed composition body. Glass sleeping eyes. Square Heubach mark on neck. 9 in. high. (*below right*) 301 One of the few coloured dolls with especially-moulded heads was produced by Ernest Heubach of Köppelsdorf. Made in several sizes. This doll has sticker on body, "Hills of London". Pierced ears with original ear-rings. Marked on head, "Heubach Köppelsdorf 390.16". 7¼ in. high.

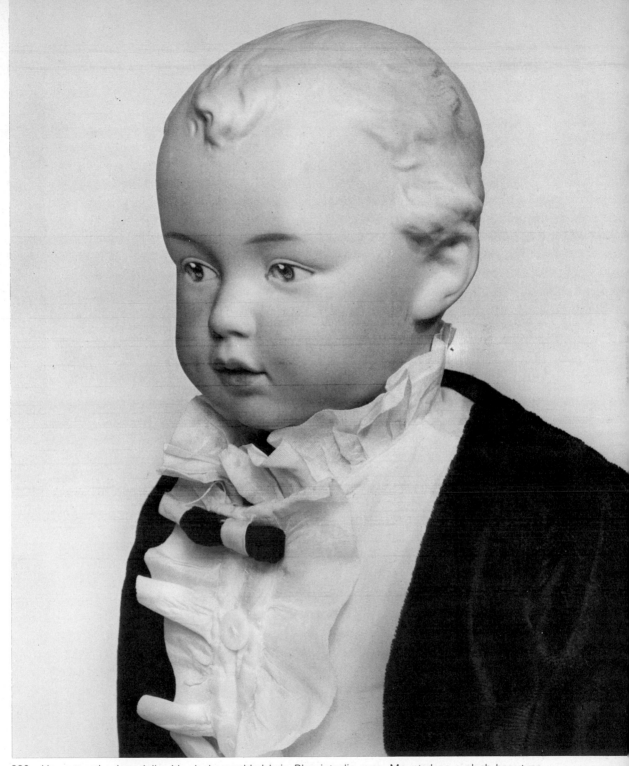

302   Very attractive boy doll with nicely-moulded hair. Blue intaglio eyes. Mounted on a plush bear-type
body. Wears black velvet suit. Probably Heubach. 16½ in. high.

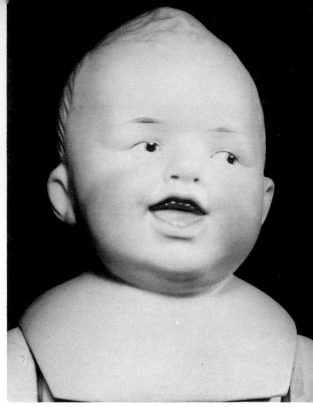

(*left*) 303   Boy doll with sideways-glancing intaglio eyes and open-closed mouth. Marked "Made in Germany" in blue circle on torso. "5" incised on neck. Probably by Heubach. 15 in. high.   (*right*) 304   Character babies on shoulder heads are much rarer than the socket type. Sideways-glancing intaglio eyes, open-closed mouth. Mounted on bent-limb composition body. Square Heubach mark on shoulder and "No. 8306". 15 in. high.

A very large number of small firms made dolls, and many heads are at present completely unattributable as records are lost, partly as a result of war damage, and partly as a result of the division of Germany. These unattributable dolls have to be assessed on their interest value. Almost any closed-mouth double-jointed doll is well worth buying, as they were not as popular when new, and fewer were made. German heads that have pierced ears are also worthwhile purchases, as they tend to be fairly early and made in the period when children's ears were still sometimes pierced. The painting of the face should be regular and delicate on a doll of good quality, and the eyebrows should preferably be moulded. Simon and Halbig dolls are liked because they often have both moulded teeth and pierced ears, though other dolls made by little-known makers are sometimes of even better quality.

The manufacturers obtained eyes mainly from Lauscha, and these also vary greatly in quality. The best are filamented, but some have a very unpleasant, flat, pale effect that is hardly attractive. Not all the dolls were originally given eyelashes. Many of the glass eyes were simply given the painted and wax-dipped lids that enabled the eyes to move easily. One doll in boxed condition had one eye with lashes, and one without – a reminder that despite the fact that dolls now

422

305 Amusing googlie-eyed doll. Head marked with square Heubach mark and "Einco" above, being the trademark of Eisenmann and Co for whom these heads were especially made. Googlie eyes moved by wire lever. Original costume. 14 in. high.

(*top left*) 306 Googlie-eyed doll marked on neck with the trademark of Strobel and Wilken. Straight-limbed composition body, white moulded socks with brown shoes. A rather shiny bisque. 7 in. high.

(*top right*) 307 Dolls produced by Gebrüder Krauss often look rather French in appearance because of their large eyes and heavy brows. Double-jointed composition doll. Marked on head "GBR 165K8". 22½ in. high.

(*right*) 308 Straight-limbed toddler-type girl doll. Open mouth with teeth. Whistling tongue. Head marked "Heubach Köppelsdorf 342.3/0" 14½ in. high.

(*opposite*) 309 Baby doll in high chair, marked "BSW 2097" for Bruno Schmitt. Jointed girl doll with sleeping eyes. Wearing brown dress and pinafore marked "MOA 200 Welsch". 18 and 31¾ in. high.

(*above left*) 310   Double-jointed girl with blue sleeping eyes, open mouth. Marked "Heubach Köppelsdorf 230". 23¼ in. high.   (*above right*) 311   Very slim, jointed girl doll with unusual modelling to eyelids. Slightly open mouth. Marked "S". 21 in. high.   (*below*) 312   Pair of large jointed dolls with fixed wrists. Doll with dark hair has pierced ears, heavy brows, open mouth, marked "172". Fair-haired doll wearing a pink, white embroidered dress, has blue sleeping eyes. Marked "101". 27½ and 29½ in. high.

command quite high prices, they were originally cheap, and often exhibit the maker's carelessness. Flirty-eyed dolls are always popular, as are those with the lever or string mechanism. Any doll that can be claimed as having been manufactured for the French market, because it has a French-type body, is immediately much more desirable! The small coloured dolls and character babies made by the smaller firms are well worth buying, if of good quality or unusual in any respect.

Condition of a doll, especially one made in Germany, is obviously important, but it is unrealistic to expect the doll's body to be pristine unless it is in boxed condition, which is very rare. The dolls have usually been played with by several generations of children, and the collector should not become so involved in marks and makers as to forget that the collected objects were in fact children's toys.

Any doll that is dressed in the beautifully-hand-stitched clothes made by its original purchasers is naturally worth more than a doll nicely dressed in reconstructed clothes, but again it must be remembered that when dealers acquire the dolls, they are often dressed in a wild assortment of oddments from the last fifty years which do little for their appearance. Just as an antique chair is re-upholstered

(*left*) 313   Large baby doll with well-modelled composition body. Sleeping eyes, open-closed mouth. Painted moulded hair. Marked "14". Kestner. 24 in. high.   (*right*) 314   Flirty-eyed baby doll. Open mouth. Marked "257 JDK Germany". The clothes were made as a sampler by a trainee needlework teacher in 1911. 16½ in. high.

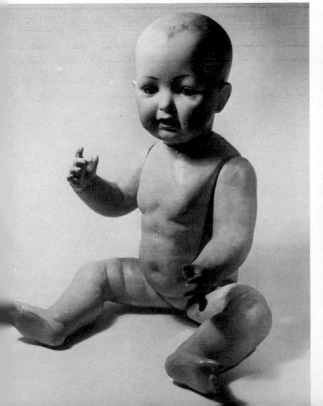

(*above left*) 315   Character baby with moulded tongue and two upper teeth. Slightly-open mouth. Marked "A.B.G." for Alt, Beck and Gottschalk. 14 in. high.   (*above right*) 316   Jointed girl doll with stick-like legs. Attractive head marked "SPBH 4000". Large brown eyes. 20½ in. high.   (*below left*) 317   Jointed girl doll in original costume marked "Max Handwerck Germany". Blue eyes. 22 in. high.   (*below right*) 318   Jointed doll in white dress. Pierced ears. Marked "Heinrich Handwerck, Simon & Halbig". 19½ in. high.

319   Pair of fine all-bisque double-jointed googlie flirting-eyed dolls. Unmarked. Dressed in original yellow dresses. 7½ and 8 in. high.

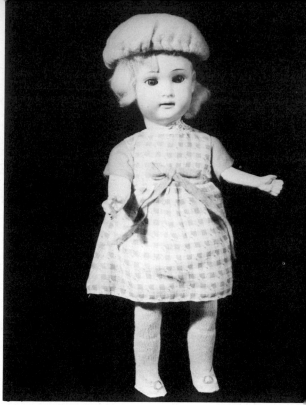

(*above left*) 320 Boy doll with moulded hair and sleeping eyes. Closed mouth. Toddler-type body. Head marked "2048", probably for Bruno Schmidt. 14½ in. high. (*above left*) 321 Doll marked "Special" in boxed state. Straight-limbed body. Blue felt beret. 11½ in. high. (*below*) 322 Jointed girl doll with pierced ears. Head marked "1362, A.B.G.", for Alt Beck and Gottschalk. 23½ in. high.

if the cover is unsightly, so it is necessary tastefully to re-dress dolls in order that they become attractive objects to have on display.

Exports of dolls, both to England and America, flourished around 1900, but the First World War stopped production of such frivolous items, and after the war bad feeling continued to such an extent that a sale of German dolls in America had to be halted because of riots. During the war, over-patriotic parents and children even burned dolls that had originated in Germany. It is fortunate that many owners were not aware of the origins of their dolls, or no doubt many more would have perished at the hands of young patriots.

After the war, the German industry was slowly reorganized and the old trade outlets gradually re-established, but a further blow was given by the galloping inflation which Germany suffered as a result of the war, and which forced many old companies into bankruptcy in the 1920s. China-headed dolls were also becoming less popular as unbreakable types were developed, and shopkeepers were not as eager to stock these fragile items when children were just as satisfied with unbreakable dolls. It is probable that several firms perished as a result of the reorganization of German industry under Hitler on military lines – thereby ending the world supremacy of an industry that had given pleasure to so many generations.

323   View of the warehouse showroom of W. H. Smith & Son, Booksellers and Newsagents in *British Toymaker*, 1916.

324   A selection of the dolls assembled by W. H. Smith & Son during the First World War. Page from *British Toymaker*, 1916.

FOURTEEN

ENGLISH AND AMERICAN
BISQUE DOLLS

American Bisques

In the period before the First World War, there was little doll-making in England and comparatively little in the United States. The German manufacturers produced well-made dolls so cheaply that any competition in the making of china-headed dolls would have been rather pointless, as the Germans had developed the skills necessary for successful firing of heads, which potteries without the relevant experience found hazardous and consequently expensive because of kiln wastage. The Americans appeared to resent the necessity for imported dolls far more than the English, and even before 1900, progress was made in establishing successful factories to produce both papier mâché and wooden dolls. As many Germans had emigrated to America, there was a core of skill and craftsmanship that was capable of being developed.

Dolls of wax as well as wood and papier mâché had been made in the nineteenth century by these émigré workers, while regional dolls such as those of corn husk, had been made in the Southern Highlands for about 200 years and are still made today. The rawhide 'Darrow' dolls that were made in Connecticut in the 1860s were also purely American in concept, and though commercially manufactured, are more reminiscent of folk items. Goldsmith, remembered particularly for his papier mâché heads, attempted in 1893 to make heads of imitation bisque by treating the basic composition with ether to give a dull finish that was intended to resemble the imported china heads. Little success, however, appears to have been achieved by the method, as is usually the case when material is tortured into an imitation of something else.

Many companies, both in England and America, registered patents for dolls that sound fascinating, but as examples are not known, it is difficult to assess whether any were actually produced commercially. The American inventors gave a great deal of attention to innovations, particularly with regard to unbreakable dolls, which were the logical successors to the work of the Greiners and the Schoenhuts. Examples of a clockwork walking doll made around 1875 by A.E. Hotchkiss have been found, but as they were of an extremely strange shape, it is not surprising that only a few appear to have been made. A. W. Nicholson of Brooklyn registered a patent for a mechanical walker; but again it is doubtful whether the design ever reached production stage.

A phonograph doll was patented in 1888 by W. W. Jacques of Massachusetts. A turntable was contained in the torso and wound from the back. The Edison Toy Manufacturing Company eventually obtained the rights of this invention and used it in a French-made doll. Edison himself experimented with phonograph cylinder dolls, but they were hardly things of beauty, and were given only to his family. Eventually a satisfactory body was created and the Edison phonograph dolls enjoyed a great success from 1891. The heads were obtained from Germany, mainly from Simon and Halbig, but like so many marketers, the Americans sold them as 'French jointed dolls' despite the fact that the heads were German and the bodies purely American. Though a very large number of these dolls were made and some were exported, very few appear to have reached England, and even in America they are now quite rare.

Doll-making formed a considerable industry in Boston, Philadelphia and New York during the second half of the nineteenth century, but it was an industry that relied on German imports for the most important part of the product. The heads used on the dolls' bodies were made by such companies as Armand Marseille. It is interesting to note that the 'ne plus ultra' joint, that was used so often by the German makers, was patented in America by Sarah Robinson in 1883. The American toy-makers were proud of the well-constructed bodies they made of wood fibres and various composition substances that were the waste materials of local industry.

Several tentative efforts at china doll-making were embarked upon during the First World War as the supply of the essential German heads suddenly ceased. An amusing attempt to make imitation bisque heads out of some kind of prepared flour was made by a Los Angeles firm, Kellow and Brown, but the heads were rapidly eaten by insects despite all efforts to treat them.

The first bisque heads were made from moulds obtained from Armand Marseille. According to American collectors, these dolls can be distinguished from the German by their inferior bisque and poor decoration. One of the companies to make use of the Armand Marseille moulds was the Fulper Pottery of Flemington, New Jersey. Their dolls are marked as having been made in the U.S.A., and the company appears to have ceased production of dolls' heads after 1920, when the German dolls reappeared on the market.

The Fulper Pottery included some all-bisque dolls among its products, such as Kewpies and the 'Peterkin' doll designed by Helen Trowbridge. Some of their dolls with moulded hair and intaglio eyes are very reminiscent of heads made by Gebrüder Heubach, while their girl dolls, though of poorer quality, are also very much in imitation of the average German product. As dolls were made by these old-established potteries for such a short time, it is not surprising that a particularly American style failed to emerge.

According to Dorothy Coleman, the Horsman Company, which had been importers and doll distributors since the middle of the nineteenth century, helped the Fulper Pottery in the making of heads. Harold Bowie, Benjamin Goldenberg and Horsman himself gave advice on the making of dolls with both jointed and baby bodies. Benjamin Goldenberg was the firm's expert on the colouring of the bisque itself, and some of the Fulper heads also bear the Horsman mark.

Fulper dolls were made in some variety and in sizes between 14 and 24 inches. In 1920, at the end of the production period, they were marketing ten girl models with socket heads and eight baby models. A variety of eye methods was also used, ranging from the cheapest intaglio to glass or even celluloid. An interesting sales ploy was that wigs had to be purchased separately!

The first American bisque dolls are generally believed to have been made by Ernst Reinhardt of the Bisc Novelty Manufacturing Company, Ohio, as some of their heads made from original moulds bear a 1914 patent mark. A wide variety of heads was made, some in the German manner with the cut-away top for the fitting of the wig. They do not appear to have made the all-bisque dolls that were becoming increasingly popular. Though the Bisc Novelty dolls are very familiar to American collectors, they are not found outside that country, as they were made purely to satisfy home demand.

Another American pottery that attempted to satisfy the wartime demand for dolls was the Lenox Company, under the management of Walter Scott Lenox. This firm made some heads for 'EFFanBEE' which had turned wooden limbs and the usual composition bodies. These dolls are very rare, as only a small number were made, and a collector's chance of finding an example is remote.

The Paul Revere Company of Boston, Massachusetts, made socket heads with open or closed mouths during the war. Most of their dolls were intended to be given wigs, though some all-bisque dolls were also made. Like the Fulper Pottery, this firm found that doll-making was pointless once the German dolls began to be imported again, though this did not take place until several years after the war. The Boston Pottery marketed dolls' heads in these immediately post-war years, as did the American Bisc Doll Company and the Progressive Doll Company of New York, who both produced the traditional range of jointed and baby dolls.

Between the two world wars, collectors' dolls were especially made by the St Clears, who ran the very famous Humpty Dumpty Dolls' Hospital at Redono Beach, California. This hospital was begun during the Depression years in the owners' chicken farm, which was empty because the stock and equipment had all to be sold. As doll-collecting was fast gaining ground in the States, even in 1929, the St Clears decided to cater for the collectors needs. Mrs St Clear had run a dolls' hospital and shop before the war, and she re-dressed her old stock of pre-war imported dolls and unpacked boxes of old spare parts.

The new service for collectors obtained a quick response and dolls were sent to the Humpty Dumpty Hospital from all over America. Wallace St Clear invented all sorts of gadgets, including one for filling bodies with sawdust efficiently. Apart from their useful work in restoration, the St Clears also employed designers to create china dolls especially for the new American collectors. A replica of the so-called 'Jenny Lind' was the first to be made, and was sold in three sizes, with a white, pink and lustre finish. Bisque as well as china dolls were made to the highest specifications necessary for luxury items.

There is an unpleasant artificiality about dolls that are especially made for inclusion in collections. They have no legitimate place in the history of dolls if considered as children's playthings, but as so many have found their way into representative collections, it appears necessary to make some mention of them. It is a pity that these well-constructed figures were so often made merely as replicas of older German dolls rather than from contemporary original models. Fortunately there are a few good exceptions. George and Martha Washington are justly the best-known creation of the St Clears. The figures were designed by Martha Oathout Ayres, who modelled the President's hands from those of her own husband. Martha Washington's wrinkled hands were modelled on those of Emma St Clear herself. The same designer also modelled an original doll, 'Danny', on her own son, and 'Modern Madonna' on her daughter. It is by dolls of this original type that the work of the St Clears should be represented in collections, though even the replica dolls are very popular in the States.

Another doll-maker who produced very collectable work is Elizabeth C. Scantlebury of Brooklyn, New York, who designed wax costume dolls and 'artistic' baby dolls in the 1920s. Bisque dolls designed by Grace Corry Rockwell are also very desirable, especially those with attractive moulded hair. More recently Lewis Sorenson of Los Angeles made quality bisque dolls, among which were figures modelled on Marie Antoinette, Will Rogers and a hobo.

The making of American bisque dolls can be seen to divide quite firmly into two sections. The first is the dolls that were made purely as play items, to replace those that had been imported from Germany, and the second those made purely as display items for collectors by such people as the St Clears. Their contribution as bisque doll-makers is therefore slender, though that of the English is even more so.

A substantial contribution to the history of dolls was, however, made by American doll designers, who created several completely new types of doll which were made in Germany to their specifications.

There were several large American doll importers including Horsman, Borgfeldt, Schwartz Brothers and Wanamakers as well as Sears Roebuck, Strasburger and Pfeiffer and Company. These importers obtained the bulk of their supply from Germany and France, but were necessarily alive to the demands of the American market. Several of these companies specially commissioned artists to design dolls, sometimes based on contemporary cartoon characters, which could be made exactly to order by such firms as Kestner.

Horsman employed Helen Trowbridge to design dolls such as Little Billie, Peterkin, Tom Thumb, Sunshine and Mischievious Pippkin. The firm was very alive to the interest shown by the public in the whimsical characters created by such illustrators as Brinkerhoff. Their 'Little Mary Mix Up' was based on a Brinkerhoff cartoon, while their Campbell kids were based on the advertising characters for Campbells Soups. Drawings by Charles Twelvetrees inspired the HEbees and SHEbees which were made completely of bisque and in sizes up to 12 inches high. The dolls had simple joints at leg and shoulder and wore short vests and very large baby shoes in order to balance the figures. HEbees wore blue shoes and SHEbees pink.

The firm was quick to take advantage of the growing popularity of character babies and introduced their own realistic Baby Bumps. Other dolls were based on characters invented by such artists as Grace Drayton, and almost every year new dolls were created to satisfy children who appear to have suddenly grown tired of the old type of conventional, sweetly-smiling little girls.

Borgfeldt also commissioned doll designs from Grace Drayton, who had been the first to use large round eyes known as googlies in her dolls. Among their other designers was Helen Nyce and Geneviève Pfeffer, who created 'splash me'. Katie Jordan also worked for Borgfeldt, and designed the well-known Happifats for them. The Happifats represented a fat little couple who appear to suffer from some unfortunate glandular disease. They had first appeared in John Martin's book and were obviously very attractive to a generation of children who appeared to relish distorted figures.

The forerunners of the American fashion for making figurines in imitation of fictional characters seem to have been the Brownies, which were made as a result of an illustration by Palmer Cox in the *St Nicholas Magazine* of 1883. All the American importers remained aware of the interest in such characters, and the number created between the wars is very great, especially in comparison

437

with England, where very few original dolls were commissioned. Mickey and Minnie Mouse are again fantasy creations that hover between doll and toy, and were also products of the American style, while even the Teddy bear originated in that country, though the Germans have a counter-claim. The English contribution by contrast is extremely conventional except for the work of Deans Rag Book Company.

A doll with a crying face known as 'Tummy Ache' was made in 1916 by Jeanne l'Orsini, whose other dolls were given names like 'Mimi' or 'Didi'. Like most bisque dolls, they were made in Germany. The Kestner Company in particular appears to have executed much of this American designer's work.

George Borgfeldt is owed a great debt by collectors as he not only commissioned Rose O'Neill, but also Grace Storey Putnam, who created the Bye-Lo Baby.

Rose O'Neill's Kewpies were copyrighted in 1909, and it was again to Kestner that the company turned for the original production, though it was necessary later for many other companies to make Kewpies to supply the tremendous demand. Rose O'Neill later designed Scootles, and just before the outbreak of the last war, Budda Ho Ho, which is quite rare, as the Oriental was understandably unpopular in America.

The most famous of all American doll designers is Grace Storey Putnam, whose Bye-Lo Baby was copyrighted in 1922. She set out to design and make an attractively realistic doll that would appeal to children, rather than a figurine based on an illustration, which would be as much in place on a piano or mantelpiece as in a nursery.

Though Grace Putnam had trained as a watercolourist, her own career had been neglected in favour of that of her husband, who was a sculptor. After divorce, it was necessary for her to earn her own living again and she became an art teacher. She developed a great enthusiasm over her project of creating a doll in imitation of a baby of about three weeks old. After searching nursing homes, orphanages and hospitals, she eventually found a baby in a Salvation Army home that was exactly suitable. The Colemans repeat an unconfirmed rumour that the model was a dead baby; but Eleanor St George states that part of the head was modelled while the baby was asleep, and when she returned three days later to complete the model, the baby's appearance had changed so much that the artist was forced to model the remainder of the head from memory. The original head was modelled to fit a body socket, but was commercially made with a flange neck on a cloth body.

Grace Putnam made several plaster casts of the head and her brother cast a wax head which she painted in oil colour. The doll was given a soft body, to make it more attractive to the doll-makers to whom she offered her design. Like Kämmer

(*above left*) 325   Girl with open-closed mouth, blue fixed glass eyes. Marked "3½, English Make, Hancocks".
12½ in. high.   (*above right*) 326   Shoulder-headed lady-doll with blue painted eyes. Marked "M & S" for
Mayer and Sherrat. 12½ in. high.   (*below*) 327   The poor-quality bisque rather than the modelling made
collectors slow to acquire English dolls, such as this shoulder head with moulded bow to hair. Marked "S.
Classic England". 11½ in. high.

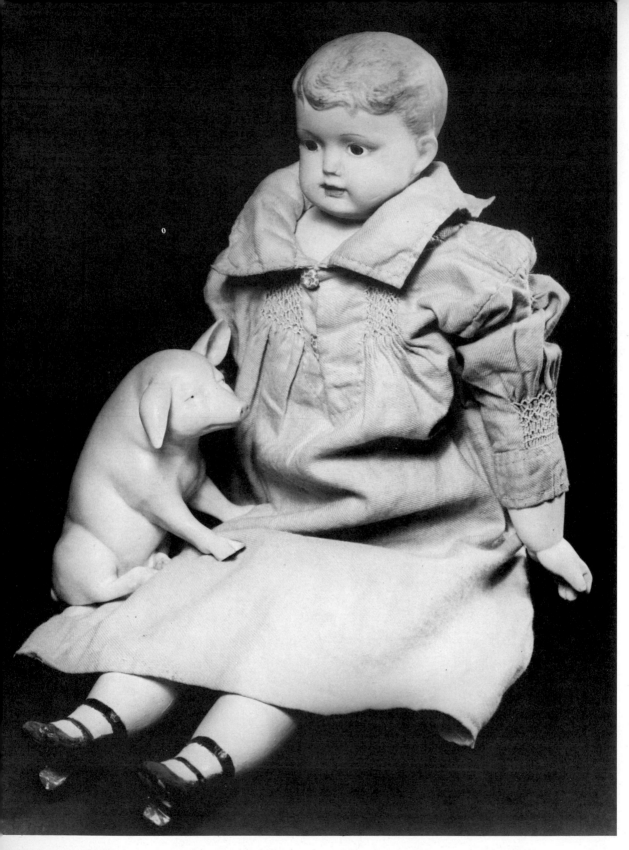

440

and Reinhardt's 'baby', Grace Putnam's Bye-Lo was at first considered to be offensively realistic, and she found difficulty in finding a maker, until the Borgfeldt lawyer was shown the doll and immediately saw its possibilities. She had originally wanted the doll to be made in rubber, to look more realistic, but Borgfeldts envisaged the doll only in German bisque.

The first Christmas the doll appeared in the shops, people actually queued to buy it, and it became known as 'the Million Dollar Baby'. The 1922 copyright describes the doll as life-size, and with narrowed eyes and a closed mouth. At this distance in time, it is difficult to understand why the doll created such a stir, as heads that were equally realistic had been imported since 1910. The first Bye-Lo Babies had bodies designed by Borgfeldts, but Grace Putnam herself designed the bent-limbed cloth bodies that are most often found. She made her rather untidily-shaped bodies in seven sizes, though the flange heads that could be bought alone for home assembly were eventually made in nine sizes.

The heads were made by a variety of makers, including Alt, Beck and Gottschalck, Kling, Kestner and even Schoenhut, who made a wooden version. Some were made as small as 4 inches, all-bisques, which are possibly the most attractive, since they are not as reminiscent of the stories about the dead baby as are the larger models. Some of the all-bisques have slippers and moulded socks, while others wear wigs. These miniature versions have both fixed and swivel necks and eyes that can be painted or sleeping. Most of the all-bisques originally carried labels on the chest which read 'Bye-Lo Baby, Germany'. The very precise marking sometimes spreads almost across the whole of the back, and reads 'Copr by Grace S. Putnam, Germany'. Some of the all-bisques even wear nappy pants threaded with moulded ribbon.

It appeared worth repeating the Bye-Lo Baby story in some detail, as it is the only doll whose manufacture has been so precisely documented. Due to the great success of 'the Million Dollar Baby', Borgfeldt persuaded Grace Putnam to create another doll. She envisaged a fairy-like doll, to be a complete contrast to its predecessor, with huge exotic wings. The design was unfortunately modified by Borgfeldt who decided a more realistic type of baby doll would be more in demand. A seated doll with rather tentative wings was made and marketed as the Fly-Lo Baby. The head was quite attractive, but the permanently-seated body was not popular and the doll did not have the realistic appeal of its predecessor. Few were actually made, as it was becoming difficult to obtain the bisque heads from Germany, since bisque was going out of fashion.

328   Boy doll carrying china pig. Shoulder head marked "D.P.Co." for Diamond Pottery Company, who also made multi-faced dolls. 15½ in. high.

The American Depression eventually forced the company to abandon the project.

Just before the last war, Grace Putnam designed a doll's house with a typically American family of very realistic dolls. The dolls were never commercially produced and the originals are now in the Bowers Memorial Museum, Santa Ana, California. Though Bye-Lo Babies are extremely common to American collectors, they only occasionally come up for sale in England, for again the American designers were creating dolls to satisfy the home demand for items that had some originality.

English Bisques

Like the American, the English contribution to the actual manufacture of china dolls is relatively small. When doll-collecting first became popular, a large variety of china and bisque heads were erroneously attributed to famous English factories as their quality was felt to be too good for them to have originated in Germany. Collectors' opinion has now swung completely in the opposite direction, and it is now fashionable to claim that no heads were made in England before 1914, a statement that appears too sweeping.

As very few shards have been found during excavations of pottery sites, it is unlikely that dolls were made in any number before the First World War forced the British government to encourage the potters to make them. It would have been very depressing for the general public had all the china dolls disappeared from the shops shortly after the outbreak of war, and several potteries were persuaded, apparently against their better judgement, to make bisque dolls' heads. It was soon found that considerable skill was needed to fire thin bisque without suffering a very large percentage of kiln damage, which meant that many heads were so distorted and misshapen that they could not be sold. Consequently, once the war ended and German dolls again began to be imported, the unwilling manufacturers were quick to abandon the uneconomical project.

With the possible exception of Hancock, the English makers were unable to make a fine bisque head, and their thickness is very noticeable when compared with the delicate German products. Most of the factories who produced dolls were really makers of domestic crockery, and were completely unused to making the delicate decorative china, such as mantelpiece figurines, which the German potteries created with such skill. The exception is the Goss Pottery, which was capable of producing extremely fine work, including busts that were better than those made in Germany. When the Goss Pottery turned to doll-making, the standard immediately dropped, and the Goss heads are of such poor quality and decoration that it is difficult to understand how they could have been marketed by the same company that made, for instance, the beautifully-tinted and modelled head of William Shakespeare.

The modelling of many English heads appears to have been done by inexperienced designers. It was possibly felt that dolls were really of no long-term interest, and only the cheapest materials and workmen were felt worth expending on their manufacture. Another possible reason for the poor standard is the number of workers who were lost to the army, which must have caused the factories some strain.

A rather short-lived publication, the *British Toymaker*, contained an interesting comment on the English trade in 1916.

The Staffordshire potteries have already come in for a good deal of attention in toy trade circles since the outbreak of war, largely because of the growing activity that is being displayed in 'The Five Towns' in regard to the manufacture of porcelain dolls' heads, a business that is destined to assume important proportions as manufacturing difficulties become less acute and labour more plentiful than is the case at present. Up to quite recently, however, with the exception of the manufacture of numerous varieties of toy tea sets, the efforts of North Staffordshire in the direction of toy making have been associated chiefly with dolls, that is to say, either dolls' heads and limbs made by competent potters, mainly in porcelain, but sometimes in earthenware, or stuffed bodies for dolls made quite independently of the potting trade by firms who have been progressive enough to realise that there is a decided opening for new and brisk business in the assembling of dolls in the district where heads and limbs will henceforward largely be made.

The reproduced account, written specifically for the toy trade, which would have been quick to point out errors, suggests that china dolls were made to some extent in the Five Towns before the war. The extent of this manufacture is very hard to assess, as the larger companies do not appear to have participated in any doll-making. Smaller factories were continually being amalgamated or taken over by other firms, and records of items that would have been rather insignificant are lost, though it does appear necessary to revise the current assertion that heads were definitely not made. If heads were made in any number, they must have been of the glazed porcelain or possibly the pipe clay type, because bisque dolls that are completely unmarked are rarely found, and the English potters were never very skilful in their utilization of this substance.

The same wartime report gives a suitably biased account of the contemporary German doll industry which, it was claimed, had been reduced to complete ruin by the war and the stopping of German exports. The writer also claimed that the Germans themselves had stopped buying dolls for their own children.

443

Representatives in the German Reichstag of all the constituencies in Central and South Germany, where the effects of the collapse are felt by former employees of toy factories, large and small, as well as by individual toy makers in the villages, have combined to urge the Imperial Government to initiate adequate measures of relief and have received a pledge to this effect from the Imperial Secretary of State for the Interior.

Gloating over the demise of the Germany Industry, the English decided that in future it would be necessary to make dolls themselves in large quantities. They obviously felt that never again would the Germans be able to supply, or the English desire, the traditional products.

Large English companies decided that it was necessary to establish their own toy-making factories to supply the variety of items they had previously obtained from Germany. The policy of W. H. Smith & Son was typical of the movement in this direction, and it is by the kind co-operation of the firm's archivist that the following report of just one leading English firm's activity in the period was obtained.

A disused glass factory was taken over for the manufacture of toys and dolls at Shelton, Stoke-on-Trent, where

A close practical attention is being devoted to the manufacture of dolls which, the writer is informed, the firm is bent on supplying in as fine a range of any to be found in the country. They are making and stuffing the bodies and procuring the china heads from the local potteries which are specialised in the manufacture of dolls' heads and limbs. The dresses will also be produced on the premises, a full set of power-driven Singer machines having been installed for the purpose.

The range of dolls, whose heads were obtained from the potteries, contained over thirty different designs and varied in price from 13s. 6d. a dozen to 21s. each. The complete range was available in August 1916. The bodies were overlock-stitched, and filled with the typical 'guaranteed' clean materials of the time. An illustration showed the wide range of dressed dolls, with those in sailor suits and Red Cross uniform very much to the fore. Several of the costumes were surprisingly retrospective and obviously made to appeal to adults. Undressed dolls were also sold. All appear to have the bisque heads usually associated with the wartime English dolls. The heads presumably only carried the potter's mark, as none have been discovered with the distributors' initials, which were probably carried on the boxes. Firms such as Cauldon, Empire, Mayer and Sherratt, and Hancock all made marked heads, which they supplied to doll assemblers.

Various efforts had been made in nineteenth-century England to make dolls in imitation of china. A certain E. E. Eaton in 1898 registered a patent for paper

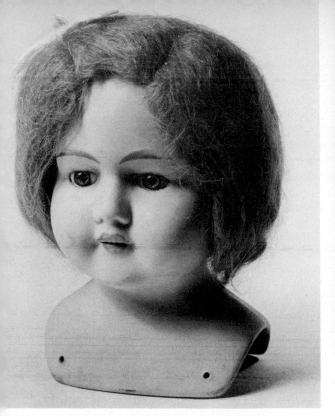

(*left*) 329   Shoulder head of typical English type marked "Melba England". 5½ in. high.   (*right*) 330   Baby doll. Shoulder head with blue painted eyes. Closed mouth. Pipe clay lower arms and legs. Marked "Regd. 654738, DP Co." for Diamond Pottery Company. 33–6. 14½ in. high.

heads that could be processed to resemble china by boiling paper for twenty-four hours, mixing it with glue and then pressing it in moulds. The process sounds as though it would have produced a typical papier mâché head, but the maker appeared to be very sure of its superiority! Florence Emily Eaton at the turn of the century had also attempted to improve upon porcelain dolls' heads by coating them with dental enamel, consisting of thin sheets of prepared India rubber or gutta-percha, which was to be moulded over the face and hardened. Presumably the aim was to give a relatively unbreakable skin-like effect, but as with so many inventions, it is doubtful whether dolls were made in any commercial quantity.

One of the more amusing English patents was registered in 1916 by E. S. A. Perks, and was for a telescopic doll whose size and expression could be varied. Twelve telescopic cylinders made possible this change of form. This energetic inventor also applied for a patent on an extremely gruesome-sounding head with interchangeable eyes. No extant examples of either doll have been discovered, and possibly the contemporary manufacturers also found the ideas a little too strange.

For many years, collectors would not buy English-made heads, as they are of a

445

much inferior quality to the Continental. But as accepted dolls become more expensive, new collectors naturally turn their attention to cheaper types, and English dolls are again becoming saleable, even being included in sales at Christie's. Though they still fetch only low prices, they are at least now judged respectable, whereas even a few years ago doll-dealers sometimes quite literally gave them away to make space.

The heads made by W. H. Goss are necessarily very desirable, both to collectors of the products of that factory and to doll-collectors. The heads are not visually attractive, as they have most of the disadvantages of the other English-made heads, including bad colouring and rather unpleasant expressions. The doll production of this factory is particularly surprising when compared with the quality of their ornamental items, but presumably the making of dolls was not taken very seriously.

The Goss factory was at the Falcon Pottery, Stoke-on-Trent, and their known dolls are of the shoulder-head variety and always marked Goss. Collectors of Goss have told me that it is the current fashion to offer them all types of inadequately-marked English heads as products of this factory, at quite high prices. Only heads that are fully marked should be bought, as it was the policy of the firm to ensure that their products were attributable. The limbs and bodies were assembled by the Potteries Toy Company, the bodies usually being of the cheap pink-cotton variety with hygienic filling. It is possible that heads were also supplied to other makers.

Goss dolls were made in a variety of sizes up to 36 inches. Heads were given stationary or sleeping eyes, and the lips are generally of an unpleasant dark red, competently decorated but in distasteful colours. The heads made at the time by Goss were described as being relatively expensive, and it was probably because of this that doll-making ceased after the war. A patent registered by Goss in 1942 does suggest that doll-making might again have been contemplated.

The Goss concern was taken over in 1934 by Cauldon potteries (who also made dolls' heads: shards have been found on their sites). The 1942 patent relates to a device for a doll's eye, which consisted of two spheroidal sections simulating eyeballs, connected by a yoke. A stem extended rigidly from the yoke, and the whole unit was to be cast in one piece from china, porcelain or other ceramic. No dolls have been found with this device, though it must be admitted that at present few dolls made after 1930 are examined in much detail by collectors.

Some of the best-quality English dolls were made by Hancocks, who used quite a good-quality bisque, but again fell down badly over the colouring of the face. Some of the Hancock heads are marked only 'English Make B.3', though the bodies that accompany heads marked in this way sometimes carry the stamp 'Made in England. H. & S. P. Hancock', proving that for at least one manufacturer, bodies were specially made. Other heads carry the mark B with a size, while one has been found marked 'Laurie Hancock English Make'. Dolls marked 'N.T.I. boy English Make' have also been found on marked Hancock bodies.

Some of the heads were given fixed glass eyes, but the more commonly found are intaglio. A number of undecorated heads without bodies have been found, and possibly these were sold off at the end of production. The undecorated heads have moulded hair and intaglio eyes. By 1935, the Hancock Company was working at the Corona Pottery, Hanley, but it is unlikely that dolls were made at this time. Dolls marked only 'Corona' are found and often attributed to Hancocks, as they used the trade name 'Royal Corona Ware' on their crockery. There is no record of the word 'Corona' alone being used by them. The trade-mark 'Corona' was used by Gater, Hall and Company of Tunstall around 1914, and it appears much more likely that these heads, which have a distinctly wartime look, were made by Gater Hall rather than by Hancocks. The 'Corona' marked dolls are either black or white and their quality is not as good as the authenticated Hancock heads.

Cauldon, Ridgway and Hancock were all involved in mergers, and remains of heads found on sites could have belonged to any of the three concerns, though no marked Ridgway heads are known.

The Diamond Pottery Company of Hanley, Staffordshire, also made bisque dolls during the First World War, marking their dolls 'D.P. Co.' Once again, the dolls are mainly of the shoulder-head type and the intaglio eyes were often painted with highlights. A self-coloured pink body was usually used for their thickly moulded heads, and the painting is often competent, but again the colours are unsatisfactory. Diamond Pottery heads have been found on a grotesque assortment of bodies, some of which were obviously commercially made to do duty either as bodies for baby or girl dolls. The design registration number is often given in full, which means that the dolls can be quite precisely dated. A few all-bisque dolls, a type not previously recorded as having been made in England, were produced at the Diamond Pottery. Some of their all-bisques were as large as 11 inches high.

The Diamond Pottery was rather more adventurous about the types of dolls it was prepared to make than the other English makers, as, besides the all-bisques, they also made character-type dolls with closed mouths and sleeping eyes on jointed bodies. Their basic dolls were similar to those made by the other companies, though they made a wider range of sizes, while jointed dolls' bodies are not generally associated with English manufacturers, H. Eckert was a producer of such bodies and possibly supplied the Diamond Pottery or their assembler.

Glass eyes had been made in the Midlands throughout the previous century, and no doubt the doll-makers were able to draw on this source. English mohair

331   Bye-Lo baby doll designed and copyrighted by Grace Storey Putman. Bisque flange head and fabric body with celluloid hands. Much of her original modelling was lost when it was made in doll form.

had also long been famous, so that the materials, if not the doll-making skills, were readily available to such companies as the British Novelty Works, a subsidiary of Dean's Rag Book Company, who are considered possibly to have produced the dolls both of bisque and composition marked 'B.N. London'. Some baby dolls marked in this way have been found on toddler-type composition bodies that are superior to the usual English-made bodies.

448

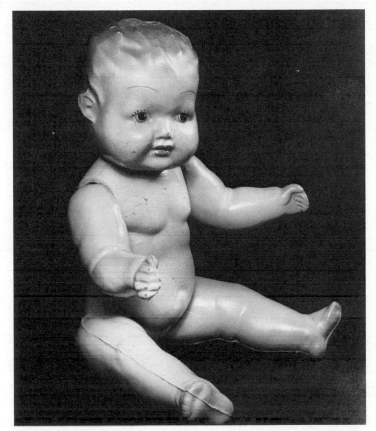

332   Baby doll made of earthenware during the Second World War.
Unmarked but probably English. Painted eyes. 14 in. high.

Among the other firms making dolls was the Willow Pottery at Longton, owned by Hewitt Brothers, who impressed 'H & L. Willow England' on heads, and G. D. Green, who made dolls of earthenware, china and 'Parian' (probably white bisque). Green registered a patent for transferring eyes on to ceramic, and another member of the firm registered a patent for colouring dolls' heads of bisque or pottery without firing, by applying a spraying apparatus such as an aerograph, a colouring composition comprising shellac and rosin with a suitable solvent and colouring matter. It is interesting to note that the manufacturers of the period were themselves calling untinted white bisque 'Parian'.

Mayer and Sherratt, of Clifton Works, Stafford, made both baby and girl dolls with fixed glass eyes that were impressed 'Melba'. Some Mayer and Sherratt heads were marked only 'M & S England', and are more attractively modelled than many other English dolls. The Empire Porcelain Pottery, Stoke-on-Trent, also turned to making dolls, which were marked 'E.P. & Co. Stoke'.

The rather pouting expression of some of their boy dolls is attractive and the original model was obviously well designed, though the quality was lost in manufacture. These dolls are sometimes found on American cloth bodies.

Playthings with its usual German bias commented in 1919 that "England, as is always her way, is attempting a huge manufacture of dolls." The publication concluded that as the dolls were of such poor workmanship, they could not possibly become popular outside that country. At this time the Germans were struggling to re-establish their industry and, fortunately, their poor view of English doll-making was shared by the English potters themselves, who were quick to abandon their government-inspired doll-making projects.

FIFTEEN

DOLLS OF CLOTH, RAG AND FELT

The oft-repeated statement that dolls were not made of fabric before the nineteenth century, as cloth was too costly for such use, bears little examination. From the time when man first wore woollen cloth, there were rags that could be rolled or roughly sewn into a doll-like shape for the pleasure of children. Being much more fragile than wood, and usually showing considerably less skill than the carved figures, the rag babies were discarded, and only those which once belonged to the most wealthy families have survived. Authenticated examples, even in museums, are rare before 1800, and are usually included in the textile collections rather than those of dolls, which is perhaps part of the reason why so many collectors claim very confidently that they were not made at all!

The collectors of antique dolls have often tended to neglect the rag-type dolls, as they are not usually objects of great beauty, and appeal more to the collectors of folk art. Some of the early examples in the Reserve collection of the Textile Department at the Victoria and Albert Museum are extremely fine, and hold their own both in construction and artistry with the wooden and wax dolls of the eighteenth century. A small black page boy, probably made originally for a baby house, is particularly evocative of its period, and is made with a clever utilization of good fabrics of the time. Small dolls were also made to decorate boxes or needle-cases, and some of these, made of imaginatively combined silks, braid, beads and ribbon, create quite sumptuous effects. Scraps of expensive fabric were looked after carefully and re-used, not only by eighteenth, but also nineteenth-century ladies. The ribbons from Queen Victoria's bonnets were regularly re-ironed, so that the royal children could use them for dressing their dolls, since ribbons were a necessary and expensive item in any lady's wardrobe. Many of the eighteenth-century dolls display fragments of very fine material, which had obviously been stored away for future use by the needlewoman, and then skilfully combined to create a lively doll, with interesting effects both of colour and texture: a type of exercise that is now seen only rarely in the work of modern rag doll-makers, who appear to consider that a generous allowance of rug wool hair is all that is needed for success.

The rag dolls of poor children have only rarely survived, though an Essex gravedigger recently told me that he had several times come upon the remains of fabric dolls in old graves. The Church was obviously not successful, even in Victorian times, in its desire to persuade country folk to abandon the old pagan customs. Too often the ugly remains of once-loved possessions are discarded as they have no monetary value and little beauty; but it seems appropriate to put in a plea that any collector who finds an old rag doll, no matter how disfigured and dirty, should at least photograph and record all the relevant details.

An early nineteenth-century child's birthday party, at which the centre of attraction was two home-made rag dolls, was vividly described by Mary Mitford. The first doll shown to the children was in the form of a very fashionable lady, of delicate construction and elaborate ornament.

> A doll of highest fashion, with sleeves like a bishop, a waist like a wasp, a magnificent bustle and petticoats so full and so puffed out around the bottom that the question of hoop or no hoop was stoutly debated between two of the older girls. Her cheeks were very red and her neck very white and her ringlets in the newest possible taste.

The glories of this fine lady were soon put completely in the shade when a second, and much more unusual, doll was produced.

> A young gentleman, habited in the striped and braided costume, which is the ordinary transition dress between laying off petticoats and assuming the doublet and hose. The apparel, however, was not the charm that fixed the attention of the young people, the attraction was the complexion, which was of as deep and shiny a black, as perfect an imitation of a negro in tint and feature, as female ingenuity could accomplish. The face, neck, arms and legs were covered with black silk, and much skill was shown in shaping and sewing on the broad, flat nose, large ears and pouting lips, while the great white teeth and bright round eyes relieved the monotony of the colour. The wig was of black worsted, knitted and then unravelled, as natural as if it had actually grown on the head. Perhaps the novelty, for none of the company had seen a black doll before, might increase the effect.

Black dolls, though a surprising delight to the English children, were very commonly made in the United States, though more often in the form of the Black Mammy doll. Several American collectors have attractive examples of such dolls, some of which are very skillfully made. These nineteenth-century black rag dolls are bought by collectors, who think little of the white dolls made

333 Felt-faced doll with the sideways-glancing eyes and well-made costume typical of Lenci. Turquoise and yellow clothes. 17½ in. high.

at the same time. It must be confessed, however, that the black fabric has usually stood the years rather better than the pink-faced dolls, which look unappealing when faded and dirty. Such home-made rag dolls were played with by children from all ranks of life, but it is very difficult to value them, as they are really items of curiosity rather than collector's pieces.

The printed rag dolls which were sold in sheet form in the last quarter of the century revolutionized the traditional methods. Several companies produced fabric dolls on a commercial scale, however, before this time: even the Montanari family are recorded as having been makers of rag dolls. The 'English Rag Babies' made by Richard Montanari and exhibited at the Paris Exposition of 1855 should not be confused with the more mundane rag dolls that the firm manufactured. The 'Rag Babies' were wax dolls with a layer of cloth drawn over the face, so that even very young children could play with them without fear of breakage. No marked examples of the basic rag dolls made by the family are known to have survived, but at the Great Exhibition, alongside their prestige display of wax dolls was a small case of rag dolls which were intended purely for the nursery and which made a clever use of fabrics. These rag dolls cost between 6s. 6d. and 30s., and were well dressed, it is to be hoped, as the prices do seem to have been high for dolls of such a simple type.

The ladies' magazines eagerly encouraged the making of rag dolls, both by adults and children, and supplied patterns for their clothes. The dolls with stitch-modelled faces that are often found on Victorian tea-cosies are so similar in construction that it would appear probable that they were commercially made. A head with a disdainful 'we are not amused' expression is seen in several collections, and is obviously believed to represent Victoria, but it is again debatable whether these were commercial dolls or home-made to precise magazine instructions.

The Housewife for 1890 commented that "Of all dolls, the rag doll is most beloved, as they can do with it as they like, without fear of injuring the doll or calling down reproof upon themselves." It was suggested that dolls were best made of old flesh-coloured silk underwear, though white twill was considered to make a more substantial doll. The reference to flesh-coloured underwear is interesting, as so little of it has survived, and we now tend to think that all late Victorian ladies wore white cotton under their dresses. The magazine also

334 Felt-faced boy doll often referred to as Christopher Robin. Original costume. Stamped "Lenci" on foot. 17½ in. high.

335 Leather was skilfully used to make this late nineteenth-century pixie doll. 15 in. high.

336 Fabric dolls soon became disfigured when played with. Seated doll in replacement dress probably Lenci. Baby doll probably Käthe Kruse. 17 in. high.

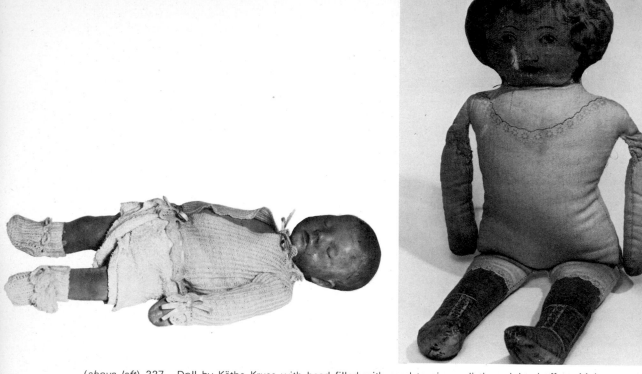

(*above left*) 337   Doll by Käthe Kruse with head filled with sand to give realistic weighted effect. Makers name in ink on left foot. 20 in. high.   (*above right*) 338   Printed fabric girl doll. Foot marked "Art Fabric Mills, New York. Feb. 13th 1900". 18 in. high.   (*below*) 339   Pickaninny, a rag doll to be cut out and assembled at home. Made by the Arnold Print Works of North Adams, Mass. and patented 5th July 1892 and 4th October 1892 in U.S. Note the interesting detail of the shoes to be sewn to base.

assumed that the homes of all its readers would have a sewing machine, and its use was recommended for the construction of the body. Gores at the sides of the head and tiny darts at chin and heels were advised for shaping the figure, and the nose, mouth and ears were to be needle-moulded and then painted. Each joint was to be made separately, but it was essential that the doll should be made of one piece of fabric to "save the creature being torn limb from limb". The hair was to be made of "single zephyr wool". The designer completed her very precise instructions by stating: "Such a doll will last for years, and be the boon and companion of its little owner, while many wax beauties, the favourites of a day, bloom but to fade and pass away."

American Fabric Dolls

The American makers, far more than the English and European, saw the need to create sturdy dolls that would stand up to nursery and frontier life, and their most successful products are those of papier mâché, wood and fabric, which did not need the careful handling that the European porcelain and wax dolls demanded. The advantages of these robust American products were extolled by their manufacturers, who saw little advantage in the fragile imported dolls.

The name of Izannah Walker is known to all doll-collectors, even those not specifically interested in fabric dolls. The quality, moulded stockinette dolls that she made are very similar in appearance to the imported German porcelains, but they are a much larger and more homely version. A characteristic is the addition of painted curls that fall to the doll's plump cheeks, though this is their only concession to frivolity. These figures suggest the hard-working, unadorned, early settlers, and the fact that they were made in the late nineteenth century is always something of a surprise, as they are constructed and decorated in a much earlier manner. Like most other American toys, the dolls were made purely for the home market, and the European collector is unlikely to find examples.

There is considerable controversy over the date on which the Izannah Walkers were first made. Family tradition maintained that some were made as early as 1855, a date that would suggest itself strongly because of their appearance, but the patent was granted as late as 1873. The Walker dolls are often claimed to be the first commercially-produced American dolls, and are therefore extremely popular with collectors, as they combine the primitive appearance of the home-made with the excitement of a commercial venture. The 1873 patent records the method by which Miss Walker worked. Cheap cloth, soaked in glue or paste, was pressed into a two-part mould. When dry, a layer of soft wadding was placed over the head, and covered in turn with a layer of stockinette held in

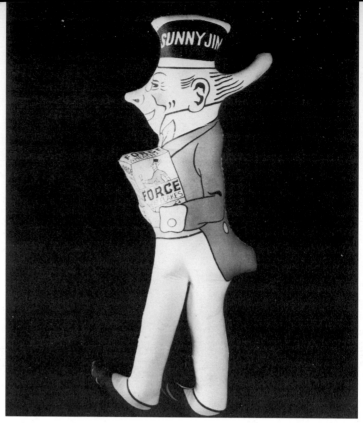

340   Aunt Jemima printed on oil cloth. An American advertising doll for pancake flour. 12½ in. high.

341   Printed fabric doll made from 1903 to the present time to advertise Force Wheat Flakes. Designed in 1902 by Minnie Maude Hanff. Sold in England from 1920. 16 in. high.

342   Diana, Aunt Jemima's little girl. Design printed on fabric. 12 in. high.

place with a few stitches or paste. The head was then placed again in the original mould to press it back into a good shape. Two pieces of wood were used to strengthen the shape, and the cavity was filled with stuffing to help the face hold its contours. The two sides of the head were then sewn or glued together. The padded layer was painted with oil colours, and the dolls have a pleasant, soft, flesh-like touch, which must have made them attractive to children. To the collector, this slightly springy surface is the hallmark of an Izannah Walker.

Her grand-niece described Izannah as a rather eccentric lady, who would have much preferred to be a man, and who demonstrated what were considered at the time to be purely masculine skills in carpentry, breeding canaries and property dealing. Her construction of dolls and doll's-house furniture must by contrast have appeared as a concession to femininity. It is typical of her character that she insisted on creating a doll that necessitated years of experiment to perfect the method. Several moulds were used for the heads, and all the dolls have individual character, as they are hand painted. The ears were separately applied, which must have called for great patience, and the hands and feet were also carefully stitched. The dolls with stitched toes were once considered to be the early type, while those with shoes were thought later, but collectors now agree that little significance can be given to this point in dating. When seen in American collections, the dolls are usually dressed in the costume of the 1860s, and, even allowing for the fact that American costume was a little behind European, it does seem surprising that the dress was so retrospective. The Colemans suggest that because of patent rules the dolls could not have been on sale before 1871, but the character of Miss Walker was such that it is difficult to believe that she would have cared over-much about rules made by governments, and it is very possible that she had already sold a large number of dolls before she actually registered an official patent.

The possibly better-known Chase dolls were made because Martha Chase herself had owned an Izannah Walker as a child, and attempted to make a similar doll for her own children. She used a rather simplified version of the mask method. A face with raised features was covered with stockinette, and the head was then sized and allowed to dry and harden. When hard, the faces were painted in oil colours, in the manner of the Izannah Walkers, though Martha Chase made use of an impasto effect to give the hair, which was usually fair, a realistic surface. Blue and brown eyes were painted, and the sizing of the heads preparatory to painting meant that they could be washed carefully when dirty.

According to the daughter of Martha Chase, the doll's torso was originally made of sateen, but the later bodies were of stockinette. The arms and legs were painted in oil colour, and early examples have joints at knee and elbow. The ears and thumbs were applied separately. The aim of Mrs Chase was to make a doll that was strong and yet light enough for a child to carry easily.

Though the dolls were at first made purely for her family and friends, they were commercially produced after Martha Chase had taken a doll to a shop to fit it with shoes, and was prevailed upon to supply a sample to the shop for sale. The dolls were so successful that she built a small factory behind her home to produce them commercially, and from this grew the Chase doll factory at Pawtucket.

Several character dolls, including 'George Washington', a coloured mammy and figures from *Alice in Wonderland* were produced. Dolls ranged in size from 9 inches to the height of a year-old child. By 1910 the dolls were given a water-proof finish, and carried the Chase trade-mark on the thigh or under the arm, a trade-mark that has unfortunately often rubbed away. Nineteen different models, including some with moulded hair, were made by 1922; many of these had very gentle, attractive faces that represented children, but the body con-struction was not very satisfactory and presented a rather ugly effect. An even more unpleasant body was given to the Chase hospital babies, which Martha Chase, herself a doctor's daughter, was persuaded to make as a teaching aid. A doll was developed that could be made in adult life-size and in four different baby sizes. The usual waterproof finish was given, but the hospital doll also had a rubber watertight interior to help it survive even enemas and douchings. Despite their very ugly appearance, it is the hospital dolls that have survived longest in production.

Moulded-face dolls similar in construction to those of Chase and Walker were patented as late as the 1920s by Charles Bloom and Lillian Shearer. Another version was made at Louise R. Kampes studios, and took the name of 'KAMKINS, a dolly made to love'. These look very much cheaper than the Chase dolls, but have soft and rather gentle faces. A sales ploy was the new outfits in which the dolls appeared each year. The dolls are very much in the tradition of the American moulded method, and have the typical round-faced placid appearance.

The Brückner dolls were constructed on similar lines over a moulded base, but in this case the face itself was applied to the fabric before construction of the head. The layers of paper and fabric to which the painted mask was bonded gave the hard and almost indestructible finish that most of the commercial concerns of the period were working towards.

Various methods of soaking combinations of paper, buckram, felt and fabric in glue to create a moulded fabric head were registered. One head was made of stockinette soaked in starch and salt, with the inner surface coated with paraffin. The usual filling of cotton stuffing helped maintain the general shape. As with dolls registered in the English Patent Office, it is often difficult to surmise how many were actually commercially produced. The Cra dolls were made by the

(*left*) 343   Charmingly-primitive stiffened rag doll made by Izannah Walker with the detail of the face painted in oil colour. These dolls were patented in 1873.   (*right*) 344   Boy doll by Martha Chase made with a moulded mask covered with stockinette and painted with oil colour. Note the scumbled paint on the head giving the textural effects of hair.

Dollcraft Company in 1922, and had waterproofed buckram pressed heads, so that they could be washed. As were many of the American-made heads at this time, they could be bought in white or black versions. Those with the black finish have usually best stood the test of time, and still look very attractive.

Rag dolls with mask-type faces were also made by Madame Alexander in the early 1920s. It is still quite possible to buy these Alexander dolls, as they were produced in large numbers and more appear to have been exported. As a girl, Madame Alexander had helped her émigré parents in the running of their toy-shop and dolls' hospital, and during the First World War she created a Red Cross Nurse figure, which was followed later by a whole series, including some baby dolls with sleeping eyes. Most of her dolls represent characters, such as those from *Alice in Wonderland* or Dickens. She painted the heads herself, and the hair was made of wool. Some of the characters, such as the Mad Hatter, are quite exciting, but the basic dolls are very ordinary, and it is surprising that they have remained so popular with collectors.

Rag dolls with painted features were also made by Emma and Marietta Adams, and are known as Columbian dolls. The heads were rather different, in that they were built around a sawdust core, and modelled by stuffing muslin with cotton waste. The heads were painted by Emma Adams herself until 1900, but afterwards by commercial artists. The clothes were made in precise detail by Marietta. At this distance in time, the dolls do not appear particularly attractive, but they were once extremely popular. Those made before 1900 carried an Emma Adams stamp. Some of the dolls were as tall as 30 inches, and the usual range of girls, boys and babies in black and white was made.

The most positive advance in the manufacture of America rag dolls developed from the introduction of cheaper textile printing methods. Doll designers and distributors, particularly Horsman, explored the possibilities of the new cheap printing techniques. Edward Peck has made a two-piece rag doll around 1884, and this figure of Santa Claus is said to have been the inspiration for those designed by the Smith sisters-in-law. Laurence and Co., Boston, who were cloth distributors and printers rather than doll-makers, produced some of the earliest printed dolls. They were sold by the yard, and could be purchased both from drapers shops and general 'dry goods' stores, so that they were very widely available. The first doll designed by Celia and Charity Smith in 1892 was made in two pieces and wore combinations and blue stockings, which were of course printed. The sheet on which the doll was reproduced bore the instruction, 'Sew together and stuff with cotton batting and sawdust.'

The dolls designed by Charity Smith were mainly produced by the Arnold Print Works of North Adams, Massachusetts, to whom she sold her patent in 1892. This firm was one of the largest manufacturers of Prints and Dress goods in America. Their advertisements for the popular rag dolls warned that the buyer should make sure that their trade-mark, which included their date of establishment in a circle, was printed on the fabric. Many amusing figures were boldly printed on white cotton, which was marked accurately with the cutting lines, and also carried the instructions for making up the doll. A characteristic of the dolls made by the Arnold Print Works was the circle of fabric that formed the base of the feet. It was necessary to back this base with paste-board in order to make the figures stand. Apart from their toy range of monkeys, dogs and hens, they made a wide variety of dolls including the "Palmer Cox Celebrated Brownies that were patented in 1892. They are twelve in number, and all come in one yard of cloth: when completed they are about 7 ins. in height and can be bent

345 Two printed rag dolls made by Deans. Big Baby, measuring 22 in. on left and an improved version, given an extra seam below chin for added realism, introduced from 1920 onwards. 20 in. high.

and twisted into any funny positions without injury." All the Brownies have large round eyes and down-turned mouths, and included such characters as 'Uncle Sam', 'Indian', 'Irishman' and 'Soldier' – all with bowed legs and bent backs. The words 'Copyright 1892 by Palmer Cox' appear on the back of the right foot of each Brownie. Other companies also produced the popular Brownies, but those made by the Arnold Print Works are considered to be the best. The Brownie Camera is said to have been so called because of the popularity of these figures. The fabric cost 20 cents a yard, out of which all twelve Brownies were to be cut.

A delightful 'Topsy' doll was made by the Arnold Print Works, which wore a long pink dress, pin-tucked and buttoned neatly at the cuffs. This doll was also made in a white version, though the coloured is much more eye-catching. The doll carried a large blue frilled picture hat. The design was patented in 1892, and was printed on a half yard of fabric that cost 10 cents.

Their 'Little Red Riding-hood' was unusual, as the doll was not cut out all round the figure, as was usually the case, but stood in a background of flowers, rather in the manner of the dolls in book form that were popular at the time. Pitti Sing, Our Soldier Boys and Piccaninny were all produced on cloth and so simple to construct that 'any Child can do it'. They were further advertised by such phrases as "so perfectly made you would think they were alive".

A jointed cloth doll, designed by Charity Smith, was given darts at neck, chin, elbows, knees, heels and ankles, so that the figure could be made to sit. It was printed with a design of high buttoned shoes, a string of beads, and underclothes. In 1893, it was sold for 10 cents. Most of these dolls produced at the Arnold Print Works, are in attractive, soft colours, though it must be confessed that, as is the case with most of the printed dolls, they look much more satisfactory as printed sheets than made up into rather tortured three-dimensional figures.

The Art Fabric Mills of New York was the other great producer of rag dolls. This company, on receipt of 50 cents, would supply a printed doll direct to the customer. In comparison, the Arnold Print Works insisted in their advertisements that their dolls could only be purchased from shops, and not on any account direct from the maker. The best known of the Art Fabric Mills dolls is "The Life Size Doll made so that babies clothes will now fit Dollie". Edgar Newell, the President of the company, obtained this doll's patent in 1900. "The material used is very heavy sateen that will not tear. Oil colours only are used – they will not crack. By means of the patent gusset, the feet protrude in front, enabling the doll to stand alone." The doll, which stood 30 inches high, was printed with red stockings and black shoes. "Every child loves a big doll, but what will they say to a Life Size one?" It was further rapturously described as "this century's model of the old-fashioned rag doll that Grannie used to make",

(*above left*) 346 Master Puck, a four-piece rag doll cut to give a profile to the face. Smallest of a family of four. In production by 1912. Dean's advertised the 18 in. sheet on which Master Puck was printed for 6*d*. (*above right*) 347 "Mignionne", designed and facsimile autographed by Pauline Guilbert. Introduced *c*. 1912. Dean's advertised the figures as "Printed on strong cotton. 12×23 in. costing 6*d*. each." 14 in. high. (*below*) 348 "Dolly Dips" wearing fashionable bathing dress for 1920. Skirt separate. "Her bathing costume displays to advantage her well-modelled figure." Original cost 2*s*. 6*d*. Supplied with improved Tru-shu feet. Made by Dean's Rag Book Company. 14 in. high.

465

and (optimistically) as "an exact reproduction of a hand printed French Creation." The workmanship and colour were claimed to be absolutely perfect. The Art Fabric Mills also made a smaller version, and 'Topsy' dolls in black or white. As alive to current favourites as the other American doll-makers, they made Buster Brown in imitation of a popular cartoon in the *New York Herald*. 'Diana', 'Newly Wed Kid', 'Foxy Grandpa' and 'Cry baby pincushion' were all among the products of this prolific firm.

Various novelty dolls were produced in rag. An obvious and simple method was to print a different character on either side, so that dolls representing 'Jack and Jill', 'Farmer and his Wife', and the ubiquitous 'Red Riding-hood and the Wolf' were made in some number. Not to be outdone, Horsman, the makers and importers, gave their dolls printed photographic faces. The upside-down or turnover-type dolls were also popular in rag, and 'Teddy Turnover', made by the Dreamland Doll Company, was given a brown or white rag doll at one end and the usual Teddy bear at the other.

A 'Wide Awake' doll was made in 1908. By turning the head and moving the hat, a new face was introduced. An amusing doll was patented in both England and America, and concerned a doll, each of whose limbs was a complete doll in itself. They were hooked on to the main torso, and the heads were covered by the dress of the largest doll. Another was given a face on either side of the head which was jointed to the body so that it could be turned. A third face was hidden beneath the first, which could if necessary be unpicked to reveal it!

'Dolly Double and Topsy Turvey' was a black or white doll, with a red skirt printed with black which was to cover the unwanted half. In sheet form, the doll was to be obtained from the Toy Department of Elms Company, New York. A multi-faced doll was also made by Chester Limbra in 1912. This doll had several faces that could be turned down at the neck and hidden under the clothes when not in use. A bandeau held the required face in position.

The 'No-Brake' life-size doll was jointed, and its dress was printed on the sack that held the stuffing to make up the doll. The great interest in photographic processes, by which actual children's faces could be reproduced on the dolls, was served by the Dreamland Doll Company, who claimed to have originated the idea. The popularity of the rag doll was such that the Butterick Publishing Company, better known for their dress patterns, produced a doll in eight colours, whose price included the patterns for its clothes.

The idea of using printed dolls of paper and cloth for advertising purposes was another area which the Americans seemed willing to exploit. The 'Sunny Jim' doll, which first appeared in 1905 as an advertisement for Force breakfast cereal, can still be obtained today. It illustrated a figure who had quickly passed from pessimism to optimism by eating Force. There is a tradition that this doll

349 "Peggie and Teddie" introduced by Deans, 1912–13. Pair from series first called the Wiederseim series after their designer, Grace Wiederseim, but later catalogues refer to them as part of the Goo-Goo series. Original cost 10*d*. each. Peggy: "No, I don't fink muvver would mind." Teddy: "No, I nevver done nuffin." 9 in. high.

was designed by the artist who also illustrated *The Wizard of Oz*, and it certainly displays more individuality than many. The dolls were given in exchange for the tops of packets, as were several other advertising dolls. Ceresota flour was promoted by a healthy-looking farmer's boy, wearing an open-necked shirt, while 'Gretchen', in imitation of a Dutch girl, advertised Malted Breakfast Food. The long-produced 'Aunt Jemina' doll advertised flour, and was for a short while accompanied by a family of 'Uncle Mose', 'Little Diana' and 'Little Wade', all of which could be obtained for box tops.

'Rastus the Cream of Wheat Chef' was a broadly-smiling coloured doll in chef's uniform, who proudly carried a packet of wheat. Puffed wheat was advertised by 'Puffy', another cut-out doll, and there was even a 'Uneeda Biscuit' doll. Other dolls were given away free with, for instance, the purchase of a gas range. (This doll was almost inevitably called 'Kookie'!) In return for a year's subscription to *Comfort Magazine*, a doll called 'Golden Locks' was presented. All these printed dolls are brash, lively and inventive, and perfectly suggest the America of the early twentieth century.

European Makers of Cloth Dolls

As the French were able to produce fine dolls of bisque, there appears to have been little interest in the creation of rag dolls until the boudoir type of the 1920s became popular. Home-made rag figures were obviously created, as were some rag-faced costume dolls, to be sold as souvenirs, but the French never put the energy of the American makers into manufacturing commercial dolls of this material. The French, it must be remembered, made quality dolls for export and for the bourgeoisie; they did not have a large working population that could afford to spend money on children's dolls, in the way that even quite humble Americans were prepared to do. The rag doll, in the eyes of the French makers, was a trivial object that could in no way be equated with their quality products.

Italy is particularly associated with fabric dolls, because of the pressed-felt dolls made by Enrico Scavini of Turin, who marketed his dolls under the trade name of 'Lenci', which was the pet name he used for his wife. A rather strange assortment of dolls was created, varying from 'Mozart' to a 'Fat Girl' and a 'Madonna and Child'. The dolls were made in the 'artistic manner', for sale to parents who were concerned for the development of good taste in their children. It was claimed that each doll was studio designed by Italian artists and painted by hand.

The faces were pressed in moulds, and had no disfiguring seam. A characteristic of the dolls is the eyes that always glance to the side. All the figures were articulated, and small dolls were given real hair. With their rather plump sturdy limbs, they do not look much like 'artistic' dolls to the modern eye, but merely quite pretty and unexciting child figures. All the characters were originally given labels or 'Lenci' marked metal buttons that are often lost so that any felt-faced doll with sideways-glancing eyes is categorized as a Lenci. As many other firms made dolls with some character and pressed-felt faces, caution has to be exercised. The genuine Lenci dolls were given high-quality clothes that were extremely fashionable. In 1921, the firm was selling 100 different character dolls, including Chinamen and Indians. They were well made and strongly con- structed, which accounts for the fact that they have often survived in remarkably good condition for fabric dolls.

Though the German manufacturers were primarily concerned with the manufacture of bisque dolls, there was a great deal of restless questioning among the intellectuals over the psychological force of the doll, and the hard-bodied chinas that had been made for some time fared quite badly in this new assessment.

The reforms in the doll trade began in Munich and spread to Berlin and Dresden. Competitions were organized for doll designers, who submitted artistic abstract dolls that were intended to appeal to the child's primitive instincts and natural appreciation of form. To their chagrin, the organizers quickly found that the children hated these consciously stylized dolls, and preferred the traditional types. In 1904, the Dresden handicraft workshops appealed for fresh designs in the traditional manner, but apart from the designs of Marion Kaulitz, little that was successful in the eyes of children was developed, despite all the activity.

One Berlin exhibition of home-made toys did produce an artist with an understanding not only of doll-making methods, but also of children. Of all German doll-makers, Käthe Kruse is the best known and appreciated. She was the wife of a sculptor, and wished to create a completely satisfactory doll for her children that was lifelike in feeling as well as in appearance. The first doll she made was a very sorry-looking object, made of a towel, a potato for the foundation of the head, and sand to give a natural weighted feeling. Her seven children responded to the doll with delight, and she was encouraged in her efforts to create a successful figure by her husband's artistic advice. She later explained that she had created the dolls so that the child could feel the pleasure of holding a real baby in its arms and develop an emotional attachment to it. She felt that many of the currently popular character dolls made of china were in too contrived a taste, and she never classed her own dolls as characters, though to the modern collector they seem typical of the type, if a little softer than some. One cannot imagine Käthe Kruse modelling an ugly doll, with its face twisted in a temper tantrum, as did the bisque doll-makers in their search for realism.

She spent four years in developing a commercial doll from the sand, potato and towelling experiment. The heads of the perfected dolls were of muslin, which was chemically treated on the back. The two halves were joined together, and the head cavity was filled with wadding. It is said that the artist's own children served as models for the dolls, while others were based on children's faces in classical paintings. All the time there was a striving not only towards realism, but also towards beauty. The faces were decorated individually and then sprayed with fixative. The bodies had layers of cotton wound around a wire armature in typical artist's fashion. The maker's name is to be found on the sole of the foot. After 1934 she also created manikin shop-window display figures, and the family tradition is still carried on today in Swabia by her children.

In 1923 Käthe Kruse wrote:

My dolls, particularly the babies, arose from the desire to awaken a feeling that one was holding a real baby in one's arms. I must say, however, that this idea did not originate in my brain, but sprang from that of my sculptor father, who all his life long was concerned with the problem involved in the effect created by plastic form. Strange to say, the consideration of the emotional effect to be aroused, and of the recognition of the necessity of working on one's emotions, is virgin soil for the doll. But it is always so; wherever there is creativeness, a start must be made at the beginning, in so far as there is a desire to solve the problem. And the problem of the doll, tantamount to education in maternal feeling, education in womanly act and womanly bliss, perhaps in a better understanding between mother and child, between mother and mother – this whole problem of the doll has certainly sufficient interest in itself.

Holding one of the Kruse dolls, rather dusty and faded from years of play, it is difficult to conjure up all the depth of feeling and serious creative activity that went into its evolution. After the intensity of its designer's emotions, it feels almost sacrilegious to question whether a child really wants a doll that feels like a baby. A fur Teddy bear or a soft velvet dog is often preferred, and the love of a child for its toy is more often an extension of its own personality than of that between mother and child, which would imply a completely different set of mature emotional values.

The dolls of Käthe Kruse suggest the virtues of German womanhood, with an inward-looking love of home and family. In comparison, those made by Margarete Steiff are aggressively outward-looking and often brittle in their concept. Some of the German soldier dolls appear sinister in retrospect, and seem to have an aura of menace.

The Steiff factory was at Giengen in Würtemburg, and is best known for the Teddy bears that have remained constantly popular. Little menace in this example of the firm's work! The years 1903–8 are known in the history of the Steiff firm as the Bear years (Bärenjahre) as the company could hardly keep pace with the tremendous demand for the lovable toys.

Felt-headed dolls were first made in 1894 by Margarete Steiff, and are characterized by the seam that runs down the centre of the face and tends to contribute to a sinister appearance, especially in the dolls with duelling scars painted on their faces to represent the students at Heidelberg. The dolls wore a button in their ear (*Knopf im Ohr*) after 1905, though dolls with plush or velvet heads had already been made for some time.

The factory developed from Fräulein Steiff's enthusiasm for making felt animals from off-cuts obtained from a nearby factory, and she claimed that her firm was the first to make soft stuffed character dolls. The dolls were enabled to stand by their very large flat feet. They were not made in very large sizes, and 21 inches is the biggest Steiff play doll known.

The firm made its presence felt each year at the great trade fair at Leipzig where they set up huge displays showing scenes such as a village school or a parade ground. After the death of 'Gretle Steiff' in 1909 her two nephews took over the firm and among the new dolls for that year were some that cried 'mama' when turned over. The Steiff Company now has one of the four largest toy factories in the Federal Republic, though its production is more concerned with toys than dolls.

English Fabric Doll-makers

Although rag dolls had been home-made, or made for local sale, in Britain throughout the previous two centuries, there was little commercial activity in this field before 1900. Frederick Sindall is one of the makers recorded as having both made and exported rag dolls around 1899, but no examples that can be attributed directly to him are known. A number of dolls that appear commercial and have silk or felt faces can be dated by their clothes to the nineteenth century, but they are usually unremarkable and only collectable if particularly well dressed.

As a result of the interest in craftsmanship and the use of simple materials that was extolled by the William Morris group and the Arts and Crafts movement, there was more activity in the creation of dolls and toys out of cloth, but it took some time for this inspiration to filter through to the commercial makers. Although there were almost as many popular cartoon and storybook characters as there were in America, the makers were not as willing to manufacture dolls in imitation of them. The delightful characters created by Kate Greenaway would have made appealing dolls, but it was left to an American maker, the Saalfield Publishing Company, to make dolls inspired by this artist.

Beatrix Potter desperately wanted to make 'Peter Rabbit' dolls commercially, as one she had made herself for a child had been so well received. She attempted to persuade one of the London toy factories to produce the doll, but found that because of the Free Trade policy the English market had been inundated with cheap German toys, and the London trade had almost been killed off. The Camberwell doll industry "that had employed skilled female labour for generations was on its last legs, the people who had once been involved in the making of dolls and toys were now unemployed." She discovered, to her fury, that the public were able to buy German-made 'Squirrel Nutkins' and 'Peter Rabbits' made from pirated designs. "My father has just bought a squirrel in the Burlington Arcade. It was sold as Nutkin."

As a result of her unhappy efforts in persuading English toy-makers to manufacture her dolls, a frustration that must have been felt by many other designers of the time, she participated in the 1910 election and campaigned for tariff reform. In a pamphlet which she herself wrote, she said:

> A few years ago I invented a rabbit doll which was in demand. I tried in vain to get it made in England. There was not a single British wholesale toymaker left who could undertake the job – my doll is now made by scores in Frau H.'s factory in Germany . . . the London toyshops are choked with foreign toys.

Beatrix Potter also laboriously produced her own individually hand-drawn posters to promote reform. The drawing showed a limp British doll: "Poor Camberwell Dolly is Dying. Killed by Free Trade." One wonders whether Dean's Rag Book Company, by this time already making soft toys, was also approached.

Against this depressing background, it is small wonder that English doll-makers were producing little work of great interest. The picture had begun to change somewhat, and an increasing number of patents were registered. Burnell and Hockley of Crouch End, Middlesex, registered in 1905 a patent for rag dolls made of printed or painted fabric, to be sewn together and stuffed – a method the Americans had been using for about twenty years. A line of stitches at hip level allowed the doll to sit down – again in the American manner. Rather predictably, Liberty and Company, who had provided such a good outlet for the artefacts of the Aesthetic movement, produced, around 1906, 'Art Dolls of Fabric'.

The First World War accelerated the production of dolls, and some rather merciless-looking 'British Tommies' were marketed by Samuel Finsbury & Co. The design of this doll is good and in a bold and explicit manner. Dean's Patriotic Pinafores, which represented the uniforms of various fighting men, had been on sale before the war, but must have become even more popular at this time. The children were encouraged through their toys to participate in the war, and toy stretchers, field ambulances containing bandaged figures and Red Cross nurses' uniforms were all considered appropriate. The Kaiser was an

350 "Charlie Chaplin", one of Dean's printed characters, also made with moulded 'Tru-to-Life' face. Originally cost 1*s.* and was not sold in sheet form. 11½ in. high.

351 George Robey, from the Tru-to-Life series that was introduced in 1920. Robey was not made until 1923 and formed part of series including the Coogan Kid. All with pressed faces. This example given to Dean's by Lady Robey. 14½ in. high.

352 When new, the Dean's mask-face dolls were most attractive. This example dressed in blue velvet and imitation fur can be identified as Dean's by the rivets fixing limbs to body that are marked "Dean's A1". The A1 dolls were introduced in 1920. 17½ in. high.

ever-near bogey-man, and a shout of "The Kaiser's coming", would rout the toughest of children. My own parents remember thinking of the Kaiser as a very positive force in their childhood, omnipotent and omnipresent.

Many English dolls dating from the first quarter of the twentieth century have a rather fey quality. One cloth doll made before the war was stuffed with lavender, rose leaves or rosemary, while an amusing venture of the 1920s was a rubber figure to be covered with Turkish towelling. It served a dual purpose as a pillow for baby or as a brush for silk hats.

A rather more practical approach was pursued by the firm launched by Samuel Dean in 1903 to make rag books for children who "wear their food and eat their clothes". This company has an almost uninterrupted history of toy production to the present day, though regrettably no dolls are now made. The work of this company is dealt with in some detail, as it has not before been covered in any depth, and the firm's products truthfully reflect the aims of British manufacturers during the first half of the century.

A booklet produced by Dean's for the 1922 Trade Exhibition stated that rag dolls were first made in book form, but, as parents disliked cutting up the books, the dolls were issued in sheet form. Examination of the company's catalogues and records bears no evidence to this effect and I know of no examples in book form. A fire at the 1910 Brussels Exhibition destroyed the Dean's exhibit of early products, so it is possible that there might be some truth in the statement. Anyone finding a Dean's doll in rag-book form would possess an interesting and important rarity.

Soft toys were made shortly after the introduction of the rag books in 1903. Well-known artists such as Hilda Cowham, Harry Rowntree and John Hassall designed figures that were marketed by the company, though most of the designers' names are unrecorded. The printed dolls, with which collectors are most familiar, were made in several sizes, and it is noticeable how few new designs were actually issued; the originals, designed well before the First World War, were still being produced in 1936, after which this type of rag doll ceased to appear in the firm's catalogues. Now, because of the revival of interest in these traditional toys, the firm is again considering their re-issue from the old plates; an edition that would obviously be of great interest to collectors.

The actual range of printed dolls produced was surprisingly limited, and cut-outs in a long outdated manner were sold alongside the flappers of the twenties. In imitation of the American makers, a 'Life-Size Baby Doll' costing 1s. 6d. was made and printed on a sheet 30 inches square. "For sterling value, this sheet comprising one Life-Size Baby Doll over two feet in height and three smaller dolls cannot be surpassed. Not an inch of the cloth was wasted . . . produced in the most delicate and artistic colours." The small dolls on the sheet included 'Old

King Cole' and 'Lucy Lockett'. The manufacturer was truthful in his reference to the colouring, which was very gentle. A mechanical printing process was used by the firm at this time whereby eight colours could be printed at the same time from hand-engraved rollers, which enabled subtleties of tone, not seen in modern printing, to be achieved.

'Big Baby' wore a frilly chemise and a liberty bodice, with knee-length buttoned knickers, in direct imitation of the clothes worn by most children around 1910. The three features of the rag dolls that were promoted by Dean's were their qualities of 'Indestructibility, Washability, and Hygienic Merit'. Wood wool or granulated cork was recommended for stuffing, so that the doll could be washed. The world-wide distribution was indicated by the fact that the instructions were printed in English, French and German, the firm's 1912 catalogue even showing the German Crown Prince with his rag book on its cover.

From around 1906, clothes had sometimes been included on the doll sheets, though separate sheets of costume did not become available until 1925. 'Betty Blue', printed on a 24-inch square sheet, cost only 1s. when introduced circa 1910. "From the top of her head to the soles of her dainty brown shoes, 'Betty Blue', whose height when formed is 22 ins., is indeed a darling dolly, while her sister 'Curly Locks' with rosy cheeks and the daintiest of underclothes is a veritable treasure for a baby." 'Curly Locks', who cost 6d., was really rather a cheat, as she was simply a small version of 'Betty Blue'!

Typical of the most romantic and artistic aspirations of English toy-makers in these golden pre-First World War years was the 'Lucky Puck' doll series. Puck, of *A Midsummer Night's Dream*, "has been brought with his family into the world of Mortal children to give them long hours of contented delight and pleasure." A new patented design was used for the faces of these dolls. A seam, running down the centre of the face, meant that a profile could be given – an advance on the standard flat-faced rag doll. Mr Puck was sewn in four sections, with seams not only at the sides, but also at centre back and front. 'Master Puck' and 'Baby Puck' could also be purchased either in sheet form or made up. Prices ranged from 1s. 6d. to a mere 6d. for Baby. The dolls were costumed in green, red or brown, and were accompanied by a discordant jingle:

> You must certainly be struck
> By the looks of Mr Puck
> He may be an ugly duck
> But will bring you luck.

Despite the firm's claim that the Puck family was "as immortal as its Shakespearean prototype", very few now survive. Dean's rag dolls can be recognized by the firm's trade-mark of two dogs fighting over a rag book, and were also marked 'certified as hygienic'.

Another typically British set was produced in the 1930s, representing Alice in Wonderland and including the March Hare and the Dormouse. It is very unlikely that any complete sets of this edition are still in existence.

The range of printed dolls had increased by 1913, and included the 'Dinah Doll' and 'Little Sambo', both black and with googly eyes. A soft woolly cloth was now used, in addition to the ordinary cotton, and the new dolls must have made much more satisfactory take-to-bed toys. 'Red Riding-hood', 'Cinderella' and a set of glove puppets were introduced, while more romantic aspirations were maintained by 'Master Sprite', a goblin with a long beard, and 'Cheeky Imp' with a face very like the present-day 'trolls', wearing a fur-trimmed suit. A new line for 1913 were the 'Knockabout Toy Sheets', on which were reprinted all the old favourites including 'Red Riding-hood', already popular in the larger series. The 3d. Knockabout Sheets were recommended as "an excellent guide for little ones' needles." The cheapest range of cut-outs, known as the 'Bo-Peep' series measured only 6 inches square and cost 1d. These were recommended not only as dolls, but also as artistic pincushions. Once again the firm methodically re-used designs, and 'Old King Cole', 'Daffey Down Dilly' and 'Little Betty Blue' all reappear in this series.

For 1s., a charming 'Nursery Land Box of Dolls' could be purchased, which included six doll sheets and all the equipment necessary for making them, complete with a German silver thimble.

In these pre-war years the great interest in character and artistic dolls was reflected in the production of the Pauline Guilbert series of dolls, tea-cosies and bonbonnières, which were introduced in 1912, each doll carrying a facsimile autograph of the artist. Strangely, the dolls were made very much in Victorian style and wore large picture hats. Each figure carried either an umbrella, a bouquet or a muff. The Edition de Luxe was printed on rich satin. The doll's skirts could either cover the nursery teapot or a box of sweets. Described as the Elite of Toytown, they were given names such as Eugénie or Antoinette.

The same year saw the introduction of another so-called artistic doll printed in bright colours, the 'Wiederseim' series. These were based on Grace Wiederseim's drawings, and have typical googly eyes. Teddy, 'No, I nevver done nuffin', and Peggy, carrying a doll while she sucks her thumb, 'I don't fink muvver would mind', are both typical of the sickly adult-directed *double entendre* used by so many toy-makers in the first quarter of the century.

An amusing advertising ploy was used by Dean's, whereby on signing a guarantee to wear an outfit on a given date, all the materials for a fancy dress costume made out of rag book and doll parts would be supplied. One colourful

(*above left*) 353 "Joan and Peter" Dean's dancing dolls from A1 Toy series. Original label but also carry stamp under feet. Introduced in 1928. Cost 8s. 6d. a pair when new. 14½ in. high. (*above right*) 354 "Miss Sue", printed Dean's rag doll made as an advertisement for Sue Flakes Beef Suet. 12 in. high. (*below left*) 355 Wounded soldier of the First World War wearing the blue hospital uniform with red handkerchief. Marked on sole of foot "Specially made for Boots the Chemist by Dean's Rag Book Co. Hygenic Stuffing". 10¾ in. high. (*below right*) 356 Part of a poster made to advertise Little Betty Oxo, a mask-face doll given away in exchange for Oxo tokens. Doll and poster made by Dean's.

Pedlar costume was designed, including a tray full of small rag dolls, while others were to be stitched to the hem of the dress. A natty hat proclaiming 'Dean's Rag Book Company' had to be worn.

The First World War obviously limited production, and few new sheets were introduced until the mid-twenties. A few patriotic figures were produced, however, including a set of rag ninepins in the form of Grenadier Guards and a nurse doll with 'Tipperary' written on her belt. At this time Wheeldons U.S. design patents were assigned to Dean's. The patent described a method of cutting out printed dolls complete with canvas backing, which could be pressed with hot or cold dies to form a moulded face. It was most probably from this patent that the famous 'Tru-to-Life' face was developed.

The company was determined in the years after the war to keep ahead of the German makers, who were again exporting dolls, and English shopkeepers were advised to 'deal with those who dealt fairly with you'. It was obviously thought advantageous to adopt the more serious attitude to dolls that had been introduced by progressive German designers, and in a booklet *Twenty Years After*, the company stated, "We shudder at the thought of what might happen to our exhibit if the news got about that it was promoted for mere idle amusement." The firm's stand at the 1922 Exhibition consisted of dolls in the costume of twenty nations. "Taken at its lowest estimate, the small collection gives the lie direct to those who vaunt the superiority of foreign made dolls, and it is confidently suggested that better dolls are not made in any of the countries here represented."

Some improvements had been made to the basic rag dolls by 1920. 'Tru-shu' feet which were given soles so that the doll could stand were now used, and 'Big Baby' was given a more realistic head by the introduction of a dart at the neck and over the back of the head. Both the Pauline Guilbert and the Grace Wiederseim series survived the war, as did the 'Bo-Peep'. The newer Tru-to-Life rag dolls were advertised as embodying all the details of the natural human features in profile relief, never before produced. "It possesses all the merits of the fragile wax or china face, but without many of their disadvantages. The face is as strong as the body. As purchased by Her Majesty Queen Mary."

The first True-to-Life dolls cost between 3s. and 9s., and some were sold with long wigs. They represented a change in the company's policy towards dolls and their entry into the market for assembled dolls. The entry was at first rather tentative, as most of the Tru-to-Life series could be bought made up or in sheet form. The designs for the faces were printed on the fabric which (in the commercially-produced examples) were then hot-pressed, together with a

357 "The Dutch Twins", made in the 1930s. A very large pair of well-dressed felt-faced dolls made by Dean's as a display piece. About 35 in. high.

478

buckram backing into a realistic face with wrinkles, moulded nose and lips. Not surprisingly, the moulded examples are the most sought after, as the flat-printed faces often have little of the intended character.

A variety of popular character dolls was made by the Tru-to-Life method, including 'Charlie Chaplin', 'The Coogan Kid', 'George Robey' and 'Buster Brown'. In 1937, both 'Lupino Lane' and 'Popeye' were added to the series. Just before the war, a particularly effective representation of Will Hay wearing an academic gown and carrying a cane was made. An attractive pair of dolls in golden velvet were produced in association with Great Ormond Street Hospital in 1937, and represented Peter Pan and Wendy. The designs for Tru-to-Life dolls were printed on cotton, felt, plush and velvet, and as most were unmarked, except for a tie-on label, there are probably many in collections that are not known to be Dean's.

The 'Mother Goose' series of cut-out rag dolls was introduced in the 1920s, which included such obvious characters as 'Mary Mary'. Pinafore dolls, all wearing a neat apron, were a feature of 1920, though 'Charlie Chaplin' (not in sheet form) costing 1s. must have been very popular. 'Cosy Kids', 'Ta-Ta' and 'Jumper' dolls were all put on the market in these post-war years, when materials were again becoming available, and the interest of the British public in home-made dolls had to be maintained.

Tru-to-Life Hilda Cowham rag dolls, known as Cowham Kiddies, were also made at this time, each with hair wig, jointed legs and mercerized stockings. Dean's had sole rights in producing Hilda Cowham rag dolls, which were given exotic titles such as 'Tantalizing Thora', 'Natty Nora' and 'Captivating Cora'. Some of these dolls were given eyes that were painted shut in a coquettish manner.

It was not only American manufacturers of dolls who became very aware in these competitive years of all the current trends. One year the scooter was felt to be fashionable, so all the Dean's toys were sold complete with their scooters. 'Gilbert the Filbert the Nursery Knut', a grotesque half-doll, half-toy, was promoted as the gimmick for another year.

Dean's A1 label was used on dolls for the first time in 1923. The 'Doll with a Disc' series also originated in that year, and consisted of a bead necklace with a gilded seal that hung from it. Many of the dolls were quite beautifully dressed, the short-coated baby doll being particularly effective. German dolls of this period were not dressed elegantly, and much effort was clearly put into the manufacture of detailed and eye-catching outfits.

'Evripoze' Tru-to-Life dolls were given what the firm described as a skeleton, then a soft inner covering to represent the fleshy and muscular tissues, and "an outer integument or skin". The utmost freedom of movement was thus obtained without a "cumbrous and complicated series of joints". 'Little Lord Fauntleroy', 'The Coogan Kid' and 'George Robey' were all made in this way.

A two-faced doll known as 'Peep-Bo' was made in the A1 series – the face not wanted was simply hidden by a cap! The usual laughing-crying or sleeping-waking varieties were made. 'Baby Bunting', whose body was completely fur covered, had remained popular for many years but is now very rarely found.

The felt-dressed Posy dolls were probably intended as the English answer to the Lenci dolls, which also had pressed-felt faces and fine clothes. The outfits worn by the Posy dolls were very cleverly designed in an up-to-date manner, but based on various flowers. 'Marguerite', for instance, was dressed in an outfit based on the white petals of the daisy. Dolls dressed in imitation of flowers often look fussy and rather silly, but the designer was most skilful, and really elegant costumes were devised. As many of these dolls have the sideways-glancing eyes usually associated with Lenci, it is little wonder that there is confusion.

From 1926, velvet-faced dolls with inset glass eyes, also with a sidelong look, were made. Some of these dolls made in black look very like those made by Nora Wellings and are sometimes seen labelled by antique dealers as made by her. The sailor dolls with ribbons around their hats, made by Dean's to be sold on board ship, are another product, often confused with those of Nora Wellings. The Dean's basic sailor dolls were sold with ribbons reading S.S. *Queen Mary* or H.M.S. *Royal George*, though special orders were also produced.

Dean's Dancing Dolls were the best sellers for 1928. 'Bunty' and 'Bobby' could be purchased separately at 4s. each, or, curiously, 8s. 6d. for the pair! "These quaint dancing figures will provide an endless fund of amusement for both children and grown ups alike. The antics and attitudes of the figures when danced either singly or in couples are beyond description. These playthings strike an entirely novel note." They are again typical of the toys of the twenties, part doll and part suggestive adult's toy. The illustrated pair were obviously not much appreciated by their child owner, as they still bear their original label. Economically, the firm sold the pair with the heads of rabbits, and in 1937 the head of 'Bobby' was replaced by that of 'Lupino Lane'.

Public interest in popular film fictional and cartoon characters was followed as closely by Dean's as by any American makers, and 'Milly-Molly-Mandy', 'Mimie and Shah' and 'Mickey Mouse' were all good sellers. A very fierce village blacksmith with a bristly black beard was made, as well as a 'By-Lo Baby', the last in clever imitation of the American 'Bye-Lo Baby'! In 1938, when it appears cami-knickers were all the rage, Dean's predictably made a cami-doll.

Several advertising dolls were made, such as 'Jimmy Whiteshine' for polish and 'Miss Sue' to advertise Sue Flake's Beef Suet. The best known was probably 'Miss Betty Oxo', sent in return for the greatest number of Oxo tokens.

482

There is little problem for collectors in the attribution of the cut-out rag dolls that are usually fully marked, but the Evripose and Tru-to-Life figures are more difficult, as similar dolls were made by other companies. Going through the firm's surviving catalogues, I was staggered at the large number of completely different dolls that were produced, and saddened by the fact that, being fabric, relatively few have survived.

Toys that were often quite similar to those made by Dean's were produced by Chad Valley. Like many of the Dean's dolls, the figures were often marked only with labels that were sewn under the foot. The shoes, usually of brightly-coloured felt in two colours, with characteristic piping between sole and upper, sometimes carried the label. Others were marked with a sewn on grey metal button while the 'Bambina' series carried a label sewn to each foot marked 'Hygenic Toys. Chad Valley'. Chad Valley made their first dolls in 1920, and later figures are typical of the period with their pert faces and fashionable clothes.

Unlike Dean's, Chad Valley made only soft dolls. The heads were heat-moulded under pressure, and made of buckram, canvas and felt. A patent taken out by the factory in 1924 referred to dolls' heads that were stiffened with shellac or starch and provided with openings into which glass eyes were inserted from within. It was claimed that the heads were virtually indestructible.

Collectors now particularly associate the firm with the drawings of Mabel Lucie Attwell, despite the fact that dozens of other dolls were made, such as boudoir-type night-dress-cases and painted flat-faced 'dolly' types. The work of this artist and its adaptation into doll form creates an interesting parallel with that of Rose O'Neill. Like the American artist, Miss Attwell claimed that her drawings were intended to appeal to adults rather than children. Like Rose O'Neill's Kewpies, the children designed by Lucie Attwell were seized upon by toy manufacturers, who were quick to realize their potential. Those produced by Chad Valley in the 1920s were described as, "An exquisite range of models in assorted Art shades." They were made in three sizes, $14\frac{1}{2}$, 16 and $18\frac{1}{2}$ inches high. "Personally designed by Miss Mabel Lucie Attwell, these delightful felt and velvet dolls faithfully reproduce the inimitable features of her well-known drawings of children." The range included a coloured doll, a soldier and a smart boy in morning dress, apart from the figures wearing dungarees that are always associated with her drawings. The dolls were sold in a specially-designed box known as the 'Bed-Bye' bed box.

Despite the fact that thousands of Chad Valley dolls were made, they are not

358 Extremely effective and well-equipped Britannia made by Nora Wellings. Label sewn to wrist. Felt head, swivel neck. Painted eyes. 33 in. high.

484

very easy to find today. As with other fabric-faced dolls, the material became discoloured and the dolls were thrown away. When found in almost mint condition, they are very appealing, and the vivid colours in which they were dressed must have made them popular. There is a marked similarity between some of the dolls produced by Chad Valley and those made by Nora Wellings. Miss Wellings worked for seven years as a designer for Chad Valley, and her influence is to be seen in many dolls that are only marked with the Chad Valley label. The illustrated smiling sailor is a typical example.

Many present-day collectors as children owned a Nora Wellings doll, for she was designing until 1959. Operations had begun at the Victoria Toy Works, Wellington, in 1926, when she and her brother Leonard established a soft-toy factory. A full range of soft toys was produced, as well as the more frequently-found dolls. In a conversation, Miss Wellings told my husband that she designed almost all the dolls herself while her brother ran the business.

When in her eighties, Miss Wellings was proud of the variety of dolls she made and was touchingly grateful to her work force of skilled local girls. Some of the costumes which her dolls wear are remarkably well made by any standard. The costume of 'Britannia' is particularly fine, with a quilted, plumed fabric helmet and a coat of mail. Many of the dolls, including this one, were made primarily as mascots, to be sold on board the great ocean liners; which is why so many small sailor dolls are found, wearing the names of the liners on their hats.

Felt, plush, velvet, and very occasionally cotton were all used for dolls' heads by Miss Wellings. A patent of 1926 related to a doll's head formed of fabric or felt and backed with buckram. The inner surface was to be coated with plastic wood. To this inner surface or moveable eyes were attached with plaster of paris. A waterproof layer was also given so that the faces could be washed, as could most other quality fabric dolls of the time, though I would not personally like to risk washing such a doll now. The heads were made in two halves with the front part strengthened by a wooden strut.

Miss Wellings insists that all her dolls were fully marked with a sewn-on label. This label can be found either on the wrist or under the foot. It can be either cream or black. As they were very firmly stitched on all four sides, they were unlikely to come away unless cut. Several dolls were made in imitation of the designer's work, and were unmarked; a fully-labelled doll should therefore be insisted

359 Deans, Chad Valley and Nora Wellings all produced night-dress cases in doll form. This example, marked "Nora Wellings", has the characteristic grinning mouth found on so many of the firm's dolls. 16 in. high.

360 A doll similar to Britannia (358) used to create the character of Bo Peep. This version, again very well costumed and wearing original child's leather shoes, is marked on the foot with the Nora Wellings label. Painted eyes. 33 in. high.

361 The velvet-faced Maori boy was made in several sizes by Nora Wellings. This version has effective inset glass eyes and a smiling mouth. Swivel head. 34 in. high.

362   Two plush dolls by Nora Wellings. The mounty smiles, but the rather Ruritanian soldier in blue grins with a sideways glance of painted eyes. Mounty with stockinette face marked with white label, felt-face soldier has brown label. 9 and 10½ in. high.

363   Nora Wellings worked for Chad Valley for a few years, and her influence can be seen in this doll's expression. Made by Chad Valley, but of a much poorer quality, with paste stiffened fabric face. Marked on white label "Chad Valley Co. Ltd". Painted eyes, sewn-on ears. 10½ in. high.

upon when buying, unless an absolutely identical marked doll is available for comparison.

The fact that many of Miss Welling's dolls were designed for the Atlantic travel route is evident, not only in the sailor dolls but also in 'Mounties' and 'Cowboys'. I owned a huge cowboy with chaps and stetson, made by Miss Wellings, when I was a child. Re-dressed in a velvet cloak and a cardboard crown, he was renamed 'Henry V' after my current hero. Sadly, Henry was ceremoniously buried after a particularly bloody Agincourt and mysteriously stolen during the night, which prevented his regular resurrection. I now have a particular fondness for the dolls that this designer created, as they vividly recall a very happy childhood.

The brown plush 'South Sea Islanders' that were made in a wide variety of sizes are at present very popular among collectors. They have the glass eyes and grinning face particularly associated with the more common dolls, though Miss Wellings was quite hurt when asked whether most of her dolls grinned; she insisted that they actually smiled.

Another quite popular doll is 'Harry the Hawk', made as a Royal Air Force mascot and sold in aid of Royal Air Force comforts during the war. Though such dolls could be purchased very cheaply, they are now becoming collectable, as many in acceptable condition are found, in comparison to the play dolls made by, for example, Dean's. As many of the Nora Wellings's dolls were made as mascots for adults, a large number have survived on both sides of the Atlantic and in good condition.

Rag dolls did not need the long and complicated manufacturing process that necessitated mass production. They were therefore designed in a much more adventurous manner. All the makers discussed created a very wide range of dolls, often with completely different faces. Even small establishments were able to produce commercially a variety of dolls that would not have been viable in china. Despite the fact that they were spurned by collectors for many years, they are now becoming more popular, as they are often much more accurate reflections of their period than those of china.

(*above left*) 364   Seated bent-limbed baby marked "Sun Rubber Co. Barbeton.O.U.S.A. Patent 2118682". Blue eyes. 12 in. high. Standing toddler is an EFFanBEE. "Patsy Jr. Doll". Blue painted eyes made *c.* 1950. 11 in. high.   (*above right*) 365   Feeding and wetting rubber doll with a stopper in buttock. Rubberized composition head. Marked on shoulder "EFFanBEE, DY-DEE Baby". 15½ in. high.   (*below left*) 366   Tin head mounted on leather body. Marked "Minerva" to front of shoulder and on back "5 Germany". Composition lower arms. Painted eyes. 13½ in. high.   (*below right*) 367   Open-mouthed glass-eyed tin head with teeth and wig. Marked "Minerva". American cloth body. 16 in. high.

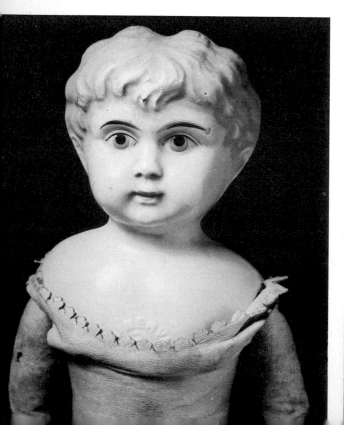

SIXTEEN

THE SEARCH FOR AN INDESTRUCTIBLE SUBSTANCE

To the planganologist, the nineteenth-century doll-makers were endowed with great skill, but also with an abundance of tasteful material out of which to fashion aesthetically satisfactory dolls. Wax, wood, papier mâché and china are all effectively different media, with the accompanying limitations and possibilities, but the manufacturers continually pursued their ideal of a doll that was completely unbreakable. It is paradoxical that the substances they invented during this search have suffered the ravages of time far more than those they sought to replace. The china doll, if it has survived at all, is still in almost original state, whereas dolls of various composition substances, even those made as recently as the 1930s, have usually faded, cracked or even warped.

Gutta-percha

Throughout the nineteenth century, efforts had been made to provide children with unbreakable dolls that were more realistic than the relatively sturdy woodens. Gutta-percha dolls had been sold as early as the 1820s, though the material did not come into regular use until the 1840s, when makers such as Edward Gatter and Richard Brooman were making moulded, stamped or embossed figures in England. It is extremely difficult, except by chemical analysis, to distinguish between rubber and gutta-percha, as both harden similarly and crack in time. The tendency for the colour to flake away is also common to both materials. The distinction is further complicated by the fact that a combination of the two was sometimes used. Gutta-percha is made malleable by immersion in hot steam or water, which enables it to be moulded when it reaches a temperature of 190 °F. Brooman coloured his gutta-percha mixture while it was in the kneading machine, which meant that painting of the 'flesh' after moulding was not necessary. In its raw state, the material is reddish white, so it is unlikely that Brooman needed in fact to introduce very much colour. The Colemans illustrate a particularly fine authentic gutta-percha head, with flowers moulded on the chest, in a manner quite unlike the porcelains with which the early rubber-type dolls are so often compared.

In their efforts to keep ahead in doll-making innovations, Maison Huret experimented with gutta-percha in the 1850s, and made heads as well as the more frequently-found bodies and limbs. At the 1855 Paris Exposition they exhibited the moulds which they used. Other French makers, such as Duclos, had already patented gutta-percha heads, but Huret was the first maker well known to collectors to use it. Long after the material had gone out of fashion, it was still used by Huret, who made *bébés* as well as *Parisiennes* of the substance. Few can have survived, as the material became very brittle and cracked, though dolls with gutta-percha arms are sometimes seen. Gutta-percha-limbed dolls made by Rohmer are also occasionally discovered, but are rare, since presumably many of the dolls that were originally given these limbs were provided with bisque replacements as they became disfigured.

In England, William Scott and Henry Plumb were also making gutta-percha dolls in the last half of the nineteenth century, but examples are not known. Mayhew commented that the heads that were hawked in the London streets in the late 1840s were not actually gutta-percha, though they were so described, but a mixture of glue and molasses. He describes these toys as

> articles which, having become cheap in the shops, find their way to the street traders and, after a brief or comparatively brief and prosperous trade has been carried out in them, gradually disappear . . . things which are grotesque or amusing but of no utility and are supplanted by some more attractive novelty.
>
> Among such matters of street trade are the 'elastic' toys called gutta-percha heads; these however have no gutta-percha in their composition but consist solely of a composition made of glue and treacle – the same as is used for printers' rollers. The heads are small, coloured models of the human face, usually with projecting nose, chin and a wide or distorted mouth, which admit of being squeezed into a different form of features, their elasticity causing them to return to their original cast. The trade carried on in the streets in these toys was at one time extensive, but it seems now to be gradually disappearing.

Such toys would have held great appeal for adults of the period, as well as children, and it is surprising that none have survived, even in the form of prints, from which much of our knowledge of fragile toys is derived.

Rubber

Le Blond exhibited indiarubber manikins at the 1853 New York Exhibition, and early rubber dolls generally are very much the province of the American collector, as they are very rarely found in Europe. The rubber heads were made in the manner typical of the 1850s and 1860s, with plump shoulders and round faces. The hair is often styled in plump ringlets which fall to the shoulders. It has often been suggested in the past that many china and rubber dolls were taken from the same moulds, but, as china dolls were almost exclusively made in Germany and rubber dolls in America, this seems very unlikely. There is the obvious possibility of American designers having copied pleasing china heads, though the more likely reason for the similarity is popular taste, which demanded dolls made in a certain style.

The early rubber dolls have great charm, despite the fact that the surface paint has often flaked away to reveal the raw substance beneath. The earliest known rubber dolls were made by Charles Goodyear as early as 1839, and by the 1850s rubber was used, though to nothing like the same extent, in France and England. The European makers, especially the French, used rubber instead of leather or china for dolls' limbs, though eventually Steiner, Delachal and Bru were to make complete rubber *bébés*. Bru made some rubber heads in the 1860s, though the jointed hard rubber dolls were described as 'new' by the firm in 1879. A few of the French rubber ladies' heads of the 1860s were given enamel eyes and mounted on wooden torsos with rubber limbs. The rubber *bébés* were proudly guaranteed as unbreakable, and others were suitable as bath-time toys, Bru for instance making 'bathers' in the 1870s.

Derolland was one of the most important makers of French rubber dolls. This firm made a wide variety of dolls in the medium, including besides the standard dolls, soldiers, 'Punches', and solid rubber dolls with squeakers. The bathing dolls, with a whistle inserted in the back, have remained popular to the present time, though the whistles in old examples were usually lost as the rubber contracted with age. The Derolland dolls were particularly commended for their variety of expression, though again examples are virtually impossible to find.

Dolls produced by the Goodyear Rubber Company are among the most desirable of this substance. It was this American company that made possible the development of rubber as a commercial doll-making material by inventing the vulcanizing process for hard rubber in 1851. There is a story that Goodyear discovered the method by accidentally dropping a mixture of rubber and sulphur on a hot stove. Rubber heads are found marked with the Goodyear patent, and are characterized by the fact that lashes are usually painted only on the lower lid. As other companies also made dolls which were marked with the Goodyear patent, it is difficult to be certain as to origin. Most of the Goodyear dolls have rather plump faces, and a few rather square-faced boy dolls were also made in the shoulder-head manner of almost all dolls of this period. A dark green rubber was used, and the dolls had painted eyes, in contrast to the better-quality 'French ladies', who were often given eyes of glass.

Soft rubber was pressed into a two-part metal mould to make a head. The two halves of the mould were then clamped together and placed in a vulcanizing bath. When the moulds were opened, the heads were complete, except for a little trimming and the actual painting. Some were decorated with moulded flowers and even hair nets, again in imitation of the porcelain dolls. Like the china dolls, the rubber heads were also sold separately to be made up at home.

One of the firms whose dolls carried the Goodyear patent mark was the New York Rubber Company, which operated during the second half of the nineteenth century. By 1897, this firm was making all-rubber dolls in both black and white. Some of their 'bather' dolls differed from the usual, which were made with moulded clothes, as they wore knitted outfits which appear to have been a somewhat unnecessary addition to an already satisfactory product.

When in reasonable condition, the dolls of the India Rubber Comb Company are also attractive. Made in the years after 1850, their dolls were given black or blonde moulded hair, some being as tall as 23 inches. The heads are marked 'I.R.Comb Co.' and are very much sought after by collectors. A red basic rubber was used, and the heads were always modelled with centre-parted hair. Other American companies made rubber dolls, but they were really only imitators of the methods and designs already used by the India Rubber Comb Company.

Various novelty-type rubber dolls were produced through the second half of the century. Their appeal was mainly to adults, though a few, such as a rag doll with an inflatable rubber lining made by Dean's before the First World War, were intended specifically for children. A baby doll intended purely for the amusement of adults was advertised in the *Graphic* in 1881; it could be obtained from the 'Facsimileograph Company, Brighton'. The 'Yankee Rubber Baby' dressed in a long white dress cost 14 stamps; boys or girls could be supplied, or twins at 2s. The doll would fit into a waistcoat pocket but could be inflated to life-size. "Like the real article, it coos at pleasure, yet screams awfully if smacked." For some reason the advertisement was directed only at adults.

When toy baby dolls with bent limbs became popular, the manufacturers quickly seized on the realistic qualities of rubber to make lifelike baby dolls. The 'Dydee' baby, which was designed by a schoolmistress, utilized very fully the possibilities of the substance. The doll 'drank' from a bottle and appeared to wet its nappy when a rubber stopper was removed from the buttock. It was obviously felt that too accurate positioning of the outlet would have been distasteful to parents! The Dydee dolls were given rubberized composition heads, a combination that was far more successful than most experiments of this kind, as the heads are still usually in nice condition. The bodies however have often shrivelled with

(*above left*) 368 Girl doll with pale yellow hair and fixed celluloid eyes. Marked with turtle symbol and the numbers "38/56" and on body "52/58". Straight legs. 21 in. high. (*above right*) 369 Dainty French celluloid girl doll marked with the eagle symbol for Petitcollin. Fixed eyes. 14 in. high. (*below*) 370 Well-costumed celluloid doll probably sold as souvenir. Straight legs, moulded socks. Painted eyes. Moulded hair under applied wig. Marked with eagle's head. 11 in. high.

493

age, and when undressed the babies present a rather macabre appearance. 'Betsie Wetsy' was brought out in 1937 by Uneeda to compete with the 'Dydee', but it never became as well known.

The Germans were not very interested in rubber as a doll-making medium, and the examples originating in that country usually date from the early twentieth century, when it was used merely to keep German dolls abreast with American developments. Kämmer and Reinhardt made some dolls with rubber heads and limbs. The substance must at first have appeared ideal for limbs, as it was soft enough not to damage the child and unbreakable. As late as 1932, Kämmer and Reinhardt were registering patents for soft rubber dolls' heads with strengthening supports of hard rubber around the eyes, mouth and neck.

For about fifty years after the introduction of the Goodyear patent, the makers of rubber dolls appear to have been content to produce items in a very similar manner; they either made shoulder heads or moulded complete figures which often look more like mantelpiece ornaments than play dolls. The Museum of Childhood in Edinburgh has a moulded figure of this type, which depicts a little girl who is seated and holds a King Charles spaniel. A few innovations were patented in these years, such as a method of inserting hair into the rubber scalp, but little significant advance was made until around 1900, when doll-makers became aware of the new possibilities of all the materials available to them, and created some very complex figures.

In 1918, Emanuel Cervenka revived the old idea of gutta-percha heads that could change expression when squeezed, but he made his dolls of rubber. Others were made to cry when they were squeezed. The Baumann Rubber Company made a two-faced rubber baby, with the usual laughing and crying face. This particular doll was quite complex, as it also contained a crying voice box, the volume of which could be varied according to the pressure with which it was squeezed. Madame Alfred Fayaud also patented a two-faced rubber doll, whose head was turned by pressing it down on a compressed air ball. The Radium-Gummiwerke made inflatable rubber dolls that must have been as easy to store away as the plastic reindeer and Father Christmasses made in this way today.

Probably the most complicated rubber doll was that patented by Munyard of London, which was provided with a mechanism that produced changes of expression when the doll was picked up and rocked. The eyelids and eyeballs were moveable, and glass teardrops were fitted into recesses in the eye sockets. Eyebrows, lips, cheeks and tears were all connected to a bar and pendulum.

371   Celluloid boy doll with delicately-moulded hair wearing sailor suit. Bent-limb baby body. Brown intaglio-type eyes. Marked on shoulder with turtle symbol. "SCHUTZ MARKE 45. Germany" for Rheinisches Gummi-und-Celluloid-Gesellschaft. 19 in. high.

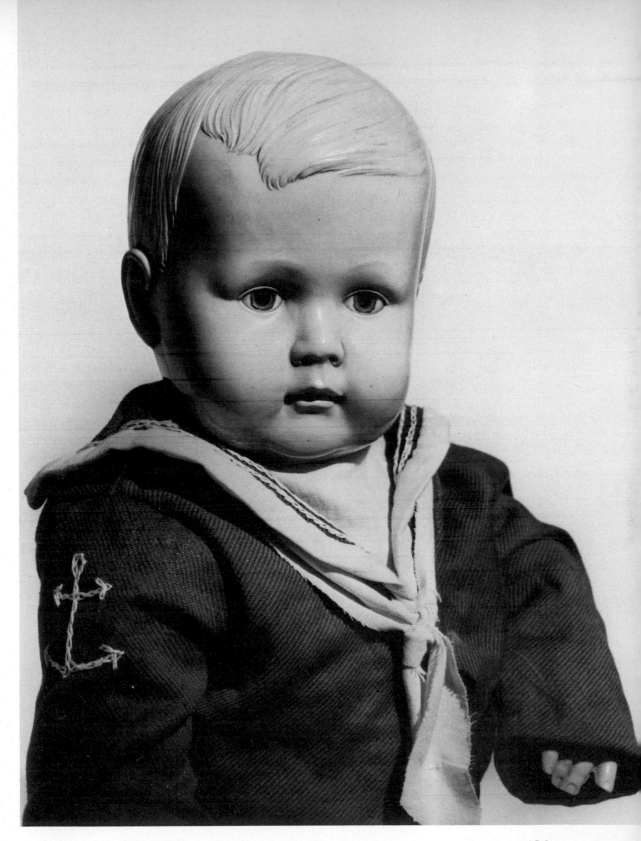

When in the 'normal' position the doll's face was fretful, but when the doll was rocked in the child's arms, the pendulum swung, moving a rockbar which raised the eyebrows, withdrew the tears and caused the lips to part. When laid down again, the face assumed its original fretful expression.

Hot-water bottles made in the form of dolls were popular from the 1890s, when they were first made by S. L. Wilson. The Metropolitan India Rubber and Vulcanite Company of London manufactured similar bottles for many years, and they are a form of utility toy still popular today.

Many firms have continued to produce rubber dolls almost to the present time. Dean's still included some rubber dolls as late as 1956, such as a black doll dressed in fur and a 'Musical Coon' and 'Musical Indian Boy', both with rubber heads and musical movement, in their range. Many of these dolls, though made comparatively recently, were produced for a very short time, and should, over the years, become interesting collector's pieces, providing they are stored carefully. The 'Magic Skin' dolls, which had a soft rubber surface over a padded filling, must have appeared the ultimate in realism, but even this was only a short-lived success, and the doll buyers for large stores expected something new the following year; although it is probable that children themselves, if free from advertising pressure, would have continued to play happily with long-outmoded dolls.

Metal

The rubber doll was attractive to children because it was soft and very safe to handle. A baby could chew off an arm or an ear without coming to any great harm himself and the doll hot-water bottle made a lovable bed-fellow. In comparison, metal dolls were cold, unyielding and subject to disfiguring damage, as the paint chipped away if the doll was roughly treated. Although metal dolls, particularly those of silver, had been made since the Middle Ages as gifts for princesses, there had been no great interest in the indestructible qualities of metal until the last quarter of the nineteenth century.

Several of the French makers used metal for the hands of *bébés*: a sensible choice, as the composition fingers broke much too easily. A few, extremely rare, pewter heads are known, which were made in the 1870s, and wear the hairstyles of that period. The pewter shoulder heads are mounted on wooden jointed bodies, rather like the Grödnertals of the first half of the century. With their moulded flowers, ornate hairstyles and necklaces, these dolls are very valuable collector's pieces.

Brass, zinc and copper were all used for making dolls' heads (René Paulin, of Paris, made painted copper heads with inset glass eyes). All these metal heads were painted or enamelled, and many are now completely unattributable and

496

(*above left*) 372   Heavy-quality black celluloid boy wearing white sweater and red trousers. Brown painted eyes. Jointed only at shoulder. Schutz Mark. 18 in. high.   (*above right*) 373   French celluloid boy doll with lashed sleeping eyes marked with eagle head for Petitcollin. 16½ in. high.   (*below left*) 374   Celluloid heads were at first used merely as a substitute for bisque by firms such as Kammer and Reinhardt. Sleeping eyes, head open at top as in bisque, open mouth with teeth. Marked "K & R 406" turtle mark. 20 in. high.   (*below right*) 375   Celluloid boy doll showing the fine modelling possible in this medium. Unusual pearlized effect to hair. Turtle mark for "Rheinisches Gummi-und-Celluloid-Gesellschaft". 18 in. high.

have to be valued on quality and condition. Rather more boys' heads were made in metal than in china, so that the former are less sought after.

In the Germany of the 1880s, a large number of dolls were made of sheet metal, brass, zinc or tinplate, but again most were unmarked, except for a number. An interesting phonograph doll was made by Giebeler-Falk in 1919: the crown of the head was hinged and could be lifted off to reveal a horn and turntable. As the actual mechanism was fitted in the dolls body, it could be cranked from the back. Records of the doll singing were supplied in $3\frac{1}{2}$- and 4-inch sizes to fit inside the crown of the head. The same firm experimented with jointing methods, in an attempt to create a model figure that could assume human poses.

The collector is most likely to acquire dolls of tin or aluminium. Better examples were so well finished that at a distance they can be mistaken for bisque heads. Often the metal heads were used on jointed wood and composition bodies, but a few more interesting examples are found which are completely made of metal. The Swiss maker Bucherer made an amusing assortment of metal-bodied dolls, which were given composition heads representing various characters. Even the feet of these well-constructed figures were jointed. An American maker made an all-metal doll representing Jiggo in *Bringing up Father*. The most commonly found are the shoulder heads, often mounted on home-made bodies, or the socket heads that were used instead of bisque.

The shoulder-headed type are often considered to be earlier than the socket heads, but both types continued to be made as late as 1930. The boy dolls with moulded short hair lent themselves best to the material, though they are often very badly damaged. The makers' theory was that if a head was dented, it could be removed from the body and the dent pressed out, but they omitted to state that in the process an unsightly crack would be left in the surface paint. Though the moulded hair can sometimes be satisfactorily restored, the matching up of the flesh paint is extremely difficult and often unsatisfactory. The 'tin' heads are therefore very moderately priced today, as they are not often objects of great beauty, though of interest as a stage in the development of the doll. Broken bisque heads were sometimes replaced by metal heads at toyshops and dolls' hospitals, and it is often difficult to decide whether the head is actually original or not.

Heads marked 'Minerva' are the most commonly found in Britain. They were made at the turn of the century by A. Vischer in Germany, though Buschow and Beck also used this name on their metal heads. Some of the Minerva heads were made of brass rather than the usual tin, and were coated with a 'new process combination celluloid washable enamel'. The heads were usually of the shoulder type that could be bent to fit the body of (perhaps) a porcelain doll whose head was broken. In 1912, Minerva dolls that shed real tears were advertised, though

376   Probably the most famous of all composition dolls was that made to represent the 1930s child actress
Shirley Temple. Here with facsimile autographed photograph and Shirley Temple badge. Original boxed state
with hairnet. Green sleeping eyes. Marked on head "Shirley Temple CDP Ideal". 18 in. high.

existing examples must be very rare. Sears Roebuck and Company in the United States distributed a 'Knock-About Grade' of these dolls in the 1920s. The arms of these dolls were of wood, though metal would have seemed the more obvious choice, if slightly more expensive.

This unbreakable quality of the metal heads appealed more to the Americans than the Europeans, and of course was a suitable product for the vast American tin toy industry. The Metal Doll Company, run by Vincent Lake, made their ball-jointed dolls entirely of metal and gave them snap-on interchangeable wigs. A New Jersey firm, the Amor Metal Toy Stamping Company, made their own types of doll, some of which walked. The Atlas Doll and Toy Company was yet another firm that made heads of metal in America, though the majority were still made in Germany and bore names such as 'Diana' or 'Juno'.

The French makers were not as interested in metal as they had been in rubber, though some French patents were registered as early as the 1860s for copper and zinc heads. Paën Frères were putting metal heads on some of their dolls in the 1880s, but the foremost doll-makers obviously gave little consideration to the material's potential. The makers' interest swung away from metal when doll manufacturers, particularly in America, ceased to rely on the waste products of other industries for their doll-making materials and began to use substances, such as the various types of composition, that were especially adapted to the work.

Celluloid

Celluloid was a much-insulted substance that was at first used imitatively, and its potential as a material in its own right was almost ignored. Objects were made to imitate ivory, tortoiseshell, coral and wood, almost in the way that plastic is tortured by modern manufacturers. The difficulty of using it as a doll-making material lay in the extremely glossy surface which it gave to dolls' faces, a surface that was obviously unacceptable to children accustomed to the more natural effect of bisque. Various methods were tried to limit this 'unpleasant' effect, and some effort was even made to persuade celluloid to look like wax.

One maker attempted to give a matt finish by rubbing the completed head with a fine pumice stone or powder. Kestner claimed that all their celluloid dolls were of the soft matt-finished type, and had the added advantage of colour that would not fade in the sun, this being another quickly discovered disadvantage of the material. The shoulder-type heads, which tend to be the earlier, are often found with a wan, rather bleached look to their features, caused by over-exposure to light.

Though celluloid had been invented in England in the middle of the century,

(*above left*) 377   1922 Poster in background shows original Campbell Kids. In foreground, plastic doll made by Ideal Toy Company in 1952. 8 in. high.   (*above right*) 378   "Betty Boops" modelled and copyrighted by Joseph Kallus. Based on animated cartoon by Paramount Pictures. Made in 1932 by the Cameo Doll Company. Wood and composition. 11½ in. high.   (*below*) 379   Edgar Bergen, the American ventriloquist had two dolls, Charlie McCarthy and Mortimer Snurd. Charlie, seen here in doll form, has a pull string at back of neck. Marked "A Reliable Doll, Canada". Patented by Ideal in 1939.

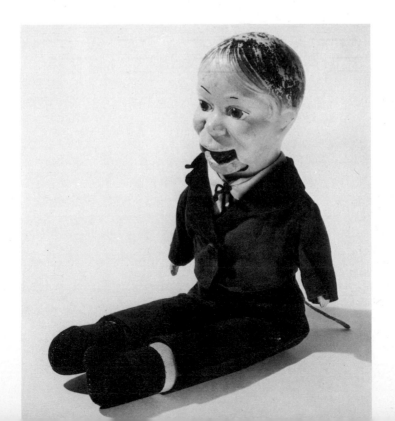

it was first used for dolls by an American company in the 1860s. Hyatt Brothers of New Jersey, working under the trade name of the Celluloid Novelty Company, used this mixture of camphor and cellulose nitrate for their products. The celluloid, in solid state, was laid in two-piece metal moulds. Hot air or steam was then blown into the mould under pressure, which forced the celluloid to soften and conform to the shape. When cooled, the mould was removed and the two parts of the head were joined with ether. They could then be decorated with paint, which was often not very permanent, and the dolls have usually lost most of their original complexion. The early shoulder-headed celluloids, such as those made by Valmore Boitel, were made in imitation of the traditional china and wax dolls, and mounted on kid or fabric bodies, a practice that continued into the 1920s. The collector quite often finds well-made bodies with what appear to us as very cheap heads, but it must be remembered that, like most new substances, celluloid was at first much more expensive than the traditional materials, and was used for dolls of reasonable quality. It was only after 1900 that the making of celluloids became really cheap, and millions of these dolls were made in America, France, Germany and, of course, Japan.

Perhaps the best-known celluloid dolls of reasonable quality are those carrying the 'turtle mark' of the Rheinische Gummi und Celluloid Fabrik, which was established in the 1870s. As the name is remarkably ponderous, collectors refer to these dolls simply as 'the turtle mark'. Many reputable companies were provided with heads of celluloid for composition bodies by this firm. Kestner and Kämmer and Reinhardt are among the most famous, and though celluloid dolls are now regarded with much less interest than the bisque dolls, they were at first very adventurous. A high-quality walking doll was made by K & R, which usually had a celluloid head mounted on a composition body. The rigid legs moved from the hips on eight wheels that were set in metal plates under the feet. Most of the turtle mark K & R dolls were made from the models originally used for bisque dolls, so that a few rare 'baby' dolls marked 700 are found in celluloid, as well as several of the other 'doll-faced' double-jointeds. For some reason, the more attractive 'character' toddlers were not made in celluloid, or at least are not yet known to have been made! Some good-quality all-celluloid dolls were made for K & R, and two basic types of body were used: one with very short plump legs to represent a very young child and another type with a much slimmer body and long straight legs. Some of the heads for these all-celluloid dolls were made with moulded hair, but others had wigs. Completely undamaged dolls of this type are not often found, and are worth buying, especially as they are still so much cheaper than the more beautiful china dolls.

380 Appealingly-modelled composition negro baby. Marked "H.W.4" on head. Bent-limbed baby body, glass sleeping eyes. 15 in. high.

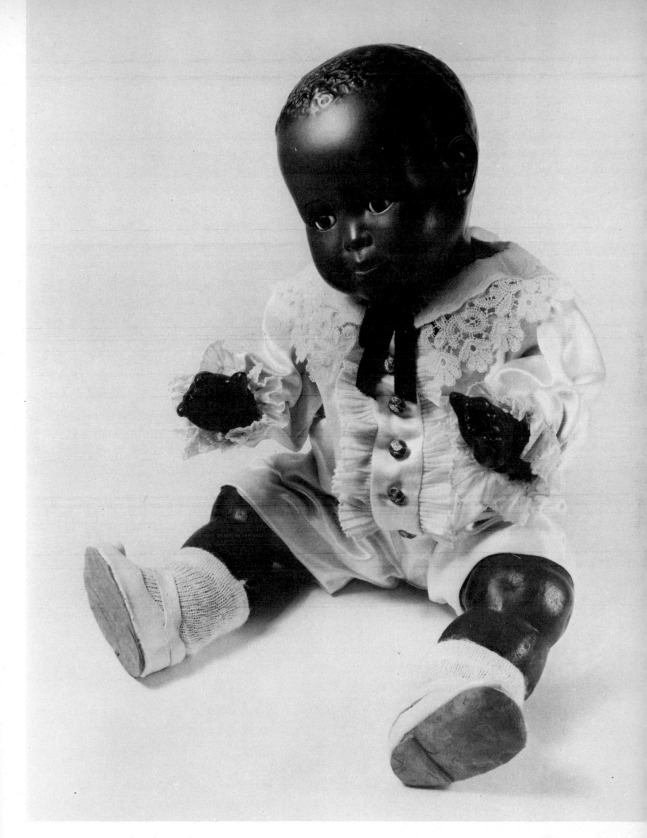

The fate of most celluloid dolls was to be squashed. As a child, I remember a treasured pre-war fairy doll of my mother's that was carefully brought out each year at Christmas. The doll was of the stiff-limbed variety, with huge painted eyes, made by the million in Japan. As a collector I now rate such dolls very low, but as a child I gazed at the tinsel-dressed figure in wonder. The weight of stored tree decorations eventually crushed this doll, but most were broken during play and very little can now be done in the way of restoration.

Some of the celluloid eyes that were used for the later dolls were of an excellent quality not approached by the makers of modern plastic eyes. Some of the black celluloids with moulded hair are also of a high standard, and the colour has not been subject to as much damage as the pink used for European dolls. An attractive black doll dressed in moulded clothes is illustrated, which makes good use of the material in its own right. Too often the celluloid dolls were made to imitate the older bisques.

The celluloid substance is of great interest, as it is the first man-made plastic material used for doll manufacture. Great concern was expressed because of its highly inflammable qualities, and as early as 1907 one New Jersey company was claiming to make fireproof celluloids. Despite their dangerous quality, the sale of these dolls was not banned in Britain until the 1960s, though because of the adverse publicity, many dolls must have been thrown away by anxious parents long before this time. Even some doll-dealers are anxious about selling collector's items that are a potential danger.

Celluloid Mabel Lucie Attwell dolls were found among the toys of most British children before the Second World War, often made by the London Cascelluloid Company. Kewpies must have been equally popular in America. An attractive pair of 'Hottentots' were sold wrapped in a blanket with their eyes looking in opposite directions. Some of the simple two-piece moulded doll's-house figures of adults made in the 1920s have an excellent period feel, with their shingled hair and clinging dresses, though they fall over at the least movement. A character celluloid was made to represent Emma Haig as she appeared in a play *The Rise of Rosie O'Reilly*, and the doll, like so many more of the period, carried a facsimile autograph of the star.

Probably the most collectable of the celluloids are those with interchangeable heads. One doll was provided with five possibilities, including a cat's head, all of which were to be screwed into place. Few have survived complete with all the heads, and those that have are, therefore, much more expensive than the ordinary celluloids. Hermsdorfer Celluloid Warenfabrik made an all-celluloid drinking baby in 1923 that would also be a good acquisition. This firm used a ladybird trade-mark, which was probably meant to deceive the casual buyer into thinking he was buying one of the turtle mark dolls, as they were very similar.

(*above left*) 381 "Dancerina" made by Mattel. By turning the plastic knob on the head the doll's dancing is controlled. Runs on battery and dances, predictably, in time to the 'Sugar Plum Fairy' from *The Nutcracker Suite*. 24 in. high. (*above right*) 382 Composition flange head on stuffed pink cloth body. Made in England, 1947–8. Original costume. One of the first dolls available in quantity after the war. Selected by myself as a child from a large number. Considered extremely beautiful by original owner. 16½ in. high. (*below*) 383 Composition doll representing Scarlet O'Hara. Made by Madam Alexander. Teenage-type body. 11 in. high.

Though the turtle mark had originally been used to indicate longevity, it could not have been more inappropriate than on celluloid dolls!

As the material was light and could be washed easily, it was eminently suitable as a material for bath-time toys. The Industrielle de Celluloid Cie made a bathing doll that was cleverly weighted to float in a standing position, with its head and shoulders above the water and its hands outstretched. When the arms were placed to the sides of the figure, the doll could lie in the water with just a small weighted part keeping it in position.

Many of the brightly-coloured bathing dolls made in imitation of nursery-rhyme and story-book characters originated in Japan, but some were made in England. An ingenious hinged celluloid ball was made by A. B. Knight in 1893: when the ball was thrown to the limit of the piece of string to which it was fixed, the sides opened and a doll was propelled forward on a spring, rather like a sophisticated Jack-in-the-Box.

Although the French and German doll-makers were on the whole content to use celluloid in place of bisque without exploring new possibilities, some quite good dolls were made, many of the celluloid costume dolls in particular being dressed exquisitely. Several French companies, such as Boitel, Parisienne de Cellulosine Cie and Anel et Fraisse, were established to make dolls of the new material, though their production was only a fraction of that of the turtle mark company.

Some of the famous Grace Putnam Bye-Lo Babies were made of celluloid, while it was commonly used for the hands. This method of using celluloid hands or lower arms was very popular in the 1920s, and though it now appears to have been an unnecessarily complicated method, it must have held great appeal for the doll-makers of the time. The modern collector often thinks these celluloid hands indicate a recently 'made-up' doll, but many actually left the factories in this state.

The light celluloid dolls became known in the United States as 'Parcel Post Babies', and this cheapness of transportation must have done much to popularize the use of, for instance, the celluloid hands by other makers. One American firm, the Celluloid Collar Company of Ohio, is reputed to have turned to doll-making as a means of using up the scraps from the manufacture of imitation stiff collars, so that when these went out of fashion the dolls also ceased to be made.

Products of factories that worked for short periods, character-type dolls such as one made in Italy to represent Charlie Chaplin raising his hat, and figures made in imitation of popular cartoon or fictional characters are all worth buying. With the exception of these interesting dolls, the basic celluloids should not at present cost a great deal of money, as they are not yet generally accepted by established collectors, whose taste affects price. No doubt in ten or twenty years' time these dolls will be selling for considerable amounts, and they are a promising but fairly long-term investment.

Great care should be taken in the storage of these dolls, which need almost as much attention as wax. They should not be kept in a strong light which might bleach the faces, or in heat which will soften or warp. A doll's dressing-case of this material was rescued in the nick of time from the floodlights used in photographing dolls for this book, again indicating the care needed in handling the material.

The celluloids with moulded hair are usually more popular than the wigged examples, and the black dolls are particularly liked. Celluloids are one of the few types of relatively old dolls that can still be picked up at jumble sales; they should not be despised, as their manufacture marked yet another stage in the search for a durable, hygienic doll.

Indestructibles

In the manufacturers' efforts to create an indestructible doll, metal heads were experimentally coated with celluloid, in an attempt to achieve the advantages of both materials. Some of the heads marked 'Minerva' were coated in a similar way with both celluloid and enamel. The degree of success achieved by these methods is debatable, as the makers were continually trying to make unbreakable heads that looked just like china. When efforts were concentrated upon making them unbreakable rather than imitative, more success was achieved.

Spanish craftsmen in the 1880s had tried to treat papier mâché in a special way to make it look like china, while English makers were painting the same material with celluloid in the early years of the twentieth century in an effort towards the same end. The early makers of composition described the material as 'Imitation china, washable and sunproof'. The Biskoline made by Parsons Jackson in America was described as being similar to celluloid: 'Will never break, crack, surface chip or peel.' A generation of children was growing up who were no longer satisfied with the gentle doll-play under adult supervision that had pleased their parents, but expected to take their dolls into street or garden without the trauma of a smashed friend. In the efforts to provide children with unbreakable dolls, one maker even created a complete figure of pumice stone!

Despite all their activity, the manufacturers were only able to make relatively indestructible dolls. The damage that a child's hands failed to do was carried out most effectively by time, and when found, most of these heads have either cracked, faded or discoloured so badly that they are quite unacceptable as collector's items. A few rather better-quality composition heads were made by German companies, such as Armand Marseille, and some of these heads, if in good condition, are very acceptable to new collectors. American collectors are naturally more interested in the indestructibles, as they are the logical culmination of the work of Greiner, Schoenhut and Ellis. Most of the real advances in the creation of twentieth-century indestructible dolls were also made in America, so it is little wonder that examples of the various types are often included in good collections.

Several patents for indestructible heads were registered in England, but there are only a few makers whose products are often found. The French doll-makers saw many advantages in unbreakable dolls, and in 1890 the Bru advertisements were claiming such heads as new. Fleischmann and Bloedel also made 'pâte incassable' heads for their dolls, as did S.F.B.J. The substance used by the French doll-makers was known as Fiberloid or Fibrolaque. The S.F.B.J. heads made of this material look very poor in comparison with china heads made from the same model, but perhaps when new the difference was not as great.

Most of the composition mixtures were based on the combination of wood fibre with various binding agents. Lignum fibro was made of a mixture of fibre, flour and glue, a fairly successful combination, since finished dolls were extremely light in weight. In 1892 Solomon Hoffmann was claiming in America to be the sole maker of composition dolls. His products were marketed as 'Can't Break Em' dolls, 'hand painted by trained artists'. Other patents for the basic mixture included combinations of plaster, linen, glue, whiting or even stone! The Ideal Novelty Company went so far as to claim that their dolls could be dropped on stone floors without breaking, a feature that was demonstrated in small American stores by their salesmen. All the companies used slogans such as 'looks like bisque, feels like bisque' in their sales promotions, though all sorts of trade gimmicks were used to sell the dolls of individual companies.

The glue that was used as a binder for most of the composition substances was regarded with great distrust by progressive parents, who were becoming much more aware of the possible danger of many toys. Horrific tales abounded of the unpleasant raw materials obtained from the slaughter-houses, used in making glue, and many doll-makers were at pains to point out that their products were free of animal waste and made only with 'chemical binders'. Because of the great suspicion of glue, the 'American Glueless Doll Company' was set up in 1918. Their dolls, it was claimed, would not peel or chip, and could be thoroughly washed without danger as their products were jointed rather than strung.

Various formulae were registered for the manufacture of unbreakable materials. Adtocolite, a composition that has usually cracked badly, was used by many American makers. A very ingenious method which combined almost all the known doll-making ideas was registered in England in 1924. A cardboard head was to be covered with cotton, coated with celluloid and then decorated with paint applied with a rubber stamp. While it was the glue used in doll-making that particularly worried the American parents, the English mothers were more concerned over the actual stuffing used in the dolls. In the Victorian period, horsehair and straw had both been popular and often became infected with insects. A great deal of time was therefore spent in working out new and effective methods for cleaning vegetable fibres and cotton waste to make them not only hygienic but non-inflammable too.

Just as nineteenth-century makers had sometimes marketed dolls under the names of famous stage or music-hall artistes, so the makers in the 1930s took advantage of the great effect the cinema was having on ordinary children. Dozens of characters, such as 'Felix the Cat', or 'Mickey Mouse' were represented, not always as toys, but often as mascots for adults. Several versions of Charlie Chaplin appeared, including a moulded example by Louis Amberg, marketed as 'Charlie Chaplin doll. The world's greatest comedian'. 'Shirley Temple', made by the Ideal Toy Company in the 1930s, sold one and a half million copies. This little-girl doll was supplied complete with hair nets, an instruction booklet and a facsimile signed photograph. This doll, though hardly beautiful, is bought by many established collectors who would decline to buy other types of com-position doll. The Shirley Temple cult exerted a great influence on the lives of many children in the 1930s. One collector, when a child, was inspired to begin collecting dolls because she saw a photograph of Shirley Temple herself with her own collection of dolls.

Other, less immediately suitable, characters served as models for dolls, including Deanna Durbin, Jane Withers and Jackie Coogan. It was probably inevitable that after the success of the Shirley Temple dolls, 'Judy Garlands' should also be made. 'Glenn Hunter', as he appeared in *Merton of the Movies* came complete with his facsimile autograph. EFFanBEE made 'W. C. Fields', whose jaw could be moved by a wire that protruded from the back of the neck, and 'Charlie McCarthy' was made in a similar way by another company. The search for celebrities to perpetuate in doll form even spread to the Dionne quins, who were reproduced by the Alexander Doll Company. Fictional characters were also made, such as 'Samson, Uncle Sam's Firstborn' claimed by Louis Amberg to be the first wire-jointed composition doll to be made in America.

Firms like Amberg employed first-rate designers, Grace Drayton, Helen Trowbridge, Aaron Cone and Joseph Kallus, to create their dolls. Joseph Kallus was first employed to transform Rose O'Neil's Kewpies into doll form, but he later trained specifically as a doll designer, and eventually set up his own doll company in 1916. Many American collectors consider 'Bo Fair', made by his firm, the Rex Doll Company, to be his best product in these early years, though other creditable dolls were made by the Cameo Doll Company, of which he became president later.

Throughout this progressive period, the doll-makers strove to produce a doll in the Käthe Kruse manner, which would engage the child's motherly instincts. It is strange that in the period when woman's emancipation and equal education for girls was so much in the air, the doll-makers were concentrating their activity on the production of baby dolls on which the little girl was expected to exercise her mothering instincts. The fact that little girls played with baby dolls often in imitation of adult behaviour, rather than with a flowering mothering instinct, did not occur to them, and the makers' favourite slogan of the period was 'Dolls like children are dolls children like.'

Titles such as 'Baby Beautiful', 'Next-to-Nature Babies', 'Baby Grumpy', and crying babies that uttered when the doll was rocked, all pandered to the accepted longing of the little girl to have a baby of her own to love. The fact that little brother, when he arrived in person, was often a tolerated intruder rather than a person upon whom she lavished her love and affection was tactfully forgotten!

One doll, which bore the label 'Mother's darling, quiet and good, requires no nursing, attention or food', was surely intended to appeal to the harassed mother herself. . . .

American Beauty made "New American Baby dolls, with those marvellous eyes, roguish eyes that roll, flirt, blink, wink and sleep. Toddles when guided." EFFanBEE's advertisement in the *Ladies' Home Journal* for 1925 recommended 'Rosemary', the specially-made Christmas doll. 'Every child wants me for Christmas – the doll with the golden Heart.' The golden heart was a necklace which the doll wore, with a heart-shaped pendant reading EFFanBEE. The little girl was told, "You can play with Rosemary like a real baby. Dress and undress her, take her for a walk or dance with her. When you put her to sleep she closes her big blue eyes with real eyelashes. When you take her up she says 'Mama' as plainly as a child." As though this eulogy were not sufficiently tempting, extra ploys were used, again very typical of the doll-makers of the period. "You can tell Rosemary by her little golden heart necklace. Every EFFanBEE Doll wears one. Rosemary wants every little girl to have one too. Mail her this coupon and 6 cents for postage and she will send you a necklace."

In accordance with the growing twentieth-century belief in motherhood as a science rather than a natural state, the doll-maker also supplied a booklet, *The Proper Doll for my Child's Age*, "which mothers find of great value. It has many helpful hints on using dolls for character-building play. It shows Rosemary's flocks and flocks of pretty sisters."

The advertisements of the 1920s obviously attacked at all levels, possibly even more subtly than those of today.

Many of the early composition dolls were made almost in imitation of the shoulder-headed bisques. Lower arms and legs were of composition and the head was mounted on a shoulder plate, narrower and shorter than that needed for the heavier china heads, but in much the same manner. As the indestructible dolls developed, flange necks were found to be more suitable, and often the whole of the arms and legs were made of composition, leaving only the fabric torso to act as a simple means of joining the various parts. Later, complete bodies were made in composition, which made the doll less cuddly but much stronger. Babies' bottles, nappies to be wetted realistically, teething rings and (of course) dolls' prams were all made for baby play, and Dean's Rag Book Company in England even made specially-printed bibs for baby dolls.

One of the first 'copyrighted' dolls was 'Billikin', made in composition by Louis Amberg. It represented a semi-human figure with its hair drawn to a peak rather in the Kewpie style, but with slanted eyes. Composition Kewpies were themselves made often dressed to represent characters such as soldiers. The surface of these dolls frequently has a rather rubbed look, which detracts considerably from their value. Happifats, Campbell Kids and Bye-Lo Babies were made in the new material, though they are now valued at considerably less than the bisque versions.

Large googly eyes, which Grace Drayton popularized, were used by her for 'Bobby Blake', which she designed in 1911. All the American makers, in contrast to the majority of English manufacturers of this period, were remarkably adventurous. The English were generally content to go on producing pretty 'little-girl' dolls in the traditional manner, while the Americans made use of all kinds of simple but eye-catching innovations, such as threading ribbon through slots cut in the doll's moulded hair. Dean's, whose rag dolls were so inventive and progressive, did not make composition dolls until the 1930s, when they announced their 'Bye Bye Baby' with sleeping eyes and a soft cloth body. Some of their subsequent baby dolls, such as 'Cherub', were sold lying neatly upon a pillow. The firm relied more upon the beautiful dressing of its dolls than upon any particular innovations, though the clothes themselves are often worthy of note. 'Stormy Weather', a toddler type, was dressed in Wellington boots, sou'wester and mackintosh, all very well made. In contrast, 'Sandy' wore a swimsuit and carried a bucket and spade.

Toddler dolls with mohair wigs that could be washed and combed were made by Dean's in the 1930s, and given names such as Christine and Gwendoline. Their moulded baby heads at this time were marketed as 'New-Born Nigger' and 'New-Born Baby', the black doll being by far the more attractive. Both these heads were sold loose for home assembly, a method of doll-making that does not seem to have survived as long in other countries.

The composition substance could be moulded in one of two ways. The old method, used since the eighteenth century, was to use cold presses. The mixture was spread in the mould, pressed into shape and allowed to dry slightly before removal and later assembly. The new method, of which the doll-makers (according to their advertisements) were very proud, was the 'hot press'. The composition was placed in electric- or gas-heated two-part moulds, which moulded and dried in one process, and meant that heads could be immediately passed to the decorators and a much faster production maintained.

The pressure of advertising campaigns, especially in the United States, meant that dolls of this type were often utilized either as give-aways or as straightforward advertisements. A doll dressed in denim overalls and known as 'Buddie Lee' was used as a shop-window display piece and given a new outfit each year. Aunt Jemima was made in composition as well as rag, and represented a coloured woman carrying a slogan 'I'se in town, honey'. 'Dolly Drake', a girl doll carrying a cake and wearing a baker's hat, was used by Drake Brothers. The Cubeb smoking doll was a rather elegant, all-composition jointed lady with moulded high-heeled shoes. It was used to promote the smoking habit among women at a time when respectable women didn't – or at least, not in public.

Many English makers imitated the ideas of the Americans, so that a Snaresbrook manufacturer made 'Goo Goo' dolls as well as 'Gigglies'. 'Baby Dimples', 'Wob-Li-Gob' and 'Bathing Jeff', the last made by the Art Toy Manufactory of Fitzroy Street, are all reminiscent of American doll titles.

Apart from the popularity of dolls based on stage and screen characters, many dolls were based on the creations of popular newspapers and writers. Phyllis May, who appeared in the *New York Evening Mail*, was represented in doll form based on the original drawings by Hazel Drukker. 'Little Nemo', dressed in his best nightshirt, was based on the cartoons of Winsor M'Cay, while 'Bobby Bounce', created by Grace Drayton and used as a printed design on baby crockery, was made as a doll by Borgfeldt.

The First World War inspired several military dolls, such as 'Liberty Boy' wearing a soldier's uniform and 'British Tommy' and 'Army Nurse', both made by Horsman. Several unmarked dolls representing soldiers in officer's

(*top*) 384 "Little Brother" whose genital realism raised eyebrows in the 1960s. Marked on head "Clodray, 7324. Made in France". On box "Ceji Compagnie du Jouet. Fabriqué Clodray". 15 in. high.

(*bottom left*) 385 Teenage girl doll in brown vinyl. Made by Lesney, England. Miss Matchbox Disco Girl. Has a variety of commercially-made outfits. Action flex legs. 9 in. high.

(*bottom right*) 386 One of the most attractive of modern dolls to collectors is that designed by Sasha Morgenthaler. Made by Trendon, England. 16½ in. high.

uniform and carrying sticks were made at this time by English makers but are unmarked. Many Red Cross nurse dolls were supplied, some complete with little stretchers.

The North Pole expeditions encouraged the making of a doll by Horsman in imitation of Cook, while another doll of the period was 'Arctic boy'. As news appeared to have remained fresh for a much longer period than it does today, the makers had time to make and market their dolls before popular interest was lost.

Some two-faced indestructibles were manufactured, such as 'Soozie Smiles' by Ideal, who also made 150 different walking dolls. Independent moving sleeping eyes were another innovation that had a brief success, but by the late 1930s the makers seem almost to have exhausted all possible innovations and there was a return to a more basic doll.

Early compositions can be recognized by their closer affinity to the china dolls. Some have the ball-jointed bodies that seem to belong particularly to the bisque dolls. There is little that can be done to improve the appearance of these composition dolls when they are disfigured, as overpainting gives them a very odd, bedizened effect. A chalk-like substance was used by many English makers in the 1940s, but this was even more prone to scratches and chips to the surface.

The cost of many of these poorly-made dolls in the 1940s was astronomical and, even taking into account the relative value of money, many ordinary parents during these years spent more on their children's dolls than the wealthy French merchants who bought lavishly equipped *Parisiennes* for their children in the nineteenth century. A few years after the war, I was taken to see the first really big doll display at Christmas in a local store. All the dolls wore flowered muslin or striped cotton dresses and bright red shoes. I thought them beautiful, with their bright yellow hair. Now, looking at the doll bought for me that day, I wonder at a child's bad taste.

Latex foam or froth dolls, with a non-porous outer surface, were made in the 1930s by Latex Processes of Guernsey, though toys of this type did not become really popular until after 1950. The Bendy dolls and toys are familiar to almost every modern child and irresistible to teething babies!

The first plastic dolls are believed to have been made by the firm of Riedeler in the German Democratic Republic in 1948. Many early twentieth-century patents refer to 'plastic' substances, but the term was used at that time in connection with almost any mouldable material. The plastic dolls of the 1950s and 1960s really plumbed the depths of unattractiveness. Every figure seems to have been made in imitation of curly-haired red-lipped movie stars. A few of the Rosebud and Pedigree dolls were better than average, but as yet are only worth buying as an investment for the year 2000, though no doubt they gave great pleasure to their owners.

Despite the fact that the modern dolls are made of the most permanent material yet used, their life is often very short, as they are frequently discarded after minor damage. It is sometimes difficult to locate examples of dolls made just a few years ago; even Baby Brother, whose genital realism caused raised eyebrows in the late sixties, is not easy to find. As dolls are becoming more hazardous as a business venture, several firms have gone out of operation, and children with examples of these firms' work would be advised to keep them.

A few of the vinyl dolls at present on sale are much more attractive than the dolls of the sixties. The pensive-faced 'Sasha' dolls, designed by Sasha Morgenther, with well-constructed bodies and quality clothes, immediately come to mind. A sales assistant in a very large toy store explained to me that if children are allowed a completely free choice, they rarely select these well-made dolls, but prefer the gaudily-frilled and curled figures in fancy boxes.

Various innovations have been introduced in recent years. Mattel made a dancing doll known as 'Swingy', and also 'Dancerina', a ballet dancer, and the first doll in the world to toe-dance: surely a collector's item of the future. The movement is controlled by a switch under a crown on the head and the doll predictably keeps time with music from the 'Nutcracker' suite. An Italian company makes a doll that can speak nine languages, and an extremely clever German doll can walk at different speeds. A doll that changed colour was made in 1963. When placed in the light it developed a suntan, which was lost in the dark each night. Various baby dolls, including 'Tearful Cheerful' whose face changes expression, a crawling baby and another that belches after drinking have added to the list of doll-making inventions.

The teenage dolls, rather in the manner of the nineteenth-century *Parisiennes*, are essentially a revival of the 1960s. 'Barbie' was launched by Mattel in 1959, but did not become world-famous until the following year. Known as 'Sindy' in England, she was also provided with a fashion-conscious boy friend, 'Ken'. The cost of some of the quite poorly-made clothes that teenage dolls such as these wear is often staggering, but very typical of a period when children often have quite large amounts of money to spend on personal amusements. The latch-key ten-year-old, left alone in school holidays while mother is at work, is as typical of our age as the little factory drudge was to the Victorian. It was very obvious to me, as a teacher in a comprehensive school in a New Town, that the twelve-year-olds with the most pocket money and the largest wardrobes for their teenage dolls were usually those most personally neglected. The pendulum has truly swung, and the fashion doll with its host of accessories no longer suggests the cosseted but too often the purchased child.

387   Early Victorian home-made paper doll with two-sided dresses to slip over head. 6 in. high.

388   "The Little Girl's Doll Dressed in the most pleasing costume. Together with 8 Child's Dresses." Design printed on one side only. Richly hand-coloured. Marked "G.W.F." for Faber. 7 in. high.

SEVENTEEN

PAPER DOLLS AND DOLL'S-HOUSE FAMILIES

Paper Dolls

As paper dolls are sought not only by doll enthusiasts but also by collectors of ephemera, advertising material and books, examples do not remain long on the market. Despite the fact that in the eighteenth century, when the Protean figures were first published on a commercial scale, they were referred to as 'English dolls', the majority of those found which date from before 1840 are usually of German or French origin. The exceptions are the home-made figures and the characters, such as 'Little Fanny' published by S. & J. Fuller of London. After 1850 the scene is different, and large numbers were produced both in England and America, though the actual printing often continued to be executed in Germany, where colourful lithographed toys could be produced more cheaply and skilfully than in England.

Like rag, paper is a material that lends itself well to the home manufacture of dolls, and often in the pages of old scrapbooks are seen small figures carefully built up with scraps of crêpe paper, tinsel or even lace, on the foundation of a hand-painted paper or card body. Some very large families of hand-painted dolls were made, including maids and visiting children. Some examples I looked at recently were only 1 inch high, but were given neatly-made dresses and capes that could be changed by tabs that were attached to the shoulders. The adults in this particular set were about 5 inches high, and all would have fitted quite nicely into a doll's house. The patience expended on their construction and the skill in painting were quite considerable, as even the smallest figures were given six changes of clothes. Another home-made set with equally small figures was mounted on card, and the clothes fitted by tabs pushed through slots in the backing. Such sets are extremely difficult to value, and have to be bought purely on their appeal, though they are of interest in the study of costume before 1850. Some of the home-made lady-dolls of this type are very skilfully made and have wigs, bonnets and shawls that are usually attached with tabs, which was the easiest method for the amateur to use. Colour was usually painted on, though a few of the Regency period were given cut-out pieces of fabric as clothes. One Scottish gentleman-doll of this period was particularly well done: the jabot was decorated with strips of lace, and buttons were of applied metal. Such dolls fall on the border line between rag and paper, but as the actual figures are of paper, it seem appropriate to include them here.

Three-dimensional figures were quite often made by amateurs, such as those in the Dresden Volksmuseum, which are fully formed and made of writing paper. Books of juvenile instruction often suggested quite ingenious methods of utilizing waste materials to create effective figures, not only as dolls but also for use as menu card holders, Christmas-tree decorations or dressing-table tidies. One firm, as a sales ploy, gave away figures of card dressed in a printed chemise – figures that were to be clothed in the crêpe paper the company made.

The interest in art dolls that became so strong in the years immediately before and after the First World War involved the use of strange, and probably unsuitable, materials. Paper was an obvious choice, because of its low price and wide variety of colour and texture. Some quite exotic figures were created that were displayed as art objects rather than dolls, in the same way as window dressers now construct stylized figures for specialist displays. The work of Erna Muth of Dresden is particularly remembered in this sphere of art paper dolls. She first exhibited her work in 1919 and limited her craft to the few materials that were available at the time. Modelling silk paper over wire armatures, she created sinuous and evocative sculpture from the simplest of materials. Despite their beauty, which is evident in photographs, there is something frighteningly decadent about them, and they are very far indeed from the type of art dolls made by Käthe Kruse.

Three-dimensional paper dolls, be they home-made or the work of artists, are regrettably fragile, and have very rarely survived. Occasionally home-made figures of this type are seen in the shell houses that were made as pastimes, or even in the rooms of unplayed-with doll's houses, but they are not particularly collectable, as they are rarely in acceptable condition. The exceptions are those made by religious orders in various church vestments that were often placed reverently by their purchasers under glass shades.

389   Late Victorian lady-doll wearing a coloured petticoat. Clothes printed on two sides to fit over head. Gold decorated embossed surface. 7 in. high. .

390   Home-made Edwardian family of paper dolls some painted with more skill than others.

Doll-like figures were often included in the sheets of scraps, usually printed in France or Germany, made for use in the Victorian craze for Decalomania. One interesting set still in uncut state showed the usual basic doll wearing a petticoat and surrounded by articles of dress. The clothes were obviously intended to be laid in place in the eighteenth-century manner, rather than hung by tabs on the standing doll. Another set was produced, known as Grandpa's Rocking Chair. A series of figures could be made to sit in the large bentwood chair, the set being published by W. Hagelburg.

Following the manner of several Regency books, which included a doll that could be dressed in costumes appropriate to the development of the story, many publishers throughout the century produced their own versions of this basic idea. Warne, in the middle years of the century, produced their *Picture Puzzle Toy Books* one of which, *The Nursery Play Book* included a picture of a doll's house with gaps left plain for the affixing of pieces of furniture and dolls. A sheet of colourful scraps accompanied the book and scraps were to be selected for the appropriate positions. Augsburg printers sold sheets of prints depicting soldiers and characters in various costumes that were especially made for cutting out. The book in the shape of a paper doll was very popular by the end of the century, and these were produced mainly in Bavaria by such publishers as Ernest Nister.

Many sumptuous lithographed cardboard rooms were made, mainly by French and American publishers. 'L'Interieur de la Poupée' provided a series of elegantly-dressed dolls that were to be placed in a richly-decorated salon. In the United States, Charles, Austin and Smith published a series of similarly-made dolls' rooms, dolls and furniture that was given the title 'The Girl's Delight'. In the 1880s, the House of Hanover was reproduced in a set of paper dolls consisting of more than sixty sheets that included not only the Royal Family but also furniture, houses and towns.

In the early years of the nineteenth century, public picture-galleries were a new and excitingly fashionable idea, and model versions were rapidly produced in Germany, including a variety of paper dolls in appropriate elegant dress. Similar models included an assembly hall, a theatre and a church, all suitably occupied by dolls. The Christmas crib, which was most popular in Germany, lent itself well to a paper construction, and cribs were produced until the First World War by Augsburg engravers.

One of the earliest known cut-out dolls was printed in Germany, circa 1650. Almost every part was interchangeable and meant to be laid in place. This early method of assembly held little lasting appeal, since the costume was too easily disarranged, and the idea of attaching tabs to the various costume parts was a logical development. Most of the commercial figures made before 1860 make use of this method of attaching costume, but as the dolls became more sophisticated, back views were also provided, and in this case the costume was either slipped over the doll's head or slid across the body, to fix together at one side. There were many developments of these two basic ideas, including cleverly-folded costumes that gave a three-dimensional effect. At the end of the century, paper dolls were made with jointed limbs, interchangeable heads and sleeping eyes, all in imitation of the popular bisques. It is noticeable that modern paper dolls, such as those produced by Mary Quant, have reverted to the traditional, one-sided, tabbed method that children appear to find most acceptable.

The concept of providing boys with dolls is not as new as the current 'Action Man'. The boys of the Regency and Early Victorian periods were accustomed to figures of knights and soldiers that could be costumed appropriately for war games. Figures from model theatres and prints of actors could be cut out or embellished with coloured paper. The Epinal prints, usually associated with *Pantins*, were also available as sheets of paper soldiers that could be used by poorer children instead of lead figures. Examples both of the *Pantins* and the paper soldiers can still be obtained quite easily, especially in France. A 'Boy's Paper Dressing Doll' was published around 1850 as a companion box to those intended for girls. The title, as was often the case, was printed in French, German and English.

The packaging of the dolls made by G. W. Faber was particularly effective. Gold edging was applied to the sturdy boxes, which were brightly decorated with hand-coloured prints of the figures they contained. Titles such as 'Little Darling's Wardrobe for a New Doll', or 'The Little Girl Doll, dressed in the most pleasing costume' were given in four languages. At least eight basic costumes were provided, which were printed on one side only and were to be slipped over the head and held in place by a thin tissue backing. Items such as hats or wigs were sometimes printed on both sides, and the older tabbed method of fixing the clothes was sometimes used. Small unnecessary detail was avoided, as colouring was by hand. These dolls are richly painted and give the lavish effect of figures intended for wealthy children. They are among the most desirable of paper dolls, and are rarely seen for sale.

In the period before 1840, most of the figures were printed from engraved copper or steel plates and then hand coloured. Sometimes, as in the case of those colourists who worked for the producers of model theatres, stencils were used to speed the application of colour to flat areas, and this method can be detected by the complete evenness of colour. It is seen particularly in the Epinal prints. Around 1840, lithography replaced engravings, but was at first used very much in the manner of the old engravings, and of course colour was still applied by hand.

Paper dolls were usually produced by firms who published books or games, and I know of no maker who exclusively created dolls. The boxes or folders of dolls were an attractive sales line that could be supplied as novelty items to stationers and gift shops. As many have lost their original boxes or folders, they are often difficult to attribute except by comparison. Many of these mid-nineteenth-century figures originally fitted into a small wooden stand, but it is very unusual to find these still in the boxes.

The French were more concerned with paper dolls as fashion figures, and it is common to find French examples with both the back and the front of the dresses shown. 'Poupée A Habiller', a particularly well-dressed doll, showed off its costume in this way. One of the best loved of paper dolls is that made by Faber for the French market and given the title of 'Eugénie'. It showed the Empress in a series of the very fashionable and ornate dresses that she wore, she claimed, to encourage the French textile and fashion industry. Her elegance made a great impact on the English people, and, after her State visit, the doll also sold well in England. The French publishers produced charmingly-clothed dolls that were set in sumptuously-furnished lithographed rooms, rather in the manner of stage settings. As they were obviously fragile, these are now rarely seen outside museums.

The American contribution in the field of paper dolls was considerable, and by the end of the century some English producers of dolls used American in preference to German printers to execute their designs. In 1854, Nicholls and Company of Boston published *Fanny Gray. A History of Her Life* which is believed to have been the first paper doll to be commercially produced in the States. The popularity of the singer Jenny Lind caused her to be represented in doll form in many of her roles, such as 'Mary' in *The Daughter of the Regiment*. One 'Jenny Lind' at the Essex Institute, Massachusetts, has ten dresses and head-dresses that were two sided and fitted over the head. Other versions of the singer were made with costumes that fitted by tabs. Fanny Essler 'The Dancer of Paris' was made at about the same time, and included a similar range of costumes. Boys were provided with paper dolls in the blue and grey costumes of the Civil War. Many of these early American dolls were still printed for the publishers in Germany, as American printing at this stage was still considerably behind the European.

Godey's Ladies' Book for 1859 included a set of dressing dolls, comprising six boys and girls with their costumes. This set was probably the first to be given away in a magazine, as no English examples of the type are known that date from the 1850s. The issue of the figures set a trend that was to continue to the present time, and several sets of dressing dolls taken from American publications of the 1920s are shown. Some magazines published complete families of dolls that were issued over several years, so that a continual subscription would be maintained by the persuasion of children. A few of these families were also provided with rooms in which they could be set out. In the years 1895–6, the *Boston Sunday Herald* printed a doll supplement of one adult costume in colour each week. For 2 cents, the card figure the costumes fitted would be sent.

The *Ladies' Home Journal* produced several attractive series, from a very popular doll known as 'Letty Lane' in 1908 to a quite complicated adaptation of the basic paper doll in 1922, which was designed by Jessie Louise Taylor. The figures were known as 'Fold-A-Ways' and were intended to be glued to card and then cut out. The method was patented in 1917, but magazine examples seen usually date to the twenties. Back and front of the dolls were shown, and the one piece clothes fitted neatly together at the back by a series of ingenious tabs and slots. Each page of cut-out dolls was accompanied by a story. Characters, such as 'The Puritan Twins', were produced. At about the same time, the magazine printed a series that included a story by Sarah Addington, with cut-out dressing figures designed by Gertrude A. Kay. Some of this second series was accompanied by animals, and in one, 'Humpty Dumpty', a boy doll, was provided with a wheel chair with a patchwork quilt into which he could be slotted.

Apart from their use in persuading mothers to continue to buy a particular magazine, the dolls were also useful as advertising material. Clark's O.N.T. Spool Cotton published a two-sided doll with the pertinent message, 'If the little girl who gets this doll is sent to the store for thread, she should asked for Clark's O.N.T. Spool Cotton.' The dolls were dressed in various national costumes. A very fashionably-dressed doll that made use of a different construction technique was published by McLaughlin's Coffee. These dolls, one of which, together with costumes, was included in every bag of coffee, were popular for many years. The doll folded along lines that ran from shoulder to hem, and was thus given a conical effect. As many as sixteen figures were included in each set. Some of the men-dolls were amusing, with the typical moustaches of the period. Not as many men as women and girls were made, and as with nearly all types of paper doll, they are now the rarest, if not the most attractive. Some of the dolls represented queens, and a piece of paper furniture was included as a bonus in the packets containing them. Guidelines on some of the dolls indicated where folds were to be made, so that they could sit. The gentlemen never sat.

The 1890s in America saw the production of thousands of advertising dolls, including a few that were provided only with head and arms that were pushed through the two-sided costume. New England Mince Meat, Barbour's Irish Flax, Diamond Dyes, Overall Boys and Lions Coffee were all advertised in paper-doll form. All these figures are now very collectable, and form a specialist field in their own right. The American collectors are supplied with a much

greater variety of advertising dolls than are to be found in England, where we do not appear to have found this type of advertising as useful.

There are several American publishers of paper dolls whose products form attractive acquisitions. The dolls, like the English ones, were sold either in book form or in envelopes, and were nothing like as luxurious as the boxed sets of the fifties and sixties. Austin and Smith, R. A. Hobbs, Kernel and Foster, and (the most famous) McLaughlin Brothers all made figures of acceptable standard. McLaughlin Brothers was established in New York in 1828 as a publishing firm, but their first paper dolls did not appear until about 1860. Among the most popular of their dolls, and probably the earliest set, are 'Mr & Mrs Tom Thumb'. Included in the 'Tom Thumb' set were 'Commodore Nutt' and 'Minnie Warren'. A particularly attractive 'Topsy and Eva' set was also made, though the most famous doll produced was 'Susie Simple', a series that was begun in 1885. (It is probably worth commenting here that there was no connection between McLaughlin's Coffee and McLaughlin Brothers.) Among the other collectable dolls published by McLaughlin were the inevitable 'Little Red Riding-hood' and, in complete contrast, Madame Pompadour.

Palmer Cox 'Brownies', so popular in cut-out form, were also made in paper. The Arnold Print Works copyright was carried on the paper dolls, but they were actually produced by Thomas and Wylie, Litho Company, New York. 'Uncle Sam', 'German Peasant' and 'Student' were all issued in paper. On one side of the simple fold-back stand was printed 'Lion Coffee'. The figures were given greater play appeal by their interchangeable heads.

In 1874, H. Hart Jr of Philadelphia patented a walking paper figure. The doll was assembled in sections, and was to be held by a tab at the waistline. When the doll was pushed forward on a flat surface, the head and legs moved as though walking. Activated paper dolls were also produced by the Dennison Manufacturing Company in the 1880s. Their dolls were jointed at the arms and legs. A series of actresses of the period were made with these swinging legs and arms, and were shown dressed either in low-necked combinations or wearing a type of can-can outfit, with long black arms and legs. Both were rather more in the manner of adult amusements, rather than play toys, but they now make eye-catching collector's pieces. Animated figures of card were also made. Two sides of a figure enclosed a wheel, to which were attached five legs that rotated

391 "My Lady Betty and her Gowns". Our Pets Series No. 1. Raphael Tuck & Sons. Publishers to Her Majesty the Queen (Victoria). The type of costume is peculiar to Raphael Tuck.

392 "Dolly's Wardrobe" with blouse-type tops. Late Victorian. Produced by Dean & Sons Ltd, London.

as the wheel was pushed along by a stick. Several companies made similar dolls to this, and in 1920 one was patented as 'Daddy Longlegs'.

Many dolls sold in America, even at the end of the century, were still printed in Germany, as were most of those sold in England. A large number of the dolls designed in England by Raphael Tuck but actually printed in Germany were sold in America. It is now much easier to buy Raphael Tuck dolls in America than in England, as the export was so great. Apart from producing dolls, Tuck's main production was concerned with fancy stationery, notably Christmas cards. Sets of scraps, often including doll-like figures, were also produced, and the character heads after the drawings of Cruikshank are greatly sought after. The firm was established in 1866 by Raphael Tuck, who came from East Prussia to England already a businessman, and set up as 'A Fine Art Publisher and Picture Frame Manufacturer'. His advertisements stated that he specialized in oleographs, prints and coloured scraps in sheets or relief. It is not known for certain when the first paper dolls were made, as many of the firm's records were unfortunately lost during the bombing of London in the last war.

Keen selling characterized the establishment, and Raphael sent his two sons, Adolf and Herman, on trips around the country. At the end of each session sales would be compared, and the son with the best sales record would be given the largest egg for his breakfast. The German links of the firm were maintained, and the packages containing the dolls (and sometimes the dolls themselves) bear the words 'Printed in Germany' or even 'Printed at the Fine Art Works in Saxony'.

Innumerable paper and thin card dolls were produced by Tuck's. The figures were not dressed in high fashion as were the French, but wore fanciful outfits designed to appeal to children. Many of the dresses were obviously influenced by current fashion, but it was so much altered and adapted that the dolls might be said to be dressed in the Raphael Tuck manner. Some of the earlier dolls were made as quite fashionable men and women, and they are slim and in the French manner, but attention was mainly concentrated on the girl-women in stylized adult clothes.

The stylized clothes are of little help in dating, as many of the dolls continued to be produced for some time. The details given of monarchs in the Royal Warrant stamps are of some help in recognizing Victorian examples. One of the nicest of the late Victorian dolls was 'The Bridal Party'. The lady-doll was given the usual very splendid wedding dress, but a hideous walking costume for the honeymoon, with a Tyrolean-style hat with a feather. The bride was truly

393   Girl doll with range of costumes. Printed on thin card. Late Victorian. From Raphael Tuck's "Artistic Series III".

transformed overnight. The 'Bridegroom', the second set in the series, was in the American version given a most improbable assortment of dress including U.S. Army uniform, a cowboy outfit and a smoking jacket. It would be interesting to find the English market version of the 'Bridegroom'; one would expect an equally diverting range of clothes. Maids of honour and bridesmaids were also included in this series, and given stylish sporting outfits for cycling and bowling. The same series was also sold in sheet form, to be cut out and assembled, but the quality dolls were packed in folders or boxes.

Other true lady-dolls made by Raphael Tuck included 'Favourite Faces', dolls made as portraits of popular actresses of the time, such as Miss Maude Adams and Mrs Lesley Carter. The actresses were supplied with a change of wigs as well as costumes. Julia Marlowe and Ada Rehan were included in this series. The 'Belle' series of lady-dolls appears to have been made for the American market, as no companion set with English place-names is known. The dolls were given titles such as 'Belle of Saratoga', 'Belle of Newport' and 'Belle of the South'. The dolls could be obtained either fair or dark haired. Many of the American dolls bear the words 'Designed at the studios in New York'.

By the Edwardian period, most of the dolls were child-like. They were usually about 9 inches high and given clothes that fitted on one side only. They were supplied not only with fashionable hats and umbrellas, but also with pets, dolls, soft toys and even a doll's pram. The best collector's pieces have changeable shoes, a refinement not often seen, and the cat with shoes is particularly sought after.

'Father Tuck's Doll Sheets' were introduced after the accession of Edward VII, and came in two sizes, each of which comprised a set of eight uncut sheets. Unfortunately, when cut out, these dolls do not carry the firm's mark and are not always recognized by collectors. The 'Fairy Tales' series, as well as the 'Bride and Bridegroom', was issued in this form, and included 'Dick Whittington', 'Mother Goose' and 'Jack and the Beanstalk'.

An amusingly-named group of dressing dolls were made by Tuck's at the end of the last century. They were dressed in decidedly strange medieval-style customs and given titles such as 'Lordly Lionel', 'Courtly Beatrice' and 'Royal Reggie'. This set was sold in extremely ornate envelopes. 'Fair Francis', in the Dainty Dollies series, was dark haired, but her head tilted provocatively to one side makes her unusual. This figure wore particularly sumptuous clothes, with a muff and splendidly-decorated coat.

---

394 "Little Marjorie and her dresses. Figures have arms jointed by paper clips. Two dolls included in box. Costumes fix by tabs. Printed by Raphael Tuck & Sons, Publishers to their Majesties the King and Queen. Printed at the Fine Art Works in Bavaria." Pre-1914 war. Doll 8½ in. high.

Dresses for Dolly was a painting book that included a selection of thin cakes of paint at the top of the cover. Unfortunately, most of these figures were ruined as collector's pieces by the young artists who owned them, though any example that by chance has not been played with is worth buying. In this particular sphere, it is generally the nurseries' failures that are the collector's items.

Several patents were registered by the firm in England. One by A. Tuck and F. P. Scott was for a cardboard figure of a baby. One part represented the baby's face, and the other the arms and a bottle. The doll was then given a long-tissue paper robe and a frilly tissue cap. It is not known whether the doll was commercially produced, but home-made versions do occasionally appear. Raphael Tuck's also patented a doll show-card to display figures that wore two-sided clothes: one doll carried a mirror so that the front of the opposite doll could be seen. 'Home Sweet Home for Dainty Dolly', published by them in 1910, was presumably a cardboard room or small box-type house in which the doll could be kept.

'Little Marjorie and her dresses' was made in the 1920s, and included a pair of dolls that were given arms jointed at the elbows with paper clips. Extra realism was lent by cutting slits near the lower edge of the dresses, so that the legs appeared to stand in front of the back of the coat, an economical way of making a one-sided costume look more realistic. The doll was printed on card, and wore clothes that were much more up to date than the imaginative dress usually worn by the Tuck dolls.

In 1893, a doll with changeable heads was patented by Raphael Tuck. The figure could be either fair or dark-haired, and in some versions wore very unusual changeable gloves. The doll dressing postcards also made by Tuck's, which are still comparatively cheap, are sought after by collectors of unusual postcards. There are a large number of the Tuck dolls that are unmarked, and a good deal of work still needs to be done by collectors in comparing examples and identifying various dolls. American collectors are better organized in this respect than the English, and much useful research is carried out in the States that could not as yet be attempted in England, because of the very casual organization of most doll clubs.

The improvements in colour printing, set in motion by Baxter's work in the 1850s and by the continual lowering of the price of paper meant that after 1860 paper dolls were available to a much wider public, though such dolls were not very cheap until the 1880s. The gradual change of market for the figures is very noticeable, and as the dolls became cheaper, the costumes became more mundane. The introduction of die-sinking between 1855 and 1860 meant that embossed decoration could be added to the costumes, but as with most new processes, this was at first only found in the better dolls, and the embossed parts were usually decorated with gold. As the technique became cheaper, it was used for details such as pleats or frills on dresses. Frosted effects, achieved by sprinkling the surface with powdered glass or aluminium, were not introduced until the late 1870s; but it is an effect only occasionally seen on dolls.

Efforts were constantly made to make paper dolls appear more realistic. One doll, made by Tapeso before the First World War, had sleeping eyes that closed when a tab at the back, which also formed the support for the stand, was pulled. The method of cutting near the hem to give the doll added realism was again used in this doll, and it appears to have been a method that was popular between 1910 and 1925. It was not always successful, because it is often difficult to slide the hands through the sleeve slits, and they break easily. The sleeping-eyed doll was known as 'My Own Dolly', and the arms were conveniently folded at the back so that they could be included on the actual dresses – a method that may not seem very realistic to a child, but which made it unnecessary for the manufacturer to cut the parts very precisely.

An extremely improbable doll was produced in 1899 by W. R. Robb, which had small magnifying lenses for eyes. Microscopic information or small advertisements were to be placed behind the eyes, so that they could be read by peering through the doll's magnifying eyes!

Metal supports were sometimes used for making paper dolls more stable. Dolls, dolls' carriages and pianos were made in this way by Trufant. The figures were given backs and fronts and joined with tabs at the sides. A fashionably-dressed series was made in a rather similar manner by the British Novelty Works, a subsidiary of Dean's Rag Book Company. The figures were known as 'Hilda Cowham Kiddies', and stood 12 inches high; they were provided with metal bases and wire legs to give stability. Though examples of these attractive dolls, each of which was given a special name, are often included in doll collections, they were never intended as play dolls, but were meant to hold menus, place-cards or even calendars. Dean's catalogues were including these figures as late as 1928. They were described as 'dainty little figures in perfect miniature representations of the life size models as purchased by H.M. Queen Mary. Each miniature kiddie is about twelve inches high. 1s. 3d. each or 1s. 4d. with calendars.' Each figure was dressed quite differently.

Gibsons' paper dolls, dating to 1895, were made with the head, shoulders, and body separate. Blouse, parts of the skirt, sleeves and blouse fronts could all be applied separately and an endless number of possibilities could thus be created. The Harrison paper dolls made in 1903 were dressed in cleverly-folded tissue or crêpe paper, and in the patent drawings they look very like Christmas-tree ornaments.

In England as in America, various firms advertised their products by the use

of paper dolls. An attractively coloured advertising postcard was produced around 1900 by Germea, and showed a little girl saying her prayers before her 'Germea for Breakfast. The true health food'. The postcard included two cut-out dresses and a hat. Barbour's Irish flax threads were advertised in England by a series of dolls in imaginary costumes based on the flowers or fruits of various countries. A set of twelve was made, and six of the characters had changeable dresses. In the changeable dolls, the head and arms were slipped between the folded dress; the remaining six were simply 'fold-back' figures. This set, which was appealingly coloured, was printed in America. A complete set could be obtained by sending three penny stamps to Barbour and Sons, Lisburn, Ireland. Quite a large number of these dolls are to be found today, and it should not be too difficult to build up a complete set. As they were about 5 inches high, they are sometimes seen in the rooms of doll's houses.

Sunlight Paper Dolls were also given away. No. 1 Series, produced by the soap manufacturer, was composed of dolls that were 6 inches high. Three dolls were included in the series, each of which was given three dresses and three hats. The names of the dolls were 'Daisy Bell', 'Annie Laurie' and 'Kate O'Connor'. The dolls were dispatched in return for twelve wrappers of Sunlight or Lifebuoy soap. 'Punch and Judy' was given away in the same series, together with all the necessary scenery.

Another company with strong German roots that became established in England was that of J. W. Spear and Sons, whose dolls and games were printed at the Spear works in Bavaria. Like Raphael Tuck, they continued to produce dolls in almost the same manner for many years, and some dolls made in the 1930s had plainly been originally designed before the First World War. 'Dolly's Wardrobe' for instance, in an out-of-date though attractive style, was still appearing in the mid-thirties. The wardrobe doll was particularly effective, as it was made of strong cardboard and finished in bright colours. The wardrobe was actually made in the form of this piece of furniture, rather than being, as in the nineteenth century, merely a term for the box container. Inside the wardrobe were three dolls, twelve dresses and hats, metal coat-hangers and a muff.

395 "My Own Dolly" with eyes that sleep by movement of tab at back that also forms the stand. Soft attractive colour. Marked "Tapeso No. 391". 14 in. high.

396 Hilda Cowham Kiddies made by British Novelty Works, a subsidiary of Dean's Rag Book Company. Were originally sold not as dolls but as menu-card holders or calendars. Facsimile signed by Hilda Cowham. Each figure given a name such as Motherly Molly or Saucy Sally. Life-size versions originally produced for advertising purposes. Original cost 1s. 3d. each or 1s. 4d. with calendar. Introduced in 1920. 12 in. high.

Attached to the wardrobe door was a fine 'feather' boa and an elegant parasol. The dolls themselves were dressed in the usual simple petticoats, and the set was packed in a sturdy box embossed with silver lettering. This must have been a peak in the manufacture of paper dolls.

Cheaper figures were sold in transparent envelopes, containing dolls and their clothes in 7,000 assorted designs, so that the child could buy several packs without repeating the costumes. These envelope sets contained a doll $7\frac{1}{4}$ inches high and four changes of clothes. Included in the range of cheap dolls and cut-out figures were sheets of scraps that were to be fixed in the appropriate sections of outline pictures, very much in the manner of the Raphael Tuck scrap sets.

Also reminiscent of Raphael Tuck are 'Doll Cut-Out Sheets'. They were made in a wide variety and printed on card. The dolls and costumes were the same as those made for inclusion in boxed sets, but they are now difficult to attribute, as the dolls themselves did not carry the maker's mark.

'Quick-change Dolly' supplied the craze for dolls with changeable heads. The basic doll was provided with a range of six faces, but only four dresses and hats. The clothes were attractively coloured and detail was aided by an embossed effect. 'Quick-change Dolly' was one of those also used on the cut-out sheets, but in this case interchangeable heads were not provided.

As with all companies, the number of boy dressing dolls made was limited, and only 'Little Dick' has so far come to light. His outfit included a bucket and spade and a tam-o'-shanter. The boy doll came dressed in a vest and shorts and carrying a sponge and toothbrush. Some boy dolls were included in the cut-out sheets and given the ever-popular sailor suits among their equipment, but these were not named.

Any maker whose box of paper dolls contained an unusual novelty was bound to increase sales, and in the late 1920s and early 1930s Spear and Sons produced some quite progressive figures. Teenage dolls were again new to a generation that was very far removed from the 'Empress Eugénie' type of doll found in the 1860s, and the elegant girl dolls with their tennis outfits, fur-trimmed coats and cloche hats must have appeared quite fresh. A pierrot outfit for fancy dress parties was often included, a style of dress that was so popular that it is also seen among the outfits for child dolls.

'Daphne' was an ultra-smart schoolgirl very much in the "Abbey Books" manner and included a Japanese-style dress and fan amongst the up-to-date dresses. 'Little Gladys' was a more realistic and rather younger schoolgirl with a badly-fitting gym slip. The doll swung Indian clubs in imitation of the fashionable craze for eurythmics.

'Elizabeth' was made in the modish manner of a little girl dressed in adult clothes. The doll wore very fashionable outfits and some splendid picture hats, and was given a doll in a perambulator that now makes the set an unusual acquisition.

After the Second World War, the quality of paper dolls became very poor, and designs were often retrospective or based on nursery-rhyme characters that gave little indication of contemporary dress or interests. Very few examples are collectable at present, though any made to advertise specific products are worth buying as long as the cost is very low.

A few dolls are now produced that are completely in the modern idiom and must be collector's items of the future. Mary Quant's 'Daisy Doll' is very much a product of the 1970s, with thick platform shoes, peasant skirts, smock tops and denim battledress. Thousands of thin card *Pantins* were made in imitation of Charlie Chaplin, but so few of these can now be found in good condition that one maker finds it worth while to reproduce them. Early paper dolls are also occasionally reproduced, but in such an obvious way that they could not possibly deceive. A few good-quality reprints are sometimes issued, and if made in a limited number are almost bound to increase in value.

Doll's-house Families

Elegant and exquisitely made, the small Grödnertals that Queen Victoria dressed as a girl continued to be popular as inhabitants for doll's houses, model shops and rooms until around 1840, when they were superseded by more fashionable figures. Their shape, with slim bodies and high breasts, lends itself well to the costume of the Regency period, for which they were originally designed, and they are best suited to houses of that period, despite the fact that they were made for some years after the accession of Queen Victoria. Male Grödnertals are very rare, even in doll's-house size, while they are virtually impossible to find in larger sizes. The doll's-house men have the same body construction as the ladies, but have carved whiskers and some rudimentary carving of the hair. Some are believed to have the detail added in plaster or brotteig, but the male Grödnertal illustrated has been carved.

Penny Woodens and Wooden Tops are also found in Victorian houses, though they were often relegated to the kitchen or scullery, because their bucolic faces clearly suggested a lowly station in life. Very small versions are also seen in use as doll's-house dolls in nurseries. Some of these very minute dolls were sold enclosed in wooden eggs as 'the smallest dolls in the world' at the Great Exhibition, while others, equally small, were sold in well-built little leather boxes as 'carriage dolls' with which a bored child could play while travelling. The Penny-Wooden was adaptable, and with just a touch of black paint could be converted from a domestic to the gentleman of the house with a splendid black moustache. These figures are not easy to date very precisely, unless in their

535

397   Folding paper dolls advertising Barbours Irish Flax threads. Copyright 1895. Made in U.S.A. From a set of twelve. 5 in. high.

original clothes, as the scooped hands and well-carved feet that often characterize the older large versions are rarely seen in this small size.

Papier mâché dolls with stitched leather bodies also occasionally appear in doll's houses, but their survival is quite rare, despite the fact that so many were

398   Paper dressing doll from the 1920s cut from an American ladies magazine. 5 in. high.

made. The small sizes have much simpler hairstyles; obviously the extravagant coiffures of the larger sizes could not be rendered in miniature to this extent. The bodies, however, are almost identical, and were still given the coloured-paper bands to cover the joins between wood and leather and to prevent any escape of sawdust. The price of papier mâché dolls has escalated very suddenly over the last few years, and the owner of a doll's house that is inhabited by such figures is fortunate indeed.

It is the black-haired porcelain dolls that immediately spring to mind as typical inhabitants of nineteenth-century houses. Despite their rather daunting similarity, a few examples with a little more character do occasionally emerge. Blonde hair was not as popular with the makers, who presumably considered the combination of a chalk-white, glossy complexion with pale yellow hair a trifle insipid, but nevertheless quite a number were made, and their presence gives a little zest to an otherwise almost identical family. To represent grand-mothers or an aged nanny, the heads were sometimes left with the hair undecorated, but in this case the white hair was offset by adding colour to the face. A few were given grey painted hair, which made them even more realistic.

I recently purchased an unusual doll's-house man with hair decorated in two shades of brown and a moustache applied by the manufacturer in an almost stylized manner. Some of the more basic porcelains with very short moulded hair could adopt the role of either sex, as there could have been few children who were unable to persuade an indulgent adult to paint on a beard or moustache. Dozens of these basic porcelain heads can still be found without much difficulty, though the bodies have often long since disintegrated. They are excellent to costume for doll's houses, for the soft bodies can be dressed in some detail and decorative features even pinned in place. Lustre-decorated examples are rare, but boots or shoes treated in this way were sometimes used on figures of doll's-house size.

Pink lustre or pink-tinted dolls are also quite rare in this scale. A few of the better examples are reminiscent of those made in larger sizes by the Berlin factory, but unfortunately few makers bothered to mark these very small products. Most of the figures, whether of lustre or common white china, depend very heavily for their effect upon their costume, which was often executed in great detail: old soldiers were given campaign medals, and grandmother dolls had reticules for their handwork. One of the few pierced-eared porcelains I have seen was of doll's-house size: the ears had been pierced after glazing, and the effect though interesting was rather untidy.

'Frozen Charlottes' were sometimes called upon as inhabitants for doll's-house bathrooms that became, certainly by the Edwardian era, a necessity for every well-planned house. They are also found in doll's-house nurseries representing children's toys. When used as inhabitants for a house they are rarely satisfactory, as they are difficult to dress and more in the nature of figurines than of convincing miniature people.

Probably the most effective dolls in this context are those with white or pink bisque heads of the shoulder type. The earliest have rather flat-topped moulded hairstyles decorated in pale yellow. The lady-dolls of this type look particularly effective presiding over the tea-table, as they have a very haughty appearance. Some very small versions of this kind of doll are found that still retain scaled-down ladies' heads, and these appear to have been accepted as children. Any dolls of this size with inset glass eyes must be worth buying, since few were made.

When pink-tinted bisque became popular, these figures were made in a much greater variety, and complete families especially made for doll's houses were sold. Grandparents, children, maids and butler often appear in very humble 'two up, two down' dwellings. Any complete family of this type is very desirable, as most of the fragile figures were broken during doll's-house play. The men often have the blond, drooping moustaches associated with younger sons in the army, or black waxed beards that look as if they have come straight off the stage of a Victorian melodrama. The male dolls are again the most difficult to find, because a larger number of women were made to act as servants, aunts and elder sisters. Some of the 'elderly' dolls were given grey hair and beards, and their faces were wrinkled, so that the child could invest (perhaps) a doll with upswept grey hair with the personality of Great Aunt Emily, or regard a curly-haired blonde as a favourite music-hall actress. The individual dolls are usually well constructed and decorated, and worth buying in their own right, though a complete set greatly enhances the appearance of a doll's house. Though made in the Edwardian manner, they could still be bought in the 1920s. Several owners of family doll's houses have recounted how their mothers carefully selected the figures in these years to replace the older, basic type of porcelains with which the houses were originally peopled.

The Schwarz catalogue for 1913 advertised "doll's-house dolls for use in doll's houses. We have a large variety of small dressed dolls, such as gentlemen and ladies in different costumes. Maids, nurses, waiters, butlers, cooks, etc. The dolls measure from five to seven inches and range in price from 50c. to $1.50." The illustrations indicate that these were the German-made moulded dolls discussed, but some were made to which mohair wigs were attached, and some very rare men-dolls wore moulded hats. Because of the obvious popularity of

399   The Puritan Twins. Complicated folding method patented in 1917 as a "Fold-A-Way Toy". Designed by Jessie Louise Taylor, for the *Ladies' Home Journal* of November 1922.

The Puritan Twins

Fold-A-Way Dolls Designed by
Jessie Louise Taylor

(The story of the Twins is on page 42.)

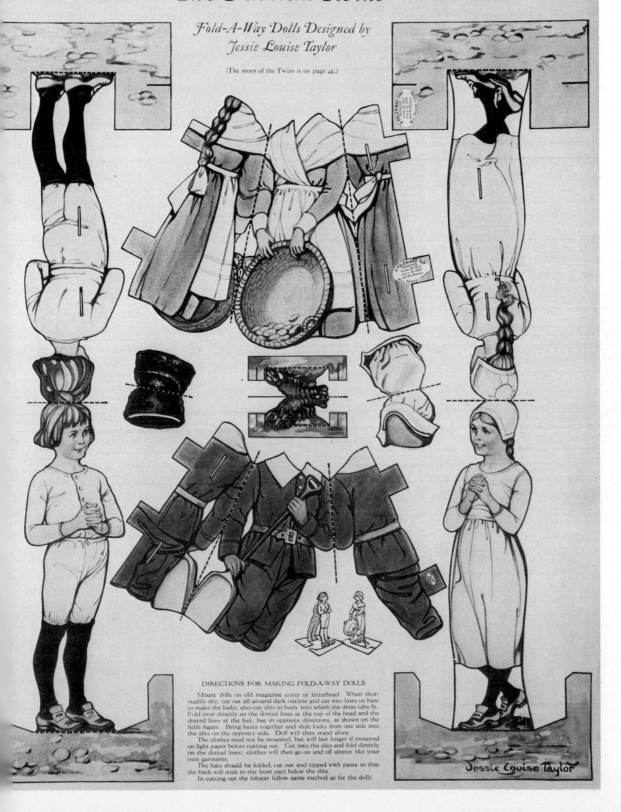

DIRECTIONS FOR MAKING FOLD-A-WAY DOLLS

Mount dolls on old magazine cover or letterhead. When thoroughly dry, cut out all around dark outline and cut into lines on base to make the locks, also cut slits in body into which the dress tabs fit. Fold over directly on the dotted lines at the top of the head and the dotted lines at the feet, but in opposite directions, as shown on the little figure. Bring bases together and slide locks from one side into the slits on the opposite side. Doll will then stand alone.

The clothes need not be mounted, but will last longer if mounted on light paper before cutting out. Cut into the slits and fold directly on the dotted lines; clothes will then go on and off almost like your own garments.

The hats should be folded, cut out and tipped with paste so that the back will stick to the front part below the slits.

In cutting out the lobster follow same method as for the dolls

Jessie Louise Taylor

(*above*) 400 "Quick Change Dolly" made by Spear's and printed at the Spear works in Bavaria. One basic figure with six interchangeable heads. 10½ in. high. (*below left*) 401 "Daisy's Fashion Wardrobe." Designed by Mary Quant. 1974. (*below right*) 402 'Tommy Lad.' Dressing doll printed on postcard marked "Dressing Dolls Series 1". Raphael Tuck. After original painting by M. Banks.

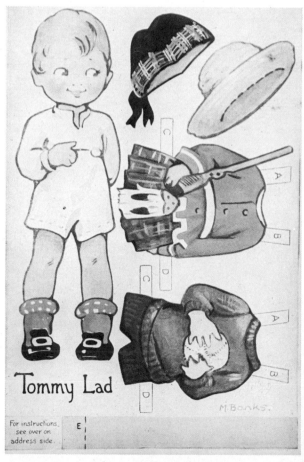

(*above left*) 403   White bisque half-doll of doll's-house size. Blue moulded bow, fair hair. One of set of four. Marked "Germany". 6 in. high.   (*above right*) 404   Pink-tinted porcelain doll's-house doll with hair moulded in coils over ears. Sawdust-filled body. Flat-heeled shoes. 3¾ in. high.   (*below*) 405   Group of basic-type porcelains taken from a doll's house *c.* 1890. Tallest 7 in. high.

these sets with doll's-house collectors, reproductions are now made, but usually with no attempt to deceive, as the quality is very different. The American-made reproductions however are extremely good, and could mislead any collector who has not handled many dolls of this type. Fortunately, makers of reproductions are becoming aware of how their work is misrepresented when resold, and are marking their work; but until all are prepared to do this, there will be many traps for the unwary.

Most of the existing rag dolls found in houses date from the eighteenth century. Presumably, if a child could afford a house in the Victorian period, the parents would also allow her to spend a few pence on the purchase of inhabitants. Some rag dolls were made, often of cloth wound around a wire shape, but they were considered of little value, and were usually thrown away when dirty. The home-made paper doll's-house families met with the same fate.

In the 1920s, a series of doll's-house characters with composition or plaster heads were made, some (it is believed) especially for a shop in the Burlington Arcade. The dolls were given wire bodies and metal feet, and the body frame was bound with silk thread. Similarly-made dolls with celluloid heads are also occasionally found, though the all-celluloid ladies with moulded flapper dresses are probably the best, despite the fact that they are easily overbalanced.

A very appealing series of half dolls was made in Germany which fitted very neatly into the rooms of larger houses, as the adults were $6\frac{1}{2}$ inches high and the children $4\frac{1}{2}$ inches. Again families were made, but of a more restrained size, and father, mother and two children were considered adequate. The figures were moulded to waist level in bisque, and the upper arms and lower torso and legs were of sawdust-filled fabric. An older couple was also made, probably to represent grandparents, but they were made as peasants and have two improbably young children dressed in German country style. The boy and girl belonging to the younger parents are sometimes found in a shoulder-headed version, but the other characters have not yet been found treated in this way. It is now thought that these dolls were marketed by Hertwig and Company, Katzhütte, Thuringia, for they appeared in an advertisement in a paper of 1911 unearthed by the Colemans during research.

The small all-bisque figures with brass wire jointing and moulded hair, often referred to by collectors as stone bisque, have plump bodies, and are used frequently in houses to represent children. Some are minute and exquisitely decorated. As I write, I have before me a $1\frac{1}{2}$-inch boy with ribbed socks and individually-defined fingers. The decoration of the head, with its pink cheeks

---

406 Soft-paste man-doll with two-tone hair and simply-suggested beard and moustache. Lady with a brilliant pink face and white hair. Man $8\frac{1}{2}$ in. high.

and blue eyes, must have called for considerable skill. Bisque-headed dolls with rigid limbs of composition are also found in houses, and despite the fact that their French and German makers did not specifically create them for this purpose, they can sometimes look convincing, especially in the salons of French houses.

With the exception of the bisque families that were marketed by companies such as Schwarz, many of the small dolls were not made specifically for houses, since only a comparatively small number of privileged children would have owned a doll's house at the time. The majority were played with simply as miniature dolls, together with a few pieces of doll's-house furniture or a cheaply-made model room.

407   Group of dolls from various periods such as were added to many dolls' houses. White bisque lady c. 1855. All-bisque boy doll with auburn hair c. 1900. Bisque immobile and white bisque baby c. 1875. Boy doll 3½ in. high.

408   Group from a family doll's house. The man-doll with moulded blonde whiskers and ecclesiastical air is particularly nice. Maid has fair moulded hair, chauffeur black moulded moustache. The rag baby doll is unusual to find in a nineteenth-century house, as few have survived.

409   These Edwardian bisque figures reflect the mood of the young of the period's approach to the increasingly-revealed human figure. Marked with symbol of Schafer und Vater of Volkstedt. 4½ in. high.

410   The porcelain figures known to collectors as pincushion ladies were made in huge variety and form a collecting field in their own right. Spanish lady marked "D683", black-haired doll with necklace, "26933", figure with clasped hands "4621", other marked "Germany".

EIGHTEEN

FIGURES FOR ADULTS
AND ALL-BISQUES

Art Dolls

A recurring phenomenon throughout the history of dolls has been a fashionable taste for doll-like figures among adults. Just as the ladies of the Regency period toyed with dressing dolls of paper or isinglass, so almost a century later the conceit again became fashionable, but in a slightly different form. The women of the early twentieth century did not need dolls on which to try out different fashions, as there were plenty of good photographs and fashion drawings available; so instead they treated their dolls as mascots and thus gave an adult title to a childish conceit.

Paul Poiret, the couturier who introduced the hobble skirt, is generally considered to have launched the idea that fashionable women should carry dolls in the 1910 season. Elegant doll-like figures were especially dressed for this purpose by Paquin and Mademoiselle Lanvin. Other fashion houses quickly copied the idea, and small figures were often made with great artistry, to be given away with expensive purchases or sold as decorative objects from exclusive French shops. Some of these dolls display great ingenuity in the use of materials and real artistic flair, but as with most fads, the examples made for popular sale fell well below the standard of those produced for the quality shops.

Although the use of 'art' dolls as related to fashion itself was an innovation, there had been a noticeable trend in this direction for some time. The waxed and composition lady-dolls, often made to look like fashionable women of the turn of the century, could not have held any great appeal for children, since their clothes often could not be removed and the figures themselves were too fragile to withstand nursery life. Presumably it was elder sisters and mothers who stood these figures on their dressing tables to be admired, despite the fact that they were marketed by their German makers as play items. The work of Marion Kaulitz was also setting a more positive trend towards an adult appreciation of the doll, which developed as an art form of its own particular kind.

The shoppers of the early twenties found the fashionably-dressed mascots irresistible, and the wealthy carried them when flying or motoring; while the average girl took her long-legged flapper doll to dances or out visiting. The cheaper dolls of the type were often displayed in a tempting array of imitation silk and gold braid at fairgrounds and seaside gift shops, and boy friends were soon tempted into buying one of the gaudy ladies for their girl friends to carry. Some were costumed most exotically, in a rather strange medieval style of dress. These are now the least desirable, as they are not really suggestive of the period. Of much greater interest are those that were dressed in contemporary style with cloche hats, long beads and Charleston dresses. As many of these figures are very lightly considered, it is an area in which a new collector could build up an interesting and varied group at a low cost.

The French boudoir dolls have more attractive faces. They were usually hand painted on silk stockinette, which was stitched over a thin cardboard shape. Slits were sometimes cut just above the eyes and long eyelashes were inserted. The treatment of the hair is often surprisingly complicated for a doll that was to be sold quite cheaply, and some awe-inspiring creations were attempted. The bodies are almost invariably cotton or muslin, and the very long arms end in plaster or composition hands that are always long and slim and sometimes wear rings. The slender legs end in moulded and painted high-heeled shoes.

The heads were sometimes stuffed with newspaper to help maintain the shape, and this often gives an indication of the country of origin. Not all the French dolls were made with silk faces: felt, for instance, was used by Giotti at Nice, and some of the cotton-faced dolls are believed to have originated in France, because of the detail in their costumes. The English makers produced a greater number of felt or fabric, but some silk-faced dolls were also made, and as manufacturing processes in different countries were by this time becoming very similar, it is often difficult to decide on a doll's country of origin.

Among the French makers of art dolls were Madame Jeanne de Kasparek, Madame Galabert and Adrien Carvaillo. In an attempt to counter the German success in manufacture, the French firms in 1902 offered a prize for the design of progressive dolls. The project appealed to many artists, and designs were submitted by the sculptor Fremiet and the painters Detaille and Gerome. As their ideas were presumably non-commercial, little success was achieved by the venture, though the artistic calibre of the entrants is significant, and current opinion was evidently beginning to see dolls in a new and exciting way.

In the 1890s several series of dolls had been made to illustrate the costumes of various countries. The characters from Balzac's *Comédie Humaine* had been recreated by Madame Martet, while other designers had made dolls in

411 A few pincushion heads were given wigs such as the red-haired lady with fan and lustre decoration marked "Germany". Figure with pink hat "1357", with cloche hat, "Foreign, A106". Flesh-tinted nude "Germany 14276". Largest 4 in. high.

imitation of great actresses of the period. The actress dolls were given wax heads that were modelled by Mlle Lifraud. Many of these specially-made exhibition dolls were eventually given to museums, and do not appear to have been made in commercial quantities. Model mannequins were also made for special use in exhibitions, and Anne Lafitte Desirat made some particularly effective models in this manner for an exhibition entitled 'L'Art Pour l'Enfance'. These figures were posed in the most elegant manner, to display their hobble skirts and huge fashionable muffs.

Chocolate boxes and gift sets were decorated with small figures in this idiom. Plaster was popular as a medium for the amusing standing figures that were provocatively dressed in knee-length bathing costumes or Charleston dresses. Very slightly suggestive poses were popular, though the doll's face was usually very demure, and appeared to disassociate itself completely from the alluring body to which it was attached. A trade catalogue of the 1920s described a similar figure: "Her fashionable and charmingly designed bathing costume displays to advantage her well-modelled figure".

A variety of strange art dolls were made, to be used as decorations for cars, hat-boxes or even gramophones, the gramophone dolls made in Germany being

549

Poupées Consuelo Fould –
DANSE MODERNE
4

LES VICTORIEUSES
POUPÉES CONSUELO FOULD BREVETEES

Poupées Consuelo Fould –
ESMÉRALDA
8

(*above*) 412 Two postcards of the 1920s showing well-made art dolls. Created by Consuelo Fould. Could assume any normal position. Winners of Diploma of Honour. (*left*) 413 Now referred to by collectors as boudoir dolls, these figures have an amusing air of decadent abandon. Pressed fabric heads with composition lower arms and legs with high-heeled shoes. One dressed in lounging pyjamas trimmed with maribou. 30 and $26\frac{1}{2}$ in. high.

particularly grotesque. Containers that included such figures are bought now by collectors of advertising material, but there still remain many cheap examples from which the doll-collector can choose.

Bernard Ravca is probably the best known art doll-maker of this period. He originally created figures with stockinette faces that represented young people, such as the group he made for a composition known as the 'Modiste's Atelier'. He felt that all dolls should be as completely individual as people, and concentrated on a method of working that enabled him to achieve this end. Silk stockinette was primarily his medium, but he also used chemically-treated breadcrumbs for miniature work. His first really popular doll was a representation of Marguerite in *Faust*. Ravca began his artistic career by painting scarves and shawls, and the progression to dolls' faces was quite logical at a time when these were also considered fashion items. He opened his doll-making studio as a result of the publicity he received when he made a pair of French character figures as a gift for an English lord to present to his wife on the occasion of their silver wedding.

Among the Ravca dolls most popular with collectors are 'Mistinguette' and 'Maurice Chevalier'. All his figures were individually made and almost frighteningly lifelike, especially as many were very large. Examples of Ravca's work are now more often found in America, where the artist lived after the last war, but they do sometimes appear in the stock of English dealers. Prices vary very considerably, for the figures have an immediate impact and are either liked or absolutely loathed; and much of the pricing in the past was based upon these criteria. As all Ravca's figures are signed, attribution is fortunately no problem.

Tastefully-made art dolls suggested themselves as a means of raising money for distressed people. Madame Paderewski opened a Paris factory in 1915 to help Polish refugees, who made and dressed dolls that were designed by a Polish sculptor. Madame Marie Vassilief, wife of a Russian nobleman, made kid portrait dolls of famous people in the same period.

A Russian lady also ran a shop in America in the 1920s, from which were sold hand-painted papier mâché headed dolls that could be made to order in either an approximate or a really close likeness. These portrait dolls, often of famous people, were very popular between the wars, and doll-makers vied with each other in producing the current celebrities in doll form. Figures as diverse as Lord Kitchener, Gloria Swanson and Lupino Lane were used to appeal as much to adult fans as children. So popular was Jackie Coogan that he was represented both by Borgfeldt and Horsman, while there are many versions of Charlie Chaplin.

Celebrity dolls were made in America, in particular by a firm known as Margaret Vale's Celebrity Creations. The dolls were made by Jane Grey, and

(*above left*) 414 Porcelain heads with flange necks were especially made for use on pincushion-type figures. Here as a commercially-made sewing companion and safety-pin holder. Head to round base 4 in. high. (*above right*) 415 Known as "Mistinguette" by its original owner, this French boudoir doll has a pressed silk face with eyelashes inserted through slits over eyes. 30 in. high. (*below*) 416 Wax-headed figure dressed in orange and green crêpe paper. Especially made to be used as table centres at banquets after film premières in the 1920s and 1930s. 13 in. high.

were hand-painted likenesses of stage or screen personalities, dressed in copies of costumes worn by them. A facsimile autograph was included with the doll, plus the name of the character and an appropriate line from the show. Elizabeth Kuzara of New York also made portrait dolls, but in a completely different vein: she created likenesses of Bolshevist leaders, Cossacks, Slovac women and café characters of Prague. Apart from these recorded makers there are dozens of small manufacturers, who made a limited number of similar figures to satisfy popular demand.

Boudoir dolls were popularly known in America as Vamps, Wobblies or Flappers. These, together with Teddy bears, were taken out for walks as mascots, and doll pendants were worn around the neck. The German writers of the period took a very superior attitude to such behaviour, and Max von Boehn commented that the women of his country were content to play with their dolls indoors and take rubber dolls with them to their baths!

To suit the young women of the new image in America, several firms made dolls that must have shocked grandmothers of the time. The N.V. Sales Company made a composition 'French Flapper', with bobbed hair and a cigarette in its mouth. It was dressed in a trouser suit of daringly masculine cut and high-heeled shoes. Konroe Merchants at the same time were marketing an almost identical figure, while other lady-dolls were made wearing monocles. One firm was actually named the Flapper Novelty Doll Company, and they produced the typical long-limbed painted-face figures. The pierrot and pierrette figures that were so popular in Europe were also made in the States by several companies; they were made in the same way as the flapper dolls, but given a masked face.

The 1920s form a strange and fascinating period with its new-found freedom and excesses, and the dolls seem to parody the people who were so aggressively gay and scintillating. The figures made by Lotte Pritzel belong completely to the mood of Germany at this time. Each of her figures was freely treated and built up with scraps of silk or chiffon and beads over a wire frame; wax heads that she carved as characters were used for the dolls, which were given titles like 'Ganymead', 'Chichette' and 'The Unveiled'. Art type objects were sometimes used as a stand for the figure and to suggest the mood of the piece. The figures were exaggeratedly slim, sensuous and rather frightening, though at the time they were considered to be the ultimate in elegance. Lotte Pritzel's first experimental figures were made with heads of chestnuts, and she also attempted to utilize ordinary jointed dolls, but found that with these it was impossible to convey adequately the mood that she found so essential in these art objects.

Despite the assertion by von Boehn regarding the fact that German women would not carry their dolls in the street, the figures were very popular in Germany as drawing-room decorations, and an exhibition devoted to them was held by Hella Bibrawicz and Clarissa Spiegel in Nürnberg in 1921. The gramophone grotesques were possibly more popular in Germany than America, and the German designers appear to have put more sincere and wholehearted artistry into their work. Many of the grotesques can hardly be classified even as drawing-room toys; they are small sculptures. Cloth dolls with moveable limbs were made, particularly by Erna Pinner, who entitled her figures 'The Resolute', 'The Elegant' or 'Woman of Today'. They were much more robust and could be played with as toys, in comparison with those of Lotte Pritzel which were purely artistic. The two extremes of doll-making were both considered at the time as art dolls: at the one extreme the realistic toddlers made by Käthe Kruse, and at the other the wispy ephemera produced by the wire sculptresses.

The English doll-makers, with a lesser tradition of doll-making than the Germans, followed very much in their wake, but found it necessary to produce flapper dolls themselves. A catalogue for 1927 commented,

> Some of the little men and women of today are very up to date . . . it is perhaps a wise dispensation that, when ladies of mature growth begin to adopt little girls' playthings as mascots, boudoir ornaments and even as companions for the dance, their small nieces and daughters should prefer 'grown-up dolls' to play with. However that may be, there appears to be an insistent call for dolls of this grown-up appearance.

Lady-dolls, especially in the form of night-dress cases, had been produced by several firms from before the 1914 war. The *de luxe* versions often had satin faces and were given silk dresses. Chad Valley made such cases, as did Dean's and many small factories in London's East End. Many of the boudoir dolls with long limbs are made with the pressed-felt or fabric faces particularly associated with Dean's and Chad Valley, and it seems likely that a few were made by these firms. There had been a trend since the beginning of the century, in England as on the Continent, towards a more adult type of doll; and the dolls designed by Hilda Cowham were typical of the type, with their long legs and mercerized stockings. Some of the dolls' heads were made with painted closed eyes. 'Natty Nora', 'Captivating Cora' and 'Tantalizing Thora' are typical of their period. 'Florrie the Flapper', in another series, was given 'real flapper cut' clothes, a tam and a flapper bag.

In 1927 Dean's produced their ultimate in flapper dolls, described as 'Elegant dolls, the Elite of Dolldom'. There were twelve different models which each stood 21 inches high. Each figure was stunningly dressed in extremely fashionable clothes. One wore a leopard-skin coat trimmed with fox fur, while another wore knee-high leather boots and knickerbockers. All varieties of fashionable hats were worn, and if the series could be collected together, we could again see all the fashions of the twenties. Velvet, plush and mock fur were used to decorate these very cleverly-made costumes. In 1928 'Smart Set Dolls' were made, including a Duchess complete with a lorgnette and wearing what was obviously the ultimate in dress at the time – a leopard-skin coat.

Dean's Dancing Darkies, known as 'Uncle Remus', 'Massa Bones' and 'Massa Johnson', were introduced in 1923 as toys that would appeal as much to grown-ups as children, and could be used as mascots or ornaments. 'Jolly Tar' and 'Billy Buttons' were introduced on a similar theme, and each carried a box in which could be placed a birthday present or a peace-offering. Boxes that were decorated with a doll's head on the lid were also produced by this very prolific firm. These small boxes can still be found in street markets and bric-à-brac shops and are often mistakenly described as French. They sometimes included the shoulders as well as the head and the box itself was covered with paper or fabric to suggest the skirt or shoulders. A Mecca box was given a black sultan wearing a turban, while 'Good Luck' was a jockey. Croquette boxes were also popular and were cylindrical and topped with the head of a pierrot or jolly minstrel. The Mecca series was also made in full figure form, and the sultans carried large baskets as containers for gifts. Others were assembled as pincushions. The bride in the pincushion series was very splendid and wore orange blossom in her hair.

Freed from the enveloping folds of nineteenth-century costume, the human figure became a thing of great decorative interest in the 1920s. It appeared on vases, china, glass, murals and cheap bijouterie, and it is difficult at this distance in time to appreciate how fresh the human form in free poses and attitudes must have seemed. The dolls, with their abandoned loose limbs and coquettish faces, are very much in this idiom, as are the pierrots with their traditional silk suits, floured faces and black calottes, giving an air of added mystery.

The dancing dolls made by Dean's were also intended as adult toys. "The antics and attitudes of the figures when danced singly or in couples are beyond description. These playthings strike an entirely novel note." The first dolls of this type represented children, but later 'Lupino Lane' was substituted for the boy doll.

The dolls that collectors lightly term 'twenties' were actually made up to 1938, when night-dress cases in the form of fashionable ladies (as well as Mickey and Minnie Mouse) were still made. In this year, pierrot was still suggested in catalogues as a motor-car mascot. Some of the traditional boudoir dolls with long legs were still in production in these immediately pre-war days, and a 'Lido Lady' with flared beach pyjamas and a big sun-hat was typical of the type of doll made; and the basic boudoir figures with long satin frilled dresses, feathered hats and fur muffs were still produced at this time.

The chocolate boxes and gift boxes that were decorated with boudoir-type heads were really an imitation of the much older idea used by the porcelain

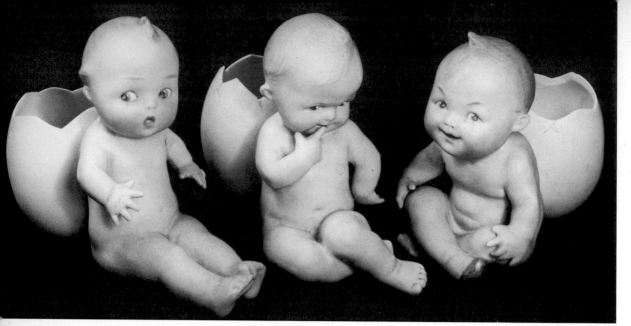

417　Easter Egg piano figures by Heubach all with square mark. Figure with shoes marked "9902", sucking finger "9903" and one with startled expression "9913". All about 5 in. high.

418　Piano figures of Dutch children by Gebrüder Heubach. Carry sunburst mark. Boy marked "3748" and girl "3964". 4½ in. high.

factories. The fine white bisque dolls' heads that were lustre-decorated were often used as tops for pincushions and gift packs, but they were soon superseded by half dolls that were especially made for this purpose.

After 1880, an extremely large number of busts, referred to by collectors as half dolls, were made by hundreds of porcelain factories both in France, Germany and later, Japan. Firms such as Limbach and W. Goebel, who also made dolls, were prolific in their output of these often quite complicated figures. A staggering assortment was made, especially when one considers how many separate pieces would have been assembled for some of the more delicate and complex figures.

The half dolls were sold very cheaply from haberdashers and novelty shops, and they were utilized by their buyers in a variety of ways, from handles of crumb brushes to tops for telephone covers or lampshades. Some of the half-doll models can occasionally be seen moulded full-figure on pin-boxes or powder-bowls.

As similar dolls, usually made in Japan, are still sold by needlework shops, some care has to be exercised in their purchase. The pretty 'Madame Pompadour' models are usually the least desirable, as they do not evoke any particular period and are still made today in the imitative manner of the porcelain factories of the twenties. Better examples often appear to have been made in the years just after the First World War, and suggest the ravaged, rather unwholesome-looking women often popularly associated with Germany at this period, with raddled and heavily made-up faces. The dolls set in alluring poses are always the best liked, especially the lady who has slipped down her bra straps so as nearly to reveal all her breasts. Spanish dancers, Dutch girls and even chubby children were all made in half-doll form, though the children were obviously less popular at the time and are now more difficult to find than the adults.

The figures made by Royal Rudolstadt, with their lush decoration in rich colours with black and gold, are particularly admired by collectors. Dressel Kister and Company also made some good-quality heads of this type that are marked. Most of the factories did not bother to mark such cheap items, but they are sometimes attributable by their decoration or colours. Firms such as those which produced fairings included these heads among their products, and marketed them in the twenties as 'flapper heads'. Legs could be purchased separately if required, and the wrong size often appears to have been bought, as a large head frequently sports a very stunted pair of legs. They were also applied in all sorts of anatomically improbable angles when made up at home. A few professional makers made use of the heads, and Emma von Sichart of Munich used Nymphenberg porcelain heads for her tastefully-made and expensive tea-cosies. One of the most sought after of the half figures is the doll that was made to advertise Walter Baker Chocolate. It was produced by the Goebel porcelain factory, and made in imitation of a painting that showed a waitress in a Vienna chocolate shop. The girl carried a tray upon which was a chocolate pot, a cup and a saucer. The porcelain half doll, made to represent the waitress, is very complicated, and wears a moulded fichu at the throat and a maid's cap.

The Meissen half doll that holds an apple in one elegantly-extended hand is another that is searched for avidly. As there is such a wide variety of these dolls, and the possibility exists of finding the mark of a good factory impressed or painted on the lower edge, they are becoming much more widely collected. Falling as they do somewhere between an ornament and a doll, many people who are primarily interested in china find them attractive, especially as large numbers can be displayed in a very small space.

The advantage of small size is shared by the bathing beauties that were made from the Edwardian period until the 1930s. These beautifully-made bisque figures of nude or semi-nude ladies were made purely as ornamental items. The bisque is often of a high quality and the decoration skilled. Hair is usually moulded, but a few, which originally cost more, wear wigs. The most frequently-found examples recline in luxurious attitudes, rather like the draped figures around Roman pools in Hollywood spectaculars. The standing bathing-beauties, especially those that still wear their original crochet bathing costumes and hats, are very pleasant acquisitions. They were made in a diverting variety of stances, one with her hand to her forehead as she gazes out to sea, another with arms raised in a diving position, while yet another sits cross-legged and pensive. Again they are usually unmarked, except for the country of origin, but consider-able skill must have been needed to produce such delicate work, which had to be cast in so many pieces.

Provocative and suggestive, these bathing ladies must have appealed most to young men and women, while older people with much less 'progressive' tastes still bought the small all-bisque figures of infants that had remained popular since the 1870s. The baby figures showed chubby infants in all sorts of positions. The tar-babies, who wear delicately-coloured, moulded clothes that they have wickedly splashed with tar, have been bought by collectors of Victoriana for many years, though it is only recently that they have come within the orbit of the doll-collector.

Many German factories included a range of figures such as these among their products, but those made by Gebrüder Heubach are the best known, since they are often fully marked. Many were produced in pairs, as were the Kewpies, and

419 Seated piano baby with intaglio eyes marked with square Heubach mark, indistinct number. 4¾ in. high.

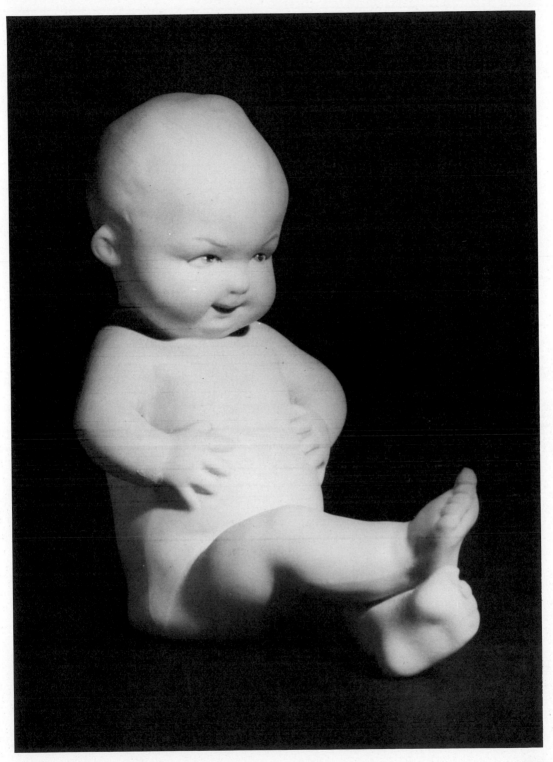

were given eyes that looked towards each other. Some of the babies wear sun-bonnets and others shoes or boots, but they are otherwise naked. The highlights on the intaglio eyes are often a feature of the Heubach figurines. Apart from the similarity of this highlighting method, there is often a minimal similarity between the figures and the dolls' heads. They were probably made quite separately and for a different market, and collectors find it very tempting to see similarities that do not really exist. The quality of the bisque is obviously similar, and the firm's use of self-coloured bisque extended into their production of figurines, but we are probably deluding ourselves if we attempt to see more than a few similarities.

All sorts of frivolous figures on the border line between dolls and ornaments were made by the German factories. In particular, there were the figures with wire jointed arms that resemble so closely the all-bisque dolls, but carry baskets or containers for either flowers, sweets or Easter eggs. Any of these which can be attributed by their marks are interesting, but fine bisque, good decoration and the complexity of the actual model have all to be taken into account when assessing value. One rather nice set that came as a family, complete in a special box, included grandmother, grandfather, mother, father and two children.

Both the half dolls and the all-bisque figures have despite their skilful manufacture a charmingly 'cheap and cheerful' appearance. They were very obviously not intended for a wealthy or even very discriminating market, but for the ordinary person who had a little money to spend at a seaside fair or a local gift shop. The surprising fact is that even with all their complexity they could be sold sufficiently cheaply to appeal to the man in the street. The pitifully low wages paid to the German workers in the porcelain factories at this time made this feat possible.

Frozen Charlottes and Bathing Dolls

Several German collectors have assured me that the 'bathing boys' or *Bädekinder* were never intended as children's toys, but were kept purely as ornaments, rather as Englishwomen kept their china baby figures on window-sills or the mantelpiece. Some of the large *Bädekinder* would certainly have made very unsatisfactory toys, being heavy, slippery to hold and easily broken, qualities which would have combined to make them rather unlovable except as ornaments.

The 14-inch size has for some time proved very popular, especially with American collectors, and commands quite high prices. At the time of writing, a positive glut of these figures has appeared on the market and has caused the price to fall, because collectors are obviously concerned whether the example they have bought could be a reproduction. Dealers explain their sudden abundance by the story that a Dutch or German dealer has discovered a shop or factory stock that he is selling, a story that causes some anxiety, for similar tales

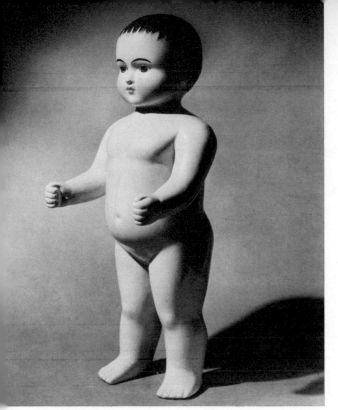
A

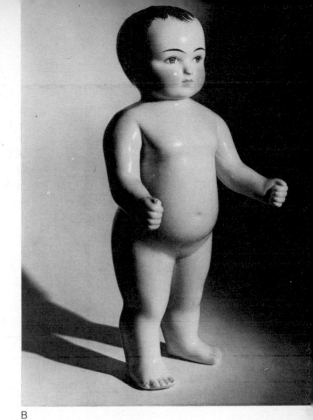
B

420 A and B   Two bathing boys showing difference in treatment of hair and eyes. One white porcelain and the other pink glazed. 16¼ in. high.

421   Unusual white porcelain bathing boy with genital detail. Marked "Germany, 4433". Very light in weight. 5¾ in. high.

were told when the London markets were flooded with reproduction fashion dolls in the late sixties.

The 'fashion dolls' were obvious fakes, but the bathing boys are much more difficult to assess, since the high-glazed porcelain would, in any case, show little wear if it had been used as an ornament or kept in original wrappings. Some of these questionable dolls have been found with the impressed mark of the firm that made fairings, but collectors are still unhappy about the sudden supply of what had been quite a rare item. The fact that there is a sameness of size in all the examples seen is also difficult to explain, as it seems unlikely that even a shop would have stocked all its dolls in the same size.

A possible explanation could be the fact that the East German government apparently advertises in state newspapers for antiques, including *Bädekinder*, and it is possible that this might be a source of supply though many are reproductions.

The better genuine examples have pink-lustre finish, pink-tinted faces and sometimes the whole body decorated in flesh colour. Despite the fact that I have purchased examples, I have never succumbed to the charm they apparently exercise, as I find them big, clumsy and distinctly unattractive, though sometimes amusing.

Variously called pillar dolls, solid chinas or 'Frozen Charlottes' after a popular American ballad, the smallest untinted examples are about 1 inch long and were originally sold to be put into Christmas puddings, on cakes or in crackers as favours. Many of these small versions are seen in doll's-house cradles, or used as miniature toys in such houses. They are too small and far too easily swallowed to have been given to young children as toys. This pudding type of 'Frozen Charlotte' is white and sometimes unglazed. They almost always have black hair, and any very small examples with blonde hair are unusual. Feet were usually bare, though a few wore painted boots. A few black-glazed chinas, though usually in slightly larger sizes, were made for the American market, and some of these negro figures even wore moulded turbans. The white-glazed chinas sometimes wear boots, garters or hats. Despite the fact that the most common type in the middle-size range has arms bent at the elbow, all sorts of varieties are found. Some wear striped bathing suits, others are crouched in crawling positions while others take up a seated pose. A few sit in china baths on a small ledge to enable them to balance; others sit cross-legged with their hands on their knees. One fine model in a bathing suit has his arms thrown back, as if breathing in the fresh sea air.

The earliest dolls were made in a simple two-part mould, and the arms were

422 Page from the *Ladies' Home Journal* for December 1925, showing drawing of original Kewpies.

Kewpieville

By ROSE O'NEILL

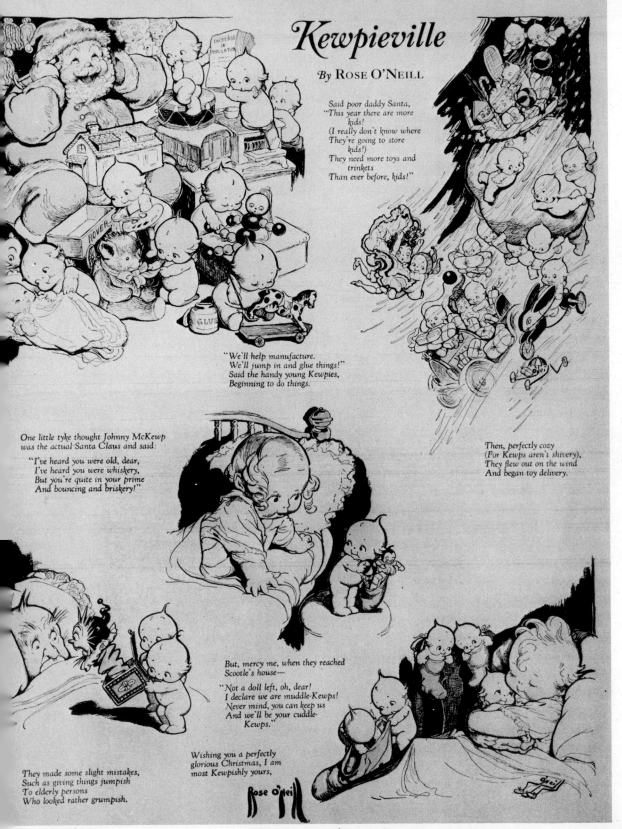

Said poor daddy Santa,
"This year there are more
    kids!
(I really don't know where
They're going to store
    kids!)
They need more toys and
    trinkets
Than ever before, kids!"

"We'll help manufacture.
    We'll jump in and glue things!"
Said the handy young Kewpies,
    Beginning to do things.

One little tyke thought Johnny McKewp
was the actual Santa Claus and said:

"I've heard you were old, dear,
I've heard you were whiskery,
But you're quite in your prime
And bouncing and briskery!"

Then, perfectly cozy
(For Kewps aren't shivery),
They flew out on the wind
And began toy delivery.

But, mercy me, when they reached
Scootle's house—

"Not a doll left, oh, dear!
I declare we are muddle-Kewps!
Never mind, you can keep us
And we'll be your cuddle-
    Kewps."

Wishing you a perfectly
glorious Christmas, I am
most Kewpishly yours,

They made some slight mistakes,
Such as giving things jumpish
To elderly persons
Who looked rather grumpish.

Rose O'Neill

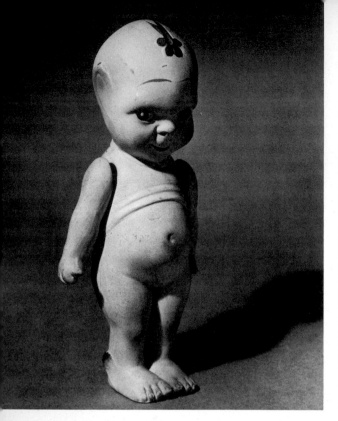

at the sides or crossed over the chest. They are often very thin and light and sometimes show granular imperfections in the glaze, especially at the back, as they were often laid rather carelessly in the kiln, occasionally without stilts. The illustrated male pillar doll is an unusual example of this type. Obvious genital organs are not often seen, and the doll might have been thought to have offended late nineteenth-century propriety. Apparently German taste at the time would have also been offended by such a doll, according to elderly Germans with whom I have discussed the figure that carries an impressed 'Germany' on the back. The paucity of surviving examples would lead to the conclusion that few were made, as they were not popular.

The pillar style of doll developed into a more complicated form, with separately applied arms, and from this simple beginning developed the figures in the quite complex poses described above. These dolls, set in poses other than standing, are often termed 'immobiles' by American collectors, so that they can be distinguished from the small figures with wire jointed arms. This term extends to dolls of bisque and composition as well as to porcelain figures.

Early examples of bathing dolls are often characterized by short, thick legs and low, sagging buttocks, presumably as an aid to balance. A few white 'Frozen Charlotte' dolls were given pink-glazed faces, but the majority are decorated in a similar way to the white-glazed porcelain shoulder heads. Any dolls with light brown hair would be considered quite unusual. Among the many makers and distributors of these glazed dolls were C. F. Kling, Pfeiffer and Company, Kestner and Bahr and Proschild.

The description 'bathing dolls' as used in old catalogues is often very misleading, for a number of different types that we would not now so classify were given this title. *Ridley's Fashion Magazine*, in 1886 advertised 'small bisque bathing dolls, finest quality with moving eyes and head to turn. Jointed arms and limbs. Long flowing hair'.

The bisque immobiles remained popular until the late 1920s, and were given a variety of decoration. Some wore *Alice in Wonderland* hairstyles with a band, others were given combs in their hair, and many wore gilded boots. The bisque versions are usually between 1 and 8 inches high, and no very large figures, like the 14-inch glazed porcelains, are known. Several of the French doll-makers

423   Fums-up Kewpie in poor-quality bisque. 7 in. high.

424   French all-bisque boy and girl in well-made original clothes. Glass eyes, mohair wigs. 3¾ in. high.

425   Group of all-bisque dolls. Thumb-sucker with open mouth for insertion of thumb. All bisque with jointed arms and bisque immobile. All marked "Germany". Thumb-sucker, 3 in. high.

advertised bathers, but whether or not they actually made them in France is debatable, as almost all that are found look very German, and the majority are marked only with numbers if at all.

Some of the bathers were sold complete with oil-silk caps, while others wore very ornate bathing costumes. A few wore only hats or bonnets. Most of these figures, unless of very poor quality, are very collectable, as a large number can be interestingly displayed in a small space. Quality is mainly determined by decoration. Some have skilfully-painted lines indicating wisps of hair; others have highlights on their eyes.

It was probably some of the larger *Bädekinder* that were taken to the bath by German ladies in the 1920s. The fact that these large and heavy figures float so well never fails to surprise. I lowered the first 14-inch examples I bought into a sink of water in great trepidation, doubting whether a monster of such dimensions could possibly stay afloat; but as Archimedes discovered, the mass of the doll was less than the water it displaced, and the figure lay, only half submerged, on the surface. It seems unlikely that the largest versions would have been played with at bath-time by children, as they would have been too easily broken by contact with the metal sides.

Kewpies

The fairy-like Kewpies also appear to have held as much appeal for adults as children. They first appeared in the *Ladies' Home Journal* in 1909 as a series of line drawings, intended primarily for the amusement of adults. In the first story, a little girl is left behind by her elder brothers and sisters, who run off to play without her. Her tears are soon dried when a host of fairy-like figures appear and play and gambol for her amusement. The illustrations have great charm, but are accompanied by quite excruciating verse. Both the illustrations and the dolls derived from them have stood the test of time and are still very popular.

The Kewpies were the brain child of Rose O'Neill, who first made a rag doll in imitation of her drawings in 1910. Borgfeldt saw the possibilities of the popular illustrations as toys, and asked her to design a Kewpie doll in 1912. Joseph Kallus was asked to advise on the modelling and manufacture of the figures. The first bisque Kewpies were made at the Kestner factory in Germany, and Rose O'Neill was sent to supervise the manufacture.

Though the first American design patent was granted in 1913, the dolls had been sold since 1912. The success of these squat figures was immediate, with their impish expressions and blue wings, and Kestner was unable to keep up with demand, so that in the year before the First World War there were twenty-one factories satisfying the needs of the American market. Some of these early

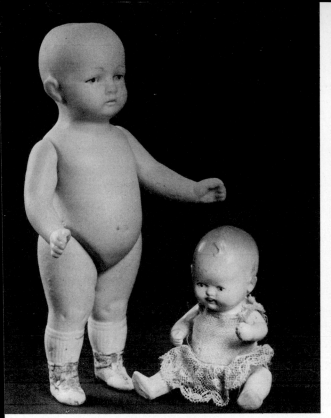 

(*above left*) 426   All-bisque toddler of self-coloured pale pink bisque. Marked on head "621—12½". Size on inside of leg. Intaglio eyes. Also small painted bisque baby. Larger doll 5 in. high.   (*above right*) 427   All-bisque girl with glass eyes and yellow ribbed socks. Marked "301—9.4". Some mark inside leg. Very good quality. 5¼ in. high.   (*below*) 428   Pair of white all-bisques with two-tone hair. Painted eyes. Unmarked but of German origin.

Kewpies were of celluloid, but later they were made in a variety of materials from rubber to ivory.

The smallest Kewpies, measuring only about 2½ inches high, are hard to find. Much rarer are the 17-inch versions, with jointed composition bodies and the usual webbed hands. The large glass googly eyes and the excellent painting of the hair on this particular model make it a fine acquisition.

Composition Kewpies were made by the Rex and Cameo Doll Companies in America, while bisque heads were sometimes given to the small composition bodies. The legs on most of the models are moulded together, but a few have separated limbs. Some late Kewpies were given jointed wooden bodies and wood-pulp heads. Though the majority have painted eyes, some have fixed glass ones that look either right or left so that pairs could be bought. A few slightly strange versions were given wigs of mohair. Even shoulder-headed Kewpies were produced, though this doll-making method was rather out of date by this time. Some were made as convention or party favours and fitted with a shank for a buttonhole.

Rose O'Neill described all these barefoot Kewpies as 'plain', and they were sold in their thousands in amusement arcades and at carnivals. The designer's name and the copyright mark was impressed under the foot or down the side of the body. Paper labels were sometimes attached to the torso, and similar labels were used on the pirated (and therefore much less collectable) Japanese versions of the dolls. The figures were so popular that they were used to decorate china and all sorts of ordinary household items.

A variation was introduced in 1914 in the form of negro Kewpies that were given white wings instead of the usual blue. After a short time the black figures were named Hottentots. A large variety of new figures then proceeded to appear, from musicians and firemen to policemen and a 'Tommy Atkins' soldier. The basic dolls remained the same, but they wore a few essential items from the costumes of the characters they represented. The army doll, for instance, wears a silver sword and a black belt with a bright red cap with visor. Some Kewpies were moulded in one with chairs, while others were sold in pairs hugging one another. Rose O'Neill described dolls that engaged in such social activity as sharing a book as 'Instructive Kewpies'. The figures that are jointed at hip and shoulder are rare, even in the States, and the English collector usually has to be content with more mundane acquisitions. In spite of the scarcity of interesting examples in England, there is quite a Kewpie cult among collectors of these amusing figures and interesting examples are discussed avidly.

429   All-bisque swivel-headed doll with brown glass eyes. High-heeled brown boots. Slim body with some shaping to chest and waist. 6¾ in. high.

568

569

'Scootles', an all-bisque boy doll, was designed as a follow-up to the successful Kewpie in 1925 by Rose O'Neill, and again Joseph Kallus assisted in the modelling. 'Scootles' was much more realistic, but possibly too like many other all-bisque figures that came from Germany, and never became as popular. Rose O'Neill said that she did not think her Kewpie figures would appeal as much to children as to adults, and this observation appears to remain true today, since the real devotees are still very much the adult collectors.

All-bisque Dolls

With the exception of figures (like the small immobile snow babies) that were made as cake decorations and Christmas ornaments, most of the German-designed dolls of miniature size appealed very strongly to the children who purchased them from their pocket money. They were sold from shops throughout the year for small sums, and children vied with one another to assemble the largest and most interesting groups. Even fairly ordinary children in the Edwardian period were able to buy many specimens that offered great play possibilities, as they could be seated on narrow ledges or placed in wooden boxes to represent dolls at school or in a house.

Though the all-bisques that were popular with children were usually under 4 inches high, some quite large dolls were also made in this way, though their life was usually short, as the limbs broke quite easily. One of the two dolls I have broken in about fourteen years of collecting was an all-bisque which I assumed would stand safely. It is little wonder that they were broken so quickly by the children who originally owned them. The method of peg-stringing, whereby elastic is held by wooden pegs that are glued in place, also gives rise to damage, as careless fathers chipped the bisque when attempting to restring. Damage of this type has to be considered as almost inevitable in figures of this kind.

Probably the most attractive of the all-bisque figures are those that were made in France and sold fully dressed. Some of them have heads almost of the standard of *Parisiennes*. Certain of the better examples have bisque loops at the base of their necks for stringing. Eyes are also of a good quality. The figures were dressed very professionally, in up-to-date children's costume, for which specially made buttons, brooches and buckles were provided. Despite the fact that they are usually unmarked, they are completely French in manner, with their tight curls and rather overdressed bodies. The bisque used was of quite a good quality and without the many imperfections seen in some of the German all-bisques. The base of the neck was often lined with fine leather to prevent damage when turned, but as many good-quality German dolls of the type are also leather-lined, this must be taken not as an indication of origin but only of quality.

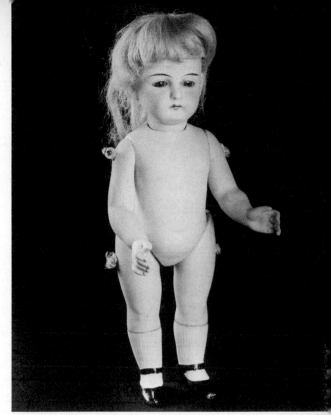

430 All-bisque girl doll. Fixed blue glass eyes. Ribbed socks, black shoes. Unmarked but probably Kestner. 8 in. high.

431 Group of all-bisques including pair in centre with swivel heads. Also sold as separate dolls. Marked "Germany". 3 in. high.

Male all-bisques are virtually unknown, except in the form of jointed jesters and goblins, some of which were made by Heubach. The jesters are notable for their moulded moustaches and beards and sometimes intricate moulded detail in their clothes. They were quite loosely jointed and wire-strung, so that the limbs would swing amusingly when the doll was played with.

One of the most sought after of the all-bisque dolls is the knee- and elbow-jointed googly. This type of body construction was obviously very prone to damage, and few of the larger versions have survived the nursery. Baby dolls are not as common as toddlers among the all-bisques, but they were made in all sizes and in a wide variety of positions. Some were quite large, as long as 14 inches. Swivel necks were given to the larger versions, while others had fixed heads, though the former, being originally more expensive, are the rarer. Some unusual all-bisques were jointed, with the legs moulded in a seated position. Babies were made with moulded caps, napkins and dummies, while others wore moulded vests and pants. Some of the best babies of this type have curved backs and limbs in different positions to give more realism. A few figures were made with a round hole in the mouth for the insertion of the thumb, and are referred to by collectors as 'thumb-suckers'.

Louis Wolf produced a well-made all-bisque baby known as 'Chubby', which was moulded wearing a ribbed suit. The arms were cleverly curved so that they would lie neatly over the doll's fat stomach. The all-bisque Bye-Lo Babies are also produced attractively and in some variety, with either painted or glass eyes, barefoot or wearing coloured slippers, and with or without wigs. As all these dolls are marked, they can be instantly identified.

The earliest type of all-bisques were made rather like the glazed pillar dolls and given moulded hair, sometimes with hats or bonnets and wire jointed arms. They are simply made, and were obviously intended to be sold very cheaply. Their diverse headgear now makes them quite collectable. Though the wigged examples were the more expensive when new, the moulded heads are now preferred. Very large numbers of these cheap figures were exported from Germany to America, but far fewer were sent to England, so that certain types that are not highly rated in the United States are rarely seen here. The American public in the years before the Depression was much more affluent, and was the main target for the novelty German items, while the more ordinary and cheaper examples were sold in England.

Another reason for the wide range of examples in America is the early twentieth-century Americans' love of the grotesque. This affection for amusingly misshapen forms has been recently seen in the popularity of Gonks and Trolls. A variety of these American grotesques were made in imitation of the drawings of popular cartoonists. Huge heads, protruding bellies, webbed feet, crossed eyes and big ears were the order of the day. This odd appreciation of the human form reached such a degree that even the saucer-like googly-eyed dolls were described as 'realistic'.

The Happifats, made in 1914, were never as popular as Kewpies. Hebees, Shebees and Chubbies were all grotesque and sold well. A whole series was made in imitation of characters drawn by Frank King. Rachel, a thick-lipped black woman with round squinting eyes was the black mammy in *Gasoline Alley*; the 'Rachel' figure itself was moulded as an immobile, but was given a swivel head. Other characters in the series were 'Lord Plushbottom', 'Uncle Walt', 'Mr Bailley the Boss', 'Skeezix' and 'Auntie Blossom', all of which were modelled in a similar way. Another group that was made with moveable heads was 'Our Gang', which included a dog. 'Chubby Chaney', the fat boy wearing a short-sleeved shirt and with his hands pushed into his trouser pockets, is the fat boy we all knew at school, and one of the most likeable in the series. A few of these characters were moulded on bases, rather like ornaments, and were obviously made partly as figurines, to appeal to adults. It would now be a satisfying but difficult achievement to assemble the complete 'Our Gang' set.

Among the German companies who produced all-bisques in great numbers were Limbach, Goebel, Stroebel and Wilkin, Kestner and Alt, Beck and Gottschalk. The Kestner Company is generally considered to have made some of the best all-bisques. Many of these more traditional dolls were sent to England and there are still plenty of examples available. Kestners are often chosen when a collector is seeking a good-quality German doll of the type. Though often unmarked, they are recognized by their vertically-ribbed moulded socks and eyes that are often lined in black, rather like the quality French *bébés*. A plaster pate instead of cardboard was also frequently used. A few have holes above the ears, believed to have been intended for the ribbon that held on the wig. Socks are usually white with a blue band at the top, but yellow socks are also seen. The mark 'K' is sometimes found on the leg, instead of on the back of the neck where it would be expected.

Any swivel-headed all-bisque with moulded hair is quite rare. Quality should be looked for, not only in decoration, but also in construction, so that a figure made in such a way as to prevent the legs splaying apart untidily when seated would be a better-than-average acquisition. Those that are articulated but have also complicated moulded clothes are effective as clever pieces of porcelain, and interesting as dolls too.

The Japanese-made all-bisques are still quite cheap. They are often of the rigid type and have no articulation, but are made in a variety of costumes and poses, and could form an interesting collection in their own right at a low cost. Many were very obviously pirated from the currently popular German dolls

573

that were such good sellers in America. Morimura dolls are often not very well finished, though the 'Queue San Baby', made kneeling or standing and with jointed arms, is popular with collectors. It was designed by Hikozo Arakici, a U.S. citizen, who assigned his design patent to Morimura. The figure wore a small hat and a long pigtail. Morimura Brothers was located in New York and was run by Japanese. At first the company copied European dolls that could no longer be imported because of the war: Hebees, Happifats and Baby Bud were all made in imitation versions. They were fond of the large painted googly eyes that had been popularized by the German makers.

A city in Japan named Usa was cleverly developed into a toy-making area, so that the American prejudice against Japanese-made items could be overcome by the legitimate printing of 'Made in USA'. The figures marked 'Nippon' are generally considered to be older than those marked 'Japan'. The china-doll trade is often said to have been ruined by these cheap products that undercut prices, but in actual fact it appears more likely that the china dolls simply became outdated, and children sought rubber, celluloid or other unbreakable toys.

The fashion for flapper dolls extended to the small all-bisques. At first long stockings were simply painted on the legs of stock models, but later moulded garters, cloche hats and high-heeled strap shoes appeared. Some moulded complete outfits were made, and those with Charleston dresses of this type are popular for use in twenties doll's houses. Some of the dolls were dressed in aviators' outfits and others as pierrots.

'Little Annie Rooney' was a doll that was very much of this period, and was modelled by Joseph Kallus from the drawings of Jack Collins. The doll was sold wearing a red hat and woollen pigtails, black stockings and yellow shoes. As the character had been played by Mary Pickford, the doll's popularity was assured. The dolls designed by Jeanne Orsini are also popular in America, and are characterized by one raised finger. These are again typical dolls of the 1920s, with their large eyes and expressions as pert as their names, such as 'Didi' and 'Mimi'. The flapper all-bisques are sometimes immobile, but at other times they were given very slim moveable limbs.

One amusing pair of all-bisque toddlers was made as a fighting brother and sister. The boy has just sustained a black eye from his sister's clenched fist, and a tear is moulded on his cheek – again an appeal directed primarily at adults.

432   Pair of all-bisque girls. Doll with wig French, with glass eyes, and doll with long painted stockings and 1920s hairstyle, German. Both 4 in. high.

433   All-bisque 1920s doll made in Germany. Painted long stockings, hole through moulded hair for bow. 6½ in. high.

434   Two white bisques. Immobile bride marked "Made in Japan" Shoulder head with bisque limbs on red fabric body, also marked "Japan". Immobile 4 in. high.

NINETEEN

ON COLLECTING AND RESTORING

Starting a collection

At the time of writing, British collectors are in the unusual position of finding that late nineteenth-century dolls are sometimes fetching higher prices here than in America. The sudden increase in price is the direct result of the large number of men and women who have succumbed to the fascination of dolls, and are competing to acquire them. There has, over the last year, been some levelling-off in the prices that ordinary dolls can command, but the finer examples have continued to escalate. Throughout this book I have deliberately avoided any reference to the actual monetary value of objects, for prices and fashions for particular types of doll change quite rapidly, and any effort to suggest a price-guide would be out of date within a few months.

For the general reader who might possess a few inherited dolls, the sensible advice is either to take them to one of the major London salerooms for an opinion, or to show the dolls to a keeper at a specialist national doll museum. There is little point in asking the curator of a local museum for help, as his knowledge could only be expected to be of the more general kind. Privately-run museums are not always reliable; naturally they wish to pay as little as possible for acquisitions. Many specialist dealers will undertake valuation at a set fee, though the client must make it clear that a valuation for selling is required rather than for insurance purposes. It is not fair to expect any knowledgeable specialist to give free valuations. His expertise has been built up over many years, and must be treated like that of a solicitor or financial advisor. If complete confidence is felt in a doll-dealer, then the item can be offered for sale and a fair price agreed upon. If a fair offer is made which the vendor refuses, the dealer might be justified in charging as for a valuation, and several shops make this

435 Head for a boy-doll. Art doll modelled from the head of a child called Elliot. Poured wax. Inset glass eyes. Modelled by Nicholas Bramble. 7½ in. high.

clear when an item is offered for sale.

The steady rise in the price of dolls has caused many collectors of moderate means to turn to buying boudoir dolls or pincushion figures that are still quite cheap. Schoolgirl collectors often see great appeal in the composition and chalk dolls of the thirties and forties, and obviously examples of this type will eventually become desirable. Many antique shops and market stalls offer items of this late date at quite high prices, on the casual assumption that 'any old doll is worth money', a statement they quickly find is untrue. Dolls of this late period should, at the time of writing, cost only a few pounds, as they are still objects of curiosity rather than of antique interest.

I am often staggered at the large amounts new collectors, with no knowledge of the subject, are prepared to risk on the purchase of a doll for which they have no developed appreciation or understanding. The sensible collector, who seeks to understand the subject rather than to dazzle his or her friends with a case of expensive dolls, starts a collection with care and only buys items that are recognized and understood.

Buying a doll just because its face or costume appeals is a good enough reason if the price is low, but a little more than a decorative figure should be looked for in dolls that are expensive. Too many very ordinary dolls are now sold purely on the basis of long, ringletted, replacement wigs and ornate but made-yesterday clothes. The doll itself is the important item, and the collector should not be dazzled by a fur-trimmed cape or a lace- and flower-decorated dress. Though it is obviously unreasonable to expect a shopkeeper to allow the undressing of cheap dolls in order to examine the body, only the most careless would buy an expensive doll without first thoroughly studying the construction. Few antique buyers would purchase a coffer or bureau without opening the lid or drawers, yet several doll-sellers become quite distrait when the buyer questions the body.

It is unfortunate that a large number of reproductions and 'made-up' dolls have caused a feeling of distrust to develop between customer and dealer. It should however be remembered that a reputable shopkeeper would not risk his reputation by knowingly selling unauthentic objects. At the same time, the collector should realize that no dealer, no matter how experienced, is infallible. Mistakes are made by everyone, and anyone claiming either to 'know the subject A to Z' or never to sell any vaguely questionable item is suffering from a most destructive form of self-delusion. Some protection is given to the buyer in the form of the sales receipt, which should be explicit. An exchange is also occasionally countenanced if the buyer becomes very unhappy about an acquisition, though this depends on the relationship between dealer and collector.

Members of the public often comment very unfavourably on the owners of private museums and doll shops who will not allow children to enter the premises. The modern child has little respect for fragile toys, and it is unfair both to the child and to the dealer to expect that he should be allowed to handle delicate objects. The comment, 'We're not buying, just bringing the children to look' is anathema to the busy shopkeeper who feels, quite justifiably, that a public museum is the place for such excursions.

Collectors themselves are often plagued and terrified by friends who bring their children to 'see the dolls', and wonder why their reception is not as warm as usual. Few parents would expect a collector of porcelain or jade to be enamoured at the thought of a few undisciplined children rampaging among his acquisitions, but because dolls were once playthings, many parents feel that it is legitimate to expect their children to be allowed to examine them. The question "Is it wax?" is often accompanied by the scraping of a finger-nail along a fragile cheek! Though it is difficult to explain to uninitiated friends that your collection is of too great a value, both historically and possibly financially, to justify the risks run in allowing children to handle it, this statement has to be made for your own protection.

Local charities often ask doll-collectors to stage exhibitions. These can only be undertaken if locked display cases are available, as the use of a barrier is not much help against a determined thief. The expense of insuring the items from the time they leave your home until they return can also often be prohibitive. Groups of collectors are sometimes prepared to arrange one-day exhibitions, where they each guard a few objects; but unfortunately the days when dolls could be stood on unguarded tables in church halls are very much past.

Regional doll clubs are often active in this type of charity work, and the membership of such societies is often invaluable to the new collector. Visits to interesting collections and talks by enthusiasts are invariably instructive. Spare parts, old fabrics for doll dressing, and helpful tips on conservation can all be exchanged. It seems a pity that so few of these clubs have any male members, who, it would be hoped, might help counteract the rather overwhelmingly feminine atmosphere that often comes across so heavily in newsletters. Before joining a club, the collector is advised to confirm the times at which meetings are held, as those in the afternoon are of little use to the man or woman who works.

Various newsletters are supplied by subscription. Some of these are helpful, especially in obtaining the addresses of doll-repairers or wigmakers or shoe-makers, though the editorial is often less informative than space-filling. Most of these newsletters depend on the advertising they carry, and it is understandable that large numbers of reproductions have to be included, though it would be refreshing if a few antiques were occasionally offered for sale.

Repairing Dolls

The British collectors who began buying dolls in the 1960s were forced to learn how to make wigs, repair, string and costume their own dolls. I still find this aspect of doll-collecting enjoyable and instructive, but the new collector has a variety of dolls' hospitals and semi-professionals who will repair and restore. Not every so-called dolls' hospital is reliable; I have seen some dreadful examples of such professional work and some fine repairs by amateurs, so it is advisable to ask to see samples of work. There are even skilled doll costumiers who will reconstruct detailed outfits out of authentic fabrics. If a doll in bad condition is purchased, it is as well to consider carefully how much the services of these specialists is going to cost, for it is often cheaper in the long run to buy a ready-dressed doll.

While they were still very cheap, it seemed legitimate to practise repairs on badly-damaged dolls, but success was not always assured, and disasters did sometimes occur. Unless the collector is sure that the doll is of little interest, it would be as well to leave the restoration to a professional. Fingers can be mended with proprietary fillers or modelling substances, and cracks in bodies strengthened with resin compounds that will prevent further warping. Eyes can be reset with a little practice, by greasing the surface and applying plaster of paris, which will contract away from the eye as it dries. This calls for some skill, and a damaged head is useful for trying out different techniques. It is as well to avoid any restoration that cannot be removed if it later becomes discoloured, or if a better method is decided upon. A badly-restored doll is worth much less to a collector than another in damaged but original state, and unnecessary repairs should be avoided.

Damaged bisque faces are difficult to restore at home, and should be sent to a professional. It is prudent to ask to see examples of a restorer's work before a good doll is passed to him, as a man who is quite skilled at repairing glazed porcelain may often find the dull flesh-coloured bisque finish very difficult. A few restorers are virtually self-styled and some of their work is dreadful. An estimate of the cost should also be obtained, if possible in writing. If a good but damaged doll is considered for purchase, it should be borne in mind that a chip or a piece out of a head is often much easier to repair than a crack which has to be ground down before filling. Few restorers would attempt to re-fire a doll's head, so that one is in effect paying for a surface treatment that can change colour over the years. I have seen several dolls that were satisfactory after restoration, but several years caused the surface to develop a different texture and the colour to fade. The temptation to buy a cheap doll because of the thought that it can be restored should, if possible, be resisted. Good restorers are hard to find and the cost of their time is high.

In the United States, a small industry has developed around the collecting of old dolls, and similar services are becoming available in England. Soon replacement eyes, teeth and hands will all be available. Though such replacements are necessary if a doll is in a ruinous state, these too should if possible be avoided. It is better to remodel a few fingers than replace a complete hand. Costume must also be treated with respect for authenticity, and re-dressing should only take place if the original costume is lost or completely inappropriate. Many jointed and toddler-type dolls were dressed by their original purchasers in outgrown baby-gowns, which contribute little to their appearance. If for some reason a doll's costume is particularly disliked, and the figure has to be re-dressed, the original costume should be retained and labelled.

Uninteresting but beautifully-stitched clothes can often be given new life by the addition of old flowers, ribbon or even a lace apron, while badly-stained cotton dresses can be dyed to cover up marks. Many modern dyes are too harsh to use convincingly, but by experimenting in mixing several colours or using less than the prescribed quantity, some softer effects can be obtained. Of course it would be unforgivable to tamper in any way with the costumes of dolls made before 1840, no matter how stained and damaged. Very fragile fabrics can be backed with fine canvas, and it is possible, though expensive, to have really good silks restored. Silk is the most difficult to repair, as it was often treated with substances such as shellac to give it body; this artificial stiffening, used from the middle of the eighteenth century onwards, has made the fabric liable to split and fragment. It is therefore much safer to back damaged silk than to try to darn. On cotton and woollen materials, however, a beautifully-stitched darn can be completely in character and even enhance the doll's appearance, providing that a convincing thread is used.

It is an unfortunate fact that many of the dolls that the collector buys are without their original clothes. New fabrics, even if meticulously sewn, always look wrong on antique dolls, and collectors search constantly for pieces of old dresses and lengths of Victorian lace that can be re-used. Fortunately, our ancestors treasured their ribbons and lace, and often at house clearance sales boxes of bits and pieces can be bought very cheaply. They also saved pieces of fur and feathers, and when relatives throw away the property of deceased elderly people, they may be persuaded to sell the boxes of bits. Jumble-sales and street markets will often produce a Victorian child's hat or a pair of shoes in just the right size, which rewards hours of patient searching.

When creating costumes, it is better to study actual children's clothes of the period and attempt to copy their design, as the women of the period would have done, than to copy the dress of another doll. There are many books on costume, and several museums feature children's clothes that can be studied and sketched in detail. As far as was possible, dolls in original clothes were photographed for this book, but many in reconstructions had to be included.

It is a great temptation when recostuming to overdress the figure. A collection of overdone dolls can look as depressing when displayed as another in tatters. Several collectors have told me that they do not like dolls' original clothes, as they are so often dirty; and so, instead of washing and preserving the costume, it is thrown away and new substituted. Another lady often re-dresses *Parisiennes*, as their clothes are not to her taste. Such collectors would do better to buy good modern or reproduction figures, as they are doing considerable harm to the objects they profess to admire.

Some care in the display of dolls made of substances other than china is needed. Wax dolls in particular should be kept from direct light, which will eventually cause the colour to fade. There is a very marked difference of colour to be seen between the faces of such dolls and the tops of the limbs that have always been covered by the clothes. Though the collector wishes to enjoy the doll, it is better to keep it in a shaded part of a room, especially as the heat of the sun can cause the wax to melt. Waxed compositions are particularly susceptible to changes of temperature, most of all those that have been restored. Ordinary variations do little damage, but if the temperature is likely to drop to freezing-point, it would be better to keep the dolls elsewhere, as cracking is inevitable. Dolls kept under glass shades or in cases are particularly vulnerable to heat, which is intensified by the glass. A spotlight trained on such a display can build up a considerable heat in a short time, while photographic floods can also be extremely damaging if left for long on the subject. It is not a good idea to leave a wax doll in a photographer's studio, as it is difficult for someone who is not used to wax to understand that a few minutes spent in answering a telephone could cause irreparable damage.

Wax dolls can usually be cleaned free of dust and surface dirt with a damp cloth wrapped around a spatula or finger. More difficult marks can be wiped away with a little soap. Great care must be taken around the eyes, since inset lashes will be ruined if wetted. Owners of old wax dolls, if they think of selling, would be advised to leave them in their original state, as the buyer usually prefers to clean the doll herself, and the price that can be obtained would not be affected by any surface grime. Cold cream is also sometimes used to clean wax heads, but it should be remembered that both this and soap act as mild solvents and should be wiped away quickly. Soft cloths must be used for cleaning wax, because any fabric with a textured surface can leave marks. If one is uncertain

436 Head for a lady doll. Poured wax with inset glass eyes. Modern art doll made by Nicholas Bramble.

of the effect, the cleaning substance should be tried out under the hair or at the top of an arm or leg.

The heads of bisque dolls can be washed quite thoroughly, and a soft brush can be used for cleaning out any small indentations. The area around the eyes must be kept dry in order to protect the lashes and the plaster of paris that holds the eyes in place. Very dirty wigs can be removed and washed carefully. Some time is needed after drying to tease the mohair back into place, and some wigs can be ruined by washing! Marks on bodies are often best left as they are; it is easy to remove the surface varnish with the mark and damage the doll.

Both papier mâché and composition dolls are best left alone even if the faces are marked, as the protective varnish, especially on the later dolls, is very thin and almost impossible to replace convincingly. Cracks in old dolls can be filled with gesso that is easy to remove if the repair is unsatisfactory or fades with time. One of the most distressing dolls I have seen was an eighteenth-century wooden whose face had been repainted. No matter how damaged a doll of this age might be, it is better (unless museum restoration is possible) to leave the face in its time-worn condition, as the quality is completely lost by insensitive reconstruction.

Display

Acquisitions are at first quite easy to accommodate on a sofa or chair, but collections grow at an astonishing rate, and since many dolls are large, other means of display have to be found. The ideal solution is a room that could be devoted purely to display, but few collectors are able to achieve this goal, and other ideas have to be sought. Glass-fronted shop display cabinets can be used, but are really only suitable for use in a very large room, as they can too easily dominate the whole area, and the collector finds herself in the position of being overpowered at all times by rows of china and wax faces. Commercially-made wall units, in which the dolls can be displayed in the glass-fronted sections customarily used for china or *objets d'art*, can be effective. Display in this controlled area means that the collection is integrated into the complete concept of the family and its interests, instead of being a private individual conceit.

Victorian and Edwardian china cabinets that once housed the cranberry glass and bisque figurines of our grandparents are excellent for drawing-room display of small *Parisiennes* or all-bisque figures. The Edwardian cabinets are still relatively cheap, and the silk or velvet lining often enhances the dolls' appearance. Quite ordinary dolls are given great importance when displayed in fine Georgian bookcases, but as these have been avidly sought for by collectors of ceramics for some time, prices are high. I partly solved my own problem by

437 Good-quality reproduction poured-wax doll made by Myrtle Smith. Inset hair and glass eyes. Kapok-filled body. 18 in. high.

438 Group of rubber-headed dolls made by a modern commercial doll-designer, Sylvia Willgoss, who is design director of Dean's.

purchasing the shelving from a Victorian Gothic library. The removal of several layers of paint from the shelving and skin from my hands has revealed the warm pinewood. As every shelf is adjustable, dolls in a wide variety of sizes can be accommodated. The disadvantage of this type of shelving is the lack of glass fronts, but few solutions are completely perfect.

If one is making specially-constructed wooden cases, it is sensible to work to a regular size, so that additional cases, when needed, can be stacked together to maintain a neat and uniform appearance. Nothing looks worse than a good collection displayed in a motley assortment of cases of irregular size and quality. It is far better to use a simply-made plastic or pine series of boxes than an assortment of junk-shop finds, whose only unity was their low cost.

Very small rooms can often accommodate triangular shelves that can be fitted neatly into a corner and given a glass door. If a case of this type is taken up to ceiling level, a large number of dolls can be attractively set out. Shallow wall-cupboards that are of little use for general storage can have the doors removed, shelves fitted and glass doors replaced to make a considerable display area. Many collectors complain that they have no room for display cases, but there is nearly always some space in a house that can be utilized, if only for small dolls. Often the fresh eye of a friend will see possibilities in a room that have been overlooked because of long acceptance.

When exquisitely-costumed figures are displayed, mirror-backed cases are often effective. A good but much cheaper effect is to be achieved by the use of the adhesive plastic 'glass' that can be bought by the yard. Other cases may be papered or painted to resemble miniature rooms or scenes, and furnished with accessories to scale. Even quite large dolls can be displayed in this 'doll's-house' manner. Too much cluttering of figures should be avoided, as the quality of the object itself can become obscured by abundant decoration. In a similar way, dolls should not be crowded together, as they so easily assume the effect of a jumble-sale. A critical examination of methods of display in some of the better museums often gives rise to ideas that can be modified to use at home. Some of the complicated lighting effects and revolving stands would look ostentatious if applied to a collection displayed in a living-room, but would be interesting if a special room were set aside for display.

Figures under 5 inches high are much easier to accommodate, even in the smallest bed-sitter, and can look effective if displayed in the type of showcases that were once used to promote chocolate or spools of thread before the Second World War. Some of these sales cases are becoming collector's pieces in their own right, but those that have lost their original lettering or need repainting are still cheap. An alternative is a shelved box covered with hessian or felt and fitted behind a good picture-frame – probably one of the cheapest methods of display. One collector utilizes baker's trays, into which shelves are fitted, while another uses partitioned wooden cutlery boxes.

A good doll can be lent significance by being placed under a glass shade. Though Victorian examples are no longer cheap, those made for modern clocks can sometimes serve. Shop display units, especially constructed for exhibition stands, can also be used and are often cheap, as they are of no use after the event. Despite all these experiments in display, no collector will ever be really satisfied, but it is this continual rearrangement that gives zest to collecting.

A prestigious group of beautifully-dressed Brus and 'closed-mouth' French dolls can leave the viewer as cold as a group of modern statuettes, while a lively and individually-chosen group of rag dolls, bought with enthusiasm and interest but not much money, can be a delight when skilfully displayed. I visited the homes of many collectors while writing this book, and was struck as much by the variety of people who collected dolls as by the range of their interests. Some lived with the dolls in a jumble and confusion that was quite frightening, and one felt that they were living dolls rather than life. In contrast others kept their acquisitions almost secretly locked away. Fortunately, the majority of collectors lie somewhere between these two extremes, and improve their displays by the discriminating purchase of figures that have personal appeal.

People are often astonished at the actual number of dolls owned by individuals. A large collection mainly composed of dolls of the same make and type can be worth considerably less than another composed of only five or six fine-quality items. One lady collector who lives in a small flat has continually bought and sold dolls until she has achieved a very small collection of French dolls of almost unsurpassable quality. Another gradually sold off all her bisque dolls to buy dolls that were of historical interest. The collection that is static is dead, and as interests change so should your collection. We all own a few dolls that have great sentimental value, and others that have been sold to us on the understanding that they would be kept safely, because the original owners had grown very old. I have several very ordinary 'A.M.s' that come into this category: one has two right legs and was bought for me as the first of my collection by my then very young and impecunious husband, while another was sold to me, amidst floods of tears for its safety, with the words, "It will be thrown out in the ashcan when I'm gone, love!" However, dolls that are acquired from dealers, and have no background history, can be resold without scruple, and the proceeds used to buy a better or more interesting doll. Every few years the sum of acquisitions should be looked at dispassionately, and the question asked, "Have I here an accumulation or a collection?" With the rapid increase in the price of dolls, fewer people will be able to hoard all their purchases, which should mean more dolls in circulation, even in the collections of the most wealthy.

As a result of this great price escalation, several doll enthusiasts have turned their attention to making good-quality reproductions that can either be given to children as a very special present, or bought as a purely decorative item. Among the makers of these dolls is Myrtle Smith, who creates wax dolls from casts taken from old dolls. So well made are some of these figures that they could be taken for Victorian examples, and to guard against this all the dolls are signed on the torso. Imitation china dolls of unbreakable resins are also made individually by this craftswoman, who has spent several years in developing a successful technique.

A few original dolls are still made both by designers, such as Sylvia Willgoss, who work for toy companies, and by artists, such as Nicholas Bramble, who works in wax. Some of his creations are sinuously beautiful, but their long emaciated limbs are a little disturbing. Each hair is separately inserted into the scalp, a process that takes a week to complete, and the dolls, being numbered and completely unique, are necessarily quite expensive. The majority are modelled on actual people, as their maker studied his medium at Madame Tussaud's and later turned to doll-making.

With the increasing interest in traditional crafts and art forms, we could in the next few years see a rapid increase in the number of doll-makers meeting a demand for a doll that has more individuality than those of plastic or vinyl. It is a sad fact that for many children of today, the period of essential innocence is no longer than it was for the little drudges of the late Victorian period. As they grow up, it is probable that they too will look for that innocence reflected in the toys of childhood's golden age, which was surely the years between 1880 and 1920 – when doll-makers' materials and methods of working were still those of traditional skills and craftsmanship, but when dolls were sufficiently cheap to be owned by many children.

GLOSSARY

As well as the terms used in this book, those in common use by doll dealers and auctioneers, when describing items for sale, have also been included in this Glossary.

ADTOCOLITE. Light, smooth-textured composition used by Aetna Doll and Toy Company.

ALABASTER. Fine-grained sulphate of lime that was ideal for carving. Also used by doll-makers to describe heads cast in plaster of paris.

ALL-BISQUE. Used only when the complete doll is made of bisque.

ALL-PUPIL EYES. Dark brown, irisless eyes.

ALMOND-EYED. Dark, almond-shaped fixed eyes used by Jumeau. Dolls with this type of eyes usually have 'early' ball-jointed bodies.

ALPHABET DOLLS. Fabric bodies, printed with letters of the alphabet. China heads.

APPLIED EARS. Ears attached separately after the moulding of the heads. Used on quality dolls.

ARMATURE. Inner frame of wire, metal or wood.

ART DOLLS. Can refer to children's dolls designed by artists or to adult, boudoir-type dolls made in stylized manner.

BABYLAND RAG DOLLS. Made by Horsman with painted faces but sometimes used to describe any doll of similar type.

BAGMAN'S BABY. Any doll sold by a travelling salesman.

BALD HEADS. Dolls with smooth, fully-moulded heads.

BARTHOLOMEW BABIES. Any type of doll sold at St Bartholomew's Fair.

BÉBÉ. Child-like doll with double-jointed or leather body.

BÉBÉ BAISER. Kissing doll.

BÉBÉ DE CHANT. Singing doll.

BÉBÉ TÊTEUR. Feeding doll.

BELTON TYPE. Bald-headed, French bisque doll. Small holes in crown, possibly for attaching wig or for stringing.

BENT-LIMBED BODY. Baby-type body in sitting position.

BERLIN TYPE. Moulded porcelain shoulder heads with soft pink glaze.

BIEDERMEIER. Porcelain dolls with a round black spot on pate. Used by German collectors to refer to any glazed porcelain dolls. Other collectors describe any dolls made between 1805 and 1840 as Biedermeier.

BISKOLINE. Self-coloured substance similar to celluloid.

BISQUE. Unglazed porcelain.

BLACK SPOT. Porcelain dolls with black spot on pate.

BLONDE BISQUE TYPE. Used to describe pink-tinted, unglazed heads with moulded hair and shoulder plate.

BLOWN EYES. Glass eyes blown into round spheres.

BLUSHING. The soft colour applied to the backs of dolls' hands and tops of feet.

BONNET DOLLS. Those with moulded hats or bonnets.

BOUDOIR DOLLS. Term to describe lady-dolls made in early twentieth century as mascots for adults.

BREVETÉ. Patented.

BROTTEIG. Mixture of dark meal, rye meal and glue water, used to make a modelling substance. Often used for detail on wooden heads made around 1800.

BUST HEADS. American term for shoulder heads.

BUTTERFLY DOLLS. Moulded head-dress in the form of butterflies.

CANDYSTORE DOLLS. American term for cheap all-bisques in small sizes.

CARRIAGE DOLLS. Very small dolls in leather cases to amuse on journeys.

CARRIAGE TRADE. Quality dolls sold to the wealthy.

CARTOON DOLLS. Bisque or composition figures made in imitation of cartoon characters of twentieth century.

CHARACTER DOLLS. First made by Marion Kaulitz in Munich, but now used mainly to describe bisque-headed dolls with realistic expressions made after 1909.

CHILD DOLL. Double-jointed or leather-bodied little girl dolls.

CHINA HEAD. American term for glazed porcelain, shoulder-headed dolls.

CHINA LIMB. Lower arms and legs of porcelain.

CLOVER LEAF. Has leaves of this type moulded as a head-dress.

CODY JUMEAU. Long-faced doll with two-tone mouth. Once thought to have been specially made to honour Buffalo Bill Cody when he visited Paris in 1887. He returned to America with a doll of this type for his daughters.

COLUMBIAN DOLLS. Painted rag. American, circa 1900.

COMPOSITION. Can refer to any mixture of wood or paper pulp with glue as binder. Papier mâché is sometimes included.

COQUETTE TYPE. Has large, sideways-glancing eyes. Painted or glass.

CORSET BODY. Fabric of body printed with a corset.

CRÈCHE FIGURES. Made for use in Christmas cribs.

CUPIDS. All-bisque figures made in Germany. Similar to Kewpies, with sideways-glancing eyes, but without wings or quiff.

CUT-AWAY HEAD. Method of cutting bisque heads at the crown. Those cut well away at a sharp angle are more highly thought of.

DAIRI HINA. Japanese Girls' Festival dolls. Emperor and Empress.

DECAL EYES. Often of metal given a transfer-type film.

DEP. – Deponiert (German) or Deposé (French). Indicates a registered design or trade-mark.

DOLL-FACED. The typical smiling little girl face.

DOLL'S-HOUSE FAMILY. Term to indicate a set of dolls that includes men-dolls with moulded hair.

D.R.G.M. Deutsches Reichs Gebrauchsmuster. (Registered Design.)

DOUBLE-JOINTED. Parts of body pivot around a wooden ball.

DUTCH DOLLS. Corruption of German word Deutsch. Used loosely to describe all types of cheap, jointed, wooden dolls but in this book only for woodens of shoulder-headed type.

EARTHENWARE. Opaque body of common clay.

ENIGMA. Once used as term to describe dolls now known as Motschmann type.

EYELETTED BODY. Limbs have sew holes that are protected by metal eyelets. Used on quality wax dolls.

FASHION DOLL. Outdated term used to describe French lady-dolls of late nineteenth century. Correctly used as a description for genuine mannequin figures.

FIBERLOID AND FIBROLAQUE. Unbreakable, composition-type substances.

FLANDERS BABY. Name sometimes given to jointed wooden dolls.

FLANGE NECKS. Necks that open out at lower edge to be held in place by cloth bodies.

FLAPPERS. 1920-type dolls with long, shapely legs. Especially used to refer to all-bisques of this type.

FLIRTING EYES. Eyes that move from side to side.

FLOCKED HAIR. Method of simulating hair on baby or boy dolls by coating head with glue and attaching powdered felt.

FLOWER DOLLS. Porcelain heads with moulded flowers forming hats.

FOLIE. Doll's head mounted on stick. The fabric costume conceals a squeaker.

FORK HANDS. Describes fingers of early wooden dolls that are close together and stick-like.

FORTUNE-TELLERS. Any type of doll that carries an assortment of written predictions. The leaves often form the skirt.

'FRENCH' BISQUE. Late nineteenth-century doll-makers described any quality bisque in this way.

FROZEN CHARLOTTES. Immobile figures of indeterminate sex. Usually white porcelain with black, or more rarely, yellow hair.

GESSO. Fine plaster used to give a good surface for painting.

GESLAND-TYPE BODY. Jointed wire body that was padded and covered with stockinette.

GIBSON GIRLS. Correctly bisque lady-dolls made by Kestner and based on portraits of C. D. Gibson. Name also commonly used to describe any lady-dolls of Edwardian period, whose features resemble those of the ladies in *The Social Ladder* by Charles Dana Gibson, printed in 1902.

GLAZE. The glass-like finish applied to earthenware and porcelain. Impervious to liquid and smooth to touch.

GOFUN. Paste of powdered oyster shell and glue used on faces of Japanese dolls.

GOO-GOO EYES. Unnatural, large round eyes, usually sideways glancing.

GOOGLIES. As above. Good examples have eyes that move by action of lever.

GOSHO-NINGYO. Japanese court or Palace dolls.

GUSSETED BODY. Leather body with insets at joints to allow for movement.

GUTTA-PERCHA. Rubber-type substance obtained from Malaya.

GRÖDNERTALS. Jointed wooden dolls. Early nineteenth century. Usually have yellow or gilt combs in hair.

HALF DOLLS. Head and torso moulded in one to waist. Fabric upper arms and legs.

HAPPIFATS. Based on drawings by Kate Jordan. Only the arms move. Made in Germany after 1914.

HARD PASTE PORCELAIN. True translucent porcelain made of kaolin, china clay and flux.

HEAD CONES. Tops of bisque heads were left open to fit eye mechanisms and reduce weight. The gap was covered by head cones of cardboard or, in better dolls, cork. Kestner used plaster cones.

HOLZMASSE. Wood pulp.

HOOF FEET. A stylized method of carving the feet of wooden dolls in the eighteenth century.

HOTTENTOTS. Black Kewpies made after 1913.

IMMOBILES. All-bisques in fixed positions. No moving parts.

INCASSABLE. Unbreakable, but used by many French makers to describe *bébés*.

INTAGLIO – Incised. Used particularly to describe painted dolls' eyes with incised detail.

INTERCHANGEABLES. Refers usually to dolls with a choice of separate heads.

IRISH BISQUE. Term used by American collectors to describe very thin sharp bisque.

IRISLESS EYES. Pupil-less.

JEWELLED HEAD. Shoulder head embedded with glass to give the effect of a necklace.

JNE. Junior.

JOINTED BODY. Makers used term to describe any moving part, but now used by collectors to describe dolls with moving limbs.

JUMPING JACK. Jointed figure of wood or card activated by pulling a string.

KAISER BABY. Collectors jargon for Kämmer and Reinhardt model '100', known to the firm as 'Baby'.

KEWPIES. Designed by Rose O'Neill. Have small blue wings and starfish or 'webbed' hands. Hair in quiff.

KIDILINE. Imitation leather used in early twentieth century.

LONDON RAG DOLL (BABY). Wax dolls whose faces were covered by a layer of muslin. Nineteenth century.

LUSTRE. Decoration of pottery or porcelain by means of a thin film of metal.

MADAME BOURGET DOLLS. Wooden dolls made in twentieth century in style of eighteenth century.

MANIKIN. Lay figure of an artist or male doll used to display costume.

MARGUERITE DOLLS. Porcelain shoulder heads with large daisies forming their hats.

MAROTTE. Head or complete doll mounted on a musical box which is activated when stick on which parts are assembled is swung.

MASK FACE. Printed or moulded front of head fixed to stuffed fabric back.

MATRYUSHKA. Nest of wooden dolls. Russian.

MILLINERS MODEL. Term coined by Eleanor St George to describe papier mâché dolls of early nineteenth century, with moulded hair.

MOTSCHMANN TYPE. Dolls made in Europe after 1851 in imitation of Japanese baby dolls. Fabric inserts allowed movement.

MOULDED TEETH. Teeth moulded in one with the head rather than inserted as in cheaper dolls.

MOULDED TONGUE. Tongue that is either moulded in one with lower lip, as in an open-mouthed doll, or protruding slightly from an 'open-closed' mouth.

MOULDED YOKE. Decoration suggesting lace collars, etc., found on good bisque shoulder heads.

MOVING MOUTH. Several dolls patented with moving teeth or lips.

MOVING HEADS. All-bisque dolls whose heads were fixed to immobile bodies by elastic.

MULTI-FACED DOLLS. Several faces that are turned by a knob at the top of the head or by a string.

MULTI-WIGGED. A selection of wigs sometimes accompanied better-quality dolls.

NECKLACE DOLLS. Moulded necklace on shoulder plate.

NEEDLE-MOULDING. Modelling of features of cloth-faced dolls by small stitches.

NE PLUS ULTRA JOINTS. Patented in the United States by Sarah Robinson in 1883. Usually a rivet hip joint used on leather bodies, but sometimes also used at knee and elbow.

NETTLE CLOTH. Used by Käthe Kruse for waterproof dolls' heads which were stuffed with deer hair and reinforced with metal.

NODDERS. Dolls whose heads nod on a pivot. Usually mantelpiece ornaments.

OLD WHITES. American term for very white all-bisques usually with yellow hair.

OPEN-CLOSED MOUTHS. Mouths that are modelled in the open position but have no entry into the head cavity.

PANDORAS. True mannequin dolls. Usually full or half life-size.

PANTIN. A Jumping Jack.

PAPERWEIGHT EYES. Term for good-quality, early, flat-backed type of eye.

PAPIER MÂCHÉ. Paper reduced to fibrous pulp, mixed with chalk and sand. Used by doll-collectors to refer to dolls of the 'Milliners model' type.

PARCEL-POST BABIES. American term for celluloid dolls with cloth bodies.

PARIAN TYPE. White, unglazed porcelain as used for moulded shoulder heads.

PARISIENNES. French lady-dolls of the late nineteenth century.

PATE. The crown of the head.

PEDLAR. Dolls that sell from a tray or basket.

PEG-JOINTED. Can refer to pegs holding elastic for stringing or small, dowel-type jointing as used in Grödnertals or Wooden Tops.

PENNY WOODENS. Used here to describe mid-nineteenth-century dolls of similar quality to Grödnertals, but without the carved combs.

PET NAMES. Dolls that carry their name on the shoulder plate.

PIANO BABIES. Ornamental bisque figures, often immobile.

PIANO DOLLS. Small figures of wood or card with bristle legs, that appear to dance when piano keys are moved. Also known as Pigmées Musico Dancemanes.

PIGEON TOES. Usually refers to early nineteenth-century waxed dolls, with turned-in toes, caused by the structure of their fabric bodies.

PINCUSHION HEADS. Ornamental half figures of bisque or porcelain. Could be fixed to pincushions, crumb brushes, vanity bags or lampshades.

PINK LUSTRE. Very delicate, uneven pink shading to basic white-glazed porcelain heads.

PORTRAIT DOLL. Head modelled on a known person, e.g. Lord Roberts or Sara Penfold. Erroneously used to describe a miscellany of bisque and porcelain heads that have a slight resemblance to beauties of the period, e.g. Alexandra, Eugénie or Jenny Lind.

POUPARDS. Doll's head mounted on stick. Musical movement or squeaker concealed under clothes. Also a swaddling baby of wood or composition.

POUPÉE. A lady-doll.

POUTIES. Usually refers to bisque-headed dolls with a pouting expression and closed mouth.

PRE-COLOURED OR SELF-COLOURED BISQUE. Pink colouring in substance of bisque rather than applied.

PRESEPIO. Christmas crib or crèche.

PRINTED DOLLS. Refers to rag dolls bought in sheet form.

PUMPKIN HEAD. Also known as Squash Heads. Waxed composition with blonde, moulded hair. Heads made in shallow, two-part moulds and consequently present a flattened appearance.

RETRACTABLE TONGUE. Tongue pivots back into mouth when doll is laid down.

ROBINSON JOINTS. Designed in the United States by Sarah Robinson 1883. Used on fabric and leather bodies. Each section was given 'ears' that fitted the part above. Rivets, pins or even stitches held the two together. Neatened by buttons or stiffened fabric washers.

ROOTED HAIR. Set into wax or plastic material, either singly or in tufts. Lashes, eyebrows and beards could all be treated similarly.

RUPPRECHT DOLLS. Figures of Dutch origin dressed completely in fur. Were attendants to Santa Claus.

SABULAS. Coined by Jo Gerken to describe early papier mâchés that were made in two-piece moulds and consisted of head and body to the knees.

SAND BABY. A doll whose head was weighted with sand. Made by Käthe Kruse.

SCARF DOLLS. Moulded shoulder heads wearing a scarf or turban.

SCHILLING JOINTS. Method of fixed wooden or composition arms to a body of leather or cloth. 1884.

SCHUTZMARKE. Trade-mark.

SEWING COMPANION. Dressed dolls whose costume is a holder for scissors, thread, etc.

S.G.D.G. (French). Without government guarantee. (Used in conjunction with BREVETÉ (q.v.).

SHOULDER HEADS. Head and shoulder plate of same substance. Sewn or stuck to body.

SKITTLE DOLL. Carved, one-piece wooden dolls of primitive type. Skittle-shaped.

SLIT OR SPLIT HEADS. Usually refers to dolls of waxed composition with a slit cut along crown for insertion of wig. Some papier mâchés have hair similarly attached.

SNOW BABIES. All-bisque figures wearing snow suits of grog. Can be wire-jointed, or, more usually, immobile.

SPECIAL. Mark found on bisque heads. Believed to refer to a special issue, perhaps for Christmas, etc. Used by several makers.

SPOON HANDS. Embryonic hands where only the thumb is carved separately.

SPRINGFIELD DOLLS. Jointed wooden dolls made in this area.

STARFISH HANDS. Early twentieth century. Hands modelled to look almost webbed. As in Kewpies.

STE. Society (French).

STEUBER BODY. Boots and stockings form an integral part of the lower legs.

STIFF-JOINTED. Arms and legs move only at shoulders and hip.

STIFF NECKS. Terms for dolls whose heads are moulded in one with body. Usually refers to all-bisques.

STRAIGHT-LIMBED BABY. Legs modelled almost straight so that the doll can stand.

STRINGING LOOPS. Bisque loops modelled in one with limbs for neater stringing of all-bisques. Some baby dolls made by Heubach have stringing loop on neck.

SWAYERS. Figurines that sway from side to side.

SWIVEL NECKS. Turn in socket at base.

SWIVEL PEGS. The top part of the arm or leg of a Grödnertal that fits into the torso and allows movement.

TAUFLING. Unchristened babies. Used to refer to several types of folk baby dolls.

TODDLER-TYPE BODY. Plump, double-jointed body, often with shaped thighs to fit neatly against body.

TEA-CUP DOLLS. FROZEN CHARLOTTES (*q.v.*).

TELEPHONE DOLLS. Have large skirts to cover the telephone. Often given waxed plaster heads combined with bisque arms.

THUMB-SUCKER. German all-bisque with well-moulded hand. Thumb fits into open mouth. Some have rubber hands.

TOPSY-TURVY. Doll with head at top and bottom. Unwanted head covered by skirt.

UNIVERSAL JOINT. Patented in 1895 in the United States by Charles Fausel. Used on kid bodies, where a composition or china part has to swivel within a leather socket.

VAMPS. 1920, boudoir-type lady-dolls.

VENDORS. Any dolls that sell from booths, carts, etc.

WAX-POURED. Moulded heads made completely of wax.

WAXED. Heads of wood, plaster or composition coated with wax.

WHISTLING DOLLS. Mouth puckered into whistling expression. Appears to whistle when sound box in torso is squeezed.

WHISTLING TONGUE. A tongue that vibrates when the doll is moved.

WIMPERN. German for eyelashes. Found on Simon and Halbig heads probably intended for quality market.

WINKING DOLL. Made between 1910 and 1920. One eye closed. Smiling mouths.

WIRE-EYED. Eyes close by action of wire lever that protrudes from side of body or crotch. String sometimes attached to wire inside body.

WOODEN KATES. Wooden dolls with black hair and undetailed faces.

WOODEN TOPS. Cheap, jointed, wooden dolls with black hair made in Switzerland and Germany.

WOOD PULP. Sawdust mixed with a glue binder.

YEUX FIBRES. Good-quality eyes with a white-rayed iris.

MUSEUMS

Britain

Though the following museums have interesting collections, they are not always open, and the dolls sometimes not on show. If travelling any distance, it is advisable to confirm by telephone what can be seen.

ABBEY HOUSE MUSEUM, Kirkstall, Leeds
AMERICAN MUSEUM IN BRITAIN, Bath
ART GALLERY AND MUSEUM, Keighley
BARRY ELDER DOLL MUSEUM, Preston
BETHNAL GREEN MUSEUM, London
BIRMINGHAM MUSEUM AND ART GALLERY, Birmingham
BLAISE CASTLE, Bristol
BOWES MUSEUM, Barnard Castle, Co. Durham
BRITISH MUSEUM, London
CAMBRIDGE AND COUNTY FOLK MUSEUM, Cambridge
CASTLE MUSEUM, York
CHELMSFORD AND ESSEX MUSEUM, Chelmsford
CITY MUSEUM, Leeds
DARTFORD MUSEUM, Kent
DOLLS IN WONDERLAND, Brighton
FITZWILLIAM MUSEUM, Cambridge
GUNNERSBURY PARK MUSEUM, London
HEREFORD CITY MUSEUM, Hereford
HORNIMAN MUSEUM, London
LONDON MUSEUM, London
MUSEUM AND ART GALLERY, Luton
MUSEUM OF CHILDHOOD, Anglesey
MUSEUM OF CHILDHOOD, Edinburgh
MUSEUM OF CHILDHOOD AND COSTUME, Blithfield Hall, Rugeley, Staffs.
PENRHYN CASTLE, Bangor

PENSHURST CASTLE, Kent
POLLOCKS TOY MUSEUM, London
RINGWOOD TOY MUSEUM, Hants
ROYAL TUNBRIDGE WELLS MUSEUM, Kent
SAFFRON WALDEN MUSEUM, Essex
SALISBURY MUSEUM, Salisbury
SOMERSET COUNTY MUSEUM, Taunton
THE GRANGE TOY MUSEUM, Rottingdean
THE HOLLY TREES, Colchester
THE ROTUNDA (doll's-house dolls), Oxford
VICTORIA AND ALBERT MUSEUM, London
WARWICK DOLL MUSEUM, Warwick
WELSH FOLK MUSEUM, St Fagans, Cardiff
WINDSOR CASTLE, Windsor
WORTHING MUSEUM AND ART GALLERY, Worthing

America
CAMERONS DOLL MUSEUM, Colorado
CHILDREN'S MUSEUM, Brooklyn, New York
THE MUSEUM OF THE CITY OF NEW YORK, New York
DETROIT PUBLIC SCHOOLS CHILDREN'S MUSEUM, Detroit
ESSEX INSTITUTE, Salem, Massachusetts
MARY MERRITT'S DOLL MUSEUM, Douglasville
PLYMOUTH ANTIQUARIAN SOCIETY, Plymouth
SMITHSONIAN INSTITUTION, Washington D.C.
WISCONSIN STATE HISTORICAL SOCIETY, Madison

Europe
BAYERISCHES NATIONALMUSEUM, Munich
DEUTSCHES SPIELZEUGMUSEUM, Sonneberg
DANSK FOLKMUSEUM, Copenhagen
GERMANISCHES NATIONALMUSEUM, Nürnberg
HAAGS GEMEENTEMUSEUM, The Hague
MUSÉE DES ARTS DECORATIFS, Paris
MUSÉE D'HISTOIRE DE L'EDUCATION, Paris
NATIONAL MUSEUM OF FINLAND, Helsinki
NORSK FOLKMUSEUM, Oslo
RIJKSMUSEUM, Amsterdam
STADTISCHE KUNSTSAMMLUNGEN, Augsburg

BIBLIOGRAPHY

The bibliography for a book of this kind can only be partial. Newspaper and magazine articles and catalogues of toy-makers are not available in most libraries, but where reference was made to such publications, they were cited in the text. Many books on dolls in the list below are those to which both the present writer and the collector owe a debt of gratitude, especially to the Coleman family and Luella Hart, whose painstaking research into makers' marks and patents has made the attribution of so many items possible. Several background books on social history, ceramics and costume which the author has found useful are also included. Though several of the books are out of print, they can usually be obtained by local libraries without difficulty.

ASHTON, *Social England under the Regency.*
D'ALLEMAGNE, H. R., *Histoire des Jouets.* Paris, 1903.
ANGIONE, Genevieve, *All-Bisque and Half-Bisque Dolls.* Thomas Nelson, New York.
ARGYLL, Duke of, *V.R.I. Her Life and Empire.* Harmsworth Bros. Ltd, 1902.
ARONSON, Theo, *Victoria and the Bonapartes.*
ASLIN, Elizabeth, *The Aesthetic Movement.* Elek, London.
BACHMANN, Manfred and Claus HANSMANN, *Dolls the Wide World Over.* Harrap, London.
BESANT, Sir Walter, *The Queen's Reign.*
BOEHN, Max, *Dolls and Puppets.* 1932. London.
BOVILL, E. W., *English Country Life, 1780–1830.*
BROOKE, Iris, and James LAVER, *English Children's Costume since 1775.* Adam and Charles Black.
BRYANT, Sir Arthur, *The Age of Elegance.* Collins.
BUCK, Anne M., *Victorian Costume.* Herbert Jenkins.
BURY, Lady Charlotte, *The Diary of a Lady in Waiting.*
CHAPUIS, A., and E. DROZ, *Les Automates.* Neuchâtel, 1949.
CLARETIE, Léo, *Les Jouets, Histoire, Fabrication.* Paris, 1894.
COLEMAN, D. S., E. A., and E. J., *The Collector's Encyclopedia of Dolls.* Robert Hale.
CRUMP, Lucy, *Nursery Life 300 years ago. The Story of the Dauphin of France.* Routledge, 1929.

CULFF, Robert, *The World of Toys*. Hamlyn.

DAIKEN, Leslie, *Children's Toys throughout the Ages*. Spring Books.

DELANY, *The Life and Correspondence of Mrs Delany*.

DESMONDE, Kay, *Dolls and Doll's Houses*. Letts.

DICKENS, Charles, *The Cricket on the Hearth*.

EARLY, Alice K., *English Dolls, Effigies and Puppets*. Batsford, 1955.

FARJEON, Eleanor, *A Nursery in the Nineties*.

FAWCETT, Clara Hallard, *Dolls, a new guide for collectors*. Century House, New York.

FERGUSON, Rachel, *We Were Amused*.

FOAKES, Grace, *Between High Walls*.

FOX, Carl, *The Doll*. Abrams, New York.

FRASER, Antonia, *A History of Toys*. Weidenfeld and Nicolson.

FRASER, Antonia, *Dolls*. Octopus.

GARRATT, John G., *Model Soldiers: A Collector's Guide*. Seeley Service.

GERKEN, Jo Elizabeth, *Wonderful Dolls of Papier Mâché*. Dolls Research Associates, New York.

GODDEN, G. A., *British Pottery and Porcelain Marks*. Barrie and Jenkins.

GORDON, Lesley, *A Pageant of Dolls*, Edmund Ward.

GORDON, Lesley, *Peepshow into Paradise*. London, 1953.

GREEN, Vivien, *English Dolls Houses*. Batsford.

GRÖBER, Karl, *Children's Toys of Bygone Days*. Scribner's.

HART, Luella, *Directory of British Dolls*.

HART, Luella, *Directory of French Dolls*.

HART, Luella, *Directory of German Dolls*.

HILLIER, Mary, *Dolls and Doll Makers*. Weidenfeld and Nicolson.

JACOBS, F. G., *A History of Dolls' Houses*. Scribner's.

JACOBS, F. G., and E. FAURHOLT, *Dolls and Doll Houses*. Tuttle (Japan).

JAEGER, Muriel, *Before Victoria*.

JOHL, Janet Pagter, *The Fascinating Story of Dolls*. Century House, New York.

LANE, Margaret, *The Tale of Beatrix Potter*. Warne, 1946.

LOCHEAD, Marian, *The Victorian Household*. John Murray.

LOW, Frances, H., *Queen Victoria's Dolls*. Newnes, 1894.

MAILLARD, M. M. Rabecq, *L'Histoire du Jouet*. Hachette.

MAREUS, G., *Before the Lamps Went Out*. Allen and Unwin.

MATHES, Ruth and R. C., *Decline and Fall of the Wooden Doll*. Doll Collectors' Manual, 1964.

MAYHEW, Henry, *Mayhew's London*. Pilot Press.

MITFORD, Mary Russel, *Children of the Village*.

MONTGOMERY *The End of an Era*. Allen and Unwin, 1900.

MOORE, Doris Langley, *Fashion through Fashion Plates*.

MOOKERJEE, Ajit, *Folk Toys of India*. 1956.

NESBIT, E., *Long Ago when I was Young*. Whiting and Wheaton.

NICHOLSON, Harold, *Good Behaviour*.

NOBLE, John, *Dolls*. Studio Vista.

NOBLE, John, *These Beautiful Dolls*.

PHILLIPS, Hugh, *Mid-Georgian London*. Collins.

PIKE, E. Royston (Editor), *Human Documents of the Victorian Golden Age, 1850–1875*. Allen and Unwin.

PINCHBECK, J., and M. HEWITT, *Children in English Society*.

POWELL, Rosamund Bayne, *Housekeeping in the Eighteenth Century*.

PRAZ, Mario, *History of Interior Decoration*.

PÜCKLER-MUSKAU, Prince, *A Regency Visitor*. Collins, 1957.

QUAYLE, Eric, *The Collector's Book of Children's Books*. Studio Vista.

RUGGLES, Rowena Godding, *The One Rose*. Oakland, 1964.

ST GEORGE, Eleanor, *Dolls of Three Centuries*. Scribner's.

ST GEORGE, Eleanor, *The Dolls of Yesterday*. Bonanza Books.

SAVAGE, George, *German Porcelain*. Spring Books.

SCHOONMAKER, Patricia N., *Research on Kämmer and Reinhardt Dolls*.

SHINN, Charles and Dorrie, *Victorian Parian China*. Barrie and Jenkins.

SLEIGH, Barbara, *The Smell of Privet*.

SMITH, C. H. Gibbs, *The Fashionable Lady in the Nineteenth Century*. H.M.S.O.

SOUTH, Brenda B., *Heirloom Dolls*.

TROUBRIDGE, Laura, *Life among the Troubridges*.

WHITE, Gwen, *European and American Dolls*. Batsford.

WHITE, R. J., *Life in Regency England*. Batsford.

WHITTON, Barbara, *Paper Dolls and Paper Toys*. Jendrick, 1970.

WILLIAMS, E. N., *Life in Georgian England*.

WILSON, Harriette, *Memoirs*. Peter Davies.

YARWOOD, Doreen, *English Costume*. Batsford.

INDEX

Numbers in **bold type** denote illustrations;
c = colour